industrial
MARKETING

industrial
MARKETING

HORY SANKAR MUKERJEE

EXCEL BOOKS

ISBN: 978-81-7446-700-3

First Edition: New Delhi, 2009

EXCEL BOOKS
A-45, Naraina, Phase I,
New Delhi - 110 028

Published by Anurag Jain for Excel Books, A-45, Naraina, Phase I, New Delhi-110 028
and printed by him at Excel Printers, C-205, Naraina, Phase I, New Delhi-110 028

This book is dedicated to
The Almighty,
my dearest parents,
Rima and to Bhabataran,
who have given us a lot of joy and happiness.

Brief Contents

Detailed Contents

Preface

Industrial marketing has started gaining prominence in India since the last decade as a subject, especially in the B-school curriculum. More and more number of B-schools have an option of "Industrial Marketing" (often referred as "Business Marketing") in their second year.

Industrial marketing is a very vast subject. By the time, I might have completed the first chapter, it is quite possible that some researchers must have made a drastic change in another area of the subject. Modern age is an age of innovation. With information technology as a major influencing factor, it is very difficult to predict anything because technology brings discontinuity to the existing ways. After a year I might find my book to be obsolete.

However, the objective of this textbook is to develop an interest amongst the students in the subject. When I started teaching this subject, I found most of the Indian students new to the concept. All the textbooks that are currently available in the market cater to an absolutely different market structure and set up. However, the books on industrial marketing written by the foreign authors are very classy, and all have different style, objectives and viewpoints but the examples given in those books are quite different from the Indian market. Therefore, while writing the book, I had to focus on more Indian examples, keeping the students in mind and also some of the best practices of the developed nations, to give the new genre of students a feel of how different it is in the west.

Another challenge while writing this book was that the research material available in this subject for Indian markets was not sufficient. Also, I felt that there is a need to contribute to the practical aspects of the book. So, I requested leading practitioners from the field of industrial marketing to help me out in this book by sharing their knowledge.

This book is neither purely theoretical, nor purely practical, instead, I have tried to strike a balance between both the aspects. I would be very glad if students find the book interesting and will appreciate their feedback for the improvement of the book.

HORY SANKAR MUKERJEE
(hsm123in@yahoo.com or horysankarmukerjee@yahoo.co.in)

Acknowledgements

This book would not have moved an inch if the Almighty had not given me strength to think and to write. My parents, who have been my constant source of inspiration throughout my life, encouraged me to write this book.

Writing a textbook means a lot of sacrifice by the author. Going through pages after pages and trying to get the manuscript right is a tough task. I am thankful to Anish Hazra, Sales Manager of Excel Books, who kept on interacting with me and inspiring me, while I wrote this book.

During this period of writing the book, I had a chance to interact with some of the best practitioners from the field of Industrial Marketing. I was overwhelmed at their humility. I had a chance to interact with Alan. J. Zell, whose understanding of the subject amazed me. I think the best part of writing this book was the interaction with these "great" people across the globe.

I would also like to thank my student Mr. Suhail Syed, for going through the material and pointing out at areas where students would require a little more clarity. I would also like to thank Prof. Y.V. Sheshadri, for taking the trouble to edit the book.

I am thankful to Mr Anurag Jain, MD of Excel Books, whose humility and vision have made 'Excel Books' one of the best Indian management book publishers. Also my heartfelt thanks for Mr. Mahadev, sales manager and Malabi, Editor of Infomedia India Limited and to all who have contributed in making this textbook a reality.

About the Author

Hory Sankar Mukerjee has been a student of Symbiosis, Pune, and has been in the corporate sector for last five years. He has worked for Tata Infomedia and Standard Chartered. After that, he took a break for teaching and simultaneously completed his second Master's degree in economics. He has presented multiple papers in national and international conferences and has authored many articles. He is currently working for Infosys, as an Associate Consultant.

c h a p t e r

ONE

Introduction to Industrial Marketing

COMPANY PROFILE 1: TISCO (TATA IRON AND STEEL COMPANY)

Established in 1907, Tata Steel is Asia's first and India's largest private sector steel company. Tata Steel is among the lowest cost producers of steel in the world and one of the few select steel companies in the world that is EVA (Economic Value Added). Tata with the acquisition of Corus becomes one of the largest producers of steel in the world.

Its captive raw material resources and the state-of-the-art 5 MTPA (Million Tonne Per Annum) plant at Jamshedpur, in Jharkhand State, India give it a competitive edge. Determined to be a major global steel player, Tata Steel has recently included in its fold Nat Steel, Asia (2 MTPA) and Millennium Steel (1.7 MTPA) creating a manufacturing network in eight markets in South East Asia and Pacific rim countries. Soon the Jamshedpur plant will expand its capacity from 5 MTPA to 7 MTPA by 2008. The Company plans to enhance its capacity manifold through organic growth and investments. The Company's wire manufacturing unit in Sri Lanka is known as Lanka Special Steel, while the joint venture in Thailand for limestone mining is known as Sila Eastern.

Tata Steel's products are targeted at the quality conscious auto sector and the burgeoning construction industry. With wire manufacturing facilities in India, Sri Lanka and Thailand, the Company plans to emerge as a major global player in the wire business.

Tata Steel's products include hot and cold rolled coils and sheets, galvanized sheets, tubes, wire rods, construction rebars, rings and hearings. In an attempt to 'decommoditise' steel, the Company has introduced brands like Tata Steelium (the world's first branded Cold Rolled Steel), Tata Shaktee (Galvanised Corrugated Sheets), Tata Tiscon (Rebars), Tata Bearings, Tata Agrico (Hand Tools and implements), Tata Wiron (Galvanized Wire Products), Tata Pipes (Pipes for construction) and Tata Structura (contemporary construction material). The Company has launched the Customer Value Management initiative with the objective of creating complete understanding of customer problems and finding solutions jointly. The Company's Retail Value Management addresses the needs of distributors, retailers and end consumers. The Company has also launched India's first steel retail store - steel junction - for making steel shopping a happy and memorable experience.

The e-Procurement site is TATA Steel's B2B procurement platform and is one of the first, among many future-looking, initiatives being undertaken by Tata Steel to tap the tremendous opportunity offered by Information Technology, especially the Web, towards conducting business with the partners in a better way. The site offers Web based multi-directional flow of transactional business information, between transaction participants which forms the backbone of the Internet revolution as applicable in the B2B scenario. All cross-organisational elements of the Inbound Supply Chain, including Enquiry/RFQ details, Online and Offline Quotation logging. Order placement, Delivery compliance monitoring, Order amendments, Material Receipt and Payment tracking are covered and may be transacted through this site. In addition, value-added services such as Negotiation Chart Room with Bid revision tracking (Reverse Auction), Transactional correspondence (mails initiated on a transaction hitting appropriate mailboxes) and e-Mail notifications and acknowledgements, are also offered.

For Jamsetji Tata, the progress of enterprise, welfare of people and the health of the enterprise were inextricably linked. Wealth and the generation of wealth have never "been ends in themselves, but a means to an end, for the increased prosperity of India". The Times of India wrote in 1912 for the Tata.

Successive generations of Tata Group leaders have always held the belief that no success in material terms is worthwhile unless it serves the interest of the nation and is achieved by fair and honest means.

Tata Steel is driven by its leaders and believes that leadership is not just about the creation of wealth, it is about the creation of a better world for tomorrow and the building and growing of people, because business is and always has been about people; its primary concern is the privilege of making someone more happy and more useful.

Tata-Steel subscribes to the thought that there is a difference between making money for oneself and creating wealth for others and will therefore, not rest on its great achievements alone, however splendid they are, but as trustees of this wealth will administer and utilize it for the common good.

Source: www.tatasteel.com

Mind Power 1: The Winning Edge- Dr. Phillip D Hall and Frank Hurtte

Theoretically, success in business is simple. But in the real world this same success is incredibly challenging to achieve. Every piece of a complex puzzle must fall into place and remain there. The successful distributor knows that it all starts with knowing two basic things: customers and competitors.

Know your Customers

With all due respect to the famous Mac-Kay 66, we don't mean that you should know their golf scores, alma maters and favourite liquors. You need to know what they want to buy, why they want to buy it, and sometimes, what happens if they don't buy it. Customers are searching for the products and services integral to their business goals and they are going to select vendors that anticipate (and provide) what they want and need. The first step is that you must understand the customers' businesses. With this information you figure out how to provide solutions that match their needs. This concept sounds simple but many find it hard to carry out. You must use every possible means to get this knowledge. Here are some practical ideas to get you started.

Train your people to know and understand customers

The distribution industry spends the bulk of its training time on vendor led product familiarization (incorrectly labeled as sales training). Products are important and time is limited, but these sessions miss the mark. A customer focused workshop is created by adding a "3-Why" discussion to the lasts few minutes of product training sessions. Here is a dialog to get your juices flowing:

The traditional training is coming to an end and Bill Fletcher the local Acme Salesman says, "And that concludes our discussion of the Acme Power Poker." To drive customer understanding, you ask three why based questions.

1st Why, **"Why** would this product be important to our customer WC Manufacturing?" A customer service person says something about how it pokes more holes faster.

2nd Why, **"Why** are more holes faster important?" Your junior salesman answers because that way WC can make more products.

3rd Why, **"Why** is that important?" This final question leads into a discussion of increase revenue, meeting the new delivery deadlines, and dollar values associated with these increases.

Read the technical and trade magazines of your customer's industry

Often trade journals will give you an early warning sign of the general concerns of the industry. Trade journals open the door for in depth discussion. A very simple use would be to ask your customer if he believes the article reflects the issues at his/her company. The dialog that follows often will open a number of topics regarding the inter-workings of the customer. If you wonder where to start on getting these magazines, often they are found in the lobby or common areas of your customer. Electronic versions of these publications are often found online and at minimal cost. Amazingly very few distributors use this wealth of information.

Contd...

Use your customer service and technical support staff

Engineers and technical people from your customer often form bonds with your own technical support folks. Within this special relationship opinions and observaticns flow in both directions. Often these people are tuned into the dynamics of the customer's organization and understand the reason for the pressures on price, delivery, etc. Tap into this resource.

Always understand the reasons for change

Look for more than the obvious by applying the 3-Why Technique to common questions. Here are several that should always be explored.

Why did a customer switch vendors?

Why did the customer change specifications or requirements?

Why did the customer expedite the product?

Why did the customer ask for electronic parts printouts?

Customer knowledge must be a priority all the time. Remember, you are not the only one doing this.

The simple basics of business success are not proprietary information. Every firm is trying to do the same things, especially your competitors.

Know your competitors, know yourself

Business is simple; two or more firms are looking to make the same sale. The winning firm is the one that takes the profitable sale away from the rest of the industry. If you take more away than the others, you have real market growth.

You know the customer, now you want the customer to select you instead of one of your rivals. You must out perform your competition in providing the right solutions for your customer. Service, customisation, delivery timing, matching quality requirements to price, or other factors all come into play. Satisfy the customer in a manner that distinguishes you and you win.

Michael Porter of Harvard University states that all competitions can be generalized to two classifications:

Cost/price leadership and differentiation. Cost leaders can give the customer lower prices and will get selected if this is the customers' key. Differentiators do what is important better than the others and will be selected because of higher quality and service. This is basic, the ABCs. The challenge is to master the specifics of your industry, your competitors, and your customers.

Cost Leader or differentiator? Distributors suffer most when they try to "straddle the fence". The differentiator style competitor typically needs expensive in-house resources. Product knowledge does not come cheap. The ability to modify or customize inventory often requires additional resources. The sales activity associated with differentiation is much different than the action plan of a price driven competitor.

Both types of competitors need to know their customers, but often the information required to make the sale is different.

Distributor managers often report hearing their salespersons' say, "the customer likes our service and gave me last look to match prices." This scenario happens literally hundreds of times a day in the world we call distribution. Without a strategic competition factor the wrong decision could be made. It's not enough to have a general idea of where you play in the competition game. Your plan has to be well thought out, written down, and revisited often. Salespeople, customer service, and key vendors all need to understand your competition strategy and the competition strategy of other distributors in your market space. If you are in the "differentiation game", this needs to be reviewed often.

Contd...

A variation of the differentiation style competitor is the niche player. The niche strategy requires very special knowledge of the customers in a particular segment. The niche has to be large enough and experiencing a positive outlook to make it a long-term opportunity. A niche strategy is a where decision. A firm decides where to compete by customer segment, product line or both. The firm still must take on every rival for this niche and find the way to win.

Winning is everything. The successful distributor understands the customers and knows how to beat the competitors to these customers. Then the distributor acts in every specific way to implement the winning competitive strategy.

Meet the Authors

Dr. Phillip D. Hall

Phillip Hall comes with a wealth of academic credentials and awards. He has 25 years of university level teaching experience with over 15 years spent in MBA Programmes. Dr. Hall received his MBA from Cal State Sacramento and was awarded a PhD from the University of Nebraska - Lincoln (with special emphasis in Strategic Planning). While a Professor at Nebraska, Phil served as Assistant Dean of Students in the College of Business. During the 1990's Dr. Hall was recruited by St. Ambrose College of Davenport, Iowa. At St. Ambrose, he has served as the Chair of Managerial Studies as well as conducted numerous courses in the undergraduate and postgraduate curriculums.

Frank E. Hurtte

Frank Hurtte has spent his life straddling the line between engineer and businessman. Frank graduated from the University of Illinois - Champion with a degree in Computer Engineering. He worked for a leading manufacturer of automation equipment in both a field engineer and sales role. Frank had P and L responsibility in one of America's fastest growing Electrical Distributors. Today Hurtte is a nationally known author, speaker and industry consultant. As the Founding Partner of River Heights Consulting, he works with corporations and charitable organizations in defining their strategic future.

INTRODUCTION TO INDUSTRIAL MARKETING

Industrial marketing constitutes one of the largest markets. The volume of transaction in the industrial markets is more than that of the consumer markets. It is the largest market, which mostly goes unnoticed in the eyes of a normal consumer. The purchases made by the government and commercial entrepreneurs constitute a huge chunk of this market.

Often, in the classroom, if a faculty asks "What is your most coveted job, post you're MBA?" Most of the reply would be a product Manager at Britannia or handling a product line of Hindustan Lever. But, however, most of the students do not know that about fifty percent would be placed in companies, which market to business.

Business markets are markets "for products and/or services, generally used by institutions, government or business houses for consumption, use, resale or value add such products".

Let us take an example to illustrate this. Take any automobile, personnel computer or your mobile phone. Now all the component parts are not manufactured by the company. They purchase some of the components, manufacture some and then assemble them to form the final product.

So, if one manufacturer is selling its products to another business either in the form of raw materials, component parts or selling its services for consumption, use, resale or for value addition, then we would call it as business marketing or industrial marketing.

Mind Power 2: Modern B2B Marketing Defined

The focus of this blog is to discuss new ways of thinking about B2B Marketing, from best practices in lead acquisition and nurturing to marketing accountability to community-based marketing.

It is clear that traditional marketing approaches are no longer acceptable. Some reasons why:

1. ***Customers DON'T want to be interrupted:*** They DON'T want to be marketed to. And they'll let you know by finding ways to screen out, throw out, and tune out your unwanted marketing messages.

2. ***There are no more mass channels:*** Buyers (especially the young and tech-savvy) are harder than ever to reach using traditional channels and media outlets. At the same time, new technologies (especially broadband and mobile) combined with social computing have created a "Cambrian explosion" in experimentation with media and marketing channels. This fragmentation diminishes the effectiveness of traditional marketing channels while simultaneously creating opportunities to reach customers in new ways.

3. ***Marketing can't get away with not being accountable:*** New channels (like PPC search engine marketing) have raised expectations for marketing accountability. It is no longer acceptable to say "half the money I spend on advertising is wasted; the trouble is I don't know which half."

Marketers must adapt to these changes. CMOs that don't will not last long. Those who do will survive by practicing Modern B2B Marketing. Some principles of Modern B2B Marketing:

1. ***Attention Marketing:*** Buyers are in control of what information they want and their attention is a valuable, scare commodity. Marketing needs to engage with customers when and how they want to engage. This is why search engine marketing is so powerful, the customer is attentively seeking information.

2. ***Community Marketing:*** In a world where we can no longer push our message to the marketplace, marketing need to finds ways to communicate with the marketplace. The best way to do this to enable and nurture open source style communities of customers, prospects, partners, and other influencers. In other words, join the conversations that customers are already having, online and offline.

3. ***Left Brain Marketing:*** Because many of the new marketing channels are measurable and targetable, marketing is rapidly shifting towards science and away from art. Forrester Research aptly calls the rise of analytics over creativity in marketing "Left Brain Marketing". New marketing skills will include segmentation and targeting, testing and optimization, and quantitative planning and measurement. (This is not to say creativity has no place in marketing, just that the balance will incorporate more math and science than in the past. And that creativity will take a different form, i.e. thinking of creative new things to test.)

4. ***Accountable Marketing:*** Certain parts of the marketing budget are already very accountable - most notably pay-per-click advertising. As testing becomes predominant and budget shifts towards measurable channels, CMOs will be able to measure the bottom-line impact of every marketing activity. Aided by tools to aid with marketing planning, measurement and execution, they will also be able to quantify the impact of changes to their budget and to predict pipeline and revenue as well as sales can. Over time, this will raise marketing's power and influence across the organization.

Of course, there are many other forces driving the transformation of marketing today, including the changing role of the marketing organization and new marketing automation technologies. What factors do you think are most affecting B2B Marketing?

Contd...

Traditional Marketing	Modern Marketing
● Marketing needs to interrupt the customer to get attention	● Customers control their attention and marketers engage when and how consumers want
● Marketing pushes a "consistent" message to the marketplace	● Marketers join the conversation by enabling communities of customers, prospects, partners, and other influencers
● Limited set of marketing channels	● Rapid proliferation of (and experimentation with) new measurable and targetable channels
● Marketing is mostly right-brained (creativity and art)	● Marketing is mostly left-brained (science and math)
● Marketers are not held fully accountable and (as a result) are not considered strategic at many organizations	● Marketers can demonstrate bottom-line impact, justify their budget, and plan the marketing mix with quantitative rigor

Source: Posted by Jon Miller on August 08, 2006; Copyright 2007. Marketo Inc. You can visit the web at www.marketo.com. Reprinted with kind permission of Jon Miller.

Mind Power 3: Why B2B Marketers Must Work So Hard

According to IDC, B2B Marketers are being forced to do more with fewer people than ever before. The "programme-to-people" ratio, which compares the ratio of programme expense to staff expense in the marketing budget, is becoming more leveraged every year (meaning fewer people running more programmes). In 2006, the ratio hit a high value of 65:35.

At the same time, "marketing staff throughput", defined as programme execution dollars per employee, reached a high of $301,400 in 2006. This is 10 percent higher than the previous year. (Putting the two numbers together implies an average expense per marketing employee of $162,292. Presumably this includes salary, bonus, benefits, allocations, and expenses.)

Compare this dramatic growth in Marketing productivity to the overall average for US labour productivity, which grew by only 1.4 percent in 2006 (the lowest in more than a decade). This implies that Marketing productivity grew more than 7 times as fast as overall productivity! It also explains why so many marketers feel like they are being forced to "do more with less".

What It Means

1. *Marketing automation drives productivity:* The main driver of global productivity growth has been investment in technology. According to the Conference Board, the lower US productivity numbers might mean the current crop of business applications (such as SFA, ERP, etc.) have maxed out their ability to drive incremental productivity gains. On the other hand, the huge growth in marketing productivity suggests that investment in and value from marketing automation technology may actually be accelerating.

2. *Limits to gains from agency outsourcing:* The trend of outsourcing key marketing functions to agencies raises the programme-to-people ratio, since it transfers people dollars to programme dollars. Of course, there is a limit to how much can be outsourced without requiring oversight from in-house staff. Also, I question the long-term value of outsourcing strategic marketing

Contd...

functions (such as pay per click management), since it makes marketers reliant on outsiders who will never be able to react as quickly as in-house staff.

3. ***Start building the case that marketing is an asset now:*** Marketing productivity growth cannot grow faster than overall productivity over the long-term. There will eventually be a time when extraordinary productivity gains can no longer be squeezed out of marketing, when marketers will no longer be able to do more with less. Marketers who work at companies that still think of marketing as a cost center will be pressured to continue to cut to the bone, and eventually performance will begin to suffer. On the other hand, marketers who can demonstrate impact on the bottom line will be well positioned to make the business case for ongoing investment.

Source: Posted by Jon Miller; Copyright 2007. Marketo Inc. You can visit the web at www.marketo.com. Reprinted with kind permission of Jon Miller.

Understanding Industrial Marketing

There are three major participants of industrial marketing. They are:

1. Commercial Organization

2. Governmental Agencies

3. Non-profit Organizations and Charitable Institutions.

All these three categories are the sellers as well as buyers. For example, a commercial organisation like Tata Steel, may sell their steel to Maruti Udyog or to Indian Railways; Maruti, being another commercial organization and Indian Railways as Governmental agencies. What do you think, will a commercial organization market to a non-profit organization? So, all the above three categories form a part of industrial marketing or business marketing.

One question can come to mind, is that do industrial marketers cater to consumers? Yes, they do, if they choose so. For example, a furniture manufacturer like "Featherlite" may sell its furniture to offices as well as to houses, or say "HP" may sell the personal computer to offices as well as to individuals.

So is the reverse true. That is, does consumer goods company offer its products to industrial firms? Yes, it does; for example, soap manufacturers can also bid for supply to hospitals and for commercial enterprises. Consumer and industrial marketing overlap.

The basic rules of the game of consumer marketing is equally applicable to industrial markets, but the nature of market, buying behaviour, nature of demand, advertising and promotion has an absolutely different perspective in industrial marketing. Selling is more on strong bonding of the buyer and seller and relationships, than on the basis of the product. "Marketers sell relationships and not products". The reader should not misrepresent the statement. Soundness of products definitely is required, but what is more essential is "something extra" which we do not see in consumer marketing. It represents a unique situation, which is generally not encountered in consumer markets.

"Industrial markets are the flesh and blood of any market or economy. It provides strength to the entire system of economic activity and forms a foundation to the economy. It even forms a foundation to the consumer goods industry also. It is dynamic, challenging and accounts for well over half of our economic activity".[1]

Differentiating Between Industrial Marketing and Consumer Marketing

CHARACTERISTICS	INDUSTRIAL MARKETING	CONSUMER MARKETING
Competition	Oligopoly, few buyers	Monopolistic and mass markets
Demand	Derived and thus volatile	Direct and less volatile
Market Size	Larger and a global market perspective. Geographically concentrated buyers.	Smaller and a regional perspective. Buyers are geographically dispersed.
Buyer/Seller Interaction	Functional involvement, relationship oriented, stable relations, inter-personal relationships and reciprocity.	Family involvement, less technical know-how, transaction oriented, non-personal relationships.
Key Accounts	Very important	Non existent
Buying Behaviour	Large order sizes with strong buying powers and greater purchasing involvement. The purchasing decision is lengthy, complex and risks are high.	Small order sizes, with weak buying powers and less purchasing involvement. The purchasing decision is relatively shorter, less complex and risk is relatively low.
Product and Service Mix	The "PLC" is shorter, service levels are high. Also, the quality is of prime importance. Branding is of the parent company.	"PLC" is longer, service levels are less. Quality may not be vital. Branding is for individual products.
Distribution	Generally short, direct and complex channels. Great importance for product knowledge and delivery is very crucial. There are few linkages.	Longer channels and simple. Product knowledge and delivery is not very critical. There are multiple linkages.
Price	Bidding, negotiation, leasing are very common. Promotional pricing is used rarely. List prices only on standard items.	Bidding, negotiation, leasing are uncommon. Promotional pricing is very common. Only list prices.
Promotions	Personal selling, trade shows, catalogues, direct mailers; editorial publicity are some of promotional emphasis.	Advertising for the mass is the most common form of promotion.

While the basic concept in both consumer marketing and the industrial marketing remain the same, in industrial marketing, however, there is a separate set of special challenges. In this market, number of customers is small, they are well-informed as to what they need, generally do not base their decisions on emotions, are organized and attribute their buying decisions to multiple factors and multiple people in the organization. Thus, the challenge becomes unique. In consumer marketing, for example, if a television set requires to be bought, the decision-making process, would be only amongst the family members and probably with some amount of external influence acting on it. But in industrial marketing, the scenario is absolutely different. In industrial marketing, any kind of changes, whether it is in the range of products or service, tend to have a companywide implication.

In industrial marketing, not only goods are sold, but there is also an exchange of information, financial and social exchange.[2]

We would now try and understand the difference between industrial and consumer marketing in a greater detail, under the following headings:

- The Markets
- Purchasing Process
- Product, Price, Channels and Promotion.

The Markets

Industrial Markets generally have very few sellers and few buyers. But, however, this always may not be the case. The industrial markets are characterised by derived demand, which we would see in a detailed discussion later in the chapter. We will see how derived demand affects the selling to industrial buyers more volatile by nature. The industrial markets constitute a large chunk of business, with goods for three big categories viz., commercial enterprises, governmental agencies and non-profit organisations. Industrial marketers tend to geographically clustered with factors like nearness to raw materials, availability of cheap labours, and close to industrial buyers. Consumer markets on the other hand, tend to be dispersed.

Segmenting of industrial markets is not on the basis of demographics. Other criteria like end uses, markets to be served are some of the criteria used in segmentation. The involvement of purchasers is huge, because of the kind of expenditure, an industrial manufacturer undertakes to buy a product is sometimes to the tune of crores. Applications of industrial products remain the same and do not vary with buyers, although some degree of customisation may be required. Industrial manufacturers, invest heavily on research and development to give products a cutting edge. The level of interaction between the manufacturer and buyer, importance of key accounts and the level of buyer knowledge makes industrial marketing a different game altogether.

Mind Power 4: Understanding Customers: Customer is the Key to Success: - By Sanjay Limaye

We keep a close watch on our customers. But as business marketers, it's just as important to watch your customers' customer. Savvy marketers recognize that their success ultimately depends on their contribution to the entire value chain.

Unfortunately, most of the organizations think of primary customers as the only customers, relying on them for just about all their market feedback. The problem is primary customers who don't adapt to rapid changes in the markets drag their clueless suppliers down with them. Similarly satisfied big customers can blind us to the major trends that eventually dictate our business. Therefore, the suppliers who are a step or more removed from end-users in the value chain must know what that Customers-of-Customer is up to.

However knowing Customers-of-Customer (C-of-C) gives tremendous advantages. For example,

1.   Your salespeople, will have the information they need for value-added selling.

2.   Your new product will be much less likely to be obsolete the day it is launched.

3.   You'll also know which of your customers to prefer over others, because they'll succeed as their markets change.

4.   Which customers to treat as cash cows.

C-of-C know and worry about the components in the products they buy. In striving to meet their own competitive quality challenges, they'll want to know more than just the price and terms when buying from their supplier, which is your direct customer. If you, the upstream supplier, know what those C-of-Cs need, you'll be way ahead of your competitors. In addition, your smart primary customers will recognize your loyalty to their interests, when you help them sell more to their customers.

C-of-C is not a rocket science but requires discipline

Encourage salespeople to discuss long-term trends with major customers, particularly their innovative "lead-users". Study printed and online resources. Insist that a full C-of-C analysis be included in each marketing plan.

Contd...

The specific scenarios you'll address will vary by industry, but conceptually you need to know the following:

1. What drives your customers' success with their own customers? What factors do sustain their competitive advantages?

2. What's likely to be your major customer's response to each of those scenarios trend-by-trend, key customer-by-key-customer?

3. What new markets will your customers explore, or which could they vacate? How will that change, what they now buy and could buy from you and from your competitors?

4. How will economic, regulatory, technological and social trends after the importance of those competitive advantages?

Source: Copyright with Industrial Marketing Services. Reprinted with permission. Visit him at www.inmas.com.

Purchasing Process

Purchasing generally is in bulk (except for capital items) and often contracts are given for one year. Finding customers, prospecting is very selective unlike consumer markets. Generally, industrial buyers do not switch suppliers and loyalty forms a very important component of industrial marketing. Suppliers are evaluated at regular intervals on various parameters. 'Suppliers' are considered as 'partners' in industrial marketing, because any kind of changing suppliers involve "switching costs".

Industrial purchasing involves a number of members of the organisation, often called the DMU or decision-making unit. The process can take a longer time, often upto one year, because of various considerations. Taxation, depreciation, increased profitability, leasing, hire purchasing are some of the areas which the buyer might also consider.

Product, Price, Channels and Promotion

The rates of technological changes are higher in industrial markets and thereby product life cycles are shorter. In other words, the risk of obsolescence is higher than consumer markets. The industrial products are designed as per specification given by the industrial buyer and are custom built, except for supplies. Also, products might require some kind of treatment before it enters actual production process. Servicing and quality are very important in industrial markets. Also, companies with a stronger brand presence give a better edge.

As far as pricing of industrial product goes, most of it is "negotiated pricing". For government contracts and larger projects, competitive bidding is very common. Also, leasing and hire purchasing is becoming an important area of discussion.

Industrial channels are shorter than consumer markets, but are more complex. Generally, channels are direct. The industrial channels have the most critical component that has to be satisfied in delivery and service. A lot of industrial selling requires technical assistance and for that the buyer and seller must closely interact. One of the reasons why channels are generally short and direct. A lot of different set of customers makeup the market, making it more complex. Since the participants are knowledgeable in the market and it adds up to the complexity.

Sales promotion uses more of direct mail, trade shows, catalogues and editorial publicity. However, personal selling is the best form of promotion. Buying often involves solving a lot of complex problems and thus personal selling forms the key in industrial marketing.

Economics of Industrial Demand

Demand is the volume of a specific product that industrial buyers purchase during a specified period.

The table given below is the demand for steel in the United States market. Now two things can be inferred from the table:

1. The demand for steel has been fluctuating.

2. The demand could have been more or less depending on the economy and the marketing strategies of the industrial manufacturers.

Whenever any economy is in a depressed state, whether it be the US economy or Indian economy, the consecutive demand for steel goes down, as all the industries which needs steel also are in a downturn.

ITEM	1990	1995	2000	2001	2002	2003	2004
Steel mill products: Apparent supply	95.5	109.6	131.9	116.4	117.8	116.1	131.8
Net shipments	85.0	97.5	109.1	98.9	100.0	106.0	111.4
Exports	4.3	7.1	6.5	6.1	6.0	8.2	7.9
Imports	17.2	24.4	29.4	30.1	32.6	23.1	35.8
Scrap consumed	50.1	62.0	65.0	63.0	62.0	61.8	57.3
Scrap inventory	3.6	4.1	5.3	4.9	4.2	4.5	4.8
Iron and steel products :							
Exports	5.3	8.2	7.7	7.2	7.0	9.3	9.6
Imports	21.9	27.3	42.6	34.4	37.3	27.9	41.2
Capacity by steel making process	116.7	112.4	130.3	125.5	113.7	121.6	116.1

Source: http/www.census.gov/compendia/statab/manufactures - Data on the steel demand from the period of 1990-2004.

So, in any economic downturn, or due to the influence of any social, political, legal factors, the demand will fluctuate. This is very strongly visible in industrial markets. If consumers have lower disposable income to buy cars, not only the automobile manufacturer would suffer, but also the steel manufacturer, the leather manufacturer, the glass manufacturer, the tyre manufacturer and the component parts manufacturer.

Finally, it is our consumer who buy the product. They buy it for their personal use or satisfaction and not for any commercial purpose, or to make profits. The mobile set, the television, the video game, home theatre etc. This is the demand of the consumer. It is the origin of all other demands and is also called as **'direct demand'**.

However, the business buyers face a different kind of challenge known as "derived demand". It is called as the derived demand because the demand is derived by the customer or clients of the business marketer.

Derived Demand: As said earlier, that the name derived demand is used because the demand is derived. Let us take an example to illustrate this. Maruti manufactures a basic model- "Maruti 800". It is people like you and me, who buy the car. This demand for car is a direct demand. Now to manufacture the car, the manufacturer has to buy several things like paints, engine, exhaust pipes, components, plastic, glass, leather and batteries to name a few. So, if consumers are purchasing more of cars, then the suppliers of Maruti would be asked to supply more components, raw materials and others. So, the battery manufacturer say "Exide", will get more orders from Maruti and in turn, they will order for more materials required to make batteries. Thus, a chain is created. This is "derived demand".

Why Does Industrial Marketers Need to Understand Derived Demand?

1. Predicting, the individual level of demand more accurately.
2. Helps industrial marketers understand the factors that influence their sales.
3. In cases of less sales, from one segment, industrial marketers can look into other segments for more business.
4. Better understanding of the impact on price, profitability, promotion and distribution strategies.

You might have noticed that Intel Processors for personal computers, laptops and desktops are advertised on the television. It gives you a feeling that it might not be a right strategy to promote a B2B product on television. But, if you look at the finer line, this strategy to advertise to the consumers is to build a confidence amongst consumers and a loyalty for Intel Processors. It would be so strong that when you go to buy a laptop, you check whether it has an Intel Processor. This is to reduce the uncertainty caused due to derived demands in industrial markets. This strategy is more feasible when products are patented, and the industrial firm has a large chunk of the market share. Also, the end market should be a sizable chunk and would be preferable if that industry has a high entry barrier.

Joint Demand

It is very common in the industrial markets. It occurs when products require existence of other products. For example, food processors would require floor, yeast, salt, egg, in the production of bread. Industrial customers often prefer to buy joint product items or complete line of products from one supplier. Similarly, a pump would be rendered useless, if it does not have a motor.

Cross Elasticity of Demand

It is the response in the sales of one product to a price change in another. Say for example, the demand for steel may be related to aluminium. The direct relation between the price of one good and the quantity demanded of another good is very much true for industrial products.

Fluctuating Demand

Since the demand is derived, the industrial marketer must monitor the changing preferences of consumers and demand patterns. So, if the interest rates on consumer durable products are falling, there has to be a rise in the production of all related categories.

CONCLUSION

The basic fundamentals of marketing remain the same in both consumer and industrial markets, but some differences exist in the way industrial marketers look at business. The 4P's, buying patterns, markets, buying behaviour contrast the consumer markets. In industrial markets, not only goods interchange with money, but also relationships bind contracts. In consumer markets, we observe direct demands and in industrial markets we see derived demand. This makes the complete way of looking at the industrial markets, differently. We will discuss these issues one by one in greater details in the later chapters of the book.

References

1.   Fredrick E.Webster Jr., *Management Science in Industrial Markets.* pp 21-27.

2.   Hakan Hakanson *(Ed) International Marketing and Purchasing of Industrial Goods.* IMP Project Group. pp-16-17.

Mind Power 5: What Will You Do With China? – By Dan Adams

The way you answer this question depends on your mental model of China. If you see China as the next Japan or Korea, you will probably look to some familiar options. But what if China becomes to the 21st century what America was to the 20th century? There are several reasons why some experts believe this will be the case.

China... The America of the 21st Century?

Like Japan and Korea before it, China is climbing the technology ladder. It produces more than half the world's toys, bicycles and shoes, and is now rapidly gaining ground in electronics, automotive and aircraft industries. But with many of its 1.3 billion people still living in the hinterlands, it need not abandon low-technology industries as other developing countries have done. You can't ride this one out: Expect to compete with wages below $1.00 per hour for a longtime.

That same enormous population-aka "market"-has allowed China to attract more foreign investment than all other developing countries combined. When you think of Chinese competitors, don't just think of primitive shop floors run by locals. More than half of all Chinese exports are produced by foreign firms, many of whom have been forced to bring their best technologies as the price of entry into this vast market.

Protectionism won't work either, because China's success is simply in the best interests of too many consumers and large corporations. If Wal-Mart were a nation, it would be the 6th largest importer of Chinese goods. Another factor in China's success is its highly educated and successful Diaspora, a large portion of which has been returning to mainland China, fresh from success in US and European universities and businesses.

This is not to say that China does not face obstacles. Its' banking and service sectors are in bad shape, and in the midst of its burgeoning capitalism, it's easy to lose sight of the fact that it is ruled by a communist regime. The Japanese government encourages its companies to keep some manufacturing capacity outside China in case of political turmoil. But ignoring China or hoping it stumbles both make for weak global strategies.

A better approach is to seriously consider two types of competition presented by China: direct and indirect. The former occurs when your customer shows you a Chinese import that looks a lot like yours… and is priced at or below your costs. This occurred in the textile and furniture industries and can be rapid and unpleasant. According to a petition filed by U.S. furniture manufacturers, "It is no exaggeration to say that the imports from China have single-handedly forced the industry into a tailspin so swift and so deep that it may soon become irreversible".

Contd...

Indirect competition is more subtle and has, in my opinion, not received nearly enough attention. This takes place when your customers' products are attacked by low-priced imports. You feel the heat in several ways:

1.   Your sales suffer as your customers' output declines,

2.   Your customers become a credit risk, and

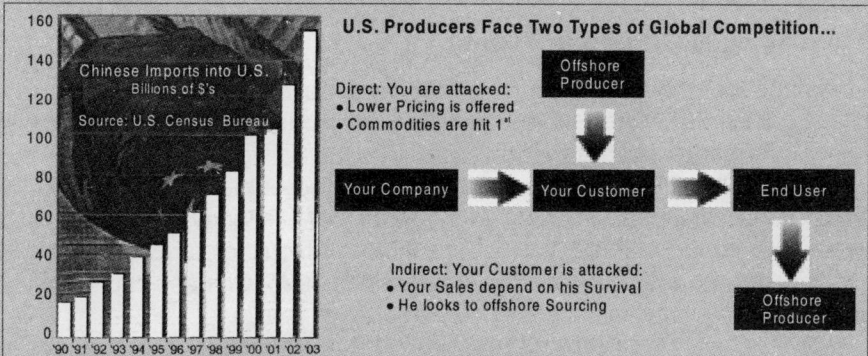

3.   Your customers look to lower-cost sourcing which ironically, may be produced offshore. Notions you had about the values of relationships and service can be dashed as your customers struggle for their survival.

Pursue a Three-Fold Strategy

Consider a three-fold approach. First, perform a 'China threat' audit on the market segments you serve. Imagine you produce resins used by coatings producers. Be nervous if those coatings are for metal parts that could be made in China. Feel more secure if your products are used to make house paint, since the substrate (house walls) probably won't be imported and the paint itself must be tinted locally. After the audit, realign your commercial and technical resources to pursue the most attractive segments. (In my view, a strategy is just an internal exercise unless though trade-off decisions are made.)

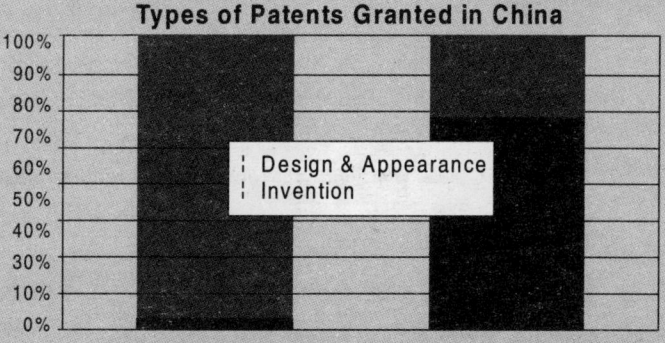

Source: China's National Bureau of statistics & Ministry of Science & technology for 2001.

"Consider how fast you can increase your presence in China. Then accelerate. Leave skid marks."

The second element is to make some products in China. This lets you (1) Follow and support your customers there, (2) Gain access to a large and growing market, (3) Understand emerging global competitors better and (4) Be prepared to defend the more commoditised portions of your product line. Whether or not you now have a manufacturing base in China, consider how fast you can reasonably increase your presence there. Then accelerate. Leave skid marks.

Contd...

The third element is to develop innovative new products that deliver real value to customers. Many companies used to talk about being low-cost producers which were fine when they compared in a national, not global, economy. But if you or your customers face Chinese competition, that's like taking a knife to a gunfight. When you develop new products with superior value, you sidestep the global shop-floor economics war, constructing a hedge against direct competition. And, because you'll attract more innovative and forward -thinking users, you will reduce indirect competitions as well.

Innovation ... The only Games in Town

It wasn't that long ago that a popular notion claimed companies could be equally successful with a strategy of customer intimacy, operational efficiency or product innovation. Pick a strategy, any strategy. As many U.S. manufacturers are now learning to their chagrin, it just isn't so. Your customers may like you - a lot - but when their survival is at stake, they'll buy from an offshore source in a heartbeat. And certainly you should improve your operational efficiency, but unless you are favoured with very high costs or capital intensity, you will find it most difficult to compete globally on this basis. And capital intensity may be a short-lived advantage. Since 1995, Chinese capital investments have led to productivity improvements in excess of 15 percent per year).

That leaves us with product innovation. Fortunately, Chinese innovation is weak today. While they may follow the Japanese sequence of imitate...improve ....innovate, relatively little true invention takes place today.

After you've completed your China-threat audit, focus your research and development resources on those market segments that are winnable and worth winning. Then vigorously protect your intellectual property through patents and well-guarded trade secrets. Unprotected innovation is just a form of philanthropy. While it is true patent enforcement is weak today, in China, this will change in coming years. In the meantime, strong patents can at least let you block the inflow of knock-off imports at the U.S. dock.

A final thought: You won't see big benefits from an innovation strategy for 2-3 years, so if you have a window of opportunity, move fast before it closes. After all, when was the last time you heard someone surprised at how slowly China did anything?

Learning More...

If you want to dig deeper into this subject, I highly recommend The Chinese Century, by Oded Shenkar, and The World is Flat by Thomas Friedman.

Source: Copyright with Advanced Industrial Marketing, Inc. Visit them at www.aimtolead.com. Reprinted with the kind permission of the author.

Mind Power 6: Lessons From Germany – By Malabi Sengupta and Shailesh Sheth

The first of the three articles, "Innovation": Last on the list?' featured in the October 2006 issue of MMT brought to light the criticality of innovation. Indian companies traditionally have pushed out 'innovation' from the priority list. But the time has come when it has become impossible to survive without research and development and innovations, if India needs to make the transition from being a "manufacturing sub-contractor to the world" to "a producer of finished products that reach global markets".

This article is all about Germany, how it manages innovation, carries out basic as well as applied research and development in a seamless manner, and lessons for India.

Contd...

Why Germany?

True that the Germans are known for their experience in science and technology, but so are the Japanese and the Americans. What makes Germany, the country to benchmark against and emulate? The reasons are quite a few, and all very convincing.

Japan

The island country is well-known for its scientific research and the production of innovative technological products. And the Japanese manufacturing concepts like lean manufacturing, just in time (JIT), Kaizen, 5S, Kanban have taken the world by storm. Yet, when trying to learn from Japan's success story you will stumble and that is because the Japanese are known to be inscrutable. They are not open and forthcoming. Also, there is a strong nexus between the Government, the industry and institutions and they all work for only the Japan Inc.

The Japanese are strong in applied research, and commercialization of innovation. It is interesting to note that basic research is, however, not Japan's core strength. Take example of consumer electronics, or even cars. The Japanese have commercialized many technologies, but have they invented it? The first quartz, non-mechanical watch was not discovered by the Japanese, but by the Swiss. The Japanese did not discover the colour TV, but they sure popularized it. So, what the Japanese did was build on an existing technology. In a nutshell, they handled the applied part of it well.

The US

The Americans are known for hi-tech innovations that beat even the wildest imagination. Their prowess is undisputed in basic and applied research and development. There is a famous anecdote on the US's technological abilities….

The US and USSR both were working on space technologies and sending man to outer space. At zero gravity, the astronauts faced a peculiar problem. The ink used in pens work under the force of gravity. So in the absence of gravity, the pen refused to work.

The Americans faced this problem in their typical industrious manner. To combat the problem, NASA scientists spent a decade and $12 billion to develop a pen that writes in zero gravity, upside down, underwater, on almost any surface including glass and at temperatures ranging from below freezing to 30 degree C.

USSR unfortunately located both the structural approach and the funds to develop such a product. So, what did the Russians do? Well, they simply used a 'pencil'.

Tail tales apart, the US surely is a big name in the area of science and technology. They however, enjoy extremely large allocation of funds, thereby giving its scientists enormous individual freedom and space. There is hardly any 'fear of failure'. In research and development this fear of failure is a very critical issue, as 99 of 100 innovations fail, while one may go on to become a commercial success. But India lacks the deep pockets the US enjoys, thereby making it unviable to use the US as a role model.

The German Industry

There are not many machine tool professionals who don't secretly nurture a wish to visit the hallowed centres of higher learning and research related to machine tools in Germany. Most machine tool professionals have grown up learning of the contributions of stalwarts like Dr. Schlesinger, Prof. Tobias, Prof. Weck and others from the technical universities of Aachen, Berlin and other places. Germany has played significant role in the development of the machine tool industry. Even today, it is considered to be the masters in engineering. True, there are small dents in its image with the turn of the century. Yet, the country stands on a solid foundation… be it innovation, basic or applied research and development, it clearly has an edge over the others, especially in the field of machine tools. And at the base of this lies a structured model that allows seamless transfer of technology from the academia to the commercial entities, aka companies that manufacture the products using the innovative

Contd…

technologies. And experts in the Indian machine and tool community feel that this German model is ideal for India to emulate.

The German Model

With Germany's long tradition of building machine tools, combined with the fact that it is among the top producers of machine tools, the study of the German model proves very interesting. Figure 1 illustrates how the German business model for research and development and commercialization technology is structured. A technology mission to Germany revealed a lot of interesting aspects.

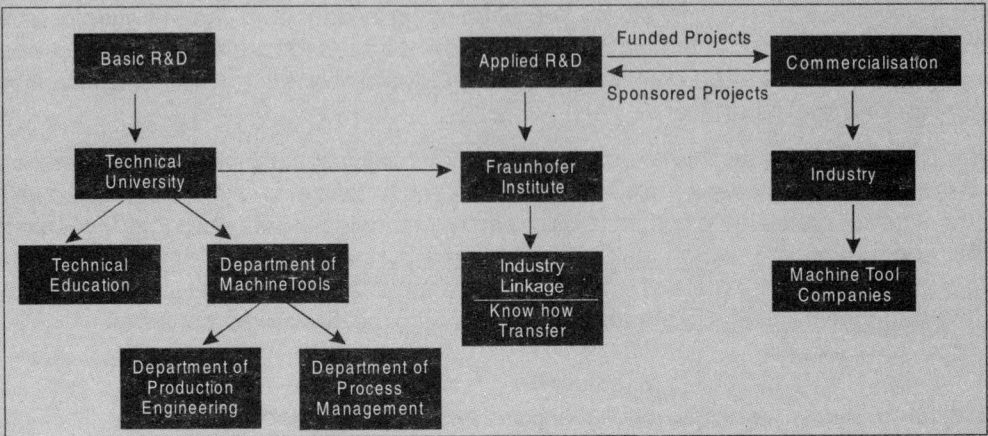

Figure 1.1: The German Model

Some of the characteristics of the German model, with special reference to the machine tool industry are:

1. Basic research into advanced metal cutting and metal forming sciences is carried out by the Technical Universities.

2. Delivering these as commercial technology packages into industry is done by the Fraunhofer Institute (60 in all), which are co-located at the Technical Universities.

3. The Universities and Fraunhofer Institutes are headed by the same professors but have its own research and development facilities and staff. There is strong synergy between the two.

4. University professors are also appointed to the boards of major corporates in Germany and so have a strong link with industry. Result Contract research work industry and funding flow to the universities and Fraunhofers. Similarly, industry experts take teaching positions from time to time.

5. The eight Fraunhofer Institutes involved in production technology operate a budget of Euro 125 m annually (Rs. 75 crores) and with staff strength of 2000.

Many Indian machine tool experts admitted that after scanning the global scenario of institutions involved in development of machine tool technology that Germany has the best business model for basic research and development, applied research and commercialization of development, which India could adopt.

What Germany does right

A remarkable aspect of technology development in Germany is the active interest the industry takes in funding basic research as well as applied research and development. Take for instance the joint funding of projects, where even competing companies come together to fund projects. If individual companies had to sponsor a project, the resources available to the company would be limited. When a group of companies jointly fund a project, such constraints are eliminated.

Contd...

A final feature that makes the German Model almost perfect is the 'apprentice training programme'. It is inevitable that trained manpower is required to receive and absorb the new technologies on a sustainable basis. Germany has a sound apprentice-training programme in place that ensures that there is no dearth of trained workforce. These apprentices spend time at the academic Institutes, then the research and development Institutes and finally return to work in the industry. Thus, from early days, they understand the link between academic institutions, research and development establishments and the industry.

Fact - file

The research and development work in Germany is characterized by the following:

1. Contract research provides one-third revenue to the Fraunhofers. Another one-third comes from publicly funded research projects. The Federal and state governments contribute the remaining third as grants, Euro 1 for every Euro 2 from contract/funded research.

2. A large part of the development projects are contracted by SMEs in Germany.

3. Individual projects can be from Euro 200 to Euro 2 million, and can take from a few weeks to 2-3 years to complete. Doing research and development in Germany need not be expensive!

4. A fascinating feature of German research and development is the concept of 'research circles'. By this, machine tool companies, users, sub-suppliers, standard organizations, even public bodies form research circles, contribute to technology development programmes, and share the results. This reduces development cost to companies, while getting together the critical mass of funding required to carry out meaningful research and development of long lasting importance. Research circles are usually long-term and are not tied to one project. While new members can apply to join, they must be voted by the existing members. Typical research circles have anywhere from 10 - 20 members or even more.

Research and Development activities under GOI's patronage

Department of Science and Technology (DST) under the Government of India (GoI) was established in May 1971, with the objective of promoting new areas of Science and Technology and to play the role of a nodal department for organizing, coordinating and promoting S and T activities in the country. All the Science and Engineering Research Council (SERC) is the apex body through which the DST promotes research and development programmes in newly emerging and challenging areas of science and engineering. A look at some of the organizations under DST's umbrella.

IRHPA: The programme for Intensification of Research in High Priority Areas (IRHPA) was launched during the 6th Five Year Plan to strengthen research in high priority areas. This is meant to set up core groups, centres of excellence and national facilities in frontline and emerging fields of science and engineering. This has had significant impact on the national and international scientific scene in terms of quality and quantity of work in important fields such as neurobiology, solid state chemistry, nano-materials, materials science, surface science, plasma physics, macromolecular crystallography and ultra fast processes.

NSTI: Nano-science and technology is receiving increasing attention all over the world in the last few years. DST assessed the importance of this emerging, highly interdisciplinary field and launched a national programmed titled 'Nano-science and Technology Institute (NSTI)". The programme focused at overall research and development in nano-science and technology with vigour so that India can become a significant player in the area and contribute to the development of new technologies besides carrying out basic research at the frontiers.

SAIF: DST provides facilities of sophisticated analytical instruments to researchers through its Sophisticated Analytical Instrument Facilities (SAIF) programme so that the non-availability of these instruments in their Institutes may not come in the way of scientists in pursuing research and development activities requiring such facilities and they are able to keep pace with developments

Contd...

taking pace globally. Thirteen Sophisticated Analytical Instrument Facilities (SAIFs) which provide sophisticated analytical instruments to users are functioning at IIT, Chennai and Mumbai; Bose Institute, Kolkata; CDRI, Lucknow, Panjab University, Chandigarh; NEHU, Shillong; Nagpur University, Nagpur; IISc, Bangalore; AIIMS, New Delhi; Gauhati University, Guwahati; IIT, Roorkee; CVM, Vallabh Vidyanagar, Gujarat and STIC, Cochin.

FIST: Launched in 2000-01, the fund for improvement of Science and Technology Infrastructure in Universities and Higher Educational Institutions or FIST provides support for basic equipment necessary for imparting quality teaching. Support is given for a period of 5 years. Support is aimed at two levels:

Level 1: Moderate funding for improving quality of teaching and research through modernization of labs and for augmenting library facilities (from relatively small but active departments).

Level 2: Substantial funding for acquiring state-of-the-art equipments and setting up labs for conducting internationally competitive research from well-established departments.

There are other organizations under DST, which provides a plethora of services. For instance:

1. Human Resource Development and Nurturing Young Talent

    i) Swarnajayanti Fellowships

    ii) Fast Track Scheme for Young Scientists (FAST)

    iii) Better opportunities for young Scientists in Chosen Areas of Science and Technology (BOYSCAST)

2. Women's Scientists Programmes

3. Kishore Vaigyanik Protsahan Yojana

4. Partial Financial Assistance for Participation in Conference Abroad.

5. Assistance to Professional Bodies and Seminar/Symposia

6. Earth System Sciences

7. Mathematical Sciences Office

8. Seismicity Programme

9. Utilization of the Scientific Expertise of Retired Scientists (USERS)

10. National Science and Technology Management Information System (NSTMIS)

The following Institutions have been set-up under Technology Development:

1. Instrumentation Development Programme

2. Technology Development Board

3. Joint Technology Programme

    i) Inter-Sectoral Science and Technology Advisory Committee (STAC/IS-STAC)

    ii) Technology Systems

    iii) Drugs and Pharmaceutical Research

    iv) Patent Facilitating Centre

    v) Good Laboratory Practice Authority

Lessons for India

A technology mission to Germany organised by the Indian Machine Tool Manufacturers Association (IMTMA) revealed that the Indian machine tool industry, in fact the manufacturing industry by and

Contd...

large has much to learn from Germany. There is a need for a structured interface between the academician, research and development institutes and the industry. Taking cue from their counterparts in Germany, the Indian industry needs to take active interest in research and development work. They need to come forward and fund research projects, instead of expecting the government to do it for them. And when a single company doesn't have enough funds, a consortium of sorts can be built, which will jointly fund the projects.

Technology spin offs

In every technology savvy country, the bulk of technological developments take place in the strategically important sectors like defence and aerospace. In most cases these technologies are not viable for civilian purposes. However, secondary technologies can often prove useful in civilian sector. Let's take the example of Uzi gun- the compact, boxy, lightweight submachine gun developed by Israel Military Industries. A special kind of cutting tool was developed to machine the barrel of this Uzi gun. And the cutting tool technology was sold to a company, which today has become a leading cutting tool player in the world. The company was Iscar.

Unfortunately such technology spin-off has not happened in India yet. Similar technology transfer can benefit the civilian sector greatly; as it would justify the large amount of money spent in the development of technologies in the defence, aerospace and other similar sectors.

Safeguarding the future

Finally India needs to safeguard its future by putting in place an apprentice- training programme similar to that of Germany. India does have industrial training institutes in form of ITI's. But its capacity to churn out trained workforce has been far from adequate. The industry laments that there is a disconnect between the skills in imparted in these institutes and the skills demanded in the market. According to a FICCI survey, the situation with regard to physical infrastructure and availability of power supply in the countries ITI's remains comfortable. However factors like non-availability of Computerized Numerically Controlled Machines (CNC), inadequate supplies of raw material and lack of focus on staff training and development are the key impediments in the way of strengthening these institutions.

Further, the fact that nearly 51 per cent of the participating ITI's reported under utilisation of seats indicates that the basic industrial traits offered by these institutes are becoming increasingly unattractive for their limited scope in terms of creating job opportunities. It is also to be noted that as against 107 trades that have been notified by the government, the maximum traits which any ITI covered in the survey offered were just 38 which reflect the deficient capability of the ITI's to ramp up their scale and offer new and more market oriented courses.

One of the key steps to revamp the ITI's is to strengthen industry- academia linkage. FICCI recommendations include:

1. Industrial visits of at least three weeks for the final year trainees should be made mandatory for all trades.

2. Industries should be associated to design need based short-term courses in the ITI's.

3. Industry should come forward to solve the shortage of raw material problem of it is by giving the job work to the ITI's.

In a nutshell, India Inc. needs to take active initiative in imparting training to the aspiring engineering students.

Taking it a step further, the Government could even introduce a law, which would make it mandatory for every company to participate in the training process. For instance, for every twenty workers that a company employs, it can be made compulsory to train one. It is high time that the industry instead of shrugging off all responsibilities by saying it is just the Government's job, comes forward and takes

Contd...

active part in the apprentice-training programme. The issue is of great importance in building an India of tomorrow and thus can't be left to mere affirmative action by the industry.

"FICCI has conducted a ground level survey amongst 100 it is identified by the government to be converted into centres of excellence. The survey, which saw participation from 69 out of a total of 100 it is to which the questionnaire was administered, is part of FICCI's efforts to highlight the key areas that require focused attention of both the government and the industry for strengthening the country's vocational training system.

Source: This article was published in the "Modern Machine Tools"-November 2006. Copyright with Infomedia India Limited. Reprinted with permission.

QUESTIONS FOR DISCUSSION

1. Intel, the largest manufacturer of microprocessors, sells a major chunk of their processors to personal computer manufacturers. However, it advertises its products to its final consumers. Why is then a large amount of money spend on advertising by Intel?

2. Discuss the concept of joint demand and derived demand, with the help of an industry example?

3. Industrial marketing is not only about exchange of products and services for money, but also exchange of information. How and why does this exchange happen?

4. The concept of industrial marketing is similar to that of consumer marketing. Do you agree or disagree on this statement?

5. Mr. Ratan Tata decides to buy a "Rolls Royce" for his personal use, and a corporate jet for his organisation. How would the buying process vary with respect to product, price, promotion, channels and buyer behaviour?

6. What is the impact of joint demand and derived demand on resellers?

7. How do we as consumers find it difficult to understand the complexities of B2B Marketing?

8. Why do we as students need to study the subject of industrial marketing?

chapter

TWO

The Industrial Markets

COMPANY PROFILE 2: BHARAT FORGE

Bharat Forge Ltd., the flagship company of the US $ 1.5 billion Kalyani Group, is a leading global **'Full Service Supplier'** of forged and machined – engine and chassis components. It is the largest exporter of auto components from India and leading chassis component manufacturer in the world. With manufacturing facilities spread over 9 locations and 6 countries - two in India, three in Germany, one in Sweden, one in Scotland, one in North America and one in China, the company manufacturers a wide range of safety and critical components for passenger cars, commercial vehicles and diesel engines. The company also manufactures specialized components for the railway, construction equipment, oil and gas and other industries. It is capable of producing large volume parts in both steel and aluminium.

Over the years, Bharat Forge has been investing in creating state-of-the-art facilities, world-class capacities and capabilities. Their facilities include, fully automated forging and machining lines, the largest of its kind and comparable to the best in the industry. Bharat Forge has built up a strong capability in design and engineering, including a full fledged product testing and validation facility, which gives Bharat Forge a Full Service Supply Capability – from product conceptualisation to designing, manufacturing and product testing, and validation.

Its customer base includes virtually every global automotive OEM and Tier I supplier. Daimler Chrysler, Toyota, BMW, General Motors, Volkswagen, Audi, Renault, Ford, Volvo, Caterpillar - Perkins, Iveco, Arvin Meritor, Detroit Diesel, Cummins, Dana Corporation, Honda, Scania and several others source their complex forging requirements including machined crankshafts, front axle beams and steering knuckles from Bharat Forge.

With significant global market share, Bharat Forge is ranked among the leading forging companies in the world. Its capabilities to manufacture complex forgings out of both steel and aluminium are a unique feature of BFL's competitiveness.

Bharat Forge is the largest manufacturer of crankshafts in India and the second largest worldwide with an annual production of over 5,000,000 crankshaft forgings. It enjoys a leadership position in the domestic market.

Bharat Forge is the largest manufacturer of Axle Beams in the world. It is a major supplier of axle beams to the world market and produces over 700,000 axle beams in a year. BFL caters to marquee OEM's in Europe and US with an US market share of over 50 per cent in class 7 and 8 trucks. Bharat Forge manufactures transmission parts for passenger cars and SUV's, used in highly sophisticated manual as well as automated transmission. Bharat Forge is a major player in the oil and gas segment, with products ranging from valves, chokes, casing heads, shells etc. in forged condition. Bharat Forge has developed forged components for high-pressure applications in the oil and gas industry.

With facilities in India and Europe, Bharat Forge offers end-to-end solutions to its global customers, based on its extensive technology, product design and product development expertise. The engineering centre processes are well-designed to adopt best practices and technology, and to continuously improve upon them to meet the growing challenges. The company also has a tool and dies manufacturing facility, forging facility, heat treatment facility, processing facility, machining facility, inspection and testing and logistics.

Our greatest strength is our ability to understand customer needs. Our ability to deliver unsurpassed quality and reliable products and services to our customers globally can be attributed to strong teamwork, continuous research and development and the dedication and commitment of each and every member of the BFL family.

Source: www.bharatforge.com

Mind Power I: Airbus in India

Airbus is one of the world's two leading aircraft manufacturers and, since delivering its first aircraft to an Indian operator over 30 years ago, has steadily grown to become the manufacturer of choice for the region. In 2005, Airbus won 70 per cent of the market share in India and this increased to 75 percent in 2006. From the early A300B2s for Indian Airlines to recent orders for the flagship A380 and the all-new A350 XWB for Kingfisher Airlines, that relationship continues to go from strength to strength, promising a bright future for airlines industry and passengers.

Airbus aircraft form the backbone of the Indian Airlines and Air India fleets, with Indian Airlines now the largest A320 operator in Asia and Air India established as the largest A310 operator in the world. They also play an increasingly important role with Jet Airways, India's low-cost pioneer Air Deccan and newer airlines such as Kingfisher Airlines, Indigo Airlines and Go Air.

Looking ahead, airlines in India are expected to invest over $100 billion in 935 aircraft with 100 seats or more by 2025. Thanks to the most modern and flexible airliner family in the world and an excellent customer support network, Airbus' expects to provide 60 percent of these aircraft.

Indian industry also benefits from close ties with Airbus, manufacturing parts and sub-assemblies, as well as providing engineering and IT Services

This began in 1988, when Hindustan Aeronautics Limited (HAL) of Bangalore was chosen to build passenger doors for the A320. This initial undertaking proved so successful that in 2004, Airbus extended the contract to cover a total of 1,000 sets of doors. Moreover, companies like CIM Tools and Maini from Bangalore have become part of Airbus supply chain, manufacturing details parts.

Airbus is also building industrial relationships directly or through its strategic partners with a number of other Indian companies including, Aetos, CADES, HCL, i2 Technologies, Infosys, Satyam, TCS, Tata Technologies and Wipro, all of whom provide Airbus with engineering and/or IT services to design and support its aircraft. In Hyderabad, Infotech opened a dedicated centre of excellence to work on technical publications for Airbus platforms at the end of 2005 and another dedicated centre on technical publications for Airbus platforms was opened by Aetos-Sonovision at the end of 2006 in Bangalore.

In second quarter of 2007, operations will begin at the Airbus Engineering Centre India in Bangalore, a fully owned subsidiary of Airbus. This will be a significant part of the EADS Technology Centre India to be set up in 2008. Focusing on high-end engineering analysis and design, the centre will be fully integrated into Airbus' global engineering network. The number of people employed at the centre will increase gradually over the next five years, with many indirect jobs likely to be created as a result of the centre's work with Airbus partners in the region. Airbus is also working with Canadian aircraft simulator manufacturer CAE to establish a training centre in the India in 2007. Such close international co-operation with Airbus contributes to the continued growth of India's economy, securing skilled jobs in an increasingly wide range of activities.

Source: www.airbus.com

Mind Power 2: New Determinants of Competitive Structures in Industrial Markets

Source: Authored by Prof. Jagdish N. Sheth Reprinted with permission of the author.

This paper suggests that the traditional theory of the firm assumption that competitive intensity is proportional to the number of competitors is not realistic. Instead, competitive structures are created

Contd...

by product and market differentiation. Four types of competitive structures are described, with examples: commodity markets, fragmented markets, differentiated markets and segmented markets.

Introduction

Theories of competition in microeconomics have been generally based on the realities of the times when they were developed. For example, in the reindustrialized age when the economy was dominated by the agricultural sector, theories of competition were based on the assumption of homogeneous products and therefore, competitive intensity was presumed to be strictly a function of number of suppliers in the marketplace. Indeed, most of the government antitrust policies and regulations related to the monopoly practices are still based on this assumption: competition is directly proportional to the number of competitors in the marketplace. The theory of the firm even provided us with such labels as monopoly (single supplier), oligopoly (concentrated few suppliers) and perfect competition (large number of small suppliers) to reflect this presumption.

With the emergence of the industrial age, it was discovered by several economists that competition and competitive structures are also a function of product or technological differentiation. For example, economists such as Chamberlain and Robinson suggested that product differentiations (real or psychological) created a certain degree of monopoly power for a supplier even when there were large numbers of suppliers in the industry. Since the traditional theories of competition could not explain this reality, it was necessary to broaden the determinants of competition to include both the number of suppliers and the degree of product differentiation. This led to a new form of competitive reality labeled as monopolistic competition.

Figure 2.1 represents this two-factor theory of competition.

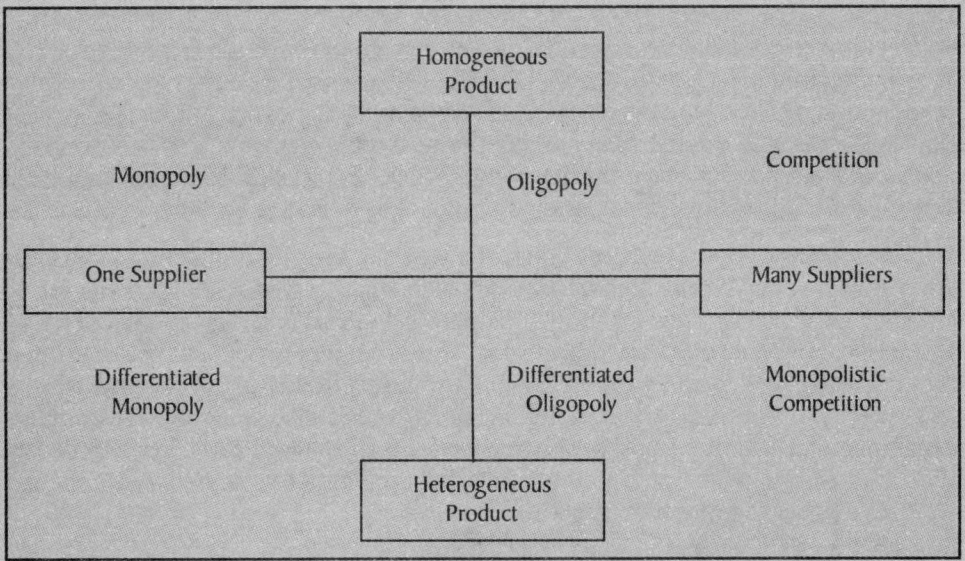

Figure 2.1: Economic Concepts of Competitive Structures

This broadening of the determinants of competition has been extremely useful to account for a large number of market realities of the industrialized economy.

First, it enabled to explain the prevalence of supplier or brand loyalty based on such non-price competitive factors as product differentiation, value-added services and even professional salesmanship.

Second, it clearly pointed out that not all monopolies are created equal and therefore, a monolithic regulatory process is inadequate. For example, it would be very difficult, if not impossible, to treat monopolies such as water and electricity which are based on homogeneity of products in the same

Contd...

category as monopolies of telecommunications and radio or cable communications which are clearly anchored to technology and value-add differentiations.

Third, it clearly demonstrated that the antitrust policies of the country needs to be amended or at least updated in light of a more complex set of determinants of competitive structures. In short, the present day antitrust laws may be outdated and unrealistic.

New Determinants of Competitive Structures

It is my contention that the revised theory of competition anchored to the two factors of product differentiation and number of suppliers is also becoming obsolete. It is being replaced by the new realities we are experiencing today as the economy shifts from the industrial to the post industrial age.

The new determinants of competitive structures seem to be anchored to the following two determinants: Product differentiation and Market differentiation. Furthermore, this is creating new and different types of competitive structures for which the traditional labels such as monopoly, oligopoly add monopolistic competition have no relevance. Therefore, we also need a new typology of competitive structures based on these new and emerging determinants of competitive structures.

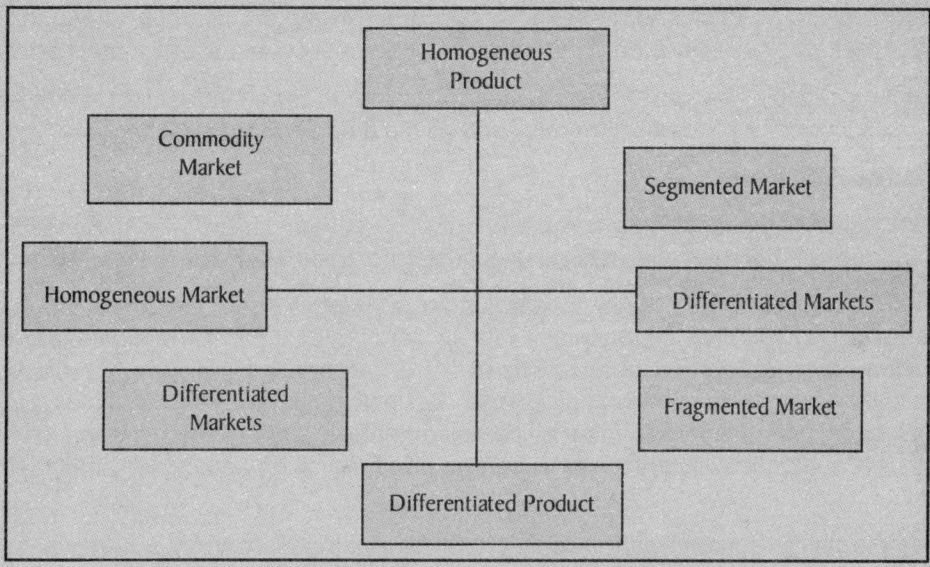

Figure 2.2: New Determinants of Competitive Structures

Figure 2.2 is an attempt to describe the new determinants and to generate a new typology of competitive structures. Each type of competition will be described and explained in some detail in the following pages. However, it is important to recognize that traditionally the most salient determinant of competition, namely number of suppliers, is conspicuously absent in the proposed typology. In other words, the new theory and its typology clearly reject the idea that monopoly is directly proportional to the number of suppliers in the marketplace. It is, therefore, possible to possess monopoly powers in an industry with a large number of suppliers and vice versa.

The four major competitive structures postulated in this paper are: Commodity market, Differentiated market, Segmented market, and Fragmented market. Each will be described below and illustrated with industrial examples.

Commodity Markets

In an industry characterized by homogeneity of technologies and markets, the competitive structures most likely to emerge is commodity markets. Commodity markets refer to the reality of a handful of

Contd...

suppliers manufacturing a highly streamlined product offering and marketing them to customers on a non-differentiated basis.

The driving force in the commodity market is cost efficiency and economies of scale with respect to both manufacturing and marketing operations. It is possible that the scale economies may favour only a single supplier in the industry resulting in the traditional definition of a monopoly situation. However, there are no presumed entry or exit barriers, and therefore, it is possible for a more cost efficient supplier to enter the market and successfully compete against the monopoly. For example, in many electromechanical industries such as tractors, earthmoving and earth digging equipment, the Japanese have successfully entered and taken the markets away from the American and European monopolies. On the other hand, it is possible for the monopolist to exit the market on a gradual basis. For example, several steel companies are presently exiting the markets due to the superior performance price ratios of substitute materials such as plastics.

Since cost efficiency and economies of scale are the driving forces in commodity competition, it is postulated that only three to four suppliers are likely to remain profitable. This is because it is likely to be uneconomical to divide the total industry capacity into smaller market shares.

The fundamental strategic issue in commodity competition is market share. Therefore, competitive strategies are likely to be designed and executed in order to protect or win a larger share of the market. These include acquisitions and mergers, price competition and share protection.

Commodity competition is becoming increasingly prevalent in many industrial markets including chemicals, semiconductors and basic metals such as steel and copper.

Differentiated Markets

Differentiated market is the most likely competitive structure in an industry where the market needs are homogeneous but there are alternate substitute technologies which can satisfy them.

Differentiated market refers to a reality in which a large number of suppliers provide specialized technologies and products to the marketplace with similar or even identical marketing programmes. There are numerous industries characterized by differentiated market. For example, the telecommunication industry is manifesting alternate technological bases between digital vs. analog PBX and between digital vs analog central office equipments. It is also demonstrating differentiated markets with respect to the cellular mobile vs central office switching and cable vs microwave local area networks.

Another example of differentiated market comes from the pharmaceutical industry in which each firm tends to have proprietary drugs which are offered to the same customers (hospitals and physicians) in the same manner.

The driving force in the differentiated market structure is strong RSD and highly proprietary products. Economies of scale and cost efficiency are less critical to competitive advantage. Therefore, the strategic issues are significantly different. The basic strategies for success are research and development acquisition, research and development and unique manufacturing expertise.

Segmented Markets

An industry characterized by a universal and versatile technology but catering to heterogeneous market needs is likely to manifest in segmented markets. Segmented markets refer to a reality in which a handful of suppliers offer a common but versatile technology to differ market segments on an application based differentiation. In general, suppliers practice highly specialized or differentiated marketing programmes for each segment, although their Research and development and manufacturing are more integrated.

The best industrial examples of segmented markets seem to be in the office automation industry. The universal but highly versatile technology of computerized data processing and data storage has

Contd...

enabled computer manufacturers to seek numerous applications specific to each segment. These include not only mainframe, minicomputers and microcomputer applications, but also manufacturing, payroll and telemarketing applications.

Another excellent example of segmented markets comes from the financial services including banking, brokerage and insurance. The applications of these universal but versatile services are quite different among business customers depending on their size and type of business.

The driving force in the segmented markets is application-based segmentation and customisation. A supplier capable of offering unique marketing programmes including industry specialized sales force and customized products or services is likely to survive and grow in this competitive structure. While market share is an important objective, it is achieved less by cost efficiency and more by value-added services customized to each segment.

The strategic issues facing a segmented market structure are market segmentation, market expansion and total systems approach. There are several good examples of suppliers following this competitive strategy including IBM and ATST.

Fragmented Markets

If a market is characterized by heterogeneous needs and heterogeneous means to satisfy those needs, the resulting structure is likely to be fragmented markets consisting of many specialists who cater to unique market segments.

Fragmented market reflects a reality of a large number of suppliers each controlling a small market share but still retaining strong supplier or brand loyalty. Each supplier has some unique technological or value-added differentiation and markets his products selectively to a target segment with a highly customized marketing programme.

It is more difficult to identify an industrial market with these characteristics. One good example comes from the large number of parts suppliers to automobile and appliance industries. Each parts supplier controls a very small share of the total market and at the same time, has a competitive advantage in terms of product or value-added differentiation. Another good industrial example comes from the custom shops for metal fabrication and metal mouldings.

The driving force of fragmented markets is niching or ultra-specialization. In fact, it is generally advantageous to aim for low market share rather than a higher market share. Both technological and application based ultra-specialization is necessary to survive and grow in fragmented markets.

The strategic forces in the fragmented markets are focus and expertise rather than market share and cost efficiency. Therefore, it becomes highly desirable to decentralize the organization which permits each unit to autonomously niche a fragmented part of the total market.

Summary

Here two new determinants of competitive structures have been identified in industrial markets. They are product differentiation and market differentiation. I have also suggested that the traditional theory of the firm which is based on the concept of competition equals number of competitors is probably obsolete. Furthermore, we need to replace the traditional typologies such as monopoly, oligopoly and perfect competitor with a new typology which reflects the new realities.

This paper has proposed the following four competitive structures: Commodity markets, Differentiated markets, Segmented markets and Fragmented markets. The driving force for a competitive advantage is likely to be different in each competitive structure. For example, cost efficiency and market share are the primary drivers in commodity markets whereas technical expertise and specialization are likely to be the primary drivers in differentiated markets.

Contd...

The theoretical speculations proposed in this paper do have a strong face validity in terms of illustrating each typology with certain industrial markets. However, it will be desirable to carry out an empirical study of all industrial markets with respect to product and market differentiation.

References

Archibald, G.C. (ed.) (1971). *The Theory of the Firm.* Baltimore, MD: Penguin Books.

Chamberlain, Edward (1933). *The Theory of Monopolistic Competition*, Oxford, England: Oxford University Press.

Meade, J.G. (1937). *Economic Analysis and Policy*, Oxford, England: Oxford University Press.

Robinson, Joan (1933). *The Economics of Imperfect Competition*, New York: MacMillan Publishing Co.

Porter, Michael E. (1980). *Competitive Strategy*, New York: Free Press.

Stigler, George J. (1946). *Theory of Price.* New York: MacMillan Publishing Co. Nissan and Mitsubishi Expand OEM Business.

THE INDUSTRIAL CUSTOMERS

As we have seen the difference between B2B and B2C marketing in the last chapter, what became clear that the kind of the business done in this particular market is different. The objectives of the buyer are completely different. The markets are characterized by huge amounts of diversity in the behaviour of the customers and products sold. Spares, components, accessories, service are only a part of this entire marketplace. What is very important in this chapter is the understanding as to how to pitch the clients and what buying process they generally do follow.

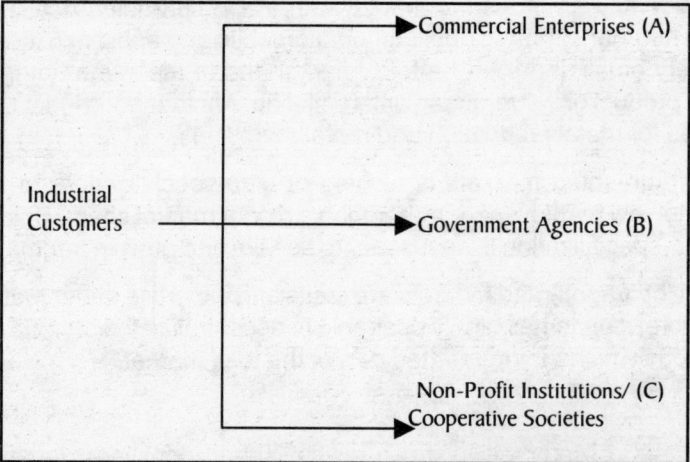

The industrial customers are divided into 3 groups. We will further understand them in greater detail.

Commercial Enterprises

Commercial enterprises such as Bajaj, Telco, Tisco, IBM and GM are companies which work for profit. They purchase goods and services, for their own use in the manufacture of final product, but do not sell it directly to ultimate customers. Since they have different purchasing purpose, it would be better if we understand it through their purchasing needs. Later, we will look into the strategies to tackle such enterprises. Broadly speaking.

We can divide the commercial enterprises into three categories. They are:

1.   Users

2. OEM's (Original Equipment Manufactures)

3. Industrial distributions and dealers

1. *User:* Commercial enterprises that purchase goods and services for consumption, may be as supplies, capital goods or materials for incorporation into their products, are known as users. The identity of the material used would be lost in the process. Let us say Indians railways buying diesel from Bharat Petroleum to run the diesel locomotives or it could be where the business or operation is facilitated with the use of such products like photocopying machines, type writers and computers.

2. *OEM:* It is also called "Original Equipment Manufacturer". When commercial enterprises buy products to incorporate in their final products, it is termed as OEM. For example, Intel Pentium chips for IBM notebooks or MRF tyres for Maruti 800 vehicles. In an oligopolistic market, OEM's are generally the largest volume users of goods. Also, an important thing that needs to be noted here is that both MRF and Intel offer products to the customers in the replacement market or after market, through industrial distributors. For example, if MRF is supplying tyres to Maruti, MRF will be called as an OEM parts suppliers. Component part suppliers must meet specification and also ensure quality, reliability and JIT delivery.

The replacement market or the after market is a huge size. These are generally the products which are subject to wear and tear, such as the headlights, steering wheels, oil filters, etc. Many component manufacturers look in for a share in the after market.

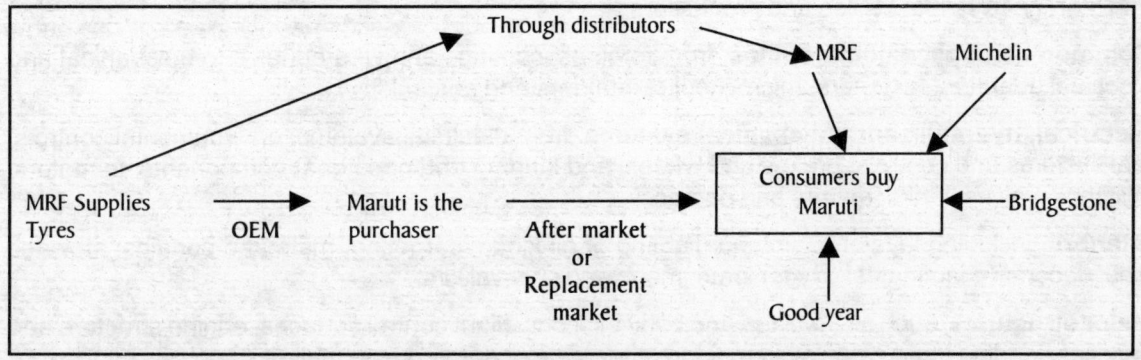

Mind Power 3: Nissan and Mitsubishi Expand OEM Business

Tokyo, April 3, 2007 — Nissan Motor Co. Ltd. and Mitsubishi Motors Corp. today announced that they have agreed to expand their current business collaboration by enhancing the OEM (Original Equipment Manufacturing) contract scope.

Under the expanded OEM agreement. Mitsubishi will supply Nissan with the "TOWNBOX" minicar at a volume of 4,000 units per year. Nissan will supply Mitsubishi with the "AD and AD Expert" Light Commercial Vehicles (LCV) at a volume of 3,000 units per year.

Mitsubishi has supplied Nissan with the "Clipper" (the Mitsubishi "Minicab") LCV and the "Otti" (Mitsubishi "eK Wagon") minicar, but this is the first time for Nissan to supply vehicles to Mitsubishi.

The agreement will allow both companies to improve productivity through expanded economies of scale, and offer their respective customers a wider range of products.

Source: http://media.mistubishi-motors.com/pressrelease/e/corporate/detail1614.html

3. *Industrial Distributors and Dealers:* When a commercial enterprise, purchases industrial goods and resells them in the same form termed as they are distributors and dealers. They are also

known as wholesalers, and act as middleman providing various kinds of facilities. Assortment of products is created by dealers. The function provided by the distributors is plenty, and may vary. (We will see this in detail, in a later chapter). They may be authorized distributors, holding products of a manufacturer or a general distributor, holding an assortment of products.

One point that needs to be clarified here is that, these categories are not mutually exclusive. If Maruti buys a machine tool for its manufacturing process, it is a user, but the some company becomes an OEM, when purchasing steering wheels for its cars. All products are viewed differently, because the purpose of purchase is different, for different class of customers.

Mind Power 4: What Boeing Buys

As the world's leading aerospace company, The Boeing Company buys billions of dollars worth of products and services each year. The goods and services Boeing buys fall into nine general categories.

Aerospace support, such as maintenance and modification labor, repair and overhaul services, spares, training services, engineering services, ground support equipment and specialized part handling and distribution.

Avionics and avionics components, including communication systems, display systems, cockpit instruments, navigation and guidance systems, mission management systems, sensors, recording and storage systems, cables and processors.

Common aerospace commodities, from forgings, castings and wire bundles to mechanical and electrical adapters, fasteners, microcircuits, retainers and sealants.

Electrical, hydraulic and mechanical systems, from electrical systems, environmental controls, fuel systems and controls, brakes and wheels and landing and nose gear components, to motors, switches, valves, tanks, meters and pumps.

Interiors, including lavatories; interior lighting of all kinds; carpeting, mats and curtains; stowage bins; decorative laminates; oxygen equipment; and survival kits.

Major structures, such as fuselage and body sections, flight control surfaces, engine structure and nacelles, landing gear, cargo systems and other large integrated assemblies.

Non-production goods and services, such as factory tools and supplies; facilities services and supplies; computing hardware, software and services; office equipment and supplies; contract labor; and financial products and services.

Propulsion systems, such as aircraft engines, liquid and solid propellant rocket engines, missile and rotary-wing propulsion systems, jet fuel starter and pyrotechnics.

Purchased outside production, including sheet metal and non-metallic products, machined parts, and tubing and ducting products and services.

As Boeing strives to improve the quality and cost of our products and services, we are constantly looking for new suppliers who offer us the best value and the strongest solutions to our customers' needs. Prospective suppliers can register their company's capabilities via the Boeing Supplier Introduction process.

Source: http://www.boeing.cora/companyoffices/doingbiz'esd//boeingbuys.html Reprinted with permission of Boeing Corporation.

GOVERNMENTAL AGENCIES

They form a major chunk of industrial purchasing groups for a nation. The purchase by the Indian government is for the various developmental projects that the government undertakes. The central government, state government, electricity boards, telecommunications, ministry of defense all from a part of government purchasing goods. The government buys every thing from pin, paper to missiles and jet fighters. They represent a huge chunk of the industrial market. They are widely dispersed, with large number of players, and over regulated. Procurement mechanisms, often through tender, with social goals as the driving force, needs to the kept in mind. Purchasing for governmental organizations is complex.

NON-PROFIT INSTITUTIONS AND COOPERATIVE SOCIETIES

Public and private institutions such as schools, colleges, churches are another important classification. Some of them have rigid rules for purchasing while other follow a casual approach. Cooperative societies are unique to India (Amul). It can be a manufacturing or non-manufacturing organization.

Mind Power 5: List of Items to be Purchased Centrally By Coal India Ltd

Heavy Earth Moving Machinery

1. Shovels over 2-1/2 cm m. capacity
2. Cranes over 30 Tonne
3. Front End Loaders above 3 or. m. Rock/3.6 en. m. Coal Bucket
4. Walking Dragline
5. Dumpers of all sizes (above 25 tonne capacity)
6. Dozers over 200 HP
7. Hydraulic shovels of all sizes (above 1 cu. m. bucket capacity)
8. Blast Hole Drills of all sizes

Underground and Surface Equipment

9. Road Headers and Dinters
10. Shuttle Car
11. Winders and Shaft sinking equipment
12. Self Advancing Supports/ Long wall Face Equipment
13. Dredgers
14. Gas Turbine
15. Captive Thermal Stations
16. Coal Cutting Machines
17. Shearers
18. Friction and Hydraulic Props and Bars
19. Stage Loaders

Contd...

20. Feeder Breaker (U/G)

21. Explosives

Capital Inputs

22. PVC Belting

23. Cement (Release and Allocation)

24. Iron and Steel (Release and Allocation)

25. Cap Lamp and its Spares

26. Billet and re-rolled 30 lbs rails

Safety Equipment

27. Environmental Telemonitoring Equipment

28. Self Rescuers

   R&D and Laboratory Items

29. Man Riding Haulage

30. Coal Analyzer

31. Infra Red Analyzer

32. Ash Analyzer

Others

33. Procurement of all equipments against World Bank Loan.

Source: Coal India Limited-Purchase Handbook-1986

CLASSIFYING INDUSTRIAL PRODUCTS

After we have seen the classification of industrial customers, we will now ask what type of goods do these customers need, when or how does a particular good enter a production process, and how are the cost of the goods affect the decision making process. "Classifying industrial goods gives the industrial marketer a better indication of the scope of the market, who is involved in the purchasing process, and what marketing factors affect the buying decision."[1]

There are 3 broad categories of industrial goods. They are:

1. Material and Parts

2. Capital Items

3. Supplies and Services

Entering Goods

These goods become a part of the finished product. They consist of raw material, manufactured materials and parts.

"**Raw materials**" consist of both farm products and natural products. Farm products would be wheat, rice, etc. Natural products would be iron ore, coal. They enter the production process with little or no alteration.

"**Manufactured Materials and component parts**" undergo more processing, i.e. some amount of processing is done to them before they enter the manufacturing process. For example, copper turned into wires or steel into sheets.

When we speak of component parts, it is the product which can directly be installed with little or no additional changes. When these products are sold, they are generally OEM. Examples would be tyres, microchips, displays and monitors.

Foundation Goods

These goods are capital items. A part of their cost is assigned as depreciation expense. They include installations and accessory equipments.

Installations are long-term investments such as factories, office buildings, generators, furnaces and computers. The demand for installation depends much on the economic climate, and also the outlook of the firm's products.

Accessories are less expensive, light and shortlived in comparison to installation, and do not form a part of fixed plant. They generally have wide usage compared to capital equipment. For example, the computers bought for all departments. Companies today are working towards leasing products to users.

Facilitating Goods

These support organizational operations, and do not become part of the finished product or support production process.

Supplies such as soaps, paper, clips, and staplers are required by organization for their day-to-day working. They are standardized and marketed to a broad cross section of users.

Services would be advisory services like management consulting, legal advisory service or could be the general maintenance and repair services of the machinery or the computer.

BUSINESS MARKETING STRATEGY

We have seen above a classification system. Now the involvement in purchasing a particular kind of product will vary from product to product. A marketing strategy suitable for one category of goods may be absolutely unsuitable for another. The promotion, pricing and distributional strategies also require to be altogether different.

Strategy for Manufactured Materials and Parts

If we remember these are the goods that we use in the manufacturing process. These goods would be either a standardized part or a customized part. In case it is a standardized part, it will include critical factors like pricing, delivery and services. In case the buyers are spread out, then the use of industrial distributors can be done. For customized parts, the best way of approach is personal selling. The sales man should be able to 'sniff' new markets and discover the uniqueness of various customers.

Strategy for Installations and Accessory Equipments

The cost and the risk involved are very high. Thus the need is a direct buyer seller interaction. For standardized products, intermediaries may be used. Negotiation generally here takes a lot of time. This buying decision will be taken on the 'outlook' of the firm on the business that they are into. Servicing support and heavy assistance from the time that deal is signed has to be maintained.

Strategy for Facilitating Goods

The supply items are generally served from multiple industries. A wide variety of intermediaries are required to cover this broad area. Personal selling here will be of very little use (e.g., think of you going to every business house and selling papers). Catalogue listing, advertising and through distributors would be the primary mode of reaching the customers. Since products in this market will be undifferentiated, branding and price will play a very important role. Assortment of goods, timely delivery and better prices would be the key for facilitating goods.

ORGANIZATIONAL BUYING

Organizational buying is a very complicated process with a broad range of customers. These customers know their products and their requirements. They are very realistic of an innate value of a product. Thus the buyers generally select suppliers who would be providing them with the greatest value. Thus, we require to know clearly as to how the buying process takes place for a diverse range of markets, products and situations.

The Purchasing Department

It is one of the most important departments of an industrial organization, because the total inventory cost at any point of time would be about 50 to 60 percent of the sales revenue. Not only this, the objectives of the purchasing department varies considerably with other departments, and clashes are seen frequently. For example, a supplier might be supplying goods to you, at a very low cost, but does not adhere to his delivery schedule, then what? To the purchasing department this might be ok, but definitely not to the production department.

Purchasing department has few most important jobs to take care of. They are:[2]

1. Uninterrupted flow of materials

2. Manage inventory

3. Control quality

4. Developing and managing relationship with suppliers

5. Achieving low costs

6. Betterment of a firm's competitive position.

This department must ensure flow of raw materials to ensure that production is not hampered at any point of time. The purchasing department also has an objective to reduce the level of inventory to its minimum, because high inventory implies high cost. To check the quality of products, so as to ensure minimum amount of defects from the final products and less rejection. (Xerox, allows only those suppliers, who are 'ISO' certified). Low cost of purchase for the inventory and better supplier relationships over a period of time also is an objective for the purchase department. One more important objective is to reduce supply chain costs and thereby creating a cost differential advantage. Working closely with suppliers and a well-integrated system helps both the seller and the buyer.

Before selling a product the marketer must realize what value does the product contain. If it is something to do with the style of the final product and the importance of the final product you sell is high, you will have better impact. For example, if you are suppliers of highest quality leather to Mercedes Benz, which acts as a fashion statement to the car, the impact will be higher.

One more recent trend that is seen is the use of Internet and Intranet facilities for procurement. Indian companies like Tata's and Ashok Leyland has such a practice in place. This reduces the overall transaction costs for both the buyer and seller. E-purchasing has a long way to go.

Purchasing in Commercial Enterprise

The goods and services purchased in a commercial enterprise depend on the nature and size of business. It will also depend on volume, variety and technical complexity of the product.

In these organizations there would be **multiple influencers** who would be playing their role in the decision-making process. Thus, multiple techniques like material planning, supplier rating, value analysis are used by buyers. The influences can be from production, engineers, accountants, middle and upper management, etc.

For example, if Maurya Sheraton would have to purchase cooking oil for the kitchen, it would be heavily influenced by the executive chef, who would be using the product. Knowledge of what a customer wants, the products which can fulfill such needs and the capabilities of competition is essential. A very realistic perception of the needs can be done through a process called **Value Analysis**.

Value analysis is an intensive appraisal of all the elements of the design, manufacture or construction, procurement, inspection, installation and maintenance of an item and its components, including the applicable specifications and operational requirements in order to achieve the necessary performance, maintainability and reliability of the item at minimum cost.[3]

The major steps that involve the buying process are:

1. Identifying the p1 electing suppliers

2. Manage Inventory

3. Control Quality

4. Ensuring the maintenance of order schedules

5. Feedback system of the supplier

The complete process of purchasing assumes a very important role in the organization. 50 to 60 percent of the revenue is spent on purchase. Thus saving of operational costs, good quality material can contribute to a company in a big way.

Ford, GM, Jacuzzi Motor, Xerox have used the system of purchasing very effectively and has given way to their companies competitive advantage.

Purchasing in Government Enterprise

They form the biggest chunk of industrial purchase. To understand the purchasing process, we must try and appreciate two most important factors. They are:

1.   Widely dispersed

2.   The procurement mechanism is complicated and time consuming

Buying in these institutions is absolutely a different game. It may be centralized or decentralized. The government agencies have set standard terms and conditions, which all suppliers must fulfill. One needs to appreciate the fact, the relative bargaining power for them is better and stronger. The process that is generally followed is:

1.   Registering the name of the company with government units

2.   A quality check is done of the seller

3.   For standard products, tenders are floated

Tenders would be open or closed tenders. In case of closed tenders, tender enquiry is sent to only a few suppliers. For open tender, it is advertised. Based on the lowest price bid, the orders are offered to the lowest bidder.

Purchasing in Institutions

They constitute the last part of business market. Institutional buyers make a sizeable market. School, universities, colleges, health care, universities, libraries, comprise this sector. They are quite similar to governmental purchases and some similar to a purchase in a commercial enterprise. Since many institutions are constrained by political considerations, a marketer needs to be very cautious in their approach.

In this market, say for example in a hospital the responsibility may quite much be on the dietician. In some other cases the purchases may be contracted out. Because of this multiple variations excessive caution, needs to be put and directing the sales force to tailor make marketing efforts to each situation.

There would be a great deal of conflict between those responsible for the purchasing function and the professional staff for whom the purchasing department is buying. The sales person, must develop a strong relationship with the professional staff.

Another important factor is group purchase. They purchase as a group to avail quantity and cash discounts. Here the marketer must be able to deal with individual institutions and also special purchasing requirements of joint purchases. The buying centers or the people taking decision will vary considerably.

Also distribution to each member should be done promptly. Thus, there is a strong need to have a strong distributor network.

Purchasing in the Resellers Market

Vendors in the resellers market are evaluated on their expected contribution towards sales volume and profits. Buyers in this market are not only interested in the products of potential suppliers but in their marketing policies as well (e.g. their choice among intensive, selective or exclusive distribution, and there attitude towards co-operative advertising and the provision of point of purchase displays).[4]

Mind Power 6: Tata Steel Ventures into Steel Retailing Launches 'Steel Junction': India's First Organized Steel Retail Outlet

Kolkata, December 13, 2005

'Steel Junction' – India's first organized steel retail store, envisions to create a unique organized, retail experience that displays the versatility of steel - from its functionality to its aesthetics. Further it will bring innovation to steel product make steel buying pleasurable. 'Steel Junction' is a midsize, specialty store, which, will retail a range of steel oriented products 'all under one roof. It will offer shopping experience, better quality of products, greater time and money value the customer through its comprehensive range, services and in-store facilities. Wide aisles, warm ambience, pleasant sales personnel will welcome the customer. The format will allow families to step in and involve more and more women in process of buying steel. Well-displayed and stocked shelves, signage, competitive prices will help them browse and choose. New designs and innovative products will engage them. Information, consultancy service and advice will facilitate right selection. Concept kiosks and displays, which showcase the product, will enable them to visualize and promote impulse buying.

Source: http://www.tatasteel.com/newsroom/press275.asp
Courtesy: Tata Steel

EVALUATING PERFORMANCE OF SUPPLIERS

Suppliers are evaluated on a continuous basis (probably an quarter or half yearly) to understand the performance level of each supplier. This data sheet is handed over to the suppler, or discussed, with areas demarcating the positive and negative aspects. Generally weights are assigned to a multiple factors considered important by the buyer. The marketer should always try and improve on areas of weakness. If a product is standardized, focus should be laid upon price. If the product is unique, focus should be more on other criteria's like servicing and on time delivery. Economic criteria for a purchase play a significant role, as well as performance criteria of a product. A more detailed discussion of this will happen in chapters to follow.

An example of a supplier rating chart is given below:

Criteria/Subcriteria	Weight					
Quality	30%					
Product Quality	40%					
Corrective Action Management	35%					
Quality Management Policies/ Practices/Processes	15%					
Document Management Quality	10%					
	Weight					
Delivery/Schedule	30%					
SPI	25%					
Schedule/Delivery Subcontract SDRLs and Product	25%					
Schedule/Delivery Services	25%					
Schedule/Delivery improvement Efforts	25%					
	Weight					

Contd...

Technical	20%				
Technical Compliance	50%				
Product Development Participation	20%				
Technical Process and Systems	15%				
Technical Project Management	15%				
	Weight				
Price/Cost	10%				
CPI	30%				
Cost Reduction Efforts	30%				
Accurate & Timely	25%				
Payment Term Flexibility	15%				
	Weight				
Management	15%				
Management Compliance	40%				
Communication	20%				
Representation	20%				
Sub-Tier Supplier Management	20%				
	Weight				
Responsiveness	15%				
Timeliness	35%				
Customer Focus	35%				
Effective Communication	30%				

Note: The percents are defaults and can be altered
Courtesy: Raytheon: Accessed on 12th January 2007
Source: http: //raysrs.raytheon.com/srsrc/dl/supplier_self_assess.xls

CONCLUSION

Customers in this market are a very diverse group, classified as commercial enterprises, governmental agencies and institution. Commercial enterprises also classified as users, OEM's and distributors. We also saw the difference between material and parts, capital items and supplies and services. Purchasing thus is a very specialised activity and requires a lot of planning and control.

References

1. George Risley, " *Modern Industrial Marketing*" (New York: McGraw Hill) ; pp 22-24.

2. Leenders and Fearon, "*Purchasing and Supply Management*", 11th edition-Chicago Irwin, pp 34-37.

3. Richard and Nicholas, "*Production and Operation management*", Section 3-406. 3; pp 567.

4. Michal E. Leenders, Harold and Wilbur, "*Purchasing and Materials Management*", pp 490.

Mind Power 7: How to Analyze the Supply Market

By Staff
Purchasing
March 1, 2007

Strategic sourcing is at the heart of the purchasing function. Yes, there are plenty of other important skills that purchasing professionals must possess, but analyzing the supplier market, identifying potential suppliers to work with, deciding how you'll work with them, planning your negotiations strategy, integrating suppliers into your business and monitoring their performance are absolutely critical for successful purchasing and supply chain management.

With this issue, we start a series on how purchasing staffs at a variety of companies organize their strategic sourcing activities. We've structured the series according to a version of the classic sourcing process described by consultant firm A. T. Kearney and used by such companies as United Technologies, which recently won the Purchasing magazine Medal of Professional Excellence. On these pages, you'll read how some of your peers try to understand the competitive pressures prospective suppliers are under and how those pressures could affect their performance.

Dive deeper

Deb Lynch, director of sourcing and supply management at outdoor products maker Toro Co. in Bloomington, Minn., says the four-quadrant supplier categorization process is the best base for any future sourcing activity. Putting suppliers into four categories (leverage, strategic, transactional, and bottleneck) helps identify overall trends and opportunities in the supply markets, she says.

"Of course, the transactional and bottleneck categories are easier to identify," she adds. "Determining which suppliers are strategic and which can provide leverage is more difficult".

Lynch says she has been doing more analysis of suppliers' cost structures than in the past. At the broader level, Toro tracks supplier industry margins and evaluate its suppliers' margins vs those typical in that industry to ensure suppliers are "profitable, but not too profitable."

"We track raw material prices and know what percentage of the product we're buying is made of that raw material, so we have an idea of when and how our suppliers are impacted," she points out. "We also track labor costs by global region—and I mean one region of China vs another—so when a supplier pushes a cost increase out we have this data available."

Lynch says one aspect that many buyers may overlook when it comes to analyzing a supplier or supply base is the outcome of the last bidding cycle in that area. For example, if the supplier that is awarded the business backs out of the contract or declares material price increases or quotes on new business at a much higher rate, it's typically a sign that the individual supplier or supply base in that area is struggling.

When a certain supply area—or a specific supplier—is not competitive enough, Toro runs joint cost-reduction programmes with the supplier(s) to improve the margins and competitiveness in that supply base that will benefit future sourcing events. In fact. Lynch says joint cost savings agreements are now standard in most Toro supply agreements.

"We agree to share continuous improvement resources and cost savings with suppliers, and they agree to do the same," she says. There are some suppliers that resist these joint cost reduction projects, taking the "if it isn't broke, then don't fix it" philosophy.

Lynch says Toro's experience with e-sourcing has taught her about supply base analysis.

"Of course, we work to understand our supply base prior to an e-sourcing event, but the events themselves provide us with a lot of information about the competitiveness in that area and which

Contd...

sourcing strategy will work best," she says. "When we issue an e-RFQ, the format allows suppliers to provide more feedback on how they would prefer to see the lots structured to provide their best price package. It also allows them to provide feedback on process improvements, or improvements in packaging or design to help us all reduce costs."

Build a team approach

Over the years, Jeff Bruett has learned that "the law of supply and demand ultimately determines market costs and prices, so his buying team can't be a 900 lb gorilla dictating terms and conditions to the supply base." That's especially important for the automotive division purchasing manager of connector maker FCI because "we have to work with our suppliers to get their best efforts, not just their best prices.

That's why Bruett's 10-member procurement staff works to engender a team approach with the 100 or so suppliers, in supervising the sourcing of $45 million in direct materials. "We know that these businesses have to make money, provide quality materials and be innovative on new products," he says. "At the same time, they have to fulfill their obligations to provide on-time deliveries of functional-quality materials at competitive prices and to have the tactical and technical ability to resolve problems when they occur and plan for the future."

Bruett is the divisional purchasing manager for North American automotive operations at FCI, a producer of connectors and interconnect systems for electrical, automotive and electronic applications. This division is a tier-three supplier to General Motors, Ford Motor and Chrysler Group. Bruett's procurement group also sources around $20 million/year in MRO materials, office products and capital equipment from an average 350 active suppliers. The purchasing organization supports automotive connector manufacturing plants in West land, Mich., Markham, Ont., and Juarez, Mexico.

"The fact is that we are analyzing supply performance for direct materials on a regular basis; if the suppliers we have are doing the job, they are selected for more business," says Bruett in an interview. "Sometimes, suppliers fall down because of competitive pressures. It doesn't matter the reason why, we have to make objective decisions on performance—whether the suppliers are doing their job or not—and, if necessary, fix the problem or change suppliers."

"We buy 65 million meters a year of copper insulated wire, enough to go around the earth twice," Bruett says.

The FCI procurement team uses standard potential-supplier evaluations of product capabilities, quality control systems, manufacturing process management and operating procedures—using standard measurable metrics. The goal, of course, is perfect quality. FCI analyzes firms for quality of products available and looks at history of on-time deliveries, whether early, on target or late; functional quality based on history of supply measured in parts per million, and quick or late response to customer complaints.

So, what FCI automotive really wants is total value from its suppliers, "meaning a combination of price, quality, delivery and service." The philosophy is that a great price means nothing if the quality is suspect. Similarly, great quality is meaningless if there's no on-time delivery. Also, service has to include value-added performance, not just resolving delivery or technical problems.

There always is an interdepartmental approach in supervising the supply base so that purchasing, advance engineering and manufacturing get feedback from the assembly operations and from the Big Three. That's important, Bruett says, because the end customers—the automakers—directed about 15 percent of which connector systems and which component suppliers are to be used. For the other 85 percent of supply, "we at FCI need to know if the companies we have selected are doing the job; that is, if they are providing what they were selected to provide," Bruett says.

— **Tom Stundza**

Contd...

Quiz your peers

After they've tapped databases and online sources, MRO purchasing professionals simply pick-up the phone and talk to people on their commodity teams and, even, colleagues at other companies to analyze the supplier market.

When he was at the Kansas City, Mo. based Hallmark Inc., Darren D. Wright, former category manager—MRO, global procurement, would solicit information from databases on his desktop, and later consult with other purchasing professionals who work for companies located nearby. He lists Sprint and Yellow Roadway as two examples, but says he contacts buyers at smaller companies as well. He calls it his local area, or regional, network. For him, 'it's typically an informal process, but he says he also meets buyers through the local chapter of the Institute for Supply Management.

"Whether positive or negative, word of mouth really helps in analyzing the supply market," says Wright. "A colleague may say that he or she wouldn't touch ABC supplier with a 10-ft. pole for a particular reason. That doesn't mean I won't consider them, but it does mean that my antenna is up to do a little more investigation."

He adds that it isn't difficult to find information on the markets for the MRO items he purchases. "However, it is hard to find good suppliers. You need to be cautious and try to take the personal or emotional piece out of the equation," pointing out that those he consults with may sometimes refer suppliers with whom they have a personal relationship.

— Susan Avery

Hold regular meetings

Purchasers at the Toronto-based electronics manufacturing services provider Celestica meet about 200 key suppliers every three months to discuss a variety of issues, including pricing trends and supply conditions, says Harvinder Sembhi, vice president, supply chain strategy and planning. The goal? Make sure Celestica is getting the best total cost of ownership from suppliers.

"At the meetings, we give them an update on the state of business and what our customers are asking for and what our price pressures are," he says. "At the same time they give us a business update as well, where they see the market going, where they see commodity pricing."

He adds that prior to the meetings; Celestica's commodity managers examine component pricing and review "purchasing associations' numbers and market reports" from researchers such as iSuppli and Gartner for commodity-specific intelligence.

"For instance with connectors they would take a look at The Bishop Report that gives specific information about connectors," says Sembhi.

In some cases, Celestica gets pricing information from its OEM customers that have contracts with suppliers and share their pricing information. In other cases, Celestica gets information from RFQs sent to multiple suppliers.

Sembhi says Celestica wants to understand the pricing pressures that its suppliers face. However, Celestica expects suppliers to find ways to deal with that pricing pressure.

"A supplier's standard answer cannot be 'my commodity pricing went up so I have to increase pricing," he says. Celestica wants to hear from suppliers what efficiency measures the supplier has taken to improve their manufacturing process and in their logistics operations to reduce cost.

Celestica also does a breakdown analysis of the parts and materials a supplier provides so it can understand their costs. "What is their material cost? What is their labor rate per hour? In some cases what are their scrap allowances?" he says.

The breakdown analysis factors in flexibility terms the supplier may provide. "Are they giving us vendor-managed inventory, shorter lead times, better payment terms? Are they rewarding you for

Contd...

getting their products into the market? We look at a total cost-of-ownership score for suppliers and decide who is awarded business," says Sembhi.

He says Celestica often can determine the supplier's margin and compare prices and margins to other suppliers.

"We aren't trying to squeeze their margins. We recognize that they have to make some money. Our point is to get the best total landed cost pricing," says Sembhi.

— Jim Carbone

Check the records

Roy Calderon spends a large part of his day trying to understand the competitive situation of his suppliers. The Latin America sourcing manager for H.B. Fuller, a manufacturer of adhesives, sealants and coatings based in St. Paul, Minn., Calderon employs a variety of strategies to find out what his suppliers are paying for their raw materials so he can anticipate any incoming price changes.

"In some countries, import records are public information, so that means I can go to the import records and see what they're importing and what prices they're using," says Calderon. "That gives me an idea of how the market is moving...how much my suppliers are paying for their basic raw materials." In nations where import records aren't available, Calderon goes to his second or third-tier suppliers to find out how their raw materials prices may be fluctuating. "Based on that information I can predict whether my supplier is getting a better or worse raw material cost, or if they're having problems getting raw materials, and that will affect my supply and demand," he says.

Suppliers' locations also come into play when Calderon considers any difficulty they may be facing. If a supplier's host nation is experiencing any kind of civil unrest or economic problem, he can anticipate whether or not that supplier will have a problem getting their materials through.

All this information that Calderon gathers is helpful to him in price negotiations, especially in debating any price increases a supplier might try to pass along. On the other hand, if he notices a price drop in a raw material one of his suppliers uses, he "proactively push[es]" that supplier about the decrease in costs and how that will be passed along to him. "Instead of me waiting for them to come back to bulk material price reductions, I am knocking on their door, saying that their raw material price is going down by 15 percent, and if this raw material is 30 percent of their manufacturing costs, I will expect at least a 5 percent price adjustment," he says.

This works both ways. If Calderon sees that a supplier's raw material costs are going up, he will anticipate the price increases coming his way up between 30 to 45 days ahead of time. In some cases, he can communicate price increases ahead of time to minimize any impact on the company's gross margin. "There are many things we can do creatively to avoid that impact, and if we know beforehand, it's going to help us."

— Maria Varmazis

Mind Power 8: "B2b" Means "Back to Basics" For Now

The e-commerce (EC) hype wave is history, but we are still in the 6th year of a 12 to 15 year e-commerce revolution. The raw fuel for yesterday's digital economy dream is still in place; the explosive growth rates will continue for chip power, Internet interconnectivity, bandwidth capacity and digital commerce software solutions.

The "next big thing(s)" for EC could still be 3 to 5 years away or never. Those applications, for example, that assume most businesses will have continuously on, reliable, big bandwidth connections

Contd...

- "webtone"- will be delayed. The telecom start-up companies that were building the digital infrastructure are crashing for lack of cash, so former monopoly companies have gone back to glacial-speed rollouts at higher prices.

Industry supply chain consortia are quickly finding out that creating new e-standards that can stay current while everyone in a given industry actually uses them is a long-term bet at best. Buyers that are using reverse auction exchanges are finding that lowest prices from new suppliers are not as good a total deal as the lowest total procurement cost supply systems from old suppliers. Local suppliers, it turns out, have customer-tuned inventory service levels and services that constantly evolve while providing shock absorption insurance for unforeseen disruptions within supply chains.

There are, however, lots of little EC applications emerging that will gradually affect distribution channels over the next 12 to 18 months. Most of these applications will be services that help traditional individuals or departments within distribution channels keep doing what they are doing more efficiently or effectively.

Examples of specific web-based applications (and vendors) that can make traditional channels more efficient in a down turning economy without disruptive side effects are:

1. Partner relationship management software packages for manufacturers that sell to and through independent channel partners, (www.haht.com).

2. Digital media and content management services that will repackage product information in databases for faster, easier access for anyone in a channel to access (www.steadyrain.com).

3. Store and access services for business documents that allow trading partners to passively adopt paperless relations *(www.webarchive.net and www.channelinx.com).*

4. Channel service utility companies that allow equipment dealers to find and buy parts faster *(www.arinet.com).*

5. Real time e-point rewards for all types of channel incentives down to the individual education and motivation level *(www.emaritz.com).*

Keeping on top of both short-term and long-term EC opportunities is important, but even more pressing amongst distributors is the erosion of basic operational profitability. Annual financial performance reviews published by distribution trade associations reveal steady erosion in profitability for all distributors over the past few years, well before the economy started turning down. Why?

BACK TO BASICS

Most businesses have been so preoccupied with both the EC and Y2K hype storms that started sequentially with the Netscape IPO in mid-'95 that they have forgotten to address the following profitability problems:

1. Hiring and keeping good employees who can in turn give desired result.

2. Measure, achieve, maintain, sell, get paid for and leverage basic service excellence.

3. Measure customer profitability to maintain and grow the winners and shape up or out the losers?

4. THEN, use the extra time, talent and profitability that results from the first three measures to take first and best advantage of the near term and then long-term EC opportunities that will arise in each distribution channel?

These basic operational opportunities can not be solved, however, until the average CEO truly believes in and puts into practice high-performance service management principles like:

1. Paying more and investing more into frontline employees to get a lot more in return. UPS, FedEx and L.L. Bean are companies known for zero errors, 100 percent on time delivery and

Contd...

good value pricing. They pay 30 percent to 50 percent more in total compensation for warehouse people and drivers than the average wage for those jobs. But, they skim the very best work ethic people from other local employers and invest in their education to cross-train them at many different service steps. Perfect service and high employee and customer retention economics allow them to achieve 200 percent of the average margin dollar per employee ratio for a great return on their employees.

When will most executives really believe their own statement that "employees are our most important asset" and pay and invest accordingly? When will most learn that "hire them cheap and work them hard" works only when the owner is the 80 hour per week foreman in a perpetually small business?

2. Wiring every employee's wallet, mind and heart into achieving basic service brilliance for one niche of customers at a time. What would the average frontline service employee say to these questions? Who are your company's 5 most profitable customers? What are those customers' most important service measurements in priority order? Where do you post those measurements everyday to insure that they happen? What can you do directly or indirectly to make sure those metrics happen? Why should you care about any of these questions, what's in it for you? If the answers are: "don't know, don't like not knowing, and nothing more in it for me", then the company has big economic upside possibilities for all stakeholders.

3. Totally informating the working environment so that every employee can be responsible for growing reinvested profits by being part of the solution to improve service and productivity goals. Playing a game with no way of keeping score or knowing how we are progressing toward some measurably excellent goal is not fun. If our occupational pride and well being is at stake, then its time to leave if we have any ambition. Distinctive service is the only competitive edge for most distributors, and it can't happen without information feedback to the people who must make it happen.

Source: Copyright with "The Merrifield Consulting Group". Visit them at www.merrifield.com. Reprinted with permission.

QUESTIONS FOR DISCUSSION

1. How does selling to commercial enterprises and governmental agencies vary?

2. How can a company be classified by some business markets as a user and others as an OEM customer?

3. You are a manufacturer of electronic items. Due to cumbersome policies and practices followed, you have avoided the governmental customers. But now, it is becoming absolutely necessary to open up new fronts? How would you approach the government customers?

4. Your company manufactures "power drills. How will you go about marketing it?

5. Your company manufactures "papers" and other accessories. How would you go about marketing them?

6. You are supplying copper to a wire manufacturer? You have just learnt that your competitors are going to approach the wire manufacture, with the objective to "kill" you? How do you defend your company's position?

7. Supplier rating forms a key component for the industrial buyer? Why?

chapter

THREE

Industrial Marketing Environment

COMPANY PROFILE 3: ACC (ASSOCIATED CEMENT COMPANY)

ACC Limited is India's foremost manufacturer of cement and ready mix concrete with a countrywide network of factories and marketing offices. Established in 1936, ACC has been a pioneer and trendsetter in cement and concrete technology. The brand name is synonymous with cement and enjoys a high level of equity in the Indian market. It is the only cement company that figures in the list of Consumer Super Brands of India. Among the first companies in India to include commitment to environment protection as a corporate objective, ACC has won several prizes and accolades for environment friendly measures taken at its plants and mines. The company has also been felicitated for its acts of good corporate citizenship.

ACC Cement is the most commonly used cement in all constructions including plain and reinforced cement concrete, brick and stone masonry, floors and plastering. It is also used in the finishing of all types of buildings, bridges, culverts, roads, water retaining structures, etc. What is more, it surpasses BIS Specifications on compressive strength levels. They have specially blended cement, produced by inter-grinding higher strength Ordinary Portland Cement clinker with high quality processed fly ash based on norms set by the company's Research and Development Division.

ACC is the pioneer of the Indian cement industry with over 66 years of rich experience in prospecting for raw materials, setting up and managing cement plants of different sizes, technologies and processes. This experience is shared by our team of talented Scientists, Engineers and Technocrats in meeting the needs of the cement industry in India and in many other countries. ACC has a successful track record in modernizing old technology based cement plants to improve their operational economy and also in the design and engineering of new technology based cement plants. Our project engineering consultancy and project management expertise has been tested against the best in the world. ACC's team of qualified geologists has over 60 years of experience in India and abroad, offering valuable services in the following areas:

1. Complete Raw Material Assessment for Cement Industry

2. Topographic Survey

3. Diamond Core Drilling

4. RC Drilling

5. Computerized Ore Body Modelling

6. Mine Planning

ACC's Environment Management Division delivers world-class air pollution control systems, equipment and custom designed solutions for a number of process industries in India and abroad.

Sustainable development is recognized by us as a process of development that "meets the needs of the present without compromising the ability of future generations to meet their own needs". We believe this constitutes balancing the Triple Bottom Line — defined as the achievement of three interdependent and mutually reinforcing goals of economic development, social development, and environmental protection.

ACC has a countrywide spread of 14 modern cement plants and a string of 13 Ready mix concrete plants. This large network of manufacturing units consumes a wide spectrum of inputs - about 60,000 different items ranging from Coal, Gypsum, Slag, Packaging material (bags), Refractory, Steel, Grinding Media, Electrodes, Cables, Bearings, Conveyor Belts, spares of various mechanical, electrical and instrumentation equipment, mining equipment and their spares and explosives.

ACC has a vendor base of more than 6000 suppliers spread across the country. A team of 144 professionals at Corporate, Region and Plant Level manages the procurement function at ACC. The function is organized so as to derive maximum value for the company through economies of scale from central pooling and procurement of some inputs at the corporate level while meeting individual operational requirements at plant level.

Source: www.acclimited.com

Mind Power I: Steel Outlook: Disagreement Reigns on Steel Price, Supply

Mills predict price hikes soon. Buyers reject that view, saying that weak demand won't recover for some months to come.

By Tom Stundza

Purchasing

February 15, 2007

Steel producers in the fourth quarter wrestled with falling prices, high supply levels and weaker North American demand. That's why carbon and alloy steel prices dropped 4 per cent in the final stanza even though they increased 5 per cent for the year. Faced with high customer inventories and record import levels, North American steel producers have reduced production and shipments and seen month-on-month prices fall short of their estimates. This quarter, though, despite the best efforts of the domestic steel mills to manage supply, prices have continued to ease because demand remains soft and imports remain high.

"Disappointment with the fourth quarter of last year and optimism for the first quarter of 2007 are consistent commentary from steel producers," says analyst Randy Cousins at BMO Capital Markets in Toronto. But, "falling demand, excess inventories and persistently high imports are taking their toll on pricing." In their latest report to Wall Street, executives at Charlotte, N.C.-based Nucor acknowledge that inventory corrections at service centers and original equipment manufacturers are continuing, as are domestic production cutbacks; saying "however, the continued record levels of imports of finished steel are delaying this inventory correction."

Looking ahead, neither the analysts, buyers nor their suppliers agree on the steel market. What's obvious is that the sharp pullback in housing and automotive activity in the second half of 2006 expanded into the production of related materials and supplies, major appliances, machinery and heavy trucks. But the demand outlook projections range from an increase of 2 per cent to a decline of 3 per cent while supply forecasts range from flat with 2006 to growth of 7 per cent. Purchasingdata.com sees a 1.4 per cent increase in purchasing activity.

Domestic output was slashed during the third and fourth quarters by domestic producers of cars and light trucks in an effort to reduce elevated inventories-particularly of minivans, sports utility vehicles and pickup trucks. Last October, light motor vehicles were assembled at the slowest pace in more than eight years.

The economic drag from this sector's inventory correction is far from ending, which is why the Big Three cut production in 2006 and will keep reducing assembly in the first half of 2007. Auto industry economists agree that 2007 assembly will be flat, to weaker than 2006.

This is being ignored by some suppliers and analysts, though. Kuni Chen at Banc of America Securities in New York, who surveys service center executives, finds them bullish about demand for finished mill products from metalworking sectors and nonresidential construction.

Contd...

"Demand is down compared to last year, but demand expectations over the coming six months are positive," he says, as the executives and managers working in the steel sector insist to him that demand trends for steel will accelerate going forward and inventories will be back to normal levels by the end of the first quarter.

However, only 17 per cent of the buyers surveyed in January expressed bullishness on near-term future demand or prices. "The steel market currently is in a suspended animation of sorts," explains Peter J. Merriam, materials manager at Interroll manufacturing in Wilmington, N.C., a maker of drives, rollers and other roller and conveyor systems components. "Demand has declined and the steel companies are doing everything possible to maintain the price levels and prevent a price slide. But, 2007 demand will remain relatively flat when compared to 2006."

There is real uncertainty about demand in early 2007 for sheet and bar steel from the motor vehicle and appliance sector as assembly plans are being revised downwards continuously. The market for structurals stayed tighter longer in 2006, but this year's demand is unclear. Also, while grades of plate and pipe headed for use in the energy sector have been tight, those aimed at manufacturing have grown in supply.

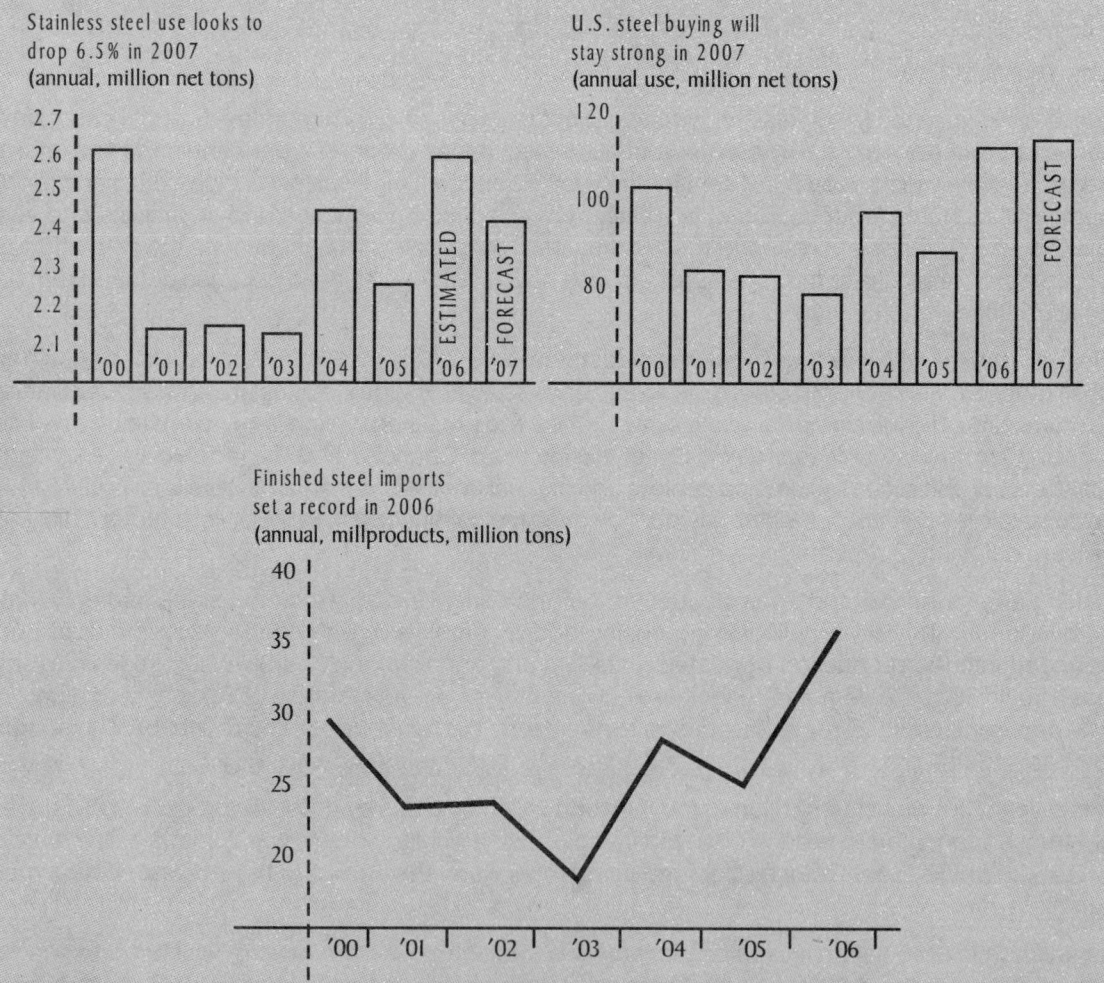

Stainless steel use looks to drop 6.5% in 2007
(annual, million net tons)

U.S. steel buying will stay strong in 2007
(annual use, million net tons)

Finished steel imports set a record in 2006
(annual, millproducts, million tons)

Source: U.S. Census Bureau

All that fits with the view of economist Zoltan Pozsar at Moody's Economy.com, who says recent contractions have been evident in factory orders for construction materials, motor vehicles, related auto parts, construction machinery, metal working machinery, computers, communications equipment

Contd...

and non-defense aircrafts. Economist Pozsar reckons that lower business equipment investment in 2007 also could reduce industrial machinery assembly. Analysts say military spending will generate demand-as metal-bearing equipment and ordnance used in the Iraqi war has to be replaced—but the strength of demand is uncertain.

John Schmitt, vice president of purchasing at the Denman and Davis steel service center chain in the Northeast, says that "carbon steel flat-rolled prices are softening (because) the push is always on reducing inventory even more". That fits with buyer surveys, which find 84 per cent maintaining a flat-to-down inventory strategy for metals.

Two-thirds of the way across the country in Denver at metal machining company Acme Tool and Manufacturing, purchasing manager Tom McSwain says "the costs of carbon steel products are down-which is good because sales volumes are down and the cost of goods sold is down and finished product availability is up."

Gazing into his crystal ball, materials manager Merriam of Interroll believes 2007 demand will remain relatively flat when compared to 2006.

"The automotive industry is still in somewhat of a slump due to higher fuel costs pushing consumers toward smaller vehicles, hence less steel," he says. "The appliance industry is performing well but more and more of the production is offshore and so we will not see any increased demand in North America from this industry."

There will be growth in many of the durable goods sectors and in general OEM manufacturing, he believes, "but not enough to offset the decreased demand in the major leagues and so I do not see that demand will be a factor in pushing prices upward but in fact may contribute slightly to lowering prices overall."

Stainless supply tight

Stainless steel is another story. Only 9 per cent of the buyers complaining to Purchasingdata.com about tight supplies of production materials in January listed steel, and 60 per cent of them homed in on stainless steel mill products. None of buyers polled were accepting what analysts Cousins terms "the mills' Pollyanna-like blue-skies optimism that supply soon will be tight and prices soon will be rising." Except, of course, for stainless steel. "Stainless steel supply is tight with long leadtimes and prices-due to alloy surcharges-continue to go through the roof," says Joe Diedrichs, director of production resources at ACI Mechanical, an engineering services and mechanical construction company in Ames, Iowa.

High prices and tight supplies of stainless steel mill products continue to irk purchasing pros like Sue Kirk, a buyer at the BandL Bolt fasteners distributorship in Portage, Mich.; George Paul, purchasing manager at Sabel Engineering, an automatic case packaging machinery maker in Sonoma, Calif.; Bill Downer, a buyer at fiber and pulp-making production equipment manufacturing plant in Glens Falls, NY; and Byron Taylor, director of purchasing and regulatory compliance at New York Blower industrial and commercial fan-making plant in LaPorte, Ind.

The Commerce Department says imports of total specialty steel-stainless steel, alloy tool steel and electrical sleet-through October were 828,803 tons, a 12 percent increase compared to the same 2005 period. Meanwhile, the Specialty Steel Industry of North America trade group reports that U.S. consumption was 2,600,277 tons, also a 12 percent increase; thus, import penetration was 32 percent.

However, the U.S. stainless market is easing, says analyst Michael Gambardella at J.P. Morgan Securities in New York, "as lackluster end demand is becoming more apparent." Economists suggest that while the energy sector is so strong that specialty steel production is hard-pressed to meet demand, construction among petrochemical and other chemical process industries' plants is weakening and is even softer for end products aimed at the consumer durables markets.

Another sign: U.S. domestic demand for stainless steel scrap appears to be receding, indicating reduced purchasing by buyers like North American Stainless, the Acerinox stainless steelmaking

Contd...

subsidiary in Carroll County, Kentucky. Purchasingdata.com's forecast is a 6.5 percent decline in 2007.

Distributor's inventories high

Structural change in steel supply has occurred through the consolidation and rationalization of the flat-rolled (sheet and plate) and long products (bar and structurals) segments. U.S. Steel, Mittal Steel USA, Nucor and Steel Dynamics pretty much own the flat-rolled segment while Nucor, Commercial Metals and Gerdau Ameristeel control steel long products-notably 73 per cent of the merchant bar market and 62 percent of the concrete reinforcing (rebar) market.

Distributor inventories hit all-time record highs in 2006; in fact, Metal Service Center Institute-member inventories in the U.S. and Canada were 17.9 million tons in November, up 33 percent (or 4,435,000 tons) year over year. Even before the recent consolidation, North America mills couldn't produce enough finished steel to meet the requirements of the domestic metalworking and construction industries.

Consequently, steel imports always have been a factor in the market. "Global steel supply is high and the U.S. is end market for much of the world's excess output," says economist John Anton at Global Insight's Eddystone, PA, offices. "Mills in the U.S. have cut tonnage produced and shipped, but all their good deeds could be undone by a global glut."

In 2006, the importers dramatically increased tonnage by 44 percent, which set all-time records and more than made up for the decline in mill shipments. Import volumes in 2006 were just about 45 million tons–36 million tons of finished steel mill products and 9 million tons of semifinished ingots and billets.

The high level of inventory in the distribution sector put downward pressure on prices. In fact, hot-rolled sheet (at $515/ton in January) was down $115 from the July/August 2006 peak of $630/ton.

There is a broadly held expectation among many steel executives and other market observers that imports are set to drop dramatically. Michelle Applebaum, the principal analyst at Michelle Applebaum Research in suburban Chicago, expects to see imports declining in coming months.

Actually, with high levels of imports, excess inventories, falling demand and softer pricing, the steel mills initiated production cuts last quarter. "Fourth quarter raw steel production declined 1.7 million tons compared to the year-earlier final quarter," calculates analyst Mark Parr at KeyBanc Capital Markets in Cleveland, "which would be down 2.4 million tons from the quarterly run rate through the first nine months of 2006." Week one of 2007 revealed another 275,000 ton year-over-year reduction, he says. Shipments, in turn, dropped from a monthly peak of 9.9 million tons last May to 8.7 million tons in October (the latest audited data).

Analysts believe the smelting cutbacks will have to be maintained or increased in the first quarter to prevent any further deterioration in pricing. Most steel mill executives arid industry analysts disagree. They believe that steel prices are very close to bottoming out late this quarter because domestic production is very disciplined, imports will fall sharply in the near term, and inventory at the service centers soon will be back to normal levels, or moving in that direction. So, looking at the second quarter, most mill executives expect steel prices to begin rising again.

Merriam, materials manager at Interroll, agrees that "the steel industry is much more adaptable and disciplined, in that they are achieving a good deal of success at matching supply to demand like never before. However, demand continues to decline though at a slower rate than during the fourth quarter of 2006 but a decline nonetheless." There is a point at which the steel companies will not be able to sustain the cooperative, or collaborative, approach to market conditions, he suggests. "This will begin a slide in prices throughout the steel industry on the order of 10 percent to 12 percent on average."

Analyst Cousins also agrees with the buyer. "The expectation of many industry participants and/or steel market observers is that the inventory issues will have been dealt with by the end of the first

Contd...

quarter," he says. 'We are not convinced." He suggests it will take 10 months to complete the inventory drawdown."

However, the mill view has advocates in contrarians Kuni Chen at Banc of America Securities and Aldo Mazzaferro at Goldman Sachs, both in New York. These analysts forecast that the market's demand fundamentals will remain strong in 2007. Chen conducts a monthly poll of 50 executives and managers working at service centers. Based on January's poll, Chen argues that steel prices are at a near-term low and are set to recover by March as inventories come back into balance. "Our poll suggests an improving operating environment going forward," Chen says, noting that 50 percent of participants in the poll expect lower inventories by March or April.

While demand is down compared to last year, more than 60 percent of those polled forecast increased order activity ahead, he adds. Meanwhile, Mazzaferro at Goldman Sachs says that "steel market conditions tighten this spring." His rationale: `Although steel prices have fallen, steel supply is falling rapidly and should result in a tighter market and higher pricing by the second quarter of 2007."

"Domestic demand for foreign steel has waned as relative domestic prices have continued to decline since the summer months," she says, "The significant drop-off in Novemberesearch and developmentecember imports takes a meaningful amount of supply out of the domestic market and in tandem with declines in production and inventory liquidation should firm up the steel market by mid first quarter." On the other hand, Cousins believes "it will take until September for imports to normalize."

Buyers remain bearish on prices

Buyer surveys see prices rising by mid-year but only by $20 to $30 per ton, depending on the product line. Nucor and other mini-mills are trying to push through $15/ton price hikes on rebar, merchant bar and light sections in February, but it's not happening. The mini-mills had been holding base prices steady but transaction tags have fallen steadily since August. The mills point to January scrap prices of $20 to $30 a gross ton from December for the bar price boosts; buyers don't care-projecting that January's $490 price will increase that $15 to $505 but not until June.

Analyst Cousins suggests that hot-rolled-which will have hit bottom in January at $515-will show only a gradual recovery, but only to $560 by the end of the year. The buyers polled agree, since their mid-year projection is $535.

Mike Napoli, purchasing manager for institutional lighting company Kenall of Gurnee, Ill, projects that the hot-rolled and cold-rolled price will be flat in the first quarter. It is stainless-steel pricing that bothers him more, suggesting that "Type 304 sheet prices will increase yet again in February." John Mathis at Trantech Radiator Products in Edgefield, S.C., says that "the cold-rolled sheet, steel market's pricing, demand and supply will remain flat or slightly down for the first quarter, but will pick up by mid-April in both demand and pricing. "He adds that business in the third quarter will be slightly higher than second quarter, "but the fourth quarter will show a drop in both spot price and demand as it seems to do every year."

Service center industry inventories in December at 16.5 million tons were a 28 percent increase compared to a year earlier (12.9 million tons). However, months of supply soared to 4.7 in December compared to 3.3 a year earlier. Analyst Chuck Bradford at Bradford Research in New York says "below three is normal and reflects inventory turnover of at least four times, the minimum for a well-run service centre."

The market "will see the inventory correction in carbon steel occurring around April and flat-rolled prices will bump up about $30/ton in the second quarter," suggests John Davis of Lozier. "We don't see much room for that to go higher unless the Chinese pull back their exports to the U.S." But, Davis doesn't see such cutbacks as likely since "there currently are boatloads of Chinese cold-rolled booked and offered on the West Coast through April at a landed price of $610/ton."

Davis believes the $610 cold-rolled price "will set and maintain the floor" at January's level for some weeks ahead. "U.S. Steel, Mittal and Nucor will try to hold back production to balance demand in the

Contd...

first quarter," Davis says, "so I don't see any additional opportunities to reduce prices since most OEMs settled their first quarter pricing in the $615 to $620 range." His forecast: A $30 bump up in the May timeframe, which the mills will lose come October.

In fact, a new report from Macquarie Bank's commodity research team in Sydney, Australia, says Asian steel will continue to flow into the North American and European markets. These analysts expect China's home-market hot-rolled sheet prices to stay around the $500/ton mark in 2007 because "the demand and supply profile in the region is reasonably well balanced." That will make hot-rolled export sales anywhere above $510 attractive again this year.

What it means to buyers:

1. Supply/demand imbalances take quite a long time to resolve.

2. U.S. economic slowdown can cut deeply into demand from metalworking.

3. Steel demand growth never recovers as quickly as forecast.

4. Higher than expected costs-for scrap, iron ore and energy-force mills to seek higher than expected prices.

5. Buyers have erratic history of accepting/rejecting price increases.

6. Mill shipments and steel selling prices generally are depressed by foreign steel.

CHINA STEEL: AISI keeps raising economic concerns about imports

The American Iron and Steel Institute (AISI) just keeps dissing China's steel industry and now U.S. economic policies. The domestic trade group is angry that buyers imported 5.4 million tons of Chinese steel last year from a total record 45 million tons. AISI says in a press release: "China-a non-market economy country that provides massive subsidies and other forms of government support to its domestic steel industry-will again be the single largest foreign supplier to the U.S. market" in 2006. In another press release, the Washington-based trade group is complaining that the U.S. risks "becoming dangerously dependent" on foreign steel because China's rising output is undermining U.S. producers' ability to compete. AISI says these rising imports of cheaper Chinese steel are harming the ability of the U.S. industry to provide materials for such military equipment as the body for the F-35 Joint Strike Fighter. AISI keeps contending that China provides allegedly illegal government subsidies to support its industry and gain global market share, threatening U.S. competitiveness. In fact, the AISI statement alleges "market distorting and often illegal, foreign government incentives and unsound economic policies at home" are undermining the U.S. steel industry's ability to supply the defense establishment with reliable supply. AISI's position is that foreign sources of supply are unreliable.

For another view, Feng Shui experts steeped in the ancient Chinese knowledge of geomancy, or natural energies, tell the Reuters News Service they see turbulence in this year's steel market because of reduced demand and excess supply. The market will be out of balance, say the Feng Shui masters in Hong Kong, simply because 2007 is a year of fire and water, and they're not in harmony. "I'm not sure about the Feng Shui, I prefer the Farmer's Almanac," says John Davis, director of purchasing at Lozier in Omaha. Neb., a manufacturer of retail store fixtures. "But I do believe that this year will be a bit more stable than last year."

STEEL: Novamerican management provides positive outlook

Executives at the Novamerican Steel service center company recently told Wall Street analysts that it had a stronger than expected start to its December-February first quarter, including solid momentum from energy, non-residential, construction infrastructure construction, railcar assembly, and some industrial end markets. This would be good news for the processing and distribution company, which operates 22 branches in the U.S and Canada, since its processed steel shipments dropped 9.5 percent in fiscal 2006 (ended November 25) and dollar-based sales rose by only 1 percent.

Contd...

In one of the first service center outlooks for 2007, Novamerican's management is pretty bullish and tells the analysts that "the decline in steel prices, resulting from weakened demand and an oversupply of steel in the fourth quarter, appears to be over." Management says that "import offerings for first and second quarter delivery are limited and the domestic mills appear committed to price stability early in 2007." Moreover, the LaSalle, Quebec-based firm's executives say they are looking for "better than expected shipments early in the new year."

As summarized by analyst Mark Parr at KeyBanc Capital Markets in Cleveland, Novamerican "indicates it has seen a stabilization of steel pricing and is witnessing ongoing discipline at the mill level. Finally the company has seen a marked fall-off of import offerings for first quarter 2007 delivery, with remaining offers at prices much higher than normal relative to domestic mill quotes." Commentary by analyst Randy Cousins at BMO Capital Markets in Toronto notes that "disappointment with the fourth quarter of last year and optimism for the first quarter of 2007 are consistent with commentary from some other steel producers."

Novamerican management provided an encouraging near-term outlook, suggesting that the inventory overhang appears to be over, says CIBC World Markets research analyst Mike Willemse. He also points to the Novamerican view that "overall demand is expected to improve in the first quarter vs. the fourth quarter based on warm weather conditions and inventory replenishments" Commentary by Willemse also notes that "Novamerican management's encouraging outlook is essentially in line with our (CIBC World Markers) forecast in light of the seasonal (springtime) pickup in demand and declining North American import activity."

Mind Power 2: Where Productivity is Growing in Wholesale Distribution

August 2006

By Adam J. Fein, Ph.D.

Wholesale distribution contributed more than 25 percent of the U.S. economy's total productivity gains over the past 15 years. Surprisingly, only four sub-sectors of the wholesale industry supplied most of the growth since 2001. Ongoing technology investments by distributors bode well for future productivity gains throughout the industry.

Productivity is fundamental to economic growth. The U.S. economy has been able to produce more goods and services over time by making production and distribution more efficient, not simply by adding more labor time. Output per hour, the most commonly cited labor productivity statistic, captures the combined effect of changes in technology, capital per worker, level of output, capacity utilization, managerial skill, and many other factors.

Productivity is also crucial to profitability in wholesale distribution because employee compensation costs-salaries, commissions and benefits-represent 60 to 70 percent of total operating expenses. As I note in an earlier column, distributors are at the forefront of using technology to reduce repetitive, low value-added activities such as order processing, billing, inventory control, delivery route scheduling and warehouse management. (See the productivity imperative for wholesale distribution)

The table below compares "output per hour" in wholesale with the non-farm business sector, which includes all for-profit business sectors in the U.S. economy. Productivity growth throughout the economy began accelerating in the mid-1990s. Yet productivity growth in wholesale exceeded the overall business sector by 1.6 percentage points in the past fifteen years and by 2.5 percentage

Contd...

points since 2001. Note that output is adjusted for price changes, eliminating the effect of product inflation.

Average Annual Growth In Labor Productivity, 1991-2005

	1991-1995	1996-2000	2001-2005	1991-2005
Non-farm business sector	1.5 percent	2.5 percent	3.3 percent	2.5 percent
Wholesale trade	3.0 percent	5.1 /0	5.8 percent	4.1 percent

Other studies of labor productivity, using different metrics, also show that the wholesale industry has made a disproportionately large contribution to the nation's productivity. McKinsey Global Institute concluded that the wholesale sector contributed 28 percent of the productivity increase from 1995 to 1999. A study by economists at the Department of Commerce found that wholesale trade contributed a similar proportion of the nation's productivity growth over the longer period from 1989 to 2001. To put these results in perspective, the wholesale industry accounted for only 6 percent of U.S. gross domestic product during the periods studied.

Unfortunately, these studies do not identify which sub-sectors of the wholesale industry contributed to productivity growth. Therefore, we mathematically decomposed productivity growth into the exact percentage point contributions of 19 major sub-sectors within wholesale distribution during the 2001 to 2005 period. This process, called growth accounting, allows us to identify how much of the 5.8 percent growth in labor productivity came from each sub-sector.

The results of our analyses are shown below. Four sub-sectors accounted for nearly 70 percent of the 5.8 percent growth in labor productivity from 2001 to 2005. These four sub-sectors accounted for only 43 percent of the wholesale industry's sales during this period.

Contribution To Total Productivity Growth In Wholesale, 2001-2005

Sub sector (by major product type)	Contribution	10/o of total growth
Computer hardware and software	1.61 percent	27.8 percent
Motor vehicles and motor vehicle parts	0.84 percent	14.5 percent
Electrical products and electronics	0.78 percent	13.6 percent
Pharmaceuticals	0.74 percent	12.8 percent
Industrial products	0.48 percent	8.3 percent
Commercial equipment and supplies	0.42 percent	7.3 percent
Office products and paper	0.21 percent	3.6 percent
Apparel and piece goods	0.16 percent	2.8 percent
Other consumer products	0.15 percent	2.6 percent
Miscellaneous durable goods	0.11 percent	2.0 percent
Metals	0.10 percent	1.8 percent
Furniture and home furnishings	0.09 percent	1.6 percent
Building materials	0.08 percent	1.4 percent
Oil and gas products	0.03 percent	0.5 percent
Agricultural products	0.01 percent	0.2 percent
Chemicals and plastics	0.00 percent	0.0 percent
Hardware, plumbing and heating equipment and supplies	-0.01 percent	-0.1 percent
Beer, wine and liquor	-0.01 percent	-0.2 percent
Grocery and foodservice	-0.03 percent	-0.5 percent
Average Annual Growth in Wholesale Trade, 2001-2005	5.8 percent	100.0 percent

Contd...

Data limitations prevent us from peering below this admittedly aggregated view of the industry. However, the sub-sectors making the largest contribution to productivity growth have some common characteristics:

1. *Faster industry growth:* Growth attracts outside financial capital, enabling investments in an IT infrastructure that can exploit latent scale economies. Early, successful innovators can capture an increasing share of the market by offering different services or lower costs than less technology intensive competitors. Even after adjusting for product inflation (pharmaceuticals) and deflation (computer hardware and software; electronics), three of the top four industries are growing quickly.

2. *Competitive intensity:* More-intense competition encourages distributors to innovate and seek new ways to cut costs or use IT more effectively. This effect appears to be even more powerful as a distribution industry consolidates and competition shifts to a national level instead of geographically separate, regional markets. The largest publicly traded distributors operate in the top contributing sub-sectors.

3. *Product characteristics:* Certain products allow physical distribution efficiencies. For example, less bulky products or products with a higher value relative to shipping costs provide greater opportunities to automate warehouse picking.

4. *Supply chain technology standards:* In each of the top contributing industries, manufacturers and distributors have agreed on common standards for product identification. As a result, distributors can invest in technologies such as warehouse management systems with an automatic product identification system, such as a machine-readable bar code or a Radio Frequency Identification (RFID) tag.

Note that total industry size did not guarantee a meaningful contribution to productivity improvement. Grocery and food wholesaling, which represented 11 percent of total revenues, actually had a slightly negative contribution to the wholesale industry's productivity growth. Although these wholesalers are information technology intensive, they face shrinking capacity utilization as larger retailers bypass the traditional channel. Wal-Mart's leading share and the growth of large supermarkets are triggering an intense shakeout among the remaining smaller stores that used to purchase through wholesale distribution. Real (inflation-adjusted) revenues of grocery wholesalers have been essentially flat since 2001.

Nevertheless, the factors driving productivity growth in the top industries are likely to continue. These productivity gains will probably spread to other sectors as distributors continue making investments in information technology.

Source: Adam J. Fein, Ph.D. is the founder and president of Pembroke Consulting, a firm that provides business and marketing strategy advice to executives operating in channel-intensive industries. He can be reached at (215) 523-5700 or on the web at www.PembrokeConsulting.com. © 2006 Pembroke consulting, Inc. Reprinted with his kind permission.

INTRODUCTION

Any business organization, work in a dynamic work atmosphere. It is not only the internal challenges, that they would be fighting against, but also against the external unknown forces, which would be constantly imposing a business with a set of opportunities and threats. Many companies overestimate their branch sales and at the end of the year, it becomes way below target. Old technologies fade away and pave way for the new.

The understanding of the environment becomes a very crucial factor in the survival of the organization. The effectiveness of the buyer-seller relationship directly impacts both organizations. Today, the marketing departments gather and analyze information on forces in the business environment. Thus the changes in the environment are well acted upon by the firms today. The need today is to be proactive, so that marketing can be developed not only to adapt to the changes, but also make changes in the environment.

In this chapter we will discuss the environmental issues, that organizations face and what strategies can be adopted to counteract them.

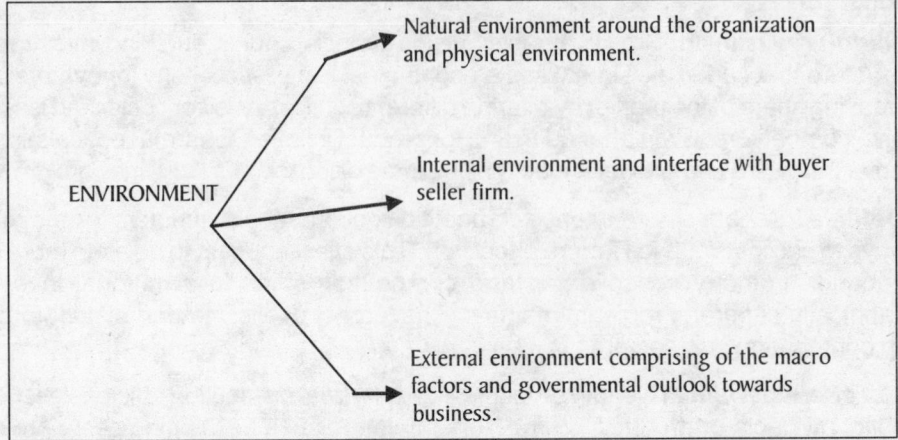

ENVIRONMENT
- Natural environment around the organization and physical environment.
- Internal environment and interface with buyer seller firm.
- External environment comprising of the macro factors and governmental outlook towards business.

Mind Power 3: Who is GeSI?

As the collective voice of its members, GeSI aims to influence the sustainability debate, inform the public of its members' voluntary actions to improve their sustainability performance, and prompt information and communicate technologies that foster sustainable development.

Our principles

Partners of the Global e-Sustainability Initiative acknowledge the need for the Information and Communications Technology (ICT) industry to take a leadership role in:

1. Better understanding the impact and opportunities offered by its evolving technology in the context of a fast growing information society, and

2. Providing individuals, businesses and institutions, with sustainable solutions to the challenge they face in their attempt to maintain the fragile equilibrium between economy, ecology and society.

Through their commitment to these principles, members of the Global e-Sustainability Initiative make a contribution to the Global Compact (GC) initiative of the UN Secretary-General.

The members are:

1. Bell Canada

2. BT

3. Cisco

4. Deutsche Telekom

5. Ericsson

6. ETNO

7. France Telecom

8. HP

Contd...

9. Lucent

10. Microsoft

11. Motorola

12. Nokia

13. Sun Microelectronics

14. Telefonica

15. US Telecom Association

16. Vodafone

Source: http://www.gesi.org

Mind Power 4: Bhopal Gas Tragedy: Relief and Rehabilitation

On a cold wintry night of 2nd/3rd December, 1984, when the residents of capital city of Bhopal went to their beds, they had no inkling that many of them were doing so for the last time. Not far from them in the factory of Union Carbide (India) Limited, a chemical reaction had already started to that end. At around midnight, this chemical reaction culminated in the leakage of deadly Methyl Isocyanite (MIC) gas from one of the tanks of the factory. A cloud of gas gradually and surely started descending and enveloping the city in its lethal folds. And soon all hell broke lose. The city of hills and lakes turned into a gas chamber. Bhopal was witnessing the worst ever industrial disaster. On the morning of December 3, the whole world learnt about the holocaust in shocked disbelief. The tragedy took an immediate toll of about 3000 innocent lives and left thousands and thousands of innocent citizens physically impaired or affected in various degrees. Livestock were killed, injured and infected. Businesses were interrupted. Environment was polluted and the ecology affected with flora and fauna disturbed. Such was the enormity of the tragedy that all available instruments in the field of health care, administration and law were found to be inadequate.

Source: http://www.mp.nic in/bgtrrdmp/profile.htm

Natural Environment

Today around the globe, organizations, especially manufacturers face public reaction and governmental interference for any kind of industries. With strong environmental laws and the need of the society, industries today are becoming very conscious of their environment. Organizations manufacturing chemicals, fertilizers, acids pose severe threat. Not only that the disposable materials also referred to as "hazardous waste" with high toxic levels have endangered the water bodies.

Mind Power 5: Tata Steel to use Dry Quenching Technology for Better Environment Management

Tata Steel in collaboration with NEDO (New Energy and Industrial Technology Development Organization), Japan has embarked upon a new approach to conserve both heat energy and fresh water and abate air and water pollution associated with the conventional wet quenching process

Contd...

during manufacture of Metallurgical Coke. A Memorandum of Understanding has been signed today by Mr. K. Koizawa, Executive Director, NEDO and Dr. T. Mukherjee, Deputy Managing Director (Steel), Tata Steel and Mr. Farooqui, Joint Secretary, Department of Economic Affairs, Ministry of Finance, Government of India, in the presence of officials of Ministry of Steel, to use Dry Quenching Technology for cooling of Coke. The new technology will use Nitrogen gas to recover the sensible heat of hot coke and generate steam which would be used for power generation.

According to this MoU, NEDO will contribute the equipment produced in Japan, under the Green Aid Plan of the Government of Japan and Tata Steel will set up the plant and disseminate the know-how to other integrated steel plants. This is the second time that Tata Steel has received Japanese technology from NEDO under the Green Aid Plan.

Majority of the electrical power generated in India is by burning coal. For producing 1 MW of power in a conventional coal fired power plant, as much as 6500 tonnes of green house gas (carbon dioxide) would be produced per year. In an integrated steel plant, huge quantity of heat may get wasted in direct and indirect cooling. In the conventional coke making process in steel plants, red hot coke is pushed out of coke ovens and quenched with large quantity of water resulting in evaporation of water into the atmosphere. Naturally the heat energy is lost in the process. In addition, quenching of coke results in air and water pollution.

The Coke Dry Quenching (CDQ) process offers distinct advantages of sensible heat recovery, conservation of water and zero air and water pollution. This is an established technology, popular in the more advanced countries. The dry coke produced in the process enhances the productivity of blast furnaces, the work horses of integrated steel plants. Annually 1 million Cubic meter of water will be saved and, almost 3 quarters of million tonnes of steam will be generated for use in power plants. This technology, commonly known as CDQ, would have favorable impact on climate change issues being addressed under the Kyoto Protocol. The carbon dioxide emissions into the atmosphere will come down by 140,000 tonnes per year.

Tata Steel believes, as always, that better environment management leads to superior and long lasting corporate performance. Its steel works, mines and collieries and the town services in Jamshedpur are ISO 14001 certified for environment management. Under the Green Millennium Countdown programme, the Company planted and ensured 1.5 million surviving trees in its mines and all other operating units.

Source: http://www.tatasteel.com/newsroom/press299asd: Report of June 16, 2006.

Here the examples of Bhopal Gas tragedy and Chernobyl in Russia can be mentioned. Methyl Isocyanite, the cause of the Bhopal Gas tragedy today has been banned in many countries.

Environmental organizations are raising their voices against the apathy of the industries towards the environment. Recent acts like the "Environmental Act" and "Right to Information" act have given strong powers in the hand of the people to make the conduct of organizations, environment friendly.

Mind power 6: US: Chevron Faces More Scrutiny in Ecuador over Pollution

By Emad Mekay, IPS News

March 15th, 2007

Leaders of indigenous communities in Ecuador are pressing their government to investigate senior executives from U.S. oil giant Chevron for an alleged environmental fraud scheme in the mid-1990s related to a long-running six-billion dollar class action suit in the South American nation.

Contd...

But the U.S. oil giant vehemently denies the accusations and says it has already been absolved by the local authorities.

Leaders from CONAIE, Ecuador's powerful indigenous federation, which represents millions of people, say in a news letter to the Quito government that the U.S. company defrauded the authorities during an environmental clean-up more than nine years ago.

The alleged operation involved bulldozing soil and organic debris on top of waste pits rather than cleaning them of poisonous toxins in the 1990s. The letter asserts that both lawyers oversaw this shoddy remediation. Later, Chevron tried to use the action as a defence in various lawsuits arising out of the ecological disaster in Ecuador.

Source: www.corpwatch.org: Reprinted with permission: "Special to CorpWatch".

PHYSICAL ENVIRONMENT

Physical Environment also plays a very important role. The ability to produce goods at a profit makes it necessary to have an ideal combination of the inputs needed. Certain areas geographically have natural blessings, like the "coal belt" around Jharkhand and West Bengal borders. Other inputs like raw material, water, power, lost cost labor and cheap transportation facilities act as a differential advantage over other competitors.

Location and transportation costs, ensures a strong relationship between the buyer and seller. With increase in transportation costs, the advantage lies to the companies who are located near to raw materials.

Mind Power 7: Oil Supply Shortages Likely After 2007

WASHINGTON - January 29 - Global oil supplies could start to have difficulty meeting growing demand after 2007, according to a recent analysis of existing and planned major oil-recovery projects published; this month in Petroleum Review.

While a flood of new production is set to hit the market over the next three years, the volumes expected from anticipated new projects thereafter are likely to fall well below requirements, the report says.

"There are not enough large-scale projects in the developmental pipeline right now to offset declining production in mature areas and meet global demand growth beyond 2007" said Chris Skrebowski, author of the report, editor of Petroleum Review and a recently appointed Board member of the Oil Depletion Analysis Centre (ODAC) in London.

"Since it takes, on average, six years from first discovery for a mega project to start producing oil, any new project approved today would be unlikely to come on stream until the end of the decade," Mr. Skrebowski noted.

Source: www.commondreams.org

Internal Environment

Internal environment analysis is carried out in successive period of time to identify the strengths and weaknesses of a company. Generally while analyzing the strengths and weakness of a particular company, the following factors are considered:

Mind Power 8: Substance Management at Nokia

Substance management at Nokia is built on the underlying guiding principle that the use of chemicals in its products and processes shall be safe to both humans and the environment. During the planning and design of its products, Nokia continuously collects and analyzes information on the materials it uses to drive the use of safe substances and materials.

Nokia's approach is based on the precautionary principle. Where Nokia has reasonable grounds for concern over the possibility of severe or irreversible damage to health or the environment, lack of full scientific certainty should not be an obstacle to triggering actions to gather and assess additional data. This may lead to Nokia voluntarily taking steps, such as substituting substances of concern with safer alternatives where feasible alternatives are available.

Source: http://www.nokia.com/A43593: Courtesy Nokia

STRENGTHS
Strong Brand Image
High Quality Products
Excellent Distribution Networks
Good Inventory Management
Strong Research and Development
Economics of Scale
Latest Technology
Comfortable Debt – Equity Ratio
Good Credit Rating
Motivated Employees
Industrial Relations
After Sales Service
Motivated Sales Personnel
Breadth of Product Line
Locational Facilities
Outsourcing Support
Effective Cost Control
Tax Concessions
Firm's Record of Achieving Objectives
Top Management Skills, Capabilities and Interest

WEAKNESSES
Poor Brand Image
Narrow Product Mix
Weak Distribution
Poor Product Quality
Uneconomical Size of Operations
Outdated Technology
Poor Inventory Management
Weak Research and Development Skills
Poor Reserves
Highly Leveraged
Low Credit Rating
Poor Receivables Management
Excess Manpower

Contd...

Hostile Industrial Relations Climate
Poor Morale
Inefficient Board
Inaccessible Location

Source: Strategic Management Text and Cases, Rao and Krishna, Pg 148 - Excel Publications.

Interface with buyer and seller firm is important for facilitating production, distribution, and purchasing. Any firm has a singular objective, i.e., to combine all the inputs, add value to it and produce an output, which is a better offer than competitors.

Input goods like raw materials and labour are supplied by organizations. The output produced forms an input for some other firm. To explain this, a little more clearly a company producing copper wires, buys copper from industries, transforms it into wires and these wires act as an input for electrical companies or motor making companies. Thus industrial sellers and buyers must monitor the activities of suppliers and anticipate the objectives.

Mind Power 9: Xerox's Paper Sourcing Policy and EH & S Requirements for Paper Suppliers

In 2000, Xerox adopted the following position on paper sourcing:

Xerox sources its paper from companies committed to sound environmental, health and safety (EH & S) practices and sustainable forest management in their own operations and those of their suppliers. Our intent is to protect the health and integrity of forest ecosystems, conserve biological diversity and soil and water resources, safeguard forest areas of significant ecological or cultural importance, and ensure sustainable yield. Companies must be committed to compliance with all applicable EH & S regulatory requirements in the countries where they operate.

Source: http://www.xerox.com/go/xrx/template/020e.jsp?view

Distributor links also play a very important and critical role because the stock inventories provide credit and advice to buyers. They also play an important role when there is a joint demand of products. In some industries, the distributors become dictators to the manufacturers.

Advertising agencies, PR firms, transportation and warehouse companies also influence the business in an indirect way. Advertising agencies act as an interface between the potential buyers and the seller, for a better business prospect. Transportation and warehousing play an important role in delivering the goods at the right time and place.

Competitors also influence the environment and a company's marketing strategy.

Thus from the above we understand that the interaction between the buyer and seller is very important. The relationship developed must be long term. Individuals from various functional areas, often meet their counterparts in other firms to have an exchange of opinion, ideas and views and act for the betterment of each other. Betterment in areas of technology, innovation, cross distribution, manufacturing and common areas to cut costs. Competition is not only at domestic ends, but also at foreign ends. Global business houses trying to have more markets and thus sustainable differential advantage have become a must for all companies.

Mind Power 10: Affecting the Business Environment

Competitors affect the way businesses are run and have severe implications on profitability. Competitors will try and gain by differentiating seeking to provide better value for money.

The social system, cultural factors also affect the way businesses are run today. They give a clear picture of human relationships. Businesses are also influenced by consumer attitudes and behaviors. The political/legal system creates the rules and frameworks within which a business operates. Government policy supports and encourages some business activities although the nature of support from countries would vary. Business houses have today become aware of the relationship between their economic activity and the effect on the environmental system.

External Environment

The dynamicity of the macro environment plays a major role in the behaviour of an organization. Shifts in the world economy, impact all manufacturers be it small or big. Forces acting in the macro environment are difficult to control in comparison to the other two factors that we have seen above. The external environment in today's world is highly dynamic and changing at a very fast pace.

If we see the period of 1980–1990 and compare it with the next decade post liberalization, we are speaking of massive differences not only in the way; businesses are run but also the outlook of the companies. Thus, a balance with the external environment is very necessary for all organizations.

"The '**Made in India**' tag is being recognized world over and is now gaining acceptance in world markets. A study by the CII and McKinsey and Co on the manufacturing sector in India, estimates that the Indian manufacturing export has the potential to touch $ 300 billion by 2015, growing at an annual rate of 17 percent, as against historic growth rates of 11 percent."[1]

Emerging economic changes worldwide has influenced the organizations capability to buy and sell. Today we are seeing quantum leaps in the business arena with "Tata-Corus" deal which expects to make "Tata's" jump to the 5th position in the world steel market.

Cultures, customs, habits and traditions also influence the way an organization function. It also influences the interaction of the buyer and seller, and also the interaction between the members of an organization. In a country like India, where there is a vast cultural difference in the way the business are run, the outlook of the owners play a very critical role. A pattern of work suitable in one location may not be suitable for another. "Japanese methods of consensual decision-making, long-term employment and the use of quality control circles have all experienced difficulties when attempted in the United States".[2]

Mind Power 11: Work Life Balance

Stress is a cost to companies because of the effect attached to these problems. People may quit because of stress and it affects their performances which have impact on the company. Fighting this is essential and companies need to be proactive in addressing this problem.

A motivated and skilled workforce are the biggest assets that will decide a firm's success or failure. Reducing the stress and providing better work life balance is a target that should be on the minds of a global professional company. Better work life balance means:

1. Increase in productivity, accountability and commitment

Contd...

2. Better teamwork and communication

3. Improved morale

4. More balance in life

5. Increased productivity

6. Better relationships both on and off the job

7. Reduced stress.

Technological changes influence both buyers and sellers, because, as technology changes profitability, acceptability in the market becomes a very key component of any organization. Since, the business is well dependent on derived demand, rapidly changing technology can create huge ripples in any industry and also holds the capability of wiping out old technologies. The sectors today that are seeing tremendous changes in technology cannot be specified. Technology is the driving force today for all organizations. Thus, the strategy required is that marketing should work in close co-ordination with research and development, for better and faster development of products.

Demographic changes also affect the way; businesses are run. With the changes in income-profile of the people, fall in the death rates, rationing or allocation of resources today is becoming a challenge in itself. Thus industrial firms must keep a track on the demographic data for short, medium and long-term planning.

Government is probably one of the most important factors that have to be kept in mind, especially for business houses in India. With a democratic form of government and a huge amount of instability, difference of opinions and outlook has caused a great damage to Indian businesses.

Government regulatory laws of taxation, funding, interest rates, safety standards, corporate governance, environment and research and development play a very important role in the process of how industrial concerns are run. Government also has to take care of the "infant" industries and protecting the society from unfair business practices. Thus the judgements of the judicial system also become a strong benchmark for the organizations. Whenever we speak of a democratic system like ours three most important criteria's come into our minds. They are:

1. Stability

2. Policies towards business

3. Trade restrictions

Decisions with regard to 'quotas' and 'tariffs' can have implications throughout the industry. Government and legislators are also responsible for:

1. Protection of consumers

2. Larger interests of the society

3. Protection from 'cut throat' competition

The industrial marketer must therefore keep a very close watch on the actions of the government.

Mind Power 12: The Business Environment that Changes

Today's business environment is characterized of market's internalization, specialization of customer's needs, hard competition and deduction of products' life cycle. Businesses' competitiveness depends

Contd...

from their ability to adapt the new conditions. New technologies allow a complete, flexible organization that leads to an efficient workflow management and to a faster response to the market's needs. It is important for the Greek businesses to realize all these changes and adapt to the new circumstances.

The new technologies alterate work in different ways. In the digital age, knowledge has a key role to the reformation and the organization of work, generating a new economy based on the occupational qualification and adjustiveness. Information systems and communication networks render work less dependent on time parameters, while changes of the professional practices constrain the concept of stable work duties. The above two factors affect the composition of life institution, like protection and adjustments of occupation.

Around all world and among all economy sectors, businesses have started using Internet for their trade offs with other businesses (B2B e-commerce) and end users (B2C e-commerce). This new technology wave spreads quickly since those that use the technologies and practices of e-commerce "enforce" their suppliers or their customers to do the same.

Source: http://www.ebusinessforum.gr/ebusinessforum/goals/index.php?language=en

BUSINESS ENVIRONMENT IN INDIA

On our Tenth Five Year Plan and after about a half century of independence, we have seen a lot of remarkable changes in the business environment of our country. With a policy, which was completely "inward looking" to a current account convertibility post 1990-91, the journey has gone through tough test of times. Being a democracy, the biggest difficulty was probably the constancy of plans, and objectives of the government.

The crumbling down of the highly regulated markets, with a lot of red tapism and bureaucracy involved, the strong regulations of FERA and the governments policy of looking down at FDI's have changed. Today, we see FDI in various sectors of the market, be it the financial markets, or industrial goods market. Our former Prime Minister Rajiv Gandhi had envisioned a technology based nation and thus focus on technological imports and foreign collaborations were allowed. Again on the other hand the state of West Bengal and Kerala due to their staunch communist outlook, saw a lot of companies switching over their bases to Mumbai; now the financial capital of the country. Strong political factors have always predominated the development in our country. West Bengal has today the largest number of industrial disputes and man days lost.

Mind Power 13: Industrial Environment Improving

KOCHI: Minister for Overseas Indian Affairs Vayalar Ravi has said the industrial environment in Kerala was showing positive signals as the workers have done away with the practice of resorting to strikes over minor issues. The workers as well as managements have a better understanding of the situation, he said at a function organised by the Kerala Management Association (KMA) here on Wednesday for distributing its Management Leadership Award, 2006.

Source: http://www.hindu.com/2006/10/13/stories/2006101301081900.htm (Internet edition - 13th Oct 2006): Courtesy-*The Hindu*

Another example that comes to mind is the ruling of the Janata Party in the mid-1970s. It was at this time that companies like IBM and Coca Cola were asked to windup. Political pressures and the atmosphere have always dominated the business environment in India.

In India, the legal factors have played another major dominant role. The laws in relation to industrial policies, selective licensing, strong trade unions, payment of wages, provident funds, are examples of some of the legal factors. Excessive control by the Central Government, having an absolute 'socialistic' pattern of government, and encouragement to trade unions, has led to business ruins in some states.

Today, the government is also cautious about the ecological factors of the nation and we see the Water Act 1974, Environment Act 1986 and the Air Act 1981 forming a key component of the corporate outlook. With the international outlook changing towards the environment, the government and corporate houses today have committed themselves to the preservation of the ecological balance.

There has been an end of communism and socialism, and companies are becoming and going global. Today companies do not define themselves as regional companies, but the ones with stronger outlook and global vision. We have seen companies like Tata, Birla, ICICI, and MRF going global. The business pressures have no more been restricted to one region, but are multidirectional. The EEC, NATA, NATO, OPEC, SAARC, LAFTA, NAM, ASEAN have contributed to the building of strong regional bonding. Today managers need to be globally oriented. About 20 percent of total India's exports are to the EEC group. Their requirement is quality.

Political risks, government effectiveness risk, legal and regulatory risk, macro economic risks, financial, infrastructure and labor market risks are risks a manager must understand today before entering into any other nation.

Industrial marketers must appreciate the environmental factors, which are associated with any business. In industrial markets, we require to be extra cautious with the environmental factors. Eliminating risks is not possible in any business; what is needed is reduction of risks.

CONCLUSION

Thus, as we have seen above, we as industrial marketers cannot neglect or avoid the influences of the environment on businesses on an organization. Marketers should try and be proactive and make necessary changes to counteract it.

References

1.   Business @ India -"Witnessing Quantum Growth", Pg 36, Vol 2 No 2, November 2006.

2.   Are foreign partners Good for U. S. Companies? *Business Week* (May 28, 1984), pp 58-59.

Mind power 14: Energy is Precious: A Study by the Gujarat Energy Development Agency

The rate at which the energy demands and prices are increasing it may be impossible to pursue the present rate of development. Developing countries, like India, will be forced to retard its development / industrialization programme for want of sufficient energy reserves. Besides this the environmental implications of haphazard energy utilization also need to be closely studied. Inefficient use of energy has stretched the global environment to its limits as can be seen from unpleasant responses of the nature. Green house effect, acid rain, smog, deforestation, shift in climatic conditions, etc., are some of the indications. Setting up additional generating capacities to meet increasing energy demands is not only a very expensive alternative but also a very time consuming approach. Additional Power

Contd...

Plants, meaning additional pollution and further degradation of the environment. While Energy Conservation, besides being a quick and economical approach has the potential to provide an effective solution to emerging environmental hazards.

Considering the scenario of the Indian Industrial sector and its energy utilization efficiency, there is urgent need to review manufacturing technologies and the present energy management approach. Owing to old and obsolete industrial technologies and machinery the extent of energy wastage is very high. Energy Conservation potential in the industrial sector of our nation has been projected between 30 to 40 percent. Energy conservation measures range from simple good housekeeping practices to plant modernization.

To know the extent of energy that is being wasted it is very essential to know what amount of energy is being consumed. Monitoring industrial energy utilization on continuous basis and relating it to the production is the first step of any energy conservation programme.

The industrial sector is a major energy-consuming sector accounting for about 50 percent of the commercial energy available in the country. The total energy consumption, including non-energy uses about 103.1 mtoe. Of the commercial sources of energy, coal and lignite account for 56 percent, oil and natural gas - 40 percent, hydroelectric power 3 percent and nuclear power 1 percent.

Table 3.1: Energy Conservation Potential in Indian Industries

INDUSTRIES	PERCENT SHARE OF ENERGY IN PRODUCTION COST	PERCENT CONSERVATION POTENTIAL
Refineries	1	8-10
Sugar	3.4	25-30
Ferrous Foundry	10.5	15-20
Textile	10.9	20-25
Petrochemical	12.7	10-15
Chloro-alkali	15	10-15
Iron and Steel	15.8	8-10
Fertilizers and Pesticides	18.3	10-15
Pulp and Paper	22.8	20-25
Glass	32.5	15-20
Ceramics	33.7	15-20
Aluminum	34.2	8-10
Cement	34.9	10-15
Ferro-alloys	36.5	8-10

Source: http://www.geda.org.in/default.htm

Mind Power 15: Retail Chains and Future of Business to Business (B2B) Trade in India

By Dr. Amit K Chatterjee

Govt of India has decided to allow 51 percent FDI in retail chains. This will certainly make the sector more attractive to foreign retailers who want a controlling stake in their Indian ventures. Retailers who are comfortable with ownership rather than franchises may look at the Indian market with greater interest.

Contd...

Entry of large foreign retail chains like Wal-Mart will have profound effect not just on small retailers and Indian retail chains but also on business to business "B2B" trade. Introduction of B2B cash-and-carry outlets by Wal-Mart, Metro and possibly other retailers will bring significant changes in large and fragmented Indian supply chain. Middlemen like wholesalers and stockiest will increasingly be under pressure. Where does small and medium manufacturers/exporters stand in this changing scenario?

What is Cash-and-Carry Scheme?

Targeted at and open only to business customers cash and carry scheme focuses on small-wholesale customers who buy in bulk and pay in cash. Unlike hypermarkets where any consumer can walk-in and buy goods, cash-and-carry outlets allow only authenticated bulk buyers to transact business. Medium-sized businesses such as retail stores, hotels, restaurants, caterers, exporters etc. can buy from cash-and-carry outlets at prices much cheaper than market rate.

In its original form, owners of cash and carry outlets (i.e., large retail chains) buy from producers directly at very high volume, dispensing with middlemen like wholesalers and stockiest. They also establish their own brands - asking producers to manufacture as per their product and packaging specifications. Volume purchase and removal of middlemen result in substantial cost reduction – a part of which is passed on to B2B customers. So, B2B customers get products of assured quality throughout the year at less than market price.

How does Cash-and-Carry Outlets affect your Business?

Large scale introduction of Cash-and-Carry outlets will definitely affect and influence various players in Indian B2B supply chain. While it may prove to be a boon for business buyers, manufacturers and producers such as small-scale units and agricultural producers' cooperatives which are not big or savvy enough to be able to dictate terms to established supply chains – it may adversely affect wholesalers and other middlemen.

De-layering of Indian distribution system may pose threat to middlemen, many of whom may be rendered redundant in the supply chain. Increase in competition and cost cutting will bring more efficiency in the market place, benefiting businesses.

Where does Small Scale Manufacturers and Exporters Stand?

Though it's too early to predict possible changes large retail chains may bring new opportunities for Indian manufacturers and exporters. While small scale manufacturers may enter into collaboration with retails chains allowing them the chance to join a modern procurement chain that thrives on efficient suppliers, it may have interesting influence on Indian exporters.

Fragmented and largely unorganized sourcing channels pose a formidable challenge to small and medium exporters in Indian sub continent. Some of the major hurdles in any export transaction are lack of assured and uniform quality standard, uncertainty about round the year availability and wide fluctuation in market price. Exporters lose lucrative overseas orders because of deficiency in supply chains, factors completely out of their control. Organized supply chains such as Cash-and-Carry outlets may bring new opportunities for small business owners.

Conclusion

Exporters sourcing from organized channels such as Cash-and-Carry outlets will benefit from more predictability in business, reducing inventory levels and competitive price. The resultant cost benefit, if passed on to buyers, can make Indian exports that much competitive.

Source: The Great Indian Bazaar (www.infobanc.com)

Mind Power 16: Five Pillars of Teamwork (Part 2) – Promote Healthy Conflict

Source: This article has been authored by Sanjeev Baitmangalkar. Copyright with Infomedia India Limited. This article appeared in the Modern Machine Tools- January 2007-pp 162- Reprinted with permission.

Failure to build trust is damaging as it can build the fear of conflict. Teams where members trust one another are capable of engaging in unfiltered and passionate debate of ideas without being veiled in their discussions or guarded in their comments. For relationships to grow and last over time: require productive conflict, be it in business, in parenting, marriage or even in friendship.

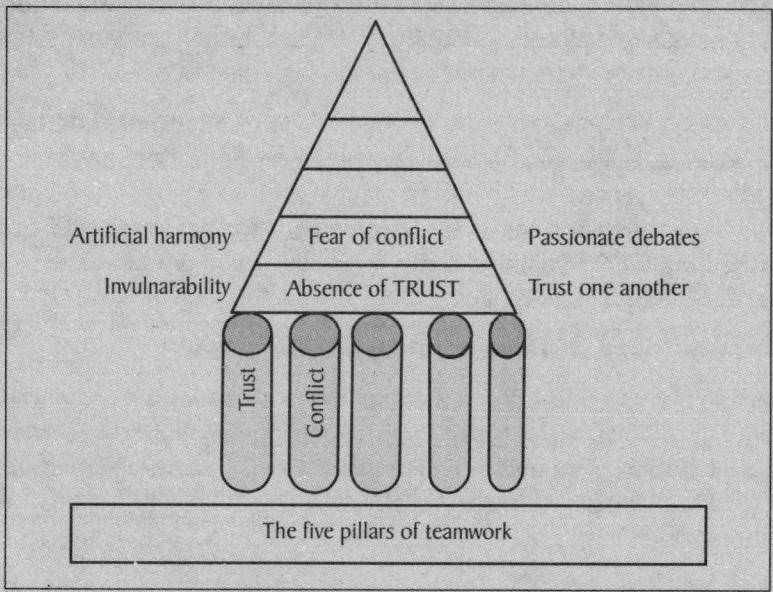

The five pillars of teamwork

Conflict is the result of differing perceptions, assumptions, and/or values, mostly understood as being argumentative and destructive. People often forget that conflicts can be constructive and productive. Many organizations consider conflict somewhat like a taboo, something forbidden and unthinkable, and hence ban it instead of encouraging it. About 20 years ago, when I visited Kirloskar Cummins, I saw passionate debates taking place on why a particular process is better, why this tool has the best chance of producing a better quality hole, why this machine is more process efficient and effective compared to other options, and so on. To an untrained eye it might have appeared as an argument, but it was a very effective discussion of ideas and finally agreed on the best solution. No individual won or lost here, it was always the team.

One must learn to distinguish productive ideological conflict from interpersonal politics and destructive fighting. Ideological conflicts are limited to concepts and ideas and avoid personality focussed, mean spirited attacks. However, ideological conflict can have the same external qualities of interpersonal conflict–passion, frustration and emotion–so much so that an outsider might easily mistake it for an unproductive argument. Successful teams know that by engaging in productive conflict it is possible to produce the best possible solution in the shortest possible time. Such teams discuss and resolve issues more quickly and completely than others and emerge from heated debates with no collateral damage or residual feelings, but with an eagerness and willingness to take on the next issue. Why do teams avoid ideological conflict? To avoid hurting the feelings of team members. But in this process, end up encouraging dangerous tension. "When two persons have the same opinion, then

Contd...

obviously one is not required there," all of you have heard this saying. So, also when team members do not openly debate and disagree about important ideas, they often tend to back-channel personal attacks, which are far nastier and more harmful than any heated discussion over issues. Healthy conflict is a time saver, but many avoid it in the name of efficiency. When you avoid healthy conflict, you are doomed to revisiting the same issues many times. A few tips on how to approach conflict:

1. The key is to view conflict as an opportunity to implement change in the way people interact and improve their problem solving skills.

2. Successful conflict resolution can result in innovations and strengthened relationships for your organization.

3. Supervisors and managers do not always have to provide the solution to the conflict, but they should be skilled in how to facilitate, negotiate, or communicate conflict resolutions.

Teams that fear conflict	Teams that engage in conflict
Have boring meetings	Have lively, interesting meetings
Create environment where back-channel politics and personal attacks thrive	Extract and exploit the ideas of all team members
Ignore controversial topics that are critical to team success	Solve real problems quickly
Fail to tap into all the opinions and perspectives of team members	Minimise politics
Waste time and energy with posturing and interpersonal risk management	Put critical topics on the table for discussion

Credit: Lenchioni's Table

It is, therefore, necessary for an organization to help the teams develop the ability and willingness to engage in healthy and productive conflict. To be able to do this, the organization must first accept and acknowledge that healthy conflict is productive. The team members must be taught that healthy, productive conflict is necessary. You can use a few methods to make this possible.

Bring out buried disagreements

One of the team members is asked to be the miner. He digs and brings to surface earlier disagreements and sheds light on them. He must have the courage and confidence to call out all sensitive issues and force the team members to work through them. This can be done only by objectivity and a commitment to staying with the team through the entire process of conflict resolution. A team member can be given this responsibility even during meetings and discussions, so that no issues are left unresolved and no ideas are left unexplored.

Drain that tension

In this process, members of the team must remind one another that this healthy discussion is necessary to find the best solution, and hence coach one another not to retreat from the healthy debate. Usually, people become uncomfortable with the level of discord when engaged in a conflict, so remind them that the process or what they are doing is important to the team. This may sound simple and somewhat paternal, but it is found to be an effective tool to drain tension from the difficult but productive interchange infusing confidence into the participants to continue.

Contd...

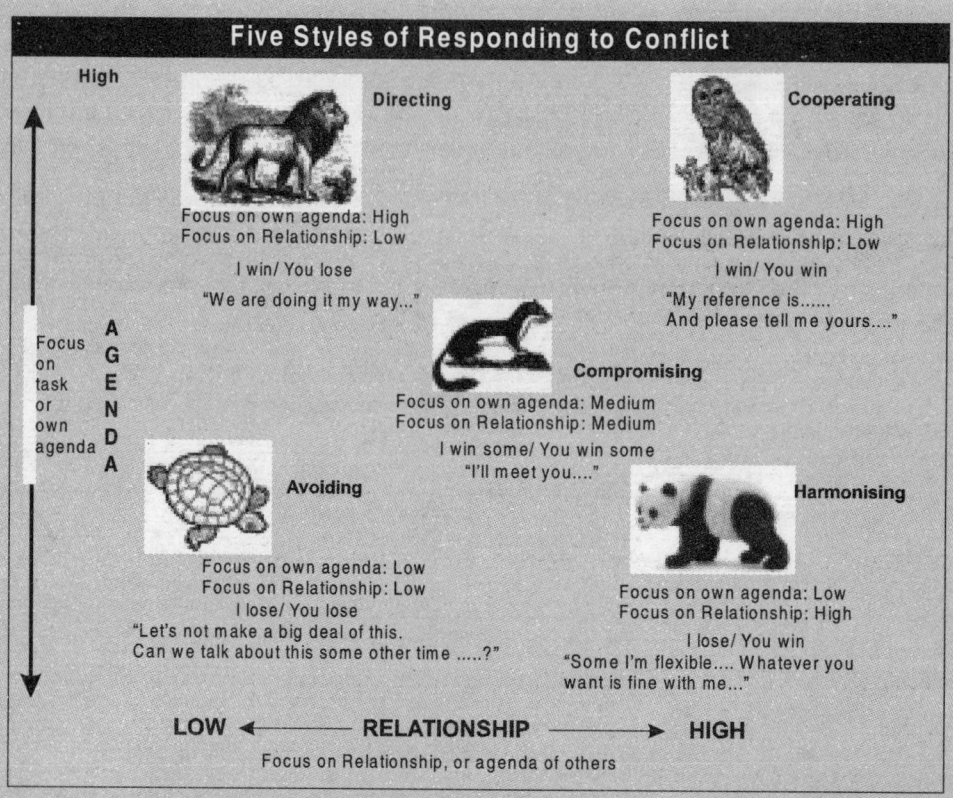

Five Styles of Responding to Conflict

High

Directing
Focus on own agenda: High
Focus on Relationship: Low

I win/ You lose

"We are doing it my way..."

Cooperating
Focus on own agenda: High
Focus on Relationship: Low

I win/ You win

"My reference is......
And please tell me yours...."

AGENDA

Focus on task or own agenda

Compromising
Focus on own agenda: Medium
Focus on Relationship: Medium

I win some/ You win some
"I'll meet you...."

Avoiding
Focus on own agenda: Low
Focus on Relationship: Low
I lose/ You lose
"Let's not make a big deal of this.
Can we talk about this some other time .....?"

Harmonising
Focus on own agenda: Low
Focus on Relationship: High

I lose/ You win
"Some I'm flexible.... Whatever you want is fine with me..."

LOW ◄——— RELATIONSHIP ———► HIGH

Focus on Relationship, or agenda of others

Others

The team members can be taught to understand the various personality styles and behavioral preferences of individuals to better understand one another. Two books I found useful reading are *Personality Plus* by Florence Littauer and *Simple Steps to Impossible Dreams* by Steven Scott. One can also take Littauers' personality test, it is simple and it is fun. Many people do not know their own personality traits and this will help them discover themselves. This also helps to understand the approaches of different styles and how they choose to deal with conflicts. The Thomas Kilmann Conflict Mode Instrument (TKI) or the Kraybill Conflict Response Inventory helps the understanding of natural inclinations around conflict, so that they can make strategic choices of which approaches are appropriate to different styles and situations. The chart of the 'Five Styles of Responding to Conflict' (credit Ron Kraybill) tells us about the characteristics of each style. Whether you follow Littauer or Scott or Kraybill doesn't matter, because all of them give an explanation of how to understand each character trait and help you understand deal with it.

Five Styles of responding to conflict	
Competing (Directing): High assertiveness and low cooperativeness…	The goal is to win
Avoiding: Low assertiveness and low cooperativeness…	The goal is to delay
Compromising: Moderate assertiveness and moderate cooperativeness…	The goal is to fine a middle ground
Collaborating (Cooperating): High assertiveness and high cooperativeness…	The goal is to find a win-win solution
Accommodating (Harmonising): Low assertiveness and high cooperativeness…	The goal is to yield

Credit: Ron Kraybill

Contd...

You can also use these essential steps to conflict resolution identified by Psychologist Dr. Dudley Weeks, PhD:

1. Create an effective atmosphere

    i)   Determine an appropriate time and place (i.e, do not meet in your office)

    ii)   Establish ground rules (i.e, take risks, maintain confidentiality, listen with respect)

2. Clarify perceptions

    i)   Talk to the right person; agree to be direct, open and honest

3. Focus on individual and shared needs

    i)   Allow for give and take

4. Build positive shared power

    i)   Use 'I' messages and practice active listening

5. Look to the future, then learn from the past

    i)   Talk about dealing with conflict in advance

6. Generate options

7. Develop 'Doables': The stepping stones to action

8. Make mutual-benefit agreements

9. Identify areas in which the parties agree

10. To meet a shared objective, build on those agreements

11. A shared level of commitment and mutual respect is necessary for this process to be effective.

The leader's role

A leader must promote healthy, productive and passionate conflicts. He must overcome the desire to protect members from harm, as it could lead to premature termination of discussions or disagreements. This will also prevent the team members from developing the skills to cope with conflict themselves. A leader must also help develop the conflict management skills of his team members and not leave them hungry for resolution that never occurs. A leader must also exercise restraint allowing a natural resolution of a conflict even if it is a vigorously contested one. This can be difficult because leaders could feel they are losing control over their teams during conflict. The leaders should only intervene when discussions become personal and issues left behind. Many executives avoid conflict when it is necessary and productive, but a true leader will encourage it.

The characteristics of successful agreements are the agreement must be balanced, clear, fair, realistic, specific, concise, forward looking and a commitment to return to discussions if there is a future problem. There are five styles of responding to conflict, as you saw from the graphic depictions earlier. The key is to be skilled in all the five styles and know when to apply each strategy.

QUESTIONS FOR DISCUSSION

1. The pollution levels of your factory have crossed the normal prescribed limit. You have discussed it with your boss. Boss says, "Manage it, or else ………." You are in a dilemma. What should you do?

2. Why should environment be a concern for industrial marketers?

3. Make a brief list of the "acts" passed by the parliament, to control the industrial marketing environment?

4. How can suppliers influence the industrial marketer?

5. Strategic partnerships will reduce price discrimination issues for an industrial marketer. Do you agree to this?

6. What are the permissions required from the governmental agencies, for establishing an industrial concern manufacturing "pumps", with respect to the environment?

7. What are the strategies for managing the industrial marketing environment?

chapter
FOUR

Industrial Buying and Buying Behaviour

COMPANY PROFILE 4: ASHOK LEYLAND

Eight out of ten metro state transport buses in India are from Ashok Leyland. At 70 million passengers a day, Ashok Leyland buses carry more people than the entire Indian rail network.

From 18 seater to 82 seater double decker buses, from 7.5 tonne to 49 tonne in haulage vehicles, from numerous special application vehicles to diesel engines for industrial, marine and genset applications, Ashok Leyland offers a wide range of products. For over five decades, Ashok Leyland has been the technology leader in India's commercial vehicle industry, moulding the country's commercial vehicle profile by introducing technologies and product ideas that have gone on to become industry norm.

The company manufactures buses, trucks, engines and defence and special vehicles.

Ashok Leyland considers its vendors as partners in progress and believes in establishing mutually beneficial relationships. Ashok Leyland provides necessary technical assistance in the form of Project and Production Engineering, to maintain quality levels. In addition, where required, Ashok Leyland also helps vendors financially.

Ashok Leyland, the Hinduja Group flagship in India, has signed an agreement with Brehon Energy PLC, Australia, for technology for the use of ecologically superior Hythane gas in CNG engines. Brehon Energy PLC has acquired and developed patents, technology and know-how for the production, storage, dispensing and use of Hythane. Since rolling out India's first CNG-powered bus in 1997 on Mumbai's roads, Ashok Leyland spearheaded the large-scale induction of this eco-friendly technology in the bus fleet of Delhi. In 2002, the Company developed India's first Hybrid Electric bus.

It is served by its own comprehensive Research and development base, complemented by collaborations with global technology leaders. Ashok Leyland has established a tradition of technological leadership and a strong reputation for product reliability. The history of the Company has been punctuated by a number of technological innovations, which have since become industry norms. It was the first to introduce multi-axle trucks, full air brakes and a host of innovations like the rear engine and articulated buses in India.

In 2002, all the vehicle manufacturing units of Ashok Leyland were ISO 14001 certified with Environmental Management System. Over the decades, Ashok Leyland's Research and development engineers have been addressing the twin concerns of fuel-efficiency and emissions. Not surprisingly, when the legislation came in 1987, limiting vehicular emission, Ashok Leyland vehicles were already meeting them. In 1992, came the more stringent norms for gaseous emissions. By then, Ashok Leyland, through timely technology tie-ups – and ahead of competition – had absorbed and was offering eco-friendly engine technology. In 1996, when the permissible levels of gaseous exhaust emissions were further tightened, Ashok Leyland again met the norms with ease. Ashok Leyland has pro-actively developed its engines to meet the progressive emission norms, including the Bharat Stage II norms.

The pan India network of Ashok Leyland serves customers in every part of the country. There are 3 streams of workshops for vehicles - Dealers, Authorized Service Centres and Highway Repair Centres - besides dedicated dealers for servicing industrial and marine engines of Ashok Leyland. Every one of these workshops and the vast network of Leyparts stores assure supply of genuine Leyparts.

The immediate Research and development priorities are to pro-actively address safety and environmental issues, harness and adopt technologies that provide value to the customer in an atmosphere enabling creativity and innovation. Powering those who "engineer tomorrows" with an enabling infrastructure has been top priority for the company. Vehicle ruggedness and longevity are a prime customer concern, as they directly impact earnings. Ever conscious of this, Ashok Leyland makes extensive use of a modem CAD set-up, a comprehensive test track facility (where cobble-stones are calibrated and reset periodically), accelerated fatigue testing rigs and rigorous durability testing facilities. Together they ensure that there is a constant improvement in the life and on-road performance of every make of Ashok Leyland vehicle to hit the roads. Ashok Leyland product development successes have come from a keen sense of anticipation and attentiveness. The company initiated research into alternative fuels well before legislative debate had even begun in the country. The result was the implementation of CNG technology ahead of the rest promising a breath of fresh air for polluted cities.

Source: www.ashokleyland.com

Mind Power I: Six Things you should know while Marketing to Engineers- Sanjay Limaye

1. Engineers look down on advertising and advertising people.

2. Engineers do not like a "consumer approach."

3. The engineer's purchase decision is logical.

4. Engineers want to know the features and specifications, not just the benefits.

5. Engineers are not turned off by jargon.

6. Engineers have their own visual language.

Engineers look down on advertising and advertising people

Engineers have a low opinion of advertising and of people whose job it is to create advertising. The lesson, for the business-to-business marketer? Make your advertising and direct mail informational and professional, not gimmicky or promotional. Avoid writing that sounds like "ad copy." Don't use slick graphics that immediately identify a brochure or spec sheet as "advertising." Engineers want to believe they are not influenced by ad copy and that they make their decisions based on technical facts that are beyond a copywriter's understanding.

Engineers do not like a "consumer approach"

There is a raging debate about whether engineers respond better to a straight technical approach, clever consumer-style ads or something in between. Those who prefer the creative approach argue, "The engineer is a human being first and an engineer second. He will respond to creativity and cleverness just like everyone else". Unfortunately, there is much evidence to the contrary. In many tests of ads and direct mailings, I have seen straightforward, low-key, professional approaches equal or out pull "glitzy" ads and mailings repeatedly. Engineers respond well to communications that address them as knowledgeable technical professionals in search of solutions to engineering problems. Hard sell frequently falls on deaf ears here especially if not backed by facts.

The engineer's purchase decision is more logical than emotional

Most books and articles on advertising stress that successful copy appeal to emotions first, reason second. But with the engineering audience, it is often the opposite. The buyer carefully weighs the facts, makes comparisons and buys based on what product best fulfills his requirement. Certainly, there are emotional components to the engineer's buying decision. For instance, preference for one vendor over another is often based more on gut feeling than actual fact. But for the most part, an engineer buying a new piece of equipment will analyze the features and technical specifications in much greater depth than a consumer buying a stereo, VCR, CD player or other sophisticated electronic device. Copy aimed at engineers cannot be superficial. Clarity is essential. Make it immediately clear what you are offering and how it meets the engineer's needs.

Contd...

Engineers want to know the features and specifications, not just the benefits

In consumer advertising it is known that benefits are everything, and that features are unimportant. But engineers need to know the features of your product - performance characteristics, efficiency ratings, power requirements and technical specifications - in order to make an intelligent buying decision. Features should especially be emphasized when selling to OEMs (Original Equipment Manufacturers), VARs (Value-Added Resellers), systems integrators and others who purchase your product with an intention to incorporate it into their own product.

Engineers are not turned off by jargon - in fact, they like it.

Jargon can actually enhance communication when appealing to engineers, computer specialists and other technical audiences. Why is jargon effective? Because it shows the reader that you speak his language. When you write direct response copy, you want the reader to get the impression you're like him, don't you? And doesn't speaking his language accomplish that? Actually, engineers are not unique in having their "secret language" for professional communication. People in all fields publicly denounce jargon but privately love it.

Engineers have their own visual language

What are the visual devices through which engineers communicate? Charts, graphs, tables, diagrams, blueprints, engineering drawings, and mathematical symbols and equations. You should use these visual devices when writing to engineers for two reasons. First, engineers are comfortable with them and understand them. Second, these visuals immediately say to the engineer, "This is solid technical information, not sales talk". The best visuals are those specific to the engineer's specialty. Electrical engineers like circuit diagrams. Computer programmers feel comfortable looking at flow charts. Systems analysts use structured diagrams. Learn the visual language of your target audience and use these symbols and artwork throughout your communication.

Source: This article has been authored by Sanjay Limaye. Copyright is with Industrial Marketing Services. Reprinted with the kind permission of the author. Visit him at www.inmas.com.

Mind Power 2: Composites bring Boeing's Buyers, Engineers and Parts Suppliers Closer

With its 787 Dreamliner, purchasing is adapting to new technology and a new supply chain that includes more than just the familiar metals suppliers.

By Tom Stundza
Purchasing
March 1, 2007

Buyers at Boeing Commercial Airplanes are flying high because of the new challenges and opportunities presented by the new 787 Dreamliner. In essence, they're working with engineering to dramatically expand the use of carbon–fiber composites–and to help develop the best fabricators of that material.

Boeing is the nation's largest consumer of heat-treated aluminum and aerospace-grade titanium, developing over the past decade a sophisticated production purchasing organization at its assembly centre in Everett, Wash. The metals buyers within the Global Partners supply organization also buy miles of other raw materials to support five active passenger and freighter jetliner production programmes.

But the use of the light-weight composites–a potential game changer in an industry saddled with high fuel costs is changing the procurement organization's focus, increasing buyer interactions with engineering and restructuring the supply chain. The buying team and its parts suppliers are getting their composite material from a single source, the Toray Industries plant in nearby Tacoma.

Since the commercial airplane group outsources the development and manufacturer of nearly all the aircraft's systems to suppliers, the 787 Dreamliner is a milestone for global development, procurement

Contd...

and manufacturing. Working together, the design and procurement team have employed such supply management techniques as:

1. Early supplier involvement in the aircraft's design.

2. Advanced sourcing practices for key raw materials.

3. And outsourcing of entire systems to suppliers.

"The major change for the '87 is that the fuselage, wing and other structural parts that used to be predominantly aluminum is carbon fiber,' says John Byrne, director of purchased outside production and common commodities. The use of composite materials will enable the new 250-passenger wide body to use 20 percent less fuel than other aircraft of similar size. This has resulted in numerous airlines, smarting from skyrocketing jet-fuel prices of recent years, to place orders already for 473 of the Boeing 787s.

Buying composite material–actually high-strength carbon fiber pre-impregnated with toughened epoxy resin– "created some real technology and engineering challenges that needed to be solved for us to have the confidence to make a whole fuselage and a whole wing structure out of carbon fiber," Byrne tells Purchasing. "Engineering wise, the fuselage and the wing going to composite was a big leap. Then, there were the design and procurement team changes that were necessitated from sourcing predominantly aluminum and titanium to buying key components from carbon fiber."

"A lot of composite materials, even though they're built to the same specification, if they are built on a different production line, they may not behave the same when a product is fabricated," Byrne explains. "So, the ability for interchangeability, the ability to source from multiple sources, changes in the composite world. This absolutely has required more coordination between engineering and purchasing."

Boeing's supply management approach always is to work collaboratively with suppliers to identify and secure new innovative composite materials that are stronger and lighter than conventional materials. However, so far, the only 787-qualified composite supplier is Toray. "So, we play an instrumental role in coordinating and aggregating demand so capacity development by Toray meets demand needs of the programme and we also work to find the best business arrangements of all involved," says Byrne. "Technically, our partners will negotiate their own contracts with Toray; we act as an integrator." That's because composites tend to be specification specific–either to a certain, often single, use or to a single producer.

Carbon fiber-based composites can be considered the biggest buy of the 787 project. That's because 50 percent of the structure is composite material, about 20 percent is aluminum, 15 percent is titanium and the rest is titanium, copper wiring and other materials. By comparison, the 777 is 80 percent aluminum, titanium and other metals with 10 percent composite material and 10 percent other materials. The fuselage is the main component of the 787," says Byrne. "But we had the design and purchasing knowledge and confidence built off the 777 that allowed us to expand its use in the '87."

Metals aren't gone

Of course, Boeing isn't eliminating lightweight metals in the new jetliner's design; it's just that they no longer will be the key material for the outer skin, wings or tail. In fact, the current manufacturing lineup–the 737, 747, 767 and 777 families of airplanes and the Boeing Business Jet–still require lots of such metals as heat-treated aluminum, titanium and some nickel-based super alloys.

"All the airplanes we're building and delivering right now have an aluminum structure, for example," Byrne says. And the purchasing systems are well established. "Aluminum and the other metals are more mature, known materials entities," he says. "The applicable aerospace alloys tend not to be proprietary and tend to be available in the general marketplace. So, there are multiple people who can make it to our specifications and deliver it as needed."

Actually, that's a good thing, since "we still have a tremendous number of aluminum airplanes being bought-with 887 ordered in 2006 alone-that also require large amounts of titanium," says Jeff Hanley, senior manager for metallic materials. Total aluminum use is growing, not declining. What's happening is that aluminum "is changing its content from the big skins that make up the fuselage and the big structural pieces-skins and, what we call spars-that make up the wings," Hanley says. "But if you look at the 787, there still is a pretty big chunk of weight in the airplane that still is aluminum, almost 20 percent."

Contd...

From a purchasing standpoint, Boeing has more options available to buyers for the traditional metals. The Global Partners organization has long-term contracts with a select number of mills and a single key distributor who handle most of the required volume for the aerospace metal by Boeing's fabrication centres and its top-tier suppliers.

During reorganizations this decade, the procurement organization at Boeing Commercial Airplanes has looked to suppliers worldwide for innovative new materials and sub-systems. If anything, the purchasing team for the 787 has expanded the collaborative approach with suppliers so they act as the master orchestrator, coordinating these disparate and geographically dispersed partners and managing final assembly and quality management.

"As we develop and introduce the 787, we are changing the baseline for structural parts on the airplane to composite material," Byrne explains. And even though there has been some use of composites in the empennage, the tail structure, of the Boeing 777 jetliner, sourcing of this material for large-scale production-and adjusting the metals buy for different future parts-has required adjustments in the supply chain and manufacturing.

Hanley notes that since the purchasing organization knew enough about the suppliers who had been qualified to fabricate composites for the 777 programme "we invited them to join development very early." That's because while the buying and design team and these fabricators "knew about composite materials for use in the tail, the applications for the 787 were so different that manufacturing techniques for structural parts would be significantly different."

What's new in the 787

The Boeing 787 Dream liner actually is a family of new, fuel-efficient airplanes that will bring big-jet comfort in a midsize aircraft. The Boeing 787 will use advanced materials, operating systems and quieter engines to provide a 20 percent improvement in fuel performance than existing widebody aircraft. The 787-8 Dreamliner will carry 210-250 passengers up to 8,500 nautical miles and the 787-9 will carry 250 to 290 passengers up to 8,800 nautical miles. Later, the 787-3 Dreamliner will accommodate between 290 and 330 passengers in routes of 3,500 nautical miles. Boeing selected both General Electric and Rolls-Royce to develop engines for the new airplane. The first aircraft will be flown by All Nippon Airways in 2008.

INDUSTRIAL BUYING AND BUYING BEHAVIOUR

Industrial Buying is an entirely a new process, when we compare it with the consumer buying process. In the last chapter, we saw how various factors affect the complete business scenario, in a dynamic industrial marketing environment. In industrial buying the purchase manager coordinates the complete set of activities, with numerous people in the organization. In fact, the purchase manager is the last person, who needs to be contacted, with reference to any kind of new purchases. For the marketer, thus understanding the entire buying process is very essential. So if we are going to sell our products to another firm, we need to understand how the process of industrial buying takes place.

Today, the business marketer works in close harmony with the various departments to provide better value to the customer. Understanding the organizational buying process is crucial for understanding the segments of the market, where we can do business profitably and how to reach the organizational buyers more efficiently.

This chapter explores the process of buying in an organization and the characteristics of every purchasing situation and what would be the implications of such buying situations, to a marketer.

ORGANIZATIONAL BUYING

Organization buying process is a set of complex events and depends on the level of experience; the firm has in purchasing that goods or service. To illustrate this, if the marketer is selling to an organization, who is making a routine purchase, would be quite different, from the way he sells it to an organization that is purchasing for the first time.

Generally, when an organization buys for the first time, the information required to them is completely different and extensive. For example if a firm is purchasing laptops for its employees, they would be interested to know about the models that satisfy their purpose and will also require high level of servicing.

The buying process within an organization is not done by a single man. It is a combination of activities.

Thus here we see two set of variables. On one hand there are a series of steps which affect the buying process, and on the other, we have the buying situations.

BUYING SITUATION

There are 3 types of buying situations. They are:[1]

1.   New Task

2.   Modified REBUY

3.   Straight Rebuy

New Task: The problem is new, to the company or the company is in an absolutely new business. It could be an additional product line or a change in consumer preferences or it could be entering a new kind of business, wherein the company had no previous experiences. Here the situation is new, and the decision makers lack the experience, product knowledge and expertise of such a situation. Here in this case a lot of information and queries will be there in the minds of the buyer. The degree of problem solving will be to a considerably great extent.

A new task would be spread over a period of time, keeping in mind the technical complexity of buying the product or it could be spread over a short period of time which would have arisen due to rapid technological change.

Guidelines: The seller must be an active participant for the buyer from the very initial stages. The seller must be able to pinpoint the needs provide a comparison statement and offer suitable proposals. For an "in supplier" i.e., who is already supplying currently to the buyer has an edge over the purchasing process, because of their relationships and rapport with the firm.

Modified Rebuy: A situation, when an organization wants to review its decisions with relation to its purchases, and they feel that there could be significant benefits such as quality and costs. The decision of modified rebuy might arise when there are external pressures to reduce costs, improve technology and quality. It could also be in a situation, when the buyer is displeased with the vendor that they are currently dealing with.

Guidelines: If you are an existing supplier already, you might have to lose some business, because of this situation. Thus careful steps must be taken to stop the process. Understanding and satisfying the customers is very essential. It could also be possible, that the buyer no longer feels that the supplier is proving too beneficial.

The outside supplier in this situation has a better edge. Thus, why the buying organization wants to change his supplier could be an important point what an outside supplier must answer. Thus, the outside supplier must focus on quality, servicing and timely delivery.

The business marketer should attempt to identify purchasing pattern that apply to a firm, study the complexity of the products and the financial risks that the buyer is going to undergo.

Straight Rebuy: This is the most common buying situation. Buyers generally have experience in buying this product and the information required is little or very less. The need to evaluate alternative proposals is not necessary. Buyers have a well-defined choice over these products. The buyers may look at new alternatives, only when there is a new technological advancement otherwise they would prefer to buy the same from the existing supplier. These are generally regular purchases and of low value.

One change that is happening for this straight rebuy situation is the process of online procurement. This not only reduces the transactional costs but is very easy to manage and operate.

Guidelines: The inside supplier should be very careful to the requirements of the buyer and maintain a strong relationship. They should be very alert to changes happening and responsive to them. Timely delivery is very essential for the needs of straight rebuy situations.

The outside supplier has to do a lot of home work, before breaking through an account. They must try and persuade buyers to reexamine alternatives and include them in the new list of suppliers.

Mind Power 3: The Xerox Supplier Diversity Programme

Based on our finding that Minority and Women-owned Business Enterprises (MWBEs) meet and surpass corporate supply standards, the supplier diversity programme at Xerox has consistently established business partnerships with MWBE companies, veterans/service disabled veterans, HUB Zone programmes, protected workshop vendors and are establishing business relationships with gay and lesbian business enterprises.

Here are some of our achievements:

1. Since 1985, Xerox has purchased more than $5.0 billion in goods and services from qualified Minority/Women/Service Disabled Veterans Business Enterprises.

2. In 2005, Xerox purchased $330.0 million of goods and services from MWBEs in the United States, approximately 10 percent more than originally targeted.

3. Total spending with MWBEs represented 24.0 percent of Xerox's annual qualified purchases. Approximately 1,000 MWBE suppliers benefited from these purchases.

Source: www.xerox.com/go/xrx/template/00.jsp?view

ORGANIZATIONAL BUYING PROCESS

When a consumer buys, the process is a lot simpler than an industrial purchasing process. The stages for a consumer purchasing process are generally:

Problem recognition, information search, information evaluation, purchase decision-making and post purchase behaviour.[2] However, the process of consumer purchase is limited to a very few number of people making the decision. The industrial purchasing process is not so.

The stages of organizational buying are:

1. Problem Recognition.
2. Determination of the characteristics and quantity of needed item.
3. Specifying the requirements.
4. Search for suppliers.
5. Acquisition and analysis of proposals.
6. Selecting of suppliers.
7. The order routine process.
8. Performance Feed Back and evaluation.

The Process of Industrial Purchasing

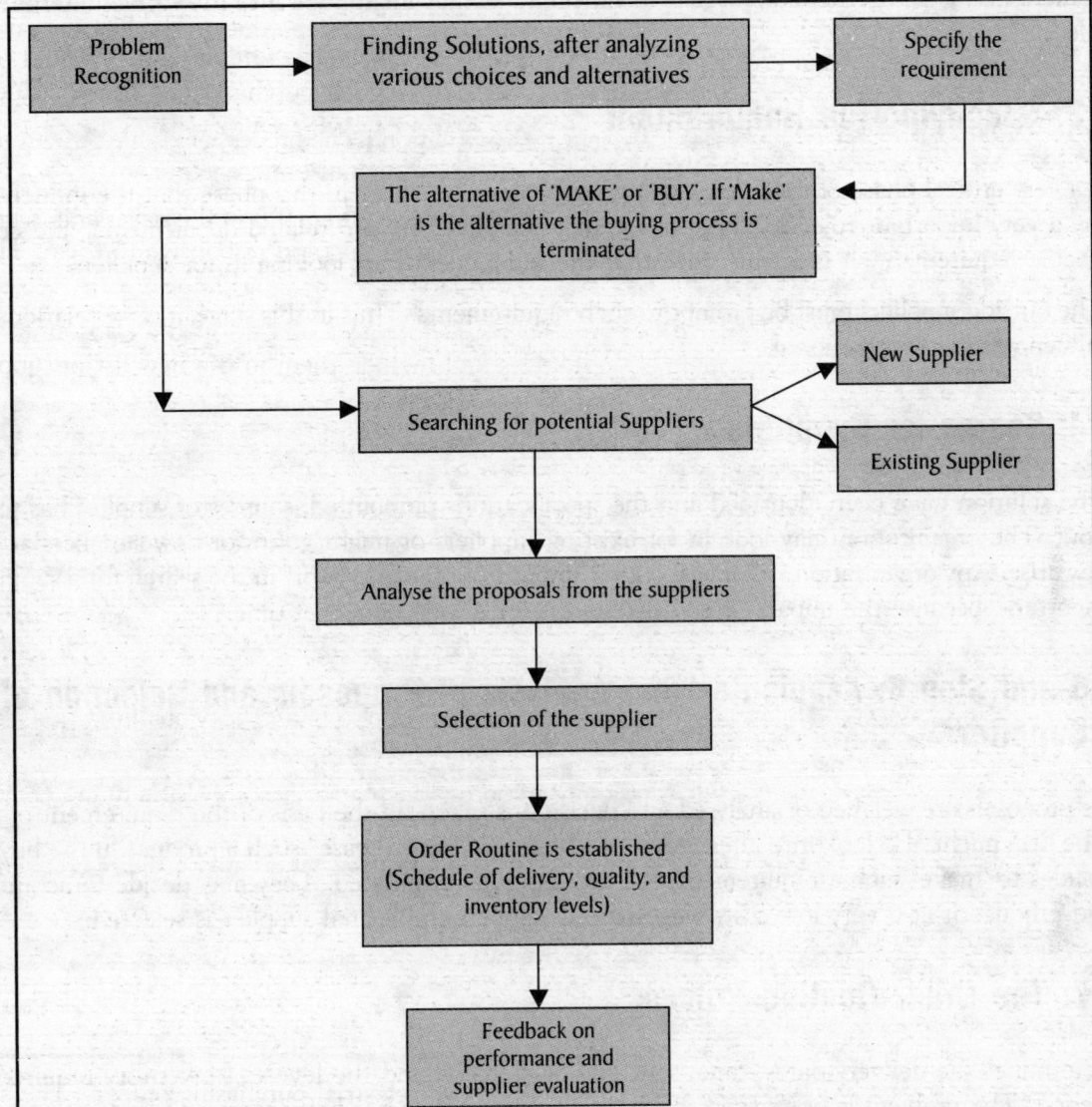

Step 1: Problem Recognition

The problem or need has to be recognized. This recognition of the problem may be internal or external. Example of internal problem recognition would be the case of equipments breaking down, or raw materials are not available in sufficient quality or quantity. An external problem recognition would be one when technology is changing and improvement of performance. Say for example, one shift of a soap manufacturing company, can generate "x" amount of soaps, with the application of new technology it can be made into "2x".

Step 2: Determination of the Characteristics and Quantity of Needed Item

Once the problem has been identified, the next step is to find a solution for such a problem. Thus the organization will try and specify the problems. Thus details like "what specification", "application" and "quantities" have to be determined. For technically complex products the engineering and research and development may join together and for non-technical items they might look into the various alternatives available in the market.

Step 3: Specifying the Requirement

This is a very critical phase of the complete buying process. It is only in this phase that the influencers will play a very important role. So, there is a joint discussion between related departments, and come to a specific requirement. It is in this stage that the influencers start looking in for suppliers.

The outside suppliers must be prompt to such requirements. Thus in this stage, a close relationship with influencers are very essential.

Step 4: Search for Suppliers

Once the solution have been identified and the specifications pinpointed, sources of supplies has to be found out. The organization may look in for existing suppliers or might go in for new suppliers as the case may arise. Any organization will invest a long amount of time and effort in the search for a supplier. It is important, because the impact of any decision is for a long period of time.

Step 5 and Step 6: Acquisition and Analysis of Proposals and Selection of New Supplier

Various proposals are weighed or analysed and decision is taken on the basis of the requirement of the firm. The firm might also look into alternatives of "Make or Buy or Lease" such a product. If the buying firm decides to 'make' such a requirement, the process gets terminated. They may decide to acquire a firm and produce it at a very low cost. Negotiations happen and a final supplier is selected.

Step 7: The Order Routine Process

This determines the delivery dates, time, schedule of delivery, and the levels of inventory required at each period. The problem is not solved fill the time the product has been received, used and gives a satisfactory performance.

Step 8: Performance Feedback and Evaluation

This consists of a formal or informal process and feedback is taken on product as well as supplier. This review may allow a purchasing manager either to continue, terminate or issue a warning to the supplier. If the supplier or his goods, is not meeting the requirements, then the ones screened earlier can be recalled back.

The flow of this model may not proceed in the same way or may be mixed up. This will depend upon the complexity of the product being bought. There is also a set of internal and external forces that acts on the buying process.

BUYING CENTRES, INFLUENCERS AND ROLES THEY PLAY

Most of the time, when a marketer goes to sell anything to a person, getting to the right person, who is a decision-maker is very important. Even any kind of communication strategy, must hit the persons having the maximum control in the decision-making process. Thus, one of the key challenges that you face as a marketer is to identify the individuals involved in the decision-making process, also called as DMU or Decision-making unit.

For example, if a tour operator want to replace its buses and are planning to bring in a new line of "Volvo" buses, who would be the person or persons involved in the process of buying.

A very small or medium organization, might have one or two persons in the Decision-Making Unit (DMU), but for larger organizations it is generally a set of people, "who share a common goal or goals which the decision will hopefully help them to achieve, and who share the risks arising from the decision".[3] These group of people, in industrial marketing are referred to as the "**buying centre**".

Thus, it would be the job of every marketer to find out the "DMU" of an industrial organization. But, before, we do that let us try and understand the role played by the buying centre members.

BUYING CENTRE ROLES[4]

Deciders

These are the people who have either a formal or informal authority to finally decide, whether to buy and from whom to buy. For a marketer the most difficult job is to find out, who the deciders are. For a technically complex product, it could be the research and development, engineering and the top management who would sit through the decision-making process.

Influencers

People who influence the decision-making process. It is not necessary that it could be only internal influences, but it could also be a set of external guys, who would typically influence, the purchasing process. A bus driver could be an indirect influencer, for a range of buses that a company wishes to purchase. It could also be an architect, who could act as an influencer in the purchase of capital machinery.

Users

They are the person, who would be actually using the product or service. Users can play a very significant role in the process of purchasing decision. They may sometimes initiate the process of purchasing. Thus marketers should not ignore the role of users, as they would be very technically competent to speak on the product.

Buyers

Organizational members, who have a formal authority in the selection of suppliers, and implementation of procedures involved with purchasing. They are generally the middle and top level managers. They play a major role in selecting suppliers and negotiating purchases.

Gatekeepers

Are members, who control the flow of information between a source and destination. They favour a particular kind of information, and filters information reaching decision-makers. Generally it is seen that the purchasing department is the least important in the process of decision-making, and they strongly act as gatekeepers, becoming a barrier to flow of information. They feel that their importance is of the highest order; they filter information reaching decision makers. They keep the management informed about developments in prices, sources and new trends in the market and expect to have a considerable influence in purchasing. Thus, an industrial marketer must act very carefully and the first step that they need to take is to meet the purchase manager at the last.

BUYING CENTRE MEMBERS

An obvious question that comes to our mind is that, who is actually involved in the process of purchase. The buying centre members are a cross departmental decision unit. People from the organization are a part of the buying centre, because of primarily 2 reasons. They are:

1. They have the authority and formal responsibility.

2. They have a strong information source.

   Now, let us see the various departments and the role they play as buying centre members.

Manufacturing

They are responsible for feasibility and economic viability of the product. Thus specifications, designs, parts and materials are confirmed in this department and equipment needs and costs are given due importance. They are generally responsible for cost reductions and quality improvements.

Research and Development

Holds a very key position, for the development of new product. The earlier, the marketer is involved in the designing stage, higher the chances of a particular product getting incorporated. They are generally responsible for the increase of efficiency and new development of products.

Purchasing

They have the least role to play, in the purchase of any kind of product. Since, they have strong negotiation capabilities and maintain the relationships with suppliers; they are strong in cases of repetitive buying.

Top Management

They generally involve themselves, when the purchase is of high significant value or a 'new buy' situation or in cases the purchase affects only the top management of the company. For example, a video conferencing facility for all the branches across the globe.

MODELS OF INDUSTRIAL BUYING BEHAVIOUR

A) A model on the composition of the organizational buying centre has been developed by Mattson.[5]

The composition depends on a multiple number of variables involved in the process of buying. The factors which determine the composition of the organizational buying centre are:

1. *Environment and Mission:* How an organization thinks, what objectives it has, how it prioritizes its tasks, how organizational authority is delegated will effect the composition of organization buying centre, i.e., who in the buying organization will be interested in the purchasing decision. Environmental factors such as economic, technological, social, cultural, legal, political, industrial structure and channel structure will also affect the buying centre and will help the marketer with clues on the buying centre.

2. *Purchase Needs:* Identifying influences and what drives the purchasing can be very key in the understanding of the buying centre composition. Organizations generally have certain objectives in mind while purchasing. It could be quality, price, servicing, and supply or could be a specific task in mind.

3. *Buy Classes and Buy Phases:* As we have discussed earlier, the buy classes and buy phases, play a very important role in the complete buying process.

4. *Dollar Value and Complexity:* With the size of organization increasing, the role played by purchasing manager reduces. This is because the purchasing process becomes compartmentalized and there are other departments who influence the purchasing process.

5. *Time Commitment and Life Cycles:* Larger the time horizon, the relationship between the buyers and sellers changes and becomes more firm. Purchasing activities will vary with harmony to the buying firm's product life cycle.

6. *Buying Centre Membership, Procurement and other Members:* Buying centre, as well as the other members play a very important role in the process of decision-making.

    Thus the industrial purchasing should be viewed as a set of complex process, which is affected by a multiple factors. Therefore every industrial marketer must approach buyers with a sufficient amount of homework.

B) Jagdish N Sheth model for Industrial Buying Behaviour[5A]

Jagdish N Sheth came out with the model of industrial buyer behaviour. In small firms or in cases of routine purchases, generally there is an involvement of one single person. But the case is not so for industrial organizations which are large. Multiple people play a very important role in the process of decision-making. Thus it forms a very important role of the industrial marketers to understand the decision-making units, power centres and how the process of buying takes place.

The model is developed using four components. They are:

1. *Expectations of the purchasing agents, engineers, users and others:* The expectations of these people are influenced by a multiple number of factors. They are:

i) The background of the individuals.

ii) The sources of information about the product or service which can be obtained from sources. They could be a salesperson from another company, from exhibitions, direct mail, press release, trade magazines or also could be word of mouth publicity.

iii) Active search is the process or way of collecting the information.

iv) *Perceptual distortion:* It is the outlook of the person who receives the information and the way and mechanism he uses to interpret such information.

v) Satisfaction with previous purchases will affect the expectations of the decision-making unit.

2. **Industrial buying process** is affected by two major components. They are:

i) **Product specific factors:** It has three variables. The time pressure, perceived risk, and type of purchase. When we say time pressure, we mean to say the availability of time in the decision-making process. Perceived risk also plays a very key and important role in the decision-making process and also the type of purchase which we have already seen earlier.

ii) **Company specific factors:** This would include organization orientation, organization size, more complex and more number of people would be involved in the decision-making process.

3. In cases of conflict how is it resolved in a particular organization? He suggests four mechanisms for the process of conflict resolution. They are: problem-solving, persuasion, bargaining and politicking.

4. Situational factors also become critical in the process of decision-making. The decision-making process can be joint or autonomous. Autonomous decisions are generally in small organizations where it is typically a 'one man show'.

This will lead to the process of choosing the supplier or a particular brand.

C) Webster and Wind Model of Organizational Buying Behaviour[5B]

The Webster and Wind model developed in 1972 is quite a comprehensive model for the organizational buying behaviour process. They speak of four set of variables:

1. Environmental Variable

2. Organizational Variable

3. Individual Variable

The above three affect the fourth variable, i.e., the buying centre variable and which in turn affect the buying decisions of an organization.

The environmental variables consists of various factors like technological factors, economic factors, political and legal factors, cultural factors, demand factors, competitive pressures and supplier information.

The organizational variables which decide or rather influences the buying centre variables are factors like: objectives and goals of the organization, the structural factors within the organization, purchasing policies that are followed by the organization, evaluation of suppliers, reward system and the extent of decentralization in the organization.

The individual variables would include personal goals, education, experience, lifestyle, income, position, values, and expertise in that field.

So, a combined force or effect of these three variables will be seen on to the buying centre variable.

The buying centre variable will thus constitute buying authority, size of the buying centre, influencers, power, involvement, communication and relationships.

The buying centre thus will affect the buying decisions of the organization. The organization will thus take a decision as to:

1. Make or buy or lease,

2. Delay the process of decision-making,

3. Search for more information, and

4. More negotiation with suppliers.

The strength of the model is that it is highly comprehensive and applicable to all buying situations.

D) Choffray and Lilien Model of Organizational Buying Process[5C]

Choffray and Lilien mention that any organizational buying that takes place is influenced by environmental factors, organizational factors and individual factors.

The environmental constraints would include physical, technological, economic and social.

The organizational requirements would be technical and financial.

These two factors will give a result to a set of alternatives and reject those, which do not meet those requirements. This will result into the formation of individual preferences for buying which will be affected by the individual responsibilities comprising of the buying centre. The buying centre judges its opinion on the source of information, evaluation criteria and interaction structure. The interaction structures of the members of the buying centre will be different and will lead into the formation of organizational preferences and finally the organizational choice for procuring the goals.

Mind Power 4: Becoming a Supplier at Phillips

Phillips' strategy focuses on leveraging their brand and core competencies in health care, lifestyle and technology to grow in selected categories and geographies. They aim to deliver products of the highest quality at attractive prices.

How Philips select suppliers

Philips will select suppliers based on competencies and competitiveness in all relevant areas. They also have legal and ethical requirements, alongside their expectations for quality and cost-effectiveness. When one becomes a Philips supplier, it is required to sign a General Purchase Agreement (GPA) and comply with General Business Principles and Philips' Supplier Declaration on Sustainability and our banned substances list. (Philips has the policy to select companies with ISO 9000-2000 and / or ISO 14001 certification as their suppliers.). All the suppliers are audited on a regular basis by Philips or third-party auditors. Their programme of global certification audits verifies that suppliers are meeting their obligations under their purchasing agreements with Philips. The audits are conducted by trained specialists and Philips constantly monitors performance and results via a Philips-wide Supplier Certification process. This enables them to provide immediate feedback to internal and external stakeholders. Relationships between Philips and suppliers are also governed by the Supply Management Code of Ethics.

Source: www.philips.com/about/businessesandsuppliers/suppliers/section-14749/index.html

OBJECTIVES OF ORGANIZATIONAL BUYING

Before an industrial marketer can actually pitch a client for sales, the marketer must be very sure of the objective to purchase. There are a certain set of **task-oriented and non-task-oriented objectives.**[6]

Task-oriented purchase will generally be factors like price, quality and services. The non-task oriented objective would be the personal objectives, goals and motivation that plays behind every purchase.

What actually a buyer is influenced by is very difficult to define. But, the non-task-oriented objectives do play a very important role in the complete process of decision-making.

Discussing a little more on the task-oriented objectives, organizations are in business mainly to make profits and the goods they buy constitute a major chunk of their total revenue. It can be about 40 to 50 percent of their total revenues. So, every buyer would be very cautious about in their approach to buying. They would be mainly looking in for factors like servicing, quality, deliver schedule, and price. Price is one factor, which is the last in the priority list. It is said in industrial marketing, that it is not "goods" that are sold for a "price", but it is a relationship. Quality of the raw materials or the goods entering the manufacturing process, should meet the minimum desired quality levels. This would be to reduce the number of defects from the final product. Generally industrial buyers do not compromise over quality factors. Probably pitching a regular supply at a low cost would work, but definitely not for the inputs in the production process. Marketers, thus must act in close coordination with the buyer, on requirement levels, and the acceptance level of quality.

Servicing the buyers is another important component that marketers have to adhere to. As we have said earlier, all relationships and transactions are for a very long period of time. So, servicing the buyer plays a very important role in the industrial buying process. These become much more important in cases of foundation goods. Where the value of goods bought is higher and the perceived risks are high, level of servicing has to be high.

Supply of goods has to be continuous; otherwise the production process can be hampered to a great extent. Proximity of buyers and sellers are very high, in these cases. Thus, the recent trend of ordering over the Internet has replaced the traditional ordering format, by quite good number of companies. Even, the contracts should be able to define the interruptions of supply due to natural or human factors. So, a buyer should decide, whether to have a single source of purchase or a mix of 2-3 suppliers, supplying the same goods.

Reciprocity is another kind of special dealing between the buyer and seller. The output for one company becomes an input of another company. Reciprocal dealings will happen when there are little differences in between products. It is a "mutually beneficial" relationship and today has become an important part. However, problems in reciprocal dealings may appear in cases when managers feel that they are not getting a better price for their product.

Non-task objectives are basically personal objectives which also play a very strong and important role in the complete process of decision-making. Power, promotion, job security, prestige are some of the internal motives that a person might have. Some people might also take up suppliers on the basis of relationship or mutual benefits. However, a marketer finds it quite challenging to handle the non-task objectives, as it defies all logic. Caution must be exercised by sales representatives, not to focus on too much of buyer's personal goals.

CONFLICTS IN JOINT DECISION-MAKING

Conflicts are bound to happen, be it industrial marketing or consumer marketing. In the previous pages we have seen that the process of purchase involves a lot of people influencing the process. We also saw the task objectives and the non-task objectives of buying. "Generally, the potential for conflict emanates from differences in expectations regarding suppliers, differences in the evaluative criteria employed, differences in buying objectives and differences in decision-making styles of the individuals involved."[7]

Conflicts are bound to happen. Some amount of conflicts is useful for the organization to grow, but excess of conflicts would have a harmful effect on the organization if allowed to persist.

Resolving of conflicts has been put across in a model devised by Day, Michaels and Purdue.[8] They spoke of five methods. They are:

1. *Competing:* This is a way in which one single person, puts the complete stress on his side, and expects everyone to follow his view or approach. They become highly uncooperative, enter into arguments and are highly assertive.

2. *Accommodating:* These are set of people, who will carry on everybody's view. They do not tend to neglect someone else's view. They believe in a perfect symbiotic relationship and are unassertive. They cooperate with others in all matters of discussion.

3. *Collaborating:* They start to satisfy the concerns of both the parties. They are assertive, but generally cooperate. They dig into issues before passing any comments.

4. *Avoiding:* They are indifferent to the concerns of the other party. They move away from the situation very diplomatically and keep on postponing issues. They are unassertive as well as uncooperative.

5. *Compromising:* They accept the middle path. They believe in setting terms somewhere in the midway. They believe in "neither yours, nor mine".

One more aspect that is generally seen is the formation of coalitions. Departments or people or members of the buying centre come tighter informally and stress their point of view. In the process of conflict resolution, power plays a very important role. The marketer thus must be able to identify the source of power for the decision-making process. Power need not be necessarily with one person or top management. Two or more groups can join together and subdue the views of the other. In a small organization, the source of power may be the "Big Boss" of the company, but for larger organizations multiple sources of power arise. Sales persons might sometimes be caught in between two power groups. Thus a very key understanding of the power capabilities must be understood and a way to bridge the gap should be found out.

Mind Power 5: Supplier Requirements at Nokia

Nokia has three supplier requirements. They are:

- Ethical
- Environmental
- Managerial

At Nokia we feel that sound environmental and social principles are an important part of sustaining a successful and responsible business

Contd...

We expect the companies in our supplier network to take a similar ethical business approach. To ensure this we have developed a comprehensive set of global Nokia Supplier Requirements (NSR) which includes specified environmental and social requirements.

NSR's environmental and ethical requirements are based on international standards ISO 14001. SA 8000, OHSAS 18001, PCMM and ILO, and UN conventions. We recognize that there are other standards and management systems in use and accept those which are equivalent to or exceed our own requirements.

In response to stakeholder feedback and as part of our commitment to continuous improvement Nokia is currently updating Supplier Requirements.

Source: www.nokia.com/link?cid=EDITORIAL 64855

EVALUATING SUPPLIERS

Once a marketer becomes a supplier to any firm, only half the job is done. The need is to consistently perform, throughout the contract period. The buyer always has a mechanism to evaluate the performance of the suppliers. The scores or aggregates or the ratings the buyer gives to a particular supplier, will depend upon whether the supplier is going to continue or not. Whenever, supplies are concerned some basic considerations like-service, flexibility, delivery, quality, and price is taken into consideration. Two methods which are very common for evaluating suppliers are:[9]

1. Weighted Method
2. Cost Ratio Method

Weighted Method

There are certain parameters, to which weights are assigned. The parameters generally vary from company to company. Now, the weighted score is calculated. Suppliers are generally given a minimum benchmark level, which they are supposed to achieve. Companies prioritize themselves amongst the factors and then weights are assigned to each factor. For example, if servicing and quality is the highest ranked amongst the companies's list of parameters, then the weight given to them would be higher than the others.

The advantage of this particular method is that, a number of variable factors are there upon which the evaluation can be done. The suppliers are also on their toes to perform, otherwise they might lose the account.

Factor	Weight (w)	Performance (p)	Score (= w x p)
Servicing	40	0.9	36
Quality	25	0.9	22.5
Price	20	0.8	16
Delivery	15	0.6	9
Total			83.5

Cost Ratio Method

It is used on the basis of the cost analysis that is done for evaluating suppliers. The interesting factor of this method is that all costs are taken into consideration. When the ratio of costs to the various parameters is low, the supplier is rated high. When the ratio is high, the supplier is rated low.

Costs include everything possible from rejection of materials, to the frequency of telephone calls made for delivery. It also includes paper works, emergency deliveries, manufacturing time lost due to defective parts, etc. What this method of supplier rating cannot account is the intangible factors that are associated as costs. The reason is the quantification of such data. It could be factors like location, financial stability, etc.

CONCLUSION

Thus in this chapter we see that, it is a very complicated process when an organization is purchasing. It is not only task-oriented objectives, but also non task-oriented objectives that play a very key and important role in the complete decision-making process. We saw the buy grid and the buy phase models and other ways how the complete process of industrial purchasing is affected.

Thus marketers should understand the role played by each member of the buying centre, the power centres so that they tailor make the situation as per the needs. We also saw the ways and means of conflict and resolution methods.

After a supplier has been selected, we saw how his work is being evaluated by the buyers. Thus, it becomes the job of the supplier not only to get the order, but also maintain a level of standard with the buyer.

References

1. Robinson, Faris and Wind, "Industrial Buying and Creative Marketing".

2. Phillip Kotler, "Principles of Marketing", Prentice Hall, pp 252-260.

3. R.D. Buzell and others, "Marketing: a Contemporary Analysis, 2nd edition, McGraw Hill-pp 62.

4. Webster and Wind, "Organizational Buying Behavior", Prentice Hall-1972- pp 77-80.

5. Melvin R Mattson, "How to Determine the Composition and Influence of a Buying Centre", Industrial Marketing Management 17, 1988, pp 200, 214, Elsevier science Publishing Company Inc.

5A. Sheth, "A Model of Industrial Buyer Behavior", Journal of Marketing 37, October 1973, pp 50-56.

5B. Webster and Wind, "Journal of Marketing 36", April 1972- pp 12- 17.

5C. Choffray and Lilien, "Assessing the Response to Industrial Marketing Strategy", pp 20-31.

6. Reeder, Brierty, Reeder, "Industrial Marketing", Analysis, Planning and Control, pp 97-101.

7. Sheth, "A Model of Industrial Buyer Behavior", pp 50-56.

8. Day, Michaels and Purdue, "How Buyers Handle Conflict", Industrial Marketing Management 17, 1988, pp 153-169.

9. Zenz- "Purchasing and the Management of Materials"- pp 140-146- John Wiley and Sons Inc.

Mind Power 6: Supplier Relationships: A Strategic Initiative

By Jagdish N. Sheth and Arun Sharma. Reprinted with the permission of the author.

Introduction

Firms are facing increasingly competitive environments characterized by continuous pressure on costs, large global players, continuously evolving products, customer fragmentation and emerging

Contd...

technologies. To ensure success, firms realize that they cannot be experts in all businesses and are concentrating on their core competencies. As an example, Westinghouse is selling its power and defense lines to concentrate on the broadcasting business. To enhance their performance in non-core competency areas, companies are reevaluating business relationships so as to form closer relationships with strategic suppliers[1, 2, 3]. Firms have realized that collaborative business relationships improve a firm's ability to respond to the new business environment by allowing them to focus on their core businesses and reduce costs in business processes.

In an earlier paper, we had suggested that the source of next-generational competitive advantage will be collaborative relationships that firms have with their suppliers[4]. We suggested four reasons for this phenomenon. First, marketers or sellers are driving this change as firms have started identifying and catering to the needs of specific customers. Thus, having a relationship with suppliers will enable firms to receive better service and therefore be more efficient in procurement. Second, firms recognize that supplier relationships will allow them to be more effective. It is easier to implement strategies such as quality platforms, if firms have relationships with their suppliers. Third, there are enabling technologies that allow firms to select their best customers and suppliers. Computer programmes allow firms to calculate profitability associated with each customer or supplier. Finally, competition and the growth of alliances are forcing firms to develop better supplier relationships to maintain a competitive edge.

The purpose of this paper is to emphasize that supplier partnership will provide a strategic advantage to firms. This paper identifies the benefits of supplier partnerships and provides guidelines for future supplier partnering.

Shift in Organizational Strategy

The reason for the emerging emphasis on supplier relationships is the shift in organizational buying strategies[4]. Organizational purchasing strategies have been dramatically changing for four reasons (see Figure 4.1). First, global competitiveness had made firms realize the competitive advantages of creating and managing supply chain relationships. Second, emergence of the Total Quality Management philosophy has encouraged "reverse marketing" starting with external customers and moving backward into procurement processes. For example, Demand Driven Manufacturing or flexible manufacturing and operations have been instituted in order to serve the diversity of demand with respect to form, place and time value to customers. The role of suppliers is critical in this regard. Third, industry restructuring through mergers, acquisitions and alliances on a global basis has reorganized the procurement function from a decentralized administrative function to a centralized strategic function. This is further intensified by outsourcing many support functions such as data processing, and human resources. Finally, uses of information technologies have restructured the buying philosophy, processes and platforms by allowing firms to share market information and use market information to schedule design and manufacturing of products better.

Fundamentally, the consequence of changing paradigms of organizational strategy is likely to result in a two-dimensional shift as shown in Figure 4.2. Organizational purchasing strategy shifts from a transaction oriented to a relational oriented philosophy and from a decentralized domestic sourcing to a centralized global sourcing process.

Contd...

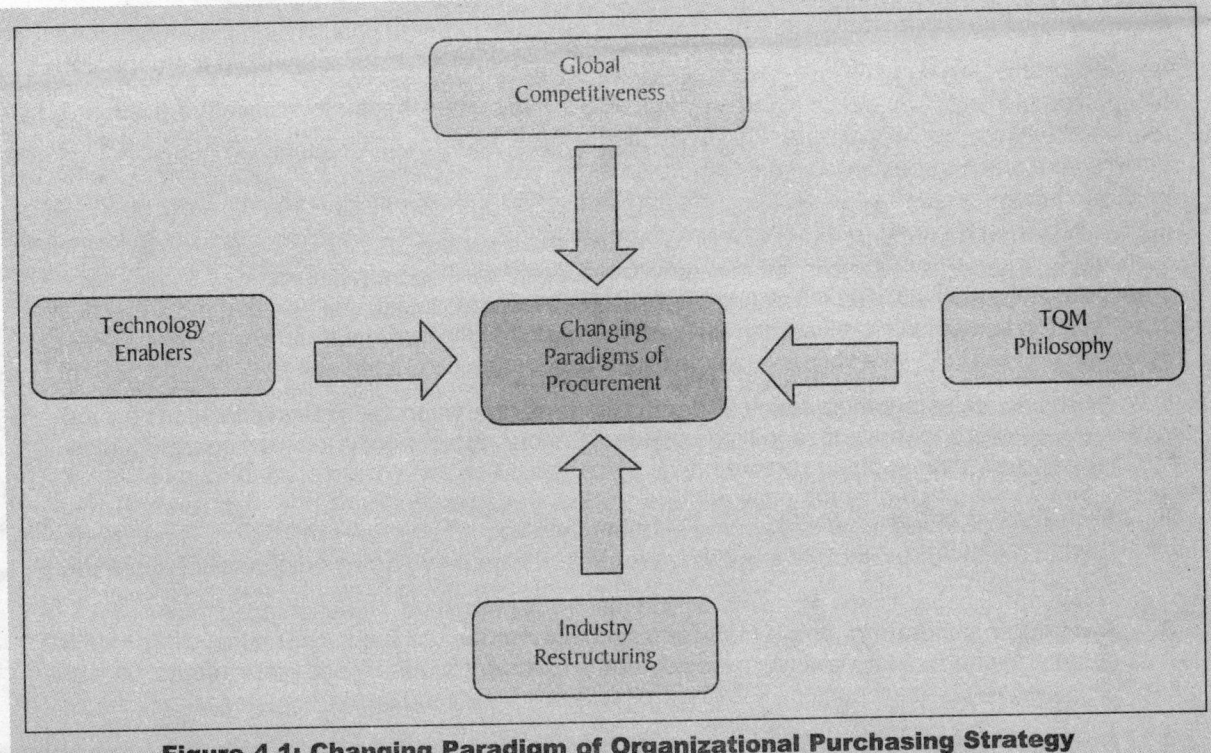

Figure 4.1: Changing Paradigm of Organizational Purchasing Strategy

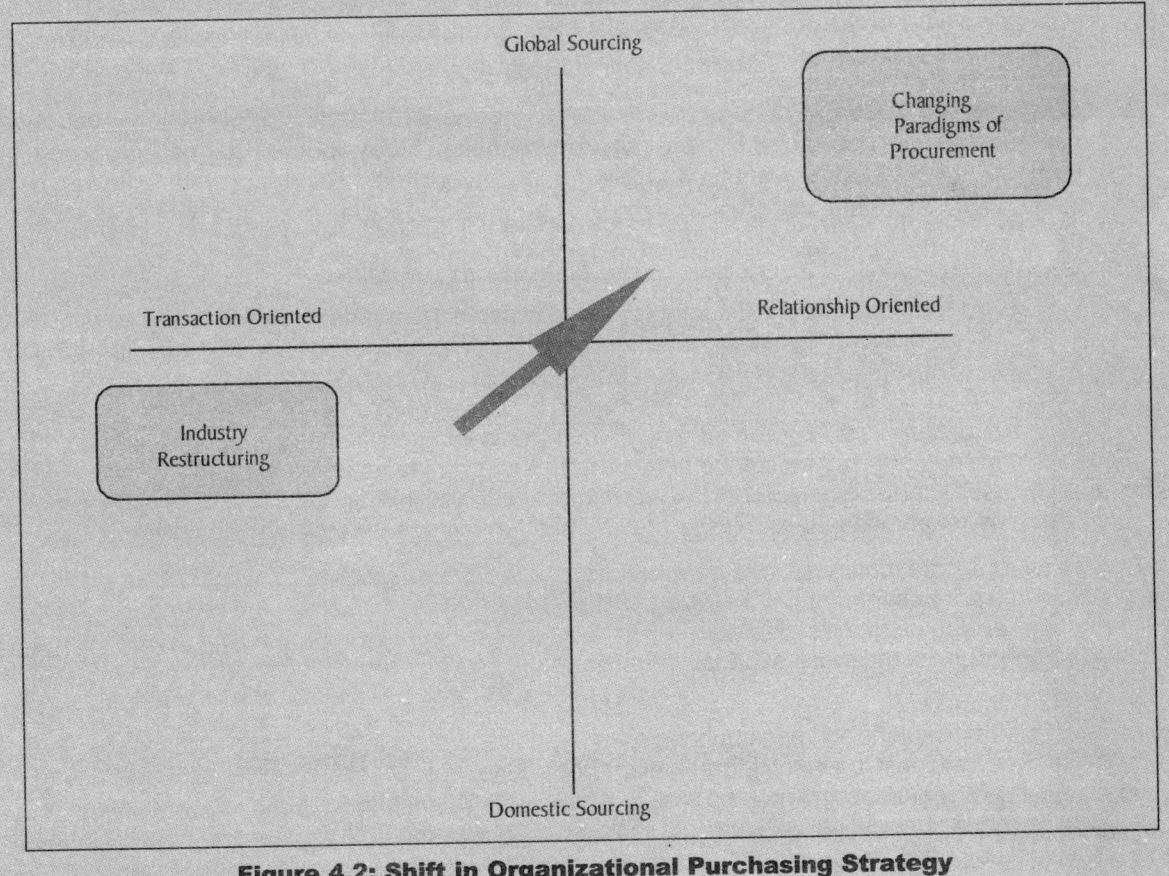

Figure 4.2: Shift in Organizational Purchasing Strategy

Contd...

Relationship with Suppliers

As stated earlier, we suggest that developing relationship with suppliers will be critical for the effective functioning of firms. This trend is reflected in Table 1 that shows that large firms have substantially reduced their number of suppliers. This trend also suggests that some suppliers would be exclusive to firms. The primary reasons are that corporations are becoming leaner. The procurement function is becoming more centralized while the profit and loss (P & L) responsibility of firms is becoming less centralized. Business unit heads are raising more questions about the way things are bought. And as vertically integrated companies – those that have complete internal capabilities and are self-sufficient – become relics and outsourcing of operations become a reality, more opportunities to partner with suppliers will arise. Taking advantage of these opportunities is increasingly important for several reasons:

1. *Declining market prices:* Nobody expects prices to rise anymore. There is going to be a tighter squeeze on the margins of customer companies. They would like to get that margin reestablished by working with suppliers.

2. *Rising competitive intensity:* With the restructuring of the world economy, the formation of the World Trade Organization, and greater economic integration within and between regions, global and regional consolidation is clearly taking place and resulting in greater competition.

3. *Advanced technology enablers:* Electronic commerce and networked computing are here. Dramatically reduced cycle times are becoming an ordinary achievement. These require partnering with suppliers.

4. *Reverse marketing strategies:* The traditional process flow – from Research and development and sourcing to manufacturing, sales and service – is becoming a thing of the past. Today, market-focused organizations are organizing into reverse marketing starting with the end users. Partnering with suppliers is critical to this strategy.

5. *Strategic positioning:* In the past, companies partnered primarily for operational efficiency (i.e., just-in-time procedures or zero-inventory models). Today, intense competition is coming from existing rivals, new entrants and the threat of substitutes. Partnering with suppliers is an increasingly important way of minimizing the competition's negative impact on an industry.

Reduction in the Number of Suppliers

Company	Number of Current	Suppliers Previous	Percentage Change
Xerox	500	5,000	90.00 percent
Motorola	3,000	10,000	70.00 percent
Digital Equipment	3,000	9,000	66.66 percent
General Motors	5,500	10,000	45.00 percent
Ford Motor	1,000	1,800	44.44 percent
Texas Instruments	14,000	22,000	36.36 percent
Rainbird	380	520	26.92 percent
Allied-Signal Aerospace	6,000	7,500	20.00 percent

Example of Companies Benefitting from Supplier Relationships

The major research regarding the advantage of supplier relationships comes from a study of the Japanese automotive component industry[5]. They found that the average length of the relationship between suppliers and buyers was 22 years. In addition, the major customer bought about half the

Contd...

output of the supplier firm. About 26 percent of the supplier's development effort was devoted to a single customer. Competition was restricted to 2-4 other suppliers. Finally, the quality of delivered product was very good. The data would suggest that supplier relationship enhanced the design efforts of the buying company and reduced uncertainty and costs for the supplier company.

Eastman Kodak, Ford Motor Company, Levi Strauss, DuPont, McKesson and Bose corporation demonstrate that some savings can be achieved by supplier relationships[2]. These firms as well as examples of other firms using specific tactics to benefit from successful relationships are discussed next:

Eastman Kodak Company: Eastman Kodak Company has outsourced its data and information processing system to IBM. Kodak has achieved substantial cost savings through reducing personnel, assets and capital expenditures in an area that is not its area of core competency. This shift toward asking data processing and systems management consultants to manage the information and data processing of a firm has accelerated as major firms such as Xerox and Ryder have outsourced their internal data processing systems.

Ford Motor Company: Ford formed a relationship with one of their own clutch suppliers. Ford examined the production process of their supplier and was able to reduce the cost of the clutch by 20 percent benefitting both Ford and the clutch supplier. Similarly, based on their past experience with Donnelly, Honda picked Donnelly as an exterior mirror supplier, although Donnelly had no experience in the area[3]. Honda sent its engineers into Donnelly's plant, and engineers of Honda and Donnelly reorganized the plant and reengineered the product process. Sales are expected to be $60 million in 1997 and costs are expected to decline 2 percent annually benefitting both Honda and Donnelly.

JC Penny and Levi Strauss: JC Penny and Levi Strauss are linked with an Electronic Data Interchange (EDI) that allows Levi Strauss to obtain sales data. Levi Strauss obtains data on the exact size of jeans sold in individual stores. This data allows Levi Strauss to better plan the production process as well as better control inventory and delivery. This saving leads to a reduction in costs and prices benefitting both JC Penny and Levi Strauss.

DuPont: DuPont has reduced the costs of each purchase transaction in the maintenance and repair supplies division from $120 to $16 by working with a smaller number of suppliers. DuPont selected one distributor in each region for a supplier relationship. They then implemented a paperless order, receipt and payment process. In addition to decreased costs of transaction, inventory at the maintenance and repair facilities were reduced by 50 percent.

McKesson Drug Company: McKesson a major drug distributor developed a relationship with Johnson and Johnson, one of their major suppliers. Through a joint computer system development effort, both firms receive data on inventory, point of sale, demand, and customer information. This has led to Johnson and Johnson providing better service to McKesson increasing the level of service that McKesson provides to its customers. Due to the success of the relationship, Johnson and Johnson have turned over a million dollars worth of business to McKesson.

Bose Corporation: Bose Corporation has attempted to eliminate both purchasers and salespeople by bringing suppliers into the manufacturing process. Suppliers have access to Bose's data, employees and processes. They work with Bose's engineers on present and future products. The reduction in personnel reduces costs for both sides and a direct contact between the user and producer enhances quality and innovation.

Establishing and Maintaining Supplier Relationships

Wilson[6] suggests that the majority of alliances fail. We feel that most of the problems are associated with the selection and maintaining of supplier relationships. We present research finding from academic research, USGAO[2] and our own experiences. In order to establish relationships, we suggest that

Contd...

firms be very selective in their criteria. In addition to the normal criteria of competency and quality, we suggest the following additional factors be taken into consideration:

1. *Trust and Commitment to Long-term Goals:* Both suppliers and buyers need to demonstrate trust and commitment toward a long-term vision. Trust and commitment have been shown to be the major predictors of successful relationships.

2. *Mutual Benefit:* The relationship should be of benefit to both the buyer and the seller. If the relationship has one-sided benefits, the relationship will not last.

3. *Top Management Support:* Most successful relationships are associated with support from the top managers of a firm. As examples, the success of Walmart and Corning in forming relationships is because their CEOs have supported supplier relationships. Also, DuPont and Roadway Express have formed an Executive Board that meets at both companies to enhance their relationship[2].

4. *Compatible Organizational Culture:* The culture of firms should be compatible. This suggests that they share common values and share common reward systems. A major relationship initiative between two telecommunication firms did not work because they did not share a common work philosophy. One firm was very intense, whereas the other firm was laid back. The relationship dissolved in six months.

5. *Sharing of Information:* Relationships require sharing of information. The benefits of relationships arise from reducing the uncertainty associated with transaction oriented exchanges. Information increases certainty and reduces needless interaction. As an example, Bailey Controls, a manufacturer of control systems shares data with two of its main electronic distributors that have allowed Bailey to reduce inventory and costs[3].

6. *Strong and Open Communications:* Strong and open communications reduce misunderstanding and enhance the quality of relationships.

Maintaining Successful Relationships

The following aspects are regarded as important for the successful maintenance of relationships.

1. *Simple and Flexible Contract:* Simple and flexible contracts enhance relationships as they are used as guides rather than specifying all contingencies. For example, when Kodak outsourced their computer support services to IBM, they used an eleven-page contract[2]. In contrast, typically simple business contracts run to about 30 pages.

2. *Intensive Management Involvement:* Cross-functional teams from both the supplier and buyer organizations that meet periodically to enhance their relationships. For example, Ford uses salespeople to provide suppliers with consumer feedback[2].

3. *Periodic Performance Monitoring:* We have found that performance monitoring is critical for relationships. Suppliers also appreciate a formal performance evaluation method. As an example, Motorola evaluates and generates a scorecard for all of its suppliers[3]. The supplier's next order is based on the supplier's previous performance. Suppliers appreciate this knowledge and compete better.

4. *Internal Controls:* It is intuitive but companies need to protect access and distribution of confidential information with rigorous internal controls.

5. *Problem Solving Procedures:* Companies need to establish problem solving procedures that reduce conflicts or prevent conflicts. One of the simplest forms is frequent communication at all levels of the customer and supplier organization.

Organizational Changes Need to Establish Supplier Relationships

As stated earlier, as we traverse from a transaction and domestic orientation to a relationship and global orientation, firms will need to emphasize the development of relationship with suppliers. This

Contd...

emphasis of a relationship orientation toward suppliers will lead to an expertise in many aspects of business buying. These areas are highlighted in Figure 4.3, raised in our earlier paper[4] and discussed as under.

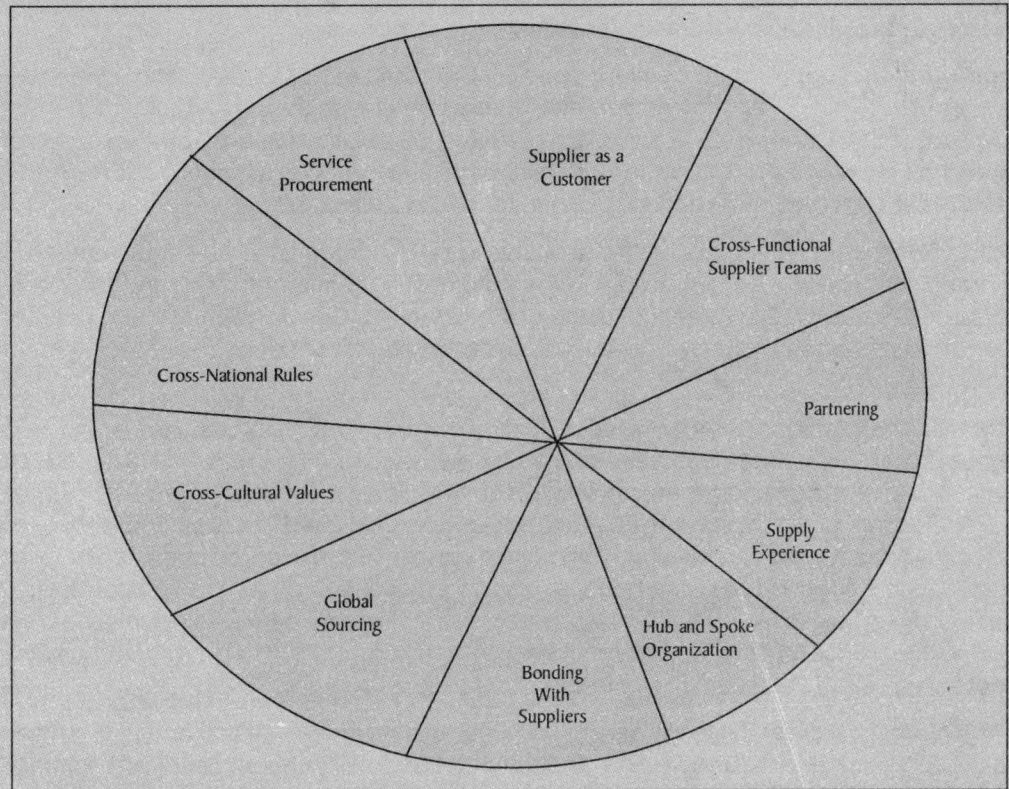

Figure 4.3: Emerging Areas of Expertise in Supplier Relationships

1. ***Supplier as a Customer:*** As discussed earlier, there will be a thrust toward developing and maintaining relationship with customers. However, firms' understanding in this area is very limited. Firms will need to develop commitment, trust and cooperation with their suppliers. Firms will need to invest in mutual goals, interdependence, structural bonds, adaptation, non-retrievable assets, shared technology and social bonds to ensure successful relationships[6].

2. ***Cross-Functional Supplier Teams:*** Marketers have used interdisciplinary teams to contact and maintain relationships with their customers. As individual suppliers relationships become more important we expect a similar thrust toward cross-functional teams that are dedicated or focused on their key suppliers. The importance of individual suppliers is expected to increase because of the emergence of sourcing on a global and relational basis with a few key suppliers. Firms will need to change goals, reward structure and group norms of the purchasing function.

3. ***Does Partnering Pay?:*** Firms will need to monitor the return on investment in establishing relationships with suppliers. Therefore firms will need to develop a performance metric that analytically quantifies supplier relationship equity. We feel that supplier partnering with smaller share suppliers will not be economical. The cost-benefit analysis of supplier relationships should result in increased supplier selectivity.

4. ***Supply Experience Curves:*** Managing supplier relationships will not be an easy task. The task of managing relationships on a global basis will be more complex and not analogous to domestic supplier management as most business customers have realized. Therefore, in industries where supply function is a key strategic advantage, companies need to focus on creating core competency in supply side management and develop sharper experience curves.

Contd...

5. *Hub and Spokes Organization:* We expect organizations to reduce the number of suppliers in each product or service category. In addition, re-engineering has forced firms to out source internal activities. We expect the results of these two trends to lead to a hub and spoke organization in which one or two suppliers in each product or service category are the spokes and the procurement organization becomes the hub on a global basis.

6. *Bonding with Suppliers:* Marketers, specifically those that practice relationship marketing have learned to bond with their customers. Bonding relates to the empathy that the marketing organizations feel toward their customer groups. With an increasing trend toward creating, managing, and enhancing ongoing relationships with suppliers on a global basis, organizations will have to invest in supplier bonding processes and philosophies.

7. *Global Sourcing:* We expect global sourcing to be a source of strategic advantage. While several global enterprises, especially in the automotive, high technology and the aerospace industries are establishing processes and platforms, it is still at an infancy stage of practice in other industries. Firms will have to develop expertise in global sourcing strategies as well as global logistics.

8. *Cross-Culture Values:* Firms will need to be more aware of cross-cultural values. These values may be in conflict with the firm's present value system. As an example, firms in the US are accused of focusing on short-term profitability whereas firms in Japan are concerned about long-term positioning. Similarly, in some cultures, reciprocity is declared illegal and unethical whereas in other cultures it is the preferred way of doing business. What is considered as an agency fee in one country is recognized as a bribe, subject to prosecution under the anti-corruption laws. Similarly, doing business with family members and politically connected individuals are presumed to provide a sense of trust and commitment in some cultures whereas it is considered as nepotism and unethical behaviour in others.

9. *Cross-National Rules:* Firms will also have to learn about cross national rules. Specifically, the two tier regulations (one for domestic and the other for foreign enterprises) are common with respect to ownership, management control, and co-production practices in countries such as China. With the rise of nationalism in recent years, this has become a key issue for global enterprises such as McDonald's, Coca-Cola, General Electric, and Enron, especially as they expand their market scope and supply scope in large emerging nations such as India, China, and Indonesia.

10. *Services Procurement:* As organizations outsource more and more internal services, and as suppliers engage in providing value-added services to their customers, firms need to better understand and research services procurement. Additionally, as most advanced countries are services economies, services procurement will rise in prominence.

Conclusions

The paper examined the reasons for the emergence supplier relations as source of competitive advantage. The paper discusses successful relationships; rules for developing relationships and concludes with organizational strategies that will enhance supplier relationships.

References

1. Napolitano, Lisa. "Customer-Supplier Partnering; A Strategy Whose Time has Come. *Journal of Personal Selling and Sales Management*, 4 (Fall), 1-8 (1997).

2. United States General Accounting Office, Partnerships: Customer-Supplier Relationships can be improved through Partnering, Report Number 94-173, Washington, DC (1994).

3. Magnet, Myron. "The New Golden Rule of Business." *Fortune*, February 21, 60-64 (1994).

4. Sheth, Jagdish N, and Arun Sharma. "Supplier Relationships: Emerging Issues and Challenges." *Industrial Marketing Management*, 26 (2), 91-100 (1997).

Contd...

5.   Wasti, S Nazli, Jeffrey K. Liker. "Risky business or competitive power? Supplier involvement in Japanese product design." *Journal of Product Innovation Management*, 14 (September), 337-55 (1997).

6.   Wilson, David T. "An Integrated Model of Buyer Seller Relationships". *Journal of the Academy of Marketing Science*, 23, 4, 335-45, (1995).

7.   Emshwiller, John R. "Suppliers Struggle to Improve Quality as Big Firms Slash their Vendor Roles." *Wall Street Journal*, August 16, B 1, (1991).

Source: The above article has been authored by Jagdish N Sheth and Arun Sharma. This paper extends research published by the authors in *Industrial Marketing Management* (March 1997). Reprinted with the kind permission of the author.

Mind Power 7: Vendor Rating-Money wise, Effort smart – V R Kolagunta

In the current highly competitive market, vendors play a very important role. Today, vendors are considered as partners in the business of the customer, although they may have no financial stake. The very purpose of having a vendor is to outsource products/services, which otherwise will be uneconomical to process in-house.

Vendors are selected on the basis of their ability to perform value-added activities. The activities would most likely be achievement of cost effective satisfaction to the immediate customer and the end customer. Some vendors excel in this. Some develop expertise in some processes and tend to enjoy monopoly. Very rarely you will find vendors catering to a single customer. Normally vendors have many customers. The work culture will vary from customer to customer and the vendor is required to adjust to these, varying cultures. His success depends on how well he manages this diversity.

Requisites, rather prerequisite

The vendor is expected to support the strategic requirements of his customer by meeting his standards. He has to keep performance objectives – like cost, lead-time, quality, flexibility, service, reliability and communication-in sight, always.

The basic activities involved while achieving the above objectives are: *procurea storea transforma storea move*. Communication is an important allied activity connected with each of the stages. How to ensure that the vendor achieves the performance objectives while carrying out the above activities? Here is where vendor rating comes in picture.

Assessing capabilities

The parameters of vendor rating are many, both objective and subjective. They can be broadly categorized into four groups – culture, organization, technology and systems. With the importance or weight of each of the parameters varying, we need a very scientific approach to evolve a rating system. It is also not feasible to review the performance of the vendor on all the parameters at the same time or at the same frequency.

Some parameters do not require review often, like infrastructure, organization structure etc. These can be reviewed may be yearly, while a parameter like quality needs frequent review. Apart from the regular review process, certain important parameters need to be considered while initially selecting a vendor. Some of these parameters need to be reviewed periodically, in order to ascertain whether the basic structure of the organization has undergone any change, which could be detrimental to the relations.

Contd...

Pointers to perfect

Considering the several factors that are necessary to rate a vendor, there is a list of parameters:

1. *Culture:* Owner/CEO relations, employee relations, supplier relations, customer relations, decision-making, service to customer, reliability, flexibility, and customer's problems.

2. *Organization:* Organization structure and manpower, infrastructure, financial stability.

3. *Technology:* Technical competence of personnel, quality, quantity, cost, time compliance.

4. *Systems:* Systems-quality certification, systems-basic activities, communication systems.

The parameters under the culture category are subjective and not measurable in nature. It requires special skills to be able to assess them. In spite of the skills, these parameters can only be assessed on a comparative basis. This means that you have to compare the vendor's performance in comparison to another existing one. In fact, it is easier and more reliable to resort to comparative assessment even in the case of other objective type of parameters, which are measurable.

Divulging further

The parameters listed under the four categories: culture, organization, technology and systems need to be elaborated for facilitating assessment. The best way for elaboration is to prepare a questionnaire for each of the parameters. The answers to the questions will aid in deciding the gradation. It is not practical to assess all the parameters at one time. Hence, the reviews should be programmed at suitable intervals. As mentioned earlier some parameters require more frequent reviews while others like infrastructure needs only yearly reviews. For convenience, we can have three review frequencies apart from the initial assessment. It is preferable to assess all the 20 parameters, while initially selecting a vendor. Once the vendor starts the business his performance has to be reviewed periodically. The suggested frequencies and the relevant parameters are:

1. *Yearly:* Organization structure and manpower, infrastructure, financial stability, systems - quality certification, owner/CEO relations, employee relations, supplier relations, customer relations.

2. *Six monthly:* Decision-making, service to customer, reliability, flexibility, customer's problems, technical competence of personnel, systems – basic activities, communication systems.

3. *Two monthly:* Quality, quantity, cost, time compliance.

Method act

What is the methodology for conducting a review? The objects of the review are assessment and grading. Before attempting this it is essential to understand the problem - in this case the rating of the vendor by analysing the parameters. Prior to analyzing the parameters, it is necessary to structure them. Structuring consists of the following steps:

1. Elaborating the parameters by creating questionnaires

2. Grading the parameters for their importance

3. Assigning weights to the parameters

4. Preparing a matrix for easy analysis

To illustrate the same, let us consider the two monthly reviews for the sake of brevity and easy comprehension.

Elaborating the parameters by creating questionnaires

1. *Quality*

    i)   What are the weekly/ batch wise PPM levels products wise?

    ii) How much is the weekly/ batch wise rejection cost?

Contd...

iii)   Cause and effect diagrams for the top 20 percent rejections?

iv)   What is the weekly/ batch wise cost of the repetitive rejections?

2.   *Quantity*

i)   What are the weekly/batch wise percentage shortages for each of the products?

ii)   What is the weekly/batch wise production value loss?

iii)   Cause and effect diagrams for the top 20 percent losses?

iv)   What is the status of the relevant inputs to the vendor?

3.   *Cost*

i)   What are the batch wise unit product costs for each of the products incurred by the vendor/ customer?

4.   *Time compliance*

i)   What is the weekly monetary loss (notional + actual), incurred by the customer in view of delayed deliveries?

ii)   Repetitive loss values?

The above are all objective questions and the answers can be computed. In the case of the subjective ones like reliability or employee relations the questions are bound to be many to compensate for the inability to measure. This way the chances of bias are reduced. Also when the questionnaire is prepared for all the 20 parameters, there is every chance of the same question occurring under different parameters. In such a case, the multiple occurrences should be analyzed to decide the most apt place for it. Once this decision is taken it should be deleted from the other locations.

Grading the parameters for their importance

The least biased method of doing this is by the system of pair ranking. To do this, the parameters to be ranked are listed in a column one below the other.

Then, one should self-assess with help of following questions: Which is more important 1 (quality) or 2 (quantity)? Then put a mark against the one that is decided as more important - see column 2 above.

Parameters for grading

	1	2	3	4
1	Quality	. . .	1	0.4
2	Quantity	.	3	0.2
3	Cost	. .	2	0.25
4	Time compliance		4	0.15
	Total			1.0

Matrix for easy analysis

		Vendor's marks out of 10 X weight			
1	Quality	0.4	6x 0.4= 2.40	8x 0.4= 3.20	4x 0.4= 1.60
2	Quantity	0.2	8x0.2= 1.60	6x 0.2= 1.20	7x 0.2= 1.40
3	Cost	0.25	7x0.25= 1.75	8x 0.15= 2.00	8x 0.25= 2.00
4	Time compliance	0.15	6x0.15= 0.90	6x 0.15= 0.90	8x 0.15= 1.20
	Totals	1.00	6.65	7.30	6.20
	Final ranking		2	1	3

Contd...

Which is more important 1 or 3(cost)? Then put a mark against the one that is decided as more important. The process is repeated for 1 and 4 (time compliance), 2 and 3, 2 and 4 and finally 3 and 4. Thus, each item is systematically compared with every other item. Now, referring to column two of Table 1, we find that one of the items has three points followed by two, one and zero. The parameter, quality, has the highest number of points - three, and obviously the most important parameter. Time compliance has zero points and hence ranked the fourth. The ranking is shown in column three above. The next step is to assign weights to the parameters.

Weighing the parameters: Pair ranking provides the base for assigning weights. Weight is nothing but fine tuned ranks. Ranking gives a general indication of the importance of the parameter. When we assign the weights the comparison between the parameters becomes more accurate. Column four above is an example of assigning weights. The weights will vary with the circumstances and the individuals concerned, but statistically the values will not vary very much from person to person.

In the above example, we have-dealt with only four parameters. When the parameters are many it could become unwieldy. In such cases we can adopt one of the following two methods. One way is to select the top four/five from the pair rankings. The other method is to split the parameters into two groups.

Preparing a matrix for easy analysis: Using the data generated it is necessary to construct a matrix, like Table 2, before attempting to analyze. In the matrix the parameters and the weights are entered. The marks are given based on the comparative performances of the three vendors. While giving the marks each of the questions in the questionnaire will have to be considered and an overall assessment is made. For convenience, marks are awarded out of 10. The marks multiplied by the weight are the weighted marks. The overall grades are obtained from the totals of the weighted marks. The acceptable norms can be decided based on the comparative grades/marks. For example, the norm can be fixed at 6.50. The results of the review is normally shown to the vendors to enable them to contribute towards improvement in the coming months, either to reach the acceptable norms or to further improve on the current performance. This exercise also affords us to gauge the performance trends of every vendor and enable to take corrective actions where needed.

Analysis first

The methodology, for vendors, suggested above has many advantages. Our normal approach to rating gives importance to the tangible parameters, leaving the subjective ones to assessment on the basis of preconceived notions. It is true that assessing the subjective parameters is not easy, but that does not warrant them being considered less important. In fact some of the subjective parameters like reliability and owner/ CEO relations are extremely crucial for arriving at an equitable rating. If these parameters are to be assessed with least bias, there is no alternative to the method suggested.

It is an analytical approach where we structure and analyse in a logical way. The structure is the matrix. Analysis is the thinking process to arrive at the performance grades or marks. Thus, structuring facilitates and empowers the thinking process. The thinking is also tuned to be unbiased.

Some purchase executives may feel that the method is cumbersome and time consuming. They should understand that structuring which takes time is mostly a one-time process, but for the collection of relevant data, which comes from standard reports. The analysis part is a quick process leading to a very transparent, acceptable and least biased result.

Source: This article has been published in SEARCH- The Industrial Sourcebook in the August 2006 edition. Copyright with Infomedia India Limited. Reprinted with permission.

QUESTIONS FOR DISCUSSION

1. You come to know that Reliance is entering into industrial pump business. They would be starting their business, within the next two years? How do you plan to approach them as an industrial marketer?

2. You are a supplier of electrical components. You want to get associated with Boeing for their electrical requirements. How will you go about doing it?

3. You work with Volvo, India. One of the tour operators who are operating in between Mumbai and Pune is interested in purchasing Volvo buses for the first time. What are the problems that "you" are going to encounter, for the first time you meet them?

4. You have been associated with a firm for quite some time, supplying them "Cold Rolled Steel". A new person has come in, who is very insecure, does not want to take any decisions and neither passes on the information to decision makers. What would you do as a sales person?

5. You have been supplying machine tools to a company for some time now? You have come to know, that the manager taking care of purchasing, is unhappy with your delivery and servicing. How will you convince him?

6. The risk of purchasing in an industrial organization would vary. How complex would it be for the sales person, to sell a product which is of low value, to a product which is a very critical and costly?

7. Ricardo Informatics is establishing an office in Gurgaon. They want to purchase computers for their new office. Who do you think would be the members constituting the buying centre?

chapter

FIVE

Managing Customer Relationship

COMPANY PROFILE 5: MRF

In the 1960s, the Indian tyre market was completely controlled by the large multinational companies. Around this time MRF opened a tyre factory at Tiruvottiyur in Tamil Nadu. With that, came the task of recognizing an appropriate Corporate Brand Symbol: one that would distinctly represent the company's culture, and convey the same to everyone in a country of varied languages and cultures.

In this process of developing suggestions for the symbol, some enterprising employees conducted an informal market survey, interviewing people from all over the country about their expectations from a good tyre.

But one day, a truck driver at a roadside dhaba (makeshift eatery) somewhere in Western India hit upon the right idea when he said, "A good tyre should have all the qualities of a pehalwan (strong man)." And from this simple statement, the muscleman was born. MRF began manufacturing tyres after this. Over the past 33 years, it has evolved from a mere corporate mascot to a symbol of strength, reliability and durability – embodying the very qualities of the tyres the Muscleman represents. For 16 years, he grew to become India's most trusted and well-recognized symbol for tyres.

MRF has an extensive range of superior quality tyres in six production facilities in India. MRF exports its products to over 75 countries worldwide – a standing testimony to MRF's outstanding leadership. It has tyres for buses, trucks, LCV's, Passenger cars, Two Wheelers and firm service.

Funskool India Limited is a joint venture between MRF and Hasbro Inc., USA, the world's largest toy company. Since late 1991-1992 Funskool's Goa plant has been making its own moulds for a number of its products, the most popular of which are Pipsqueaks, a range of low priced baby toys. These soft colourful animal toys have their sound built into their internal construction, doing away with the traditional whistle that breaks easily.

MRF's collaboration with PIRELLI comes at a time when the Indian Conveyor Belting industry is seeking technological momentum. MRF Muscle flex offers several advantages to buyers of belting in India.

The MRF Conveyor Belt plant in Arkonam, Tamil Nadu, with an annual capacity of 3000 tonnes, is the most modern belting plant in India and is dedicated to the development/manufacture of the finest Conveyor and Elevator Belting products.

MRF manufactures specialty coatings for wide range of applications. The revolutionary 100 percent polyurethane finishes are available in formulations for application to metal, wood, plastics, paper, vinyl, textiles, ceramics and glass. The coatings have been developed for colour and gloss retention, strong adhesion and durability. They guard against abrasion, corrosion, chemicals, bad weather and ultraviolet radiation and are virtually maintenance free.

MRF Pretreads is the most advanced Precured Retreading system in India. MRF made a foray in retreading as far back as 1970. Today, we have perfected the art of precured retreading with our extensive knowledge in tyres and rubber.

The MRF Pace Foundation was established in August '87, with the legendary Dennis Lillie of Australia, as Director, with the singular mission of developing and breeding strike bowlers of tomorrow.

MRF is also into tyre care and racing. MRF's turnover crossed INR 30 billion mark in 2004.

Source: www.mrftyres.com

Mind Power 1: Industrial CRM: An Area of Neglect
By Thomas R. Cutler

"Still engineering and operations focused many senior manufacturing executives are strongly resistant and visibly uncomfortable in approaching lean CRM".

August, 2006 – With up to ten years of continued process improvements on the plant floor, back office and distribution operations, manufactures have finally arrived at front door of Customer Relationship Management (CRM).

Still engineering and operations focused, many senior manufacturing executives are strongly resistant and visibly uncomfortable in approaching lean CRM. Applying a kaizen blitz approach to sales and marketing quickly results in the obvious for most manufacturing firms: an area of neglect.

Enterprise Resource Planning (ERP) vendors are capitalizing their long-established client relationship with manufacturers and distributor by attempting to extend their reach. Some ERP vendors offer industry specific CRM solutions; many do not. Bolt-on generic CRM solutions are frequently sold by ERP vendors assisting only the bottom-line of the software firm.

Larry Caretsky, President of New Jersey-based Commence, (www.commence.com/mfg) developers of a stand alone industrial CRM solution, suggested that most ERP companies offering CRM have shortfalls. According to Caretsky, "Managing the sales cycle and sales representative performance, marketing campaign management and integration with customer support are not provided by ERP tools."

One project-based ERP vendor acknowledged that CRM was neither their strength nor focus. "CRM is not within our strength or even portfolio of modules at the moment. We do not have a complete CRM product offering. Our older ERP product had an add-on module, but it is not a full CRM module by any means. Furthermore, none of our European customers have purchased it. For customers who may require CRM near term, we are recommending third party products or services."

While many ERP vendors do fall short on the industry CRM front; some have proactively addressed this critical lean aspect of the manufacturing enterprise. Toledo-based Technology Group International (www.tgiltd.com) is an ERP vendor that has developed a customized industrial CRM solution. Rebecca Gill, vice-president of TGI noted several key reasons for purchase an integrated ERP/CRM solution. Full integration allows:

1. Access to data in manufacturing, distribution, and accounting.

2. Instant notification of credit issues.

3. Instant capability to promise data for both manufactured and distributed products.

4. Direct tie between anticipated sales and related costs.

5. Instant access to historical information like sales, returns, on-time payments, margins, and other data.

6. Integrated dashboards that go beyond the typical sales funnel; show true margin comparisons.

7. No need to reshuffle sales data, or re-evaluate, or re-key. Data is all available to dice and slice as needed.

8. No lag time between data syncing or replicating. Management staff has live, real-time sales data.

9. True 360 degree view of the customer for the organization and not just the sales representatives.

Indeed stand alone industrial CRM solutions may also provide effective lean CRM processes as long as the vendor truly understands the nuances and idiosyncrasies of the manufacturing sector; most

Contd...

do not. Offering a glorified database satisfactory to any type of organization does not address central issue facing all industrial operations.

According to Caretsky, "Smart industrial organizations gather several key data points during customer research, which all helps to define a CRM profile.

1. How clearly can customers articulate your value proposition?

2. How well do customers know products or services?

3. What is the customers preferred method of purchasing products and services supplied?

4. Who do customers consider to be the preferred supplier products and services?

5. When do customers typically purchase products and services?

6. Why do customers typically purchase products and services?

7. How do customers use products and services?

8. Who is the decision maker? Who else influences the purchase?

9. How do customers evaluate suppliers?

CRM technology must help to answer these questions.

Whether fully integrated in an ERP systems or stand alone industrial CRM, elimination of waste in the sales and marketing of manufacturers and distributors requires expertise, experience, and specialization.

Source: Thomas R. Cutler is the President and CEO of Fort Lauderdale, Florida-based TR Cutler, Inc., the largest manufacturing marketing firm worldwide - www.trcutlerinc.com. Cutler is the founder of the Manufacturing Media Consortium of twenty seven hundred journalists and editors writing about trends in manufacturing. Cutler is also the author of the Manufacturers' Public Relations and Media Guide. Cutler is a frequently published author within the manufacturing sector with more than 300 feature articles authored annually; he can be contacted at trcutler@trcutlerinc.com.

Mind Power 2: CRM: It's not just about B2C!
By Neil Davey – Editor

When it comes to customer relationship management, the Business-to-Business (B2B) world has good reason to feel hard done by. It is easy to forget that CRM is a concept with its roots in the B2B sector when it is often so poorly served with relationship techniques and examples. And with B2C 'customer champions' stealing the limelight, B2B CRM success stories rarely get a look in - indeed, outside of Dell, how many other B2B firms attract similar praise as their B2C contemporaries? As such, you can appreciate why the business-to-business field could feel somewhat short changed by customer relationship management.

Nevertheless, despite this imbalance, there is just as much benefit from customer relationship management for the B2B firm as there is for the B2C business. There are of course, some significant differences between the two. B2Cs may serve millions of customers whilst B2Bs often have only a few large customers. B2Bs also often have smaller product ranges than their B2C peers, and the purchases are less frequent but higher value. Yet despite these discrepancies, most of the principles that have proven such a success in business-to-consumer can also be applied with equal achievement in business-to-business – as well as providing the same ROI.

Elements of customer relationship management may take unique forms in B2B industries - there is 'dealer management' for automotive companies for instance, or "trade promotions management" for consumer products firms - but the overriding concepts are still the same: understand your customers,

Contd...

MANAGING CUSTOMER RELATIONSHIP

In the previous chapters we have seen that the business markets are quite different from the consumer markets. The buying process of consumer is quite different from a business consumer. The business purchasing process is much more complex decision and there are a lot more decision makers involved in the process of purchasing. We also saw that the major decision buying is done by the 'buying center'. There is also an effect of environmental factors which play a very strong role in the sustainability of business. Today business buyers are purchasing products and services through the use of electronic data or on auction sites over the Internet. The pattern of business is changing. Relationships are being built in industrial markets for longer periods of time. Today, business markets are always in close contact with its customers through online mechanism. They also share information, provide customer services and maintain customer relationships.

Today the need for a buyer is to build a strong relationship with the seller. The need is to build a strong relationship between buyers and sellers. The need is to build a "collaborative relationship".

Relationship Marketing

Generally what happens is that a smaller proportion of the customer base, accounts for more than 70-80 percent of a firm's revenue. Thus, the need is to identify key customers on the basis of two factors: [1]

1. *Life time value:* The marketer has to understand, what the buyer is going to contribute in the lifetime. The factors which generally require to be taken in to account are the estimated business generated each year, cost of acquisition and retention.

2. *Strategic importance of the customer:* Some of the customers play a very important role to the marketer. It could be due to prestige value that is created by the marketer by keeping the particular account.

Marketer should remember that loyal customers are the ones which stand in the long-run. Customers who are sensitive to prices and are looking in for only price differences are not profitable in the long-run. One more important factor that needs to the kept in mind is that, more closely a marketer is related to its customer, the more difficult will it become for competitions to break up the relationship.

A business marketer's customer let us say is Toyota Motors. They initially enter the Toyota's supplier list as "one among many" but over a period of time a business market should try and build up the relationship in such a way, that it enters into collaboration with Toyota. In cases of collaboration, what happens is that the risk of loss is quite high for both. The relationships will stand and hold good when they partner for a greater value for one another.

Transactional Approach: It will be a state of purchase, when the price of goods, play a very important part in the decision-making. For example, the supply of papers for office use, or courier used for shipping goods. When there is a very little difference between one manufacturer's goods and another, this situation will arise. This is also a case when there is not much fluctuation on the supply side, and is mostly a generic product. This kind of transactional approach increases the risk factor of the marketer and is characterized by less interaction between the buyer and the seller.

Collaborative Exchange: It is the other end of the spectrum and the market situation is highly dynamic. There are a few suppliers of those products and relationship are for a longer time and is stable. There is a close sense of partnership and high level of interaction. These kinds of exchanges are true in cases, when the technology is changing rapidly, and purchasing process is highly complex.

Value Added Exchange: It is a type of exchange, between two extremes. The interaction is more than the transactional approach. Markets must slowly and steadily try to graduate from transactional relationship. Here a business marketer will try and tailor his needs for the buyer and will be more involved in the complete process.[1A]

Mind Power 3: Komatsu and Volvo Construction Equipment in Talks on Industrial Cooperation for Components

Komatsu Ltd. and Volvo Construction Equipment have initiated discussions regarding future cooperation in the production and development of construction equipment components. Tangible outcomes from the discussions are expected by mid-year 2002.

The intention is to determine whether both companies can find ways to strengthen their cost competitiveness and to increase customer satisfaction.

"We believe this cooperation could lead us to find high quality and cost effective solutions," says Mr. Masahiro Sakane, President of Komatsu, and Mr. Anthony C. Helsham, President and CEO of Volvo Construction Equipment, in a common statement to the announcement.

In the discussions, Komatsu and Volvo Construction Equipment will not include sales, service, distribution and equity participation.

Both companies will continue to engage in business as independent competitors using their own dealer networks, brands and identities.

Source: http://www.komatsu.com/CompanyInfo/press/2002062414084001795.html

One more term that is used while referring to the buyer-seller relationships is **switching costs**. Whenever a company invests in another there is a risk and exposure which will happen. Investment in another company could be in terms of money, machine, technology, human resources and business processes. Now if a company is moving away from one seller to another, there is high amount of switching costs involved. So, whenever there is a new buyer that is selected, there is a high amount of switching costs involved. It is needless to say that switching costs will be the highest in collaborative exchanges and the least for transactional exchanges.

Now, whenever we as a marketer try and market our products we will have a mix of customers. Some of them will have very loyal relationship; some will have a very fluctuating relationship. Some customers will believe that the process of purchase is a strong buyer-seller relationship while others would not. The marketer thus must try and be able to understand the buyer's requirement and suit its strategies for the same.

Since, **transactional customers** have a very low level of commitment and switching costs being low, a business marketer should be very cautious. Here the marketer should stress on factors like price, product and other services which they would be providing. More interaction is with the junior level of sales staff. Purchases are generally repeat purchases. Even here also, the marketer must try and distinguish himself and move on to a higher relationship front. Marketers must understand, even within transactional customers, the degree of involvement would vary and thus a strategy to suit all should be avoided.

For **collaborating customers**, the relationship is build over longer period of time and there is a high degree of risk involved to both parties. For these customers, many other departments are also involved with the selling firm. In some cases, it is seen that if the customers are big, there would be a person or team deputed, for that particular account. Strengthening the relationship is very important and therefore marketers meet the buyers more frequently. For these cases, companies can also integrate their systems together and a sharing of information is possible. These relationships demand high level of commitments for today, as well as for the future.

THE LADDER OF LOYALTY[2]

The ladder of loyalty speaks of the different stages through which a customer passes before becoming a partner:

1. Prospect
2. Customer
3. Client
4. Supporter
5. Advocate
6. Partner

Prospects are the ones to whom the products would be offered to. The marketer segments the market and draws up a target market to offer its products or services.

Customer is a state when the customer is interested in what the company has to offer to him. This is a very nascent stage and it could be possible that more than 50-60 per cent of them die down, before actually transacting with the company.

Client is a person when a particular customer, has used a particular product or service for more than once. Now, this customer has moved away from a trail and has tested the product.

Supporter is a person who not only uses the product but also recommends it to others. He has faith in the products and services and spreads "word of month" publicity of the product.

Advocate: A person who works closely in accordance with the company to improve the products and services. The interaction between the customer and the company is to a higher extent. There is sharing of information, as well as confidence among parties is high.

Partner: When a person becomes actively involved in the decision-making process of the company.

A business markets must thus try and shift from a 'customer' level orientation to a partnering level of orientation. This will bring in a high level of information exchange.

CUSTOMER LOYALTY

Value to a customer would be the difference between the benefits and costs. The various benefits that he receives and the costs that are attached to a particular transaction. Thus to create customer satisfaction and to keep the relationship strengthening, we require to give better and higher values to our customers.

Generally managers do not have an outlook, towards an outstanding, long-term relationship. They highly believe in the current profits; and propagate 'selling' then 'marketing'. Creation of value for the buyers is very essential. Often, it is seen that inexperienced sales person starts discussions or pitching to his clients on the basis of 'price'. That actually should be the last thing to be discussed.

It also happens that buyers are unable to express or pinpoint their needs. And, thus there is a difference of value, of what the customers expect, and what marketers provide.

Mind Power 4: Improve Business by Solution Selling – Sanjay Limaye

Companies can earn higher margins or increased revenues by selling integrated offerings, not merely bundle their products or services. The decision to sell solutions is usually based on either ambition or anxiety. Ambitious companies know that sale of solutions will give better margins than sale of products, generate longer customer relationships, and provide access to new markets.

From products to solutions

In the broadest sense, a solution is a combination of products and services that creates value beyond the sum of its parts. More specifically, it is the level of customisation and integration that sets solutions above products or services or bundles of products and services. The two elements-customisation and integration-are more than just the glue that holds the package together: the way the elements are integrated and the extent of the customisation define the added value for buyers and earn the added financial benefits for sellers.

Benefits from solution selling

When a company offers true solutions, its investment can pay off in several ways.

Besides generating higher margins for itself and additional value for customers, it might find that it can build longer-lasting and more profitable relationships with them. Sometimes solutions open doors to new markets and even reduce or eliminate competition, in effect de-commoditising sales.

Many companies, which have tried solution selling without proper preparation, have failed. They fail typically on account of three reasons.

1. They think they are selling solutions, when they are merely bundling products that create little value when offered together.

2. Companies underestimate the difficulty of selling solutions, which cost more to develop, have longer sales cycles, and demand a deeper knowledge of the customers' businesses.

3. Companies sell solutions much as they sell products. They don't recognize the need to restructure their sales teams, their performance criteria, and their approach to dealing with customers.

In short, many companies need to look more carefully before leaping into solutions. They ought to be sure that what they are offering really is a solution. They should correctly assess the degree of integration, customisation, or both required to turn a basket of products into a truly integrated package.

Contd...

Rethink your approach to sales

Solutions take longer than products to sell; typically, three or four times as many calls are needed to close deals. The longer sales cycle means that companies offering solutions to their customers must usually change their sales teams and selling styles. Bigger the problem and the larger the deal, the more people are needed to be persuaded. In sales of a product, by contrast, only a single representative or team is typically needed to explain its value for the customer, and sales cycles are relatively short.

A team selling solutions must understand the business of the customer at least as well as the customer does while developing partner like relationships with its senior decision makers.

Many companies that succeed in moving from selling products to selling solutions retrain their sales representatives they typically structure teams around a customer relationship owner supported by industry experts and technical specialists. They target relatively small number of customers with similar business needs, and try to focus more on senior executives who have fiscal responsibility for business units and less on the buyers or technical managers whom product sellers usually approach. Having completed the sale, top performers will track not only their revenues but also the business value they deliver and the reactions of their customers. Incentives are tailored to compensate sales reps for larger deals and for working with unfamiliar decision makers through longer sales cycles.

Base prices on business value

Selling solutions create opportunities for value based rather than cost-plus pricing. Solutions are integrated, so it is hard for the customer to choose only parts of the offering, (Sometimes the seller realizes it has been marketing a bundle rather than a solution when the customer disaggregates the package and gathers competitive bids). As the solution is customized, competitors find it difficult to bid against it or even to compare its price and features with those of their own products.

Source: Copyright with Industrial Marketing Services, 2004. This article has been authored by Sanjay Limaye. You can visit him at www.inmas.com

CUSTOMER RELATIONSHIP MANAGEMENT

With large number of sellers in the market, the competition is getting very tough. The success lies in the strategy of customer retention. The business marketer should be able to retain a particular customer for longer periods of time. CRM thus forms the centerpiece of all corporate discussions today.

In B2B markets, the decision-making process being complex, marketers find it difficult to clinch every corner of the market place. The purchasing cycles are longer, and the marketer is still not sure whether they would be able to get the contract. Even if that is done, retention of the customer becomes a second great step. Business buyers today demand high level of service, responsiveness, reliability and quality consciousness from their vendors. The rise of e-commerce, Internet and the ever increasing innovation has changed the complete market place.

In B2B markets, we also see the presence of online auction sites, where a buyer can quote his requirements. Companies are today moving to JIT deliveries and reducing their stock of inventories. In B2B markets vendors are selected very carefully. Customers are getting more demanding and thus the tendency to cut costs at the vendors end, is also becomes critical.

Fierce competition for customers, raising customer acquisition costs, marketing, markets, commoditisation of many products and service through e-commerce and lower under switching costs have forced vendors to focus on building loyalty with the customers. They seek to develop and mature long-term and mutually beneficial relationships with their customers.

So, today companies in the B2B market arena have used the CRM concept to:

1. Have continuous interaction with customers.

2. Focusing on some major customers and providing them with high levels of personalized service.

3. Focus on customer's retention, and anticipate customer needs.

4. Integration of the system i.e. of the buyer and seller.

5. Creating a value proposition for the customer.

The CRM system should be able to access and use efficiently all customer information from the major customer contact points. CRM is not a software "for marketing strategies. CRM is the bundling of customer strategy and process, supported by relevant software, for the purpose of improving customer loyalty and eventually, corporate profitably.[4]

To develop responsive and profitable customer strategies, special attention must be given to five areas. They are:[5]

1. Acquiring the Right Customer

2. Crafting the Right Value Proposition

3. Instituting the Best Process

4. Motivating Employees.

5. Learning to Retain Customer

Acquiring the Right Customer

The customers that a marketer brings in should be carefully studied. They should be profitable and should have future profit potential. There are some customers, who give a good weightage to the services and technical supports provided and do not mind paying a premium for it. But, on the other hand there are some customers who would be extremely price sensitive. Thus, a marketer should be very careful in acquiring the customer.

Crafting the Right Value Proposition

As a business marketer, it is very essential to understand what kinds of value proposition that needs to be given to a customer. It could be in term of services, ideas, solutions. These value propositions would be on the basis of the business environment and customer needs. As a marketer we need to understand what is it clearly that the customer needs today and tomorrow.

Instituting the Best Processes

Highly personalized services, technical support and customer services need to be given. Marketer also needs to work in close coordination with other support divisions.

Motivating Employees

Employees must be motivated and should have a service bent of mind. Importance and focus to training must be given and providing employees with an excellent path for growth and challenges. Employees must be taught to build customer relationship.

Learn to Retain Customer

Acquiring a new customer, would be about ten times costlier than maintaining an old one. This is due to primarily one reason. They tend to develop a mutual trust and understanding amongst themselves, and therefore the cost factor reduces. High value customer must be given special attention and we must also have a system as to understand why a customer defects and switches over.

Mind Power 5: Industrial CRM – Thomas R Cutler

Manufacturers all face a similar challenge: a complex sale that often requires a team selling approach. In every industrial organization one finds internal representatives, outside representatives, managers, technical specialist, distributors, and customer service professionals. Often this team manages several product lines with thousands of specific items and interacts with numerous influencers who affect the sale. During the lengthy sales process the team does their best to manage this complex environment, producing notes, sales call reports, quote logs, memos, faxes, e-mails, and customer service reports, however the information is almost always fragmented. There is rarely one central database of customer information that can be accessed and shared among the people who need it to efficiently do their jobs. As a result, acting less like a team, these people act independently when conducting business and are far less effective.

According to Larry Caretsky, President of Commence (www.commence.com/ mfg), an industrial Customer Relationship Management (CRM) firm, "CEO's of these companies often share how their new Enterprise Resource Planning (ERP) system provides them all the information they need, but fail to recognize that ERP systems provide information after the sale, not before or during the sales process. ERP systems provide no value for improving the efficiency of how to sell and service customers. This is one reason that forecast reports are always inaccurate." Industrial senior executives avoid addressing a customer-centric approach including the misconception that an accounting system provides the information needed; they provide only post sale information. The pre-sales process and information drives the sale. Manufacturers do not resist funding back-end ERP systems; however the front-end CRM solutions often make a substantial impact on reducing new customer acquisition cost and improving sales efficiency by first addressing data capture, data consolidation, and data sharing.

Access to customer Information

Access to customer information is critical when industrial companies sell and service customers. An industrial CRM system must capture data via the telephone, fax, e-mail, or the web and stored it in a unified database where it is immediately available to the people and departments that need the information. Customer information must be displayed on a single screen, providing the end-user with a 360-degree view of all pertinent information. Having immediate access to customer information significantly improves the sales process and customer satisfaction.

Sales Process Management

The foundation of any quality sales organization starts with the implementation and management of a sales process. These are the steps required by the sales representative to move the prospect from the initial introduction stage to the closing stage. Few industrial CRM systems provide manufacturers with a structured proven sales process or methodology for evaluating and managing each stage of the sales cycle. A proactive approach to managing the sales process allows the sales manager to monitor and provide guidance during the cycle, as well as help sales representatives focus on the best opportunities.

Contd...

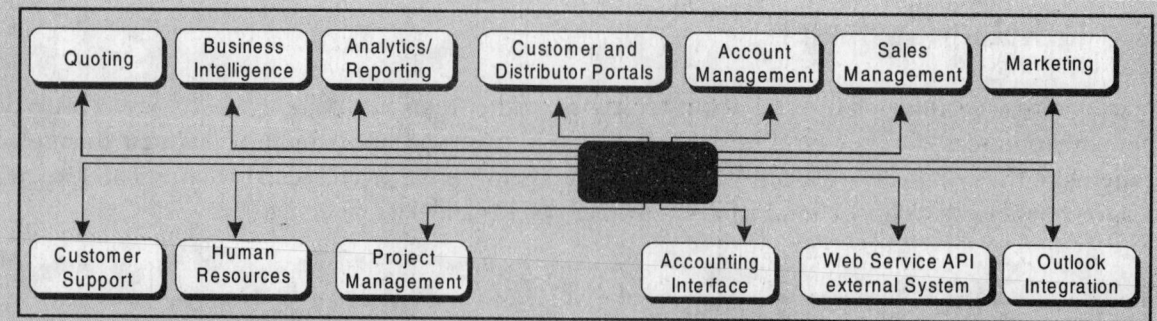

Lead Management

Between print advertising, trade show exhibiting, and other marketing outreach efforts, manufacturers spend hundreds of thousands of dollars generating leads, yet often wonder what happened to those costly leads. Caretsky suggests, "Tracking leads must be addressed via a lead automation system that automatically distributes new leads based on specific criteria such as city, state, zip code or country. A web portal capability will enable external sales people or distributors to update the status of these leads so that a manufacturer can assist during the sales process."

Reporting: And the best customer is....

Accurate and timely reporting is a key component to measuring sales performance and assisting in making informed decisions. Industrial CRM technology systems must provide analytical reports and graphs that illustrate several components including 30, 60, 90-day forecasts, won/lost reports, top ten opportunities, sales volume reports, and margin reports. As the lean initiatives trickle down to the sales and marketing arenas there will be more focus on efficient sales and marketing efforts leveraging a consistent selling effort across the organization. Better knowledge capture and retention becomes essential and achievable through immediate access to vital customer information. Industry will tune the sales approach to the specific opportunity thus assuring time is spent on deals that are winnable and profitable. Improved customer retention and acquisition will translate better serving the right customers at the right time with the right offer. A direct result will be a significant increase in internal communication because all members of the sales team, internal, external, distributors, product specialists and management will be in sync with the selling process and requirements for winning the sale.

CRM Technology for Industry Issues

While it seems axiomatic, an industrial CRM system must be easy to use and focused on alleviating the time consuming day to day minutiae and administrative distractions that rob sales people of precious selling time. Eliminating waste is a core lean principle that technology solutions must provide.

A comprehensive industrial CRM solution must offer enterprise functionality for lead capture and distribution, opportunity management, pipeline management, quoting, call reporting, forecasting, marketing automation, and customer support. It is often advantageous if the industrial CRM solution is modular in nature, allowing an organization to select only that functionality required for the business.

Industrial CRM's 'Must' Checklist

1. Address the need for data capture, data management, and data sharing.
2. Provide a structured process for effectively managing the sales cycle.
3. Enable sales people to focus on more and better opportunities.
4. Remove the pain of sales reporting.
5. Make sales management easier and more predictable.

Contd...

6.   Improve customer satisfaction and customer loyalty.

7.   Understand the complexity of selling in the manufacturing environment.

8.   Enable pro-activity at the beginning of the sales cycle.

9.   Enhance internal and external communication; allowing focus on customer opportunities and customer relationships.

10   Have proven delivery of bottom-line results.

Source: Thomas R Cutler is the founder of the Manufacturing Media Consortium of twenty seven hundred journalists and editors writing about trends in manufacturing. He is the president and CEO of Fort Lauderdale, Florida based TR Cutler, Inc, the largest manufacturing marketing firm worldwide. Cutler is also the author of the Manufacturers' Public Relations and Media Guide. Cutler is a frequently published author within the manufacturing sector with more than 300 feature articles authored annually. Reprinted with the permission of the author.

CRM STRATEGIES[6]

As we have seen above, the cost of acquiring a new customer in very much higher, than maintaining an existing customer. A CRM strategy provides a view in how an enterprise will build customer relationship and loyalty. The various steps for the development of CRM strategies are:

1.   Segment customers into categories.

2.   Understanding the strength and value of the customer relationship along two perspectives, i.e., how much customers value the enterprise and vice versa.

3.   Defining the objectives to be met and the strategies to be used

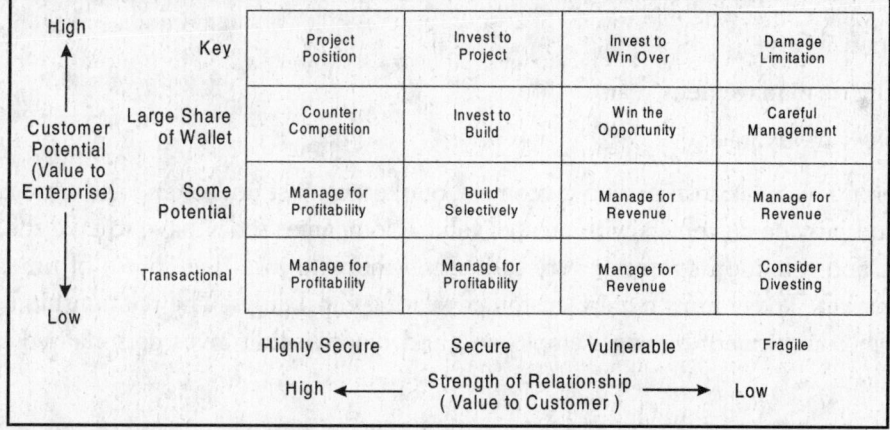

Source: Chaturvedi and Chaturvedi - "CRM- An Indian Perspective." Excel Publications pp 38.

THE FUTURE TRENDS

Today the need is for highly personalized service and customer is definitely the 'king' today. In the previous years, we had little technology and thus the preferences were not well understood. The information technology has revolutionized our outlook and has changed the way business is done today. Thus with the advent of CRM, there has been an integration of the customer directly with the enterprise.

In B2B markets, customisation is the key. With more and more suppliers and the offerings tending to be the same, it is really becoming tough to acquire new set of customers, and retaining them is a greater challenge. Thus there has been a shift to highly focussed marketing and strong after sales service.

Today companies have been seriously adopting CRM strategies to get an extra mileage and stay in business. The major reasons for adoption of CRM strategies are:

1. **Reduction of Costs:** Providing highly customized products, working in close collaboration with customers, offering personalized services, usage of technology, reduction of communication costs, less duplication of work and highly focused campaigns have led to reduction of costs.

2. **Increased Sales Revenue:** CRM has enabled to penetrate wider geographical areas and focus on to a select net of profitable customers.

3. The **margins** have increased with per unit of sales, with a reduction of costs.

4. The responsiveness to customer needs have been faster, and complaint solving has been faster.

However the implementation and success of CRM has some CSF (Critical Success Factors) attached to it. They are:[7]

1. Identifying the mission, objectives and goals

2. Identifying and prioritize what functions need to be automated

3. Gain top management support and unequivocal commitment

4. Employ technology smartly

5. Involve users early

6. Test the CRM on a small scale and on all functions, instead of the big leap.

7. Training

8. Allocate responsibility

9. Cross department management teams

10. Keep employees motivated.

To develop profitable relationships with customers, marketers must understand the various exchange relationships, try and provide customers with greater value. Companies today have to take the process of customer selection and retention strategies very seriously, otherwise in a due course of time, would be wiped out of the market. Today firms require customer relating capabilities. The relationship base should be strong, with high commitment amongst employees, and inactive that gives personalized solution to customers.

CRM DEVELOPMENT CYCLE[8]

A typical CRM lifecycle under goes through the following phases:

1. **Understanding and differentiate:** There is a need to understand the customers. Until and unless organizations build up relationship, understanding would be tougher.

2. **Develop and Customize:** "Organizations today are not able to cost effectively customize products for individual customers. The extent of customisation should be based on the potential value delivered by the customer segment".

3. **Interact and Deliver:** Interaction is the most critical component of CRM implementation. Implementation not only happens through sales and marketing, but in different ways with many different areas of the organization.

4. *Acquire and Retain:* "Successful customer retention is based on organizations ability to constantly deliver on three principles.

    i)   Maintain interaction. Never stop listening

    ii) Deliver on customers definition of value

    iii) Customers change as they move through different life stages

5. *Prioritizing the Changes:* Organizations need to prioritize. The organization should evaluate costs, overall benefits, feasibility and time required.

6. *Measuring Success*

GETTING STARTED[9]

In building a CRM vision, there are four key phases that must be considered. They are:

1. *Assess current business context*

    i)   What are the organizations current CRM practices?

    ii) Are CRM related business objectives and strategies understood throughout the organization?

    iii) What are the business and management requirements and constraints with regards to CRM? Are all customers to be treated in a similar fashion, or are some customers more valuable than other?

    iv) Does senior management understand the competitive environment?

    v)   What are the key business drivers that may change the CRM landscape that the company is operating in?

2. *Create the Strawman vision*

    i)   Which customers should they target?

    ii) How should they deal with rapidly increasing channel fragmentation and media complexity to converse with their customers?

    iii) How should they balance quality of experience, cost to serve and profitability of the customer?

    iv) What is the appropriate level of CRM integration for their business?

    v)   What is customer "insight" and how can the organization get and use it?

    vi) What should they do with unprofitable customers?

3. *Build the business case*

    i)   Business rationale

    ii) Cost to get to benefits

    iii) Pay back case

    iv) Risk analysis

4. *Prioritize, plan and transform:* This phase is about prioritizing projects and initiatives that will enable an organization to deliver its CRM vision.

CRM BENEFITS[10]

The benefits of CRM are as follows:

1. Identifying and targeting the most profitable customers and having a deeper knowledge of customers.

2. Getting more marketing or cross-selling opportunities.

3. Ability to manage marketing campaigns with clear objectives.

CRM solutions increase profitability and boosts market share through:

1. Increased revenues and reduced costs.

2. Increased return on service/support investments.

3. Increased customer satisfaction and responsiveness.

CONCLUSION

In any industrial firm, it is generally seen that 20 per cent of the business customers account for 10-80 per cent of a firm's revenue. Thus industrial marketers should identify customers, on the basis of life time value, and the strategic importance the customer has on the individual marketer.

The relationships, for business marketers should focus on collaborative approach with the integration of the supplier with customer or channel partner. We also saw, the future trends in customer relationship management and how CRM as a process should be developed and started. At the end, we saw, some of the common pitfalls in the CRM implementation process.

References

1. Shainesh, Sheth, *Customer Relationship Management*- A Strategic Perspective, MacMillan India Limited, 1st edition pp 93.

1A. Day – "Managing Market Relationships," *Journal of Academy of Marketing Science*, pp 25.

2. Shainesh, Sheth, *Customer Relationship Management*- A Strategic Perspective, MacMillan India Limited, 1st edition pp 32.

3. Krishnamacharyulu and Lalitha, *Industrial marketing* – A process of Creating and Maintaining Exchanges, Jaico Publication, pp 92.

4. Rigby, Reicheld and Schefter, *Avoid Four Perils of* CRM - HBR 80, (Jan/Feb 2002), pp 102.

5. Rigby, Reicheld and Schefter, *Avoid Four Perils of* CRM - HBR 80, (Jan/Feb 2002), pp102.

6. Chaturvedi and Chaturvedi, *CRM–An Indian Perspective*, Excel publications, pp 36.

7. Chaturvedi and Chaturvedi, *CRM–An Indian Perspective*, Excel publications, pp 79.

8. This section is adapted from Sanjay, S Kaptan. *Customer Relationship Management- Issues and problems*, Chapter 3, pp 18-20; Published in "CRM - A Key to Corporate Success, Edited by V. Venkata Ramana and G. Somayajulu Published by Excel Books.

9. This section is adopted from Stanley, A Brown and Moosha Gulyez – *Performance Driven CRM–How to Make Your Customer Relationship Management Vision a Reality*, - Copyright with PWC Consulting, Published by Wiley India, pp- 16-22.

10. This section is adapted from N. Subrahmanyam, *CRM–A Key to Corporate Success*, Emerging trends and issues, published in *CRM-A Key to Corporate Success*, Edited by V. Venkata Ramana and G. Somayajulu – Published by Excel Books, chapter 4, pp 28-29.

Mind Power 6: Large Pharmaceutical Company Implements Oracle-Siebel Solution to Improve Its CRM Capabilities

Company Background

Our client focuses on the development, manufacture and distribution of some of the most-recognized over-the-counter medications for humans. With a sales field force compromising of three distinct markets, including retail pharmacies, dental health professionals and primary/secondary care trusts, the UK division's portfolio offers 21 brands and 90 individual products.

Business Issue

Our client's existing sales force automation tool, called K and V, had been in place for several years and was no longer capable of moving with the business. The retail pharmacy field force found the application cumbersome to use and at odds with the group's visit planning and execution methodology. Customer sites, such as a pharmacy or a supermarket rarely have flat surfaces available for setting down a laptop, which discouraged use of the application during visits. Users tended to record information about their visit on lose papers or in notebooks, resulting in up to three hours of administration work at the end of the day.

The company's second field force, which included dental health professionals, had previously been outsourced to a third-party. This group was brought in-house with the introduction of the new system and needed an application to support the group's visits to dental surgeries. The dental field force suffered similar problems to the retail pharmacy group, which resulted in significant administration at the end of each working day.

As with any situation in which users feel they are re-keying information and spending time filling in data that does not benefit them directly, our client found that the quality of data was not at its highest. In addition, the excessive administration resulted in fewer average visits per day.

The third field force within the company – primary and secondary care trusts – had a stop-gap application in place and needed a system more suited to their needs.

Inforte's Solution

Our client decided to team up with Inforte to implement Oracle-Siebel Consumer Goods version 7.8, which would meet the needs of three field forces. Inforte's depth of experience with CPG processes and track record of implementing highly successful solutions in short time frames made for a perfect partnership.

A key decision was made to replace user laptops with tablet PC devices. The slimmer, more flexible device allows field force representatives to record all details about their visit. Tablets do require special consideration in that users interact with the device using an electronic pen and hold the device in one arm, portrait style, as if it were a paper notebook. In addition to normal requirements gathering and design activities, Inforte conducted a comprehensive review of each Oracle-Siebel view and set of process steps to ensure the application was optimized for use with the tablet device. Each of the three user groups had account and activity history stored in a different system. Inforte assessed this data and mapped it into the Oracle-Siebel data model. This allowed users to see their historical data in the new system, easing their acceptance of the software and providing continuity for reporting purposes.

Our client required interfaces to exchange data between the Oracle-Siebel system and other systems both internal and external. These included two interfaces of transfer orders, one interface of address modifications and one interface of marketing activity. Inforte built each interface with an aim to minimize manual intervention. Discrepancies in source data are not uncommon and require some level of correction by a business user. Inforte's solution was to add a series of business language error

Contd...

messages in addition to the maximum amount of source data. This mechanism allows business support staff to manage the vast majority of data issues independently, with no need for technical support.

Inforte envisaged and executed a training programme consisting of two full days in the classroom. The programme started with an introduction to the tablet device and all of its accessories. Delegates used role-play to familiarize themselves with the physical use of the device. The majority of the programme focused on the individual processes the field force would use in each customer visit. Role-play and exercises pulled directly from the business were heavily emphasized.

"We wouldn't be in the strong position we are in today if it weren't for you guys -your focused attention and pragmatic approach has clearly paid dividends." – National Field Sales Manager

Business Benefits Delivered

The implementation of Oracle-Siebel by Inforte resulted in a number of benefits:

1. The system is aligned with our client's 5Ds methodology used by the larger of two field forces.

2. Field forces complete visit administration during each visit, improving accuracy of data capture and allowing time each day for additional visits.

3. Product presentation materials and sales cycle objectives can be distributed electronically, eliminating costs of color printing, binding and postage.

4. Reporting of visit statistics has shifted from manual creation by 25 individuals to centralized reporting and much greater flexibility for ad-hoc reporting by field force managers.

5. The field force detail products directly from their tablet device. They appear more professional and organized using the tablet device as opposed to fumbling with papers and pen or struggling to hold a laptop in their arms.

6. Significant time savings have been realized with regard to business operations staff. For example, one of the four interfaces saves approximately one hour per day for one resource.

7. Turnaround time on transfer orders has been significantly reduced.

8. The dental field force now has visibility into the marketing activities occurring alongside their customer visits. They, in turn, appear (and feel) more aligned with the overall dental strategy and operations.

9. Marketing questions can be targeted to a specific customer profile allowing marketing and business account managers much clearer visibility of the customer. The results of these questions can be easily aggregated and reported without requiring technical resources.

The benefits produce a happier, more efficient field force that spends the maximum time possible in front of the customer. The system supports their core activities and provides information useful to the individual as well as to corporate intelligence. The field force is motivated to capture visit information which will lead to better interaction between our client as a whole and its target market, and ultimately greater market penetration.

Words of Advice

The face of the pharmaceutical field force is changing. The emphasis is no longer on making a sale in every store visit. Technology and processes must keep in step with these changes and support the field force in their objectives. Many of the applications implemented by early adopters have not kept pace with the change in the pharmaceutical business. This can be rectified relatively quickly.

Implementing a new system as well as a new piece of technology can be stressful to a user group. Attention to a change in management is key to successfully introducing two significant changes at once.

"The Oracle-Siebel implementation has been achieved in four months. This is quite an achievement. To put this into context, the KandV system took closer to 18 months to implement" – IT Business Manager.

Mind Power 7: Can PRM Power B2B Connectivity?
By Louise Druce, Staff Writer

Partner Relationship Management (PRM) is certainly not a new concept in the B2B world. But because its take up has remained relatively stagnant in recent years, it seems to have fallen off the business radar.

Even Gartner saw so little growth in the market it decided to stop tracking PRM in its own right and throw it in with the CRM lot. However, as Tiffani Bova, a research director with the analyst company points out, it would be foolish to dismiss its potential just yet.

"If you leverage the capabilities of the PRM tool you have the ability to segment your partners more effectively, which in turn can result in more appropriate communication with your partner. You know more about your partner — what are their certifications, what products they have been selling, how much they have been selling, what geography they cover and their market segments," she argues.

"Take Amazon.com. It recommends products to you based on what you've bought and suggests others you might like to buy. From a partner perspective, none of that happens. E-mails and newsletters [about products] are so impersonal. PRM allows you a much more intimate relationship with your partner."

It's a sentiment echoed by PRM expert Stephen Dent, Founder of the Partnership Continuum, who believes it is very much an emerging field driven by a need to move the focus away from short-term transactions. "More companies are becoming aware of the power of connectivity and the need for more effective partnering relationships," he says.

However, he points out: "Growing a B2B relationship into a partnership necessitates people connecting in ways that are often contradictory to the corporate cultures that exist in both organizations. Building an effective partnering relationship requires that people have the capability to understand each other's vision and then help each other to move towards that vision."

Defining the relationship

In a recent white paper, Oracle defined PRM as "a business strategy designed to automate and streamline business processes between brand owners and their partners, enabling them to work collaboratively to increase revenues, reduce partner channel costs, and improve customer satisfaction. An enterprise-wide global partner management software platform provides an environment in which the brand owner and partners within the partner network are able to communicate and collaborate in real time".

It adds that although technology is critical to an effective PRM solution, a large portion of a successful initiative centres on designing, planning and developing a customer-centric strategy for collaborating with partners and implementing accompanying best practices and processes. These components contribute to the formation of a comprehensive PRM solution that is focused on improving the way a brand owner enables its partners in their customer interactions.

The reason PRM is often lumped together with CRM is because they can complement each other as a comprehensive customer strategy. But, as Dent explains, they really need to be viewed as separate entities. "CRM tends to focus on understanding customer buying patterns and increasing sales and customer loyalty. The understanding is based on data from previous transactional history with the business and from information around customer experience with a business," he says.

"More companies are becoming aware of the power of connectivity and the need for man effective partnering relationships." Stephen Dent - Founder of the Partnership Continuum.

Contd...

"PRM is a way of interacting with another business within a partnering relationship context. The relationship itself, and the mutually beneficial business objectives the organizations can accomplish together because of their partnering approach, is the focus of PRM. B2B partners are invested in creating a mutually successful outcome in their relationship. The stakes are often higher in PRM than CRM."

Although most of the PRM examples Dent has seen mimic its CRM cousin, designed around collecting data on performance. "This methodology fails to take advantage of the relationship to enhance the strategic potential of both businesses," he continues.

"When partners do meet face to face, the time is usually spent on solving issues and reviewing performance indexes. Very little time is spent on thinking about the future and how the partners wish to position themselves in the marketplace. Often, this is because they have focused on the transactional relationship and not on the strategic benefits of partnering. It is far easier for people to focus on transactions, and it takes less time and brainpower."

The perfect couple

When PRM is successfully implemented, Dent sees expanded resources as a primary benefit. This isn't in the traditional sense of increased manufacturing capabilities or distribution, for example, but rather information and knowledge. With open disclosure and trust between companies, the shared information and collaboration can lead to more innovation and creativity.

He is currently working with two large health care providers in the US that have formed a 10-year relationship. They had a contract in place but Dent says the relationship was not delivering on expectation fast enough. "When we delved deeper into the relationship it was amazing what each party did not understand about that partnership, even internally within the organization," he explains.

"Once we were able to clarify the objectives internally it became easier to build on the commonalities that each party brought to the relationship. Helping them create a mutual strategic framework was the first step. Once they understood and agreed the vision, mission and strategic directions of the relationship they were able to stop the conflict and focus on the objectives."

Ultimately, Bova highlights, successful PRM boils down to the end result that every company strives for: improved customer satisfaction. Customers feel more comfortable knowing what they can buy and communication is more targeted to their needs, which brings about effective lifecycle management.

Making a connection

Of course, PRM isn't without its downside. Bova admits that, in most cases, the volume of data organizations hold makes it difficult to access everything the PRM tools need to work effectively. Then there is the fact that the expense and huge undertaking to clean up all the records to make CRM more efficient or even an option puts PRM immediately on a back footing.

Also, says Dent businesses need to understand that PRM isn't just about technology, it's about dealing with people. "The biggest pitfall I have witnessed is the inability of a business to move beyond a transactional relationship. When an organization reduces its business partners to transactions it dehumanizes those partners. When people feel dehumanized, they do not perform at their highest level" he emphasizes.

"The key to improving a B2B relationship is to spend time making human connections. Building mutual trust and agreeing on where both partners want the relationship to drive the business is critical. Enabling people to learn the interpersonal skills necessary to achieve this objective is crucial to success."

"Go into PRM with the understanding that you have to be committed to gathering all the appropriate data and getting all the internal organizations to agree its importance." Tiffani Bova, Research Director, Gartner

Contd...

Bova offers this advice to companies who may be considering implementing PRM: "Go into it with the understanding that you have to be committed to gathering all the appropriate data and getting all the internal organizations to agree its importance. Capture as much partner information as you can and use the tool to better segment, communicate and sell to your existing partner base."

Dent recommends starting with identifying the nature of the partnership you are looking for and understanding its limitations. Next, companies need to understand their internal needs and how business partners are expected to satisfy them. They then need to make sure there is a cultural fit and that management structures, philosophies, decision-making styles around handling challenges and opportunities, communication mechanisms and reward structures are aligned to achieving objectives.

The last step is to create a mutual, strategic framework. Not only does this provide direction for the relationship but it also builds commitment between both parties to meet the agreed upon objectives.

The underlying foundation, however, is mutual trust in the partnership. "A crucial key to success is helping people to understand the importance of building and sustaining trust in the relationship," Dent adds. "Information flow is based on trust. If you cannot build trusting relationships with your strategic partners, you may as well not have them."

Source: Copyright with Sift Media 2007. Visit them at www.mycustomer.com. Reprinted the permission.

QUESTIONS FOR DISCUSSION

1. The cost of acquiring a new customer is higher, than maintaining a customer. Discuss.

2. Air Deccan has all its aircraft purchased from Airbus. How can Airbus prevent Air Deccan to switch over to some other aircraft manufacturer?

3. The objectives of every business marketer, should be to have a collaborative relationship, than a transactional one? Discuss.

4. Acquiring the right kind of customers is very essential otherwise a business marketer will lose money than earning? Discuss.

5. All CRM strategies would fail, if the employees are not motivated. How are the employees the pillar of success for all customer relationship management?

6. Commitment on the part of the industrial marketer is essential to maintain and retain customers? Why?

c h a p t e r

Strategic Planning Process

c h a p t e r

COMPANY PROFILE 6: FINOLEX CABLES

The Finolex Group is one of India's leading business conglomerates with interests in diverse areas such as Telecommunications, Petrochemicals, Irrigation and Education. The group's range of products covers Electrical and Telecommunications Cables, Optical Fibre Cables, Rigid PVC Pipes, Suspension and Paste Grade PVC Resins, Continuous Cast Copper Rods, PVC Sheets, Electrical Switches and CFLs. All these products are available to the customers through a well-established and dedicated countrywide distribution network.

Finolex Cables Ltd., the flagship company of the Finolex Group was established in 1956 in Pune. Today, it is India's largest and leading manufacturer of electrical and telecommunication cables with a turnover in excess of Rs. 6275 million (about US $ 134 million).

The company started its operation with the manufacture of PVC insulated electrical cables for the automobile industry. Since then, the company has constantly endeavoured to augment its product range to include, PVC insulated electrical wires and Flame Retardant Low Smoke electrical wires, PVC insulated single core and multicore industrial flexible cables, PVC insulated winding wires and 3 core flat cables, power and control cables, polythene insulated jelly filled telephone cables, Auto and Battery cables; Co-axial and CATV cables, LAN Cables, Switchboard cables, Fibre Optic cables and others.

Finolex Industries Limited (FIL) was incorporated in 1981 and since then it has been in the plastics business. Beginning as a modest rigid PVC (Poly Vinyl Chloride) pipe manufacturer, FIL went on for backward integration and now manufactures PVC too.

FIL is the largest PVC pipe manufacturer in India. The Pipes division of FIL is the first Indian IS/ISO 9002 manufacturer. Production capacity of the Pipes division is 40,000 metric tonnes per annum spread over its two ultra-modern plants at Pune and Ratnagiri. FIL offers a wide range of PVC pipes and fittings, for diverse applications in agriculture, housing, telecom, industry, etc., ranging between 20 mm diameter to 400 mm diameter. FIL also manufactures speciality pipes and fittings, namely SWR (Soil, Waste and Rain water) pipes and fittings for construction industry. The company is into cables, PVC sheets, PVC pipes and fittings, copper rods and switches. The pipes division of FIL has iron the PLEX COUNCIL "Top Exporter Award" on five occasions.

The Hope Foundation and Research Centre is a Public Charitable Trust. The Pipes division of FIL has won the PLEXCONCIL "Top Exporter Award" on five occasions. Mr. P. P. Chhabria in 1979 (The Year of the Child). The Foundation is largely funded by the Finolex Group and pursues its charitable objectives in the twin fields of medicine and education. The Hope Foundation was a pioneer in the establishment of a well-equipped Kalpana Mammography Centre in Pune for early detection of breast cancer.

Now the Foundation is assisting University of South Florida, USA and Ruby Hall Clinic, Pune, –in a project to build local capacity and make Indian Medical Scientists self-sufficient to conduct activities independently through training and research. The goal of this project is to continue and strengthen medical, public health, bio-medical and behavioural training programmes to further Infectious diseases and HIV/AIDS research and prevention in India.

Source: www.finolex.com

Mind Power I: Strategy Deployment: Tools and Technique

Today, firms are operating in a new competitive landscape, one shaped by globalization and technological revolution. Survival involves building a complex portfolio of competencies that include

Contd...

the ability to forecast customer preferences, optimize resources, keep pace with technology and manage and motivate a culturally diverse workforce. The formula is clichéd, but simple: Success equals strategic advantage, which, is achieved when an organization employs an action plan consistent with its previously set strategic objectives.

In response to this changing landscape, management gurus and strategists have formulated several tools and techniques to help organizations translate strategies into tangible results. Irrespective of the model a company chooses, the writing on the wall is clear: In an increasingly flat world, no one can afford to play their game by the rulebook alone.

Road map for strategy implementation

In the strategic management space, deployment is a logical sequence to strategy development. The two stages are not mutually exclusive. The deployment or implementation process commences with the development of an action plan. The subsequent stages include resource allocation, modification of the action plan to fit circumstances, performance measurement and goal alignment.

Planning the action: The popular "Define, Measure, Analyze, Identify, Control" (DMAIC) model comprises a step-by-step representation of how strategic decisions are executed. These include:

1. D : Define the vision and strategic direction of the organization

2. M : Establish measures or benchmarks for all strategic objectives

3. A : Analyze the data resulting from measurement of objectives

4. I : Identify gaps and devise plans for improvement

5. C : Launch a control action to monitor progress of the improvement plans and rectify variances

Deploying deployment: The process of strategy deployment is context-specific. However, the core objective of strategic deployment remains the same, irrespective of the organizational backdrop. Simply put, it is to traverse the distance between business strategy and goal attainment. Hence, one can trace a common pattern followed by all entities.

1. ***Step 1 -Taking stock****:* Transformation, as the saying goes, begins with self-awareness. The first step in strategy deployment is to undertake a systematic self-assessment utilising appropriate checklists. The Malcolm Baldridge criteria are among the most popular and comprehensive assessment models. It suggests that key performance measures for tracking progress on action plans should reinforce organizational alignment, covering all deployment areas and stakeholders. Specific tools such as the Balanced Score Card (BSC) are used to quantify goals.

2. ***Step 2 - Linking the measures to individual and organizational goals:*** The next step is to align the measures with Individual goals, and re-evaluate the organization's strategic objectives. This process also involves benchmarking the measures with those of the competitors. Gaps if any are addressed and the strategy adapted accordingly.

3. ***Step 3: Getting to the roots:*** Strategy does not run an organization, people do. The most important aspect of strategy deployment is communicating the organization's strategy, to its people. This involves 'cascading' the strategy across all organizational levels and fostering a culture that is focussed on holistic objectives.

Contd...

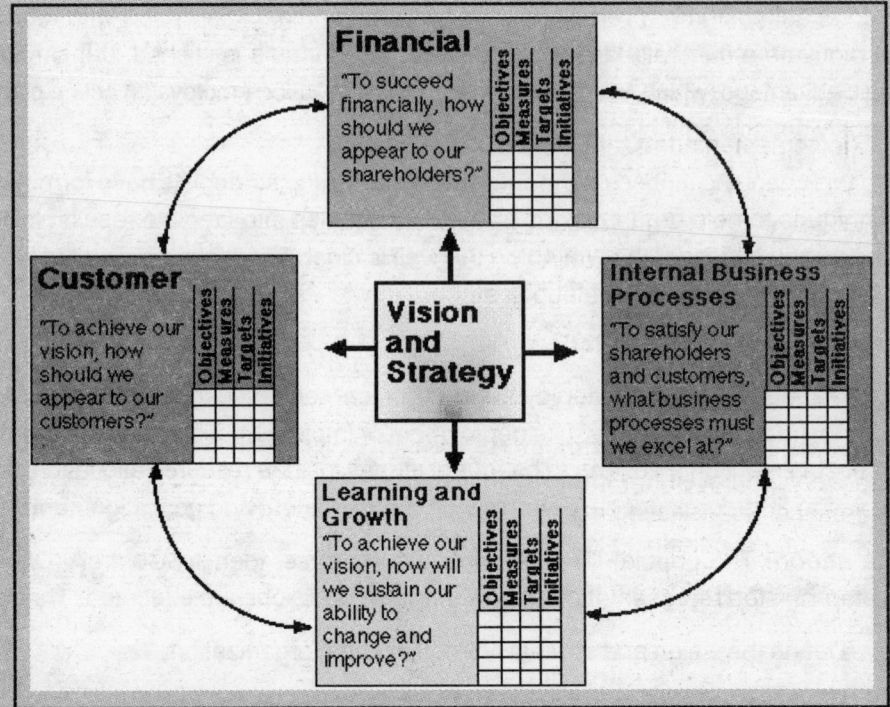

Source: www.balancescorecard.org

Theories, tools and techniques: 'Do not repeat the tactics which have gained you one victory, but let your methods be regulated by the Infinite variety of circumstances." These words of wisdom were offered by Sun Tzu, the Chinese military strategist to his generals, 23 centuries ago. It was in the 1960s that management experts across the world began to specifically address strategy development and deployment. While many of the theories from that era still impact organizational decision-making; new models, in response to the changing business environment, are prolific.

Strategic Intent theory: Gary Hamel and C K Prahalad revolutionized strategic management with the publication of the strategic intent concept in 1989. They suggested that organizations rise to global leadership through an obsession with success, fired by strategic intent which is described as an ambitious and creative dream that energises; and provides energy for the journey to the future.

The three steps that characterize the Strategic Intent (SI) process are:

1. **Setting the three attributes of SI:** viz, sense of direction, sense of discovery and sense of destiny, in the organization.

2. **Setting the challenge:** Identifying challenges and conveying them effectively across the organization.

3. **Empowerment:** Switching to a bottom-up mode of communication to incorporate creative ideas and solutions emanating from all levels in the organization.

Hoshin Kanri: Developed by Japanese companies in the 1960s, Hoshin Kanri literally means policy deployment. The model evolved from Management by Objectives (MBO), involves every level and element of the organization in defining and attaining strategic goals.

The Hoshin process involves:

1. Identifying problems and challenges facing the organization

2. Formulating strategic goals to address these problems

Contd...

3.   Developing supporting strategies for goal attainment

4.   Establishing performance measures

5.   Implementing these measures.

The process is implemented at the strategic as well as routine management levels on an annual basis.

Balanced scorecard: Drs Robert Kaplan and David Norton, who devised the BSC (Balanced scorecard) in the early 1990s, envisaged it as a complete management system. Traditionally, organizations analyzed their strategy from a limited financial perspective, thus missing the larger picture. Kaplan and Norton sought to balance this perspective with the BSC.

The four diverse vantage points offered by the BSC model are learning and growth, business process, customer and finance.

1.   ***The learning and growth perspective:*** The concept of learning organization has come of age. Today, every employee is a knowledge worker, and corporate strategy is all about knowledge management. The learning and growth perspective emphasises on employee training and corporate culture, pertaining to individual and corporate enhancement.

2.   ***The business process perspective:*** Measures based on the internal business process enable decision-makers to evaluate their organization's performance and monitor alignment with customer requirements.

3.   ***The customer perspective:*** An organization may have a healthy financial status, but customer dissatisfaction could indicate imminent doom. The BSC analyzes how customers perceive the organization's processes, products and services.

4.   ***The financial perspective:*** The traditional 'hard' financial data does not lose its place in BSC's scheme. The financial perspective includes revenues, funding, expenses, cost-benefit and risk assessment.

Quantifiable measures from these four perspectives collectively form the BSC. Further, its credo reiterates the importance of objective-measurement. "You cannot improve what you cannot measure." BSC is a very popular deployment tool, utilised by an estimated 40 percent of Fortune 1000 companies. In India, the Tata Group has implemented the BSC model with remarkable success.

Six Sigma: Devised by Bill Smith of Motorola in 1986, it was originally conceptualized as a metric for measuring manufacturing defects and improving production quality. Today, organizations have started exploring its potential as a powerful strategy deployment and change management tool.

The approach uses two key methodologies: DMAIC for enhancing the performance of an existing business; and 'define, measure, analyze, design, verify' (DMAD) to design new products and processes. The model identifies five pivotal roles within every organization:

Executive leadership: The top management team which is responsible for setting up a 'Six Sigma Vision, and empowering other role holders to contribute creatively to organizational improvement.

Champions: Responsible for implementing and integrating Six Sigma across the organization.

Master black belts: In-house trainers for Six Sigma implementation black belts.

Black belts: Those who execute specific Six Sigma projects.

Green belts: The other employees who play a supporting role. At the core of Six Sigma strategy deployments are statistical measurement techniques and feedback mechanisms. General Electric, Honeywell, DuPont and Caterpillar are among the increasing tribe of organizations who swear allegiance to Six Sigma as a vehicle for deploying strategy to ensure sustainable growth.

Contd...

People planning - The human resources aspect

Performance is all about people, the organization's most valuable resource and it is also the most vulnerable. Any strategic decision or change in an organization has huge implications on its employees. The 'Malcolm Baldridge Criteria for Excellence' states that action plans for deploying strategy should include human resource plans that are aligned with and support the overall strategy'.

Human resource strategy operates at two levels. One is the individual level, addressing issues such as job specifications, performance indicators, assessment and compensation. The other is the organizational level, involving the structure and broader issues like ethics and corporate culture. For strategy deployment plan to succeed, it is imperative that strategic decisions are communicated across levels. This is why many organizations are turning to deployment and measurement models for HR-strategy implementation.

Companies that made strategy work

X-rays for IBM: In 'The World is Flat', the epic of the globalized world, Thomas Friedman comes up with an interesting analogy. He states that the best companies stay healthy by 'getting regular chest X-rays: Friedman cites the example of IBM where the business consultancy division periodically analyzes every business component of the company in terms of whether it is a cost to the company, a source of income or both. This diagnostic process helps IBM identify its core competencies, which the company should focus on. Areas that are identified as less differentiating are usually outsourced. This strategy has helped IBM maintain its competitive advantage in a highly turbulent industry.

The-new Microsoft: Bill Gates' decision to step down as CEO of Microsoft created shock waves in the international business media. For Gates, who will take over as the company's chief software architect and also devote more time to Microsoft's charity work, this is part of a strategic response to changes in the business environment. The new strategy, Microsoft Vision 2.0, includes an organizational structure which divides the company's product development into three pairs of divisions. Each pair focuses on a specific group - corporate leaders, home PC buyers and Web surfers respectively. The new vision also empowers programmes to develop programmes that do not revolve around the Windows software. The strategy is expected to enable Microsoft to stay focussed on its customers and thus improve its already outstanding performance.

Ranbaxy's prescription for success

Ranbaxy Laboratories is India's largest pharmaceutical company and one of the world's top 10 generic drug companies. The company, which was established in 1961, markets its product in 125 countries and recorded sales of $ 1178 million in 2005. Ranbaxy maintains its competitive advantage by investing heavily in research and development. Through integration of research and development and pharmaceutical production, the company has consistently developed generic drugs, many of which became best-sellers - remember, this was much before the dawn of globalization. By scanning the international scenario for opportunities, Ranbaxy also made forays into the US and Europe. Today, more than 70 percent of the company's revenues come from overseas markets.

Voltas - staying cool: From a market leader to an ugly duckling and back - the Voltas story illustrates how a company can reinvent itself by deploying the right strategic moves at the right time. Voltas, founded by the Tata Group in 1954, was a pioneer in the Indian cooling appliances business; an unchallenged leader until the mid-1990s. Then came globalization, and with it a number of national and international players. Voltas suffered its first loss in 1996, and was soon relegated to the backseat in the cooling business. That was when the company launched a massive restructuring exercise.

The main problem area was its unwieldy workforce, 80 percent of which was unionised. In spite of stiff resistance from the workers' unions, the company launched 'zero budget' under which employees considered inevitable were identified - the others were encouraged to avail of VRS. In order to boost employee morale, Voltas introduced performance-based incentives and hiked starting salaries. In a

Contd...

bold move, the company introduced on-line systems for performance appraisals and salary processing to ensure transparency across all levels. The human resource interventions were complemented by changes in finance and marketing strategy. Results began to show within a year and the company regained much of its market share in the air-conditioner segment. Today, Voltas is back on the profit and growth trajectory.

Conclusion

Organizations create strategy; people create success. Globalization and the information revolution have resulted in a dynamic and competitive business environment. The key to strategic advantage in these circumstances is integration of strategic formulation and deployment. The survivors will be those who script their own success stories and play it out till the end.

Source: The article has been authored by Suresh Lulla. It was published in the **Chemical World**, in the Nov-Dec 2006 *Edition:* Copyright with Infomedia India Limited. Reprinted with permission.

Mind Power 2: "Kaizen" or Continuous Improvement - But How?

Since the mid-80's, we have been hearing a lot about the Japanese objective for continuous improvement called "kaizen" (ky'zen). Although this concept is as old as civilization, only a minority of individuals and corporations seem to continuously improve. A saying for non-growing adults is: "dead at 40 and buried at 85." And, if firms don't change with the times and improve at a greater rate than competitors, then they deteriorate quickly these days.

Most everyone wants to improve, but few do, perhaps because only a few people completely understand the process for how we grow and change. If so, then leaders have a two-fold challenge: first, to learn how to grow themselves to serve as role models for the rest; and second, to understand the growth process so well that they can teach it to others.

A gem of a book that addresses this challenge of growth is Mastery by George Leonard (Dutton, 1991). His diagram for growth is below:

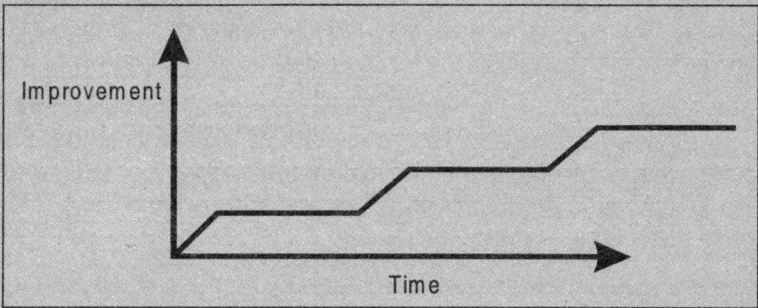

The diagram suggests that for any chosen area of growth - psychological, parenting, leadership, spiritual, or golf all progress must occur in stair steps instead of a steady climb. And, most of the time is spent on plateaus which could be frustrating for impatient achievers. If lengthy plateaus are, however, a fact of life, perhaps we should look for the good within them. Plateaus are, for example, where all the learning occurs and where the critical, and-often overlooked details that support sustainable success reside.

How Do We Learn?

On a plateau where we must identify all of the critical sub-elements that must come together to make a bigger accomplishment happen. There are, for example, over 10 elements to a perfect golf or tennis

Contd...

swing. After mastering each chronological part of a swing's kinetic-chain and converting them all into habit, a person can then work on a higher level of problems like rhythm, timing and control. With perfect strokes, a person's game can continue to improve. If there are flaws, then the quality and consistency of the stroke output will be forever suboptimal especially under pressure or after even short layoffs.

The improvement diagram above doesn't seem to allow for quick-fixes or shortcuts. If we skim over some of the sub-elements, they will create a flaw in the structure which will later undermine it. Many fast-growth companies get lots of media hype on the way up mostly for stock-price and money-raising reasons. But, when the industry matures or the economy turns down, many-high-fliers crash, because they were hastily and poorly built organizations all along.

The fastest way to relative success can often be to know and stick with the right path of improvement. Remember that many individuals and firms aren't learning and growing, but managing and repeating the past. And, many of the forward-chargers are going down wrong paths. It pays to: do some research and planning; hire the best teachers who have already been down the right path and know how to explain it; and be patient with mastering each plateau. Steady growing turtles usually beat fast, misdirected hares in the long-run.

Plateau learning also involves lots of failures. When we try new things we will fail and look foolish to non-growers, but it is important not to care about their misguided opinions, because there is no other way to learn. We must continuously repeat a cycle of:

1. Asking questions;

2. Proposing theories or solutions for those questions;

3. Testing the theories with cheap, well-designed experiments;

4. Learning from mostly failed experiments which start the cycle over with new questions.

These learning cycles allow us to creep along the plateau towards the next breakthrough and integration point.

Applications for this Learning Theory

Mastering sports is a best, first application for the improvement process, because sports are visible, measurable and familiar to many. Technique-rich, life-sports like golf, tennis and martial arts have ways to score the milestones individuals pass on their lifetime journey towards perfection.

Everyone who is physically able should consider pursuing some athletic craft as a healthy habit, but also to practice the improvement process. Too many athletic participants are obsessed, however, with results and comparative, competitive standings instead of the joy, intrigue and rhythm of the process. If more people pursued the improvement process, they would find that their competitive results would improve faster as a by-product.

If we can master the improvement process through sports, then we could next apply it to personal improvement areas like psychological maturity, leadership and parenting ability which are all heavily interlinked. These areas aren't so visible or measurable. Good coaches are hard to find, and then they can only provide guidelines for us instead of modelling the exact techniques found in sports.

In business, we could next try to coach followers to improve themselves in alignment with corporate direction and programmes. Teaching the improvement process and the philosophies that go with it, is the best way to better learn it for ourselves.

Conclusion

Continuous improvement is the way to go for both individuals and firms, but we need to know how the improvement process works and have faith in its long-term advantages. Leaders can not start to

Contd...

transform their businesses until they can continuously transform themselves in multiple areas. Then, they can start to become credible models and skilled teachers who can help followers transform themselves. Self-growing followers will add up to corporate transformation ability and sustainable profits instead of failure in a fast changing world.

Source: Copyright with Merrifield Consulting Group Inc. Visit them at *www.merrifield.com.* Reprinted with permission.

INTRODUCTION

Industrial businesses are highly challenging these days. The competition is not only from domestic sources, but there is a worldwide force, directly or indirectly hitting a business. Thus any kind of decision that has to be taken by the industrial marketer must be taken with great care and caution. The objective is simple. With the use of limited resources, we have to maximize our output, in the most profitable way.

In industrial marketing, strategic marketing plays a very important role. We have seen in the earlier chapters, the complexity that is involved with industrial marketing. Thus every industrial marketer will try and draw upon a plan, with a set of objectives, and allocate resources to it, to achieve the set of objectives. Thus strategic planning is to effectively utilize the resources, to gain the objective that has been set.

Strategy

It means "the art of the general". The term "strategy" although used from historic times, however today is used in every management discipline. The objective of any marketer (here industrial marketer) is to envision a long-term objective and thus achieve some goal. It is a set of key decisions made to meet objectives. It refers to a complex web of thoughts, ideas, insights, experiences, goals, expertise, memories, perceptions and expectations that provide general guidance for specific actions in pursuit of particular ends.[1]

Any industrial firm must have a strategy, because that would lay down, the path to achieve the objective. The market place has become very dynamic, and the industrial market place is no different. Thus, there is always a necessity, to outwit the competitors and lay down the course of action in a ever changing environment.

A strategy is a must for industrial marketer, because the need is to function effectively and efficiently and we must as industrial marketers ask ourselves:

1. "What is the business we are in?"

2. "Which is the market we serve?"

3. "Who are our competitors?"

4. "How do we differentiate ourselves to other competitors?"

Strategic Planning In Industrial Markets

Industrial marketing pose a special challenge for marketers and there is quite a significant difference between them. The differences arise out of the following issues:[2]

1. Industrial marketers have a diverse range of channels through which the product is marketed. This is unlike consumer markets.

2. A successful strategy in industrial marketing would be highly dependent on other functional areas. Any kind of planning work that we need to undertake in industrial organizations has to be

supported by other departments. Thus, it requires high degree of collaborative effort and a close relationship with overall corporate strategy.

Although, there is a great need to work in close collaboration, but still many a times in industrial marketing this is not seen. Planning is highly concentrated in the marketing department and the need for interdependency is neglected. This is "functional isolation" in industrial marketing.[3]

Mind Power 3: Who's Driving Your Company?
- Gabriel Steinhardt

Introduction

Every company claims it wants to deliver value to its customers, be profitable, and establish leadership in its core markets. Such assertions seem only natural and one would expect to be presented with a corresponding corporate strategy that supports such goals. However, closer inspection reveals that many companies often employ product delivery strategies that lead these companies far away from their business objectives.

Delivering products is a process that begins with a combination of innovation, technology, and market sensing. Each of these driving elements contribute to the initial product concept and its development, but over time and depending on the company, some driving elements will demonstrate a stronger and more lasting impact on the product concept and its roadmap. This is not necessarily due to merit or market forces, but more commonly is an outcome of the corporate culture and business perspectives which dominate the company.

Certain corporate functions that embody the aforementioned driving elements take charge of directing the company's overall product deliver strategy. For example, in one U.S. software firm, a business unit manager noted, "Marketing has had a relatively limited role in the past: technology is what has driven this company. We're a technology-oriented firm." In contrast, in a U.S. packaged-goods firm, a marketing manager said, "Engineering has absolutely no sense of the consumer. They're a group of educated technology scientist, who can do amazing things, but they need focus."

Corporate business goals and wants are relatively similar across diverse industries, but the methods they use to reach their goals vary greatly. Let us explore these different approaches to product delivery strategies, known as technology-driven, sales-driven and market-driven.

Take my road: Technology-Driven

Some companies believe they know what is best for the customer. They operate under the notion that they can develop technology; design products based on that technology, and have entire markets buy their products because they are "technologically superior." These technology-driven companies, whose product delivery strategy is determined by their engineering departments, often, create products without thoroughly researching the market and without fully understanding the prevailing market requirements.

This sounds somewhat detached from end-user needs, and may very well be so, but a technology-driven approach has its advantages. It enables a company to rapidly deliver products to market since it skims/skips lengthy traditional market research, and consequently bases product design decisions on internal company expertise.

An example of a company who chose to strive forward with a plan to launch a new product in the market without having conducted market-research first is that of Sir Clive Sinclair, a British entrepreneur who was also a brilliant engineer and consummate salesman. Sinclair trusted his intuition for all his product decisions. At the time, he believed that the moment had arrived where the general public was

Contd...

sufficiently interested in electronic wizardry to provide for a completely new market of inexpensive and relatively simple-to-use computers. Without conducting any market research whatsoever, in 1980 he ordered 100,000 sets of parts so he could launch at high-volume his new ZX8O computer. By 1982, Sinclair's company revenue was £30 million, compared with £4.65 million the previous year.

Sinclair and his engineers had intuitively succeeded in assessing the combined potential of technological developments and changing consumer needs, as opposed to researching the market potential for an innovative product. Sinclair's business decisions proved enormously successful, yet very fortuitous.

Technology-driven products are often advanced and therefore appeal to early adopters and niche markets who seek the latest technological developments.

Additionally, technology driven products may also become a high-risk, high-reward venue to be favoured by speculative investors. Such products await a triggering event that causes a dramatic surge in demand. Those events may range from the hypothetical (for example, future governmental legislation that would promote vehicles with fuel cell engines to the actual sales of survival gear when people were confronted with the spectra of Y2K or the tremendous demand for security equipment post 9/11.

But this is the problem with being technology-driven; it is a risky approach to delivering products. Adopting a technology-driven posture has, over time, proven low growth potential due to failure to implement proper marketing activities and because of the isolated manner in which products are managed. Many technology-driven products are characterized by having complex features or unnecessary features, and some technology-driven products are realistically unneeded.

At the 2004 Consumer Electronics Show (CES) in Las Vegas, Nevada; Gerard Kleisterlee, the CEO of Philips, quoted data from a Yankee Group survey:

"30 percent of all recently introduced home networking products sold today were returned because the consumer could not get them to work; and 48 percent of potential digital camera owners were delaying their purchase because they perceived the products to be too complicated."

The conclusion is quite obvious. Although some may succeed with a technology-driven approach to product development and management, there is a bigger chance that driving the best technology to customers will not yield a prosperous outcome. This is simply because the company and its products are focused on providing better technology; and not on closely matching customer needs and abilities with that technology.

A cruising taxi: Sales-Driven

A technology-driven company is focused on its technology and a sales-driven company is focused on maximizing short-term return on investment. Accordingly, the prime responsibility of most corporate departments in a sales-driven company is to help the sales channels with knowledge, ways to sell, and sales support.

Like a taxi driver cruising city streets looking for passengers who are heading to different locations, sales-driven companies cruise their markets seeking ideals with customer, who very often have different needs. Such as with the proverbial taxi driver who will deviate out of his way to accommodate the passenger going in the opposite direction, so will these companies alter their product's features in order to accommodate the particular wishes of a specific customer.

There is nothing fundamentally wrong with being sales-driven and providing custom work. Generations of tailors have sewn fitted clothes to people of different shapes and sizes; and scores of taxi driver's worldwide, transport passengers to their varied destinations.

The advantage of being sales-driven is less risk because there are always unique business opportunities and individual needs to satisfy. A sales-driven product strategy can be a lifesaver and used as a

Contd...

survival mode tactic if market segments start deteriorating or are in a chaotic phase which precludes targeted marketing programmes.

The downside is that a sales-driven product strategy is a short-term approach that does not build highly-sustainable product lines. Without those sustainable product lines it is very hard to build market leadership and promote company growth.

The eventual outcome of a sales-driven approach in high-tech companies is a plethora of product variants (produced via modification of core products) which are sold to different customers. These product variants are full of highly-individualized custom features that are developed, tested, documented and supported. This situation invariably leads to resource duplication, wasted effort, loss of distinctive competence and great difficulty in implementing product roadmaps. Due to market dynamics, the majority of sales-driven companies struggle in the long-run because there is nothing much to differentiate them from the competition, other than price, which becomes their primary marketing tool.

Driven to success: Market-Driven

To gain a status of being market-driven, a company has to engage its customers and listen to their needs. It is all a matter of timing since asking customers what they want during the sales process is not considered actually listening to the market.

Only by taking a long hard look at end-markets and paying attention to customer's demands before proceeding to develop a technology platform or products, can be regarded as a market-driven approach to product development and management.

A case of sales-driven culture posing as market-driven happened to Big Blue. IBM®, was the dominant force in the technology industry and synonymous with innovation and cutting-edge technology. IBM achieved its leadership position through a market-driven approach by using its massive sales force to determine customer needs. However, the company ran into trouble when-it stopped listening for-needs and began telling customers about its latest-new product or technology.

Applying a market-driven approach demands commitment and discipline as it is a very procedural approach. Companies with an informal work culture and lose organizational structures fail at applying this methodology and so do companies eager to rush into the market because of the time involved in executing all phases of the market-driven process. But when properly applied, the result is a product that will solve a pervasive market problem in an established market segment, and for which customers are willing to pay. Experience has shown that rewards do come for those who patiently follow the course. Market-driven companies produce sustainable products with visibly notable targeted value. The biggest reward is that a market driven product helps establish market leadership and revenue-growth potential.

Conclusion

A study conducted several years ago by querying top marketing executives working at one-hundred leading U.S. technology companies, showed that despite all the talk about being market-driven and customer-focused, 54 percent of respondents viewed their company as actually being technology-driven. Companies do understand which approach they should follow and publicly declare it, but indeed it is hard to mend ways and transition because becoming market-driven will demand a painful shift in corporate culture and business practices.

For those who take the path, success is lasting. In the high-tech world (e.g. Microsoft®) and consumer goods industry (e.g. Procter and Gamble), a leadership position can be established and maintained by being a very effective market-driven organization that has superior skills in understanding, attracting, and keeping valuable customers with products that deliver real value. This is not just a cliché but a formula for success.

What ultimately prevails in companies is the understanding that product value is always determined by the customer, not by the company or its technology. This understating in turn leads to the realization

Contd...

that finding technology that solves known market problems is easier and more profitable than finding or catering to buyers of that technology.

THE DEVELOPMENT OF STRATEGIC MANAGEMENT[4]

PHASE 1: *Financial Planning:* When a company is operating in this phase, the vision is very narrow. Although the business strategies are very sound, but it is reflected in the budgeting procedure. The plans are made by the top management on the basis of their current products and services. They try to figure out what competitors are doing. However as the company grows larger, the complexity of the various products and services increase. Documentation is required to make the strategy of the organization. Every function of the organization is highly dependent on the budgetary allocation. There is an existence of functional focus in these organizations. However, to make a long range planning, companies need to move ahead.

PHASE 2: *Forecast Planning:* When a company is in phase 2, it is under a traditional long-term planning. They will try and answer two main questions. The first is where the company is and the second would be where it would like to go. However in this state, the planning is in a very elementary form. There are 4 concepts on the basis of which, the long-term planning is done. They are: Monitoring, Forecasting, Goal setting and Implementing. Now, the trend of the business, which is of importance to the particular organization, is first monitored. The next step is to understand, as to where would the future of such trends lie. However the industrial marketer must keep in mind that a trend may not take a long-time before it bursts. The chances of it being short lived are very high. The step three would be to set the goals in harmony of the trends in the market place. The goals that have been set up, are on for a long-term and short-term goals. The last step is to look into the implementation plan and the means of achieving the particular goals. The company, at this stage needs to ask, what it needs to do, to bridge the gap between the current state and the plans. The following step is to monitor the actions and policies.

Although this way of planning is highly dynamic, but still it fails to provide adequately in certain areas. The ever changing dynamic environment is not considered in phase 2 of planning.

PHASE 3: *Externally-oriented Planning:* This is an advanced stage for planning and it is well-understood that the environment plays a key factor for forecasting. Scientific tools are used for forecasting and the defects from the previous phases are removed. Inputs from the environment are added into the planning process. This is adjusted to the dynamic nature of the planning process. The model starts with the scanning of the external environment, to aid the company in understanding the threats and opportunities that are associated to the business. The trends are studied and analyzed and a sketch is drawn to understand the impact that it would have on the organization. Then forecasting is done, on the understanding of the future using various techniques. The last step is to monitor the particular issues, and the need to add or alter additional issues. In this phase, environment is given a great deal of importance. Any drift or policy changes can make the forecasts obsolete.

PHASE 4: *Strategic Management:* The merger of the phase 2 and phase 3 forms the strategic management model. The organization sets up the goals, analyzes the resources and environment, with this model. This model consists of six stages.

They are: Environmental scanning, evaluation of issues, forecasting, goal setting, implementation and monitoring. The dynamic environmental factors are merged with the planning system, to increase the effectiveness of the planning. We call this process strategic, because it provides the best possible way to respond to the environment. The resources and objectives of the organization become very clear. It involves anticipating of the future environment and current environment. The strategic planning process and the operational decision making are joined together. Thus the objective of effective allocation of resources for future goals is achieved. Thus the long-term objectives of the organization can be understood from this model, where does it stand today and where the organization has to go in the near future. Although at a glance, the process looks to be complicated but an organization with a stronger vision and focus, needs to adapt to and appreciate the changing business environment.

Crafting and Executing Strategy[5]

As we have discussed earlier that the biggest challenge to the manager is to design the journey of the organization. Questions relating to product, customers, market and technology are always in the minds of the managers. There are a lot of choices that a company needs to make in terms of various options that are available to them.

Top management's views and conclusions about the company's direction and the product, customers, market, technology and focus constitute a strategic vision for the company. Thus a strategic vision is a road map showing the route a company intends to take in developing and strengthening its business. It paints a picture of a company's destination and provides a rationale for going there.[6] It is more than just merely a statement; it provides a very clear image of what a business is going to look like in the near future.

One hand we have the vision statement, which speaks of the what the company is going to be, the mission statement is to satisfy buyer needs, the customer groups and market segments it is endeavouring to serve and the resources and technologies that it is deploying in trying to please its customers.[7]

On the process of the journey and serving the markets, the company speaks of its values. That is, the beliefs, principles and the best practices they plan to carry along with them.

The strategy that an organization will follow will depend on the collection of all strategic actions, across departments. In an organization, with multiple levels and layers, the strategy making process will be different at each level. Three distinct levels are generally seen. They are:

1. *Corporate Strategy:* This would include managing the complete business portfolio and taking decisions that would have company wide implication. For example diversification, JV's, amalgamation, mergers or entering into foreign ventures. This is generally the responsibility of the senior management. Even business unit heads, may equally influence such decisions.

2. *Business Strategy:* The objective would be to strengthen market position for a single business line. It would be the various divisions that the company would be having. Decisions would include improving market positions and is the sole responsibility of the man heading such business. Now the business level strategy should orient themselves to the corporate level strategies and to the vision and mission of the organization.

3. *Functional Strategy:* It is for particular functions, processes or departments. They generally provide with a plan to support the complete business level strategy. These strategies are taken care of by their respective functional heads. This also includes effective utilization of allocated resources. It is a very short-term strategy and aligned to the business level strategy.

External Analysis of Industry

For a strategic vision to be successful, the organization needs to understand the dynamicity of the industry within which it works. When, managers are able to understand the opportunities and threats, if becomes very easy to take strategic decisions.

Opportunities come in when companies can use such conditions to formulate and implement strategies to make it more profitable. Threats arise when conditions are not favourable to the organization.

One of the most popular models that help a manager in the analysis of his external environment is the Michael E. Porter's five forces model.[8]

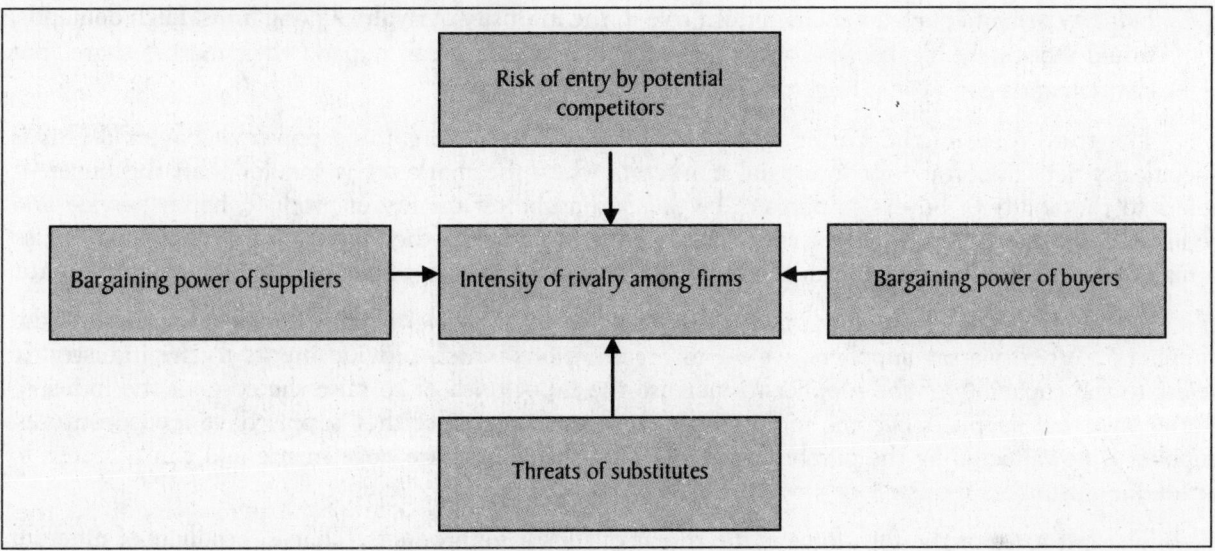

Source: Adapted from Michael E. Porters- "Competitive Strategy"-New York: Free press 1980

The first force that is acting on any business is companies that are particularly not in the industry, but at any point of time many enter the business. Whether or not a competitor will enter a particular market, will depend upon the barriers to entry. Existing competitors would try and prevent companies from entering the existing marketplace, as it would erode away the profits. High entry barriers may prevent potential competitors entering a particular market. Porter says that barriers to new entry would be:

1. *Brand loyalty to a particular product:* Brand loyalty makes it quite difficult for new competitors to come and take away market share.

2. *Absolute cost advantage position:* It is when the established companies have an advantage over new entrants because of its low cost structure.

3. *Governmental laws:* Government regulations play a very important role in the barrier of entry. Companies like Bajaj, Indian Airlines enjoyed monopoly in their respective markets for over 30 years.

4. *Switching costs:* Costs involved for a customer to switch over to another product, offered by an entrant. Higher the switching costs, lower are the chances of shifting to a new company. This is very true for industrial marketers and they should try and increase the cost of switching, by partnering with their buyers.

The second force that we have is the rivalry, which is already existing within an industry. This rivalry is power struggle and market share struggle in an industry between established firms. Higher the level of competition within an industry, lower would be the prices and the costs would be higher. The intensity of rivalry is dependent on 3 main factors. They are:

1. *Competitive structure* of an industry refer to the number of companies and their size. It could be a fragmented or a consolidated market. In some extreme cases could be monopoly.

2. *Exit barriers* are various factors that could prevent companies from moving out of an industry. They could be economic, strategic or sometimes emotional factors. In these cases of high exit barriers, excessive productive capacity is seen, which leads to rivalry and price wars.

3. *Industry demand* plays a very important role in the intensity of rivalry among firms. High demands, would reduce rivalry, because all the competing companies can expand their market share. But low demands can pose a huge threat to the industry rivalry.

The third force of the Porter's five force model is the "Bargaining power of buyers". This is specifically very important for industrial marketers when the marketer is smaller than the buyer. It refers to the ability of buyers to bargain, by demanding better quality of product, better service and reduction of price levels. If the buyers are few or large in numbers, then buyers would dominate. If also a major chunk of orders come from the buyers industry, then there would be a tendency to dominate.

The fourth competitive force in the Porter's five force model is the "Bargaining power of the suppliers". When we say suppliers, we mean organizations which provide inputs to the industry. It refers to the capability of the supplier to increase the input price or to raise the costs of the industry. Porter says that suppliers become more powerful when the product they supply have few substitutes, supplier is not affected by the purchasing company and suppliers are huge in size and can threaten to enter the customers industry.

The last force or the fifth force is the threat of substitute products. That is, products of different business can satisfy similar customer needs.

Many others have spoken of a sixth force, which they call it as **complementors.** They are companies who sell value added product and these products tend to perform better when used together.

There are also other set of forces that fall on the industry structure. These factors are the political and legal environment, the social and cultural environment, macro environment factors, demographic environment and technological environment. These are the factors, which are externally acting but are very strong forces. These forces can have significant impact on any industry and can change the complete business scenario and the strategy making process. Not only this, the external factors also play a very important role in international markets where there is a vast difference of culture and people.

Internal Analysis of Industry

Once we have done the external analysis of the industry and the various forces we now turn into the internal analysis of an organization. An organization will have its own set of strengths and weaknesses. Thus, when we see the complete picture of the internal and external analysis, it would give us a very clear understanding of the complete scenario.

Managers in an organization must understand the process by which companies create value for customers and profits for themselves, and they need to understand the role of resources, capabilities and distinctive competencies in the process. Second they need to understand how important superior efficiency, innovation, quality and responsiveness to customers are in creating value and generating higher profitability. Third, they must be able to analyze the sources of their company's competitive advantage to identify what is driving the profitability of their enterprise and where opportunities for improvement might lie. In other words they must be able to identify how the strengths of the enterprise boost its profitability and how any weaknesses lead to lower profitability.[9]

When any organization has profitability, which is greater than the industry average it would be called as "competitive advantage". When this phenomenon is over a period of years it is "sustained competitive advantage". An organization will have certain unique strengths that make a company to differentiate itself and to achieve lower costs. These are the "distinctive competencies" of a firm. The distinctive competencies that a firm has, is a sum of two factors. They are:

1.   Resources

2.   Capabilities

Resources are the human, technological, capital, physical factors that a company possess which allow a company to create value for its customers.

Capabilities are the skills of coordinating various activities, which would help the company become more productive.

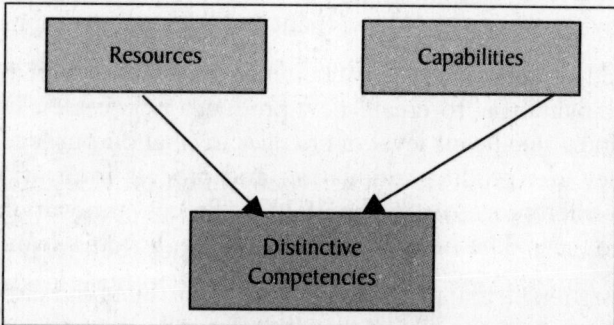

Once the organization is aware of its distinctive competencies, it would be able to build up its strategies on the basis of these competencies. These strategies, aligned with the competencies would generate "competitive advantage" which would be a source of greater profitability for the organization.

The Value Chain[10]

Organizations have a chain of activities that transform the inputs into outputs, which customers would value. This process is supported by a lot of primary and secondary activity that adds value.

The set of primary activities are the ones with designing, manufacturing, delivering the product. They would include:

1.   Research and Development

2.   Production

3.   Marketing

4.   Customer services

The set of secondary activities are the supporting activities that facilitate the primary process. They would include:

1.   Materials management

2.   Human resources

3.   Information system

4.   Infrastructure

Building Competitive Advantage

Quality: When a customer perceives the value of a product superior, compared to the same attributes in the product of its rival company, it would be called as superior quality. Any product is a bundle or collection of attributes. The attributes could be features, style, design and reliability. Out of these factors, however, reliability would be ranked at the highest, that an industrial marketer would look in for. This is because, reliability means doing a job consistency with speed and accuracy. Total quality management- a Japanese philosophy in the 1980's is to increase reliability of a product. Thus quality products would be the ones that are reliable, which increase perceived value and are differentiated by various attributes.

Efficiency: Organizations convert various inputs into outputs. Inputs are the land, labor, machinery, technology and capital. The outputs are the final goods and services that an organization produce. Efficiency would thus be a ratio of outputs over inputs. Thus the requirements of inputs are reduced as and when the efficiency increases. Here productivity of employees is considered to be very important. Because employees are the life-line of any organization. Organizations exist because of employees. One more area that needs attention is capital productivity. The output that is generated per unit of capital invested.

Innovation: We would discuss this in greater detail in the later part of this book, but a slight prelude would be good. Innovation is to create new product or processes. Even improvement in the performance would result in to significant level of changes in final output levels. We generally speak of 2 types of innovation. They are: product innovation and process innovation. Example for product innovation would be Intel microprocessor in the 1970's. Process innovation is development of new processes for producing products. The best example would be Toyota's lean production system.

Innovation is the biggest strength that the company can have, to build and sustain competitive advantage. However the success rates in innovation could be very low. But still organizations must try and innovate, to beat the competitors, create uniqueness, differentiate and charge a premium price for its products.

Customer Responsiveness: The faster a company is able to do a job, better than the competitors to satisfy a customer's needs, greater would be the customer responsiveness. Customers also needs to be provided with customized goods and services to meet the unique demands that they would have. Customer response time is the time that it takes for a good to be delivered or a service to be performed. Slow response time is a major cause of dissatisfaction for customers. For a manufacturer of machinery, response time is the time it takes to fill customer orders.[11]

But how long an organization would be able to hold back competitive advantage? Thus the durability of competitive advantage needs to be questioned.

Mind Power 4: The Largest-scale ERP Implementation in Japanese Manufacturing Industry Komatsu Completes Total Implementation of ERP

Komatsu has recently completed the total implementation of ERP (Enterprise Resource Planning) towards building a global network. This is the largest-scale implementation for primary ERP function (planning, procurement, manufacturing, sales, logistics and accounting) in Japanese manufacturing industry and approximately 5,000 users at 9 sites in 8 countries will use the system.

Contd...

Since establishing a local overseas subsidiary in 1967, Komatsu has grown into a global operation with 28 construction and mining equipment plants worldwide. Within the intensifying global competition, Komatsu has actively constructed a global supply chain based on ERP due to the necessity of cross-sourcing, where products are efficiently exchanged among the various production bases, and to achieve more prompt and accurate responses to drastic changes in the business environment.

In 1997, Komatsu organized the Information Strategic Committee to introduce information technology, through digital engineering implementation, supply chain reformation and other measures via cross-organizational activities, which was cutting edge for the manufacturing industry. Furthermore, in April 2000, the company established the "e-KOMATSU Division" to extend global business development and pursuing corporate operations by exploiting information technology.

This completion of ERP implementation within the domestic manufacturing operations has enabled Komatsu to realize a centralized control organization for the production system all over the world. By completing a global supply chain that allows all data from each base to be grasped in real time. Komatsu is successfully and dramatically reducing its inventory and lead-time. This completion will enable Komatsu to extend global business operations and accelerate competitive advantages using IT.

"iBaanERP" of Baan Japan Co. Ltd., which has abundant functions for the manufacturing industry, has been selected as this ERP package. The enterprise server "IBM @ serverz Series" by IBM Japan, Ltd., equipped with self-management functions, has been utilized as the platform for this system.

Source: http://www.komatsu.com/CompanyInfo/press/200206241401801694.html

Functional Level Strategy

As we have discussed earlier, functional level strategies are to improve the effectiveness of a company's operations and thus ability to obtain superior quality, efficiency, innovativeness and responsiveness. We will discuss this with slightly greater detail.

Quality: They do the job, for which they have been designed, and are perceived by customers as the one that generates greater value. Quality allows a firm to differentiate and distinguish it from the competitors and if quality is maintained, the level of defects is reduced and therefore efficiency and productivity increase. Deming, Juran and Feigen Baum defined "total quality management" and the need for adopting standards. This concept gave the Japanese companies a great boost and gradually got spread to the West. However, the catch here is that no organization would be able to achieve it, until and unless there is a complete organizational commitment to quality. Thus, although quality is a functional level strategy i.e. at an operational level, but it must be driven down the organization by the top management. Without resource dedication and commitment, it would not be possible.

The wants and expectations of the consumer could be entirely different from what the organization has to offer. This could pose as a severe challenge to the organization and the need is to bridge the gap between the two. Quality also needs to be measured, otherwise the purpose of it gets defeated. The measurement could be in terms of defects or wastages or could be the number of "flying hours" for an Airbus. Employees need to participate in the development of quality. Concepts like "quality circles" have been a wide subject of debate in management sciences.

To produce products of better quality, one more key is quality of raw materials and component parts. Thus many organizations are today looking in for a long-term relationship with their suppliers. Suppliers on the other hand can become hesitant if they feel that the company is not willing to support a long standing relationship.

It is important to understand that competitors would not stand quietly, who would also be in the process of improving its quality. Thus for the sustainability of a product, strong research backing and strong quality is necessary.

Efficiency: As we have discussed earlier, the job of a company is to convert a set of inputs into outputs, and the ratio between the output and input is efficiency. So, higher the efficiency, lower would be the requirement of inputs. We would see some mechanism that a company can deploy to increase the level of efficiency.

1. *Economies of scale:* The higher the output, the lesser is the per unit cost. Thus if an organization achieves economies of scale, it would be able to keep the prices down and increase its volume. Two ways, to keep the prices down are either to increase the production in large volumes, to achieve greater division of labour and specialization or else to spread the fixed cost over a large volume of goods produced.

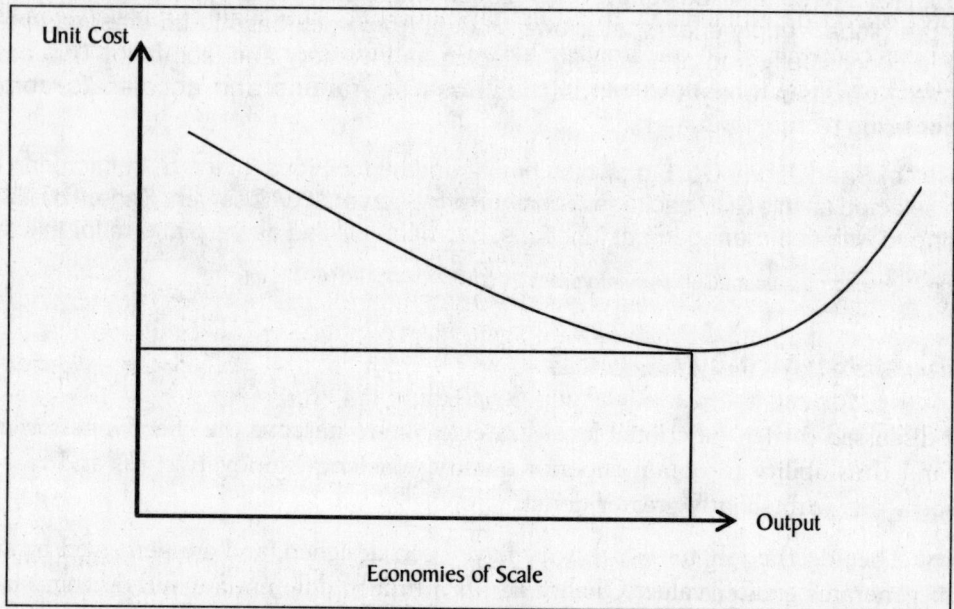

Economies of Scale

2. *Experience 'curve':* During the life time of the product, there would be a subsequent decrease in the cost structure and therefore unit cost reduction. This is called as the "experience curve". The significance of the experience curve is very important. The higher a company is on the experience curve, higher would be the volume and lower would be its cost structure.

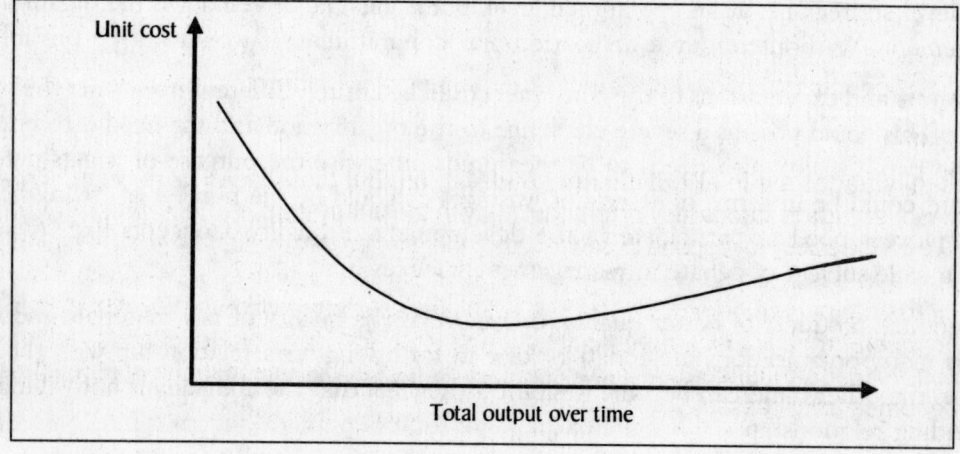

3. *Flexible manufacturing:* It is an arrangement to reduce the time to set up complex equipments, increase the use of individual machines through better scheduling and improve quality control at all stages of manufacturing process.[12] It helps the organization to achieve a wide array of products at low cost.

4. *Materials management and JIT:* Materials management is a process of getting the necessary inputs for the production process; get it into final set of goods, and then reach it to the final set of consumers using a distribution channel. Materials constitute 50 to 60 percent of the revenue and thus the potential to reduce cost and there by increase efficiency is the tremendous. Reduction of material costs can significantly give boost to the productivity. JIT or "just in time" is the process of holding inventory system to facilitate the process of material management. Thus the goods enter the production facility "just" when it is required.

5. *Internet:* The rapid growth of Internet has seen the reduction of transaction costs of business and greater operating efficiencies. In industrial marketing, the relationship between the buyer and seller has come closer to one another because of Internet. Better transparency has also increased the level of efficiency. Companies like Dell use the Internet to lower down the costs and pass on the benefits to the consumer.

Mind Power 5: Just-in-time Manufacturing- Bang on time!

Just-in-time manufacturing (JIT) is evolved into a highly sophisticated exercise that requires coordination between several different techniques and methods. In contrast to the mass production push system, JIT pulls material down the production line. Items are produced only when they are required. Operators signal their readiness for the material and hence avoid the accumulation-of work-in-process (WIP). With no WIP or buffer stocks, a defective part cannot be replaced and the operator must stop the production line. Such a system requires control over manufacturing process and quality.

Beyond call of beauty

Successful product design entails the preparation of specifications, which break down into three groups: performance specifications, design specifications, and sales specifications. But JIT implications of design do not finish when the product leaves the factory. Reliability can be regarded as the life aspect of quality. And quality criterion does not mean that the product performs satisfactorily, but also that it continues to give satisfactory service throughout its design life. It is essential that the probability of failure be also taken into account. Production can be considered in two categories: produce in demand (pull system) and produce to forecasts of demand or make to stock (push system). JIT abiding company would attempt to use pull as far as possible into the process. The advantage of the push system is predictability in the scheduling and machine loading. This task is usually assigned to the computers. Computerization makes it possible to produce plans involving the production of variety of products that could not be worked out using simulations and literature process.

Tiny hitch

The disadvantages are in all but the near perfect plan. But those plans rarely work in practice. The main disadvantage is inaccuracy of forecasting with the pull system. It is less dependent on computer and more on the ability to respond to sudden and unexpected demands. This is the principal advantage of the Kanban system. The principal advantage of the pull system is the risk of not being liable to respond to unexpected demands. The pull system places great demands on those responsible for maintenance of machinery. Machines must be in good working order at all times when demand is expected. Planned maintenance is essential. Process capabilities must be such that inspection of parts becomes unnecessary.

Contd...

Stickler for perfection

JIT requires defect levels measured in parts per million levels. Defects in parts per million cannot be achieved through the application of the traditional methods such as sampling and batch inspection. It requires the intensive application of the quality sciences. JIT depends upon involvement and participation and requires a concentrated and continuous drive at all level's towards making the company more successful than before. Dr J M Juran, Quality Pioneer, states that all problem-solving, all breakthrough follow a sequence of events. All successful projects follow the sequence.

Symptom - Cause - Remedy

In the breakthrough sequences, the theories will be identified using the brain storming process. The brain storming process is very revealing and many ideas are brought to the surface. Ishikawa or fish bone diagram is used when specific cause has been located. The symptom or effect is written in a box on the right hand side. Instead of machine, it may be better in some situation to use equipment, apparatus or tooling or instead of method other terms might be job instruction, procedures or specifications.

At each stage of process analysis with the fish bone diagram, the problem is broken down into its specific elements. Once the true cause has been identified, it becomes necessary to consider possible remedies.

The bathtub curve describes three phases in the life of a typical product - when plotted against time. A knowledge of reliability concepts and underlying theories of planned maintenance, preventive maintenance and reduction of work in process is an asset. Failure mode and effect analysis has become a basic requirement of reliability specifications.

The basic objective is to list every type of failure under the wildest variety of environmental conditions and to consider their effect. It is then necessary to assess the probability of such events occurring.

Quality manual should include the following:

1. Statement of company's quality and objectives

2. Administration of quality management function

3. Quality related functions during design and development

4. Administration of vendor surveillance, appraisal, rating and goods inward control

Keeping close tabs

JIT is based on stringent methods of inventory control. Close contacts with suppliers are essential for JIT to succeed. Production teams include representatives of different firms in the supply chain. The primary goal of JIT is the achievement of zero inventory – not just within a single organization but also throughout the supply chain. Product changes are of two kinds, planned and unplanned. Planned product changes normally occur in a predetermined cycle. These changes should have little effect on stock holding and inventory levels.

Based on past experience, stock of replacement parts and tools with obsolete designs can be calculated and held on an economic basis related to company policy. Unscheduled product changes cause the biggest problem of JIT factory. Costs associated with these changes go far beyond the cost of the changes themselves. In the ideal JIT factory operating the pull system, there will be no finished goods warehouse. Following the final operation, the product is loaded on to a pallet shrink wrapped and placed into a lorry destined for the customer.

Big task

JIT cannot be achieved without proper motivation. Motivation must be considered in three categories:

1. Motivation for control

2. Motivation for improvement

3. Motivation for involvement

Contd...

Motivation has to be at all levels—upper management, line management, off-line management, technical specialists, trade unions, supervision, outside sales, suppliers, purchasing, maintenance, administration and the work force. JIT requires continuous involvement and considerable visibility by upper management. JIT involves massive cultural change. This means a changed relationship between managers and subordinates for job evaluation, appraisal, team briefing and communication. JIT cannot be achieved in an environment where management manages and people do.

People skills

Relationships with the work force must be such that stoppage is virtually non-existent, motivation level high and skill levels at least adequate for the task. All operators must be skilled in problem-solving. Where push is required, the aim should be to keep batch quantities at the lowest level, frequent small batches being the target. This puts demands on management to ensure the quickest possible tool changes.

Good collaboration with the leaders of organised labour is essential if JIT is to be achieved. Properly implemented JIT can have phenomenal effect on productivity, efficiency and profitability of the company. For JIT to be achieved effectively, it requires collaboration right through the supply chain. Customers are not only concerned with their suppliers as well. Agreement with the Unions involves broad range of issues like participation in quality circle, profit-sharing from improvement, job rotation and job enlargement, communication, and team briefing and no strike arrangement.

In many organizations, design team has to be formed. The principal activities of the design team will be:

1.   Design the structure for the programme

2.   Design the structure for quality council

3.   Lead the strategic team, workshops

4.   Design team leader training courses

5.   Conduct counselling sessions and assist team leaders to develop projects

The team will be headed by the chief executive and contain senior executives from key functions such as marketing, distribution, finance, research and development, production and personnel. In small and medium size company, this may be the only formal organization necessary. The quality council accepts several responsibilities such as: set clear general objectives, identify major projects, create project teams, authorise expenditure on key requirements, set budget and goals, and audit and review the progamme.

Busting problems

Problems must be segregated into two categories – chronic and sporadic. It is the chronic problems which provide the greatest opportunities of JIT improvements. The improvement process is fundamental to the achievement of JIT. It applies at all stages in the product life cycle.

Planning for JIT can be effective through the selection of key individual to conduct detailed study of the concept prior to start up. The study team would be required to make proposals for these principal considerations:

1.   Evaluate alternative approach

2.   Prepare cost estimate

3.   Produce on line plan

Source: The article has been authored by K P Banerjee. It was published in the **SEARCH- The Industrial Sourcebook**, in the January 2006 edition. Copyright with Infomedia India Limited. Reprinted with permission.

Achieving greater efficiency cannot be a piecemeal approach. The complete organization should be able to support the commitment to increase efficiency, especially the top management.

Innovation: Innovation is one of the major tools to build competitiveness. Building skills in research and encouraging a work atmosphere of creativity can create changes in the way businesses are run. Although, we would be discussing innovation at a greater length in the later part of this book, but few points need to be made here. Innovations success lies with the strong cross functional integration in between the departments. It should be ensured that product developments are driven by customer needs, they should be designed for ease of manufacturing, time to reach the market should be reduced and costs should be kept under checks. For successful innovation two factors must be kept in mind. They are:

1. Management Commitment

2. Research and Development Effectiveness

Responsiveness: Manufacturing products what customers want, at a price which is competitive as well as profitable. The differentiating factor is very important and a strong loyalty can be inbuilt. Customers should be given more value for money. Focusing on customers, listening to them and driving down the culture of "customer first" need to be brought into the organization. Customer demands should be responded promptly.

Business Level Strategy

Business level strategy is an organizational specific model to gain competitive advantage over rivals in business. Michael Porter speaks of three generic strategies. They are:

1. Cost Leadership

2. Focus

3. Differentiation

	Competitive advantage	
	Low cost	Differentiation
Broad Target	Cost leadership	Differentiation
Narrow Target	Cost focus	Differentiation focus

Competitive Scope (between Broad Target and Narrow Target)

Source: "Competitive Advantage of Nations" – Michael Porter- pp-39- The Free Press.

Low cost strategy is the ability of a company to produce goods more efficiently and at a less cost than its competitors, with the same perceived quality.

Differentiation is the factor to provide the customers with something unique or greater value like quality, special features and after sales service.

When low cost strategy and differentiation are aimed at a niche, then it would be called as a cost focus or differentiation focus. Cost focus is a low cost competitive strategy only to serve a specific group or niche. Cost is a major factor of differentiation in this strategy. Differentiation focus on other hand also targets a very niche segment or market. Serving a specific target more effectively than others is differentiation focus.

Low cost strategy is for a broad market and requires economies of scale, high volumes and reduction of costs. Because of the low cost structure, it is able to earn greater profits than its competitors. It is a strong defense mechanism in an industry with high competition levels. The company would have better bargaining powers and will be a barrier to entry to new firms.

Differentiation is also aimed at a broader market and it creates a product or service that is unique. This enables the company to charge a premium for its products. Differentiation could be in its various forms, like image, design, technology or customer service. This strategy provides better returns to the organization and due to strong brand loyalty; it acts as an entry barrier.

Following the above strategies, however, is not a guarantee to succeed. Each of the strategies has its own set of risks. Cost leadership may not be maintained because of low cost technologies and competitors also may imitate such actions. Similarly, differentiation cannot be sustained, because of imitation or could be due to less importance of differentiating factors to the buyers. Focus strategies may be disturbed with new players coming in, imitation of strategies and demand disappearance.[13]

Corporate Level Strategy

Corporate strategy is all about giving direction to a business. Decisions like flow of resources, planning, product lines and strategic business units. This is applicable to all kinds of companies be it small, medium or any large MNC. The task of the corporate strategy is to align the various units, so the business becomes success as a complete unit. Three key issues that the corporate strategy deals with are:[14]

1. The firms overall orientation towards growth, stability or retrenchment (directional strategy).

2. The industries or markets in which the firm competes, through its products and business units (portfolio strategy).

3. The manner in which management coordinates activities, transfers resources and cultivates capabilities among product lines and business units (parenting strategy).

Directional strategy: It is to give every business an orientation or direction. Every business must ask itself question on - Expansion, Diversification, Growth and Retrenchment. If the company is pursuing a growth strategy, it would be in terms of sales, profits and the assets of a company. A company may choose to grow, through a merger or an acquisition or a strategic alliance. Some of the businesses would be working in industries or markets which have become mature and thus expansion in such industries has no meaning. Corporations thus can choose to diversify in such cases. Diversification could be of two kinds. They are related or could be conglomerate or unrelated diversification.

Today expansion into global markets is also a form of growth. This is generally done to reduce dependency from home markets. It could be through joint ventures, licensing, mergers, acquisition, turn key projects and management contracts.

Some of the corporations may also look in for closing down specific units or business when profits and sales are very low. Corporations may decide to focus on businesses, cut down on areas which are not doing well.

All these strategies would be pursued under directional strategy.

Portfolio strategy: Companies have multiple product line ups or business units which contribute to the profitability of the overall performance. Business managers' greatest dilemma is, how to allocate resources amongst the business units. Top management always prefers to keep changing the mix of business, to get the maximum rate of return. Two approaches are generally adopted for the same. They are:

1. BCG Growth-Share Matrix
2. GE Business Screen Matrix

BCG Growth Share Matrix

A company would have a wide range of product portfolio. This is plotted on a matrix on two scales i.e. market share on the 'x' axis and growth rate on the 'y' axis. The market share in consideration is the relative market share and the growth rate is in percentage terms.

Business Growth rate (Percent)	Stars	Question marks
	Cash Cows	Dogs

Relative competitive position (market share)

We see in the above diagram, four parts of the matrix. They are:

1. *Stars*: They are at the peak and are relatively in a high market share and high growth region. They generate enough cash to maintain high share in the market.

2. *Question marks*: These are areas, where the management is in dilemma. These are relatively new products, with a great potential to succeed. But a lot of monetary resource is needed for their development. They are in areas of relatively low market share but higher growth rates.

3. *Cash cows*: Products in their maturity and decline stages. The business growth rates are slowing down, but hold a strong market position. They need to be "milked" and the cash generated to be invested in other businesses.

4. *Dogs:* They have low market share and low potential to bring in money. They should be sold off, and further investment need not be made.

However, the BCG Matrix has its own share of limitation. This is due to several reasons:

i) Attractiveness cannot be a function of only business growth rate.

ii) Smaller competitors are ignored.

iii) It is a very simplistic model and industry dynamics are ignored.

iv) Relationship between market share and profitability can draw upon arguments.

GE Business Screen Matrix

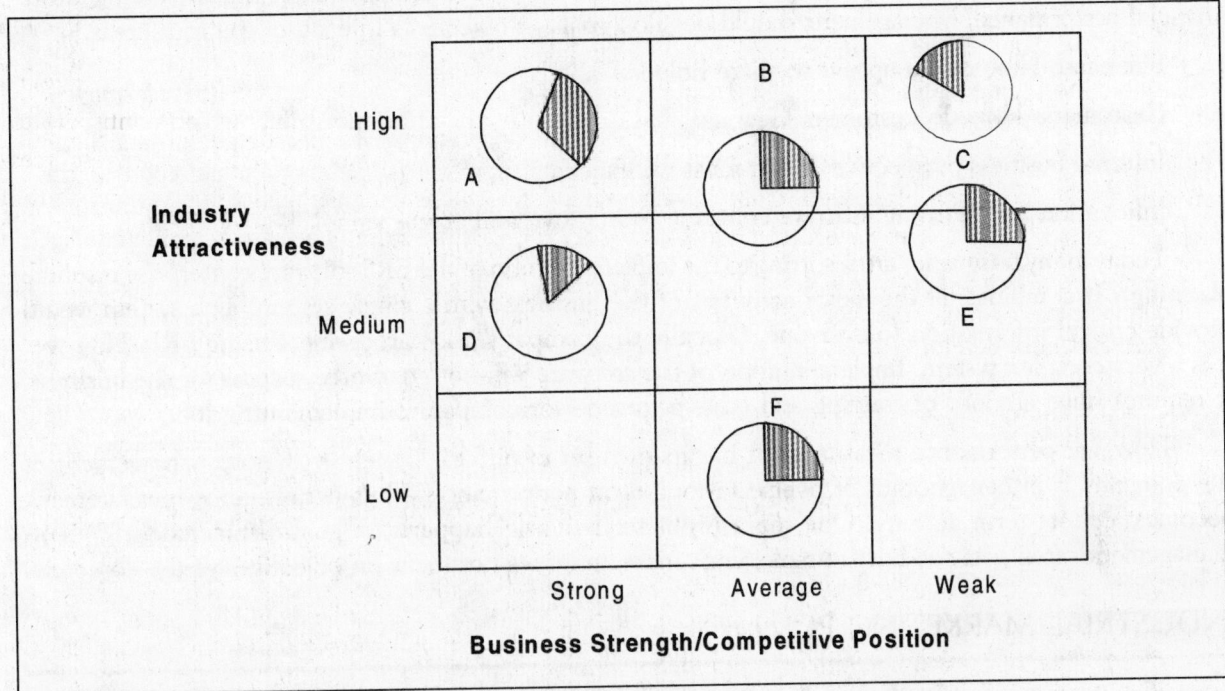

The model was jointly developed by GE and McKinsey and is much more complicated than BCG matrix. Two factors are taken into consideration in the matrix. On the 'x' axis there is "business strength/competitive position" which includes a multiple factors like technology, market share, profitability and size. On the 'y' axis, we have "industry attractiveness" which includes market growth rates, market growth rate, profitability, pricing and threats. The individual product lines are assigned an alphabet. The area of each circle is proportional to the size of the industry in terms of sales. The shaded areas, within the circle, depict the market share of each product.

Although this model is much more comprehensive than the BCG matrix, but still it becomes a highly complicated and cumbersome model, and it would be difficult to place new products within the matrix.

Parenting Strategy[15]

Corporate parenting is to define a corporation in terms of the resources and capabilities that can be used to build business unit value and generate synergies across business units. Thus obtaining synergy amongst business units, providing resources and coordinating the activities.

PERFORMANCE MEASUREMENT

It is the performance that matters at the end of any organizational activity. Now to measure the performance and to understand whether the objectives have been achieved organizations require "measuring rods" or scales against which the performance can be measured.

The measurement can be in terms of traditional financial measurements like EPS or ROI. One more approach that is seen in the recent years is the use of "balanced scorecard". It combines financial measures that tell the results of actions already taken, with operational measures on customer satisfaction, internal processes and the corporation's innovation and improvement activities, the drivers of future financial performance. Management should develop goals or objectives in each of the four areas:

1. Financial: How do we appear to share holders?

2. Customers: How do customers view us?

3. Internal business perspective: What must we excel at?

4. Innovation and learning: Can we continue to improve and create value?

Today many businesses are resorting to the implementation of the ERP software (enterprise resource planning). It combines all the major activities of the business with a single system. The system would provide critical information to everyone. Globally the company also can connect using ERP. However it is a very complex system. Implementation of the software will not guarantee success for the business. It requires huge amount of training and costs a fortune for companies implementing it.

However performance measurement has its own set of pitfalls. Generally the top management of the company is either ignorant or averse to long-term performance. Thus performance measurement becomes a short-term activity. One more problem that also happens is "goal displacement".[16] Top management often gets too busy to make ends meet and does not focus on objectives of the company.

INDUSTRIAL MARKETING PLAN

The role of the marketing department is very critical. It is not only about generating revenues, but also about generating ideas, opportunities, plan, and achieve results. The role of marketing in every step is thus very critical. We shall see step by step, the process of the industrial marketing plan.

Step 1: Situational analysis

Step 2: Setting up of goals

Step 3: Strategy making

Step 4: Implementing strategy

Step 5: Control

Step 6: Marketing audits

Step 1: Situational analysis will through a light on the current market position, market size, prospects of growth, profits, future projection for the current markets. It would also include the SWOT analysis of the products and the macro environmental factors that act as a guiding force. The situational analysis also needs to take into account the competitive situation in the market and their objectives and strategies.

Step 2: Setting up of goals: Goals specific to the marketing department in terms of sales, profitability, market share, and where we need to go ahead in the years to come.

Step 3: Is the strategy making process, where an organization selects the target markets, positions itself. It also decides on its marketing mix strategy and of its strategic alternatives, like diversification or reviewing of the SBU's.

Step 4: Is implementation where in plans are made on training, making budgets across business and product lines.

Step 5: Is control mechanisms which are to keep a check on the established objectives and performances and differences if any.

Step 6: Is marketing audit which is an extension of the control mechanisms. It is a systematic and periodic assessment of the marketing plan, with respect to objectives, strategies, activities and people.

CONCLUSION

The strategic planning process is perhaps, the most important activity of any organization. It gives direction to an organization. Poor strategy making process can result in consequent poor performance of an organization. One more area which needs a clear understanding is the level of conflict that is there in between various functional areas.

We have seen the development of strategic management as a process and what is the mechanism to formulate a strategy, and execute it. Three distinct levels of strategy making process i.e. corporate, business and functional level strategies, its importance and pitfalls. How an organization analyzes its environment– its external and internal environment.

At the end, we have studied control mechanisms and the performance measures and the role of marketing in the strategic planning process.

References

1.   Kachru. *"Strategic Management"*. Concepts and cases. pp 5.

2.   Charles Ames. *"Marketing Planning for Industrial Products"*. HBR, (Sep-Oct 1968).

3.   Wind and Robertson. *"Marketing Strategy"*. New directions for theory and research. Journal of Marketing 47 (spring 1983). pp 13-25.

4.   Gluck, Kauffman and Walleck. *"Phases in the Development of Strategic Management."* Adapted from Kachru. *"Strategic management."* Concepts and cases, pp 16-20.

5.   Thomson Jr, Strickland, Gamble. *"Crafting and Executing Strategy."* The quest for competitive advantage, pp 17-43.

6.   Thomson Jr, Strickland, Gamble. *"Crafting and Executing Strategy."* The quest for competitive advantage, pp 17-43.

7.   Thomson Jr, Strickland, Gamble. *"Crafting and Executing Strategy."* The quest for competitive advantage. Pp 18.

8.   M. E. Porter. *"Competitive Strategy."* New York: Free Press 1980.

9.   Hill and Jones. *"Strategic Management."* An integrated approach. pp 76.

10.   M. E. Porter. *"Competitive Strategy"*. New York: Free Press 1980.

11.   Stalk and Hout. *"Competing Against Time."* New York: Free Press 1990.

12.   Nemetz and Fry. *"Flexible Manufacturing Organization."* Implications for Strategy Formulation. Academy of Management Review 13 (1988). pp 627-638.

13.   Porter. *"Competitive Advantage: Creating and Sustaining Superior Performance"*. The Free press. pp 21.

14.   Wheelen and Hunger. *"Concepts in Strategic Management and Business Policy"*. Pearson Education Asia. pp 137.

15.   Wheelen and Hunger. *"Concepts in Strategic Management and Business Policy"*. Pearson education Asia. pp 156.

16.   Wheelen and Hunger. *"Concepts in Strategic Management and Business Policy"* Pearson Education Asia. pp 258.

Mind Power 6: Information and Knowledge Management— Share and Grow

In recent years, globally competitive companies have discovered the importance of an organization-wide Knowledge Management System (KMS). This system provides employees with instant access to knowledge gained throughout the organization, thereby enhancing business effectiveness. From being a hygiene factor, KMS has now evolved into a 'must-have' component for customer-facing units or departments. And for organizations that are spread across the globe, this is a necessity.

Customers contact the firm at various touch points, i.e., physical office or branch, the telephone and Internet access 24´7. They expect instant resolution for a bulk of their queries, if not all of them. Successful companies utilise the opportunity of constant contact to build loyalty. How? Simply by giving its frontline staff, rapid access to adequate customer and product information, thus speeding problem resolution.

As an example, in the mid 1990s, Citibank India changed the rules of competition with its campaign 'The Citi never sleeps'. It was the first bank to introduce phone banking to the Indian customer where he could call and transact anytime - day or night. By announcing that it worked 24´7 for its customers, in striking contrast to its competitors who operated strict business hours, it raised the bar so high that it enjoyed unassailable, competitive advantage and high brand recall for a very long time. This was made possible by ensuring information availability to employees at all times.

The main source of competitive advantage therefore lies in a firm's ability to effectively utilise corporate knowledge and learn faster than others in their field: The management and distribution of collective corporate knowledge thus becomes a powerful tool in global organizations.

Shared knowledge

A huge amount of business intelligence resides with employees. When they exit the firm, they take with them this knowledge of products, procedures and most importantly, customer feedback with them. With the right KMS in place, the hemorrhaging of this expertise and experience can be plugged. Vital employee knowledge can be retained even if the employee cannot.

What does KM involve? Step one is the aggregation of the employee knowledge about business practices, products, customer and industries. Step two involves leveraging this collective corporate intelligence to gain a competitive advantage in terms of customer retention, reducing time to market, slashing turnaround time and improving cross-sell opportunities. What ties all this in, is the continuous process of updates, assimilation, review and data availability. Developing such a knowledge warehouse helps a firm build on its competitive intelligence-eliminate redundant employee research across departments and establish best practices across the organization.

Another major benefit - aggregating such employee knowledge can reveal, over time, any lurking inefficiencies, omissions, gaps or lack of expertise inherent in the organization. KMS can also give insights into customer behaviour, identify industry or customer-specific peculiarities, and throw up best practices and lessons learned by others in the organization and help build on competitive intelligence. It can reveal hidden opportunities that can be tapped for new business and cross selling.

Take for instance, a hypermarket, which one spots in most Indian shopping malls. Such outlets stock thousands of products whose inventory management needs to be efficient and cost-effective. Inventory decision making involves assessing the stock out rates of various products, safety stock needed, reorder point, quantity to be ordered in addition to balancing order-processing costs with inventory-carrying costs. Here, a KMS finds application and could be used to move from an anticipatory-based supply chain to a response-based supply chain. The former indicates that the hypermarket orders and holds quantities based on sales forecasts, while the latter is customer-triggered in that

Contd...

fast-selling items are continuously ordered, stocked, sold and re-ordered. More importantly, spending patterns could be analyzed and opportunities for cross selling could be exploited.

The KM initiative

An organization can kick start its KM initiative in three steps.

Identification of the business requirements: Who are the employees that need information? What is the quality and depth of knowledge needed by each of them? At what frequency and how soon? Where is it needed - across local or remote locations?

These questions need to be examined before commencing the KM exercise. Understanding the organizational business strategy will yield:

1. Key business processes and procedures.

2. Information flow from one department to another

3. Who needs the information and at what level

For instance, a front-desk customer-interface employee needs a snapshot of the customer account while answering queries whereas an operations employee will need a detailed history of the customer to resolve complaints. A sales executive, on the other hand, might need information on, say, a PDA from a remote location. Thus, various departments in a single organization require different subsets of the base data in different formats.

Data definition: Once the business requirements are defined, the organization needs to work backwards and identify the data that needs to be part of the KMS. This is an extremely crucial step. Every organization houses two kinds of knowledge - explicit and tacit knowledge. Explicit knowledge refers to reports or informations meant for public consumption white tacit knowledge is information confined within the organization that others are not privy to.

For example, consulting firms consider their project knowledge in terms of approach used, strategy formulated, benchmark data utilised, client, information and lessons learned as tacit knowledge. This information goes into their KMS and is accessible, with appropriate access rights, only to its employees, whichever part of the world they may be. However, published reports from Forrester/ Tower Group research or RBI annual publications like the 'Trends and Progress of Banking in India 'or' Currency and Finance Report are explicit knowledge. This too needs to be constantly updated into the KMS.

Definition of data architecture: Once the users are identified and the data is defined, the next step is to define the data architecture and design the database. This is usually the domain of the Chief Technology Officer (CTO) and the IT department which has to map the relationship between different user requirements, identifies the inputs and outputs of the database, introduce search facilities depending on user type and initiate multiple levels of access rights to the database. It also needs to develop measures to ensure that the knowledge fed into the KMS is accurate, timely; reliable and confidential. Once the KMS is set up, the constant process of review, updates and management of the knowledge assets must be institutionalized.

Key success factors for KMS

Can a firm convert the KMS into a sustainable competitive advantage? Yes and here's how.

Top management support: A KM initiative has to necessarily be driven by the top management. A top-down approach works best in raising awareness and, emphasising the importance of constant updates to the KMS.

Ownership: A dedicated KM team is required to drive this effort. This team is responsible for ensuring continuous and consistent absorption of research, employee knowledge, (earnings and new information

Contd...

into the KMS). This team can spot duplication of efforts across departments, if any, and thus eliminate wastage of resources.

Infrastructure: If different departments of a company were to use disparate systems, information gets isolated, resulting in islands of knowledge instead of organization-wide business intelligence. A KMS integrated with the organization's IT systems allows effective and efficient utilization of knowledge assets.

Deployment: This refers to the technology deployed for KMS in the organization. It has to be flexible to adapt to existing company information systems for greater user acceptance. If it is markedly different from what the employees are used to, they may shy away from accessing, sharing and contributing to the KMS.

Resources: Managing information can require a significant commitment of resources as the sources of data and information grow dramatically. The expanding use of electronic information necessitates that the KMS keep pace with changing business needs and new technology solutions. Major resources include a strong IT team, finances and top management support.

Industry best practices

1. Ford India initiated knowledge management efforts as early as 1997 and implemented a KMS at the corporate level. The initiative is owned by the Chief Knowledge Management Organization and supported by shared infrastructure. Using the KMS helped Ford save substantial costs, by quickly transferring project learning from its economy car models to premium cars. The value derived by Ford India from its KMS is continuity of customer relations, which is in turn leading to increased orders and greater customer satisfaction, finally resulting in greater customer loyalty and product leadership.

2. Hyundai Motor India Ltd. (HMIL) is another organization that has implemented a KMS. The dissemination of knowledge is done through formal (through IT-based networking and a structured feedback system) as well as informal processes. Through KM, HMIL was able to implement its 100 PPM programme for vendors, resulting in higher quality standards.

3. Connecticut-based Xerox Corporation has implemented a KMS called Eureka that enables the organization's 23,000 engineers from around the globe to input product solutions into a knowledge base. This knowledge base holds over 50,000 problem/solution entries. If an engineer encounters a unique situation where a solution does not exist in the knowledge base, he will voluntarily input the solution into the system once the problem is resolved. To make the interface accessible everywhere, all service engineers are provided with a laptop that is loaded with a Eureka interface, as well as electronic documentation, electronic training and diagnostic tools required for the service engineers to do their jobs.

4. An autonomous body under the Railway Ministry, the Indian Railway Catering and Tourism Corporation (IRCTC), offers online train ticket bookings with a home delivery facility. Its website displays information on trains plying different cities, distances, important stations along the routes, ticket availability, tariffs and so on. For the captive traveller who books tickets on the website, the IRCTC is set to launch tourism packages that will offer one-stop service for travellers. It plans to tie up with local tour operators, hotels, government resorts and ground transport providers to offer a start-to-end package. It also plans to start a national call-centre to provide a one-stop enquiry system for train timings, reservation status, arrivals and departures and even for booking tickets. KM helped the IRCTC tap its knowledge base of highly frequented destinations, popular travel circuits, peak and lean seasons of various railway routes to expand the scope and scale of rail travel.

Conclusion

KM helps organizations leverage their knowledge assets - product and customer information, employee knowledge and organization learnings to their best advantage. A KMS facilitates easier sharing of

Contd...

knowledge across departments and geographies. As the nerve centre of the firm, it improves efficiency, increases customer satisfaction and ultimately even transforms the way they do business. No, Christmas has not been advanced, and this is not Santa's big surprise. All this and more is promised, only and only if the firm gets its IT act together, its employees motivated and the top management involved.

Source: The article has been authored by Suresh Lulla. It was published in the **Electrical and Electronics**, in the Nov-Dec 2006 edition. Copyright with Infomedia India Limited. Reprinted with permission.

Mind Power 7: Lean in Financial Domain

There are many activities that add wastage to the final product or service. Some of them are...

Over-processing

Over-processing is adding more value to a service or product than customers want or will pay for. The basic premise of over-processing is doing more work than is absolutely necessary to satisfy or delight customers. There are two fundamentals to over- processing:

1. *Not knowing what customers want:* For example, a credit card company including an envelope along with their invoice is considered as a value added service by those who pay by cheque, while those who pay by automatic transfer consider it as a waste.

2. *Redundancy:* Consider a process that involves a number of approval steps. Would customers think that each of those steps is adding value? Hardly. Rather than requiring five managers to sign off on a decision, why not develop a process and guidelines so one manager can make the call?

By developing a check list of information and documents required one authority could be authorised to process the requirement instead of many. By eliminating unwanted or irrelevant information the non-value added work could be eliminated.

Transportation

Transportation is unnecessary movement of materials, products or information. Too much physical movement back and forth is one of the problems that plague many financial areas. Excess transportation is important to recognize and eliminate because every move from one activity to another adds time to a process, and world-class organizations are passionate about reducing time.

Yet, in many service processes, we see paperwork go back and forth several times... waiting in queues. Transportation in service processes almost always manifests itself as materials are being collected or delivered, or the actual or virtual chasing of information, For example, - ("Who has that expense figure? Ram? Okay, I'll ask Ram.... Ram says Lakshman has it..."). At one end of the spectrum, eliminating excess transportation involves combining steps to eliminate the back and forth movement of information or paperwork. Cutting the movement path of information or paper in half by eliminating the unwanted steps generally cuts the queue time in half. At the other end is the option to rearrange the workspace to match the flow of the process.

Motion

Needless movement of people – while 'transportation' refers to the movement of the work, 'motion' involves movement of workers. Both are much harder to see in service environments than in manufacturing. Motion may show up as people constantly switch between different computer domains or drives, or simply having to perform too many, keystrokes to accomplish a computerised task. Solutions can involve everything from rearranging people's desks, to purchasing ergonomic furniture and equipment, to using software that performs tasks offline, so information is waiting for the staff rather than vice versa.

Contd...

Inventory

Any work-in-process that is in excess of what is required to produce for the customer can be termed as extra inventory. The evils of inventory were first recognised in manufacturing because that is where the inventory itself is most visible. It is hard to ignore a room full of half-completed assemblies – a very visible reminder of millions of rupees the company could be putting to better use. Inventory in service areas is just as big a problem, but more dangerous because it is not as readily visible. Look for physical piles of forms (in-boxes, for example), a list of pending requests in a computerised e-mail programme, callers on hold, people standing in line, etc. This excess inventory is often the result of overproduction. (As discussed later in the article). The goal, from a lean standpoint, is to have on hand only what is needed immediately or in the short-term. (To find solutions to inventory problems, read upon Lean practices such as pull systems.)

Waiting

Any delay between the time one process step/activity ends and the next step/activity begins. One of the biggest tribulations in today's marketplace is to make customers wait for delivery of a product or service, because chances are a competitor will be able to get it to them quicker. Anything in a process that makes a work item to be processed wait should be eliminated. Because so much of the work in a service process is invisible to the naked eye, process-mapping techniques (flow charting, value-stream mapping) are essential for identifying delays in a process.

Defects

Any aspect of the service that does not conform to customer needs - Producing work that customers are not going to pay for – or that makes them seek out other companies to do business with - is one of the more obvious forms of waste. Statistical methods such as Six Sigma practices have long been structured around minimizing the possibility of producing defects. In a service, these methods translate to prevent the possibility of missing information, thus improving the possibility of making deadlines.

One clue to studying defects is to recognize that their impact is usually felt far downstream from where they occurred. Customer-service staff, for example, is likely to receive the complaint calls from customers upset about something that happened in an entirely different part of the process. The defect has to be traced back to where it happened, where the incorrect information was put into the computer system, for example, in order to find a solution that will last.

Overproduction

Production of service outputs or products beyond what is needed for immediate use. In one of Lockheed Martin's procurement centres, buyers purchased items for 14 or more different facilities. The way the computer system was initially set up; it was incredibly cumbersome for the buyers to switch from one facility to another. So they naturally processed all the requests from one centre before moving on to the next, even if there were urgent or priority requests in queue from other facilities. As a result, non-priority requests from one centre would be processed before priority requests from another facility. This batch processing and delivering a service before the customer needs - it is a type of overproduction common in services. The solution to overproduction is to examine the process and see why the staff does not work in a way that reflects actual customer needs, and then make changes accordingly. (At Lockheed Martin, the solution was to change the computer system so buyers could see priority requests from all facilities simultaneously.)

The better the Lean practitioners in financial services recognize these forms of waste, the more effective their improvement efforts will be.

Source: The article has been authored by Sanjeev Baitmangalkar. It was published in the **Modern Machine Tools**, in the November 2006 edition. Copyright with Infomedia India Limited. Reprinted with permission.

Mind Power 8: Lean Manufacturing as a 'Competitive Strategy' – Money Mind, Strategy Lean

Through one of its subsidiaries, Boigon Pty in Australia ordered over a dozen different components on AV Engineers*, a company that specialised in manufacturing a particular family of parts. The initial supplies made were of acceptable quality. But over time, their deliveries and contractually obligated conditions began to falter. At Boigon, they rated the supplier low on effectiveness and response. The supplier eventually lost the export contract.

Fragrance Engineers* dialogued with an Australian dealer for regular supply of certain types of machines. They sent over their product information - literature and price. The buyer was willing to look at buying these machines against the Chinese machines that he was trading. The customers in Australia have accepted the Chinese machines for the application, and so the product has an acceptance in terms of expectations on performance and price. The buyer was willing to test market these machines as the initial price indications matched the Chinese. In the discussions that followed, the Indian machine was re-quoted in bits and pieces, eventually culminating at twice the price of the Chinese machine. Posturing on the Indian side was, let the buyer buy the basic machine from India and the accessories and tooling from China. Now, do you honestly, think this is going to work? We analyzed what could have gone wrong and found-that Fragrance Engineers worked on the RM/FG ratio of almost 1 /10! This meant that either the conversion efficiency was very poor or the manufacturing is not cost effective (even though the domestic customers pay more to buy these machines), rendering the product not saleable in the global market space. It is of little surprise then, that in the last two years Indian exports were only six machines in that category (as per published figures on IMTMA website). Efficient manufacturing can make the product competitive and profitable by adapting the right strategy irrespective of size and volumes. Fragrance Engineers clearly did not have a competitive strategy and lost out to more efficient manufacturers.

When the Japanese manufacturers were gaining market share from the Americans, it took the Americans a while to realise how and where they were being beaten. Reluctance and rigidity to accept change only made them lose more. But they did learn and by changing their thinking to lean concepts, they were not only able to bounce back, but regain lost space.

Traditionally in India, the machine tool industry has only looked at the immediate market (domestic) and they seem to be satisfied with the results. Satisfaction leads to complacency. Today's markets are global and that is how any senior management should look at it. Contentment in a market devoid of brisk competition is more of a threat. Contentment with only immediate markets could also be because of lack of a good competitive strategy in global markets. After the global recession of the 1980s; having predominantly exported over 80 percent of their produce to Europe and America, MKL Hubli saw its market share dwindle. They knew that to increase their market share, they had to re-assess their competitive strategy. In what ensued as a vigorous strategy workshop, they decided to lock into lean manufacturing as their competitive strategy, and that is how they turned their business around – from closure to abundant demand even during the lean times.

Today's customers not only evaluate the products by design, quality and price; but they also emphasise on two performance dimensions – responsiveness and effectiveness. Responsiveness is how good you are at meeting customer requests and effectiveness is how good you are at meeting your commitments. Already some industries are affected by these performance parameters. Soon, emphasis on responsiveness and dependability will increase leading to more customers demanding these measures.

For the top management, the business model is becoming more complex and challenging, especially with issues of how to increase profits and market share, ultimately leading to the inescapable question – What is the right manufacturing strategy for us to follow?

Contd...

An important aspect to consider in formulating such a strategy is the company's ability to implement an effective competitive strategy. The various operating problems such as delay in delivery, locked up working capital, slow inventory turns, slow response, high costs, etc. are some of the identified culprits that can spoil the best of strategic intents. Yet, these are only suggestive of the more serious underlying problems in the flow of material and information, which is often the result of poorly designed processes. In practice, the processes that govern the flow of material and information are typically not the issues that are focussed by the senior management, although these should be a priority.

Changing the rules

Even without an in-depth understanding, some managers are less hesitant on IT investments, and attract a common criticism– 'expected returns on investment were not achieved'. The reason for this failure is because the focus was on the wrong issues. Basically, the problem resides in the way many managers think a manufacturing organization should be run. This thinking of the management endorses the rules and operating logic that people follow on a day today basis and can defeat the effective implementation of a competitive strategy. This is especially true when inaccurate and poor flow of information and interrupted material flow, is allowed to exist.

A common reaction from managers in detached manufacturing environments to the possibility of adopting lean manufacturing in their own organizations is an 'it won't work here' kind of attitude. Lean manufacturing clearly defies the logic of their detached operational environment. Instead, what they need to do is challenge the existing approach or method. Understand and accept that the old, agreed-upon operating logic with its agreed-upon but poor rules are, in fact, outdated. The difficulty in changing mindsets, at all levels of the organization, should not be underestimated; but the bias must be changed or you will not succeed in achieving the levels of performance of true lean manufacturers.

The long-accepted traditional method of manufacturing allows the flow of information and material to be interrupted many times in its path. Now, this takes up time – cycle time – and significantly increases the operating expense. Even with computers that can process data at the speed of light, most of a company's information and material flow processes are loaded with the worst kind of time – waiting time. It is not at all unusual to find information and material waiting for up to or more than 90 percent of the time. When you pause and think that, central to effective competitive strategy are responsiveness and dependability, then cycle time reduction in the flow of information and material is of prime importance.

Is it worth it?

We can learn from the organizations that have walked this path before (refer The Lean Mindset – Indian Management, November 2004). Developing the most dependable and responsive operation can make the difference between winning and loosing. This by itself should be enough to at least initiate a thorough investigation of a lean strategy. Both west and east, a number of companies, large and small, have successfully adopted lean manufacturing as a business strategy with astounding results. Your business case may point to improvement potential that may look like this (depending on where you presently are):

1. Reduction in lead times 50-90 percent.

2. Overall reduction in cycle times 60-90 percent plus.

3. Reduction in inventory in excess of 50 percent.

4. On time delivery 99 percent plus.

5. Quality improvement - over 90 percent.

6. Reduction in floor space 40-75 percent.

7. Material cost reduction 5-15 percent.

8. Cost reduction 25-50 percent.

9. Growth in profits – from doubling to well over 10 times at base prices.

Contd...

Such results are more than enough for any senior management team to certify lean as the most sensible of strategies.

Consider the potential of a 10 percent increase in throughput. If overhead expenses are fully absorbed at the current rate of output, then usually the only major cost to manufacture is the direct material. With cycle times reduced by 60 percent or more and on-time delivery exceeding 99 percent, most sales managers will agree that market share will increase. If the increased output is truly scalable, then at least 20-40 percent of every additional sale rupee is increased profit, since the only additional expense is direct material. Just imagine what can be the saleable throughput increase and the difference it can make on your company profits. One client CEO once said, "I'll be happy with half of that" and understandably so.

There are many other valid viewpoints. For example, a considerable amount of overhead activity costs are a direct result of the company's inability to consistently and dependably respond in meeting customer requirements. The amount of schedule misses and changes create a high overhead activity cost, as the organization scrambles ineffectively to meet customer requirements. Without an ability to consistently meet customer-requested schedules, overhead activity costs increase rapidly with the organization's inability to meet plans and schedules. Most cost accountants burry these as overheads. The fact is that these costs are unnecessary.

A large part of these unnecessary costs is often the true and unknown cost of expediting an overhead activity with a ripple effect that ultimately impacts the income statement and balance sheet. Want to know how? Think of the resources consumed, missed shipments, lost sales, higher production costs, quality problems and sales expense among other things. The question 'is it worth to switch to lean?' is, in most cases, easy to answer with an overwhelming yes. The consequences of not adopting lean manufacturing as a business strategy are so costly that it should become a high priority strategic objective.

What should you do?

It is always better to embark on this journey with the help of a Sensei or Teacher, who has already been where you want to go (refer: Lean Manufacturing - Why aren't there more successes? in MMT Feb-Mar 2006 issue and Trim Wonders in Machinist Jan 2006). As managers learn more and more about lean manufacturing and lean supply chain management as a competitive strategy, understanding and acceptance of improvement potential from lean evolves. Consequently, management will want to determine and understand how good their company could really perform, if the old, agreed-upon operating logic was changed to a lean strategy. At that time, management should consider an expert, guided and focussed assessment of the 'as-is' condition versus what will be required to achieve a 'could-be' state of lean manufacturing. This focussed assessment should have the objective of quickly evaluating what improvements are needed and when and what is the potential impact on the overall business performance. The end result of this assessment should be a game plan that specifies the improvement actions and measurable performance improvements. Certainly, nothing drives the adopting of the new and better way of doing business better than a very compelling performance improvement potential.

Once management's understanding and acceptance evolves to setting your company on a lean strategy course, the real work begins. Introducing the technology of flow, while Challenging will be easily superseded by the challenge to change the old mindset. Long established value and belief systems are going to be 'upset' as the long, management-endorsed rules and operating logic are challenged to be unfit and 'scheduled' to be discarded. This is the critical point in the lean adoption cycle where only management's leadership and dogged persistence will assure that lean actually happens.

Most of us do not recognize an opportunity until we see it working for a competitor. Yesterday's struggles are either today's success or lost in history. With manufacturing gaining ground in India, sustainable business growth - as the markets become more competitive – will come from the ability

Contd...

to sustain continuous cost reductions and yet make continuous profits. By far, lean manufacturing is the best competitive strategy to make any business successful. Accept it, adapt to it, implement it and profit from it.

(*Name changed. For a copy of The Lean Mindset; you may mail your request to, the author.)

Source: The article has been authored by Sanjeev Baitmangalkar. It was published in the **Modern Machine Tools**, in the January 2007 edition. Copyright with Infomedia India Limited. Reprinted with permission.

QUESTIONS FOR DISCUSSION

1. "Implementation of marketing strategies should be proper, for an organization's success"? Discuss.

2. Porter spoke of "cost leadership" as one of its generic strategy. Would it always be possible for industrial marketers, to hold on to such a strategy?

3. Effective control mechanisms should be in place, to check the soundness of a corporate strategy? Why?

4. Study an industrial organization's product line. Place the products on the BCG framework. What is the interpretation of the products did you derive?

5. How would strategy implementation for consumer goods be different from an industrial good?

6. How would you allocate your resources to a new product line of a chemical company? What are the factors would you consider?

7. Competitive analysis is very essential for success in your business strategies. How would you use your competitor weakness as your strength?

chapter

SEVEN

Industrial Marketing Research and Demand Forecasting

COMPANY PROFILE 7: PAPER PRODUCTS LIMITED

The year 1935 saw a young visionary herald the era of modem flexible packaging in India. The next 66 years saw this dream of PPL's founder, Shri Sardarilal Talwar, transform itself onto a reality, which totally revolutionized the packaging industry in India. With consumer packaging sales revenue of Rs 3500 million in the year 2002, PPL is India's leading Consumer Packaging Company.

Today PPL offers a wide portfolio of packaging solutions that include **Flexible Packaging**, **Labelling Technologies** and **Specialized Cartons**. And all this supported by the **Packaging Machine Division** to provide the customer with Total packaging solutions. With three state of the art, fully integrated manufacturing facilities at Thane, Silvassa and Hyderabad, it meets the packaging needs of almost the entire range of FMCG segments including personal products, personal wash, laundry, foods, sauces, beverages, bakery products, spices, chocolates and confectionery, dairy, etc., and also for seeds, specialized chemicals, electronics and many other specific specialized uses including anti-spurious packaging.

The Package Protection and Decoration products range includes latest leading edge technologies - Shrink sleeves, Wrap around, Heat transfers, Pressure sensitives and Metallized paper labels.

With highly skilled and experienced staff, PPL is capable of working with the customer from product inception to the super market and with complete control and confidentiality.

Today, they have an impressive client list that includes, Levers, Nestle, Cadbury, Britannia, Glaxo Smith Kline, Coca Cola, Perfetti, Dabur, Marico, P & G...........In 1999, PPL became a member of the Huhtamaki Packaging Worldwide, a global leader in consumer packaging.

PPL has its International Business Division (IBD) set up as a separate business group servicing large Multinational accounts across 4 continents and over 50 customers worldwide. Today, our customers across South Asia, Africa, Middle East, Europe and Central America will vouch for us as a worthy competitor to European and South East Asian companies operating along side us.

PPL has a rich history of recognition of its achievements in the numerous awards that they have won across national and international forums of India Star, Asia Star and World Star. These awards represent the highest excellence in the fields of Packaging and Labelling applications amongst the best in the business. In the last decade PPL has won 9 Asia Stars and 7 World Stars in addition to a large number of India Stars. In 2001 PPL won the Asia Star for Pennzoil - Lube Oil System and the World Star for Timken Holographic Pouches. In 2002 they won the Asia Star for Britannia - Pure Magic Cartons and the World Star for MICO Bosch Holographic Cartons in keeping with their tradition of pioneering works done in the field of Packaging. PPL was the first Indian company to get recognition for its work in the field of "Holographic Packaging" and labelling solutions by winning the International Hologram Manufacturers Awards (IHMA) in the year 2001 for MICO Bosch Cartons and Nestle Cap Sleeves, and in the year 2002 for Holographic Zipper Lock Pouches.

The company achieved sales of Rs. 373.99 crores during the nine months representing a growth of 17.7 per cent, over sales of Rs. 317.80 crores in the corresponding nine months of 2005. Continued focus on the company's innovation programme NASP "New Applications Structures and Products and Processes" helped to achieve better sales.

Source: www.pplpack.com

Mind Power I: Market Intelligence vs. Marketing Research

Many companies use the term "market intelligence" inter-changeably with the term marketing research. A search on the Internet using the term market intelligence clearly demonstrates this trend, with the search returning page after page of marketing research companies advertising their market intelligence capabilities.

So is market intelligence the same thing as market research?

Absolutely not! Market research is a well-defined discipline with a long history of application in the business world. It takes many different forms, and its ultimate goal is to enhance a firm's understanding of the market and customer, but it is not market intelligence. Market intelligence is a much broader term that can be defined as an ongoing, holistic knowledge of all aspects of the marketplace. One way to visualize market intelligence is to picture a pyramid. Each face of the pyramid represents an aspect of market intelligence. The three faces of the pyramid-are information, communication, and people processes. Each of these faces is built upon a foundation of basic capabilities, with movement "up" the face of the pyramid representing increasing capabilities and proficiency Market intelligence is the culmination of each of these areas at their highest levels.

The differences between marketing research and market intelligence are as follows.

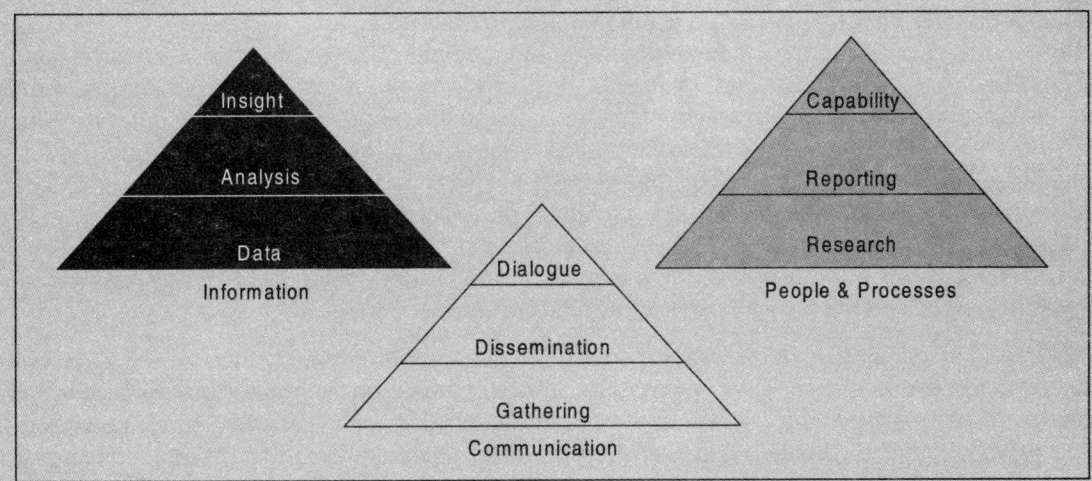

Figure 7.1: The Three Faces of the Market Intelligence Pyramid

1. Market intelligence is all-encompassing. Data gathering is just one aspect of market intelligence. It is a key building block for the information face of the pyramid, but it is not the only building block.

2. Market intelligence analysis requires different skills vs marketing research. Market intelligence analysis requires a broad set of analytical skills including business analysis skills. It requires integrating a broad array of information, which extends beyond traditional marketing research data. The analyst must understand the market, key competitors, the financial dynamics of the industry, and the entire business value chain. Often, the best market intelligence analysts have a financial or product management background; whereas many of the best marketing research analysts come from behavioral science or mathematical backgrounds.

3. Market intelligence requires integration with all aspects of the business. Whereas marketing research is highly focused on customers, market analysis encompasses the entire view of the market and requires integration into the companies forecasting process, product development process, and other business systems.

Contd...

The best way to discuss the difference between marketing research and market intelligence is to focus upon each face of the market intelligence pyramid. The information face of the market intelligence pyramid is built upon a foundation consisting of four basic areas: competitor information, product information, market information and customer information. This is depicted in Figure 7.2.

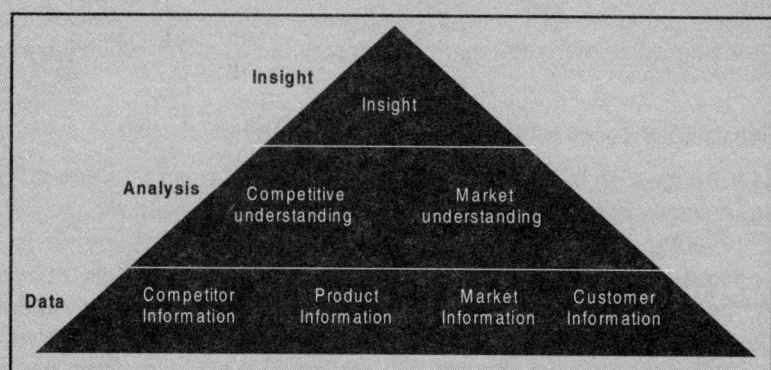

Figure 7.2: The Information Face of the Market Intelligence Pyramid

Product information refers to an understanding of the products in the marketplace, how they are priced, and what tactical marketing activities (promotions, advertising, etc.) are being used with the products. Competitor information refers to the understanding of competitor's strategies, organizational structure, product investment portfolio, and future product plans. Market information encompasses a view of the market at a macro level including the current market size, market segments, market share trends, and the forecasted growth of the market and the respective market segments. Finally, and perhaps most importantly, customer information (the traditional focus of market research) involves fully understanding the customer preferences, drivers of customer behaviour, brand loyalty, satisfaction rates and any other customer views that impact their behaviour in relation to your firm's products or services. It is important to note that each of these areas of knowledge can be a unique discipline in and of itself. However, the real power of the information lies in combining all of these areas to create a complete view of' the market, the market intelligence view.

Market intelligence yields an ongoing and comprehensive understanding of the market. Each of the four knowledge areas – competitor intelligence, product intelligence, market understanding, and customer insight – interacts to form a complete understanding of the market. Each competitor's strategies will impact their product actions, the overall trends of market growth and segment interaction will impact the strategies, and underlying all of this, the customer's behaviors and attitudes will ultimately drive the market dynamics in terms of growth rates and product acceptance. This integration of all four knowledge areas is the ultimate deliverable for market intelligence. Marketing research is a critical and significant source of information. However, it does not encompass all of the information areas which are covered by market intelligence. The scope of information covered is one of the key differences between marketing research and market intelligence.

When examining the communication face of the market intelligence pyramid, the most important difference between market intelligence and marketing research is that good market intelligence involves a dialogue between the market intelligence analyst and the client/decision maker. Conversely, marketing research provides an assessment of a specific issue, or measures a specific market dynamic. While it clearly involves communication with the client/decision maker, it typically consists of limited interaction versus the full dialogue of market intelligence.

The third and final face of the pyramid deals with people and processes. This can be the most defining difference between marketing research and market intelligence. By its very nature market intelligence is a process. One which constantly captures information from many difference sources, assesses it, and then uses the information during the ongoing business decision-making process.

Contd...

Marketing research is typically focused on answering specific questions, or tracking specific issues. While it can benefit from good processes, it is a finite "task" (or series of tasks). Market intelligence is a process, an ongoing interactive process.

This process should be a closed-loop system with a feedback cycle from the executives to the market intelligence team. The executive's feedback will guide the market intelligence team in future analyses by providing insight into the key issues the executives are facing. At the same time, the market intelligence teams are constantly capturing, monitoring, and synthesizing information that will ensure that the executive team is not surprised by market developments or competitive actions.

In his book *Business as war*, Kenneth Allard makes a parallel between the business environment and the intense and ever-changing environment associated with a battlefield. In this battlefield environment the intelligence on your enemy's activities is vital to winning, and it must constantly be monitored and updated due to the fluid nature of the battlefield. Obviously, the stakes are lower in business vs war. We are not fighting for our lives like the brave soldiers in the field of battle.

However, we are fighting for territory (market share and customers) against multiple enemies, all of whom have strategies focused on taking territory from our firms. Building a solid market intelligence system is vital to having the information necessary to compete and win in your business battleground. If your firm's focus is only on marketing research, your view of the battlefield is limited and potentially threatens your position in the market. So what about all of these companies listed under the heading of "market intelligence" in our Web search? A quick examination of these companies' Web pages reveals that most are offering a traditional set of marketing research survey services, as opposed to complete market intelligence services. While market intelligence is an oft-promised capability, frequently companies are simply delivering traditional marketing research services.

So how does one develop a true market intelligence capability? It would take much more than the space in this article to address this question. At a very high level, it involves:

1. Having a vision for your market intelligence function. Do you want it to be world-class? What do you want your market intelligence function to excel in? How would you define success for your market intelligence team?

2. Obtaining buy-in from your market intelligence team for your vision. This requires a clear articulation of what you are trying to accomplish, providing the team the opportunity to talk about the vision and to actually impact what the final vision is. Working as a team to craft a mission statement that clearly articulates the vision.

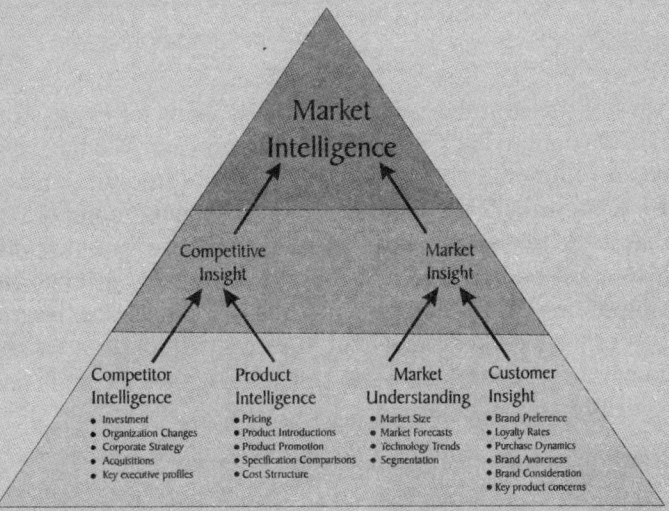

3. Mapping your vision to a set of core competencies required to fulfill your vision. Identify the competencies that are unique and which represent significant added value by your team. Perform

Contd...

an audit of your market intelligence function in order to ensure your vision maps to your client's needs, and to identify gaps between your market intelligence vision and your team's current capabilities and deliverables. Build a plan to address and fill in the gaps, keeping in mind that this doesn't happen overnight – it can easily be a two-to-three-year process.

4. Increasing the focus on building your core market intelligence competencies by outsourcing those elements (i.e., competitive product cost tear-downs, etc.) which are not essential to the core. A great example of this is to utilize outside vendors and information distribution technologies to outsource the collection, summary and dissemination of market news data (competitor price changes, promotional activities, etc.). Another example is to use outside marketing research vendors for all non-core aspects of marketing research projects (including sourcing, fielding, project management, and basic statistical and cross tabular analysis). Then your analysts can focus on structuring the initial research project based on their understanding of the business need, and then identifying what the research results mean in the context of the business issues and decisions at hand.

5. Creating a process that bridges functional groups to capture information from many different business areas to provide the information foundation for a complete market intelligence picture.

6. Ensuring the market intelligence staff has a consulting versus a project management focus (which of course, has implications for the skill sets of your market intelligence staff). This includes measuring the results of decisions made based upon your market intelligence and then fine-tuning future work in order to drive better results.

7. Obtaining the mandate of and access to your executive team in order to integrate the results of market intelligence analysis into the business decision-making process, and to capture the feedback, which will drive future market intelligence inquiries and analysis.

Of course, this is much easier said than done. However, with the rigorous application of market intelligence discipline, techniques and principles, you can create a true market intelligence organization that will not only be an integral part of your business decision-making process, but which will also play a key role in shaping your firm's strategic direction.

Source: This article has been authored by Ed Crowley. He has founded the Photizo Group (www.photizogroup.com) as a consulting resource for clients who are focussed on driving sustained business growth. He has over 20 years of experience. Reprinted with the kind permission of the author.

INDUSTRIAL MARKETING RESEARCH AND DEMAND FORECASTING

Introduction

In the previous chapter, we saw the strategic planning process. Now for every strategic planning process to be successful, we need strong data to back up the planning process. We have also seen in the previous chapters how competitive and unpredictable the business environment is and any good performance would depend on analysis of information gathered from customers, competitors and other external sources. Not only in the strategic decision-making process, but also in any kind of decisions that the industrial marketer needs to take, he needs to conduct a research, to validate himself, before jumping to any conclusion. Today more and more industrial firms use marketing research for their strategic planning process, as well as any major decisions that the company wishes to take. In this chapter we will try and understand how industrial marketers use research to their benefits and how do they predict demand for future years on the basis of past data.

There are 3 types of decision makers in any organization. They are:[1]

1. Intuitive decision-makers

2. Standardized decision-makers

3. Visionaries

Intuitive decision-makers are the ones who take decisions based on the past experiences that he has with such a similar situation. They rely heavily on secondary date sources and from the base tier of any research. Today, organizations should not and cannot afford to follow this procedure, other wise the organization will not be able to predict the environments and business trends accurately.

Standardized decision-makers are the ones where some of the decisions are only backed by research. These firms still use tested and tried methodologies excluding others that might be appropriate. In these organizations the data is not accessible to all the members in the organization.

Visionaries are the companies where every business decision taken is on the basis of research. These companies develop proprietary methodologies and are highly innovative. The complete organization has an access to the data findings and employers are encouraged to back their planning with data. As Mr. Narayan Murthy of Infosys says "Where is the data?"

INDUSTRIAL MARKETING RESEARCH

Research explores the unknown world, applications of theory and is used in building a strong base of knowledge giving practical solutions and application. "Through the process of identification, critical examination, generalization and dissemination of useful practical experiences, management research helps us to develop relevant approaches for successful management of organisations."[2]

Marketing research consist of "systematic design, collection, analysis and reporting of data and findings, relevant to a specific marketing situation failing the company".[3] Research data are used for multiple purposes in the organization. It is used to analyze, forecast and also find out the sales potential of any particular market or region. The data is also used to study the behavioural aspects of firm or an individual and also for purposes like product acceptability in the market.

USES OF INDUSTRIAL MARKETING RESEARCH

1. *Studying the business trends:* In business markets as we know that it is highly fluctuating and demand is mostly joint and derived, thus studying the business trends become very essential. For example, if a company wants to launch a new product in the market, the company should be well aware of how the market is and whether the market is in a maturing or a declining stage.

2. *New product studies:* An industrial marketer, before launching a new product must try and understand the applicability and acceptability to the users. If a new product is introduced in the market, how would buyers react to it? In case the product comes with a superior technology but a higher price tag, would buyers be willing to accept such a product.

3. *Sales quota determination and DD forecasting:* Industrial marketing research would also be used to find out, how much each area or region can generate and fix a "target" for branches or for individual salesperson. Industrial marketing research is also used for forecasting demand in an industry, how much would be the growth rate in the market and what chunk of share does a company want to have.

4. *Market potential and market share analysis:* An industrial marketer would be interested to know, what is the potential of a particular product in terms of sales volume and profits in today's scenario and in the near future. This information would help the company draw inferences on how much to allocate on each product. If a product is, say, on a maturity or a decline state, then the allocation of resources to such a product would be less than a growing market.

A marketer would also be interested to know the strategic moves of the competitor and how it would affect the industry and business on general. He would also like to know the impact of environmental factors on the market share. Based on the market potential and market share, the company can set its future goals.

Mind Power 2: Intelligence in Iraq: L-3 Supplies Spy Support By Pratap Chatterjee, Special to CorpWatch

August 9th, 2006

The official headquarters for a 300-person intelligence support operation in Iraq is discreetly located in a two-story red building in a business park in Chantilly, Virginia, just outside the border fence of Washington DC, Dulles airport. From its nondescript corporate offices, Government Services Incorporated (GSI) supplies staff for an operation that spreads over 22 military bases in the Middle East.

Walk through the entrance and to the left of the reception desk, next to a glass case showcasing electronic surveillance gear is an announcement congratulating employees on winning a $ 426.5 million intelligence contract from the Pentagon last year.

GSI is a major subsidiary of L-3 Communications, a Fortune 500 company. Retired Lieutenant General Paul Cerjan took GSI's helm, in May, after spending a year running Halliburton's multi-billion dollar military logistics contract in Iraq and around the world.

GSI is only one of several L-3 subsidiaries enjoying the Bush administration's largesse. On March 10, Titan won a no-bid contract worth $840 million over 12 months to supply translators for intelligence and regular military operations in the "global war on terror." Yet another L-3 subsidiary, MPRI, manages the recruitment of U.S. military advisors to key Iraqi ministries such as defense and interior.

Military "prime" contractors such as L-3 extend the complex web of contracts by farming out work to smaller subcontractors, sometimes disabled- or minority-owned businesses. Its partners on the intelligence contract include Florida based disabled-owned Espial Services and Virginia-based Gray Hawk Systems. Both are currently advertising for interrogators. Other L-3 subcontractors on the project include Future Technologies Incorporated, a South Asian-owned company which is hiring Middle East regional intelligence analysts; and Operational Support and Services, an obscure North Carolina company seeking counter-intelligence agents.

"The government is desperate for qualified interrogators and intelligence analysts so they are turning to industry," says Bill Golden who now runs IntetligenceCareers.com, one of the biggest intelligence employment websites in the business. "Over half of the qualified counter-intelligence experts in the field work for contractors like L-3."

Who Is L-3?

Despite being in business for less than a decade, L-3 is now the sixth-largest military contractor in the nation. Based in Manhattan, it is headquartered on the upper floors of a skyscraper on Third Avenue, a few blocks from the United Nations.

The company was created as a spin-off of several Lockheed Martin and Loral manufacturing units that specialized in advanced electronics. These small business units were having a hard time selling their products to major military manufacturers such as Boeing, General Dynamics, Northrup Grumman and Raytheon, because of perceived competition with Lockheed. L-3 was created as an independent "mezzanine" or middle company, not linked to Lockheed or Loral that would supply advanced electronics to anyone.

Contd...

The deal was engineered in 1997 by Wall Street investment bankers, the Lehman brothers, with the help of two former Loral executives, whose name coincidentally began with the letter L: Frank Lanza and Robert LaPenta. (L-3 stands for Lanza, LaPenta and Lehman).

Source: www.corpwatch.org: Reprinted with permission: "Special to CorpWatch"

DIFFERENCES IN INDUSTRIAL AND CONSUMER MARKETING RESEARCH

In the earlier chapters, we have seen that there is a vast difference in the consumer and the industrial marketplace. Differences in terms of industrial demand, buying process and the general business environment. All these factors result in a difference in approach to the research process.

Industrial marketing consists of highly technically complex products and the research agency should be well averse with such products and technology, which is not so for consumer research. In industrial marketing, since they are geographically dispersed, it is a highly time consuming process. Industrial research also consumes a lot of time, because of difficulties in meeting the industrial respondents. In a developing country like ours, often accurate and reliable data becomes a problem. Let us look at the differences in a tabular format.

Industrial Research	Consumer Research
• The population size in industrial research is small and thus a small sample size.	• The population size is large and sample size is also large.
• Accessing a respondent is difficult due to work schedules and preoccupations.	• Accessing is simple and easier.
• Research personnel should be trained and technologically oriented.	• Needs to be trained but needn't have technical orientation.
• Secondary data forms a very important source and it is relatively difficult to find accurate data in developing nations.	• Focus mostly on primary data.
• Generally personal, in-depth interview is followed.	• There are other methods.
• It is very difficult to define respondents, because purchasing would involve lot of people.	• Defining respondents would be simpler.

THE INDUSTRIAL MARKETING RESEARCH PROCESS

Marketing research as a process would be about gathering marketing information to help in strategic planning and control. Industrial research provides a lot of benefits to the firm in terms of what it needs to do and how to react in a particular situation. Now the next question, that comes up in the minds of marketer is how to conduct the complete research process.

Generally, the process of marketing research involves five distinct steps. They are:

1. Identifying the problem and research objectives

2. Develop the research plan

3. Collect information

4. Analyze the information

5. Presentation of the findings

Step 1: Identifying the Problem and Research Objectives

When we use the term problem, it need not necessarily be a problem. It could also be an opportunity, which an industrial marketer is looking forward to. One more important thing here is that, sometimes the industrial marketer might not exactly be able to pinpoint a particular problem. It is quite possible for him to make vague statements. Often a problem is not clearly defined and research agencies need to probe deep down inside to find the exact statement of the problem.

At this stage, generally the research company asks the industrial marketer as to what is called as the "research brief". This research brief contains all the possible minutest details, which will serve as a guide to the industrial researcher through out the research project. This research brief will also be used by the researcher in formulating the research plan and the following steps.

Once the marketer has identified the problem, the research objectives follow after that. Research objectives generally set limits or boundaries to the research problem. These research objectives should be jointly reviewed by individuals. If the problems are not well defined, or the research objectives are not well set in, it would require the call for performing an **exploratory study.** It would help in the discovery of ideas. The objective is to clarify concepts, put more focus on the problem and suggest suitable solutions.

Descriptive research would be one to understand the objectives and would need a descriptive study.

When we want to study the cause and effect relationships, for example, when we reduce price how would sales be affected, it would be called as a **causal research**.

Step 2: Develop the Research Plan

Once the problem has been identified and research objectives formulated, the next step in the process, for the researcher is to develop the research plans or the research design process. The essential steps are:[5]

1. It is an activity and time-based plan

2. A plan always based on the research question

3. A guide of selecting sources and types of information

4. A framework for specifying the relationships among the study's variables

5. A procedural outline for every research activity

In this step, the researcher needs to determine the information that needs to be collected. He also requires identifying what would be the sources of data- whether it would be backed by primary or secondary data source. As we have discussed earlier, that getting primary data for industrial marketers is quite a tough job and thus a heavy reliability on secondary data. The researcher also outlines the research approach that he is going to take, the methods of contact, sampling plan and instruments that he is going to use to collect primary data.

Step 3: Collect Information

Once the research plan has been formulated, and what kind of information is required has been determined, the next process is to collect information. This process of data collection has to be logical, highly sequential, so that the researcher can reach to some definite conclusion.

Let us say, that the researcher wants to collect some information on the potential of a new product, which will be introduced. For this research, complete dependency on secondary data sources would not be helpful. There would also be need for primary data.

How do we distinguish the two?

Primary data is a data which is collected by the researcher, for a specific purpose or study. They are original by nature and are generally conducted by means of survey.

Secondary data is a data source, which has already been collected by some sources, could be private or government. This data is primary for the agency that collects it and secondary for the one who is using the data. They can be obtained form various sources.

Primary data	Secondary data
1. These are data collected for the first time by observational or questionnaire methods.	1. They are data which has already been collected by some other agency, for some other purpose.
2. The data collected is in a raw form, original and for a specific purpose.	2. The data is in its final form, has been collected by some other agency and used for decision making.
3. Highly time consuming, costly and more efforts need to be put in by trained people.	3. They are less time consuming and less efforts need to be put. People need not be highly trained.
4. Accurate data.	4. Data accuracy depends upon the reliability of the source from which data is taken.

Secondary Data Sources

Secondary data sources could be a published, as well as an unpublished source. The sources of secondary data are multiple. Today, it is not difficult to find out secondary data, which is reliable. The general sources of secondary data are:

1. Publications of the central, state governments.

2. Historical records, public records and other sources.

3. Technical magazines and journals.

4. Books and newspapers.

5. Reports and publications of various international bodies like ILO, UNO, and IBRD etc.

6. Reports published by scholars and economists.

When we speak of unpublished sources, it would be various data that is collected by trade unions, labor organizations. However these data could have problems of bias.

But before any sort of secondary data that is used by any researcher, he must ensure 3 important things:

1. *Quality of data:* Data should be of high quality and accuracy. The data that is used from a secondary source, shouldn't bring out errors in the results of research process.

2. **Suitability of data:** The data gathered should be suitable for the purpose for which it is being used. The data should be comparable. For example living standards in USA and India, would be on two currencies. Thus they must be brought to one common measure.

3. **Adequacy of data:** The data should be adequate for the purpose for which it has been taken.

Primary Data Sources

Generally for industrial research, three widely used methods are used for collection of primary data. They are:

1. Observation

2. Questionnaire

3. Interviewing

Observation: This technique is generally used for observation of work. It could be used in cases:

1. The shop floor managers, helping a technician perform his job in a much faster and accurate way.

2. Conversations between sales person and his clients to improve the effectiveness.

Using this method of data collection, the process of bias is eliminated. This method can be used in industrial research for improving effectiveness of sales personnel, customer response to a product. However the major problem with this technique is the time, which the investigator has to wait. The investigator must be highly trained to observe and record, the conversations.

Questionnaire: This is a very popular method in industrial research to gather information from a set of people, who is an expert in his field or has the information, which requires to be collected.

The major advantage of the questionnaire methods is that it gives a wide spectrum of information and the questions can be generated as per the specific requirements. This method solves a lot of problem and enables the researcher to go deep. Problems like time consumption are lesser when compared to observational methods.

However the questionnaire method has its own set of disadvantages. They are:

1. The respondent may be unwilling to provide the necessary information.

2. Respondents may not speak accurately in terms of "past data" and also on factors like rivalry within an industry.

3. Biases may set in, while answering and overstatement of facts could also be a problem.

4. When international research is conducted or research wherein the language of the questionnaires has to be changed, semantic difficulties may arise. Two words may not mean the same, when translated.

Interviewing: Getting primary data through interviewing and survey methods is the most popular way of data collection. The data can be collected by personal interviews, mailed questionnaire or telephonic interviews. The interviewing method can be done in two basic ways. They are:

1. **Structured framework:** Answering a set of predetermined questions. In this method, very specific information is collected. With this method, the data collected is accurate and the data can be quantified with very little problem.

2. **Unstructured interviews:** Enable the respondents to answer with greater amount of flexibility. There are no predetermined responses and the researcher has a great amount of flexibility. However quantification of such interviews become very difficult, and the researcher should be well-trained to handle such an interview. Since these are "in-depth interviews", the time taken could be very long.

Two more interviewing techniques, that needs mention here are:

1. Focus group interviews

2. Delphi technique

Focus group interviews: These are the ones wherein there is a group of six to ten or more persons and the researcher acts as a moderator of the group. This discussion could last for something around 1 to 2 hours. The discussion is recorded by means of an audio or video. They from a very cost effective way of conducting a survey. They are generally used for obtaining information before the actual survey. They also help generate a wide range of responses and different views come out of the discussion. This technique though more widely used in consumer research, is also now being used by industrial researchers.

Delphi techniques: Experts from the industry or outside the industry are interviewed. The people who are interviewed are highly specialized in their own fields of operation. Each individual expert is asked to project future trends or react on particular situations, till a consensus is reached. These are then reviewed, averaged and commented upon. Problem to these techniques are heavy chances of bias. Selection of experts also forms a very important issue in Delphi techniques.

Step 4: Analyze the Information

Today with multiple software packages in the market, it has led to easier and high usage of research methods for analyzing the data. Once the data is fed in, it becomes very easy on the part of the researcher to interpret it.

Now the variables that we obtain from the data collection can be analyzed in three different ways. They are:

1. *Univariate:* When a single variable is analyzed, for example, finding out the mean median and mode.

2. *Bivariate analysis:* When an association or relationship between two variables has to be established, tools like regression analysis and correlation can be used here.

3. *Multivariate analysis:* When two or more independent variables form the basis for estimating the value of a dependent variable. Tools such as multiple and partial correlation and regression, discriminant analysis and ANOVA are examples of multivariate analysis.

Step 5: Presentation of Findings

The last step in the process of any research is to present the findings. The research needs to be well summarized and communicated in a form that is useful to the management. The report needs to carefully written so that it gives a very clear cut picture to the organization.

Before writing a report, certain guidelines need to be kept in mind. They are:

1. Since the audience need not necessarily have a technical background, jargons and technical language should be avoided.

2. The research should be very clear and concise.

3. The researcher should not try and satisfy the likes of a particular individual of organization.

4. An executive summary should be given so that the readers have a total idea of what the report contains. The summary is for the decision-makers who would base their judgment on this summary.

The Sampling Plan

Sample is a small part of the entire population or universe. When we use the term universe, we mean, all the items under consideration which are pertinent to the particular research project and objective.

Now, it would be ideal to use the population for every study, to reach to the correct figures. But if the case is such that, the population is very huge, it would be very difficult to survey with the complete population. Thus the various reasons why sampling is used are:

1. Restraints of cost, time and labour for population surveys and hence sampling is more economical.

2. There could be cases where observations would be obtained by destruction of units, say - the life of a lamp. In such cases, sampling has to be used.

3. The quality of data collected by the sampling method is of much superior grade than that collected of census.

The process of sampling involves certain steps. The complete process is to lay down a plan, as to how to carry out the complete process.

Step 1: Defining the population, which is pertinent to the current research objective.

Step 2: The sampling frame needs to be identified. The researcher needs to list down the complete population units.

Step 3: Select the sampling unit.

Step 4: The sampling method needs to be selected. There are basically two types of sampling methods. They are:

1. Probability sampling method

2. Non-probability sampling method

Step 5: The researcher needs to determine the sample size.

Step 6: The selection of final sample.

Let us look into the various sampling methods. As said earlier, they can be divided into two categories:

1. Probability Sampling Method

2. Non-probability Sampling Method.

Probability Sampling Methods

A. Simple Random Sampling	:	This process includes drawing the sample in such a manner, that each member has an equal chance of being included in the sample.
B. Cluster Sampling	:	The population is divided into clusters. Then with a random selection a few clusters are chosen and again a few members are chosen within them.
C. Systematic Sampling	:	Selecting a unit will depend upon the selection of previous unit.

D. Stratified Random Sampling :   The population is first classified into strata or groups on the basis of some characteristics, and then a simple random sample is drawn from them.

Non-probability Sampling Methods

A. Convenience Sampling   :   It is left at the direction of the researcher. Depends on the convenience of the location or cooperation of sample.

B. Judgment Sampling   :   The judgment and opinions of experts form the basis of sampling.

C. Quota Sampling   :   Groups or categories are identified and a fixed quota is interviewed based on convenience or judgment.

Once the process of sampling is over, data is collected with help of trained field officers. The modes to collect data could be a personal interview, or a telephonic interview or a mailer survey. The questions that are generally put forward could be an open ended or closed ended a question. But before the actual survey is carried out a pretesting of the questionnaire is done, to remove errors or to refine the questions. This pretesting brings out the weakness of the questionnaire. Once the data is collected, it goes to the next step, that is tabulating and analyzing the data.

DEMAND FORECASTING

Demand forecasting and sales forecasting is a very key part of the strategic planning. Errors in forecasting would result into problems relating to production, inventory, finance, promotions and profits. Whether a company has large scale operations or a small one, forecasting influences planning and budgeting in all areas of the organization.

So what does an inaccurate forecasting mean to a company?

1.   It would create high production, which would lead into high amount of unsold goods. If forecasting is too low, then demand would not be met and consumers would switch over.

2.   There could be situations of cash shortages or idle cash lying. Business promotions can become a waste, if forecasts are too high.

3.   If the forecasts are higher, it would lead into lower unit profit as expenses would be high. Prices may be forced to reduce, due to excess products, in the market.

However the process of forecasting becomes a headache to all organizations because forecasting is done on historical data. Not only that, in industrial markets the demand being a derived one, complex becomes more complex. However, the point of matter is that, we need to study them, as it will help the manager with a tool to analyze his decisions in a better way.

In industrial marketing, demand forecasts are subject to a set of:

1.   Controllable factors

2.   Uncontrollable factors

We have discussed this in greater detail, in the previous chapters and an industrial organization must try and reduce the risks.

LEVELS OF FORECASTING[5]

Generally when we speak of the forecasting concepts, we use five terms in this respect. They are:

1. *Market capacity:* It is total number of products that can be used in a particular period of time. For example, the total number of cars that can be used in India in 2007.

2. *Market potential:* It is the highest amount of sales expected in a certain period.

3. *Sales potential:* It is the maximum amount of sales that a company can expect during a particular period of time.

4. *Sales forecast:* It is the expected amount of sales by a company, during a particular period of time.

5. *Sales quota:* Industrial targets for the sales person.

Generally whenever any forecasts are done, two specific ways or methods are used. They may be "top down" or "bottom up". When we use the former methodology, we try and understand the general economic conditions and break it down for operational planning and budgeting purposes. However, the top down approach also have a different meaning. If the top management takes the task of forecasting and forces it down at bottom levels of the organization, it is also called as top down approach.

A bottom up approach or a build up approach is when sales people are asked, what would they bring in the coming period of sales or check what customers are expected to buy and then sum up all of them to get the forecast. However in Indian companies, this is a very rare approach. It is almost, the top down approach that is seen in Indian companies.

In industrial marketing, sometimes mailers are sent to prospective and existing clients. A good response gives a very clear idea as to what would be the forecast figure.

The common forecasting techniques are:

1. Non-quantitative methods

2. Quantitative methods

The non-quantitative methods include: Executive opinion, Delphi method, Sales force composite, Test marketing and buying intentions.

The quantitative methods include: Moving averages, Exponential smoothing, Box Jenkins method, Econometric models, Input/Output models and regressional methods. We will discuss them one by one.

NON-QUANTITATIVE FORECASTING METHODS

Executive Opinion: It is one of the simplest way of forecasting, where a group of executives from the company are expected to put ahead their opinion. Generally the top management from various departments are combined together to project the forecast. Now the problem, with this method is that in a dynamic business environment, it is very difficult to predict without data. One more problem that arises in this method is that, since top executives from various departments join together, all might not be equally competent to pitch in the figures. In case there is unavailability of data in some industries, this technique could be used. However, small and medium sized companies with limited resources may use his technique, where in the employees have contributed some years to the company.

Delphi Method: It was developed by the Rand Corporation and popularly known as the "Delphi Method". This is a modified version of the previous one. In the previous, executive opinion method, members from the same organization brought the forecast figures. In this method, it is a group of experts. The group of experts gives their individual opinion on the demand forecast figures. These are then send to the coordinator. Then an average value is obtained and sent to others for discussion. The process continues till a final figure is reached. The advantage of this method is that, there is no way a single person can dominate a particular group.

Sales Force Composite: As we have discussed earlier, sales persons are asked to project the next year's sales, in the particular region he works. This forecast is then added and then adjusted by a branch head and forecasts from other sources are compared with this figure. The advantages of this method are that the sales person would be responsible for their future targets, results tend to be accurate and sales persons have a confidence to achieve over the figures. The disadvantage is that sales person often underestimates this figure so that it becomes easily achievable. Sales person are not trained in such forecasting jobs and they put very little effort in this work or find it monotonous.

Test Marketing: This is specifically done for new products. When a new product is launched or a product, which is completely different from the existing products, test marketing is used. Generally an area is fixed and sales figures for this area are observed. These can then be scaled up for the complete market. The major disadvantage of this method is that, competitors often try to distort results and it takes time to complete the process.

Customer buying Intentions: Customers are often asked about their intentions to buy various products over a period of time. These are then combined together to have the total figure. The figure is then broken down as per region, customers or territory for industrial customers. It forms a very important forecasting technique because:

1. Customers are few numbers.

2. The demand can be forecasted with certain degrees of accuracy.

3. Business customers often decide on, with past buying experiences.

The disadvantage of this method is that customers may not respond, the requirements may shift depending on the economic conditions and is a costly method to forecast the demand.

QUANTITATIVE FORECASTING METHODS

Moving Average: This approach is based on the average of various sales figures over a period of time. This average is calculated so as to balance the extreme values at both points. For every period, a new average is calculated. This is called as the moving average. However, it becomes very essential to understand what would be the optimal period that needs to be included. The moving average brings down seasonal variations in the data and thus gives very reasonable forecasts. In periods, where there is very high level of fluctuations, it can minimizing those. However one drawback of this method is that, when a strong trend exists, moving averages lag behind.

Exponential smoothing: The moving average is not reactive to recent sales trend and this is where exponential smoothing plays a very important role. This method is generally used for short run sales forecasting. The focus on this method is recent figures and not the past figures.

One of the most important factors is to choose the smoothing constant, which has a value of 0.00 to 1.00. Generally, when sales are stable, a smaller "alpha value" is used. In cases of period with greater fluctuations, high values of alpha are used.

One great disadvantage of this method is, selecting the value of the smoothing constant. Since the value is selected with much subjectivity, errors in forecasting may come in.

Box Jenkins: A highly mathematical model, which uses computer analysis to predict the demand. It is an expensive procedure which requires high degree of expertise. It also requires large number of historic data. The results of this method are almost the same as that of other methods.

Econometric models: Econometric models are basically to capture the complex relationships between multiple variable many companies like GE, GM, have developed models which suit them for their particular purpose. The disadvantage of this model is that, it is highly expensive and is complex and it can be incapable to measure all the changes in the economy. The advantage of this model lies in the fact, that many finer points get captured in this model and uncertainties can be predicted to quite a great extent.

Input output models: A very popular form of forecasting of industrial demand forecasts. They are matrices which show the amount of input that is required from each industry that is for a specified output of another industry. It is an expensive model to build.

Correlation and regression analysis: Various variables are studied simultaneously to see the interrelation between the various factors. This is called as correlation. The values can range from -1 to +1. The higher the values, more correlated the variables are. Regression analysis is to find out the cause and effect relationship between two variables. How the change of one particular variable will result into a change of another variable.

QUANTITATIVE OR NON-QUANTITATIVE?

After going through all these methods, a question that can obviously rise in our minds is that which is the one that needs to be used? On one hand, we have highly complex models and on the other hand, very simple non-technical models. But before any one them is also used, some points must be kept in mind.

1. Highly technical models might not be interesting to the sales persons in the job. In order to raise confidence among them, simple and easier methods would be preferred.

2. The forecasting should give accurate results to quite some great extent. We have already seen, that in case if forecasting is wrong, the problems that would arise.

3. Highly technical methods require high data and time. Managers might not be willing to provide for such data and time. Not only that, data is a big problem for some companies.

4. Skilled people are required for any kind of forecasting. The forecasting should be flexible enough and should not be too costly for an organization.

Lastly, it is ultimately the sales representatives at grass root level who will bring in the sales. They must be brought in confidence.

CONCLUSION

In this chapter we have seen how research works for industrial markets and the basic differences between consumer research and industrial research. We also saw the process to go ahead with the research.

The second part of the chapter focused on demand forecasting, its importance and the various quantitative and qualitative methods adopted to forecast demand. It is not only important to forecast demand, but to drive it down and earn the confidence of the sales person, who would be responsible to achieve the same.

References

1.   Cooper and Schindler. *Business research methods*. Tata McGraw Hill, pp 10.

2.   Bhattacharya. *Research methodology*. Excel publication, pp 22.

3.   Kotler. *Principles of Marketing*. Prentice Hall, pp 139.

4.   Cooper and Schindler. *Business Research Methods*. Tata McGraw Hill, pp 139.

5.   Anderson, Hair Jr, Bush. *Professional Sales Management*-Second edition. McGraw Hill, pp 120.

Mind Power 3: A Market Intelligence Primer

So what is, Market Intelligence? In its broadest sense, Market Intelligence is the capturing of information relevant to a company's markets. In a more practical context, it is the gathering, analysis, and dissemination of information that is relevant to the market segments your company participates, or wishes to participate in. As the diagram below shows, this encompasses four cornerstones: Competitor Intelligence, Product Intelligence, Market Understanding, and Customer understanding. Market Intelligence is not just data.

Each of these areas can be a discipline in and of itself. However, their true power comes from the integration of all four of these disciplines. For example, you may know that a competitor is pricing a product below their normal pricing range (Product Intelligence). However, when you also know that this company is planning to replace this product with an entirely new line of products (again Product Intelligence) the reason for their pricing action becomes clear. When this information is combined with the knowledge that the companies board of directors has challenged the CEO with growing market share (competitor intelligence) and that they have a strategic goal of entering into a new market segment (again competitor intelligence) this information becomes much more valuable.

Knowing that a competitor has reduced pricing in order to prepare for the entry of a new product line in order to gain share in a new market segment is valuable. But how valuable is this market segment. And what will it take to be successful in the market segment? This is where market understanding and customer understanding comes in. By analyzing secondary data regarding the market, market share trends, and other market data, one can understand whether this is a segment that will "fuel the competitors" growth or whether it will be a drain on their resources (market understanding). Market research provides tailored insight into the key customer requirements, loyalty of customers to existing vendors, and other factors which will impact a firm's potential for success in a new (or existing) market segment. It's this combination of data and analysis that generates information which is relevant to making decisions.

So what does it take to deliver world-class Market Intelligence? There are four key ingredients for a world-class market intelligence organization.

1.   Data sources and 'field' resources

2.   Analytical skills and processes to pull the data together

3.   Technology foundation and platforms to deliver, store, process, and distribute the information

4.   The support of, and access to, top management

Data gathering and field resources are the foundation for any Market intelligence organization. This is the set of individuals, processes, and information services (often third party companies such as IDC) that provide the basic data on product shipments, competitor profiling, and other data relevant to the market. A world-class MI organization finds ways to turn the entire organization into one large intelligence gathering unit. By the use of incentives, education, and existing information infrastructure

Contd...

(such as e-mail) the entire organization including Sales, Purchasing, Finance, and Development can become a source for gathering competitive and market information. For example, one Fortune 500 Company offers its Sales people a monetary incentive to turn in competitive tips. As a result, the sales people are always on the lookout for new products in customer and reseller locations. In some cases, these Sales people have even encountered pre-introduction beta or evaluation products in customer locations. These "first looks" at competitive products can be invaluable in planning pre-emptive actions to attack new products from your competitors.

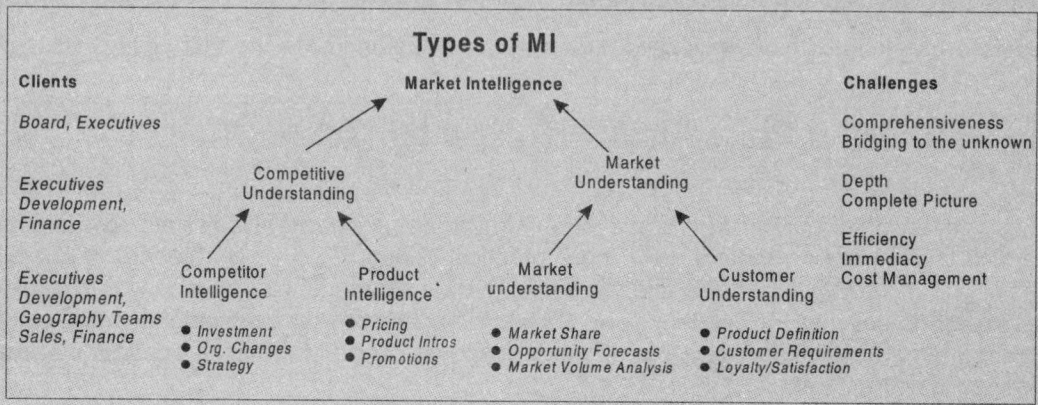

However, gathering the data is not enough. Without rigorous analysis and insightful reporting the data remains simply... data, it never becomes useful information. In order for Market intelligence to be useful, different types of data (market share, competitor product cost data, etc.) must be merged together into information which is relevant to key decision-makers and the decisions they are making. The ultimate test of the data and the analysis is whether it provides the right information in order to let the decision-makers make decisions with confidence.

For example, reporting to the executive team that the company is gaining market share in a specific market is important. However, that data is only marginally beneficial. The data's true power is unlocked when it is combined with information about competitor's actions, sales and channel activities that mace resulted in competitive advantage and a succinct and accurate definition of all the other factors that are driving the market share gains. And it will only have impact if it is presented in a concise and well-articulated report or presentation.

Another key aspect is having the right information infrastructure to support the flow of information in and out of the analytical team and to ensure that the 'data' is processed with as little manual intervention as possible. For example, often at times the data on market share provided by large market data providers such as IDC (International Data Corporation) or DataQuest is not in the right format or is not defined in such a way as to be useful to the ultimate marketing decision maker. For example, it may be composed of product segmentation based on processor speed (in the case of PC's) when the decision-maker uses segments based on customer types. In this situation, an investment in developing a database to convert the data provider's segments into the segments used by the decision-maker is critical. Without this investment in automation very experienced market analysts must spend considerable time making manual conversions using spreadsheets, pivot tables, and Power point slides! This is a very inefficient use of valuable market intelligence resources.

Finally, it is very critical that the Market Intelligence group has access to top decision-makers. This can be a challenge for many reasons. Often this is clue to the decision-makers believing that Market Intelligence has little value relative to their own 'gut' instinct. Sometimes the Market intelligence or organization has historically provided 'low impact' Market Intelligence and thus has little perceived value with the decision-makers. And in the worst case it can be the result of missed expectations in the past resulting in low credibility for the Market Intelligence organization.

Contd...

No matter what the current state of the Market Intelligence team's access to decision-makers is, it is possible to improve the situation. And the more this situation improves, the better the Market intelligence team will understand the key decision-maker's needs. This, in turn, will result in better analysis and information being provided to the decision-makers, which in turn will result in greater access to these same decision-makers.

Creating boundaries for Market Intelligence: It is also very important to understand what Market Intelligence is not. Market Intelligence is not a crystal ball into the future! While predictability is improved with good Market intelligence, there are far too many variables in the market place to ever provide 100 percent accuracy into the future actions of competitors or customers/markets. It is also important to understand that the Market Intelligence agency is not the decision-making team. In fact, while the Market Intelligence team needs to have an intimate understanding of the issue at hand, to understand the information needs of the decision-maker, and to provide recommendations, they should not be the decision-maker. Why? Because once they become the decision-maker, they have a vested interest in the outcome and lose objectivity. One of the key functions of a good Market Intelligence organization is the ability to monitor the firm's progress versus the market after decisions. This monitoring is important in order to determine if mid-course corrections are needed. In order to provide unbiased monitoring and complete objectivity in developing recommendations, it is critical that the Market intelligence team does not 'own' the ultimate decision or have a vested interest in the outcome.

A true-life example: In a recent assignment for a Fortune 500 technology company, I was challenged with turning a division-level marketing research organization into a world-class market intelligence group. While the Marketing Research team had a significant amount of talent, it was not seen as key to the division's business-making process. By leveraging the existing talent within the team, investing in database development and automation, focusing on key executive information needs, and reaching across organizational boundaries to integrate all types of market intelligence sources. This division-level research team became the premier Market Intelligence organization for the corporation. A few of the key actions that enabled this change are as follows:

1. The first step was ensuring that everyone on the team is sharing a common vision for what the Market Intelligence group should be, what it should deliver, and what are the key focus areas for improvement. It is important that the entire team is involved in this process, and that they feel ownership for the final results. Our efforts in this area resulted in a very actionable mission statement annual group objective, and the definition of career development paths. As a result, the entire team was brought in to the process and focused on achieving world-class status.

2. We invested significant time and financial resources in building databases and tools to automate the analysis process. In fact, at one point, one analyst spent about six months of full time effort managing the development of these tools. This was a difficult investment to make since the team was already understaffed. However, as a result of enabling these tools we were able to go from having three staff members spending 80 percent of their time in generating one global market share report on a quarterly basis, to having one staff member and two interns spending 50 percent of their time in generating 42 highly-segmented (and impactful) market share reports over the course of a year. As a result of this significant productivity improvement, the team is able to spend significantly more time in developing customized analysis, which is highly-tuned to the executives needs.

3. Our team began-hosting worldwide/cross-divisional summits for the marketing research and competitive analysis units within the corporation. These summits resulted in significant collaboration across teams and a better flow of information and analysis. This improved the information flows and the entire organization's analysis.

4. During the early stages of this assignment, and on a regular basis thereafter, the team should meet the executives and internal clients to understand what information they needed, what they

Contd...

were not getting, and what was working well. As a result of these meetings, and following through with information tuned to the clients and executives needs, the team became the source for market information. From the board level, to other marketing intelligence teams, to the clients, this team became the source for critical market information. In fact, this information gathering and analysis process became a critical and required component of the decision-making process.

Over the course of three years, this team transitioned from a very effective marketing research team to a world-class Market Intelligence organization, which is a model and resource for the entire organization. In fact, the team became so effective that they began driving corporate-level issues such as developing a corporate-wide market-forecasting model. This model has become the foundation for the executive strategic planning process.

In summary, there are many critical elements to building a world-class Market Intelligence team. And it is not a quick process. However, with time, investment, and patience, the development of a world-class Market Intelligence team is possible. And this team can become a strategic asset to the company.

Source: This article has been authored by Ed Crowley. He has founded the Photizo Group (www.photizogroup.com) as a consulting resource for clients who are focussed on driving sustained business growth. He has over 20 years of experience. Reprinted with the kind permission of the author. All rights reserved.

Mind Power 4: Building a Competitive Intelligence Capability

The Market Intelligence concept, and how MI is the critical weapon in the business battlefield and the four basic building blocks for MI: Competitor Intelligence, Product Intelligence, Market Understanding and Customer Understanding are the main areas of discussion.

The topic of this article is the first building block, Competitor Intelligence. Competitor Intelligence involves the science of capturing information about your competitor's current activities, analyzing their past behaviour to develop predictive models of future behaviour, and obtaining insight into their current and future product strategies. This is one of the most critical building blocks in the Market Intelligence (MI) process. Why? Because developing a complete understanding of the competitive environment and how competitors can be expected to react to your firm's activities is a critical component in your business 'battle plan'. Without this understanding, even the best marketing plans and activities can be nullified by unexpected competitor reactions (Or even pre-empted if your competitor has a strong Competitive Intelligence Capability).

Whether you are a global firm with large multinational competitors, or a local firm competing with other local or regional firms; understanding the competition is essential to your success. Like each of the building blocks, competitive intelligence can be considered a discipline in and of itself. There are many techniques and strategies for building Competitive Intelligence (CI) capabilities, and many organizations that specialize in providing (CI) services and even outsourcing.

The first place to begin in building CI capabilities is to perform a CI audit. This audit should provide an objective view of the firm's capabilities in each of the following areas:

1. ***Requirements:*** Who are the key internal clients for CI? Are they satisfied with the information they are receiving? If not. What do they-need to meet their needs?

   If they are satisfied, what could be done to increase their-satisfaction level?

Contd...

2. ***Staffing:*** Who is responsible for CI? Is it a full time role or part time, what is their experience level, and what training would improve their capabilities?

3. ***Sourcing:*** What sources is the firm using to gather CI information? Are there existing sources (i.e. the supply chain or sales organization) that could be used, but which are not being utilized? What programmes can be put in place to enhance information gathering?

4. ***Reporting:*** How is the CI information disseminated to the internal client base? Are clients satisfied with the timeliness of the information? Is the information delivered in a format that is convenient and effective?

Market Intelligence Building Blocks

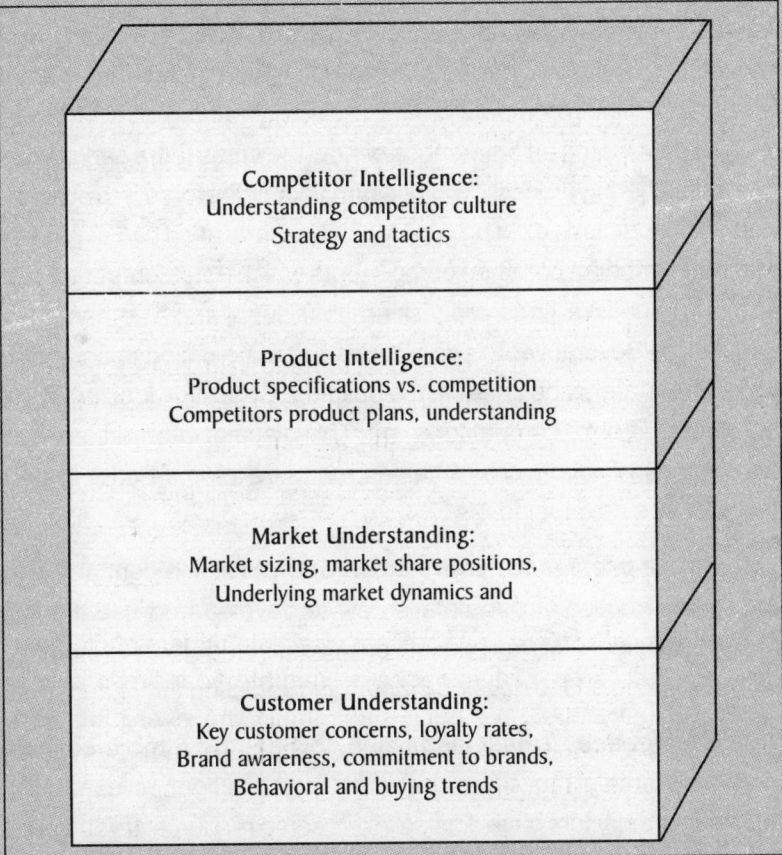

This CI audit should inspect every aspect of the Competitive Intelligence process. The diagram below provides an overview of this process and some of the key areas to examine. After completing the CI audit, the firm should develop a long-term CI plan that identifies how the firm will build its CI capabilities. One of the most common pitfalls to developing an effective CI capability is to believe that you can develop this capability without dedicating resources and budget to the effort. For most firms, my first question would be, "Do you have a dedicated competitive analyst?"

If the answer is no, there is a good chance you are constantly being surprised by competitive activity, not fully anticipating their reactions to your marketing activities and operating "in the dark" from a competitive perspective.

Some tools and techniques, which you will want to consider in building your CI capabilities include:

Contd...

Begin publishing a weekly (or ideally) daily "briefing" of key competitive activities

While this requires some investment of time and resources, it is often the most sought after deliverable from the CI function. By providing a brief synopsis of information from industry publications, internal sources, and news retrieval services such as Lexus-Nexus you can provide timely information which will be highly sought after within the organization and which has a high perceived value. The key is to make sure each summary includes a very brief and to the point snap shot of why the information is important and what it means. Clients should be able to quickly browse this briefing and be able to hone the topics for which they would like more detail.

Developing 'existing' organizational capabilities for capturing CI information: Many firms do not realize the sources of competitive intelligence, which are already available (but unused) in their firm. Perhaps the best, but least used information source is your sales force. With just a little focus on offering incentives for providing competitive tips, providing training on what to look for in customer sites and resellers, and developing an awareness of how the sales force can play a critical role in the competitive information gathering process, you can turn your sales force into an information gathering powerhouse. Additionally, your firms existing supply chain organization can play a key role by querying industry vendors on the number of common components which your competitor is buying, or looking for feedback on what competitive firms are visiting your suppliers. The same holds true for your development organization. Several years ago I happened to be sitting in a vendors lobby in Japan when I noticed some other Americans entering the building. By quickly looking at the visitor log, I was able to determine they were from a competitor's firm. This piece of information (in addition to several other insights from our sales / supply chain) helped me to develop a better understanding of what products this competitor was developing.

Developing key executive profiles for your key competitors: A recent article in the Intelligence Briefing newsletter by the Photizo Group details how to develop and use this tool. In essence, it involves developing profile folders for key executives at your competitors in order to understand their framework for decision-making and to develop models for predicting their future behaviour.

Hiring competitive intelligence firms: Often times, this can be a more cost effective approach versus building in-house staffing to support competitive intelligence capabilities. The primary disadvantage is that your competitors have access to this same resource. If you build these capabilities with in-house staffing, it becomes a competitive advantage that your customers do not have.

These are just a few of the methods and approaches for developing competitive intelligence information. Again, this field is a discipline in and of itself. However, with intelligent investments in this area, your firm can create one of the essential building blocks for Market Intelligence, the key resource for making intelligence marketing decisions.

Contd...

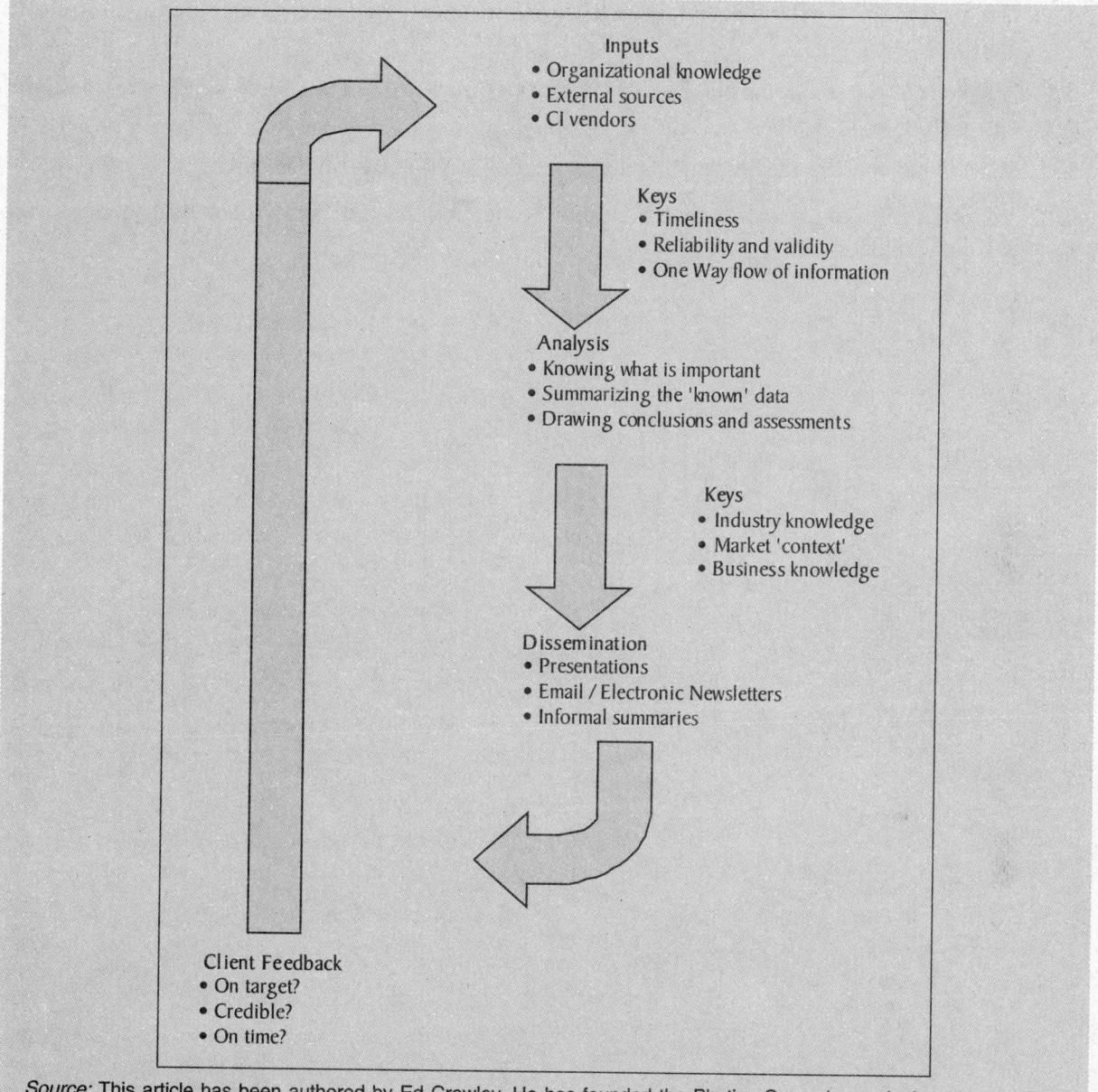

QUESTIONS FOR DISCUSSION

1. What is the difference between industrial and consumer marketing research?

2. "Marketing Intelligence" is an area, where industrial marketers today are focusing on? Why?

3. Quantitative forecasting techniques are too complicated for smaller industrial marketers to implement? Discuss.

4.   Is it possible to forecast demand, with the rapid pace of change happening in the industrial marketing scenario?

5.   What are the possible errors that you might confront in a "sales force composite" method of forecasting sales?

6.   How would you use the Internet as a tool for industrial marketing research?

7.   "Market potential or sales potential cannot be determined just by mathematical models". What is your opinion on it?

chapter

EIGHT

Segmenting, Targeting and Positioning

COMPANY PROFILE 8: BILT (BALLARPUR INDUSTRIES LIMITED)

BILT is India's largest paper company and the only Indian company to rank amongst top 100 paper companies in the world.

BILT is the undisputed leader in the Indian paper industry. It is also India's largest manufacturer and exporter of paper, with a strong presence in all segments of the usage spectrum that includes Writing and Printing Paper, Industrial Paper and Specialty Paper. Complementing this is a diversified production infrastructure with six manufacturing units spread across the country.

In recent years, **BILT** has evolved as a more dynamic, knowledge driven organization focused towards creation of stakeholder value. In the process, it has also transformed the paper industry from its traditional 'commodity market' mindset to a branded one. A concerted programme of innovation and technological excellence helps it proactively respond to the needs of each individual segment. Today, BILT not only has the range, but also a well entrenched distribution network that enables it to reach customers, any time, any place.

As the industry leader, **BILT** is committed to developing its business towards ecological, social and economic sustainability. Community development and upliftment of the marginalised class have been identified as focus areas. BILT has joined hands with Pratham, an NGO that runs primary education programmes all over the country. A key initiative in environmental accountability is the BILT Farm Forestry programme that has covered more than 7500 farmers.

BILT has been developing Farm Forestry since 1990 through its subsidiary company **BILT** Tree Tech Ltd. (BTTL). Since its inception in 1989, BTTL has concentrated on developing core competency in forestry and is manned by experienced forestry professionals.

BILT has taken a special care to target marginal land belonging to farmers below poverty line. Farmers covered under this scheme are assured purchase of their pulpwood produce by BILT at declared support price or market price which ever may be higher. Tailor-made bank loans on long-term basis are made available to the needy farmers.

Ongoing research and development activities aimed at tree improvement and clonal development are already contributing to increased returns to farmers through improved productivity. BTTL has initiated site-specific forestry research projects to identify and produce high yielding clones of pulpwood species like Eucalyptus, Casuarina and Leucaena leucocephala. Plantations raised with high yielding clones of Eucalyptus have achieved substantial increase in yield giving significantly higher returns to formers. The company plans to progressively increase usage of high yielding by adopting tissue culture route. BILT Tree Tech Ltd. has also established high quality seed orchards of above species to improve availability of good quality seed and ensure better productivity of its farm forestry programme by adopting tissue culture route.

BILT is responsible to continuously enhance shareholders wealth; it is also committed to its other stakeholders to conduct its business in a responsible manner that creates a sustained positive impact on society".

BILT believes in synergising business interests with environmental accountability. All manufacturing units follow stringent environment management systems and are moving towards ISO 14001 certification furthering its drive towards protecting the environment and reducing pollution.

BILT has demonstrated a tradition of leadership across six decades and three generations. Over the years, it has only emerged as a more dynamic, focused corporate leveraging its vast asset and knowledge pool to enhance shareholder value. In the year 1945, Ballarpur Paper and Straw Board Mills Limited incorporated. First brand names 'Three Aces' for paper and "Wisdom" for stationery. In 1969, Shree Gopal Paper Mills Limited merges with Ballarpur Paper and Straw Board Mills Limited. In 1988, they entered into industrial paper segment. In 2001, they acquired Sinar Mas Pulp and Paper (India) Limited acquired and renamed Bilt Graphic Papers Limited (BGPL). In 2003, BILT Graphic Papers Limited merged with BILT.

Source: www.bilt.com

Mind Power I: Customer Segmentation- To Sell More Products at Profit— Sanjay Limaye

Customer Segmentation is the subdivision of a market into discrete customer groups that share similar characteristics. It also divides customers into groups based on the distinct underlying needs or characteristics driving their purchase decisions. Segmentation is a powerful marketing tool to identify unmet customer needs. Truly distinct customer segments respond to different value propositions and require different strategic approaches. Customer Segmentation is most effective when a company tailors offerings to segments that are the most profitable and serves them with distinct competitive advantages. This prioritization can help organizations develop marketing campaigns and pricing strategies to extract maximum value from both high and low-profit customers.

Customer Segmentation also serves as fundamental basis for allocating resources to product development, marketing, service, and delivery programmes.

In other words, if strategy is the art of allocating scarce resources, then segmentation and the understanding it provides about your core customer groups–is part of the science informing that allocation.

How should segmentation be done?

Customer Segmentation requires managers to:

1. Divide the market into meaningful and measurable segments according to customers' needs, their past behaviours or their demographic profiles.

2. Determine the profit potential of each segment by analyzing the revenue and cost impacts of serving each segment.

3. Target segments according to their profit potential and the company's ability to serve them in a proprietary way.

4. Invest resources to tailor product, service, marketing, and distribution programmes to match the needs of each target segment.

5. Measure performance of each segment and adjust the segmentation approach over time as market conditions change decision-making throughout the organization.

However, one should remember,

1. *Segment only on what truly drives purchase behaviour*

   Customer segmentation divides customers into groups based only on those needs and factors actually driving purchase decisions. A common mistake is to segment customers based on peripheral characteristics that, while interesting, provide no help in achieving the fundamental goal of segmentation: selling more product/services more profitably.

2. *Think profit, not revenues*

   That being said, improved profits (not just revenues) should be the goal of customer segmentation. A common pitfall of companies defining target segments is to focus on revenue potential instead

Contd...

of bottom-line profit potential. This myopic view can lead a company to go after the wrong customers, growing sales even as the bottom-line suffers.

Companies can use customer segmentation to:

1. Prioritize new product development efforts.
2. Develop, customized marketing programmes.
3. Choose specific product features.
4. Establish appropriate service options.
5. Design an optimal distribution strategy.
6. Determine appropriate product pricing.

Source: Copyright with Industrial Marketing Services 2005. Reprinted with the kind permission of Sanjay Limaye. Visit him at www.inmas.com.

Mind Power 2: How's Your Market Segmentation? – Dan Adams

How are wars won? Military historian Basil Hart said, "All the lessons of war can be reduced to a single word: concentration. But for truth, this needs to be amplified to the *concentration of strength against weakness.*"

Can this lesson be applied to business? Let's substitute market research for reconnaissance, business strategy for battle plan and resource allocation for troop deployment. Could it be that new product launches and other business initiatives fail largely due to lack of concentration?

Napoleon concluded, "It is impossible to be too strong at the decisive point." Great military leaders throw the weight of their force at the critical point in the battle front. Losing generals spread their forces thinly, unable to muster an effective attack, always on the defensive. I find many business leaders fail to (1) thoroughly understand their battle fronts, (2) determine the decisive points to attack, and (3) follow with an overwhelming assault.

Napoleon concluded "It is impossible to be too strong at the decisive point"

Define "Market Segment"

Think of a business leader's potential battle fronts as market segments to pursue. Let's define "market segment." Some companies define their markets by their own organizational structure, sales territories, product lines, etc. But this is inside-out thinking and quite flawed. I believe a market segment is a *cluster of customers with similar needs.* Thinking in this outside-in fashion requires more effort, but leads to a host of benefits.

Ultimately, everything your business does should be about efficiently delivering value to customers. Now if you choose any segmentation approach *other* than clustering like-minded customers, you can't deliver value efficiently. You won't be able to *focus* on common market segment needs; these needs will be randomly observed by different people in your company at different times under different conditions. This forces you to one of two paths:

Good Segmentation Leads to Good Concentration

"All the lessons of war can be reduced to a single word: Concentration. But for truth, this needs to be amplified to the concentration of strength against weakness." (Basil Liddell Hart, Military Historian)

Proper market segmentation requires 3 disciplines:

- Market research (reconnaissance)
- Business strategy (battle plan)
- Resource allocation (troop deployment)

Contd...

1. Develop new products for one customer at a time, or

2. Develop "averaged" products for dissimilar customers that don't fully satisfy any of them. The former makes you reactive and vulnerable; the latter mediocre.

When you cluster customers into market segments you gain tremendous efficiencies. You can discriminate between segments, placing your troops where they will count. For attractive segments, you can interview customers in-depth to understand market needs far better than competitors. You can collaborate closely with key market players, establishing yourself as a supplier of choice. And you can launch your product with rifle-shot promotional tools. So both "early-stage marketing" (understanding needs) and "late-stage marketing" (promoting solutions) work better. After all, marketing should be about... *markets*.

You Have Choices

As I work across many different industries (all B2B), I see three common patterns: (1) The typical B2B company has many potential segments it *could* serve, (2) these segments vary substantially in their potential for profitable supplier growth, and (3) due to poor segmentation, enormous value is missed.

It can be tempting to begin product development without understanding your market segment. Tempting, but wrong. Any number of unseen problems could plague you: global competition, unfavourable regulations, competitive backlash, etc. You will eventually learn of these problems, but your cost of doing so could easily increase one-to-two orders of magnitude if you learn by experience instead of investigation. Ultimately, your market sets your project's ceiling: Beautiful product development in an ugly market simply makes no sense.

Market Segments or sub-Segments	Attractiveness Criteria						
	1. Size of Revenue Opportunity	**2.** Market Segment Growth	**3.** Market Segment Profitability	**4.** Unmet Customer Needs	**5.** Likely Power of Value Proposition	**6.** Likelihood of Technical Solution	**7.** Current Market Presence
Marine coatings	B	C	B	A	A	C	C
Maintenance coatings	A	C	B	B	B	C	C
Aircraft coatings	A	A	B	A	A	B	B
Bridge coatings	C	B	A	A	B	C	B
Railcar coatings	B	C	C	C	A	B	C

A: Very Attractive
B: Moderately Attractive
C: Unattractive

Figure 8.1: Screen Market Segments for Attractiveness

A.   Very Attractive

B.   Moderately Attractive

C.   Unattractive

Many companies don't understand their customer clusters well enough to do full-blown market segmentation yet. That's OK: Start where you are by screening possible segments (Figure 8.1). Gather secondary research about each segment so you can make a "stoplight" assessment. Segments that look most attractive—in this fictitious example, aircraft coatings—should be pursued with customer interviews to uncover needs and trends. Sure, you could do a more sophisticated analysis with

Contd...

weightings *and* points... but how good are your decisions until your data come from customers, not colleagues?

After you've gathered market data—with secondary research and customer interviews—you're ready for a market segment-portfolio analysis. I like to use the approach shown in Figure 2. In this example of a different fictitious business—adhesives—market attractiveness is driven by segment growth and other factors, while competitive position is driven by relative market share and other factors. All of this can and should be quantified.

You generally want to improve your competitive position in attractive segments, i.e., move top bubbles to the right. But if the enemy has amassed troops at this point of the battle front—say solar panels— you must deliver *significant* new product value to win. To understand your chance of success, you'll need reconnaissance through customer interviews and competitive benchmarking. The only military move worse than spreading forces thinly is attacking blindly.

Four Market Segmentation "Rules"

First, don't define segments too broadly lest you "average" the needs of customers, giving an opening to a competitor who targets more narrowly. Second, organize your business by market segments; many companies begin by establishing market-focused teams which later "morph" into market-focused businesses. Third, manage segments globally. Regional organization silos set you up to be blind-sided in our dynamic global economy.

Finally, once you've completed the analysis in Figure 8.2, be *bold* in piling on resources for the "Attack" segments. Too often I see this part of strategic planning end with a whimper. Your reconnaissance is complete. You've got a battle plan. Now it's time to concentrate your troops.

Figure 8.2: Strategic Market Segment Portfolio

Learning More

Figure 2 is based on traditional Boston Consulting Group and McKinsey matrices. Each of these firms offers helpful insight into the practice of market segmentation. I also recommend Jim Hlavacek's book, *Profitable Top-Line growth for Industrial Companies*. Finally, at Advanced Industrial Marketing, Inc. we provide hands-on training in market segmentation that includes customer interviewing and competitive benchmarking.

Source: This article has been authored by Dan Adams. Visit them at www.aimtolead.com. Reprinted with permission.

SEGMENTING, TARGETING AND POSITIONING

Introduction

The business marketer should be able to understand and analyze the attractive business segments. 80 percent of the complete business comes from 20 percent of the customer. So choosing the right customers for business becomes very important. Companies tend to select a "set of potentially profitable customers". These customers form their platform for business. These set of customers are then:

1.   Provided with a distinct and unique value proposition.

2.   Servicing them, nurturing them and developing them as profitable customers.

Industrial marketers can probably compete in the complete market. But what makes more sense, is to choose its customer base on the basis of certain characteristics. Choosing the segments is not an easy decision to be made, as every segment looks to be equally attractive. In this chapter, we will try and look in to how to develop the segment, create a value proposition for the customers, and develop and nurture them over a long period of time.

We have also seen in the previous chapters that the markets can be divided into commercial enterprises, government and not for profit organizations. All these organizations have a varied approach to the buying practices. Some of them may believe in a long-term collaborative relationships, others might believe in a short-term and transactional business focus. Thus choosing the right set of customers is a key to success in industrial markets.

SEGMENTING THE MARKETS

Wind and Cardozo define a market segment as "a group of present or potential customers with some common characteristics which is relevant in explaining (and predicting) their response to a suppliers marketing stimuli."[1]

As we said in the first paragraph, that it is only 20 percent of the customers who contribute about 80 percent of the business. Now if we try and understand the profitability of each customer we will be "shocked" to find out that many of the customers are not contributing anything to the company. The marketer loses more money in servicing such customer. Thus the importance of segmentation lies here.

Industrial customers are different from consumers in term of their needs, attitude towards purchase, decision-making etc. Thus marketing segmentation will help a marketer identify, groups of firms whose requirements are similar.

The difficulty in segmenting the industrial customer is that there is a great difference in the approach that each customer shows. Users and uses vary considerably. For example, customers who are buying steel may have different requirements. Some buyers would look for shine and some for strength.

Another difficulty that arises in industrial segmentation is from the fact that the purchasing process is different in different organizations. People come from various backgrounds having different set of objectives. Thus grouping of customers become a very tough task for industrial marketers.

But the segmentation process has to be carried out so that resource can be allocated efficiently to get a desired set of objectives. The marketer would also look in to some a serve a set of customers, which are the least served segments in the markets, so as to carve out a niche for them.

CHOOSING THE MARKET SEGMENT

The factors that need to be considered for choosing the market segments are:

1. *Measurability:* Marketers should be able to the find out about buyer characteristics, buyers either through primary on secondary data sources.

2. *Substantial:* The segments should be "substantially" big enough to be worth investing resources into.

3. *Compatibility:* The marketer's business strengths should match the competitive and technological state of market.

4. *Accessible:* The marketer should be able to focus its effort on the chosen segments.

The objective of market segmentation is to increase the returns and allocate its resources more efficiently to that segment. However this becomes difficult, when there are few sellers in the market or it is a fragmented industry and quite a major chunk is unprofitable or otherwise too many players are already operating.

Along with the process of segmentation, two more important considerations that a business marketer must keep in mind are:

1. Competitive Environment

2. Technological Environment.

Competitive Environment

Competitive Environment plays a very key role in the segmentation basis for industrial marketers. Industries which are heavily cluttered with players like the personal computer, cellular phones, generally have very small product life cycles. These markets are highly threatened by more innovative and competent firms in terms of technology and resources. Thus a business marketer should be well versed with the risks of a highly competitive market, and keep the competitive environment in mind before the segmentation process.

Technological Environment

Technological environment must be assessed before segmentation of the markets. Changes happening in technological fronts can lead to paradigm shifts in the product markets. New technologies, products and services create new opportunities. These might wipe out old business. So marketers should be well informed about the technological changes happening in the markets, so that they would be able to generate greater value to their customers.

SEGMENTING INDUSTRIAL MARKETS

There are two major categories for segmenting industrial markets. They are:

1. Macro Segmentation

2. Micro Segmentation

Macro Segmentation

Macro Segmentation consists of identifying macrovariables and centers on organizational and industry characteristics. These data can be easily the obtained from secondary sources and also a marketer's information system.

Let us discuss this in a greater detail:

Macro Segmentation		
1.	Industrial Variables	– Types of industry, we should market our products to – Types of customers we should look into?
2.	Organizational Variables	– Organization size, business (Big, Medium or small) – Size of the business operating
3.	Customer Variables	– Customer location? – Technology and competitive factors? – Purchasing decisions? – Industry growth rate?
4.	Application Variables	– General use or specific use of products

The basis for macro level of segmentation has been given on the table above.

Industrial Variables

Products and services can be targeted to various industries. For example, IBM's main frame can be of interest to multiple industries. Similarly a steel manufacturer can look in for diverse segments like packaging, automobiles, general engineering etc. So a business marketer must list down the set of industries the product or service can be sold to. The requirements of a particular product will be different across industries. It is also not correct to conclude that within a particular industry the requirements would not vary. For example, requirement of photocopiers at banks would be different than at offices. Thus a little more of subdivision is always better to pinpoint at the particular area the marketer would be looking at.

Under the industry characteristics one more factor that needs to be looked into, are the type of customers. Would it be commercial enterprises, governmental enterprises or not for profit organizations. How much of revenue, that we expect is also to be considered. The growth factors of those enterprises must also be taken into considerations.

Thus to obtain a very clear picture of the market, a little more effort into the marketers part, would be very helpful.

Organizational Variables

In the organizational factors two key points need to be noted. They are:

1. The size of the business we are planning to operate with; and

2. The size of their business.

It is very important to understand the size of the business, because larger the organization more different will be their purchasing objectives and criteria. Now to respond to the purchasing objectives, a marketer needs to tailor make the marketing objectives to suit the buyer. A bigger buyer would look in for a collaborative exchange, with large quantity of purchase and high levels of service. On the other hand the smaller would look at purchase from a transactional approach, with frequent price negotiations.

Customer Variables

In industrial markets delivering on time is very important. Thus customer location plays a very key role in the segmentation of the market. In industrial markets, since customers are dispersed, local regional players may find it difficult to access the complete market, because of locational factors and resource problems. Location of customers also effect transportation cost and warehousing costs. In a competitive market where every one tries to "cut costs" these become a very important aspect especially in industrial marketing.

The level of technology and automation that a particular customer works with can form a very important basis of customer segmentation. If marketers do not match up to technological changes of an industry they would lose business. Thus a marketer must genuinely look into their strategic strengths and then think on the markets to choose.

The level of competition in the customers industry also plays a very key role in the basis of segmentation. If the competition levels are higher, the market might be unattractive to new players. Similarly the rate, at which the particular industry and the competitor are growing, also should be considered. If the industry is stagnant or in a declining mode, marketers should be very cautious in entering such markets.

If the purchasing decision is centralized or decentralized it will determine the way to approach a customer.

Application Variables

A specific industrial good may be used in multiple ways. For example, ball bearings may be used in machineries to cycles. Another example would be springs which would be used from purposes like machines to automobiles. Thus each user group will have a special application of a particular product, and the marketer would be better equipped with various requirements.

Another macro level base of segmentation is the purchasing situation. As we have studied earlier, the new task, straight rebuy or modified rebuy, the buying understanding would be different. Understanding the process or stage of buying is a very key factor for an industrial marketer.

Micro Segmentation

Micro segmentation requires greater focus, better understanding of markets, market knowledge, decision making units and their criteria. There are further subdivisions on the basis of specific organizational knowledge that is related to purchasing process. This requires the gathering of high quality primary data. It can be collected either through the salesforce or a research with the help of an agency.

Micro Segmentation		
I. Purchasing Objectives	–	Transaction orientation or collaborative orientation,
	–	Inventory requirements, policies of purchase.
2. Criteria for Purchase	–	Quality, Delivery, Service or price
3. Decision Making Unit	–	Centralized or other wise
4. Innovativeness	–	Innovator or Follower
5. Organizational Factors	–	Resources, PLC stage and buying situation
6. Personal Characteristics	–	Decision-making, risk, demographics

Once the macro variables have been identified, the marketer has to divide each macro variable into smaller dimension, i.e. a micro variable. These micro variables are an integral part of the macro variables. Just by relying on the secondary sources would not help the marketer but a large deal of primary data is also necessary to study these variables. The bases of micro segmentation are given in the above table.

Purchasing Objectives

The objectives of purchasing would vary from organization to organization. Companies differ in their philosophies towards buying. Smaller organizations would look in for better bargains, whereas the larger buyers would stress more on quality and service.

Inventory requirements play a key role in the buying process. If manufactures are using JIT or MRP inventory systems, they would have an altogether different impact. These organizations would require sales person who are highly skilled and have great technical as well as human orientation skills. Supplies on time, quality and servicing play a very important role. If marketers cannot meet the requirements of the buyer, they should avoid such customers.

Policies of purchasing would also affect the micro segmentation bases. Government organizations would consider tendering and bidding unlike commercial enterprises. Some organizations would also like to lease, if the industry has frequent technological changes.

Criteria for Purchase

Across organizations, product categories and situations the criteria would vary. Smaller organizations would look for better bargains unlike their larger counter parts. Lehman and Shanghnessy speak of five buyer's choice criteria.

They are:[2]

Performance criteria : Improve the performance standards or maximize the performance.

Economic criteria : The cost involved in buying, storing and usage of the product.

Integrative criteria	:	The efforts needed to integrate the buyer's need by the seller.
Adaptive criteria	:	The buying firm may need to adapt its plans about uncertainties about the capability of the supplier to meet the buyers' requirement.
Legalistic criteria	:	Impact of purchases on legal issues.

Decision Making Unit

We have seen in the previous chapters that buying in an industrial organization are done collectively by a group. There is a multiplicity of factors that play an important role in the process of decision-making. Buying center could involve people from marketing, production, engineering, research and development and also purchase. Thus when marketers understand the process of purchase involvement, it can lead into the identification of meaningful segments.

Innovativeness

The buying needs can considerably vary according to the technological innovativeness within the industry, as well as within the buyer organization. Organizations would likely to the influenced by the innovation practices that are there in the industry. Examples would be the semiconductor industries or the personal computers. The more innovative a firm is or more technological changes if seen within a particular industry it would be more likely, that more people would be involved in the buying decision-making process. Organizational innovativeness and industry innovativeness can draw a very clear picture on the micro variables.

Organizational Factors

Organizational factors can play a very important role in the micro segmentation process of industrial markets. In the previous chapters, we have seen that how a buying situation influence the purchasing process purchasing process and how marketers must react to it. In a new task situation, the marketer should be in a position to assist the buyers through all stages of implementation. The buy grid frame work that we have discussed earlier forms a basis for micro segmentation.

The level of customer experience affects the decision-making process and thus the marketers strategy also. One more factor that plays a very important basis for segmentation is the interaction needs between the buyer and the seller. Products which are complex or very important to a company, the level of interaction plays a very important role in such places. It is seen that often buyers are not able to express their needs and are highly dependent on the suppliers. If buyers are not clear, on their requirements, high level of interaction is needed in between marketers and buyers. If buyers can state exactly as to what they want (for example, purchasing laptop, for their expatriates) the decision-making process will be much more shorter. Thus the process of interaction can be a useful process used by the marketer for segmentation.

Personal Characteristics

Human beings are complex and it is finally "people" who take the decision. Although organizational factors, policies play a considerable influence, personal characteristics also play a very important factor in the process of decision-making. Thus it is also possible to segment the markets by characteristics of individuals involved in the purchasing situation (For example, demographics, personality, non-task motives, individual perceptions and risk management strategies).[3] Thus in many organizations, it is more of social relationships and in others it is a partnering or a collaborative relationship.

One problem that arises while segmenting through personal characteristics is that, the data would be literally impossible to obtain. It would be only obtained through sales person. Not only that, from individual to individual it would vary.

SEGMENTING THE ORGANIZATIONAL MARKETS

A) Wind and Cardozo's Approach to Segmentation[4]

It combines the macro variables and micro variables and gives a series of steps to segment organizational markets. The data involved in the macro segmentation is obtained from secondary sources and in cases the data is not sufficient, then it becomes necessary to turn to primary data. The cost of research proportionately increases with micro segmentation.

The first step is to identify the macro segments on the basis of organizational characteristics. Once we have obtained a selected set of acceptable macro segments, marketers need to evaluate the selected segments. The evaluation of the selected segment would be about understanding the firm's resources and capabilities and response to the firm's marketing programme. Once we have evaluated and selected each segment we need to select the desired target macro segment based on the costs and benefits analysis. If the macro segment matches our target segment, then the process is completed.

In case the macro segment does not match the target segment then we need to identify the micro segments, within each macro segments, based on DMU characteristics.

Segmentation involves costs. The deeper we dig, the more costly it becomes. Selecting a particular market segment, must be with extreme care. Once a segment has been selected, a marketer will put in a lot many resources into the particular segment. Resources would include manpower, services and financial resources. In industrial marketing long-term resource commitment, means for a long number of years. In consumer marketing, it is comparatively easier to switch focus, but in industrial markets it's not.

B) Bonoma and Shapiro's Nested Approach[5]

A basis for segmentation has been divided by Bonoma and Shapiro, also referred to as the "nested approach". There is a hierarchical structure, and the segmentation bases move from the macro to the micro level variables. Five variables have been used. They are:

1. Organizational demographics consisting of industry, company size and location.

2. Operating variables consisting of technology, user, non-user status, and customer capabilities.

3. Purchasing approaches comprised buying centre structure, purchasing policies and purchasing criteria.

4. Situational factors consisting of urgency, application and size of order.

5. Personal factors consisting of motivation, buyer-seller dyad, and risk perceptions.

The above model forms a very practical base for segmenting industrial markets.

C) Morris – Cost-Benefit Approach Industrial Market Segmentation[6]

Morris proposed a model to industrial market segmentation on the basis of cost-benefit approach. It consists of three major blocks, trying to answer, various queries.

The first block is questioning the "approach to segmentation" and whether it is appropriate. It gives questions like whether the segments are measurable, accessible, homogenous and consistent to market approach the company follows.

The second block applies the cost-benefit analysis to the micro and macro bases of segmentation. The benefits would include revenue, company image, protection from competitors, economies of scale and better control. The costs would include research and development, production costs, overhead costs, transportation cost, storage costs and risk involved.

On the basis of the first block and second block, we reach the third block, which answers "the allocation of resources to the segments". The segments with the greatest benefits receive the highest allocation of resources.

EVALUATING THE SEGMENTS

Once we have segmented the markets, we need to quantify the segments. The marketer must know the profitability and the level of competition in such segments. We would also like to know the growth potential for each segment. To do that a marketer would implement certain forecasting methods. These forecasting methods are for two main reasons. They are:

1. Understanding the profitability from the segments chosen.

2. Level of competition in those segments.

Refer back to the chapter of demand forecasting. To understand the profitability of the segments we would use the same techniques that we had used to forecast demand. They are:

1. *Qualitative Methods*

   i) Executive opinion

   ii) Delphi method

   iii) Sales force composite

   iv) Test marketing

2. *Quantitative Methods*

   i) Moving averages

   ii) Regression and correlation analysis

   iii) Input/output models

   iv) Econometric models

   v) Box Jenkins method.

Understanding the level of competition is very important. A segment which apparently looks to be very attractive may turn out to be a high competing market space. Not only this but also the marketers must be able to understand "the weaknesses" and "the strengths" of the competitors. Competitor's ability to respond to any changes, Research and development capabilities, sales force, technology, distribution, promotional factors must also be considered.

Mind Power 3: Insight: Improving Target Marketing to Maximize Customer Relevancy

Target marketing is one of the most important, though often overlooked, components in developing a sound marketing plan. Targeting recognizes the fact that most companies have limited resources and therefore, need to "place their bets" where they will yield the highest return.

Many companies are reluctant to select a defined core target segment, fearing that excluding certain groups will decrease an important source of volume. In turn, companies try to serve all customer groups equally, which can result in a diffused offering, that no one group finds appealing.

Marketing Target vs Consumption Target

"Speak to the target, but let others listen," as stated by advertising legend Leo Burnett, distills target marketing down to an actionable insight.

More adept marketers understand the important distinction between (1) the more narrow "target market" (think center of the bulls eye); and (2) the broader "consumption market" that falls outside of the core target, though often finds the offering appealing.

The following illustrates this important distinction:

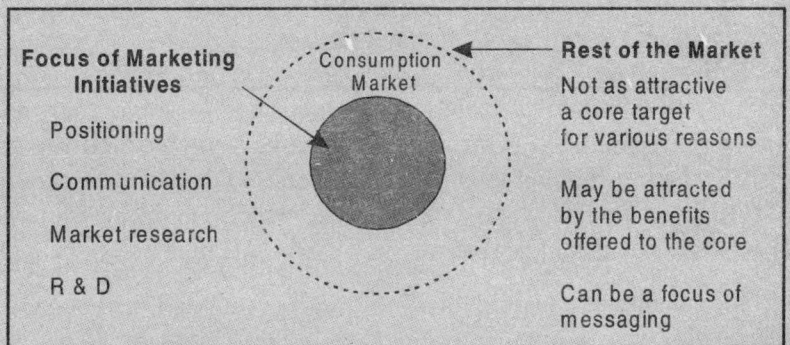

Figure 8.3: Marketing vs Consumption Targets

Target Marketing in Practice

Apple has expertly targeted iPod and iTunes, selecting a specific market appealing to a much broader group. By selecting younger, hard-core music aficionados as their marketing target, Apple was able to concentrate its early product development and marketing dollars on a fairly defined core target that would set the highest expectations for the brand. While Apple understood the much broader, market potential it initially focused on capturing heavy users of music, to establish a strong, loyal customer base. This core target then extended the brand through strong word-of-mouth and viral marketing. Eventually, a much broader consumption market began purchasing iPod, and sales skyrocketed. Still, Apple has maintained its narrow targeting strategy throughout, recognizing the 'aspirational' nature of its core marketing target, which the broader consumption market also finds appealing.

Other examples of marketing vs consumption targeting:

1. Nike focuses its product development and marketing budget on performance athletes, though the weekend warrior is a strong consumption market.

2. Gatorade emphasizes "rehydration" benefits in targeting athletes and young adult males. Much broader consumer groups use Gatorade across a variety of usage occasions.

Contd...

TARGET MARKETING

Once the segmentation of the market has been done, and we have understood the growth potential, profitability and competitive factors, marketers must now be able to devise a strategy for the segments meeting the marketer's criteria. The marketers must decide which would be the segment that they would pick to serve. These segments would be the "targeted market". Three broad strategies are available. They are:

1. Concentrated Marketing
2. Differentiated Marketing
3. Undifferentiated Marketing
4. Niche Marketing

Concentrated Marketing

Companies do have a restriction or limitation to the resources they have. The restrictions could be in terms of manpower, finance, technology or location. When the marketer feels that they have restrictions and would not suit the complete market needs, they may choose for a large share of one market or a few markets. This would also be true for firms entering into industrial markets for the first time. Once the firm starts gaining knowledge about the market place, and starts getting a strong foothold into the concentrated market and beat the competition, they would be in a position to expand to other unexplored market segments. The concentrated marketers generally tend to operate in highly localized area, probably one or two states with highly selective promotional strategy. However concentrated marketing strategy involves risk, as bigger players may use their "might" to overrun the markets. The business opportunity for this segment could decline, so companies following this concentrated strategy must try and spread the risks to multiple areas, so that dependency on one single sector is reduced.

Differentiated Marketing

Here marketers select to offer its products or services to a number of diverse segments whose needs, usage of the product or market responses are different. Take the example of a pump manufacturing company. They would have various ranges of pumps (HP-HORSE POWER) to cater to individual houses, skyscrapers and also for agricultural purposes. However, the marketer has to develop a wide range of products, modify them, upgrade then and market them to a wide range of customers. This involves cost. Differentiated marketing is best when company wants to increase its sales, reduce dependency on one single market, needs of each segment varies. Here the marketer wants to have a strong position in the chosen market segments. However multiple product lines, which the company cannot handle and products to directly counter competitions (without any special features) should be avoided.

Undifferentiated Marketing

The products are highly standardized and there is a single product or service catering to the complete market segment. The firm has a single marketing programme, which appeals to all. This could be due to lack of analysis and planning. The advantage of this method is that economies of scale can be achieved. Advertising costs, inventory costs and production costs can be achieved. Advertising costs, inventory costs and product costs can be kept down. But with this kind of strategy where the product is a near commodity, it could pose a big threat to the company. Competitive firms can easily wipe off such markets, with better offerings. Chances of losing business are higher. Companies following such strategies should try and differentiate them.

Niche Marketing

Niche marketing is a narrowly defined customer group, more homogeneous customer groups with specific product requirements catered to individual needs and services. The products are specifically tailored for customers. It is gaining importance in industrial markets and forms a key strength to marketers. In today's highly competitive market place, marketers are focusing heavily into segments which they can successfully compete in. If the niche is large enough, marketers should be able to promote a unique product to cater to that segment. It is an age of information. The buyers in industrial marketing arena have become more demanding as they have availability of information. Similarly industrial marketers with great amount of information are being able to identify and satisfy specific needs of the customers

Business customers in this segment are willing to pay a premium to their suppliers. Not only that competitors find it difficult to attack niche positions. The business marketer must offer unique and tailor made goods, to sustain itself in the long-run, in this segment. However the problem is that big giants can challenge such positions.

Mind Power 4: Improve Business by Branding – Sanjay Limaye

Recently I had an opportunity to meet a group of industrial sales and marketing professionals. The meeting was to review the product offerings of their competitors' products. One competitor stood out from all the others: he charged more and seldom discounted. Detailed analysis showed that the

Contd...

competitor did nothing special in terms of manufacturing, product design, performance or even distribution. Still he was rapidly gaining market share. This success was attributed to "a marketing ploy." Actually, there is no trick or ploy, just good marketing practice. It's called branding!

Branding explains why some products command higher prices and intense loyalty from customers.

To many industrial marketers, branding is something for consumer products. They don't explore opportunity of branding for industrial products.

Brands vs Products

Industrial organizations tend to be more products focused. Look at your own organization and count how many "Product Manager," or purely product- focused roles exist. Probably no "Brand Manager" role, which may explain why there are so few brands and so many products. There is a difference between brands and products.

Products are defined by the physical properties of what they are and what they do. They have prices, specifications, performance, delivery period etc. Product attributes are communicated relatively easily in a variety of ways. Product marketing is all about understanding what people need, and aligning key attributes of products to meet these needs.

Brands are almost the opposite of products. Where a product has a physical presence, brands exist in the hearts and minds of people. Brands convey a character, a promise, and a vision that connects with consumers. Where product attributes can be communicated quickly, a brand's character requires time to mature.

Many Industrial marketers believe creating a unique name and logo for a product is creating a brand. It's not true. These symbols are virtually meaningless if they do not reach out to users with some kind of connecting force. At best, logos and trademarks make it easier for buyers to remember your product and nothing more.

What Great Industrial Brands Do?

Unlike consumer brands, industrial brands may be household names in some industries and unknown in others. Some great brands on my list, such as Hewlett-Packard, Fisher-Rosemount, DuPont, 3M, Cummins, and Millipore, may not be on yours. Regardless of the industry, consumer and industrial brands must succeed on several levels. They are:

1. *Long-term perspective:* Great brands are not trendy, or even "cool." They evoke unique values in users' minds and remain there for decades. Companies that own great brands constantly work to build and maintain this sense of worth. Short-term decisions to cut cost or gain a few points of market share can hurt a brand if they conflict with the brand's character. Remaining relevant over the long-term is based on a commitment to quality.

2. *Defined character:* Great brands have a defined character, and the people who manage the brand are very aware of what it is. The process of defining brand character involves understanding what end-users like and dislike, and what values they associate with the core of the brand concept. Using this knowledge, smart managers decide what not to do.

3. *Invention:* Great brands invent or reshape categories. Just as DuPont created the man-made fibers category, when it invented Nylon. As Apple reshaped the personal computer category, 3M reshaped the engineered materials category and Cummins reshaped the OEM engine market.

4. *Emotional attachment:* The common link between great industrial and consumer brands is the ability to tap into consumer emotions. Nike is a master at tapping into consumer emotions. Nike commercials are works of art; they inspire. The shoes are almost incidental. Industrial products sometime achieve an emotional tie-in too. Philips is one good example of such emotional appeal.

Contd...

5. ***Design consistency:*** Great consumer brands have a consistent look and feel. All Nike shoes, for example, have a distinctive look. Great industrial brands also maintain design consistency. For example, everything about HP has a consistent design. There is a consistency of design in General Electric's industrial products, even across divisions. For example, GE's industrial turbines carry design elements of its medical imaging magnets and aircraft engines.

Branding takes time and dedication

Source: Copyright Industrial Marketing Services. Reprinted with the kind permission of Sanjay Limaye. Visit him at www.inmas.com

POSITIONING

Once the target markets have been selected, the marketer should try and create positioning strategy for each target market.

Remember the famous line of Tata steel- "We also make steel" or "India's no. 1 car manufactures". All these are unique positions that a company takes. A question that comes up is that "What is a unique position?"

Positioning is a distinct place a product occupies in the minds of the target customers vis a vis your competitor products.

In the words of Al Ries and Jack Trout[7] – "Positioning is not what you do to a product. Positioning is what you do to the mind of the prospect."

For industrial markets, positioning is equally important. This can be achieved using the tools of marketing mix and set of competencies that an organization has. But still many industrial marketers are not able to successfully understand and employ positioning.

To develop a positioning strategy, the industrial marketer must first:

1. Identify the unique attribute to differentiate and then
2. Communicate the positioning to the target market

To differentiate the product than that of the competitor, four factors are used:

1. ***Product variable:*** It includes factors like product quality and performance.
2. ***Service variable:*** Marketers offering superior pre-sales and post-sales servicing. The tag line used could be "the largest number of engineers to make your machine run free from trouble".
3. ***Personnel variable:*** Differentiating from the competitors, by recruiting better people and arranging training at all levels.
4. ***Image variable:*** The way a customer perceives a company. It takes years together to build such an image.

Once the differentiating factor has been found out, to distinguish the products from its competitors, it needs to be communicated to the target segment. Here in industrial marketers, it is done through personal selling, advertising and trade shows.

Mind Power 5: Identity: Aligning Positioning and Messaging for Clear Communication

The strongest brands have at their core a clear, succinct expression of the brand's positioning, supported by a portfolio of messages that align with that positioning.

Contd...

Brand Positioning Defined

A brand positioning is the conceptual place you want to own in the target customers mind — the benefits you want them to think of when they think of your brand.

Classic positioning examples include Volvo and "Safety," Crest and "Cavity Protection," and Miller Lite's dual, benefits of "Great Taste. Less Filling." The chart below shows alternative positioning strategies, including sample taglines intended to capture the essence of the brand:

Alternative Positioning Strategies	
■ Position and own the category Benefit - Volvo: Safety - Miller Lite:Great Taste, Less Filling - Disney: Magic	■ Position the product and the consumer - U.S. Army: Be all you can be - Budweiser: For all you do; this Bud's for you - Pepsi: Pepsi generation
■ Position how the company does business - Burger King: Have it your way - United Air Lines: The friendly skies of United - WalMart: Always the lowest price	■ Position against the Competition - Avis: We're#2. We try harder - Seven-up: The Un-cola - Apple: Think different

In order to increase competitive insulation over time, a brand positioning should remain consistent. However, a positioning *may* need to change or evolve to reflect changing market conditions, including new competitors, new technologies and new target customers. Over the years, Crest, for example moved beyond "cavity protection," to encompass "beautiful, healthy smiles," given its expanded benefits (e.g., teeth whitening), new customers (beyond kids) and an expanded product set.

Importantly, a brand should only have one positioning at any one time, to ensure clarity and consistency. Remember, one brand equals one positioning.

The Role of Messaging

Communicating a single benefit, however, can limit a brand's appeal, particularly for higher involvement purchases, where customers seek multiple benefits. (Volvo has a clear positioning, though doesn't sell nearly as many vehicles as Toyota.) In these cases, a messaging framework should be developed to align a broader *portfolio* of messages with the core positioning.

Messaging Framework

In communicating multiple messages, it is important to think about the role that any one message may play in the overall portfolio. The chart below illustrates three specific types of messages and the corresponding roles they play:

Message Type	Role
Ante	Required to gain entry to considered set
Driver	Key benefits that differentiate products and services and drive preference
Reassurance	Elements, often times emotive, that solidify the bond with the customer

Here are some examples:

Contd...

1. ***Message Type 1:*** "Ante" Benefits include the most basic benefit (s) that a product or service may offer. This may be "taste" for food products, "low rates" for financial services or "efficacy" for prescription medications. An offering must deliver on these table stakes" to be part of the consideration set of acceptable brands.

2. ***Message Type 2:*** Driver Benefits often serve as the basis for positioning the product or service. Here, the benefits extend beyond antes to incorporate benefits that drive differentiation and purchase. This might include relationship benefits for a financial services company or extended release for a prescription drug.

3. ***Message Type 3:*** Reassurance Benefits provide an emotional connection with the brand. These benefits often need to be communicated implicitly vs. explicitly. Telling a customer to "feel" a certain' way for using a brand can be off-putting. It's often better to handle reassurance benefits through product delivery and tone and manner.

Source: Copyright with Equi Brand Consulting. All rights reserved. Equi brand is a management consultancy committed to driving profitable growth. You can visit them at www.equibrandconsulting.com. Reprinted with their permission.

CONCLUSION

Resources for any company are limited. Capabilities vary from organization to organization. Customers differ, and buying needs differ. There are too many competitors in the business markets. Thus segmentation is absolutely essential for business markets both at macro and micro levels. The organization must also look in to the cost factor for a segmentation strategy.

Once segmentation is done, the marketer must choose an undifferentiated or differentiated or concentrated market selection strategy. Then the marketer should position himself within the market space.

References

1. Wind and Cardozo (March 1974), "*Industrial Market Segmentation*", Industrial Marketing Management 3, pp155.

2. Lehman and Shaughnessy (April 1974), "*Decision Criteria used in buying different Categories of Products*", *Journal of Marketing*, 38, pp 36.

3. Reeder, Brierty and Reeder, "*Industrial Marketing Analysis, Planning and Control*", pp 227.

4. Wind and Cardozo (March 1974), "*Industrial Market Segmentation*", Industrial Marketing Management, 3, pp 153-166.

5. Bonoma and Shapiro (1983), "*Segmenting the Industrial Market*", Lexington Books, DC Health and Company.

6. Morris 1992), "*Industrial and Organizational Marketing*", MacMillan Publishing Co, New York.

7. Ries and Trout, "*Positioning – The battle for your mind*".

Mind Power 6: A Look at Clarity in Positioning Steve Johnson

Pragmatic Marketing

Positioning is a process that focuses on conveying product value to buyers, resulting in a family of documents which drive all outbound communications. Yet in recent years, it seems as if positioning has 'devolved' into a document of vague superlatives that convey nothing as they attempt to trick the customer into buying the product. The best positioning clearly states how the product will solve specific customer problems.

The why of positioning

Agencies report that companies who have completed positioning documents will save 30 percent to 50 percent of their agency costs. Just as your local video store profits from late fees, the hidden costs of agency work come from all the re-work. Agencies often include an upfront cost allocated for discerning positioning from executive interviews. They interview the VP of Development and learn about company innovation; they interview the VP of Sales and learn about customer intimacy; they interview the company president and learn about stock performance; they interview the product managers and get product specifications. From these varying viewpoints, they attempt to write a campaign theme. On seeing the campaign, the executives say, that's not it. I don't know what I want but I'll know it when I see it."

Does this sound familiar?

Positioning results in a series of well-crafted documents that focus on the buyer and how our solutions improve his life.

The trick to positioning is to understand the value of the product to the buyer. In other words, what problems can you solve for the buyer? Do you know the benefits your customers achieve with your products and services? Not sure? Ask.

Insincere positioning

"The great enemy of clear language is insincerity."

-George Orwell in *1984*

Much of the writing we see in marketing materials seems obscure due to insincerity. It's as if the writer wants to fool the reader into thinking the product is more important than it is, or that the product solves problems better than the competitor's when it doesn't really. If your product is clearly inferior, you cannot fix it with positioning. A product must be adequate for the market need to succeed; no amount of marketing can overcome it. (I can hear some of you thinking about Microsoft. Remember, Microsoft products are not inadequate; they are wonderfully adequate, and backed by strong marketing.)

For those who are stuck in writing jargon and buzzwords, check out *Bullfighter*, an add-in to Microsoft Office that rates your writing for its "bull." It's particularly handy as a non-partisan comment on the writing of others. Run your company and product messages through Bullfighter to see how much is content and how much is nonsense.

Many organizations create cute or clever taglines that don't convey meaning. But cute doesn't work in B2B (and maybe not in B2C either). What does General Electric Company (GE) expect us to think about their "Innovation at Work" tagline? Can we use GE products to be innovative while working? Are their products only good in the workplace? Or perhaps are they working to be innovative in the future? A Google search for this phrase generates over 5,000,000 pages. How meaningful is the phrase to consumers of GE products?

Does anyone believe an enterprise solution will "make your dreams come true?" A Google search for this phrase generates over 3,490,000 pages.

Contd...

For what it's worth, I think that SAP does messaging pretty well: "The Best-Run Businesses Run SAP" and "Innovative Solutions to Innovate Business." The latter phrase results in fewer than 5000 Google hits, all related to SAP.

Solving problems vs speaking specs

As an industry, we wallow in technical jargon and assume that the reader can connect the specs to their problems. Or we hope that our sales people can connect the dots. How unfair to both buyer and seller! The positioning, and thus the marketing materials and sales tools, should explain the value and use specifications to support our promises (if necessary for the buyer).

Compare these two product descriptions posted on eBay for the same product.

First the specification-oriented listing

This is a trailer mounted z-boom model # is TMZ-34/19. This is a 2000 model Genie. This is a great value and innovation in the trailer mounted boom market. It is all electric, which is economical, it has 4 new batteries and new tires. It has a spare tire. The working height is 40 feet. 19ft horizontal reach, articulating jib has 130 degree working range, Compact 34 inch width, 500 lb lift capacity, Large 8 in outrigger footpads, Junction box, shelf and tie down attachment points to accommodate generators up to 2500 W,-Non-marking footpad covers, AC outlet in platform. It also has Surge Brakes, Parking Brake, Horn.

I am the original owner and this has only been used about 40-50 times. It is in excellent working conditions: I own a sign shop and have used it when working on billboards. If you have any additional questions you can call me during the day or e-mail me and I will get back to you. I will also be willing to meet someone within a 300 mile radius of [my hometown] if purchasing with either cash or cashiers check.

Now-a problem-oriented listing (for the same product)

This is a great lift because you don't have to maintain a gas or electric engine. You just hook it up to your vehicle and tow it into position, drop the four outriggers and up you go. Great for trimming trees, construction, or any job where you need a 40-foot reach!

This unit is a 1999 model that was factory refurbished (including new batteries) in 2002 and has been stored inside a hangar since then. It has been used about 10 hours since it was overhauled. The tires have about 300 miles on them including a new spare tire. It looks and operates like new.

This lift has a 500-pound capacity but is narrow enough to fit through many man doors. Plug it in, charge it up, and you are ready for a full day of power lifting!

You can pick it up or I am willing to tow the lift to one of the Shipping firms in [town name] who can flat bed it to your location. All shipping arrangements and fees are the responsibility of the buyer.

For more details and specifications go to <link to manufacturer's product page>.

You don't have to look too closely to notice the specification and jargon in the specification-oriented listing versus the listing talking to the buyer in buyer language. The problem-oriented message left the specs out but provided a link to the manufacturer's spec page.

And the results? The specification-oriented description was listed for two weeks with no bids. The problem-oriented listing sold for the same price as the competitor's minimum bid in four days and three hours.

Focus on the buyer

Most technology companies use a template and often a formula for positioning. The best positioning is put in the context of solving a problem for a specific buyer. That means that there are multiple positioning documents, each conveying product value in terms that resonate with the specific buyer.

Contd...

Start with the generic problem in the industry and the ideal generic solution (which is basically what your product does). Then provide a short primary message, 25 words that you want the buyer to remember, followed by a more detailed product description, again in terms of the buyer's need. Finally, describe the three to five features that are relevant to this buyer profile.

It takes many different people within an organization to make a purchasing decision for a complex product. Typically, we see a financial buyer, a technical buyer, and one or more user buyers. Each of these buyers has a different primary goal and sees product information through a different lens. The user buyers want to know how the features will make their daily job different and better. The financial buyer obviously wants to know how the product will save money for the company, while the technical buyer is primarily concerned with how the product will fit into the existing technology environment. Of course, all buyers want to be assured that the product will satisfy the needs of the users of the product.

How can we use one message to communicate to multiple buyers? Obviously we cannot. We'll need different articulations of our message that resonate with each buyer type.

In Pragmatic Marketing's Practical Product Management® seminar, we illustrate the differing viewpoints in positioning with a sales force automation product. A positioning document written for a salesperson should emphasize the features that reduce his paperwork while the document for the sales manager emphasizes the value of centralized territory data.

Company, family, product positioning

One company quadrupled sales of services just by positioning them using the same process. In fact, aren't services products just like software and hardware? Services should be defined as repeatable offerings that are consistently communicated, sold, and delivered-just like software.

Products and services, as well as families of products, all follow the same method. Within the company's overall message, we articulate how the product, service, or product family solves problems for each type of buyer.

For example, I assume that Microsoft has positioning documents for Microsoft Word (product), Microsoft Office (product family), and Microsoft Corporation (company). It must be true, as each positioning message is so clearly consistent with the others.

Ideally, a product positioning must amplify the company positioning. It may not matter if you do product or company first, but the product positioning must support the company positioning. Every product should integrate with the company message or the product should be spun off into a different company.

Positioning has two main benefits. The one obvious to all marketers is the consistency of message. Each marketing and sales piece communicates exactly the same message. A less obvious benefit, but perhaps the more important one, is that the positioning process forces Product Management to identify and spell out clear benefits for each type of buyer. Without a clear message, most products are doomed to failure.

Mind Power 7: Niche Marketing

Many businesses think that by focusing on specialty products they will become a "niche operator", and that there is something inherently profitable about a "niche business." Finding and creating a successful niche is a more difficult and dynamic challenge than most think. The guideline that follow may help to further explain the what, why and how's of niching.

Contd...

What is a Niche?

1. It is a target market which has needs sufficiently different from a broader market that a firm employing a focused, specialized strategy can achieve a low-cost and/or a unique capability for servicing that market.

2. Although often smaller in size than the general market, there is not necessarily a size constraint (For example, IBM in mainframes up until 1986) or a geographic limit (Rolls Royce has a global niche).

3. It should not be likely to be absorbed into a broad line supply situation like PC's and laptop computers have been.

4. It should be a lasting opportunity (supercomputers) and not a fad (wine coolers) with lower barriers to entry.

5. Ultimately, it should be a game that you can win and be a Dominant No. 1 or a Strong No. 2; otherwise, redefine the boundaries to create a game you can win.

Why is niching possible and preferable?

As the free world economy grows wealth, human beings identify more micro-needs (niches). As economic trade expands, it also becomes more competitive for the 80 percent (+) of all purchases which are mature commodities in the eyes of experienced repeat buyers. You can:

1. Go after volume commodities as a low-cost, high-volume, acceptable service leader selling on price to large or thrifty customers. Competitors with the most capital or ego always think they can win; this is a tough game for firms that are private, profit-oriented or risk-adverse.

2. Strive to be the best service supplier and risk not getting paid for it, because strip-n-shoppers are successful or service is desirable but just unaffordable.

3. Or you can find a new niche with no competition and win that game.

How Do you Niche? Skills That Are Generally Necessary

1. *Get good at marketing:* Look at the 4Cs (Customer, Cost, Channel, Competition) and the 3 Ps (Product, Price, Promotions). Whether you start with a customer need or a product-solution looking for a need, analyze all of the other Cs and Ps to make sure they are included and consistent with one another.

2. Value is a customer perception: You must identify your target customers and know them and their important needs. Meet the critical one(s) perfectly.

3. Focus on market creation

   i) This means filling unmet (existing, articulated) needs instead of trying to-win market share from entrenched, existing competitors.

   ii) Each environmental change can cause new niche possibilities.

   iii) Rapid industry growth creates general or sub-segmented niches.

   iv) Lazy, unfocused, or volume-oriented firms abandon niches, unintentionally; exploit their carelessness,

   v) You must think, act, and move like an entrepreneur, not a shopkeeper or a try-harder traditionalist. Small firms are inherently faster and more flexible for doing this, but most won't change.

4. *Add service-value to commodities:* Even more training maybe needed to be able to sell the added values. Keep focused on:

   i) The benefits of basic service value.

Contd...

    ii)   Insuring great service encounters.

    iii)   Selling the benefits of supply systems that reduce total procurement cost.

5.   ***Sell Value to Value-needers and Buyers:*** Structure and protect against aggressive strip-n-shop value buyers. Don't bother with the (5 percent-10 percent) pure price-buyers. Most ad copy is selling price on generic products instead of special benefits on specialty items for total purchasing or usage value.

6.   ***Constantly improve standards***

    i)   *Newer, better, faster, prettier, etc.:* It always sells to about a third of all buyers - the "what's-new crowd."

    ii)   *Faster service:* Credit check, Cash-them-Out, delivery, etc., seems at first unnecessary, but customers then begin to expect and "need" it.   .
    List every differentiable element you now have and rate it against competitors; improve the ones that matter to your target customers.

    iii)   *Be forward-looking and listening:* Know and change with the "living edge" of customer needs and expectations. Don't be preoccupied with selling volumes of yesterday's products and services. Be quality and profit-growth oriented.

How Do You Look for Niches Appropriate for You?

1.   ***Be realistic:*** You can't be good at everything in an exploding technology/changing world. Downsize, outsource all peripheral activities and focus, specialize, persist and excel at what you do best; enjoy most; and/or is the most critical value-added for controlling the target customers.

2.   ***Audit*** your strengths and rank them.

3.   ***Brainstorm on niches that flow from your strengths*** and from your best customers articulated, unmet needs. If you can't think of 10 or more, try some more. Keep looking – new niches open up every six months with every new environmental change and competitive shift.

4.   ***Narrow the list*** to the two or three niches that seem the most attractive and fit your strengths the best. Test them against all of the other guidelines listed here. Recycle through all of them regularly.

5.   ***Determine how to strengthen your competitive position*** for the best niche; get coach (es) to help. Simultaneously start to cut or harvest losing aspects of your business.

6.   Believe you can be a niche leader and go for being a No. 1 or a strong entrenched No. 2 at the target game. If you wait to imitate what everyone else is doing you are not niching.

Be Watchful of Pitfalls

1.   Don't fall short on achieving a sustainable advantage for the target segment, especially because the opportunity never existed, because it was based on a hunch and not good customer-based surveys.

2.   Don't under-invest and under-persist in selling your story to the target customer. It isn't different and valued until the customer is sold on it in his mind.

3.   Competitors will imitate your successful strategy and may out hustle you even though they were second to the market.

4.   Competitors may out-focus you and split your target market even finer.

5.   Technology may eliminate your barriers to entry.

Contd...

Some Thoughts on Marketing

1. *Be aware of a product's life-cycle:* Win by the changing environment and then lose because of it. Constant listening and adaptation is key. Today's specialty is to tomorrow's commodity; 2-7 year life-cycles.

2. *Don't be ahead of the leading customer:* Fill existing not future needs which they don't yet see or understand. Keep in mind bell-shaped curve of adaptation.

3. *Don't offer wildly exaggerated differentiation at ridiculous prices* unless you are in a wildly exaggerated neighbourhood.

4. *Don't do extra services and neglect the basics.*

5. *The future is not to those who "buy better" and cheapen the product and service, but rather to those who sharpen their marketing needs analysis and fulfillment.* Customers want perfect, individualized options of flawless quality tangibles and perfect distinctive service at competitive prices for total best value for them in their minds.

Marketing has gone from "allocation" marketing, to mass marketing of black phones, white refrigerators, etc., to "segmented" marketing, to micro, niche, one-on-one database marketing. Example: "Dear Mr. Merrifield: As an active tennis player, we thought you might be Interested in our sensational new type of (micro-niche tennis gear)..."

Source: Copyright with "The Merrifield Consulting Group". Visit them at www.merrifield.com. Reprinted with permission.

QUESTIONS FOR DISCUSSION

1. What are the macro factors, which the industrial marketer would use for segmentation?

2. Can industrial services market be segmented? Explain with an example.

3. Take an industrial product and segment the market. If you were the industrial marketer which segment would you have targeted and why?

4. How does customer experience affect market segmentation?

5. While an industrial market is entering in to a new market segment, it involves more commitment than his counterparts in consumer goods industry. Why?

6. What are the limitations of market segmentation?

7. "Niche Marketing" is becoming more important – Why?

chapter NINE

Industrial Products, New Product Development and Services

COMPANY PROFILE 9: ONGC (OIL AND NATURAL GAS CORPORATION)

ONGC is Asia's best Oil and Gas Company, as per a recent survey conducted by US-based magazine *Global Finance*. It ranks as the 2nd biggest E and P company (and 1st in terms of profits), as per the Plan's Energy Business Technology (EBT) Survey 2004. It ranks 24th among Global Energy Companies by Market Capitalization in PFC Energy 50 (December 2004). ONGC was ranked 17th till March 2004, before the shares prices dropped marginally for external reasons. It is placed at the top of all Indian Corporate listed in Forbes 400 Global Corporate (rank 133rd) and Financial Times Global 500 (rank 326th), by Market Capitalization. It is recognized as the Most Valuable Indian Corporate, by Market Capitalization, Net Worth and Net Profits, in current listings of Economic Times 500 (4th time in a row), Business Today 500, Business Baron 500 and Business Week.

ONGC today, is repositioning itself to foster the principle of relational enterprise through partnerships/strategic alliances/joint ventures with preferred partners and adopt a business strategy which relies on company skills and positional assets with focus on core business areas and opportunity specific diversification. ONGC has recognized the need to expand its business through profitable ventures related to petroleum and energy sectors by entering into joint ventures with other Indian and foreign companies. ONGC-Joint Venture Group (ONGC – JVG) has been formed to give impetus to joint venture activities in areas other than E and P. Petronet Lng Limited is in place with ONGC having 12.5 percent equity interest for import and marketing of LNG in India. Other partners in this venture are IOC, GAIL and BPCL each with 12.5 percent equity. The Exploration Contract Monitoring (EXCOM) Group is the exclusive business face of ONGC for jointly operated oil and gas exploration and production ventures within India. It is the nodal agency of ONGC for single window E and P business communication with companies and the government Oil and Natural Gas Corporation Ltd. (ONGC) is engaged in E and P activities both in Onshore and Offshore. The Corporation is now venturing out to new areas, i.e. deepwater exploration and drilling, exploration in frontier basins, marginal field development, optimization of field development plan field recovery and other allied areas of service sector. Engagements in these areas will require best-in-class technology, processes and practices and savvy use of the research and development assets to their fullest advantage.

Everyone who works at ONGC is responsible for protecting the environment, health and safety of the people and communities worldwide. Commitment to SHE performance is an integral part of business, and achieving cost-effective solution is essential to long-term success.

The dedication to the causes of environment and safety in ONGC is amply demonstrated by the fact that a separate institute named **Institute of Petroleum Safety, Health and Environment Management (IPSHEM)** had been set-up way back in 1989 to deal with these issues.

ONGC is playing an important role in strengthening the fabric of society. This flagship Company in India's corporate world has a finely tuned sense of moral responsibility towards the community of people where it operates and the country at large.

Local population is the one which is benefited most as a result of the ONGC operations in the region. It generates employment and business opportunities, which in turn improves the overall economy of the region and the living standards of the community. ONGC operations provide the necessary boost required for the industrial growth of the region. The requirement of the physical inputs for ONGC's operations results in setting of ancillary industries and vendors network, generating a lot of economic potential.

Oil and gas production ushers an era of growth, many core sector industries like power, fertilizer and transport, thrive as a natural consequence of the oil and gas availability. Apart from this, grants-in-aid, help in building schools and hospitals. Villages are adopted and several health and community welfare programmes are organized in the area.

Apart from benefits accruing to the region from the primary function of the corporation, i.e., exploration and production of hydrocarbons by way of direct and indirect employment and fiscal contributions to the exchequer of both State and Central Governments. ONGC has been extending full support in the overall development of the areas around its operations all over the country.

Source: www.ongcindia.com

Mind Power I: A Strategic Approach to Product and Process Development – Kenneth Crow

Introduction

In our globally linked economy, product development capabilities are the basis for successful competition. Successful product development requires fundamentally improved approaches to organizing the development process, reducing waste, and providing products to meet customer needs in order to respond to global competition in our own markets as well as compete effectively on a global basis. Integrated Product Development practices (IPD) and time-to-market are key elements in competitive success. IPD orients product design to customer needs and the company's production capabilities. More broadly, it enhances integration of product and process design with strategic objectives, improves organizational effectiveness, and provides a framework for effectively implementing design technology.

The traditional approach to improvement in U.S. manufacturing has been to break down the enterprise into more understandable functional units and work centers, study each one individually, and then optimize the operations of each unit. The optimization of individual units has been at the expense of sub optimization of the whole enterprise. This functionally oriented thinking has resulted in barriers between departments. This is exemplified by the "wall" between Engineering and Manufacturing with designs being "thrown over the wall" to manufacturing without adequate regard to producibility. IPD requires that the enterprise be viewed in a more integrated manner. This integration considers three dimensions:

1. Strategic integration to tie decision-making and the pattern of enterprise activities to a focused direction that allows an organization to distinguish itself in the marketplace.

2. Functional integration which organizes and links the various functional areas of an enterprise to work together more effectively and optimize the whole.

3. Logistic or supply chain integration which extends integration concepts beyond the manufacturer's four walls to its customers and its suppliers.

Since product and process design have such a major influence on the competitiveness of the enterprise, it is especially critical that the design function be better integrated with the other functions of the enterprise. This means integration within the engineering function (For example, integration of both product design with process design and integration of electrical, mechanical and software design), integration of the design and engineering function with the rest of the enterprise, and integration of the engineering function with external organizations (customers and suppliers).

Contd...

This integration will result in the release of more mature product designs which can be more effectively produced within a company's existing or planned production system and more effectively supported. New product design and introduction lead time or time-to-market will be reduced to meet rapidly changing technology and customer demands and increase enterprise flexibility. More specifically, the objectives of Integrated Product Development are:

1. The design of products to better meet customer needs and quality expectations.

2. The design of processes or the consideration of process capabilities in designing products in order to produce products at a more competitive price.

3. Reduction of product and process design cycle time or time-to-market to bring products to market earlier.

4. High productivity through release of producible designs and minimization of disruptive design changes.

The accomplishment of these objectives requires an integrated approach to product and process design which considers the company's business strategy. This integrated approach to product and process design rests on:

1. Alignment of product development with business strategy;

2. Organizational integration using product development teams or integrated product teams as a way to organize development activities;

3. A well-defined and optimized development process;

4. Integrated design automation tools oriented toward creating, analyzing and using digital product data to move a product into production;

5. Optimization of the product and process design to enhance manufacturability, testability, affordability, reliability, maintainability, etc.

In applying these tools and concepts, the organization must be restructured, cultural issues considered, and communication among different functional units improved.

Integration of development with business strategy

The enterprise's product and process design approach must be linked to the business strategy. Hayes and Wheelwright define five dimensions to competition: cost, quality/performance, flexibility, dependability and innovativeness. A world class manufacturer must be effective in all five dimensions, but can only excel in one or two dimensions. An enterprise's strategy must be considered in the approach to product and process design. For example, the low cost producer must optimize the product design to the company's production system and consider high volume, highly automated production processes. The flexible producer with lower production volume would develop flexible production processes and a design engineering function with greater degrees of design freedom and flexible, automated product and process design capabilities.

In any case, a general strategy for manufacturers is to move toward focused factories which concentrate on doing a few things well. This implies focused product and process design which further implies standardization and simplification of products and parts within each focused facility. (If the product has been designed intelligently, it will be possible to provide a great deal of product variety through combining assembly modules and adding product options late in the manufacturing process.) Through standardization and simplification, a company will be able to focus its attention on the producibility of its preferred parts and products. These standardized families of parts and products will require a more limited set of manufacturing processes. A company can then focus on developing these products and processes considering its selected dimensions of competition such as follows:

Contd...

Basis of Competition and Product and Process Development Implications

Cost	A strong emphasis on target costing, design-to-cost, value engineering, and design for manufacturability, minimum product variety. Significant manufacturing and accounting involvements in developing. Suppliers are well-integrated into the development process. Factory uses high volume equipment specifically-oriented to the product; automated material handling.
Quality/Reliability/ Dependability	A disciplined and rigorous product development process. Strong focus on understanding customer needs and providing products that meet those needs. Use of techniques like FMEA, FTA, FRACAS, DOE, Taguchi methods, poke-yoke, and reliability prediction. Heavy emphasis on testing and qualification. Processes are oriented to self-checking and adjustment use of computer-aided inspection and test equipment.
Time-to-Market	Use of modular design approaches. Sufficient resources to undertake development processes underway. Continuous surveillance of the marketplace and understanding of customer needs. Well-defined development processes based on tightly integrated design automation tools. Well-planned and managed programmes with clear definition and acceptance of responsibilities. Process equipment to handle a wide range of work envelopes; FMS; quick set-up and changeover
Innovativeness/ Technology	A technology plan and roadmap based on the business and product strategy and plan. Effective technology management. Process to review new technologies developed outside for applicability internally. Effective process to deploy new technology to development programmes. State-of-the-art design and analysis tools to support requirements of new technology. Policies to invest in training and development of personnel to master new technology. Culture, open to new ideas and taking risks. Investment in new process technology.

A starting point is to define and understand the company's marketplace, customer needs and competition. Based on this assessment, the company's primary competitive dimensions can be selected and a strategy defined to develop and enhance these competitive dimensions. Once this is done, product and process design based on IPD can be oriented to implement this strategy

Source: Kenneth A. Crow is president of DRM associates, a management consulting and education firm focusing on integrated product development practices. You can visit them at www.npd-solutions.com. Reprinted with permission.

Mind Power 2: Are you Squandering Research and Development Resource? – Dan Adams

Most industrial companies are. Funny thing is that many large corporations already know they are squandering at least half of their tens-to-hundreds of millions of research and development dollars. (Multiple studies show companies waste 50-75 percent of their research and development on unsuccessful new products.) They just don't know which half. Well, they actually do know, but not until after the money has been spent.

It's not that the labs are filled with technical people who can't find the right answers. They're just being asked the wrong questions. Questions that are unimaginative, being asked at too many other labs and—if they can be solved— create too little value. Questions that is too obvious.

These questions fall into one of two camps: wrong-market questions and wrong-need questions. The former occur when scientists and engineers are asked to develop products for market segments that are either unwinnable or not worth winning. This is an outrage, a terrible waste... and the subject of another paper. For now, let's consider wrong-need questions and the ensuing footrace.

Contd...

What Footrace Are You In?

Does this sound familiar? An important customer tells your sales rep what they want. That starting pistol shot begins the race, and your sales rep quickly drops the request off at research and development's doorstep, properly packaged and labeled of course, research and development may ask the rep to go back and ask more questions, but once he's handed the baton to them, his leg of the relay is pretty much done.

Since the customer is clever, it's a good bet that several other sales reps brought back the same request to their companies. Terrific, Now you're all in the same footrace, with the customer waiting patiently to see who crosses the finish line. If more than one of you makes it, you can forget that price premium you were hoping for.

What if you ran a different race? This time, you choose the race time and place by targeting an attractive market segment opportunity... which you pursue with a programme of in-depth customer interviews. A two-or-three person technical-marketing team uses advanced probing to uncover customers' *unspoken* needs. And since your team knows how to engage the customer in collaborative brainstorming, it will probably bring back some *unimagined* needs as well. The race is on and your competitors don't even know it.

The new product you develop is like nothing the customer has seen before (nor will they for a long time if your patents are in order.) It delivers real value, which the customer shares with you by paying a fair price premium.

Moving into the NO-Zone (Non-Obvious)

Patents are only granted if they are useful, novel and non-obvious. So we already appreciate the value of non-obvious science. What about the value of non-obvious market demand? If you'll work through this with me, you'll see this value can be enormous.

First, imagine your customer has obvious and non-obvious needs that you can learn about both, and that these needs are equally important. If you could pursue any of the four product types shown in the figure below—Me-Too, Long-Shot, Leading or Dominant—which would you pursue? It's a question of risk and reward where (a) risk is driven by the *likelihood* you'll find a technical solution and (b) reward is greatly boosted if you are the *exclusive* solution supplier.

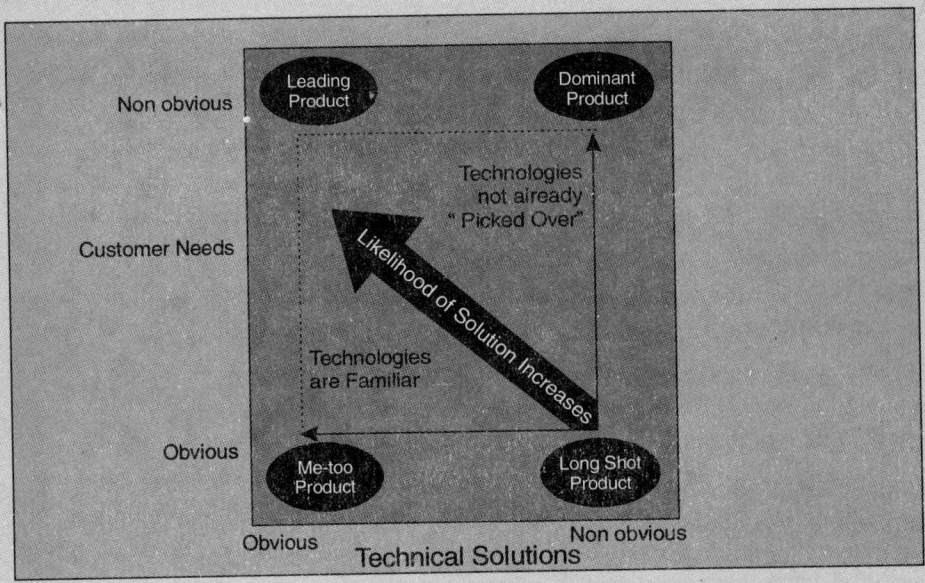

What is the Project Risk?

Contd...

In the previous figure, you'll see the likelihood of technical success increases as you move to the upper-left—obvious solutions for non-obvious needs. Of course, the vector points left because you get to use tried-and-true technical solutions. But it also points up because you're trying to answer a question that hasn't been asked before. This means the technical solutions haven't been picked over by others like the bones of a long-dead wild beast.

That's the risk profile. The reward profile is determined by how much value you bring the customer and whether or not you are the exclusive supplier of this value. This last point is huge. You might bring new value to the customer with your product and share it on a 50/50 basis. But if your competitor figures out how to deliver the same value, nearly all of it can quickly swing to your customer.

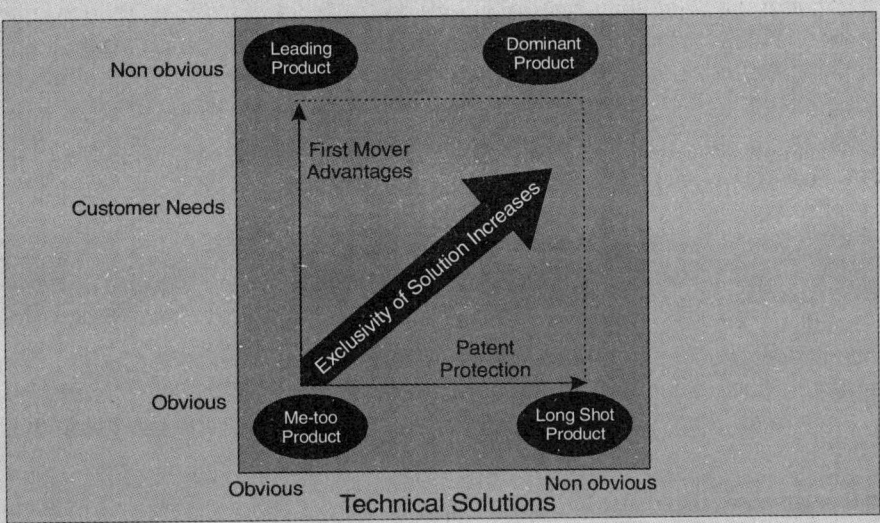

What is the Project Reward?

In the above figure, your exclusivity increases if you can patent a non-obvious technical solution. But it also increases if you are the first to discover and satisfy a non-obvious need, even with an obvious technical solution. You'll have "first-mover" advantages—industry reputation, branding, early learning-curve experience, the ability to set industry standards... and perhaps a patent based on application.

Since a project's attractiveness is a combination of its risk and reward, the profiles can be added together. By dealing with non-obvious customer needs (the NO-Zone), you'll be the first to pursue important needs. This makes it more likely you'll succeed technically, and gives you first-mover market advantages if you do.

So Which Projects Should You Pursue?

I believe most companies can help themselves greatly by spending less time in the O-Zone. It's far too crowded and frankly, it's just plain *hard* to win here. But under the right circumstances, there's room for each project type:

1. *Me-Too:* These won't bring you much value, but some may be needed to fill out your product line.

2. *Long-shot:* While these can be a resource sinkhole, they can be worthwhile if you have likely technical path.

3. *Leading Product:* Make this your first line of attack in most cases. Only move off this if you can't uncover any non-obvious needs or obvious technical solutions.

4. *Dominant Product:* These can give you blockbuster value, but don't start here: What's the point of a patented solution if competitors find an obvious solution to the same new need? Pursue this if you need more product benefit than you can get with obvious technology alone.

Contd...

Shifting Your Workload

By moving into the NO-Zone you can get much more out of your research and development organization without adding more resources. But you will have to shift the workload... specifically by shifting work forward and outward. You'll shift the work forward in time by conducting in-depth customer interviews before the costly product development stage begins. And you'll shift work outward by spending more time talking to customers. But the pay-off will be in far greater research and development efficiency. Your cost will be a fraction of what you would have wasted.

When you do this, you'll be adding a dimension to your thinking that your competitors lack. They'll be working on project portfolios in the O-Zone, balancing Me-Too and Long-Shot projects, completely missing the dimension of non-obvious needs. They'll be squandering resources in the zone of lowest possible research and development-efficiency. Meanwhile, you'll be competing where your competitors are *not*... by asking better questions. And you'll be running a footrace by yourself. Now that's a footrace you can win.

Source: Copyright with Advanced Industrial Marketing Inc. Visit them at www.aimtolead.com. Reprinted with permission. Learn more at www.newproductblueprinting.com.

Mind Power 3: Product Strategy Doesn't Just Happen – Ed Crowley

What is a successful product strategy? A successful product strategy is the use of a firm's product-related resources in such a way as to maximize growth and profitability opportunities. Sounds easy, doesn't it? In reality, developing the product strategy is one of the toughest challenges that companies face.

Product strategy development

There are several challenges in developing and executing product strategy. The major challenges include:

1. The product strategy consists of both a planning (defining the strategy) and execution (developing the products) phase. If either planning or execution is flawed, the product strategy is likely to fail;

2. The development and execution of the product strategy takes place within a complex market environment and success can be heavily influenced by external variables (the competition, the economy, and even regulation); and,

3. Developing a realistic product strategy involves multiple functions within the company, and close collaboration between these functions. These functions often have conflicting objectives (for example: Development wants to meet schedule while reducing cost, however, Marketing may want to add features which will increase product cost and increase schedule risk).

I believe that most individuals involved in the New Product Development (NPD) process will agree to these challenges. However, my next statement may not find as much agreement. I believe that without a process for managing the product strategy, 99 percent of all product strategies are doomed to failure! And without a successful product strategy, most businesses will ultimately fail.

What do I mean by a "process for managing the product strategy"? In its simplest form, this process is a repeatable, measurable methodology for defining and managing the company's product strategy and product portfolio. Firms will often have a "product roadmap" which undergoes annual reviews among a few key executives during which time resources are allocated and priorities are set. However, having a roadmap does not constitute a product strategy process. A product strategy process must be measurable, have definable checkpoints, and must involve all of the stakeholders in the process. In addition, it must have mechanisms for incorporating the external factors (competitor strategies, new product announcements, market trends, and market forecasts the "marketing intelligence"

Contd...

functions) and internal factors (funding, human/development resources, access to technology, and paths to markets) which will impact the success of the product strategy.

Product strategy traits

It's very important to recognize that "one size doesn't fit all" when it comes to product strategy. Depending on the competitive intensity within your industry, the intellectual property landscape, and your internal resources, your product strategy process may be very simple or it may be very complex. The product strategy process must be crafted to suit the needs and abilities of your specific organization. However, I believe that most successful, product strategy processes share several common traits:

1. They have a method for incorporating external market information early in the process as a basis for setting basic product strategy priorities. Good product strategy processes are not formed in a vacuum. They incorporate a keen understanding of the market needs, market dynamics, and market trends.

2. They encourage collaboration among corporate functions including Development, Marketing, Supply Chain/Manufacturing, and Finance. This implies that the process is well known, and understood by all functions. Additionally, there must be a method for resolving disagreements and conflicting priorities in a constructive manner.

3. Someone "owns" the product strategy, process and holds final responsibility for ensuring the strategy is complete, and that all parties are in agreement to the final product strategy. I have seen this work successfully when either development, marketing, or corporate strategy groups are the "owners" of the product strategy. The key issue is to ensure there is an "owner" who is responsible for gaining consensus and publishing and maintaining the product strategy.

4. Successful processes are followed religiously and are gates/foundations to other corporate processes. While the strategy itself may change during the year based on internal or external factors, the product strategy process happens every year according to a pre-defined time table. Other key deliverables (such as the annual budget) depend on the completion of this product strategy definition before they can occur.

Product Strategy myths

When developing a product strategy process, it is important to avoid falling into the trap of believing common myths regarding the product strategy process including.

Myth 1: Product strategy is only for large multinational companies with massive budgets and "armies" of internal resources

Unless you have a product/service which doesn't have any competition (and never will have), you need a product strategy process—regardless of the size of your company. You must be constantly adapting your portfolio to achieve or sustain a competitive advantage.

Myth 2: I have product roadmap-therefore, I have a product strategy process

Wrong! While a product roadmap is a valuable deliverable from the product strategy process, much of the value of the product strategy process comes from assessing the market on a regular basis, collaborating with the different functions to develop the "best" strategy, and rigorously validating and invalidating your assumptions about the market. You can have a roadmap without having an effective product strategy process.

Myth 3: Our company —— (founder, visionary, development guru......you fill in the blank) knows exactly what products we need so he/she can define the product strategy without the need for a product strategy process

Contd...

This is one of the easiest and most dangerous myths. Regardless of how intelligent this individual is, they are not infallible. And, as time goes on, the original founder, visionary, etc., often becomes less effective and more subject to being blindsided by "disruptive" competitors because they have a significant tendency to focus on those customers/products/services that made them successful in the first place.

Myth 4: An outside consultant cannot help with our process because they don't know our company/industry

Okay, many consultants probably deserve the rap they get for bringing in a "cookie cutter" approach to solving each business' issue without really understanding the firm's business or industry. The truth is no consultant will ever know your company as well as you do. However, they can bring a keen understanding of the market and a different set of eyes for a fresh perspective (note, I didn't say unbiased. Let's face it; everyone brings their own set of biases to the table). Most importantly, they can assist in developing the process itself because of their ability to assess how your current process (or lack thereof) is working without having a stake in the "turf wars" often found inside companies. A good consultant will focus on what you want to achieve with your process (as opposed to selling you a "canned" approach) and will take ownership in ensuring the process is a success.

Myth 5: A good product strategy process will use X software or X number of steps

A good product strategy process does not have to be complex, or have a certain number of steps, or use a certain piece of software. A good product strategy process will "fit" your organization, your organization's culture, and will deliver measurable results. This means that one size doesn't fit all and your process will need to be designed to fit the unique aspects of your firm.

The goal for any business is to drive profitable, sustained growth over the long-term. Meeting this goal requires a product strategy process, regardless of your company size. Keep in mind that this article addresses the issues facing a "manufacturing products" firm, but similar challenges face the services company, too, although some of the dynamics are different

Source: Ed Crowley has founded the Photizo Group (www.photizogroup.com) as a consulting resource for clients who are focused on driving sustained business growth. Mr. Crowley has over 20 years experience in the high tech marketing field including positions with Lexmark International, Texas Instruments, IntelliQuest, and VTEL. You can contact Ed at **eacrowley@phottzogroup.com**. All rights reserved. Copyright with Photizo Group.

INTRODUCTION

In the previous chapter, we have seen the importance of analyzing the market place and selecting a suitable market. Now to get success in those markets would require suitable products. The product forms the core of the marketing mix, as that would be the one, which would be giving the customer, satisfaction. So, the products form the most important component of the mix, making it very difficult for the marketer. They need to make a product which is acceptable. Thus venturing into new product lines, developing new products becomes very risky, as the success rates are very low. In order to understand potential products, a marketer must evaluate the various opportunities he has, the competitive factor in the market and its own strengths and weakness. The problem of designing a suitable product becomes much more complex, for industries which rapidly change in terms of technology.

Thus we see that product forms the most important of all in terms of the decision, that a company needs to take. The marketer will align his resources to achieve organizational goals. The product also influences other three variables of the mix-namely price, place, promotion. One more point that needs to be looked in here is that all the departments of the organization will play a key role in the success of the product. In cases of failure, all the departments would be equally responsible.

In developing product strategies, an organization has two primary goals:[1]

1. The product mix should be in line with the organizational objectives.

2. To set guidelines for developing product lines and items.

Mind Power 4: Defence and Technology

Laptops, mobiles speak of the rapid turnover in the technological arena. It only takes few months before a smaller, sleek model comes to market, asking consumers to replace their old ones that are still working, especially in nations which are potentially growing. People are convinced with new models coming in. How does a critical industry, such as defense sector, cope with technology?

Replacing sensitive framework in defence takes long time and becomes a huge financial risk. Not only is it a trouble to assemble systems but also train the operators with the new systems.

Investing on advanced technology can cost a fortune. Government agencies insist on confidentiality, quality and performance. Defence technology should survive in rugged terrains and secure from poor environmental condition.

Industrial Products

Product is just not the physical properties. It is a complex relationship with multiple factors of influence between the buyer and the seller. The relationship could be economic, personnel, technical or legal.

Now, when an industrial buyer purchases a product, he is looking in for three things. They are:

1. Basic features

2. Enhanced features

3. Augmented features

Basic feature would be the characteristics for which they have been purchased. They are the fundamental benefits that the customer is looking in for.

Enhanced features are the additions to the basic features that make the product differentiable. It could be colour, quality, design, style and feature. For example if an organization is buying computers for its employees a lot many other factors like software, ease of operation, would be looked into.

Augmented features are the benefits given with the purchase of a particular product. Examples would be after sales service, availability of spares, technical assistance, delivery, financing etc.

Mind Power 5: From the A300 to the A380: Pioneering Leadership

Some of the advances incorporated in the Airbus product line have been groundbreaking, while others were incremental. All have contributed to making Airbus aircraft the most advanced on the market.

Airbus' reputation for innovation started with the A300 - the cornerstone of its aircraft family. When it entered service in 1974; the A300 was the airline industry's first twin-engine wide body aircraft. Its optimized fuselage cross-section was retained for the A330 and A340 airliners that followed, providing wide body comfort for passengers and accommodating industry-standard LD3 containers side-by-side in the lower-deck cargo hold.

Contd...

The A300 was equipped with Category IIA autoland capability in 1977, allowing the aircraft to land in limited visibility. In the early 1980s, the A300 became the first twin-aisle aircraft to have a two-crew cockpit with all instruments in front of the pilots, using the latest in digital technology. Soon after, Airbus introduced advanced cathode ray tube cockpit displays and composite materials in secondary structures on the A310.

By 1985, composites were applied on primary structures and in the innovative drag-reducing wingtip devices that were being introduced on the A310-300. Today, composites are used throughout with the A380, the sole aircraft employing them in the centre wing box and rear fuselage.

The world's first carbon-fibre keel beam for a large commercial aircraft was built for the A340-600, and Airbus' 21st century airliner – the 555-seat A380 – is continuing the tradition of innovation with the increased use of Carbon Fibre Reinforced Plastic (CFRP), and the first application of glass fibre-aluminium laminate on a civil airliner. Airbus was also the first to introduce laser beam welding on a civil aircraft—a technology that began on the A318, and which is now used extensively on the A380.

Airbus broke new ground in 1988 for aircraft systems with the introduction of electronically-managed fly-by-wire flight control and side-stick controllers on the A320 - advanced features that have become favourites of pilots around the world, and which are employed across the Airbus family of aircraft.

Further advances in systems have been made on subsequent Airbus aircraft, with innovations for the A380 including high-pressure hydraulics and variable-frequency electrical generation- both of which reduce weight and boost system performance. Other advances for the A380 include an Autopilot Traffic Collision Avoidance System that offers additional protection when compared to conventional TCAS systems, and the Airbus-patented "Brake-to-Vacate" technology, which allows pilots to select an appropriate runway exit when landing and regulate the aircraft's speed and deceleration accordingly.

Source: http://www.airbus.com/en/corporate/innovation

One point that one needs to remember is that buyers whether B2B or B2C do not purchase the basic features. The buyers look in for something extra, some kind of value addition to the original product.

The expectations of buyers are rising and competition is becoming global. Thus the product which the marketer wishes to offer has become a priority to all organizations. Thus, quality of a product is becoming a very strong determining force for the success. Companies like Xerox Corporation insist that the suppliers to maintain quality standards as a prerequisite for qualification. Although Japanese companies are champions in managing and delivering quality, the American counterparts are not way behind. India, also is working towards developing global products which are as superior to their western counterparts, although a lot has to be done in that regard.

A marketer can find it beneficial, if the product they offer is more superior in terms of the value, in comparison to competitors. Thus value generation has two important components, i.e., quality and price. The quality will also depend on two factors, i.e., product and service.

Service forms a very key component in the total value to a customer. In cases wherein a marketer, has to customize his products might require close coordination in between the various departments. Post-purchase servicing is very essential in industrial marketing, as we had discussed earlier. The objective is to generate higher value than competitors.

PRODUCT POLICY

Products are for customer's need satisfaction. Thus changes in consumer needs, preferences, technology, government policies and product life cycles play a very key role in the firm's product offering. Industries which see rapid changes in technology, require keeping themselves aware and acting accordingly. Changing laws, rules and policies also have an effect on the product offerings to the market. PLC also plays a key role in the product policy. As products are introduced in the markets, proactive companies invest for future products. Most products reach the decline stage and for the company to exist and compete, the introduction of new and successful products is very essential. Thus the product policies and strategies will depend on four important factors. They are:

1. Changes in customer needs and preferences

2. Changes in laws, rules and policies

3. Changes in technology

4. Product life cycle

The product line for industrial products can be divided in to four categories. They are:[2]

1. *Proprietary Products:* Products which are offered with set configurations and produced in anticipation of orders.

2. *Custom built Products:* Products with numerous options available to buyers to modify alter for their requirements.

3. *Custom designed Products:* Products made to meet the needs of a specific set of customers. For example, Arms and ammunitions.

4. *Industrial services:* Services like guidance, consultancy, operation and maintenance.

All of the above mentioned products are unique and will have their own set of challenges. Each of them requires separate set of strengths that the marketer must possess.

PRODUCT LIFE CYCLE STRATEGIES

The product life cycle theory is to determine what strategies a marketer needs to follow, thought the life cycle of a product. Any product, be it a consumer product or an industrial product passes through a series of period, and shows a set of typical characteristics, before if finally ends or becomes an obsolete technology. The strategies that a marketers needs to follow at every stages would be different. This is to maximize sales and profits. In industrial marketing, where innovations are faster and changes are more frequent, marketers must appreciate the concept of PLC. Moreover, in certain industries where technology changes are very rapid, the need is to appreciate the changes and tailor make the strategies to suit the stages of the PLC.

The question that comes up is whether the PLC is of any value to marketer. Can we pinpoint a product in the PLC? In case a marketer can do that, what would be the course of action at that particular stage?

Introduction

Here in this stage, the acceptability of a product is determined by the market. Products which bring in a paradigm shift, and a new trend in the market place. It takes time to gain confidence amongst industrial buyers. However determining the product acceptance is a tough job, because the buyers have a preconceived notion and also has a set perception of the value he wants to receive. When the products gain easy acceptance in the market, the marketer should try and beat the competition. They should bring in early brand awareness in the market. The marketer should try and generate trial in the market, and these products generally carry with them high levels of margin for the distributors.

Growth

Once the stage of creating trial passes off and sales start picking, it would be very necessary to establish a strong presence in the market. The focus of the marketer should lie to build on designing, distribution and servicing. An aggressive promotional strategy should be followed. In case of rapid increase of competitors, the marketer must suitably take advantage of the price benefits which would be due to the experience curve and economies of scale. This would create a strong point for the marketer to regain its strength in the market.

Maturity

When the demand for the product reaches the maturity stage, the strategy for the marketer should be to either focus on a set of customers or find a new set of buyers or else can enter new markets with alterations to the product. In this stage, relationships with dealers play a very key role and the marketer should get ready to phase out the product and bring in a new product to the market.

Decline

This stage may come in due to various reasons. Marketers need to take a stand to phase out the product or to maximize the profits and let the product die down a natural death. However, most industrial marketers at the maturity stages, tend to pass the product to countries which are technologically less superior.

However, the PLC will take a different shape for technological and high tech products. In these industries, technology grows at a fast rate, the risk of obsolescence is high and research and development costs are skyrocketing.

Locating Industrial Products in their Life Cycles

Locating an industrial product in their life style is a tough task. It is not possible to accurately pinpoint. It depends on number of factors like industry growth, profits, total units purchased. However on a general note, to locate the product:

1. A trend analysis study needs to be done.
2. A study of competition, with focus on their product performance.
3. Estimation of future sales and profitability data.
4. Analysis of data trends in similar industries and products.

Developing Product Strategies[3]

When we speak of developing product strategies we mean dealing with multiple numbers of issues. An industrial company would be having a number of products with them. But if we take a close look at them, all the products might not be performing at their fullest potential. Some need to be phased out, some need to be shifted and others needed to be altered. Thus an organization would have to decide how to maximize profitability and sales from the range of products that they have.

Product Evaluation Matrix

Once a marketer has the data relating to a particular product (as we have discussed earlier) he can combine all these data into a product evaluation matrix.

As we all in the above figure that we have three major factors. The company, sales, industry sales and market share. An industrial marketer may have its products on any part of the matrix.

Let us say a product P_1 which has reducing company sales. The products industry share is also reducing. The marketer at this point may decide to phase out these products.

A product P_2 which has stable company sales and stable industry sales. The product is also dominating in the market. The marketer can choose to focus more on the product to expand the pie in the market.

Company sales		Decline		Stable		Growth	
Industry sales	Market share	Below Target	Above Target	Below Target	Above Target	Below Target	Above Target
Growth	Dominating Average Marginal						
Stable	Dominating Average Marginal				P_2		
Decline	Dominating Average Marginal	P_1					

Some strategies that could be followed by the entire product line are:

1. Maintaining the product and strategy in current form
2. Only change of strategy
3. Dropping a product
4. Altering a product
5. Adding newer products

Perceptual Mapping

It helps the marketer to understand the position of competing brands relating to one another. It tells the marketer about the strengths and weaknesses of a product when compared to competitors.

Let us say, there are three products A,B,C. Product 'A' is our product range and the other products are competing directly against us. Two characteristics are picked for comparisons, i.e., quality and price. Product A is a low-priced and medium quality product. So what should the marketer do? He has options of both raising the quality as well as price, as well as both. He can also make a high quality, high price product to compete directly against B. So here the marketer needs to decide, where is he ideally going to locate the product or is the current position, perfectly all right.

Revitalising and Eliminating Products

Many a times industrial marketers would confront themselves to two set of questions. Do we need to revitalize our product line and do we need to eliminate some of the products from the line? These questions could come in mind, when the sales volume, profitability, industry growth and market share is falling, or the performance is unsatisfactory. Thus to revitalize a product or a range of product would mean to take precautionary and corrective measures for the product to perform at its fullest potential. It would also be possible at times, that it is impossible to raise the performance to a particular product. The marketer at that time may decide to eliminate such product from the line.

A question obviously comes into the mind, is that why do products perform badly. There could be multiple reasons as to why a product can perform poorly in the market. Some of the major reasons are:

1. High cost of manufacturing due to obsolete technology

2. Problem relating to production

3. High cost of distribution

4. Superiority of competitors product

5. Poorly designed or poor customer feedback.

However, the earlier the marketer is able to trace such problem, the easier it becomes for him to track and correct the mistakes. Proactive actions need to be taken and the marketer should look into ways to reduce cost and improve profitability. The marketer must also try to reduce wastage and improve servicing, quality and features.

Sometimes, the marketer may decide to eliminate some products of the business line. This might happen mostly due to profitability factors and growth factors. However, alternative substitutes to customers should be made available. Now to decide on to the eliminating factor, some of the essential points that a marketer will keep in mind are:

1. The potential for new products in capturing market share

2. Actions of competitors

3. Customer relations

4. Impact on profitability

In a very dynamic and complex world, eliminating of product is and will become a very common feature. Investment in research and development of new products, will give the competitive edge to fight battles.

Systems Marketing

Today, with a drive of every company to reduce their cost levels, many companies are procuring a package of products from single suppliers. These products are generally related products. It is not only a set of products that the marketer is selling, but also associated services along with. It is a highly personalized and tailored service, bringing the buyers closely to work with sellers, giving higher set of values and reducing costs severely. One more key benefit that the marketer would have is the uniqueness in its product offerings. Beating the competitive strategy becomes easier. Systems marketing also enable the industrial marketer to reduce costs in terms of promotional activities and thus increase the productivity per employee. Buyers reduce inventory costs, through better services of the business marketers.

Mind Power 6: Are there Differences between Major Shipping Companies? – By All Business.com*

The "big three" shipping services—Airborne Express, United Parcel Service (UPS), and FedEx—are similar in many ways. All three provide worldwide service using their own fleets of aircraft and delivery vehicles, shipping centers, support facilities and thousands of private drop boxes. Each shipper offers a selection of guaranteed delivery options, ranging from same-day services to second-and third-day delivery.

The U.S. Postal Service (USPS) also offers next-day Express Mail delivery in addition to its traditional mail and parcel shipping services. Unlike the big three, however, the USPS provides mostly domestic Express Mail service along with delivery to a handful of major European and Canadian cities.

Each service touts its own special capabilities. UPS is the oldest (and biggest) private shipping company, and it also offers non-express parcel delivery service to virtually every part of the world. FedEx is the largest express delivery service, operating more than 500 aircraft and nearly 91,000 vehicles world wide. Airborne Express, while smaller than its competitors, boasts a private airport in Ohio with its own foreign trade zone and aircraft maintenance center. And although the post office is a relative newcomer to the express delivery market, it still boasts the world's largest delivery organization.

The shipping market is high competitive, and all of these companies, offer similar services at comparable prices. You may find that one company offers better corporate rates for regular customers, or that

Contd...

one offers more convenient pickup service in your area than its competitors. If you ship a lot of packages that don't require express delivery, for example, UPS may be your best choice. FedEx may be a good option for companies that do a lot of international business and the post office is a good choice for next day domestic service. In fact many businesses use more than one shipping company, giving them the best mix of price and service options.

Source: Allbusiness.com provides resources to help small and growing business start, manage, finance and expand their business. The site contains forms and agreements, business guides, business directories, thousands of articles, export advice, and business blogs. Material copyrighted by AllBusiness.com.

Industrial Services

The services sector is the strongest driver in the world economy today. Be it the US economy or the Indian economy, contribution by services sector is maximum. More than 55 percent of the GDP of the Indian economy is the contribution of the services sector. Four factors account for the growth of business services. They are:[4]

1. *E-business*: Internet has been the driving source for the growth in today's business. Reduction of costs has led corporations to reach amazing heights.

2. *Out sourcing*: Companies today are outsourcing their non core activities to various kinds of services providers, for better efficiency and management of resources.

3. *Innovation:* Today with rapid changing technology, innovation has become one of the most key divers of increasing service demand.

4. *Manufacturing growth*: Manufacturing is growing and also are the industries associated to manufacturing.

Services when we strictly speak of B2B markets can be broadly classified into two types. They are:

1. Product with service
2. Pure service

In the first situation, generally certain amount of services is attached to the product. The degree of service and nature of service would vary. These would be like services post sales or consultancy services post sales of hardware or software, training programmes for shop floor employees on a new machine installed etc. One point that must be clear to a marketer (which we have discussed earlier) is that product alone won't sell. To create a sustainable differentiable advantage in the market place requires giving customers, additional values and benefits. These are derived from services.

Pure services are the ones, which are not associated to any kind of product. Insurance, consulting, financial services, transportation, banking etc, would form a part of pure services. With growth of businesses a significant percentage of corporate opting for services are increasing.

The Challenges of Service Marketing

Services by nature possess certain key characteristics. They are:[5]

1. Intangible
2. Inseparable
3. Non-standardized
4. Perishable

Intangible: Anything one cannot touch or feel. On one side we see hard core products such as machinery, pens and papers and on the other side we have pure services like consulting and training. Some of them might be in the midway, with a mix of goods and services. Marketers need to understand that the offerings they make in the market place are a mix of goods as well as service. Marketers should be able to read the buyers as to what is it that he (buyer) is looking for. If the buyer is looking for greater service, marketer needs to be careful as the marketing tools would not work in these cases. A service is an "experience". It would work more on faith and past experiences.

Inseparable: Services cannot be stored and it is produced and consumed simultaneously. The quality of service would depend on past experiences and interaction between the marketer and the buyer. Since services are produced and consumed simultaneously lost revenue cannot be gained.

Non-standardized: It depends on the person offering the services and thus the quality may vary every time. For offering a service the human element, needs to be considered. Thus "quality" becomes a major cause of concern for service providers.

Perishable: Since services cannot be stored, the demand is highly fluctuating. When demand for a particular service is low, human resources would be wastage. When demands are high the resources need to be balanced uniformly. This is the most challenging part for any industrial service provider.

Most of industrial services firm, do not reach their potential clients through advertising. It is spread mostly through word of mouth. However, personnel selling form a very important component of industrial services promotion. Many industrial service providers, market their products to their own employees. This is done to:

- Motivate them
- Perform better and
- How the service needs to be provided.

Buyers of industrial services go strongly by word of mouth publicity. A service provider should be very careful to promote the word of mouth publicity. This is generally done by:

- Use of referral schemes
- Encouraging potential customers to talk with existing customers.

Since, the services cannot be stored and the demand heavily fluctuates, **pricing** of services become very difficult. So marketers may charge, different prices for lean seasons and busy seasons. One more area that can be looked upon is the **"bundling of services"**. Bundling means two or more services packaged together for a special price.

The **distribution** of services is also a very key area of discussion. Although direct sales may be one of the most prominent methods, however industrial service providers can also offer it through the Internet or through channel members. Companies like Cisco, HP, Dell, offer a lot of services to its customers through the Internet. Channel members may be used for services, like maintenance, repair and installation services.

Failure of Services

The services introduced into markets, fail quite often. The two main reasons for failure:

1. **It is just another "me – too":** The services provided by one firm in comparison to another are with little or no differences.

2. **There is severe lack of market potential:** Services which have no additional value die down. Even services enter into markets with very restricted potential.

Services thus would be successful, when as industrial service providers; we understand the specific needs of the buyer. Services thus should be highly innovative and customized to suit the client.

Defections and Quality

In services, customers who will never come back are defections. It has very strong effects on the industrial service provider, not only in terms of revenue loss, but also in terms of "bad publicity". Industrial service providers will only gain in the long-run, when the association with a particular buyer increases. Thus, industrial service providers should be careful in reducing the defection rates and improve the quality standards every time, a service is being delivered.

Now, the question arises – How to improve quality, and how to sustain quality in services. Industrial service providers should be very careful in maintaining standards of quality and invest on quality improvements wherever necessary. Quality is prime importance in service as this would lead to satisfaction, and market share. Checks should be provided on quality standards of every individual, and set up a benchmark for every process.

Mind Power 7: The Price is Right: Optimizing Industrial Companies Pricing of Services – David Rickard

Industrial companies are leaving millions of dollars on the table—and missing a terrific opportunity to cement customer loyalty and encourage repeat purchases of their equipment—by failing to think systematically and strategically about how they price their services. This issue becomes increasingly important as services become a core lever of profit growth for many manufacturers. Over the course of working on the issue of service pricing with leading companies in a wide range of industries, we have found that two sets of activities play critically important roles in successful pricing: understanding—and exploiting—your strategic pricing parameters, and leveraging your tactical pricing opportunities. Conducting these activities systematically can have a powerful impact on your company's pricing decisions. In the end, the rewards for getting the pricing of services right are higher profits, better customer service, and improved customer retention.

Understanding—and Exploiting—Your Strategic Pricing Parameters

The first step in service pricing is setting the fundamental strategic direction of your pricing activity by exploring the five key strategic pricing parameters: your company's objective in offering the service, your customers' value proposition, your basis of competitive advantage, your competitive environment, and your full cost to serve. These five parameters define your strategic playing field.

Your Company's Objective in Offering the Service

Typically, industrial companies offer services for three primary reasons: to improve the performance of the company's core product and promote repeat purchases, to achieve stand-alone profits on the service itself, or to stimulate *pull-through* sales of equipment. These three objectives dictate different approaches to pricing.

To enhance product performance and promote repeat purchases, companies frequently employ bundling, in which a certain level of service is included in the initial equipment sale. Conversely, pricing of services that aim to achieve stand-alone profits can be independent of new product sales.

Contd...

And companies seeking pull-through sales can offer attractive pricing of services on competitors' installed equipment, with the intent of switching the customer over to their own equipment when the installed equipment requires replacement. For example, a major industrial component manufacturer, recognizing the challenge of displacing incumbent competitors' components, used very aggressive service pricing as an entry point to build relationships and ultimately displace its competitor's equipment when it required replacement.

Your Customers' Value Proposition

Why do your customers buy services? Most often, their motivation is either to cut costs or to get better performance than they could if they provided the service in-house. Knowing which of these motivations is the primary value proposition for each of your customers is key to pricing your services most effectively. For customers seeking cost savings, your pricing flexibility will be constrained: your price must be lower than what it would cost the customer to conduct the service in-house. In contrast, for customers seeking better performance, you have an opportunity to set prices to reflect the true value you are providing each customer.

For example, a large HVAC-controls company had traditionally offered episodic services priced at cost plus. By developing a detailed and documented understanding of the value of preventive maintenance and of the optimal repair/replace cycles of its installed equipment, the company was able to transform its service business, creating fixed-term contracts. The company's customers benefited from superior performance (in terms of less downtime), while the company itself reaped new, long-term revenue streams.

Your Basis of Competitive Advantage

Whether your competitive advantage in your service offering is based on scale and experience or on skill and capability will play a key role in how you price the service, particularly when the offering is a new one. For services in which scale is a significant source of advantage, such as the remote monitoring of building security and equipment functionality, prices should be set as low as possible initially in order to ramp up scale quickly. Conversely, for services in which competitive advantage is based on skill, such as IT integration and aircraft engine maintenance, pricing should reflect the degree of differentiation between your capabilities and those of your competitors.

Your Competitive Environment

This one is fairly obvious: the degree of competition in your relevant market space is the key element in setting and negotiating the pricing of services. What are your customers' alternatives, and what is the true competitive situation?

Take the case of a distributor that was a rush-order specialist. For years the company had benchmarked its prices relative to the leading—and low-price—bulk-order specialists. This approach to pricing was particularly challenging because the company had a hard time delivering rush services at bulk-order prices. Through detailed customer research, the company discovered that, for the vast majority of its customers, it served as the only quick-turn specialist; in truth, these customers had few alternatives. Armed with this knowledge, the distributor was able to raise its prices significantly to reflect its higher-service-level niche position. It boosted its profits solidly—while maintaining its customer base.

Your Full Cost to Serve

Effective pricing requires a sound understanding of your company's true and full cost to serve, not only on average but also for specific offerings and kinds of customers. Full costs and cost drivers can be critically important in setting pricing floors and identifying more attractive customer segments to target.

Consider the on-site maintenance of equipment. Two-critical cost drivers for this kind of service are response time and local market density. Service level agreements (SLAs) that either call for faster-

Contd...

than-normal response times or address markets with lower-than-normal local-market density can drive up costs significantly.

For SLAs based on response time, it is critically important to consider not only average response-time requirements but also the actual frequency distribution of those responses. Without that specification, simultaneous or correlated service requests across customers (for example, service requests that cluster seasonally or on a given day of the week or month) can have a crippling effect on costs, so the company needs to factor that pattern into its cost structure up front. Similarly, low local-market density—meaning that customers are widely separated geographically— can significantly boost costs by increasing driving time and reducing the number of accounts a service agent can handle. Companies that look only at average costs and densities may choose pricing that is highly profitable in one market and deeply unprofitable in another.

Leveraging Your Tactical Pricing Opportunities

After setting the strategic direction for your pricing based on a solid understanding of the five parameters outlined above, you should explore several key tactical pricing opportunities. These opportunities vary with the type of service you offer, how proprietary it is, the ticket size, the frequency of purchase, and the length of the customer relationship.

The Type of Service

Services generally come in three types: required, unplanned service for which the need is immediate; required service for which the need is not immediate; and general discretionary' service. Naturally, suppliers' pricing power is highest when the need is most urgent and lowest when the service is, discretionary. Companies generally capitalize on, this pricing power by levying various surcharges for urgent or unplanned services. Classic examples are same-day surcharges and rush-order fees. The elevator maintenance industry, for instance, has recognized the incremental customer value created for unplanned emergency services and typically charges additional fees for immediate service.

The Proprietary Nature of the Service

The degree of service differentiation, including the service provider's proprietary capabilities, is a critical dimension in optimizing the pricing of services. The more distinctive the service, the greater degree of pricing power you have. Common applications of this principle include the use of certified service providers or parts, as well as warranty clauses that require authorized service. Auto and farm equipment OEMs deploy this strategy, specifying that their customers use factory parts and certifying certain dealers or service shops as authorized repair locations.

The Ticket Size

The dollar amount of the actual service ticket can play a key role in setting and changing list prices. Companies and individuals alike share an interesting bias when it comes to prices, discounts, and ticket size. People tend to see discounts in relative or percentage terms. That is, a discount of $5 off a $10 item will motivate a buying decision, whereas a discount of $5 off a $1,000 item will have little or no impact. Conversely, when price increases are specified in percentage terms, people tend to be more sensitive to increases on large-ticket items than on smaller-ticket ones. For example, people will be more sensitive to a 20 percent increase on a $5,000 item (which comes to $1,000) than they are to a 20 percent increase on a. $5 item (which comes to only $1). Understanding, these common perceptual biases can suggest tactical pricing opportunities.

The Frequency of Purchase

How frequently a service is purchased is an important factor to consider in setting the price of services. As frequency of purchase increases, purchasers become more astute and price sensitive than they are toward services that they purchase infrequently—and particularly those that they buy erratically, such as unplanned disaster-recovery services.

Contd...

The Length of the Customer Relationship

Whether a relationship is new or well-established can be an important factor in negotiating the pricing of services. Early on in a relationship, the supplier can think about investing in that relationship, provided that there is reasonable "stickiness" to relationships within the industry or segment. Then, as the relationship matures, pricing can reflect the buyer's increasing confidence and comfort, and recognize the service provider's earlier investment. Initial or entry pricing used across industries reflects this principle.

Next Steps

To understand whether digging deeper into your current service pricing might create value for your company, consider the following questions:

● Is your current approach to pricing aligned with the overall objectives of your service organization?

● Do you fully understand your customers' value proposition, and have you designed the pricing of your services to reflect that perspective?

● Do you have a clear understanding of your full cost to serve various customer segments and markets?

● Is your service organization competing on scale or on skill, and does your pricing structure reflect your actual basis of competition?

● Does your service pricing take into account differences in purchase characteristics, such as the urgency or frequency of purchases or the size of the ticket?

● Do you differentiate your pricing over the life cycle of each customer relationship?

If you can't answer yes to most of these questions, it may be time for you to revisit your service pricing. By taking a more strategic look at how you set your service prices, you not only can boost your profits but also can provide better services and cement customer loyalty.

Source: This article has been authored by David Rickard. He is the vice president and director in the Chicago office of The Boston Consulting Group. Copyright with The Boston Consulting Group, Inc.2006. Reprinted with permission.

Innovation and New Product Development

Many industrial firms earn a significant profit, from new product development. In an industry, which is highly competitive, survival is of the fittest. Firms try and create this edge over their competitors by innovating and staying ahead in market. However, it is one of the most challenging tasks that the firm faces because the risks of failure are high, investments are huge. It also tests a company's capabilities, resources, competence and ability to create a place for itself in the marketplace.

Mere innovation would not work. What is expected more from firms is the edge to stay competitive? Along with product innovation their tools and techniques must also be strong. Moreover, today the product life cycles are very short, high rate of technological obsolescence and thus firm's ability to change with such speeds is essential for success.

Mind Power 8: Intel Technology Allows Nurses to Spend More Time with Patients

Intel and Motion Computing pilot new device at leading hospitals around the world

SAN FRANCISCO, Feb. 20, 2007 – Intel Corporation today announced the Mobile Clinical Assistant (MCA) is ready to enable nurses to spend more time with patients, do their jobs on the move while

Contd...

remaining connected; and manage the administration of medications. Motion Computing's C5* is the first product based on Intel's MCA platform and has earned the support from clinicians and nurses participating in pilot studies around the world.

As Intel's first platform built specifically for health care, the MCA is an important step in the company's efforts to better connect clinicians to comprehensive patient information on a real time basis. The light weight, spill-resistant, drop-tolerant and easily disinfected MCA allows nurses to access up-to-the-minute patient records and to document a patient condition instantly enhancing clinical workflow while reducing the staff's administrative workload.

Some of the Motion C5 features designed to ease the nurse's daily workload include: wireless connectivity to access up to date secure patient information and physician's orders; Radio Frequency Identification (RFID) technology for easy, rapid user log on; a digital camera to enhance patient charting and progress notes, to keep track of wounds as they heal; and Bluetooth technology to help capture patient vital signs.

Source: Adapted from http://www.intel.com/ca/pressroom/2007/0220.htm

Innovation

Companies like 3M, IBM, Intel, Dell, Apple computers and AT and T have been innovators for their life time. They have pioneered the best products and services for the market place. As James Quinn says, "Innovation tends to be individually motivated, opportunistic, customer responsive, tumultuous, nonlinear and interactive in its development. Managers can plan overall directions and goals, but surprises are likely to abound".[7] Innovation and technology management is becoming the key to success. The top management must heavily focus on innovation and it must be reinforced by the people throughout the company. The top management must take keen interest in the process of innovation.

The challenge is not only to develop new products, but develop products keeping the customers in mind. Between 33 percent and 60 percent of all new products that reach the market fails to make a profit.[8]

Industrial Product

Booz, Allen and Hamilton have spoken about six categories of new products. They are:[9]

1. *New to the world products*: Products which are entirely new to the market place.

2. *New product lines*: A set of new products, to enter into a new market space, which was untouched by the company previously.

3. *Addition to existing product lines*: New products which competitors might be offering and placed directly against them.

4. *Improvement or revisions to existing products*: Products modified to provide better performance.

5. *Repositioning*: Existing products targeted to new market segments.

6. *Cost reductions*: Products with same performance at reduce costs.

New Product Development Process

Ideas for new product may come form a multiple sources. The sources could be well within the organization or external to the organization. Since new product development represents risk, it requires people from various cross functional areas to come and work together.

This section will focus on:

1. Environment scanning and sources of ideas.

2. Focus that drive a firm's new product performance.

3. Process of new product development.

4. Developing an innovative culture within an organization.

Environmental Scanning and Sources of Ideas

Companies need to scan their environment to understand the latest development of technology in the market place. One point that needs to be kept in mind is that for environmental scanning, we need to focus on the complete industrial market and not only in the same industry, where the firm is operating. To lean more on the technological developments the best possible idea is to locate a part of company's research and development in location where there is a strong impact on product development. The other sources that a business firm can look in for product improvements are its customers, suppliers and distributors. The above are the external environment scanning. The company must also look into a series of internal factors. These would be the internal environmental scanning. The following questions that need to be asked to understand the internal factors are:

1. Does the firm have the resources?

2. What is level of innovating culture in the organization?

3. Are employees interested in new ideas?

4. Does the company allow employees to take risks?

Once we have taken stock of our internal and external factors, we must try and understand where ideas generate from. In the last paragraph we have spoken about distributors, suppliers and customers. A lot of idea is generated from them because they gain the maximum from the success of such innovations and development. However there could be outside sources also like researchers, and competitors.

Ideas from within the Company

Entrepreneurships what we call it in management parlance, is one of the hottest topics of discussion. Companies like 3M, have used it to make world class product like "Post-it-Notes". These companies allow their employees to build upon and develop their ideas, with help of resources from across the organizations. Management is required to be highly supportive.

Ideas from lead users

Research shows that customers are one of the best sources of ideas. A way to commercialize a new technology is through early and in depth involvement with a firm's customers in a process called "co-development".[10] This type of customer is a lead user. All new product ideas must finally satisfy the customers and thus focus should be more on them. Even as the market sees new technological change, the process of new product development starts. The industrial marketer should also be very sensitive to buyers in oligopolistic markets.

Market Research

Market research is one of the ways to generate new product ideas. However customers might not be in a position to speak on radically new inventions.

Forces that drive a firm's new Product Performance

Three factors are identified which drives a firms new product performance. They are:

1. Product Development Process
2. Resource Commitments
3. New Product Strategy

Product Development Process: There should be individual attention given from the stage of idea generation to final product launch. The valued firms should have certain characteristics which are absent for other firms. Valued firms, emphasize on market and technical assessment, before they move into the process of development. These firms also have a very clear understanding of the concepts, benefits, target markets and positioning strategies for the product. The product process is flexible and certain stages are skipped.

Resource Commitments: Any firm, in the process of developing new products needs to commit resources. However, this can only happen with the commitment of top management. New products also require reasonable research and development budgets and cross functional team needs to be developed exclusively for the purpose.

Product Strategy: The industrial marketer should have clear cut goals from a new product. Firms, who are successful, set aggressive goals for their new products.

Process of New Product Development

There are no set series of steps for the product development process. Ideas must be generated on one hand; products manufactured and should satisfy the customers for success. There is a mix of cross functional teams or departments, who pull in their ideas for the new product development. However, we will try understanding the process in a series of steps. They are:

1. Idea generation and screening
2. Concept development
3. Business analysis in a preliminary state
4. Test marketing
5. Business planning
6. Commercialization

1. *Idea generation and screening*: We have seen the start of idea generation and the sources of idea generation. However, this is a very important step towards the foundation of a strong company. Companies who create a difference through their process of innovation. Customer benefit is primary and thus any product that a firm plans to develop has to target in that area. One more point that needs to be considered is that the focus should be on the firm's key strategic areas. The objectives, core competencies, complementary assets must be kept in mind to achieve the set of goals.

From all the idea that has been generated, we need to filter, pick and choose ideas. Ideas will fall of, if it is costing a fortune and if the competitor is way ahead in the particular area. Now, the ideas that are dropped may not and shouldn't be completely deleted off. Probably on a long-run, companies can try and develop such ideas. The ideas that pass through are understandably within the capabilities of most firms.

2. *Concept development*: Ideas that pass through the screening process, need to be developed and tested. If the idea has been generated internally, all such projects need to be ranked on the basis of criteria's such as strategic objectives, resources required and the business it would generate. However ideas which come from third party source should be first studied for feasibility of such projects. Two aspects that need to be kept in mind is **technical feasibility and customer satisfaction**. Whenever we are trying to test a concept we are trying to understand in that in customer terms. The concept testing process can be through a series of steps of prototype building and testing or using there dimensional models.

3. *Business analysis in a preliminary state*: When we try and do a preliminary business analysis, we try and understand about customers, competitors and business potential of the product in the market. The business analysis will generate projected figures for about 3-4 years with details regarding cost of development, required investment and profitability-market share analysis. The conversion of an idea into a product involves high level of costs. Thus pilot testing for the product is also very essential. It is important to note here that projects might get rejected at this stage due to lack of resources (mainly financial) or technological needs.

4. *Test marketing*: The research and development department develops a prototype of the idea, as a product in the step three. This prototype is to ensure technical feasibility, cost structures and performance. Once the prototype has been developed, it is made in a small quantity and given to a set of customers to check the performance and also to check whether it matches the product objectives or not.

   Price also plays a very important role in industrial products. In case of a significant change that the product can bring in, buyers would be willing to pay a premium price. However it should be kept in mind that the costs need to be controlled to a very great extent. Good products might get rejected from the market place, if buyer perceives the product to be costly.

   Once we start the test marketing of the product, the feedback given by the users is very critical. It would be very useful, in these situations, if the marketer establishes direct links with the users. As we have said that the feedback is very critical, the products might need to be redesigned or altered. However, there could be delays by the buyer, as they would resist change due to the cost implications. But if a product is strong it would be accepted in the market in due course of time.

5. *Business planning*: Once the test marketing is done, and the results are encouraging the next step in the process is to generate a business plan. This business plan will discuss the financial aspects of the particular product in a greater detail. The business planning would also include a marketing plan and a tactical plan. The marketer also has to draw a sketch on competitor reaction on the new product.

   The business planning would also require detailed pricing analysis of production costs, competitor's prices, margins and elasticity of demand. Details of distribution like agreements, shipping orders, training and new distributor appointments are some of the areas that need to be touched upon.

   As far as advertising goes, factors like total budget, advertisement schedules, direct mailers and other strategies needs to be discussed. The sales force also requires being determined, hiring of new people, sales forecasts, establishing targets and training needs to be provided.

6. *Commercialization*: It is launched into the target market, with a definite action plan in place. It will also include support services, distribution and promotional strategies in place. However the product at this stage might fail because of reasons like improper training to sales staff and distributors, lack of advertising not focussing on right set of customers or poor customer service and spares availability.

Mind Power 9: Post-it® Notes ...Little sticky notes that Revolutionized Messages

The product had its root as a solution looking for a problem."

Since the introduction of Post-it® Notes in 1980, the sticky yellow notes have become one of the best known of all 3M products. In a twist to the tradition of innovation, the product had its root as a solution looking for a problem.

3M research scientist, Dr. Spence Silver, first developed the technology in 1968 while looking for ways to improve the acrylate adhesives that 3M uses in many of its tapes - but he found something remarkably different. Silver knew that he had invented a highly unusual adhesive but what was he going to do with it?

Contd...

The invention of 3M's Post-it® Notes began with Art Fry's frustration at how his scrap paper bookmarks kept falling out of his church choir hymnal. With an intense curiosity and a penchant for practical solutions, Fry was intrigued by Silver's strange adhesive. His initial business application for the adhesive, a bookmark for his hymnal, was just the beginning of a long effort by Art and teams of colleagues to bring more than 200 Post-it® products to a world of users.

Canadian advertisers are using Post-it® Notes to deliver their sales messages with exceptional results. 3M Post-it® Notes are popping up on the front pages of newspapers across Canada. Research indicates that advertising with Post-it® Notes increases product recognition and awareness and as they're often posted on refrigerators or computer screens, the advertisement has a longer shelf life.

One year after its introduction, Post-it® Notes were named 3M's outstanding new Product. And today, loyal customers can't imagine how they ever got along without them. Post-it® Notes are best sellers worldwide.

Source: http://cms.3m.com/cms/CA/en/I-30/rFzeEA/view.jhtml

Developing an Innovative Culture within an Organization

Any organization, keen to create a difference in the market place and to do well in business, needs to innovate. The corporate structure and culture must be suitable for such practice and the top management must be committed towards it. If business firms are hierarchical, with little or no flexibility, innovation is a distant dream. Firms must bring in a culture of entrepreneurship within an organization. Firms must be flexible in its approach. Rogers in his book "Diffusion of Innovation" speaks of the characteristics that an organization should possess to promote innovation. They are:[11]

- Positive attitude towards change
- Decentralized decision-making
- Complexity
- Informal structure
- Interconnectedness
- Organizational slack (unused resources)
- Large size
- System openness

A large corporation that wants to encourage innovation and creativity within its firm must choose a structure that will give the new business unit an appropriate amount of freedom, while maintain some degree of control at headquarters.[12]

CONCLUSION

We have seen in this chapter, what is industrial product and service and what are the characteristic features. This chapter also spoke on the product life cycle for industrial products and the various strategies that a marketer has to adopt for each stage. We also understood the different structure of the PLC for a high tech product and how to develop product strategies. All products in the market would not be generating good revenue.

We have discussed the revitalizing and eliminating product decision.

Like products, industrial services also play a very key component. The typical characteristics i.e. intangibility, inseparability, perishability and non-standardized have been discussed.

We then came to product innovation and the importance of innovation. We also saw how industrial firms develop a new product and what needs to be done to create an innovating culture within an organization.

References

1.   Lazer and Cully, *Marketing Management*, pp 476.

2.   Shapiro, *Industrial Product Policy–Managing the Existing Product Line*, pp 37-39.

3.   Wind and Claycamp, *Planning Product Line Strategy: A Matrix Approach*, pp 2-9.

4.   Hutt and Speh, *Business Marketing Management*, pp 328.

5.   Zeithmal, Parasuraman and Berry, "*Problems and Strategies in Services Marketing*", Journal of Marketing, 49, (spring 1985), pp 33-46.

6.   Guiltinan, "*The Price Bundling of Services*: A normative frame work", Journal of Marketing, 57, (April 1987). pp.74.

7.   Quinn (May/June 1985), *Marketing Innovation: Controlling Chaos*, HBR6, pp 83.

8.   Schilling and Hill, *Managing the New Product Development Process: Strategic imperatives*, pp 67-81.

9.   Booz, Allen and Hamilton, *New Product Management for the 1980s*.

10. Neale and Corkindale, *Co Developing Products: Involving Customer Earlier and More Deeply*, pp 418-425.

11. Rogers (1995), *Diffusion of Innovation*, 4th edition, NY- Free Press.

12. Wheelen and Hunger, *Concepts in Strategic Management and Business Policy*, Pearson Education Asia-Eighth edition, pp 291.

Mind power 10: Listening to Potential Customers: Building Tomorrow's Products Requires Listening to the Market – Barbara Nelson

Pragmatic Marketing

Although product knowledge is important, spending time listening to the market is where the real learning takes place, and the quicker you become acclimatized, the more value you add.

What is your comfort zone as a product manager? Is it the product? The technology? The competition? The customer? When you first became product manager, how did you get up to speed on the job? Unfortunately, many new product managers gravitate towards their comfort zone: the product. They learn about "the product" by reading the user guides and brochures, going through the tutorial, attending formal training, surfing the web, and sitting through product demonstrations on sales calls.

Although it is important for a product manager to learn the product, it is imperative for you to get out into the market as soon as possible to learn what's going on there. Your objective in listening to the market is to become, a *market expert.* This series of three articles will focus on how to become a market expert by listening to 3 constituents in your market: customers, evaluators, and potential customers.

Let's define the three groups within our market.

Customers: At some point in time, members of this group realized they had a problem to solve and bought your product to solve the problem.

Evaluators: This group recognizes they have a problem to solve and are actively looking to solve a problem with your product or your competitors' products. This is where your sales channel spends its time during the sales cycle.

Contd...

Potentials: This group is within your identified market segment but they have not bought your type of product (from you or your competitors) and are not currently looking at these types of products.

Most companies think they listen to the market. What they typically do is listen to the noisy 20 percent of the customers and listen to evaluators during sales calls. (Actually, they are busy 'talking most of the time, not really listening.) They rarely (or never) listen to the third group, potentials: those who have not bought the product and are not looking. The danger in only listening to noisy customers and active sales leads is that you might build products that only appeal to noisy customers and active sales leads. You might have some initial success, but eventually the size of the market you have created is not enough to support your business. The future of your product (and your company) lies in also understanding the quiet 80 percent of your customers, knowing why evaluators buy from you or why they bought the competitor's product (through win/loss analysis), and learning why inactive potentials aren't looking and haven't bought anything.

For each group we must learn:

1. **Who** are they and how do we find them?

2. **What** are we trying to learn?

3. **When** do we listen?

4. **Where** do we listen?

5. **How** do we listen?

It is important to balance your visits with all three groups in the market to get a good perspective on the market and where your company fits. We need to use a different process to listen to each group to get the information we need.

In the first part of this series, we are going to focus on listening to potentials because this group is most neglected.

Who are potentials and how do we find them?

"Sales sometimes call hot leads or prospects." The group we call potentials are those in our market who have not bought one of our types of products and are not currently looking. Think of them as inactive prospects.

Your 'first objective is to find potentials' and set up an appointment to visit them. If you have additional resources to assist you in getting the appointment, use them. But don't outsource the appointment itself.

Source	How you find them	How to engage them
List	Talk to your direct marketing group and ask, "If you were to send a direct mail piece to our market segment, what list would you use?" This is the list you would start with. Then, remove customers and anybody in the sales pipeline (evaluators). What you have left is potentials.	Call them-I am a product manager for XYZ company. I am researching how to deploy our development resources over the next year." If you have domain expertise, say, "I used to do what you do. I am trying to learn what has changed since I was a [job title]."
Trade Show	Trade shows are usually targeted to a market segment (such as construction), a technical platform (such as Linux or Windows), or a type of problem to solve (Customer Relationship Management or CRM). As a product manager, you might already be signed up to attend the trade show. Talk to the trade show coordinator and make sure you will have time at the show outside the booth.	In the booth-ask qualifying questions. Sort visitors into customers, evaluators (these are the hot leads we give to sales), and potentials (they might be tire kicking or just want the tchatchke). Contact the potentials when you get home (You stopped by our booth. I know you aren't currently looking but I am a product manager? [similar script as above]). Work the show-go to the pretzel or coffee stand. Start up a conversation with other attendees. "I am a product manager?"

Contd...

Conference	Speaking engagement—collect business cards	Contact people who came to your session." Remember me? I'm the one that gave the speech at XYZ conference. Can we meet?"
	Go to sessions. Listen to the questions from the audience	After the session, "That was an interesting question you asked. I'd like to learn more?"
Trade Association	Join the local trade association for your market segment (usually vendors can join as associate members). Go to the meetings	At the meeting, get to know the members. Make sure they know you are not a salesperson, but that you are a product manager trying to learn more about your market.
Executive Introductions	Ask your executives to introduce you to executives at other companies in your market	These are the decision makers. Don't abuse the introduction by taking too much time. (Below is a discussion of what you're trying to learn from decision makers)
Friends and Family	Ask your friends and family if they know anybody in the markets you serve. You might find a friend of a friend who is the perfect candidate. Ask for an introduction. Get to know people at your kid's soccer games, at cocktail parties, anywhere groups of people meet.	People you meet personally or through a mutual friend are usually the easiest to engage. This is the method many sales people have used for years to cold call prospective customers

What are we trying to learn?

This is qualitative market research. Essentially, you are trying to learn how they are surviving without your technology. Why haven't they bought your product or your competitors products? Is it because:

- They don't know about you?
- They have a slightly different problem?
- They have a dramatically different problem (where you need to re-architect the product)?
- They don't have the problem?

Until you know why they haven't bought, you-won't come up with the right solution to get them to buy in the future.

Once you get the appointment, learn about the key players. For complex business-to-business solutions, there is usually a decision maker, key user, and technical reviewer. It is important to listen to each of these players.

Decision Maker: What keeps him or her up at night (not just in context of what you do)? You are competing not only with your competitors, but also for mind share and resources against everything else the decision maker has to deal with. If the final decision maker is the CEO, you are competing with both internal and external forces over which you have no control., The CEO can decide to spend money on internal infrastructure systems, more personnel, benefits, office space, security, sales, marketing, development, services, (and the list goes on?). Why should he/she buy your product? What kind of ROI is he/she looking for? If you focus your business on solving critical problems, your product will be more likely to be recession-proof.

Key User: what problems does he or she face every day? This is the person for whom you will be building the solution. But keep in mind; the problems might not be large enough that the decision maker will pay to solve them.

Technical Reviewer: This person can veto the decision if it doesn't meet the technical expectations, but generally this person isn't choosing which solution to buy. If the solution is a threat to his/her job, they could cause a roadblock, however. Understand how to get on his or her side. Also, learn what cool products they have seen lately. You might become aware of new technologies earlier than you would have on your own.

Contd...

Other things you are trying to learn:

- Do they know you? What is their level of awareness or perception of your company?

- Where do they buy products like yours, what process do they go through, what channels would be acceptable (direct, distributors, VARs, web, catalog), what kind of pricing constraints might there be?

- Who is your competition and what do they think of them?

- Who do they go to for advice about products such as yours?

When do we listen?

Becoming expert on your market is not a one-time project. It should be an ongoing process. When you first begin, immerse yourself in this activity. Spend one month visiting 10-12 sites to give you a jump-start. Then, on an ongoing basis, visit one potential a month so you can stay in touch with what is going on in your market. In high technology, things can change relatively quickly, and if you don't stay in touch, you might miss a new trend or shift in technology.

Use every opportunity you have to visit potentials. You might already be traveling to a trade show or conference. Meet potentials there. When you do a speaking engagement, be sure to collect business cards and make an appointment later in the day or the next morning. If your travel budget is constrained (and whose isn't), don't overlook potentials that might be in your own neighborhood.

Don't forget to stay in touch with those you are able to engage. When you need an outside view, call them to test ideas, positioning, names, and feature possibilities. However, be careful not to skew your results by only listening to the same few.

Where do we listen?

Visiting potentials onsite is by far the best scenario. Viewing them in their natural habitat is where you will learn the most and have the best context of their situation. But if you are not able to always do this, it's all right to also listen to them at the trade show or conference, or on the telephone. If you have usability labs at your office, observe non-customers using your products and then listen to them one-on-one afterwards to get more information.

How do we listen?

Don't outsource this part of the process! Own it! This is where the market-expertise lies. And don't take sales with you. This is not a lead generation or selling activity. It is a market research function and a listening exercise, not a talking exercise. Your objective is not to drum up new business by talking about how great your products are, but to learn about the problems in the market and how your products fit in the landscape.

Here are ten tips on listening to potentials:

1. Observe them doing their job in their natural habitat.

2. Spend a "day in the life" with the potential. Follow him or her around doing the job.

3. Ask questions: "Why did you do that? Who needs that information and why? What purpose does that function serve?"

4. Keep the questions open-ended. This kind of market research is qualitative, not quantitative and should not be conducted like a formal survey.

5. Don't interrupt – let the subject finish a thought. You might be thinking, "Our product will solve their problems!" Save that for later. You will probably still learn something by letting them talk.

Contd...

6. Don't talk about your product – At the very end of the interview, if it turns out that your product is a perfect fit, you might say, "We actually have a product that might fit your needs. Are you interested in learning more?" If the person says, "No," you need to respect that. The problem is probably not urgent enough if this is the answer (which tells you a lot).

7. Get the tour. Many companies offer a formal tour of their facilities. If so, take it. It can be very enlighten you about their business, about what they are proud of, and how they do things.

8. Go with a buddy – Whenever possible, do these interviews in pairs. What you don't see, your partner might. One person can take notes while the other observes and asks questions. Perhaps you should pair up a senior product manager with a less experienced one, a product manager with marketing manager, or the product manager with a development lead.

9. Document the interview in a call report right away. You won't remember details from one visit to another unless you do. This will become a body of knowledge you can share with others on your team.

10. Debrief with someone on your team right after your interview. This helps you remember, analyze, and share the information you have learned.

This activity takes self-discipline to make it a part of your everyday routine. It is so easy to slide back into tactical, urgent activities, but becoming expert on the market is very strategic, and the future of your company depends on it. It helps you figure out what you need to build 12-18 months from now.

Out of the 3 groups you should listen to in your market, potentials are the hardest to engage. Why? Because it requires you to get *outside your comfort zone*.

However, becoming a market expert can be the most valuable of all activities you can do as a product manager. Only you can make it happen!

Source: This article originally appeared at http://www.pragmaticmarketing .com/productmarketing/. Reprinted with permission. Copyright with Pragmatic Marketing, Inc. All rights reserved.

Mind Power II: Improving Time-to-market through Planning and Resource Management – Kenneth Crow

Introduction

Rapid time-to-market is important for the competitive success of many companies for the following reasons.

- Competitive advantage of getting to market sooner;

- Premium prices early in life cycle;

- Faster breakeven on development investment and lower financial risk;

- Longer market life cycle; and

- Greater overall profits and higher return on investment.

The key process requirements for rapid time-to-market are:

- Clear understanding of customer needs at the start of the project and stability in product requirements or specifications;

- A characterized, optimized product development process;

- A realistic project plan based on this process;

Contd...

- Availability of needed resources to support the project and use of full-time, dedicated personnel;

- Early involvement and rapid staffing build-up to support the parallel design of product and process;

- Virtual product development, including digital assembly modeling and early analysis and simulation to minimize time consuming physical mock-ups and testing; and

- Design re-use and standardization to minimize the design content of a project.

Recent studies as well as our own experience have identified that in many companies; development projects are often started at the beginning of a fiscal year or based on marketing needs without regard to priorities or resources. Further, there is often little or no project planning and little or no consideration of risks or project uncertainty. This has resulted-in development-personnel being over committed on average by 75 percent. Further, over 75 percent of development project cost and schedule estimates are inaccurate by 10 percent or more. Finally, less than 25 percent of companies have adequate resources to undertake all their planned development projects.

Benchmarking best practices has enabled us to identify a number of key issues related to project and resource planning and management that have a major affect on rapid time-to-market. These best practices and an approach to benchmarking and assessing an organization's product development process in order to develop an action plan for improvement will be covered in the balance of this paper.

Product planning

There are two types of product development environments. The first is a company that undertakes a relatively small number of major projects involving complex products. In this type of environment, product planning involves the consideration of each product development project, to a large extent, independently of other development projects. The decision to go ahead with the project implies that it is the highest priority programme for investment by the company and that whatever resources are required, will be obtained to support the development effort.

The second situation involves companies with small or moderate-sized development projects (For example; less than 50 people). In many of these organizations, development budgets and headcounts are planned on a fiscal year basis at a nominal and relatively constant level. There are often a number of product lines and many competing needs for development projects. In this situation, a product plan is critical to:

- Define an overall strategy for products to guide selection of development projects;

- Define customers, markets and competitive strengths;

- Rationalize these competing development projects and establish priorities for development projects;

- Estimate development resources;

- Provide a high-level schedule of various development projects; and

- Balance project resource requirements with a budget in the overall business plan.

In the simplest terms, the product plan can be viewed as the equivalent of the production plan used to guide manufacturing activities. While a product plan is generally prepared on an annual basis, it should be reviewed and updated at least quarterly, if not monthly. Market conditions will change, new product opportunities will be identified, and new product technology will emerge, all causing a potential impact on the product plan. These opportunities need to be evaluated and the product plan changed if needed. These changes may result in re-prioritizing development projects or making a decision to hire additional development personnel to undertake a new development opportunity.

Contd...

Planning and execution strategy

The product plan embodies an overall strategy and the critical success factors of the business. As a general rule, Integrated Product Development practices (IPD) suggest concentrating resources at any one point in time on fewer projects in order to get those projects done as quickly as possible. As these projects are more rapidly finished, resources are assigned to the next highest priority project.

A second strategy issue involves the level of development resources. If the company's objective is time-to-market, this would imply that development activities are a high priority and that the organization must maintain a sufficient level of resources to support requirements, even though the resources may not be highly utilized at all times. The benefits of time to-market in this case can outweigh the cost impact of having a higher level of development resources. If the organization's objectives are to develop a low cost product (where the per unit development cost is a relatively large portion of product cost) or to develop a product within a tight development budget, this would imply that development resources be staffed at a minimum level to insure high utilization and little downtime, even if it delays performing a development activity.

Project planning

As an organization establishes a more mature product development process, one of the steps in this evolution will be to fully characterize and understand the process. This would include defining and understanding the process steps including the inputs (information and resources) and outputs. Of course, this process should be as standardized as possible. Defining the development process is important in order to have a basis for planning a development project.

With a standard development process, it becomes possible to establish a standard project plan template (including resource estimates, task precedence, and task duration) which further eases the effort in developing a project plan. Even with a standard process, it is appropriate to tailor the process to the unique requirements of the development project. For example, a product upgrade is a less complex project than developing an entirely new product for a new market. Therefore, this standard planning template will need to be tailored to address these unique project requirements.

Team involvement in planning

Who develops the project plan? Often, this was done by a programme manager or a product line manager and then given to the team. This approach resulted in the team members not developing a good understanding of the plan, not clearly understanding the critical path and task interactions, and not being fully committed to the plan.

Empowering development personnel to create a project plan enhances their understanding of the plan and increases their commitment to the plan. When all disciplines are involved in the project early and included in the planning process, a sounder, more comprehensive, better integrated plan results. The plan should be reviewed in a team meeting so that each product development team member clearly understands his or her responsibilities. Since project conditions change and performance doesn't always go according to plan, the plan needs to be periodically maintained and revisions reviewed with team members.

Staffing strategies

There are several key staffing strategies to facilitate rapid time-to-market. These include:

- Plan based on early involvement of functional disciplines to support the parallel design of the product and the process.

- Use full-time, dedicated personnel where possible. Part-time personnel and task-switching affect productivity and slow down development activities.

- Support rapid staffing build-up to insure the project gets off to a good start.

Contd...

- Consider delaying the start of the project, if needed personnel and resources are not available.

- Maintain the core integrated product team into production to resolve transition problems until stable production is achieved. This provides resources to quickly solve problems and

- It provides direct feedback to development personnel on lessons learned.

Resource planning and management

The timely development of a new product requires that all required personnel resources to support the development effort are available when needed. This requires planning resource requirements by developing a realistic development plan which includes a time-phased schedule of manpower requirements (by discipline and position/skill level). Other indirect activities need to be included in the resource planning to properly project all requirements. The earlier this resource planning occurs prior to the start of a development project, the greater the flexibility to respond to resource constraints.

Since development projects can be affected by unanticipated issues and tasks that take longer than planned, this resource plan needs to be maintained on a regular basis. While an earned value system will recognize potential task overruns, most commercial organizations with small and moderate-size projects do not have earned value systems in place and rely on feedback from product development teams to adjust project resource requirements.

The resource plan is the basis for obtaining personnel commitments to support the product development effort and extending or changing personnel commitments. It is a basis, along with other departmental requirements, to plan overall manpower requirements (see resource planning example).

With a product development team's need for resources from different departments, it is likely that resources from one or more departments will be constrained and unable to respond to the project's requirements in a timely way. While resource planning should provide some higher level visibility to take action to alleviate significant resource constraints (bottlenecks), it is difficult for an organization to always balance its resource requirements with its available personnel in the short term.

There are a number of actions that can mitigate these resource conflicts in an integrated product development environment. One action to alleviate these likely resource constraints is to maximize the flexibility of development personnel so that they can perform tasks that are not normally their responsibility. As people become broader generalists through exposure to other disciplines on teams, through training, and through team member collaboration, a balancing of work loads will occur naturally. When a "can-do" environment is created, people understand the importance of stepping in to perform tasks normally outside their responsibility. By allowing engineers and designers to operate equipment in a lab, this avoids having to wait for a lab technician who is backlogged with work. When flexible, easy-to-use design and, analytic tools (For example, FEA) are provided, this may mitigate the need for an analyst or specialist who may not be available. It is important to emphasize training and personnel development to create this type of broadly skilled workforce.

However, when the development projects planned or underway create a significant overload on development resources, all projects are stretched out, affecting time to market. Further, individual development personnel make decisions on project priorities which are not necessarily in line with enterprise priorities. Finally, this overload causes development personnel to take shortcuts, undermining the desired process. When this overload situation is indicated, the organization must take one of two actions: add resources, whether permanent hires, contract labour, or subcontracting; or change the resource requirements by deferring project starts.

Risk management

Another common issue is consideration of project risks in project planning. Human nature being what it is, most projects are planned assuming everything will happen as intended. Except for large projects with sophisticated programme management processes, most companies do no adequately consider or address project risks. As a result, projects are often unprepared for risks that arise, delaying development, increasing costs, and impacting customer satisfaction.

Contd...

Development processes need to include process steps to identify, track, and manage risks. This is a product development team's responsibility. As the team is involved in planning the project and includes the needed functional disciplines to support an IPD approach, it will be in a better position to assess and monitor these risks. In addition to identifying these risks, the team needs to take steps to mitigate these risks. This is an area that management may be needed to support the teams efforts. When risk tracking and risk reduction are subjects of phase gate and design reviews, it will force the team to pay attention to these factors. This risk management process need not be cumbersome nor complicated (see risk management plan example).

From a project planning and resource management perspective, it is important to recognize that higher risk projects increase volatility of planning and the potential need for additional resources and additional schedule. This should be factored into the project plan and a risk reserve provided in the form of budget and the resources to address risk issues.

Requirements management

Another factor affecting the project plan, the resource requirements and time-to-market is the ability to manage customer requirements and the product specification. It is important to establish a complete set of requirements at the start of the project and avoid proceeding into development before requirements are completely defined. Further, requirements need to be tightly managed to avoid creeping elegance and its impact on time-to-market. While rapidly evolving market needs may cause consideration of changes to requirements after the project is underway, these changes need to be carefully evaluated with a formal process to fully assess the impact on the development projects cost and the impact on time-to-market before a change is made.

Benchmarking and improving the process

In its effort to improve time-to-market, there are many potential steps for a company to consider. Where should it start? What are the most important actions for a company to take to improve its development process? What best practices should be adopted? To answer these questions, a company should start by assessing its strengths and weaknesses. Next it needs to consider its critical success factors - what is important to be successful in its market. Then by focusing on the "gap" between where a company is and where it needs to be, priorities can be set for making improvements.

The Product Development Assessment methodology and the supporting Product Development Best Practices and Assessment (PDBPA) software developed by DRM Associates provides a thorough review of the development process based on approximately 250 best practices that have been identified from studying companies' product development activities around the world. This level of detail allows identification of specific strategy, organizational, process, methodology and technology issues to address as part of an improvement programme. These best practices are organized into categories for summarization and reporting purposes.

Associated with each of these best practices is a set of questions to aid in this assessment process. A company's product development activities are evaluated with respect to each of these best practices, and a quantitative rating is developed. This evaluation is supported by a verbal description of the characteristics of the organization's product development approach as it evolves toward a world class approach to IPD.

In addition to the performance rating against each best practice and for each higher level category, an overall performance rating is developed by again assigning a weighting factor to each category based on their importance given the nature of the business and the product. This performance rating, when compared to that of other companies, gives an indication of the urgency of improving the development process.

Gap analysis is then employed to focus attention on the improvement opportunities that will yield the highest payoff. The categories with high weighting factors (indicating their importance to your product

Contd...

development success) and relatively low performance ratings yield the largest gaps between what is important to the organization and what it does well. These are the areas that require the highest priority in improving the development process and will likely have the largest payoff. On the other hand, categories with low importance ratings and relatively high performance ratings indicate low priority areas not deserving as much attention.

This gap analysis becomes the basis for identifying implementation actions and priorities. The concept is to pick a manageable number of improvement initiatives to focus your attention on. Once the large gap categories are identified, an examination of the individual best practices with lower performance ratings will help identify the specific areas that require attention. This then becomes the basis for developing priorities and, eventually, an improvement or implementation plan.

Summary

While formal project and resource planning and management processes may be in place for larger product development projects, many companies do not adequately use these tools and suffer the consequences. Even when formal project and resource planning and management systems are in place, management often avoids the hard decisions regarding overloaded resources. Significant opportunities exist to reduce time-to-market by a better focus on product planning, project planning and resource management. Specific steps and strategies include:

- Align project requirements with budgets and establish priorities in a product plan
- Focus on fewer projects at any point and concentrate resources on these projects
- Realistically plan projects based on the tailored development process
- Involve team members in project planning to enhance their understanding and commitment
- Assign people full-time to the project and build-up staffing rapidly
- Plan and manage resources; don't overload personnel
- Address risks and recognize the potential need for additional resources

Source: Kenneth. A. Crow is the president of DRM Associates, a management consulting and education firm focusing on integrated product development practices. You can visit the web at www.npd-solutions.com. Reprinted with the permission of the author.

Mind Power 12: New Product Incrementalism and the Death Spiral – Dan Adams

When a company relies heavily on new product "tweaks" - offering scant new value to customers— the downward spiral doesn't always lead to its death. Sometimes the condition is more akin to life support. The business still exists, but is marginalised and irrelevant within its industry. In either case, the end result is often irreversible, usually predictable and always unpleasant.

The Risk Paradox

Some producers incrementalise because they don't appreciate how risky this behaviour is. Imagine two scenarios. In the first, you've been asked to lead a team responsible for developing a new product. Your team could either make some minor modifications to an existing product... or "swing for the fence" with a blockbuster new product, based on new technology. Which do you choose? If you want to minimize your risk—just do your job now and avoid an inquisition later-you'll start tweaking.

The Risk Paradox: A business that relies on low risk, incremental new products is at great risk

In the second scenario, you've been promoted to general manager over this business, which has several new-product projects in the works. Here's the question: To minimize your risk, should all of

Contd...

the projects be low-risk new product tweaks? Absolutely not. This is the Risk Paradox: "A business that relies on low-risk, incremental new products are at great risk."

The Death (or Life Support) Spiral

Let's think through what happens when you simply crank out new products that look like your existing products. Over time, your products also begin looking like your competitors' products. Since your customers' purchasing agents didn't just fall off the turnip wagon, they move to commoditise your products. They deem the products they buy to be interchangeable and force you to drop your price... lest they interchange you out of the picture.

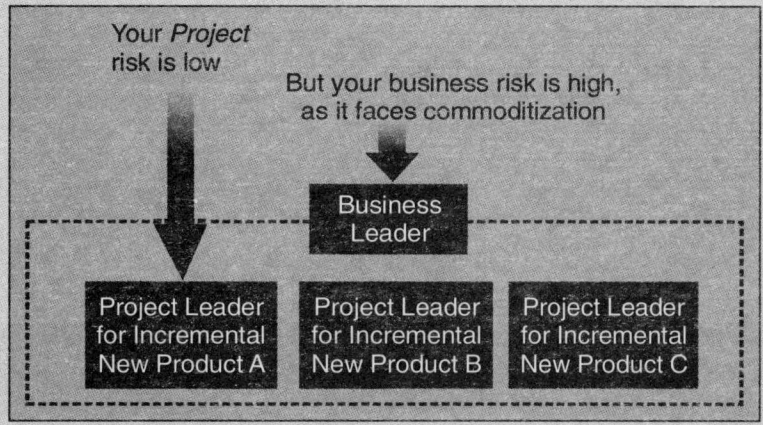

The Risk Paradox

Now it's time to budget for next year. Declining prices have led to declining profits, and nothing in your new product pipeline will change this anytime soon. Do you hand your boss a budget that promises reduced profits next year, with the cheerful notion that he can expect more of the same in following years? I'm guessing ..... no.

You have-two choices: (1) "Buy" market share by dropping your prices, hoping competitors won't match you, and (2) reduce your costs. Since the first approach can turn a death spiral into a death plummet, you opt for-door number two. But what costs to reduce? Surely nothing that's going to hurt business in the near-term.

Do you hand your boss a budget that promises reduced profits for next year?

How about research and development? After all, we're not really sure what these people do anyway, right? I worked for a large company once in which the president got lost in an unfamiliar building. All he saw were rows of labs, until finally he spotted an research and development director. On seeing a familiar face, he brightened up and said, "So this is where you research and development guys hang out." The research and development director replied (perhaps too hastily), "Actually we live in the surrounding hills and just come out at night."

So, if you cut some research and development costs and hit your budget next year, where are you then? Year by year, your capacity for pulling out of the death spiral diminishes, as the resources to produce differentiated new products are reduced. At some point, the spiral can become irreversible. Sadly, more than a few companies have reached this point.

"Great Hope" Projects

Many companies understand this spiral and want nothing to do with it. So they make sure they have a few "Great Hope" projects. Now these are **big** research and development projects. One of my

Contd...

customers once had a voice-mail message that said, "I can't come to the phone right now because I'm in the lab pushing back the frontiers of modern science."

The problem with such projects is that they often fail. Most seasoned executives have had bad experiences with these black holes. They can absorb millions of dollars, tie up valuable resources, divert management attention for 2-3 years and end with a whimper... usually from a fatal flaw that should have been found *much* earlier.

Need to "Get Out" More

So, if both incrementalism and "Great Hope" projects are too risky, what's the answer? I believe we need to "get out" more. Most companies are too internally focused in understanding two areas: customer needs and technical solutions. To put it another way, most companies fail to reduce commercial risk and technical risk because the *knowledge that will reduce their risk only resides outside their company*. As a company-shifts from an internal to an "outside-in" viewpoint, assumptions are tested and options are multiplied. These are great ways to reduce risk, but they won't happen enough *inside* your company.

You can reduce *commercial* risk in two ways when you conduct collaborative B2B customer interviews.

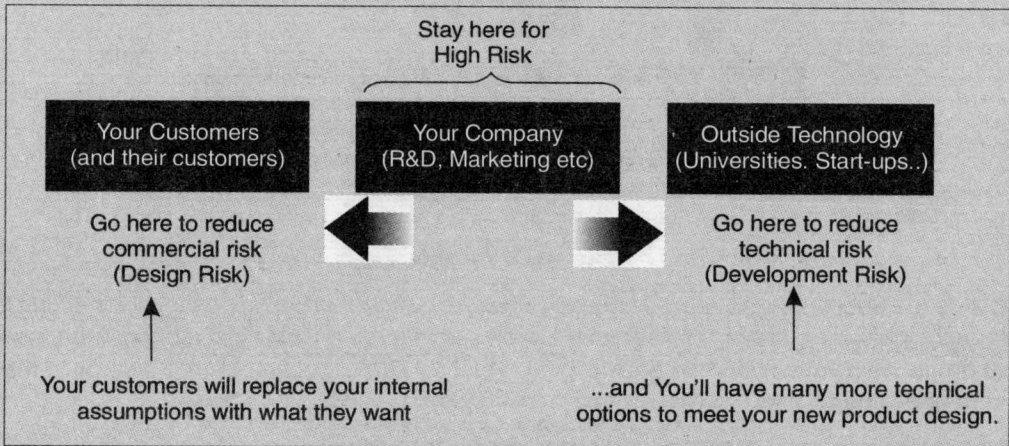

"Get Out" More to Reduce Risk

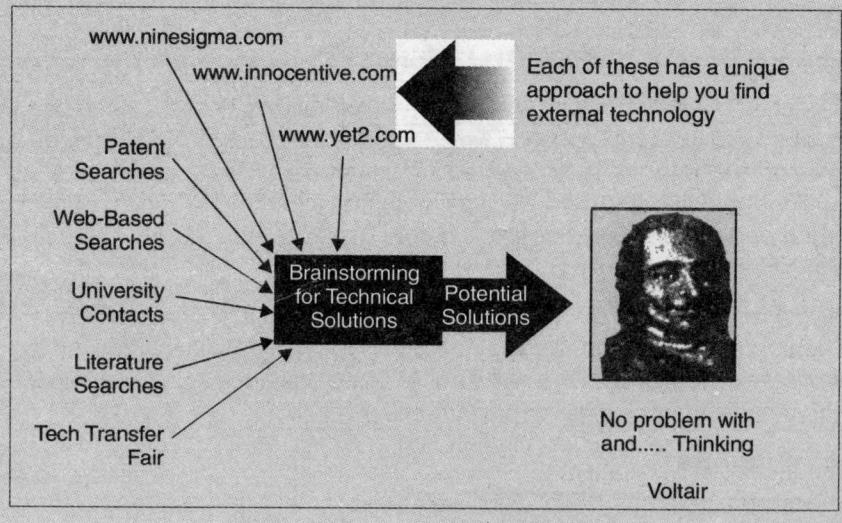

Open Innovation Sources

Contd...

First, as you enter your customers' world through in-depth interviews and tours, you'll discover unspoken needs... so your new product will make customers grin instead of yawn. Let competitors tweak. Second, you'll be able to kill big projects before they start if you learn that customers aren't interested in *your* "next big thing."

And you can reduce your *technical* risk by searching for technology that you don't have... but others do. The concept has been dubbed "open innovation" by Henry Chesbrough and is built on the notion that "not all of the smart people work for you." P and G, for instance, set the goal of sourcing 50 percent of its innovation from the outside, up from 10 percent. Their logic was simple: Approximately 1.5 million global scientists work in areas relevant to P and G, yet P and G *employs* less than 9000 of them. See Figure 3 for places to begin the process in-your company.

Let's review. Incrementalism puts a business at great risk, but simply investing in large, high-risk projects isn't the answer. We need to be more innovative about how we innovate. We need to ask questions that cannot be answered from within our company. We need to ask these questions of our customers (and their customers) to understand their unmet needs and reduce our commercial risks. And we need to ask these questions of external technologists to find novel solutions that reduce our technical risks.

Source: This article has been authored by Dan Adams. You can learn more about using customer interviews to uncover unmet needs at *www.newproductblueprinting.com*. Copyright with Advanced Industrial Marketing, Inc. This article has been reprinted with the kind permission of the author. You can visit them at www.aimtolead.com.

QUESTIONS FOR DISCUSSION

1. What is the competitive strategy, which one would follow across the life cycle of the product?

2. Augmented properties of an industrial product create a differentiation of the product. Discuss.

3. How would perceptual mapping techniques aid product evaluation decisions?

4. What are the factors you would consider, before eliminating a product?

5. "Systems marketing enables a supplier to differentiate its products from its competitors". Discuss.

6. How has technology influenced the industrial marketing scenario for over the years?

7. How would you facilitate new product development in your organization?

chapter

TEN

Marketing Channels

COMPANY PROFILE 10: L AND T (LARSEN AND TOUBRO)

Larsen and Toubro Limited (L and T) is a technology-driven engineering and construction organization, and one of the largest companies in India's private sector. It has additional interests in manufacturing, services and Information Technology. L and T has an international presence, with a global spread of offices. A thrust on international business over the last few years has seen overseas earnings growing to 18 percent of total revenue. The evolution of L and T into the country's largest engineering and construction organizations is among the more remarkable success stories in Indian industry. The company was founded in Bombay (Mumbai) in 1938 by two Danish engineers, Henning Holck-Larsen and Soren Kristian Toubro – both of whom were strongly committed to developing India's engineering talent and enabling it to meet the demands of industry.

Engineering and Construction - Projects

L and T's engineering and construction track record consists of successful implementation of turnkey projects in major core and infrastructure sectors of Indian industry. L and T has integrated its strengths in process technology, basic and detailed engineering, equipment fabrication, procurement, project management, erection, construction and commissioning, to offer single-point responsibility against stringent delivery schedules. Strategic alliances with world leaders enable L and T to access technical know-how and execute process-intensive large-scale turnkey projects to maintain its leadership position.

Heavy Engineering

L and T is acknowledged as one of the top five fabrication companies in the world, with engineering and manufacturing capabilities that are among the most sought after in industry. Operating at the high end of the technological spectrum, L and T has led Indian industry in introducing new processes, products and materials in manufacturing. L and T also has the logistics capabilities of fabricating and supplying over-dimensional equipment to tight delivery schedules.

Construction

ECC – the Engineering Construction and Contracts Division of L and T is India's largest construction organization. Many of the country's prized landmarks – its exquisite buildings, tallest structures, largest industrial projects, longest flyovers, highest viaducts, longest pipelines – have all been built by L and T.

Electrical and Electronics

In the electrical segment, the Company is India's largest manufacturer of low tension switchgear, and is rapidly establishing itself in international markets. Its products are widely sold in markets in Europe and Australia. Recently, L and T set up a new manufacturing base for high-end air circuit breakers in China. L and T also manufactures custom engineered switchboards for industrial sectors like power, refineries, petrochemical, cement, etc.

Information Technology

Larsen and Toubro InfoTech Limited, a 100 percent subsidiary of L and T, offers comprehensive, end to end software solutions and services with a focus on Manufacturing, BFSI and Communications and Embedded Systems. It provides a cost cutting partnership in the realm of offshore outsourcing, application integration and package implementation.

Machinery and Industrial Products

L and T manufactures markets and provides service support for critical construction and mining machinery - surface miners, hydraulic excavators, aggregate crushers, loader backhoes and vibratory compactors.

The company has also worked into areas of health, education, disaster management, environmental conservation as a part of their CSR.

Source: www.larsentoubro.com

Mind Power I: The Power of Balance between Partners – By Adam J. Fein, Ph.D.

In the strategic turbulence of today's industrial distribution channel, it is tempting to focus only on the "big picture" trends – electronic commerce, consolidation, or integrated supply, to name just a few. Yet, the forces of change still require distributors and manufacturers to pay close attention to the fundamentals of sound relationship management.

Manufacturers and distributors continue rely on each other's actions and resources. Simultaneously, each side struggles to maintain autonomy and control over its own operations in this era of dynamic uncertainty. This mutual dependency creates conflicts about direction, strategy and commitments. Business relationships between manufacturers and distributors are not altruistic, nor should they be. Both parties need to perceive a benefit from the relationship. But how can manufacturers and distributors work together, especially in situations when one party feels vulnerable to the other's actions?

The power of balance

Exhibit 1 shows a stylized diagram of four possibilities for a manufacturer-distributor relationship. If neither party is dependent on the other, then there is likely to be little benefit to coordinated action within the supply chain (lower left box). This type of situation occurs very rarely in industrial channels of distribution.

In the upper-left and lower-right boxes of Exhibit 1, either the manufacturer or the distributor can dictate the terms of the relationship. These extreme conditions represent relationships in which bargaining power is exercised to shift margin from one party to another, This type of zero-sum game does not create long-term competitive advantage for customers.

The upper right box, labeled Effective Relationship, represents the situation in which channel partners are bound together by a web of mutual obligations and opportunities. To build these relationships, manufacturers and their distribution partners should strive for the pourer of balance. In a balanced relationship, each side makes self-imposed commitments that create incentives to honor their agreements. Counterbalancing commitments stabilize the relationship.

Contd...

Exhibit 1: Effects of Mutual Dependence in the Distribution Channel

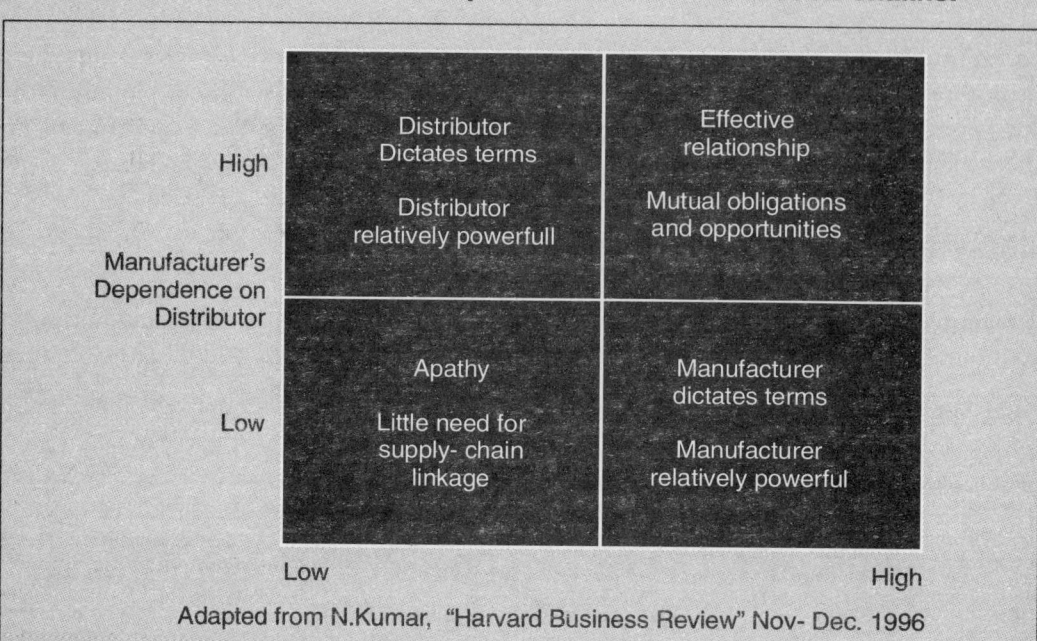

Adapted from N.Kumar, "Harvard Business Review" Nov- Dec. 1996

Each side in a channel relationship can demonstrate commitment by doing things that constrain their own opportunities and impose a cost on themselves if the relationship declines or terminates. By balancing exposure, the more exposed party receives some assurance that its vulnerable position will not be exploited.

The party that agrees to take on the counterbalancing risk both reassures its partner and obliges itself to live up to promises made. If both sides in a manufacturer-distributor relationship have self-imposed incentives to honor their agreements, then the relationship can become self-maintaining.

How balance works

To illustrate the power of balance, we can look at selective distribution agreements. A manufacturer can make a commitment to a distributor by limiting the number of distributors representing its brand within the distributor's market. Conversely, a distributor can make a commitment to a manufacturer by limiting the number of competing brands carried in the manufacturer's product category.

Using the power of balance, distributors should give a greater degree of brand selectivity to suppliers that give them greater territory selectivity, and manufacturers should give greater territory protection from intra-brand competition the more that distributor refrains from selling competing brands. Relationships remain stable and promote effective exchange when manufacturers and distributors restrict their alternatives in reciprocal fashion.

Consider the risks when there is no balance. A distributor that grants brand selectivity (at the limit, exclusivity) is at risk if the manufacturer decides to act in a self-interested way. For example, the manufacturer may not honor its agreement (explicit or implicit) to provide ancillary support because it knows that the brand is shielded from competition in the category. Thus, a one-way commitment from the distributor creates distrust and fear, limiting the effectiveness of the relationship.

Conversely, a manufacturer is at risk when it grants a territory to one or a few distributors. Restricting market coverage in a prescribed geographic area (ultimately, to a single distributor) places the manufacturer in a tough bargaining position with the distributor. For example, the distributor could charge above-market prices for the manufacturer's brand in the territory while continuing to offer an assortment of competing brands at various prices. The manufacturer suffers from the resulting decline in unit sales because the profits are not necessarily passed along through the distribution channel.

Contd...

Using the power of balance, we can see that a manufacturer-distributor relationship will be stronger when both parties make reciprocal, complementary decisions about selective distribution. A manufacturer and a distributor strengthen an unbalanced relationship by, paradoxically, weakening their own position.

When a distributor agrees to limit brands in a category, the manufacturer can reassure their distribution partner by making a reciprocal pledge of territory selectivity (at the limit, exclusivity). The manufacturer's commitment enhance its own incentive to maintain a relationship with a distributor that grants brand selectivity and is one of few suppliers for a geographic area. Limiting market coverage for its brand within a territory excludes a manufacturer from other distributors and their customers.

Similarly, a distributor's countervailing commitment also aligns the incentive structure within the relationship. Even though the distributor may gain some pricing flexibility, it must derive all category sales from fewer (at the limit, one) brands. This provides incentives for a distributor to support the brand because the distributor has deliberately cut off alternative suppliers and potentially limited its appeal to customers.

There are many other situations in which we can apply the power of balance to strengthening channel relationships. Consider investments made by the distributor to sell or service a particular manufacturer's brand. The distributor could lose much of the value of these investments if the relationship ends or if the manufacturer terminates the distributor. A voluntary commitment of exclusivity by a manufacturer protects the value of the investments made by the distributor in the manufacturer's brand. The distributor gains greater pricing flexibility due to the reduction in competition and is protected from competing distributors who may seek to free ride on market development and education efforts.

Other sources of relationship instability

Characteristics of your channel partner can heighten the perceived potential for undesirable or distrustful behavior. A commitment from the other member acts as a hedge against the heightened threat of self-interested behavior.

- **Customer pull:** Either a manufacturer or a distributor can enjoy a favorable position, or pull, with the ultimate buyer, the customer. From the distributor's perspective, the possibility of being supplanted by a manufacturer is heightened when the supplier's brand name is strong. For example, the brand may have unique attributes and be hard to replace. A strong brand can also generate positive effects for the distributor in other product categories by creating demand pull effects. Hence, the distributor which believes the brand name is powerful requires a commitment of territory selectivity as reassurance that the supplier will not use its brand power to squeeze the distributor. This commitment creates a self-enforcing agreement that benefits both sides.

  Conversely, the power of the distributor increases when the customer relies on the distributor for information or other value-added and transactional services, to make a purchase decision, such as integrated supply agreements between customers and distributors. The supplier is less able to bypass such a distributor and is more affected by the distributor's effort (or lack thereof) to generate brand demand. Hence, the supplier who perceives it is facing a distributor that "owns the customer" should insist on a countervailing pledge. Brand selectivity to ensure that the distributor will not opportunistically use its bargaining power or will not give its full support.

- **Direct sales:** Direct sales are sales to the potential customers of it distributor made directly by the manufacturer to a customer, bypassing the distributor. The level of direct sales is an ongoing source of tension in any manufacturer distributor relationship.

From the distributor's perspective, the motive for these sales is not clear. The manufacturer may simply be surrendering to the demands of high-volume accounts that have bargaining power. However, the distributor is unsure whether the supplier may be "cherry picking" the best customers or is preparing to do so in the future.

Contd...

For example, the supplier may be developing the capabilities that will allow direct competition with independent distributors, or even the elimination of the wholesale distribution channel in favour of a manufacturer-controlled electronic channel. This type of forward integration is perceived by a distributor as an ominous act by the manufacturer that could seriously damage the distributor's business.

Since it is difficult for a distributor to discern whether a supplier's motives are innocent or not, there will be considerable tension in the relationship. Distributors will be reluctant to invest in educating customers or supporting a brand if they believe that the sale will ultimately be made from an alternate, direct channel. Therefore, a manufacturer can demonstrate a commitment to the relationships by granting some type of exclusivity in exchange for allowing direct sales.

Implementing the power of balance

Strong relationships do not spring up quickly, easily or frequently. Instead, they are crafted slowly, passing through several stages in which the partners must deepen their investments and prove their trustworthiness and commitment.

I suggest that manufacturers and distributors can develop truly effective relationships by recognizing and exploiting their natural dependence on each other. By using the power of balance, both parties can receive some assurance that vulnerable position will not be exploited and that everyone has a positive incentive to live up to promises made. Eventually, these relationships can become self-enforcing; with limited need for extensive formal contracts that attempt to spell out every contingency. Unfortunately, too few channel partners see the power of balance, which often leads to litigation when a relationship ends.

Over time, trust and personal contacts can limit the need to craft these balanced relationships. But people and situations change, in the dynamic world of industrial distribution today, both manufacturers and distributors should work together to ensure a profitable and effective supply chain in the future by crafting effective, robust, and self-maintaining channel relationships using the power of balance.

Source: © 2002 Pembroke Consulting, Inc. Adam J. Fein is president of Pembroke Consulting, Inc. A strategy and marketing consulting firm. He can be reached at (215) 523-5700 or on the web at www.pembrokeconsulting.com.

MARKETING CHANNELS

Marketing channel is a very complex process of interaction between customers and businesses. The marketing channels deliver everything– from pins to machinery. Thus a marketing channel is defined as "a set of interdependent organization involved in the process of making a product or service available for use or consumption[1]." The objective is singular. Getting a particular product or service for use or for consumption.

The typical thing, however, is that although the goals of the organization and of the channels members are different but still there exists a symbiotic relationship between the two, for common goals. There are certain specific characteristics that we need to understand of channels. Channels will have their objectives to achieve a certain set of goals that an organization envisions. So business marketers are often posed with the question of selection of channels. "Which one to select?" The challenges lie in the fact that: (1) Different business would have different set of requirements, (2) There are a lot of options that are available. Today, thanks to Internet and reduction of transaction costs, marketers are constantly reviewing their channel decisions, to provide better value to their customers.

One more challenge that as a business marketer one would face, is managing the channels. The challenge lies in managing conflicts, power struggles legal requirements, performance evaluation etc.

This chapter on industrial marketing channels would thus be discussing on the above mentioned issues.

BUSINESS MARKETING CHANNELS AND PARTICIPANTS

Marketing channel is an interaction between customers and businesses or manufacturers. Now let us say that a manufacturer is making a particular product "x". Now he would be interested in reaching his potential buyers. The buyers would be located across various parts of the globe. They also would be having their individual set of needs. The challenges that the manufacturer will encounter are to negotiate, provide credit, transporting, storage, servicing and others. This task is sometimes quite difficult for the manufacturer himself to perform, and that is where the need for channels come in. We have two sets of channels. The first one is – Direct, where the manufacturer himself takes charge of the complete functions and the other is Indirect where there is an intermediary which acts as a "dealer" of such products. A question that immediately comes to our minds is — When do we use "direct" and when an "indirect" channel. We will discuss that shortly, but before that let us see the various options of channels structure.

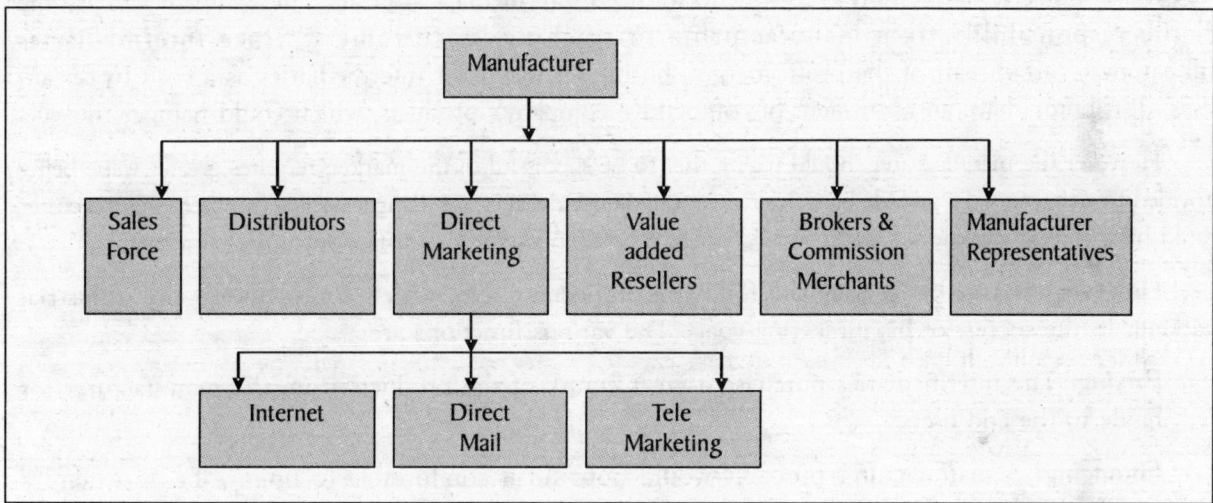

DIRECT AND INDIRECT DISTRIBUTION CHANNELS

Most of the manufacturer uses a mix of direct and indirect distribution channels; however it depends on a number of factors.

Direct distribution is when; there are no intermediaries between the manufacturer and its customers. In direct distribution, as we have said earlier that all the functions are to be taken care by the manufacturer. This direct distribution is necessary when:

1. The customers are large and their volume and value is high.

2. The negotiations run for a long period of time (setting up production process or a turn key project).

3. Customers require products which are highly complex, requires time and he needs to provide tailor-made solutions require direct channels. It requires huge amount of professionalism, strong selling and negotiating skills, and relationship building. Sales happen on mutual trust and understanding.

Indirect distribution is one, when at least one intermediary is used. This is used when the product is:

i)   Relatively simple and inexpensive.

ii)   Markets are fragmented and geographically dispersed.

iii) Buyers prefer multiple options.

However indirect distribution has its own set of advantages. The ultimate thing that an industrial customer wants is service. This job is quite well done by indirect distributors.

WHAT ROLE DOES INTERMEDIARY PLAY?

We can ask ourselves a question as to why do we need intermediary after all? The company can assume all the responsibility from manufacturing to reaching its customers. Since intermediaries will eat away certain part of the profit margin, businesses may treat intermediaries as a cost. In certain cases, distributors have an assortment of competitive company's products, which could hamper the sale.

However the manufacturer should realize that to be successful in the market, requires greater value being provided to customers. To provide better values require better delivery, servicing aspects. Also every manufacturer would have certain weaknesses, which would act as a bottle neck to the satisfaction of the customer.

However intermediaries play the following important role, which complements the industrial marketer in the success of his marketing goals. The various functions are:

1. *Buying:* The intermediaries purchase a great chunk of the products from the manufacturer for resale to the end users.

2. *Financing:* A manufacturer probably would not find it comfortable to finance i.e. to extend a credit period to its buyers. This job is well-performed by the intermediaries.

3. *Warehousing and Grading:* Since the manufacturer would not be spread across all geographical areas, warehousing forms a very important aspect of logistics. It is to ensure that goods reach the customers in a good condition. Also depending on the type of buyers and the quality of products, intermediaries grade the products as per various specifications to facilitate easy interaction.

4. *Transportation*: Logistical support is provided by the intermediary, to get the goods from the warehouse to customer's location. Sometimes buyers attach a great deal of important to prompt delivery, specially organizations who practice JIT.

5. The intermediary also performs other services. They are to provide technical assistance, especially for high involvement products. Also the intermediary would do promotion on behalf of the manufacturer.

CHOOSING THE DISTRIBUTOR

Choosing a distributor will form one of the key tasks for a manufacturer, because the success will depend upon building a strong relationship over the years, between the distributor and manufacturers. While choosing the distributor, some of the key considerations would be:

1. Size and type of distributor

2. The role they would play

3.   What are the products they would sell?

4.   Policies, rules and regulations

Size and type of distributor: It plays the most important role as sometimes the distributor is bigger than the manufacturer. They may carry a greater responsibility of the product through better service and also carry higher inventory. But however, they can also pressurize the manufacturer for better margins per unit sold. Also, such distributor over a long period of time can start commanding over the manufacturers decisions. The large distributors are beneficial in cases, when a product has weak market strength or a particular segment needs to be focused. However smaller distributor firms remain more committed and dedicated, and growth for the manufacturer and distributor will ensure larger growth over a long period of time.

The role they would play: Although we have discussed this in the earlier point, an addition to that is required. Depending on the size of the buyer and level of service required, manufacturers would decide the role of the distributor. Distributors would be given additional responsibilities of warranty, servicing, advertising, trade shows and credit.

What are the products they would sell: Generally manufacturers fragment the product lines, on the capabilities that the distributor possesses. Buyers generally look in to buy from a single source and thus fragmentation of the product line needs to be done carefully. In case of products being highly technical or complex, it is always better to handle the products using sales representatives.

In case of multiple channels how sales should be divided: This depends on the size of the market and market share that a channel member holds. Generally for smaller cities a single distributor is used, but in major big areas multiple distribution is essential.

Policies, Rules and Regulations: There is a lot of room for conflict in any kind of distribution (we will see later) and thus it becomes very essential to set the policies rules, standards and regulations in place. Clear instructions must be given, leaving little scope for ambiguity, as this forms the major source of conflicts. One more point that needs to be clear is that, the growth has to be beneficial to the both. Although, distributors and manufacturers have different policies, but it would be beneficial only with understanding and cooperation. Issues like manufacturers powers and of distributor's responsibilities have to be very clear before choosing the distributor.

PARTICIPANTS IN BUSINESS MARKETING CHANNELS

Usage of indirect channels in industrial marketing is a very common phenomenon. The performances of the intermediaries play a very important role for the success of a manufacturer. Thus understanding the various participants is very essential for any organization.

Distributors

Forms the most important way of doing business, amongst all channels. They are the most important force of a distribution channel. As said earlier, the size of distributors may vary considerably. Profits are mostly on volume of sales. Profits are low as percentage of sales. Most of the industrial manufacturers use them to sell some kind of products. Mostly they are used for maintenance, repair and operations supplies. They generally do operate from a single branch or multiple branches. However in distribution, the large ones tend to gain due to their size and also due to their reduction of sales and administrative expenses. They complement the manufacturer in the kind of work they do, specially handling wide range of products, technical assistance, credits. Distributors, often occupy greater importance to buyers. Distributors are gaining importance, with their job merely moving ahead of selling assorted products. More value added services are being provided by the distributors today, with their engineers partnering with buyers.

Distributors can be of three broad types. They are:

1. *General distributor*: They carry a broad range of industrial goods.

2. *Specialist distributors*: The focus on complementary related lines. A specialist distributor would be handling products from a related industry. This is because of more quality consciousness of buyers and technical complexities involved.

3. *Combination distributors*: They operate in two markets, i.e., industrial and consumer.

Manufacturer's Representatives

When products are technically complex and the buyer requires personal selling, manufactures, representatives or reps are used. They are also called as agents, sales agents or manufacturer's agent. They work only on a commission basis which is given only when a sale is realized. They are generally appointed for territories with lower potentials, where the cost of employing a direct sales force would be very high. They generally represent several companies in the same area and sell non-competing but complementary products.

The representatives know the technicalities of the product in and out, but generally do not carry any kind of inventory, except for a minimum level of inventory. Product knowledge, relationship with buyers and understanding buyer needs are his strength. They form a very strong arm of the manufacturer. They are highly experienced to offer technical advice and also does "end to end" selling i.e., building prospects to the final sales. They also keep the buyers informed about trends and innovations in the marketplace. They are paid commissions, which vary from industry to industry. So higher the sales, higher their earnings and this is what the manufacturer looks for, to cut down on costs of direct sales representatives. Reps handle fewer product lines compared to distributors. They form strong alternatives for a direct sales force, especially when a manufacturer is not willing to risk on a company employed sales force.

The biggest challenge that a manufacturer might find while using a representatives is to keep him motivated and not to lose control over him. Representatives also often complain about the unproductive work that they do, like follow up of payments, routine paper work and research work, as the time spend on these activities do not generate revenue for them.

Reps are generally used by small and medium firms and because of one single most reason of high cost of maintenance of an own sales force. Companies which are large also use reps like Monsanto and Mobil. Using reps is also beneficial, when the overhead costs need to be cut down. This can be achieved because there is no fixed salary or perks and very little training. They are useful in less concentrated markets especially the smaller cities and they can also be used to service distributors.

BROKERS: They occupy a less important position and may represent both a buyer and a seller and provide information on requirements. The relationship is for a shorter period of time. The broker may be used, to sell off the excess stock to other people, mostly through negotiations. They work on commission. They deal with standardized products, like raw materials etc. They tend to be useful when information to sell the "excess" is not available.

VAR (Value Added Resellers): They deal with specific market segments. They customize the needs to solve specific problems or meet specific requirements. They are specialists in their segment and provide value to both buyer and seller.

DESIGNING THE CHANNEL STRUCTURE

Designing the channel structure can be very challenging as a lot of success would depend on the right kind of design of the channel. Two important points that need to be made clear is that either the manufacturer is interested in modifying existing channels or the business marketer is interested in developing new channels in areas, where there is no existing channel. It is thus a very difficult task, which involves a lot of planning by the management. These plans should be in line with the goals that the company has set for themselves.

Designing a channel is a series of steps that the managers must understand to make sure that the entire dimension has been evaluated. When we try and design the channel structure, we look into the number of levels, intermediaries and the linkages. Today manufacturers are also faced with problems of vertical integration, i.e., to own some or all of its marketing channel has an enduring influence on its ability not only to distribute but also to produce.[2]

The process of designing a channel involves the following steps:

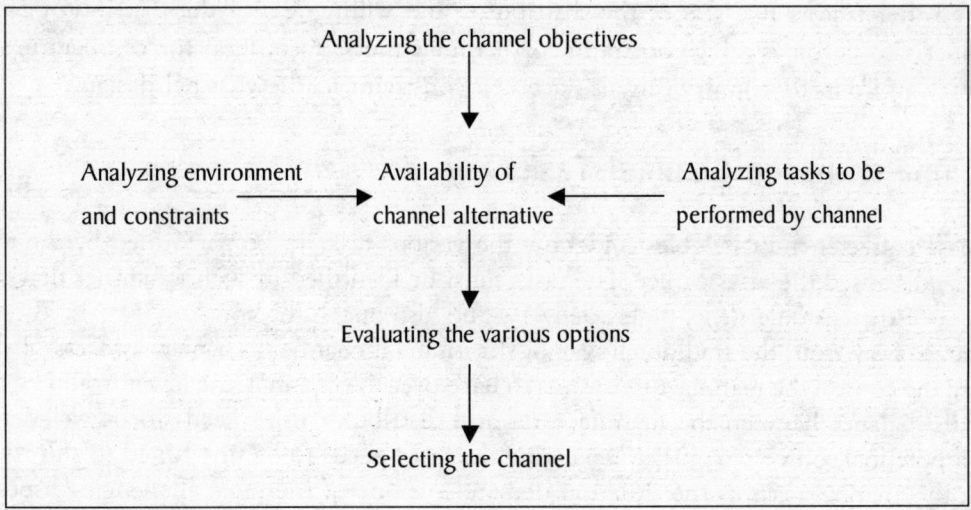

Step 1: Analyzing the Channel Objectives

Any business will have an objective with regard to sales and these objectives will come from channel objectives. Business will have their resource constraints and on the basis of which, the objective of either to appeal to a select segment or earn a certain level of profit will arise. Also the channel objectives would vary in terms of the product. That is, it would be a different channel objective for a high value, high involvement product than a low value, low involvement products. Products that are not highly differentiated, like steel products, availability of such products form a key objective for the marketer.

If the company is employing a manufacturer's representative to a direct sales force, the cost of making a sales call to a customer might reduce, but the degree of involvement would vary. Channel structure must be in line with marketing strategy.

The marketing and distribution objectives are a very strong factor of influence to the channel design. The structure must be designed in such a way, that it reduce costs, i.e., cost of maintain the channel and reducing of administrative costs.

Step 2: Analyzing Constraints

While analyzing constraints, it sometimes becomes quite difficult for the manager to decide on. The constraints could be multiple and often leaves the manager with very little choice. Some of the factors are:

1. *Customers location:* If the industrial marketer have small customers located across India, it will have problems in selecting its channel.

2. *Competitive forces:* Often competitive forces pressurize competing companies to establish a channel, quite similar to them.

3. *Company constraints:* The manufacture would have constraints in terms of financial power to afford a company sales force only to a select few regions.

4. *Products:* Greater the complexity, higher chances of establishing a direct channel. Often products which require high servicing and technical assistance may call for local distributors taking up the job servicing.

5. Some other factors like size of the distributor and willingness of the distributor to accept the product also becomes a big constraint for manufacturers. Also, legal forces operating within the country and outside country can also act as a constraint to the channel design.

Step 3: Analyzing the Channel Tasks

The business marketer must be able to identify the various tasks to be performed by the channel. We have already discussed the tasks earlier. The tasks must be identified in such a manner that, it meets the requirement of the customer (e.g., timely delivery) and also match the company's goals. Today managers need to move away from the traditional way of describing a channel as a mere process of distribution. Here, more the control the manufacturer wants to have over the channel, the lower would be distributor's margin. This balance between the manufacturer and distributor roles needs to be well-defined and is generally a potential source of conflict. Analyzing the tasks needs to be fine tuned to suit the objectives. Designing the channel tasks as the situation demands, is one of the most challenging aspects.

Step 4: Channel Alternatives

Once the manufacturer is clear on the objectives, constraints and the tasks to be performed by the channel, the next step is to look into the various alternatives that are available to a manufacturer. The various issues that need to be discussed while tackling channel alternatives are:

1. Direct or indirect channel

2. Types of intermediaries

3. Number of intermediaries

4. Other issues

1. *Direct or indirect channel*: Whether the marketer wants to have a direct or indirect channel has been discussed earlier. A marketer might choose from a number of alternatives that are available to him. Depending on the various segments that have to be served, an industrial marketer will base his decision.

    The length of a business marketing channel is influenced by availability of capable intermediaries, market factors and customer characteristics.

2. *Types of intermediaries*: A business marketer has a wide array of intermediaries to choose from. It could be a VAR's, manufacturer-rep, broker or commission agent. Depending on the need and the situation, will the marketer decide of the intermediary. We have also discussed, what is the situation when manufacturer representatives are used and when to use distributors. Now, depending on the market segments the intermediaries would be chosen. When the buyer account is large, products are complex, direct sales force is employed. In case of standardized products, distributors can be employed.

3. *Number of intermediaries*: Business marketers have shifted from the traditional role of distribution, to a market which is more demanding. There are three possible options available.

    a) *Exclusive distributor*: When a distributor does not carry competing products and there is only handful of intermediaries for the manufacturer's goods. This is exclusive distribution.

    b) *Intensive distribution*: Standardized products, low–priced and low–involvement products, which require low degree of servicing, but high degree of availability, requires intensive distribution.

    c) *Selective distribution*: It is when to choose channel members for a particular geographic area. The nature of purchase and product determine the selective distribution.

4. *Other Issues:* Issues such as the legal issues also considered at this juncture. Managing of key accounts, defining the geographical areas, restrictions to make sales call in some territories, competitor product handling, maintaining a certain level of inventory are some of the consideration that has to be given due consideration while deciding on to channel alternatives.

Step 5: Selecting the Channel

Before we select a particular channel, the step that we need to take is to evaluate the various alternatives that are available. Stern and Sturdivant recognize eight steps to evaluate a channel. They are:[3]

*   Determine customer requirement

*   Evaluate potential intermediaries

*   Analyze costs

*   Specify constraints

*   Compare options

*   Review constrains and assumption

*   Evaluate gaps

*   Implementation

Selecting a particular channel would happen only after we have evaluated the various alternatives. The selection would then be made on the basis of economic considerations, adaptation and amount of control that the marketer would exercise on the channels.

When we speak of economic considerations, business marketer would be interested to know of the level of revenue it would generate. They also would be interested in the financial strength of the distributor and whether they would be able to carry inventory requirements.

Adaptation is very important in the long-run, especially when the market conditions are changing. Small distributors would not be able to respond to competitive challenges and changes in the market place.

Control over the channel members is a very important issue of discussion as most of the conflicts arise due to control issues. It is generally seen that an industrial distributor is keen on pushing the fast moving products, there by neglecting other product lines. Having different objectives, manufacturers and distributors can often lock themselves on issues of control.

VERTICAL INTEGRATION

A question that comes in to the mind of the manufacturers is whether they should do all the work, i.e., from manufacturing to reaching its customers. This is because the moment a manufacturer decides to own the marketing channel, it would have a strong influence not only to distribute, but also to produce.[4] This would benefit the manufacturer also in terms of information about customers and competitors. The scope of vertical integration, although tremendous but quite depends on the outlook of the organizations.

The decision to integrate vertically, will have long-term impacts on the manufacturer and therefore should be a well calculated step. When the decision of vertical integration takes place, the cost benefit analysis must be done. Costs would be in terms of distribution costs, warehousing costs and of the personnel. Sometimes, findings out managers to handle these channels are difficult, as they would either be busy with manufacturing or few in number to handle distribution function. However the benefit is "control" over the channels. The question that comes up is that control itself has no use. In terms of profitability the manufacturer must gain.

SELECTING INTERMEDIARIES

Selecting the intermediaries and negotiating with them form a very important work for the manufacturer. They also need to be motivated and also conflicts arising must be solved.

Once channels have been selected, some of the channels may not perform or perform very poorly. Now, they require to be removed and new channels must be put to replace the old ones. It often becomes tedious and continuous tasks. The selection of intermediaries depends on market situations and product situation. Companies also have their own specifications for selecting an intermediary.

Mostly, all industries in India have an association. They have a list of potential distributors. Often manufacturers can solicit for new distributors through advertisements. Manufacturers would often use criteria like coverage, manpower and financial strength before short listing. Similarly distributors also evaluate the manufacturers specially profit potential and growth prospects.

MOTIVATING CHANNEL MEMBERS

The manufacturer has a long-term relationship orientation towards the market, but the distributors and manufacturer representatives are short-term profit oriented. This brings in a different in terms of their approach and their outlook varies greatly. Thus manufacturers must try and bridge this gap and bring all of them at one single common platform. Thus manufacturers must try and understand the intermediaries' perspective and must be able to generate suitable motivational programme that will help manufacturer achieve his long-term objective. The manufacturer will be able to guide the channel member behaviour, when the later becomes dependent on the manufacturer.

Partnership: Manufacturers must provide channel members with assistance, so as to build a sense of partnership. Increasing levels of trust, improved communications, training programmes and feedback will help generate a long-term partnering relationship. The objective is to build greater value, reduce cost and thus improve mutual benefits.

Dealer councils: Companies do have the facility of bringing all the channel members together periodically, discuss the plan and share information with them. Channel members generally utilize their opportunity to speak on their behalf about the problems they encounter. The inputs provided by the channel members, provide strong key insights and benefit the manufacturer to understand the loop holes and weaknesses in their product and system.

Margins, commissions and discounts: No doubt compensation plays a major motivating factor for the channel members. Compensation to channel members, must be highly market driven if not better than industry standards. This would be help the manufacturer, drive the channel members in harmony of their objective.

CONFLICT MANAGEMENT

Conflicts are bound to arise due to difference in objectives and perception of the manufacturer and channel members. Channel conflict arises when the behavior of a channel member is in opposition to its channel counterparts. It is opponent centered and direct, in which the goal or object sought is controlled by the counter part.[5]

Reasons for conflict could be multiple. Some of them are:

1. Increase in compensation
2. Maintenance of inventory levels
3. Difference of objectives and outlooks
4. Overlapping of boundaries/territories
5. Handling of customers
6. Use of Internet to bypass the distributors.

However the above list may not be exhaustive and there could be other reasons for channel conflicts. However the important issue is to solve the channel conflicts in an amicable way, otherwise the manufacturer would lose business, if the channel member threatens to call off. This conflict management can be done by better cooperation, coordination, building trust and relationship, and increased transparency. Sharing of information with channel members, joint goal setting can bring in the high level of trust and confident amongst the members. It is only then the channels would be able to perform better and the manufacturers achieve its objectives.

EVALUATING MEMBERS AND INCREASING EFFECTIVENESS

The channel members need to be evaluated periodically on their performance. This would give the manufacturer a very clear picture on the member and would enable a manufacturer to take a decision on whether to maintain the member or eliminate them. Channel members performing well, needs to be heavily rewarded to keep them motivated. Evaluation of the channel members can be on various qualitative and quantitative factors. The factors could include:

1. Sales delivery

2. Customer feedback

3. New customer generation

4. Inventory level carried

5. Overall performance

Scores are given against each factor, and weighted average can be obtained to find out their performance levels. However for different channels different benchmarks can be followed. Members in the border line or the ones performing poorly, can be given additional support and discussed. If the performance still does not improve, they can be eliminated.

If the manufacturer wants his channel member to be effective, certain areas need to be highlighted for a better enhanced performance. They are:

1. Setting up of unrealistic goals by the manufacturer would do no good for its channel members.

2. Better transparent relationships between the manufacturer and its members. Poor communication leads to distrust, and this becomes a major issue and source of conflict. Companies should have clear cut set objectives, better transparency in bringing out effectiveness.

3. Training and support must be provided to channel members. Areas of weakness should be highlighted. Distributors would require training to increase sales effectiveness. Also as we have earlier discussed, the issue to support one another. Manufacturer's image is very critical for channel members to succeed and the channel members services to the customers, will determine the manufacturers success. Thus a true symbiotic relationship must exist in between them.

CONCLUSION

Marketing channel is one of the most important challenging and dynamic aspects of business marketing. Although a manufacturer might have the best product, but the success depends greatly on the middleman or the channel member. Manufacturers also have a lot of options to choose from and that is what makes it challenging.

The managing, appointment and designing the channel form the key job. This altogether has lot of complexities involved in them. Better transparency, communication, build stronger relationship amongst channel member and manufacturer.

We have also seen the various options available and the respective advantages and disadvantages of the same. Channel management is an ongoing task to achieve the marketing objectives.

We have also seen the sources of conflict ways to resolve conflict and also the need to motivate channel members. Increasing effectiveness by better relationship management, better support, realistic goal setting, brings in a sense of commitment amongst channel members. The success lies with the manufacturer and his ability to control, manage and build the channels over a platform of trust and commitment.

REFERENCES

1.   Coughan, Anderson, and Stern, Ansary, *Marketing Channels*, 6th edition, Pearson Education Asia, pp 3.

2.   Coughan, Anderson, and Stern, Ansary, *Marketing Channels*, 6th edition, Pearson Education Asia, pp 161.

3.   Stern and Sturdivant (July/August 1987), *Customer driven distribution system*, HBR 65, pp 34-41.

4.   Coughan, Anderson, and Stern, Ansary, *Marketing Channels*, 6th edition, Pearson Education Asia, pp 161.

5.   Coughan, Anderson, and Stern, Ansary, *Marketing Channels*, 6th edition, Pearson Education Asia, pp 238.

Mind Power 2: The Redistribution Advantage

Want to offer your customers thousands of more products without expanding your warehouse or making a huge financial investment? Then maybe it's time to turn to redistributors — manufacturers as well as distributors are calling upon redistributors more and more these days.

In fact, redistribution in the foodservice channel alone is a $5.5 billion industry in the United States, according to Technomic Inc., a Chicago-based marketing research firm serving the food and foodservice industries. Technomic forecasts a robust 16 percent compounded average annual growth between now and 2010 for the foodservice channel, says Gary Karp, vice president. This growth is driven primarily by the impact on the industry of the redistribution initiative of Sysco, which will open its first redistribution facility in 2005," Karp says. He also adds that because channels like retail, club and convenience stores are more mature, their growth rates have stabilized.

Houston-based Sysco Corp., the nation's largest foodservice distributor, is building a network that will feature a system of regional distribution centers designed to handle all of the less-than-truck load (LTL) volume that flows from manufacturers to the local Sysco branches.

Redistribution is an effective tool for handling cost-to-serve issues for high-cost customers whose volumes are low or who require extra special handling of things like mixed pallets or less than pallet loads, essentially anything resulting in a reduction of efficiency, Karp says.

Redistribution has evolved to the point that most foodservice manufacturers and distributors recognize its value. The majority of foodservice distributors, both large and small, purchase from redistributors; nearly every major manufacturer has likewise taken advantage of the benefits offered by redistributors.

As a result, the foodservice volume handled by redistributors has grown at a pace that far outstrips the industry-and managers in other food industry channels are beginning to take notice.

While Dot Foods, Mt. Sterling, IL, is the clear leader in food redistribution, with national service across all temperature classes, other companies offer redistribution services by focusing on limited product lines and/or geography. These include the Rochester, NY-based Empire Beef Co. Inc.; Foodservice Center Inc., St. Louis: Honor Foods inc., Philadelphia; and Don Greene Poultry Inc., Opa Locka, FL.

There are also many foodservice distributors who dabble in shipments to other distributors, without offering sales reporting and other services provided by the major redistributors.

Manufacturers, Distributors Benefit

Successful redistributors have grown because they are uniquely positioned to provide great value to both manufacturers and distributors.

To the **food manufacturer**, it sound redistribution strategy will yield:

* Outsourced management: of small, high cost-to-serve customer orders;

Contd...

- Access to additional customers of whom they might not now be aware;
- Reduced credit risk;
- Simplified logistics;
- Additional sales support; and
- Accelerated sampling response.

Food distributors likewise benefit from:

- Faster turns;
- Shorter lead times;
- Weekly deliveries;
- No minimums per manufacturer; and
- The efficiency of one order, one delivery, and one invoice for many different manufacturers.

The problems solved by redistribution are not unique to the foodservice street channel. Food manufacturers and redistributors are beginning to develop creative approaches to systems distributors, bakery/deli specialists, vending and convenience store distributors. As a result, a new crop of sales, marketing, finance and supply chain people are working to figure out how redistribution fits into their strategies.

For manufacturers, key considerations revolve around which customers to steer toward "redi" (redistribution), which products to offer through redi and the financial ramifications of a redi program.

Distributors who struggle to meet minimum order weights, or who submit small and infrequent orders, are obvious candidates for service through redistribution.

Those who buy in truckload quantities clearly are not. Most manufacturers consider distributors who average less than one-half truckload per order as potential redi candidates, although as we shall see, the economics of filling the smallest orders is quite different: from the economics for the larger orders.

Influencing customers to buy (or not buy) from redistributors requires a combination of disciplined pricing practices, healthy working relationships between the manufacturer and redistributor, and sales force buy-in to the redistribution strategy.

The question of which products to offer through redistribution likewise bears careful consideration. In general, a manufacturer's product choice will be driven by the distributors it serves through redistribution. The system works best for all parties when a distributor is able to source a given manufacturer's entire line via redistribution, as opposed to splitting orders between it redistributor and direct service.

This becomes problematic for some manufacturers when it comes to private label, custom-packed and special-priced products. We often hear statements like "our margins are too thin on those products to put them through redistribution." While this is an understandable concern, we usually counter with "your costs don't care what label's on the box, or what price is on the invoice." This is why it thorough understanding of "redi economics" is crucial to developing a successful redistribution strategy.

'Redi Economics' 101

Redi economics for the manufacturer starts with a thorough analysis of cost avoidance for redi vs. direct service, and proceeds through marketing value and revenue impact.

When existing business is switched from direct to redi service, a manufacturer could reduce both hard logistics costs and softer order management costs. The hard savings are in customer freight, and may also include deployment and warehousing costs if the redistributor is able to pick up at a manufacturing plant. The challenge for manufacturers is to quantify these costs for the

Contd...

specific set of customers who are redi candidates. Looking at averages or company rules of thumb is inadequate because small-order customers drive higher costs throughout the supply chain. These hidden cost drivers include higher frequency of hand-picking, excessive stop charges and reduced trailer utilization.

The order management cost offsets are more difficult to quantify, but doing the work is often an eye-opening experience. Order management costs include all of the activity from receiving and entering orders through booking loads to extending credit, billing and collecting. When the "percent of orders" is compared to the "percent of volume," manufacturers begin to see that they are often laboring like an elephant to give birth to it mouse.

Some argue that even if all small-order customers are outsourced to redistributors, there is no order management cost reduction without a headcount reduction. This argument reflects the fact that current accounting systems and practices are incapable of reflecting the cost of order management, and therefore the savings when order management activity is reduced.

In fact, this issue is responsible for the occasional bum rap given to redistribution programs by some manufacturers. The redi allowance is clear and quantifiable, while the savings are often fuzzy and buried in overhead allocations.

Even without clearly documented cost savings, however, wise manufacturers will redeploy their order management resources when they move a significant amount of activity to redistributors, while the cost reduction is not explicit on the profit and loss statement, there is no doubt that money is saved when order management activity is reduced.

Another consideration is the marketing value of having your products available through redistributors. There is no question that distributors value having a manufacturer's product within arm's reach and available on a weekly basis with no minimums and with short lead times. It is also likely that fill rates and service levels will be higher through good redistributors than with direct service. As always, the challenge for the manufacturer is converting happier distributors into more business in order to benefit from this marketing value.

Manufacturers Expand Reach

Perhaps of greater interest to manufacturers is the opportunity to penetrate new distributors that would not be available through direct service. Redistributors serve a wide range of accounts that are hard to reach via traditional supply chains. These include not only small distributors who lack the volume or space to meat order minimums, but various jobbers, segment specialists and non-mainstream distributors who are often unknown even to the local brokers. Access to this new universe is certainly worth a few margin points.

The final piece of the redistribution puzzle for manufacturers is an understanding of the revenue impact of moving volume through redis. Manufacturers who enforce strict bracket pricing will need to account for revenue slippage when a redistributor buys at FOP (freight on board) plant prices to serve existing business that was billed at the highest delivered price bracket. Special prices, bids, and trade deals all take on an added level of complexity when they are managed through redistribution. And the redistributor's pricing practices relative to the manufacturer's price list must be clearly understood in order to develop an effective program.

Distributors Improve Service

From a distributor's perspective, redistribution also provides an effective solution to several persistent problems. Bruce Merrifield, a consultant based in Chapel Hill, NC, works extensively with wholesale distributors in many channels and believes redistribution will continue to grow rapidly throughout the food supply chain.

"The distributor's bread and butter is demand replenishment," says Merrifield. "Starting with his operator customer's demands, he must constantly find ways to provide one-stop shopping, a high till rate, and

Contd...

access to unique, low-volume items. By providing weekly service on a wide range of product lines, redistributors can provide measurable improvement in many key areas."

Merrifield cites reduction in inventory cost as an obvious benefit. He adds that distributors usually also show improvement in fill rate, average payload per stop and customer satisfaction when they use redistribution strategically. In a recent study of redistribution in the industrial bearings industry, Merrifield found that "the average cost of order entry has dropped from more than $5 per line to less than 30 cents (again, a difficult-to-measure hidden benefit). One distributor customer reported "inventory investment reductions of 25 percent with significant increases in fill rates, because stock inventory can be replenished and re-tuned weekly." Distributors have further found that dramatic improvements in the lead times for special orders have saved old business and won new orders. Certainly food distributors who use redistribution are realizing these benefits as well.

Pitfalls to avoid

Successful programs are based on a solid understanding of the principles outlined above, development of a sound strategy and persistent implementation. When addressed in a halfway manner, redistribution programs are subject to risks and challenges that can undermine their value. For manufacturers, failure to truly understand costs and cost: offsets can make redistribution look like a bad decision (or even worse, can drive a truly bad decision).

Occasionally, manufacturers get heartburn when the wrong distributors migrate to redi service. It can happen that a large, low cost to serve distributor elects to add a manufacturer's line to his redi order, creating a delicate situation if the manufacturer has to incur added cost. These situations are easier to prevent than to reverse, so a shared understanding of the target market is essential.

Other manufacturer concerns include putting all the eggs in one basket syndrome, where they fear giving up control of their business to a third party. This fear is worsened if sales people and brokers are allowed to fall into an out of sight, out of mind attitude toward the distributors who buy through red is. It is incumbent on manufacturers to maintain close business building relationships with distributors, even when the order fulfillment role is filled by a redistributor.

Finally, some manufacturers make the mistake of accounting for redi allowances as a trade expense. This practice fails to recognize the cost savings realized in the supply chain. Charging a proportional amount of the allowance to the supply chain group not only provides a more accurate reflection of the business, but also ensures that supply chain people are involved in program development as well as ongoing redi optimization.

Smart manufacturers and distributors are putting together a redistribution strategy which addresses all of the above issues, and are thinking well beyond the food service street channel as they seek to improve results. A sound program based on well-understood cost savings and marketing value is the start.

Diligent management of the redi channel is also necessary to maximize return on investment. Food manufacturers and distributors who excel at both will continue to reap all of the potential benefits of redistribution.

Source: This article has been authored by DeWalt, president of Franklin foodservice Solutions, Franklin, MI, has been working as an independent solution provider for foodservice manufacturers. For more information visit *www.franklin-foodservice.com.* Reprinted with permission.

Mind Power 3: Redefining B2B Channels – By Richard Vurva

The bloom has faded from the rose. Just a few short months after opening their doors with great flourish and fanfare, online marketplaces are shutting down, laying off employees or restructuring their business plans. Many online marketplaces (OLMs) – once touted as the new way for buyers to purchase MRO products – have either abandoned the idea of a public marketplace or relegated it to a lesser role.

Contd...

For example, MROLink, formerly IndustrialAmerica.com, is now focusing on developing print catalogs and custom onsite catalogs for distributors. Excara, which recently changed its name from PurchasingCenter.com, closed its marketplace in mid-December and will devote its energies toward helping manufacturers digitize content for Internet use. And supply FORCE, the online marketplace that members of Affiliated Distributors hoped would gain them entry into the world of e-commerce, now plans to focus exclusively on the national contract side of the business.

What caused this sudden change in direction? Why, in a span of less than 12 months, did companies surrender their plans to assemble marketplaces for one-stop shopping?

In large part, OLMs failed to accurately gauge the readiness of the end-user customer to buy online.

Results of a new study of Fortune 500 companies' shows less than one-third of these businesses order strategic goods from online suppliers and many have no idea how well their electronic procurement systems perform. The majority of companies responding to the study did not know the actual number of purchases they made from online suppliers, according to the study by the Hurwitz Group, a Boston-based consulting and research company.

One reason buyers aren't doing more transactions through marketplaces is because they don't want to stop dealing with their traditional suppliers.

"The trends are pointing away from public marketplaces where unlimited buyers and suppliers connect to each other, searching for the best deal and analyzing offerings of multiple suppliers," says Bill Eisele, an analyst with the Hurwitz Group. Instead, the trend is moving toward building private marketplaces between customers and existing suppliers.

"Buyers want to connect to the same suppliers they were dealing with before," he says. "Suppliers want to keep up with the changing times and stay connected to buyers they're already working with. At this point, companies on both sides are comfortable simply automating the transactions they were already doing. They're not looking to reach a whole new spectrum of business partners."

Not dead, just delayed

Just because OLMs have failed to catch on in the industrial community doesn't mean the concept of electronic procurement is doomed. More likely, the timing is wrong.

Bob Segal of Frank Lynn and Associates says there are four reasons online marketplaces haven't succeeded. No. 1, there are too many of them. Each OLM is scrambling to build an identity, causing confusion in the marketplace. No. 2, sources of capital have dried up. This is true not just for OLMs, but for most dot-corn start-ups. No. 3, and perhaps most important, the OLMs have done a bad job of explaining their short-term return-on-investment value proposition.

"Virtually none of the marketplaces made a compelling argument that says we're going to charge you 2 to 3 percent to process transactions, but we're going to reduce your costs by double or triple that," he says.

The fourth problem OLMs face is a lack of data standards. There are no common standards for describing product attributes. It cost the OLMs much more of their venture capital to create product databases than they thought it would.

Where's the pain?

Why aren't customers and their existing suppliers migrating more quickly to the Internet? For most buyers, it's still easier to do business the old-fashioned way. When they want to make a spot buy, they pick up the phone or check a catalog. It's even simpler for customers to make repetitive purchases. Thanks to the popularity of distributor bin stocking programs on the manufacturing plant floor, end-user customers rarely place their own orders.

"Small-dollar repetitive items are in free issue. Distributors order that stuff for the customer," says Doug Ruggles president of Martin Plant Services, the integrated supply division of Martin Supply

Contd...

Company. "Many customers don't have to do anything to order those items. Will they use e-commerce? No. They have no cost to procure this stuff today."

Who will move first?

Most distributors expect their large customers will be the first to make the move to online procurement. But Ruggles says Internet ordering won't catch on even with large customers until it is tied into the enterprise resource planning systems those companies utilize.

"When that becomes seamless, that's when e-commerce will take off," he says. "But it will take longer to get there than what most people think."

Two things prevent most distributors from embracing e-procurement. The first is money.

"For us to get the benefits of the Web, we have to change our software," says one distributor. "Unless we're ready to make that investment, we're not going to be e-commerce ready. A software conversion is not only expensive, it's a hassle."

Distributors investing in e-commerce capabilities today are placing bet on a horse that not only hasn't left the gate, it's still in the stable.

"In most cases, distributors understand they're not buying immediate results. They're buying the ability to offer better customer service to their current clients who are beginning more and more to request c-commerce capabilities," says Albert Cassola, director of marketing for Thomas Regional. "They're also buying some piece of mind because by being proactive and choosing to engage in c-commerce, they're positioning their business to remain strong."

A second stumbling block for distributors is a fear of losing their identity. On the Internet, all distributors look alike.

"Online catalogs don't do justice to their products." says Eisele.

Small and mid-sized distributors struggle with how to differentiate themselves on the Web. It's difficult to translate unique service offerings to an automated catalog environment. Until marketplaces give sellers a good chance to differentiate themselves, at an affordable price, distributors aren't likely to sign on with them in large numbers.

Despite the failures of some online marketplaces. Segal says the concept is still sound.

"Rome wasn't built in a day." he says. "It looks messy right now. Many, if' not most of them, will be out of business. But the alternatives look even worse. The concept is good; it's just going to take a little while to get there."

E-commerce adoption rates will likely follow the same pattern that all technology takes, Segal says. The large, technologically savvy companies, particularly in the automotive, electronics and energy industries, move first. Change then migrates to the rest of the business world. But it's a slow-moving process that could take years.

Mind Power 4: Guidelines for Changing Channels of Distribution

Many manufacturers, who have been going to market through established channels that date back to the late 60s or earlier, are experiencing, today, growing stress with their channel partners which usually includes reps, distributors and/or dealers. These relationships have been historically cemented together by the memories of the good years together in the 60s and 70s when growing up with America was easier and more profitable. During this period, partners steadily invested resources in supporting one another to reach significant levels today which are difficult to abandon. And, the top managers are often close friends who grew up doing business together.

Contd...

The stress within these relationships has been caused by a number of trends that accelerated in the 80s:

1. World supply of manufacturing capacity aimed at the U.S. market has continued to outpace a domestic demand that has leveled off. The U.S. has created the first post-consumer society in which a majority of people have run out of waking hours to consume. Total consumption of all things is dropping towards the 1 percent growth rate of the population.

   Instead of a growing demand pulling products through the channel profitably, many manufacturers are now trying to ram-and-jam too much supply through channels even at losses thinking perhaps that someday they will make it up on volume.

2. Channel power has switched from manufacturers to end-users. Consumers, for example, had to buy white refrigerators and black phones at book prices from authorized sellers until the late 60s. These were symptoms of supply being less than the demand.

   With today's global-glut supply and saturated demand, end-users express their growing power in many ways. We, as consumers for example, now expect perfect quality goods and service, unconditionally guaranteed forever. We want over choice in product selection, and we want flexibility in the types and quantity of services available. We want convenience, user-friendliness in buying, speed in delivery, and lower prices. We are steadily getting more of these needs met by more suppliers.

3. Manufacturing technology and methods continue to move towards the make-anything, in-any-quantity-now factory. This will please end-users, but it creates the growing problem of how to market micro-segmented products through traditional commodity channels and mass media.

4. New manufacturing suppliers, often foreign, who can't find qualified intermediaries to distribute their products aren't hindered. "Channel blocking" stills keeps U.S. firms out of Japan and other markets. In the U.S. the new entrants might: sell direct, set up their own distribution in the biggest markets, or sell a new breed of intermediary that traditional suppliers are afraid to sell for fear of retaliation from existing partners. The U.S. business infrastructure is so accommodating and Americans are so quick to experiment with new brands and new intermediary suppliers that penetration happens and competition escalates.

5. With too much supply, and not enough demand all players in the channel are experiencing profit erosion, so consolidation of players at each step in the channel continues. Instead of selling through lots of small, independent agents, distributors and retailers that could be controlled, manufacturers are faced with selling big chains or cooperative groups that control market share or shelf space and can push the manufacturers around.

6. Intermediaries used to have to please just the manufacturers and pass the prices, policies and terms on to the end-user. Now the big end-users are dictating terms too; the intermediaries are getting more anxious about who and how to serve.

7. Progressive manufacturers would like to sell their fragmenting line of goods to more and smaller segments of potential customers which their existing intermediaries haven't pursued and may not be geared to serve. The logical solution should be for the manufacturers to sell niche products through alternate channels that some of their intermediaries might create. Many intermediaries, however, don't see the need to change or don't want to change and threaten retaliation if manufacturers should sell alternate channels. Other manufacturers will then, unfortunately, sell their equally excellent products to the alternate channels. Traditional-thinking intermediaries are, in other words, asking progressive suppliers to join them in putting their heads in the sand, managing the past, and also suffering market share decline.

Conclusions

Because of the enormous diversity in both products and the channels through which they are sold, there are only a few specific conclusions that can apply to most stressed channels:

Contd...

1. Manufacturers and their partners should stop being volume and product-driven and become end-user or customer-needs driven. If partners can more precisely target segments of customers and give them exactly what they want in products and services, then they will be able to penetrate and retain them better and more profitably than the competitors. Volume and market share will then grow as a by-product; partners must make volume the caboose not the engine.

2. All partners must become niche marketers. If manufacturers can successfully micro-segment both end-users and their matching product lines, then they will probably have to use new marketing methods for reaching specialty buyers.

3. Let the end-user be the final arbiter of what and how they want to buy. If Intermediaries understand these niche customer needs, then they should be glad to reinvent themselves to be part of the solution or stand aside and let their manufacturing partners sell in alternative ways.

4. If channel partners can stop managing the past and share a common strategic understanding of what it takes to succeed in a global-glut, post-consumer demand economy, then they can work successfully with the trends. If one or more partners are still operating with outdated, unspoken assumptions for how the partners should be going to market, then tough decisions will have to be made. The partners who push on with forward-thinking strategies do not, however, usually suffer much retaliation. The resisters, instead, begrudgingly start to follow along and can eventually become quite enthusiastic about the new order of business.

Source: Copyright with Merrifield Consulting Group, Inc. Visit them at *www.merrifield.com.* Reprinted with permission.

QUESTIONS FOR DISCUSSION

1. What are the factors that an industrial manufacturer would consider before preparing his products channel of distribution?

2. What are the various tasks performed by distribution channels?

3. What is the ideal channel of distribution for an industrial manufacturer?

4. How is Internet changing the channel structure and strategies?

5. Contrast between manufacturers' representatives, sales persons and distributors?

6. "Intermediaries increase the prices of the goods. B2B manufacturers must try and eliminate them" – Discuss.

7. What factors would you consider for a direct distribution channel and an indirect distribution channel?

chapter

ELEVEN

Marketing Logistics and Supply Chain Management

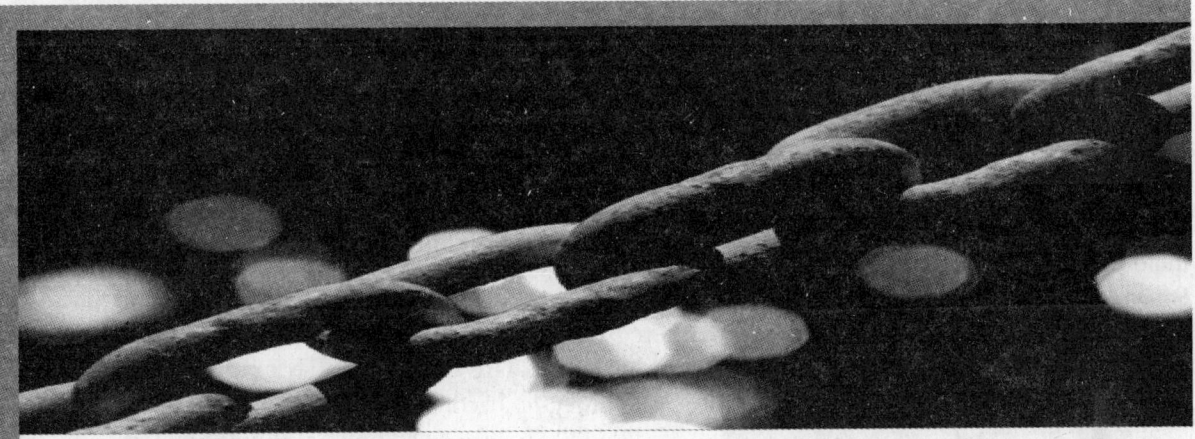

COMPANY PROFILE 11: BHEL (BHARAT HEAVY ELECTRICAL LIMITED)

BHEL is the largest engineering and manufacturing enterprise in India in the energy-related/ infrastructure sector today. **BHEL** was established more than 40 years ago, ushering in the indigenous Heavy Electrical Equipment industry in India – a dream that has been more than realized with a well-recognized track record of performance. The company has been earning profits continuously since 1971-72 and paying dividends since 1976-77.

BHEL manufactures over 180 products under 30 major product groups and caters to core sectors of the Indian Economy viz., Power Generation and Transmission, Industry, Transportation, Telecommunication, Renewable Energy, etc. The wide network of **BHEL's** 14 manufacturing divisions, four Power Sector regional centers, over 100 project sites, eight service centers and 18 regional offices, enables the company to promptly serve its customers and provide them with suitable products, systems and services–efficiently and at competitive prices. The high level of quality and reliability of its products is due to the emphasis on design, engineering and manufacturing to international standards by acquiring and adapting some of the best technologies from leading companies in the world, together with technologies developed in its own research and development centers.

BHEL has acquired certifications to Quality Management Systems (ISO 9001), Environmental Management Systems (ISO 14001) and Occupational Health and Safety Management Systems (OHSAS 18001) and is also well on its journey towards Total Quality Management.

BHEL's operations are organized around three business sectors, namely **Power Industry** - including Transmission, Transportation, Telecommunication and Renewable Energy - and **Overseas Business.** This enables **BHEL** to have a strong customer orientation, to be sensitive to his needs and respond quickly to the changes in the market. BHEL's vision is to become a world-class engineering enterprise, committed to enhancing stakeholder value. The company is striving to give shape to its aspirations and fulfill the expectations of the country to become a global player.

The greatest strength of **BHEL** is its highly skilled and committed 42,600 employees. Every employee is given an equal opportunity to develop himself and grow in his career. Continuous training and retraining, career planning, a positive work culture and participative style of management – all these have engendered development of a committed and motivated workforce setting new benchmarks in terms of productivity, quality and responsiveness.

BHEL lays great emphasis on the continuous upgradation of products and related technologies, and development of new products. **BHEL's** commitment to advancement of technology is reflected in its involvement in the development of futuristic technologies like fuel cells and superconducting generators. **BHEL's** investment in research and development is amongst the largest in the corporate sector in India. Products developed in-house during the last five years contributed about 7 percent to the revenues in 2005-06.

Towards meeting its Quality Policy, **BHEL** is using the vehicle of Quality Management Systems, which are certified to ISO 9001:2000 series of Standards by Internationally acclaimed certifying agency, BVQI.

Corporate Quality and Unit level Quality structure enables requisite planning, control and implementation of Company-wide Quality Policy and Objectives which are linked to the Company's Vision statement. Corporate Quality derives strength from direct reporting to Chairman and Managing Director of the Company.

As a result of its thrust on quality and technology, BHEL enjoys national and international recognition in the form of **Product Certification** by International Bodies like ASME, API etc. and Plant Approvals by agencies like Lloyds Register of Shipping, U.K., Chief Controller of Explosives India, TUV Germany etc.

Source: www.bhel.com

Mind Power I: Synchronization: Key to Supply Chain Supremacy

Supply chain synchronization broadly addresses the three constituent's viz. buyer or customer, manufacturer or trader, and vendor at the end of the supply chain spectrum - combined with service providers that enable a smooth functioning.

The importance of any supply chain synchronization process predominantly depends on the benefits that it brings to each of its constituents. For the customer, he is assured that the product is pristine and adds a definite cost advantage, as the supply is closest to demand. At the other end, the vendor can manage his costs effectively while the manufacturer or the trader stands to gain as there is no obsolete inventory, no unnecessary processing and other related cost and additionally trading is close to demand. The visibility improves for the service provider enabling him to improve service standards.

Seven Strategies

Moving forward, to understand the process better, one has to remember seven different aspects of the supply chain that can be effectively synchronized to achieve the highest level of true supply chain synchronization and benefit. These seven dimensions are a compendium of various individual supply chain strategies, which are to be now combined on a multi-company basis for greatest success and effect:

- Complete process and delivery timing
- Product/information linking
- Order timing and unitization
- Information movement and synchronization
- Physical movement and modal optimization
- Process exception monitoring and reporting
- People communication, co-ordination and education

Bang on Time

The first dimension of supply chain synchronization is the development of complete process and delivery timing or the actual supply chain schedule. This development is somewhat an art in itself as it is different for each supply chain studied and involves the mapping and understanding of the current supply chain flows and timings followed by the development of the new or optimized supply chain synchronization model.

The interesting aspect of this comes from the fact that the diverse flows and eccentricities of multiple companies are coming together presenting simultaneous multiple challenges from cube, weight, density and compatibility standpoints, all within the associated cube and weight capacity parameters of the transport mode selected.

On top of this, it is also important to note that due to capabilities and limitations of various firms this schedule will almost always vary between different participants and ultimately require ongoing change and modification as these capabilities and technologies change over the life of the programme.

Contd...

Scouring for Info

The first step in the synchronized design is mapping of the current process to be synchronized from start to finish, including volume and timing aspects for all potential participants. Once this is completed, a number of trends and levels of competency within the group of players will become apparent. As well current start to finish supply chain timing can be compared with the potential optimal timing model to develop a comparison of the current reality to the proposed vision and identify the rough magnitude of the opportunity at hand.

Spotting

Based on the optimal model developed, the new process flow and timing should then be defined allowing appropriate variance in timings for the different levels of players identified.

Initially, it is always better to error the safe side when setting delivery lead times for given firms to ensure that the schedule is consistently met, which lead times can subsequently be tightened should improved capabilities confirmed.

Once this schedule has been developed for each player, all associated volumes and density information can then be overlaid to define the entire supply chain flow. After all have been combined, minor adjustments may be required to fine tune, but now a relevant model will be in place from which expected delivery frequency determinations can be made on the newly synchronized supply chain.

This will also now provide the information to go back to the participants and define specifically for each, their requirements to become part of the new synchronized process.

It will also become apparent over time as volumes grow the levels at which additional delivery days can be added to the programme. Additionally, as other potential destinations are investigated as shipping locations for the programme, similar specific process models will be required for each.

Information movement and synchronization activities

It must be developed in parallel to the overall effort and the collection and monitoring process streamlined as much as possible to minimize additional data collection. In other words the data collection should take place as a by-product of the supply chain process and not become an activity.

This is partially completed by the two items – the barcode symbology (or RFID in advanced cases) and the purchase order. As the two key data stream, collection can be easily integrated into the supply chain synchronization processes by integrating scanning into the handling process and by collecting electronically at source all of the purchase orders generated for all movements in the process. This indeed is a large and valuable body of data, but collected in this fashion can be almost transparent and non-invasive to those carrying out the process.

A sequence of rules can be developed to effectively test each of these items as they move through the process and flag those requiring attention/action as exceptions, the management of which exceptions represents the next dimension of synchronization to be discussed.

Physical movement and modal optimization

It is the actual physical movement of the product successfully, on time and undamaged that defines the success of the supply chain. Synchronization can help this process to be as cost efficient as possible, but it is important not to lose sight of the overall aim.

And in the end it is final execution to the customer, which will be remembered by clients, not the beautifully attempted synchronization of the process, which in their case perhaps failed to deliver. Physical movement and modal optimization is the process that must be synchronized to deliver in this regard and whether services are provided directly by the synchronizing party or by another supporting carrier, they must in either case be bullet proof.

Contd...

The first step in defining the physical movement process is to determine the required service level or delivery lead-time that is desirable or minimally acceptable to the supply channel participants, as this is the base level of service provision required. Once this determination is made and a mode selected, the next step is to determine optimal load mix density based on the total usable cube of the vehicle and maximum allowable transport weight.

Through this process, one should then be in a position to define the optimal or perfect trailer as the goal of the load optimization process, which methodology can then be built into load building algorithms in the provider's system. This programme will be based on the total order flow cube, density and quantities for all products moving to a given destination in the same service timeframe.

Process exception monitoring and reporting

It is key to actually maintaining the order the synchronization process has put to all of the supply chain activities, which are involved in the total process. There are a number of exceptions to both scheduling, format, unitization and base data sets which will generate relevant exceptions that must be acted upon in some cases and collected for monitoring, reporting and improvement purposes in others.

If all of the above dimensions have been properly synchronized, the remaining exception levels should be manageable. However, if there are gaps, flaws and inaccuracies in earlier information used to build the synchronized system, then these will become readily apparent. These exceptions require immediate attention and correction or the entire process will be in jeopardy and will rapidly deteriorate back into a chaos perhaps worse than the original supply chain flows merged into the process.

There is reporting at two levels, one immediate where exceptions are flagged and delivered for immediate attention to the supply chain partner required to act on correcting the exception, which can be done either electronically through Internet messaging or via equally effective auto generated faxes in less sophisticated implementations.

The second level of reporting is on a cumulative basis, period-by-period of the key metrics monitored to maintain and enhance the synchronization process to the key movers and shakers at the partner firms. These are the reports, which will point out the significant ongoing issues arising within the process for correction as well as identify perhaps uncooperative players who are not meeting their part of the program objectives.

There only remain two dimensions to complete the synchronization octagon and they relate to the actual physical aspects and transportation mode issues, which equally require the synchronizer's attention for complete success in this area. And finally the need to maintain a dynamic process for continuing adjustment and improvement of the synchronization process to ingrain ongoing change and optimization as the total supply chain changes.

An important dimension for supply chain synchronization is dynamic process adjustment and optimization, which is the art of developing or defining rules and methods for the successful, ongoing adjustment and optimization of the process given the number of rapidly changing variables, which can impact the supply chain.

Also, the ability to switch to varying size and capacity of containers should volume fluctuations on a given lane and given day so dictate. As well, active analysis of cubic imbalances should be maintained and active solicitation of new partners to balance these should be pursued. Finally, as the supply chain synchronization effort proceeds and grows, so do the destinations, complexity of service and opportunities for greater synergies among the players, and these should also be actively monitored and acted upon when appropriate.

There is no doubt that the continual addition of critical mass to such a program will at some point hit justification levels for advanced handling and automation equipment to speed and simplify the process. In the end, it is through careful monitoring of these optimization opportunities, which will make the appropriate timing for such initiatives readily apparent.

Contd...

People communication, co-ordination and education

It is mandatory to mention that people communication, co-ordination and education is the most important dimension requiring synchronization as a key foundation for the success of the supply chain synchronization process. Without the support of motivated, interested and educated people not even the worthiest of supply chain ventures will succeed even in half measure. Synchronizing people to ensure the synchronization of process, information and supply chain activities can be one of the most challenging and time consuming activities around, but the results can lead-to greater synergies and levels of integration than have ever been previously achieved.

The first step in the people synchronization process is education and literally explaining in as simple terms as possible what the synchronization process is. What it intends to achieve, how it intends to achieve it and what is the individual's or group's part in making it all happen. This level of direct communication must be continued throughout the process in order to facilitate the gathering of needed information and the development of the detailed linkages required between the employees of participating firms to ensure success. Additionally, once the information has been gathered and analyzed, direct facilitation between the parties must be carried out to ensure product, ordering and systems information are correctly updated to support the coordinated scheduling upon which supply chain synchronization is based. Again it is the people aspects and diligence of those involved, which support this.

Beyond this level comes the actual execution layer when after implementation, effective communication is needed to tweak and fine-tune the synchronized supply chain. Often this occurs when faced with unforeseen difficulties, and it is the strength of prior personal contact and buy in to the vision, which makes the difference in motivating individuals to make the rapid changes required to keep the initiative on track.

In short, without effective synchronization of the people involved, you are probably doomed to failure or at best mediocre success. The people aspect touches all of the other dimensions in supply chain synchronization.

Concluding, although supply chain synchronization along the seven dimensions is a relatively new entrant to the supply chain supremacy race, there is no doubt that some firms are poised to make rapid progress in these regards. Achievement in this area on behalf of clients has a special meaning and value, which can result in the development of longer term, and more integrated provider/customer relationships, the likes of which have only been rarely seen in the world of manufacturing and other similar endeavors.

Synchronizing a supply chain is akin to the tuning and skilful playing of an instrument, which art takes significant training and personal hands on practice, and we hope that the song defined in these seven dimensions will allow more practitioners to jointly advance in the art of true supply chain synchronization.

Source: The article has been authored by Srinivasan H R. The article was published in SEARCH, the industrial sourcebook, January 2006. Copyright with Infomedia India Limited. Reprinted with permission.

Mind Power 2: Supply Chain Trends: What's In, What's Out – By Randy Littleson, VP of marketing, Kinaxis Inc. Manufacturing. Net - February 6, 2007

Supply chain professionals are always evaluating possible inefficiencies and shortcomings of their supply networks to improve their ability to deliver to the customer. This is especially true in today's fast-paced, highly competitive environment where supply chain performance can provide manufacturers with a necessary edge.

Contd...

As business dynamics continue to intensify, manufacturers are faced with the implications of growing global competition, shortened product lifestyles, distributed/outsourced operations and volatile demand – all of which make the supply chain increasingly integral to a company's success. So, while there is an escalating acknowledgement and appreciation for the role of supply chain management, many would argue that the job itself has never been more difficult.

While the challenges are many, leaders in the space are distinguishing between "what's out and what's in", what used to work versus what manufacturers need to do moving forward to remain at the forefront of supply chain innovation and enablement.

Demand Driven Supply Chains

OUT: Forecasting Demand
IN: Responding to Demand

Aligning supply and demand in today's complex and dynamic manufacturing environment can be challenging at best. Many companies spend an inordinate amount of time and resources in an attempt to better predict demand. Yet, in spite of the significant investment, static forecasts are often out of date within hours of creation, making some question the real value of traditional planning tools as it relates to near-term demand volatility. Today, a key capability for manufacturers is to be able to rapidly respond to what is happening at that moment.

As such, manufacturers need to transition from a supply chain driven strictly by forecasts to a demand-driven one. Companies are looking to establish a Response Management competency, whereby action teams throughout the supply chain are empowered with the right visibility and tools to quickly and effectively respond to demand changes as they happen – leading to such benefits as more accurate order promising, lead time reductions, and lower inventory levels and risk.

Visibility

OUT: Static Visibility.
IN: Actionable Visibility

According to a survey by the Aberdeen Group, the most important challenge facing supply chain professionals is supply chain visibility—as reported by nearly 80 percent of respondents. However, achieving visibility only solves a portion of the fundamental problem.

Many of the "visibility" solutions touted in the marketplace only offer limited access to a subset of data. With separate, a fixed view of information that cannot be integrated or manipulated, this type of visibility is far too passive.

Visibility must be holistic and supported by appropriate decision-making tools that can help turn information into action. Providing information does little good without the capability to do something with it. Information, in this context is only powerful when it can be:

● Consolidated for a multi-enterprise view across the complete supply network;

● Analyzed by frontline staff using real-time manufacturing and supply chain analytics and data modeling for "what-if" scenario simulations; and

● Shared and collaborated on with parties internal or external to the organization.

Collaboration and Coordination

OUT: Single-Silo Decision-Making
IN: Collaborative Decision-Making

As manufacturing becomes more complex in light of distributed operations, outsourced manufacturing and a multitude of partners around the globe, effective collaboration becomes a strategic imperative. Collaboration is routinely thought of at the transaction level - but collaboration amongst people is key to a responsive supply network. In such an environment, one person's actions will impact countless others both within and outside the organization. Given this reality, decisions cannot be made in isolation.

Contd...

Without collaboration, there will be a poor balance of opinion and limited insight into the impact of proposed actions, resulting in biased or uninformed decisions. In an outsourcing relationship in particular, this can be of particular concern as brand owners can make a decision with little or no awareness of the impact on its Contract Manufacturing (CM) partner, and no idea if and how it can be executed, and most importantly, at what cost.

When effective and efficient collaboration can be established, all parties can explore the options, wrestle with the trade-offs and develop a shared understanding and mutual commitment to the resolution. Collaborative decision-making can empower the brand owner and CM partner relationship and drive the ideal behaviour quickly.

Responsiveness as a Competitive Differentiator

OUT: Competing on Product and Price
IN: Competing on Responsiveness

There is a leveling of sorts happening in the industry given the transparency across the growing global competition that offers little leeway for companies to differentiate themselves solely on the traditional aspects of product and price. In an industry characterized by cutthroat competition and impatient, fickle customers, a company's success is dependant on its ability to meet the aggressive wants of their customers before the competition. Today's customer expects the products they want when they want it, and will choose a competitive offering if it meets this need. This commands a responsive supply chain.

By establishing a strong Response Management competency, organizations are armed with a key competitive differentiator. Having the process and technology in place that can demonstrate a company's ability to offer superior responsiveness (and therefore superior operations performance and customer service) to changes in demand, supply and product is an extremely compelling value proposition given today's marketplace.

Higher Consideration for Software ROI and TCO

OUT: Perpetual Software Licenses
IN: Subscription of On-demand Software

Long gone are the IT spending heydays. Today's mantra? "Make do with less." With much of the focus on keeping ERP running, IT departments have little interest exploring uncharted IT projects that require large dollars and precious resources they simply do not have.

A paradigm shift is underway that is changing the way companies acquire, deploy and use software, so companies can continue to benefit from solutions that can serve a unique purpose and offer capabilities beyond what's available in-house. The future is all about Software-as-a-Service (SaaS).

Unlike traditional enterprise applications, SaaS or on-demand services require no user-owned or managed infrastructure (software or hardware), reducing risks and costs by eliminating the need for upfront capital investments and ongoing IT resources for maintenance and management. In addition, with a simpler deployment process that requires less time and resources, customers are able to realize a compelling time to value.

On-demand services are accessible from a web browser making it instantly available to unlimited employees and partners around the globe, which is imperative for today's extended supply network and near impossible to deliver with on-premise, stand-alone software solutions.

MARKETING LOGISTICS AND SUPPLY CHAIN MANAGEMENT

Whenever we use the term logistics we mean management of physical movements of goods and materials. This concept is definitely not a new one and is being used in war, from time immemorial. Howsoever good your products might be howsoever strong your channels might be, but if products are not delivered in right time, quality, quantity and in proper condition, there is every chance that the industrial buyer would switch suppliers. Logistics involves cost, and manufactures would try at their best of the levels to keep down the logistics cost, but definitely not compensate on the timely delivery and service levels.

However we often get to hear the term "physical distribution" and "logistics" buying used interchangeably. But is that correct? We will try and understand that in this chapter. We will also see in this chapter, that how logistics and Supply Chain Management (SCM) has been clubbed. SCM not only goes to the factory where the goods are being manufactured but also to the "supplier's supplier". Logistics is thus a part of the SCM process. SCM over the last decade have revolutionized the way businesses are done. It has cut costs and made a channel very dynamic, productive as well as effective.

Logistics and SCM are very powerful tools in the hands of business marketers to cut costs. This is also a highly technical field, with lot of exposure needed into operations research. However, business marketers must focus on to this area for improving the productivity of the business. In industrial marketing the schedules for production are strict. The losses to the manufacturer could be huge. Thus, a buyer would always insist on timely delivery of his material. Thus, customer service becomes a very essential part of the industrial marketing operations.

This is also one more area, which requires a lot of concentration by the business marketers for automation and cut costs. Delayed deliveries to buyers can lose business and also buyers would be instigated to develop other sources of supply which is totally uncalled for.

IMPORTANCE OF LOGISTICS IN CHANNELS

A lot of research has been done in the last decade on logistics management. It can help the organization not only to reduce the cost, thereby increasing productivity but also to deliver higher value to customer. Using plant capacity level at the maximum, reduction of level of inventory and closely working with suppliers are some of the benefits. In industrial markets, servicing the customers has become a major source of differentiation. Thus under a logistics management regime the goal is to link the marketplace, the distribution network, the manufacturing process and the procurement activity in such a way that customers are serviced at higher levels and yet at lower costs.[1]

Logistics will involve the processing of goods, inventory management, transportation and delivering it to customers. However, it is a great problem in fast changing industries, such as personal computers, wherein a product can easily become obsolete in one order cycle. (The time taken from receipt of an order to delivering of goods). The losses are enormous. Not only the accounting loss of the value of the inventory but also the opportunity loss of the order that might have been.[2]

Thus logistics is to improve service levels at the lowest cost possible and improve effectiveness.

LOGISTICS AND PHYSICAL DISTRIBUTION

As we have told earlier the word "logistics" have been associated with war. For the success of any war, distribution system needs to be strong. The success would lie in the success of logistics. Gradually over the years we have used this term in management.

Thus, whenever we refer to any logistical activities we refer to, making raw material available for production, making of the product and giving the final products to the final consumers, as they desire.

So we see that logistics is the sum of two activities. On one hand is the raw material supply, components and supplies to the production process. This is called as the "physical supply". Once the finished goods have been manufactured, they are delivered to the customers, thorough various channels and intermediaries which we have earlier seen. This process is called as the "physical distribution".

Different customers will have different requirements, on delivery. The manufacturing will have multiple products. Managing them, coordinating the flow, so as to ensure timely delivery to customers which becomes very critical.

Mind Power 3: Using Eco-Friendly Wind to Pull Cargo

In Vienna, where they have a very progressive recycling problem, people recycle everything from pizza boxes to the plastic caps on my toothpaste. Which is why I was intrigued when I recently saw a Discovery channel documentary on how wind was used to move the giant bricks that built the pyramids of ancient Egypt. I wouldn't have believed it if you told me, but using a simple demonstration the scientists attached a massive kite to a two-ton block and it actually moved several feet. So what does this have to do with supply chains you ask? Well, coincidentally, a company called Sky Sails has been gaining some press attention about a recent demonstration using kites or paragliders to pull cargo containers to reduce fuel costs. The upfront costs for the equipment aren't cheap, but the savings are significant. According to SkySails the kites can generate 6,800 horsepower and reduce annual fuel costs by between 10 percent and 35 percent under normal conditions with 50 percent under extreme wind. There is another company called CargoLifter using giant hot air balloons to also move cargo all across Europe. This is real brilliance and I hope it becomes more then just an exercise.

Source: By Christopher Sciacca at http://supplychainsrock.blogspot.com. Reprinted with permission of the author.

WHY LOGISTICS MANAGEMENT?

By now, we have understood that logistics management is to coordinate the flow of activities, to ensure desired level of service at the least possible cost. Thus, the scope of logistics is from management of raw materials to delivering the final product to the consumer.

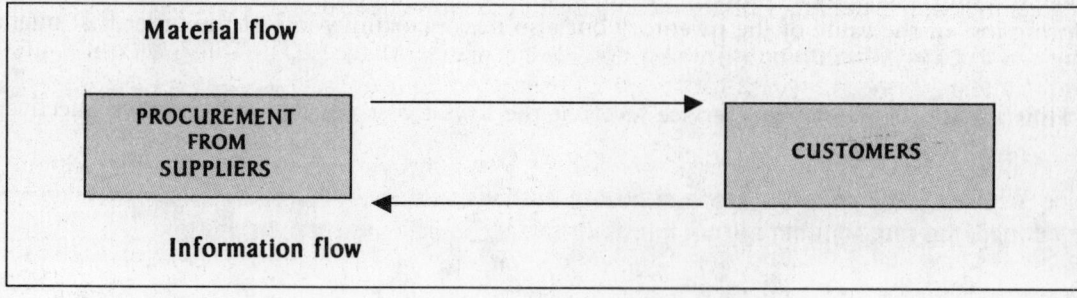

The above process involves a lot of coordination in terms of material flow and information flow. In conventional organizations, however this was not the same. Few decades ago, marketing and manufacturing were two departments which were "up in arms" against one another. However with time the scenario has changed. Previously the companies were production driven. But today, the challenge is completely different. In today's turbulent environment there is no longer any possibility of manufacturing and marketing acting independently of each other. The internecine disputes between the 'barons' of production and marketing are clearly counterproductive to the achievement of overall corporate goals.[3]

Thus, over the years we have changed dramatically with increased focus on quality and servicing along with concepts like Material Requirements Planning (MRP) and JIT (Just in Time).

Today in any organization logistical activates are under scanner. Thus it plays a very critical process in creating and sustaining competitive advantage. (Dell) It involves integration of the process and requires planning and coordination for its success.

Dell, after opening its business through its website, was clocking up Internet sales of $1 million per day.[4]

Thus, concluding the above discussion, logistics involve certain primary and secondary activities. The **primary activities** of logistics would include processing of orders, servicing of customers, managing the inventory levels and the transportation.

Secondary activities include warehousing, production scheduling and material handling. Thus logistics management is to achieve desired levels of service, at least cost.

Mind Power 4: Moving Forward... With Reverse Logistics – By Anita LaFond, News Editor, Manufacturing.net Manufacturing.Net - January 8, 2007

Manufacturing is a forward-looking process. Designing products, manufacturing them, and then getting the products out of the door to the customer are all geared towards moving products through the supply chain for profit.

But remember the "backwards" movement of products, aka "reverse logistics", can also add to your bottom line.

Mark Vigoroso, chief research officer and senior vice president, Service Chain Management, at Aberdeen Group, a research organization, defines reverse logistics as "the return, exchange, repair, refurbishment, and/or remarketing of products - basically any asset that can break." Gailen Vick, president of the Reverse Logistics Association (RLA), a trade group for third party service providers, refers to reverse logistics as "all activity associated with a product or service after the point of sale."

Reverse logistics is not just about fixing broken products, however; it's managing the return and exchange process to maintain customer satisfaction and control costs.

"Many manufacturing executives are not even aware that reverse logistics is happening in their company, because their main job priority is to concentrate on moving products out of the plant," Vick said. "But that's not the end of the manufacturing process; returned products can also affect a company's profits."

According to Aberdeen's latest Benchmark Report, "Revisiting Reverse Logistics in the Customer-Centric Service Chain," while 61 percent of companies surveyed admit that reverse logistics is important, 60 percent of the respondents are not satisfied with how their companies handle it.

Contd...

The RLA estimates that reverse logistics account for 3 percent to 35 percent of a company's bottom line. "A company really needs to get the 'C-level' executives to think in the reverse world if reverse logistics is to become a profit center," Vick explained. "Companies cannot afford to miss this opportunity."

As forward logistics became more sophisticated and economical it developed into what we now know as supply chain management, noted Tony Sciarrotta, director of returns management for Philips Consumer Electronics. Now, reverse logistics is evolving, too.

"An even better description for reverse logistics is returns management," Sciarrotta said. "Returns management should be part of a company's culture. It's not just about servicing or repairing products. Returns management is geared towards delivering a better product that won't be returned."

The smart manufacturer will pay attention to the "whole" supply chain - not only what goes out of the plant, but also what comes back in. For manufacturers, reverse logistics is really about keeping up good customer relations and understanding what is happening with products once they leave the plant. The point of reverse logistics is to quickly replace or repair a returned product.

"Supply-chain optimization does not end when the product is shipped," said Vigoroso, who co-authored the Aberdeen report. "If a customer can easily return a product to get a new one or have the product repaired, you have a satisfied customer, and hopefully that customer will continue to do business with you."

Yet many companies do not have any real process for handling returns; returned products languish on a shelf, or management may not even be aware of what or why certain products are being returned. Manufacturers are missing out on learning about their products if they don't understand why products are returned.

"Recovering failed products is really 'asset recovery,' noted Vigoroso. "Many customers will just throw out products that did not work, or buy from another manufacturer, or even buy a new product from the same manufacturer and never tell the manufacturer there was a problem with the original product."

Visibility into the supply chain is the key to successful returns management, counsels Warren Sumner, vice president of Marketing and Strategy for Clear Orbit, a provider of supply chain software.

"In the forward supply chain, usually large quantities of the same product, pallet or load are shipped to one place and one time," said Sumner. But it can be difficult to control the return of products, since they tend to come back individually, at different times, from different locations. "What can be controlled," Sumner said, "is the information about the returned products and how they are handled once they are returned."

At Philips Consumer Electronics, the "Out of Box Experience," or "OOBE," as Sciarrotta calls it, is helping the company to market products that won't be returned. Under this programme, once a product is developed and before it is marketed to consumers, senior staff members are given the product to take home. They test the product, use it, follow the instruction manual and make recommendations on how easy or difficult it was to get the product up-and-running.

"With the 'OOBE' programme, Philips can make design changes or rewrite instructions before the product goes to market, and hopefully prevent any returns," Sciarrotta said, "This is returns management at its best."

Vick believes that with a returns management programme such as Philips' can help avoid the turmoil of different departments blaming each other for product defects. "Good reverse logistics finds out where the problem is and works towards resolving the situation, to make sure the customer is satisfied," Vick said.

Meanwhile, manufacturers are discovering new profits in post-sales service.

Contd...

"By providing 'World Class Service' upfront, it can help to sell more products and build a service revenue stream," explained Vigoroso. "Some manufacturers even charge premium prices because they offer excellent reverse logistic services."

Lee Norman, senior manager of Enterprise Returns Management at ClearOrbit, agrees that in today's marketplace, reverse logistics can be a competitive advantage if efficiently appropriated. "Companies need to ask themselves, 'How do I extract dollars out of these assets when they are returned?'"

But don't just "tack-on" reverse logistic functions to the forward supply chain process, warns Vigoroso.

"Although reverse logistics should be part of the supply chain process, it must be looked at as a separate function with its own personnel set-up and manager for it to be successful," Vigoroso said.

He suggests manufacturers look at existing partnerships to see if they can be helpful with the reverse logistic process. Transportation providers, repair depots, and 3PLs (third-party providers) can all enhance the reverse logistics process, along with software systems that will help a manufacturer manage sales, warranties, contracts, and communication with customers.

PHYSICAL DISTRIBUTION AND MARKETING

Logistics, in the early years was merely taken as a cost of doing business. But today there has been a dramatic shift in the way we see logistics. It has become a critical strategic weapon that competitors are using to outperform others. Business marketers are using logistics to create competitive advantage. Many business firms today are very specific on logistical issues and use it as a strong marketing tool, to maintain superiority. Logistics planning and management can create significant benefits and create value for the business marketer.

Along with technological advancement, business marketers are looking ahead to reduce costs, by better inventory management, reducing inventory and by becoming more efficient. In cases of products being used as an input for the manufacturing, buyers often face quite some problems like storage, order processing, stock management and control. For heavy equipments, it would be more of delivering goods on schedule and thus require low logistical services.

The importance of logistics has lead to integration of the sales, marketing and the logistics function.

As we have told earlier, that logistics has certain set of primary and secondary activities. Now, the interesting thing is that, all the variables are interrelated and any change on one of the variable, will imply a change in another variable. If the supplier is unsatisfactory, buyers have greater chances of carrying high levels of inventory, developing secondary sources and in some of the worst cases may change the suppliers.

TOTAL COST APPROACH

In the management of logistical system, reducing costs is the key. Also, the job of transferring the products from production to purchase efficiently is very critical. Thus two variable needs to be considered:

1. Distribution costs

2. Degree of logistical services that has to be provided.

We require to design the system in a manner that provides best levels of service, yields profits, but still maintains low levels of cost. The logistical costs in industrial markets vary. This is due to two factors. The first one being nature of product and the other is the level of service. Depending on industry estimates, costs can be 35 per cent of each rupee sales. Thus, costs on logistics can be significant. Business marketers would always try and manage logistical costs.

The "total cost" approach also known as the "trade off" approach, offers a proposition that the costs in the firm and channel are minimized. Any logistical costs, as discussed earlier are interactive. A change in one variable, will lead to changes in other variables. Thus, business marketers are concerned with the management of the complete system, rather than seeing logistical costs as a piece meal approach.

The interactions among logistical activities are described as cost trade offs because a cost increase in one activity is traded for a large cost decrease in another activity, the net result being an overall cost reduction.[5]

Logistical costs interact in a very typical manner. For example, a company in order to maintain lower inventory levels, to reduce costs can suffer due to stockouts, or poor production runs. Thus, whenever we analyze logistical costs, we count on the efficiency of the complete system.

CUSTOMER SERVICE

Customer service acts as a differentiator in many industries. While increasing service levels to customer can and will increase costs, but it also attracts premium to the product that the marketer wishes to sell. On time deliveries will have positive impacts to business, as it will not result in the shutdown process of production. Service though generates costs, but still needs to be performed religiously. Customer service is basically to give 'utility' in the transfer of goods from seller to buyer.

La Londe and Zinser[6] had done a study on views of customer service. They said, customer service can be viewed under three heads. They are:

1. Pre-transaction elements which include customer service policy, accessibility, organizational structure and flexible system.

2. Transaction elements include order cycle time, inventory, responding to query.

3. Post-transaction elements which include complaints, claims, warranties, and spares availability.

Industrial buyers wanted to look in for the above, and if met would be happy. However the relative importance given to each factors from organizations would vary. Also, one more point that needs to be made here is that, distributors play a very critical role in customer servicing. But however due to different standards, it is difficult to maintain and measure data in this area.

Thus, we see that there are three important and clear cut junctions of the customer service element, i.e., before transaction, along with the transaction and post transaction. Depending on the nature of the product, the service levels would vary. Also business marketers should also have a close watch on the level of service, the competitor is providing.

Today, in industrial market, you see a lot of complication, because of two main reasons. The first is the buyers trying to cut down upon the number of suppliers and also the constant pressure to follow 'just in time' strategies.

SETTING CUSTOMER SERVICE PRIORITIES RIGHT

It would have been a real ideal case, if all the customers would have been provided with equal levels of service, but unfortunately this is not possible. In this context, however the rule of 80/20 provides a very strong basis. The customers may be divided into 3 groups, according to the profitability portfolio they have to the business marketer. So, the best category of the customers, providing the maximum business and profits can be termed as "A" category. The following ones could be "B" and "C" thereby a matrix can be drawn to determine the service level requirements.

	Hi		
Volume **(By SKU)**		(1) Seek cost Reduction	(2) Provide high availability
		(3) Review	(4) J.I.T Delivery
	Lo		
		Lo	Hi

Source: Christopher. *"Logistics and supply chain management – Strategies for reducing cost and improving service"*, 2nd edition. Pearson education. pp 58-59.

Profit contribution (By SKU)

Business marketers should also set standards for themselves on the servicing aspects. Achieving, perfection would be a difficult job for the business marketer, but definitely not an impossible job. Matching customer expectations and going beyond that, would probably be a dream for business marketers. Setting up of service standards is thus very essential in business marketing. Some of the factors are enlisted below:

- Availability of a product

- Order cycle time

- Information requirements

- Handling emergencies

- Frequency of delivery

- Documentation

- Completion of an order

- Post sales and technological support

Often, while providing service, it is seen that the end user is not satisfied. There lies a gap between the market perception and the needed desire. This gap can be fulfilled or blocked, if we are able to locate the drawbacks in the existing service procedure. This can be done by service audits. Changes in policies, involving logistical management will have an impact on channel members and users. The use of the audit would be used to realign the strategies, and focus on the neglected areas and on the areas important to the customers. This is the importance of service audits.

TRANSPORTATION, WAREHOUSING AND MANAGING INVENTORY

Mind Power 5: Road Freight between Major Cities (in Rs per 100 kgs)

	Calcutta	Chennai	New Delhi	Mumbai
Calcutta		1900	2200	2700
Chennai	1600		2900	2000
New Delhi	1400	2150		1800
Mumbai	1850	1200	1600	
Bangalore	1600	600	2600	1900
Hyderabad	1300	750	2300	1000

Source: Compiled from various sources

Transportation

The timely and effective management of goods is very critical. Without using the right kind of transportation, it is impossible to get the right products at the right place and time. Selecting of the transportation facility is as critical as choosing other functions, that a business marketer needs to take.

Whenever, we use the word transportation we mean four major critical components:

1. *Inbound logistics*: This necessarily involves all the goods, coming to the manufacturer for production of the final goods.

2. *Outbound logistics:* The link between manufacturer's establishment and his customers.

3. *Intraorganizational movements*: These are cases, when a business marketer has multiple productions and warehousing location.

4. *Reverse flow:* When a business marketer, dispatches off a good to a buyer and the goods are returned back.

Mind Power 6: NASA Plans to Outsource Shipping to Space

An article in the December issue of Popular Mechanics writes that NASA is going to outsource the logistics of shipping water, food, clean clothes for the International Space Station. The so called 3PLs getting the business aren't 3PLs at all, but NASA partners, SpaceX and Rocketplane Kistler, who are each getting $100M in seed money to essentially develop a transportation vehicle to deliver shipments in space. Can you imagine this scenario, "Hi, this is Captain Smith of the International Space Station, we are running low on water and I was wondering were package #47382749273892 is in route"? Operator, "Hello, Captain Smith, that package is just passing the Ozone layer and should be docking at 15:00."

Is FedEx Space around the corner? Will we be seeing Brown Space Shuttle's leaving from Cape Canaveral? What do you think?

Source: By Christopher Sciacca at http://supplychainsrock.blogspot.com. Reprinted with permission of the author.

Warehousing

The chances that business marketers, customers are geographically spread are higher and thus the needs to store the manufactured goods, in key strategic locations. This also ensures customer service in case the business marketers have a wide range of products. This is also one area, which can be worked upon by the business marketer for cost cutting and savings. Warehousing has direct impact on sales volumes and distribution costs. Cases, where warehouses are not properly located, customer services would suffer, and also the cost of the transportation would increase.

The objective of warehousing is thus to increase efficiency and timely delivery of products to customers. The location of the warehouses and the number of warehouses would be a function of the channel of distribution. If there are industrial distributors, the need could considerably reduce, than that of the distribution channel dependent on manufacturer's representative.

While choosing a warehousing, some of the areas that business marketers must look into are:

1. The requirements of the warehouse, the facilities to be made available and the nature of job that the warehouses would be performing.

2. The facilities available, proximity to markets and transportation access.

Warehouses could be located near to the final customer, to provide with higher service levels. But however, this would depend on mutual dependency of the two firms. Also, warehouses might be chosen, in a strategically central place, when the range of products or spares is high and a wider market has to be served.

Inventory

Inventory management is one of the highly challenging areas for any business marketer. This has a lot of impact on customer service as well as the cost associated. Inventory management is a big challenge to most of the business marketers, because forecasting demand is very difficult. This results into uncertainties. Delayed shipments; break down of machinery can create havoc. Thus maintaining an inventory of finished goods is very essential. Also, there are issues relating to "economics of scale" and "transportation" which also validate the needs for inventory management.

Thus, the objectives of inventory management are as follows:

*   Minimize financial investment in inventories.

*   Short-term and long-term planning of inventory.

*   Customer service and timely delivery.

*   Flexibility in production scheduling.

*   Reducing surplus stock.

INVENTORY HOLDING COSTS

They represent one of the highest costs and associated with storing an item in inventory. It is proportional to the amount of inventory and the time over which it is held. It is generally expressed as a percentage of the total inventory value. One major problem, which arises here, is the difficulty to account, since they are subtle. There are generally six components associated with inventory holding costs. They are:

- Cost of capital tied up in inventory
- Insurance cost
- Pilferage cost
- Obsolescence cost
- Storage cost
- Handling cost

Now, inventory is a very catchy situation. One hand, if a marketer carries very low levels of stock, it could hamper customer service. On the other hand if the marketer carries higher stock levels it would be costly. There is however no rule to arrive at the magical figure, as we have earlier discussed that predicting demand is quite next to impossible. However, certain techniques are there, which gives a fairly good idea, as to the amount of inventory that needs to be carried. One of the models we would discuss here is the EOQ (Economic Order Quantity) model. (You must have studied this in detail in production management).

EOQ Model[7]

It is the size of the order representing standard quality of material and it is the one for which the aggregate of the costs of procuring the inventory and costs of holding the inventory is minimum.

The assumptions for EOQ model are:

1. Annual demand, carrying cost and ordering cost for a material can be estimated with precision.

2. Average inventory level for a material is order quantity divided by two. This implicitly assumes that no safety stock is utilized. Orders are received all at once, materials are used at a uniform rate and materials are entirely used up when the next order arrives.

3. Volume discount do not exist.

4. There are no stock out costs.

5. Lead time is known, as well as fixed, and is equal to or greater than zero.

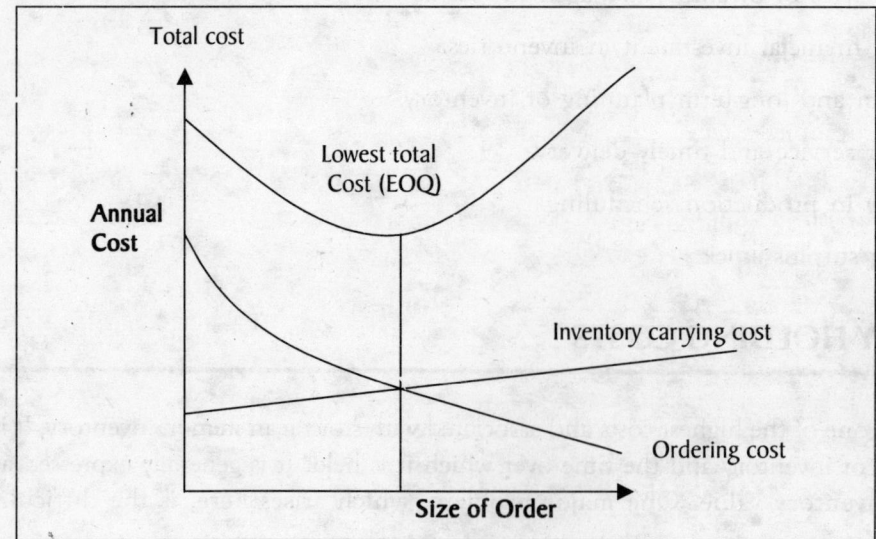

However, the EOQ suffers from some controversy. Over a period of time, it has been modified. The limitations of this model are:

1. The demand is not known with certainty.

2. Ordering cost is difficult to measure.

3. Annual demand cannot be predicted with accuracy.

4. Inventory generally does not arrive instantly.

5. Replenishment time can never be zero.

6. If the demand is falling, applying this formula would lead to obsolescence inventory.

SUPPLY CHAIN MANAGEMENT

Supply chain management includes all activities associated with moving goods from raw material stage to the end user. It has been defined by Handfield, Nicholas as:

"**Supply chain management** is the integration of activities associated with the flow and transformation of goods from raw material stage, to the end user, as well as associated information flows. This is achieved by improving supply chain relationships, to achieve a sustainable competitive advantage".

When we use the term SCM, we mean a variety of firms who are engaged from the time of processing the raw material, making component parts and also the ones engaged in wholesaling. There are a lot of functions of SCM. It includes sourcing, procurement, scheduling, manufacturing, processing of order and customer servicing. The key of success lies in integrating all these functions to give the business marketer a competitive advantage. When we integrate this complete process, better relationships can be managed, with better information flows to cut costs.

WHAT DOES SUPPLY CHAIN INCLUDE?[8]

The supply chain includes three functions. They are:

1. *Internal functions*: They include different processes in transforming the input provided by the supplier network. In the case of an automotive company, it includes all of its parts manufacturing, which are eventually brought together in their final assembly operations into actual automobiles.

2. *Upstream suppliers*: They are to perform the flow of material between all of the upstream organizations in a supply chain. Companies have managers who ensure that the right materials arrive at right locations, at the right time.

3. *Downstream customer*: They encompass the entire downstream distributions channel, processes and functions that the product passes through on its way to the end customer. In case of an automotive company's distribution network, this includes its finished goods and pipeline inventory, warehouses, dealer network and sales operation.

Mind Power 7: Creating Innovation in the Supply Chain

Many supply chains struggle to improve their level of innovation and in many cases it doesn't have to be as challenging as it might sound. The solution starts with management and how they define supply chain innovation. Does supply chain innovation have to be a new algorithm that can distribute goods more efficiently or can supply chain innovation be something as simple as using a "Lazy Susan" or carousel that can rotate a PC in 360 degrees so assembly line workers can build it faster. It can be both. While the research and development department might be the only qualified team with the mathematical skills to develop a complex algorithm, everyone from manufacturing line workers to delivery drivers can also be innovative simply by sharing their ideas on how they get their job done. Several years ago, a truck driver at one of IBM's 3PLs suggested that we put the shipping label on the same side of the box before it gets loaded on the truck, eliminating the time it takes him to search for the packing slips. After sharing this with the rest of his team and other delivery drivers it considerably improved shipping and reduced the frustration that came with searching for the label.

The main thought here is everyone in the supply chain and the company for that matter should be given the goal to improve innovation. Here are some tips to help get you started:

1. Make innovation something every person does everyday.

2. Focus on collaboration as to share ideas and approaches.

3. Provide support at the local level.

4. Continuously celebrate innovative ideas and those that create them.

Source: By Christopher Sciacca at http://supplychainsrock.blogspot.com. Reprinted with permission of the author.

PARTNERING AND MANAGING RELATIONSHIP

The major function of supply chain is to integrate the activities involved. All firms across the supply chain would be exposed to a set of very sensitive information about customers demand, sales and plans of the company. In SCM, joint planning is very essential and there is a need for a free flow of communication. Success of SCM will lie in the fact that integration not only happens in the departments within an organization, but also across other departments in partnering organization. Managing relationship is perhaps the most fragile job and can lead to break down. Poor relationships between any participating members of the entire supply chain can cause havoc, and great damage. For example, a defective spare part, can cost a business market a fortune, because it has every capability of halting the production process.

Organizations must develop better understanding of their process in order to serve their customers. Developing a strong communication network amongst the partnering members is also very essential. However, it is a very sad state of affair, that till today many organization have not partnered and there is no ground or base for a strong relationship. These business marketers are merely existing entities and would very soon fade away.

Whenever in any organization, the traditional approach to manage product and information is followed, it is highly expensive and time consuming. Traditional process not only creates inventory, but also bears excessive lead time. There has to be a common platform for the supply chain partners, to be able to enjoy the benefits of integration.

One of the major issues is sharing of information across partners in the supply chain. Whenever, firms know about their customers demand position, they have the chance to act accordingly. The ideal state would be when two organizations have aligned their process. But, however it is a distant dream in India. Sharing information is not in our blood, and is a cause of major problems in organizations.

As communication increases, informal information is also shared. This leads to the sharing of data, material requirement planning and good management practices.

In many American industries true "supply chain networks" like those found in Japan may not develop as reality. Firms are often geographically distant, and there are not as many small, family owned suppliers as in Japan.[9]

Howsoever different might be the outlooks, there is a need for process integration. This will ensure better focus on customers and markets and thus on creation of values.

Schmitz, Frankel and Frayer have developed a model on supply chain alliances. The model has three different components:[10]

- The strategic component
- The process component
- The operational component

Strategic component, process component and operational component are the vertical components of the model. Strategic component means as the alliance develops, how strategic expectations and evaluations evolve. The process component vertical is for implementation and assessment of an alliance. The operational component is for search, selection and benchmarking standards for an alliance.

In this model, as we go down from top to down, managers need to be considering the strategic, process and operational model at the same time. According to them, there are four levels of developmental stages. They are:

Step 1: Alliance conceptualization: This is a stage when a firm feels that collaboration has bigger and greater advantages, than the current system in the organization.

Step 2: Alliance pursuance: The firm decides to form an alliance and the firm determines its strategic and operational considerations.

Step 3: Alliance confirmation: Partners are selected and confirmed. Meetings are held and relationship is bound.

Step 4: Alliance implementation: It is a feedback mechanism to assess and administer the performance and take a decision on the future course of action. The relationship or the alliance may be sustained, modified or terminated.

One more issue that is very serious in any supply chain relationship is the factor of "trust". It is a factor, very difficult to measure, and until the firm shows confidence amongst its members, relationship would not be built.

SUPPLY CHAIN DRIVERS AND OBSTACLES[11]

Chopra and Meindl say that the main drivers of supply chain are:

- *Facilities*: These are the places where products are stored, assembled or fabricated. The two major types of facilities are: production site and storage site. Decision regarding locations, capacity and flexibility of facilities have a significant impact on the supply chains performance.

- *Inventory*: Raw materials, processed and finished goods constitute inventory. Efficiency and responsiveness can be greatly changed by altering inventory levels.

- *Transportation:* Products can be received or send through various modes. Faster a mode greater would be its cost. However significant costs are involved, as well as responsiveness from customers, who would be expecting their goods on time.

- *Information:* We have discussed it earlier consisting of data and analysis with reference to facilities, inventory, transportation and customers throughout the supply chain.

The major obstacles that have been discussed by Chopra and Meindl are:

- Increasing variety of product

- Decreasing product life cycles

- Increasingly demanding customers

- Fragmentation of supply chain ownerships

- Globalization

With mass customization in industrial goods and wide range of products, business marketers are faced with the biggest challenges that come across them. Not only these B2B customers have become more demanding, with high focus on better quality, reliability, service and lowest price. With respect of the above demanding situations, today supply chain has become one of the most critical components, for any business marketer.

Also, along with this globalization, removal of barriers across nations, companies focusing on only their core areas, supply chain has become less profitable. It is putting more strain on supply chains.

OBJECTIVE OF SUPPLY CHAIN MANAGEMENT

Supply chain is primarily, to enhance performance for a business marketer, through integration, coordination and cooperation between multiple firms. Every firm therefore has a huge role to play for the success of the supply chains. This integration is definitely not a sufficient enough reason for supply chain's success. Better coordination and integration is definitely required. Some of the objectives of supply chain management are:

- Demand forecasting

- Waste reduction

- Cost reduction

The above mentioned here are not the exclusive list of supply chain management objectives, but is an indicative list. We will discuss the above three in a greater detail.

Demand forecasting: This probably is the most difficult job for any firm and specifically for business marketers, because the demand is fluctuating as well as derived demand. This poses a special challenge. Let us say for example that Intel is supplying its processors to Compaq. Now, Intel would be very much interested in knowing and predicting as to what exactly would be the number of processors that they require to manufacture for each unit of computer sold by Compaq. If Intel or Compaq individually tries to take this decision, results definitely would vary. When both the companies make a forecast collaboratively, the forecast is much more accurate.

Some decisions that utilize forecasts and can be enhanced through collaborative forecasting among supply chain partners are:[12]

- **Production:** Scheduling, inventory control, aggregate planning, purchasing.

- **Marketing:** Sales force allocation, promotions, new product introduction.

- **Finance:** Plant/equipment investment, budgetary planning.

- **Personnel:** Workforce planning, hiring, lay offs.

Waste reduction: This is generally achieved in a supply chain by reducing duplication of work, better harmony and quality. There is maintenance of minimum level of inventory that is carried and is maintained only at few crucial points. With all the members, with intentions of simplifying operations and achieving uniformity, better harmony is seen. Quality of products, work and operations also form a very important link and objective of supply chain management.

Cost reduction: One of the major objectives that are achieved through supply chain management is better cost reduction. The cost per unit for the end customer reduces. Now on one hand, the firm is able to predict demand quite accurately, and it also tries to reduce wastage and improve quality and harmony. Cost of servicing are very high, and the level of service that a firm requires have already been discussed earlier. The business marketers' objective should always be to cut costs on one hand but maintain a steady or better service on the other. The principles of supply chain management are to reduce the level of costs, by eliminating activates that add cost.

Supply chain management is thus to create benefits to customers. Reduction of waste, better prediction of demand, cost reduction all aim at benefits to customers. When SCM is adopted, business marketers generally have a lower cost than competitors, better service, low inventory levels, higher profits, and better rate of returns. This is because of one single most reason "zero" duplication in work. When, this happens the logistics part of SCM, becomes effective and efficient thereby driving down the costs.

Mind Power 8: Manufacturers Look To Supply Chain To Combat High Energy Costs – By Andrea Lyn Van Benschoten, Web Editor, Manufacturing.net - January 9, 2007

Manufacturers must find new ways to offset the impact of high energy costs, and they're looking to their supply chain for answers.

The findings of Industry Directions' second annual survey focused on the influence of energy costs on the manufacturer's supply chain strategy. The survey received 139 responses from a variety of industrial companies.

The study reported that 79 percent of respondents are focused on supply chain issues as they relate to energy costs. Manufacturing executives overwhelmingly indicated that every aspect of the supply chain is being seriously impacted by increased energy costs. Warehouse management, reverse logistics, procurement and planning are being impacted at a larger portion of companies than in the previous year's findings.

"This year's findings are significant because they demonstrate that companies are not simply bearing the brunt of high energy costs in the most obvious areas of the supply chain," said William Brandel,

Contd...

Principal at Industry Directions. "Further, they now recognize that they cannot pass these higher costs on to customers or demand lower costs from suppliers."

Over four times as many respondents as in 2005, at 22 percent, now recognize that energy costs may hurt their margins. Only 15 per cent of respondents, however, believe they can pass higher costs on to customers, compared to 31 per cent in 2005. Additionally, fewer companies expect lower costs from their suppliers to offset energy costs going forward.

The study conclusion is that high energy costs are now requiring manufacturers to develop an optimized supply chain network and improved planning and execution to support global operations.

Source: Manufacturing.net. Copyright 2007. Advantage Business Media.

FUTURE CHALLENGES IN SUPPLY CHAIN MANAGEMENT[13]

Handfield and Nicholas identify some of the challenges facing the supply chain managers and identify a set of future strategies to address these challenges. These include the following:

- Sharing risks in interorganizational relationship
- Managing the global supply chain
- The "greening" of the supply chain
- Design for supply chain management and
- Intelligent information system

Sharing risks in Inter-Organizational Relationships

We have discussed it earlier, that one of major ingredient for success of any supply chain is "close coordination" and "trust". Now today, what an organization calls to be a competitive advantage turns out to be copied very soon. Pressure on supply chain is ever mounting, and thus the relationship and trust will be tried and tested.

Sharing of information, will determine the degree of success in supply chain. Information in relation to corporate level plans or business level planning or at a functional level, needs to be shared.

One more area that the author's speak of is research and development. Sharing new product information will become very important. With increased service expectation from customers and high level of customization required, it is going to get tougher.

Managing Global Supply Chain

The ruler of world trade is changing with globalization, boundaries fading out, and formation of regional trading blocks has given a new dimension to world trade. Global companies wishing to supply markets within these blocks will eventually have to set-up production inside the block if they wish to serve their markets with significant volume. One more trend that is clearly seen is that there is assembling of parts, happening at different places in the globe. With a land area one-tenth of that of California and Taiwan manufactures:

- 80 per cent of world's PC mother boards
- 80 per cent of world's graphic chips
- 70 per cent of world's note books
- 65 per cent of world's microchips
- 91 per cent of world's scanners

The brand name however on the top of the casing is likely to be a Dell, HP or a Compaq.[14] Definitely things are changing, thus world trade and to organize and run a global supply chain.

The "Greening" of the Supply Chain

Environmentally conscious firms are today looking for least wastage, recycling of materials. Consciousness about surroundings have made them today look for suppliers who are also in line with similar policies.

Design for Supply Chain Management

Coordination in supply chain is required not only for demand replenishment but also for demand generation. This can be achieved by joint development of products, sharing technology information, and creating products to capture market share. Design for supply chain extends the concept of "design for manufacturability" which refers to simplifying design for easy manufacturing. It influences production and distribution process.

Intelligent Information System

Integration of the systems, amongst partners of the supply chain is very essential. This integration has a singular objective to improve the communication levels between two companies. There are a number of such integrated systems available. With web coming in and becoming a power house of information, it acts as a very strong key to interaction.

In the years to come we will see more number of challenges that a firm would be facing in managing its supply chain.

CONCLUSION

Logistics and SCM both equip a company with better flow of products, information and services. Organizations today are able to use these tools as a mechanism for sustainable competitive advantage. Customer service is a prime function for any organization and a logistical system should support it. Poor logistics and SCM has all the capabilities to ruin an organization. Recurring wastages, zero duplication of work are some of the major objectives of supply chain management. Logistics and supply chain management run hand in hand. Logistics directs the flow of products and information. Supply chain acts upon it and gets synchronized with functions like procurement, production, order management, and servicing customers. Any change in the logistical variables, would also imply a change in the other variables. Thus, the need for logistics and supply chain management can be a reason for a strong competitive advantage for an organization.

REFERENCES

1. Christopher, *Logistics and Supply Chain Management-Strategies for Reducing Costs and Improving service*, 2nd edition, Pearson Education, pp12-13.

2. Coughan, Anderson, Stern, Ansary, *Marketing Channels* 6th edition, Pearson Education Asia, pp 505.

3. Christopher, *Logistics and Supply Chain Management-Strategies for Reducing Cost and Improving Service*, 2nd edition, Pearson Education, pp14.

4. McWilliams, Gary (7 April 1997), Whirlwind on the Web, *Business Week*, pp 132-136.

5. Hutt, Speh, *Business Marketing Management*, Thomson South Western, pp 160.

6. Londe, Zinser (1976), *Customer Service Meaning and Measurement*, National Council of Physical Distribution Management, Chicago.

7. Kapoor, *Operational Reserach–Techniques for Management*, Sultan Chand and Sons, pp12.15 to 12.19

8. Handfield, Nichols Jr., *Introduction to Supply Chain Management*, Prentice Hall, pp 2-4.

9. Handfield, Nichols Jr., *Introduction to Supply Chain Management*, Prentice Hall, pp 11.

10. Schmitz, Frankel and Frayer, *ECR Alliances: A Best Practice Model*. Grocery Manufacturers Association, Washington DC 1995, The model has been adapted from Handfield, Nicholas Jr. *Introduction to Supply Chain Management*, Prentice Hall, pp 69-73.

11. Chopra, Meindl, *Supply Chain Management-Strategy Planning and Operation*, 2nd edition, Prentice Hall of India, pp 51-66.

12. Chopra, Meindl, *Supply Chain Management-Strategy Planning and Operation*, 2nd edition, Prentice Hall of India, pp172.

13. Handfield, Nicholas Jr, *Introduction to Supply Chain Management*, 2nd Edition, Prentice Hall, pp 153-175.

14. Saperstein, Rouach, *Creating Regional Wealth in the Innovation Economy*, Pearson Education, pp 233.

Mind Power 9: The 80/20 Rule and How it Fits into every Business – Alan J. Zell, Ambassador of Selling

All business, whether they like it or not, have to live with the phenomenon called The 80/20 Rule. It is not a "rule" in the sense that someone decreed it. Its formal name is Pareto Principle, after its discoverer, Italian economist Vilfredo Pareto.

The basic rule as applied to business activity is: 80 percent of the results come from 20 percent of one's activities. In business, the 80/20 Rule can be applied in many different ways:

- *INVENTORY:* 80 percent of the business will be done on 20 percent of the selection of products or services.

- *SALES:* 80 percent of the business will be done in 20 percent of the time (year, month, week, or day) the business is open to its public.

- *SALES PRODUCTIVITY:* 80 percent of the sales come in from 20 percent of the sales staff.

- *MAJOR CUSTOMERS:* 80 percent of sales will be done with 20 percent of one's customers.

- *COMPLAINTS:* 80 percent of the complaints come from 20 percent of the customers.

- *CUSTOMER BASE:* 80 percent of the customers will come from 20 percent of the area the business reaches.

Contd...

- *ADVERTISING:* 80 percent of business from advertising will come from 20 percent of the advertising.

- *EMPLOYEES:* 80 percent of the work will be done by 20 percent of the employees.

- *SUPPLIES/SUPPLIERS:* 80 percent of what one buys comes from 20 percent of one's vendors.

- *MEETINGS:* 80 percent of important information/discussions happen in 20 percent of the meeting time.

- *PROFIT:* 80 percent of the profit comes from 20 percent of the sales or 20 percent of the customers.

There is more to these ratios than meets the eye when first read. Having the knowledge of how these ratios affect business can be put to good use. Let's examine how each of the above variations of the 80/20 Rule can be used to further the business.

Inventory

80 percent of the business will be done on 20 percent of the selection of products or services.

The logical thing to say is that if this is so, then why carry or offer things that don't sell often or don't sell at all? The 80/20 Rule is a ratio, so if the total selection is less, the total sales will be less.

For a new business selling products, this means that until one gets a track record it will be necessary to have depth in each item, line, etc. This calls for a very large beginning inventory until the "rate of sale" (or usage) can be established.

Rate of sale is something that has to be tracked very carefully, because one has to keep good selling items in stock at all times and have enough coming in, so that as the popular items sell out, more are coming in to replace them. Replacement time becomes very critical because the depth of inventory needs to cover current sales as well as sales while replacements are on the way.

Not every thing sells all the time at the same rate: Each item or style of item will have a high selling period, a slow selling period, and times when it sells somewhere in between. As the saying goes, everything has its "Christmas" selling season, but it may not be in December.

For a new business selling services, there needs to be a menu of services or choices the client can use, and they need to be ready to be performed. This calls for developing several basic files of information that can be adapted to many different situations. This is called "inventory of services." Each of these, such as with physical inventory, will have its rate of sale or usage.

Warning – "logic" would say to get rid of the some or all of the 80 percent that doesn't sell or sell well. This is "fuzzy logic" because if the overall selection decreases, the ratio still holds true and it will have a negative effect on the 20 percent that does sell well.

Better, "unfuzzy logic" says to look for ways to increase the sales of things that sell slower or don't sell. If successful, it will help increase overall sales and, since the 80/20 Rule is a ratio, the sales of the better selling products or services will also increase.

Sales

80 percent of the business will be done in 20 percent of the time (year, month, week, or day) the business is open to its public.

Some firms decrease the number of employees on hand during the slow times. This is possible, if looked upon as a yearly or weekly thing (as some days in many businesses are traditionally slow) as long as one has a trained staff or someone that can be called in when needed, much like the military has the National Guard and Reserves.

However, there are may tasks in business that get put off when things are busy that need to be accomplished and this is where the "surplus" staff may be put to work doing these activities different from what they usually do.

Contd...

Trying to boost sales for slow and non-selling products or services and looking for ways to increase profitable sales during slow times will increase gross sales and will cause the busy times to be busier.

Sales productivity

80 percent of the sales come in from 20 percent of the sales staff. So, fire the ones that are not producing?

It may not be the fault of the salesperson, it may be the fault of how territories are set up, a difference in industries, materials not suited for the potential client base, difficulty in delivery, etc. The question to ask, possibly, is what the sales per customer or order are.

Major customers

80 percent of sales will be done with 20 percent of one's customers.

It is widely practiced that businesses divide their customers into A, B, and C categories by the amount of business these customers generate. Often, it is the A customers that do the most and are highly targeted by the sales and marketing departments, while B customers are treated halfheartedly and C customers are almost entirely ignored. What is also well-known is that in a 10 year period A customers become C customers or go out of business and C customers grow to be A customers.

Source: Reprinted with the kind permission of Alan J. Zell, Ambassador of Selling, Portland, OR. Copyright 2002-2007. You can visit him at www.sellingselling.com

Mind Power 10: Third Party Logistics (3PL): The Smart Movers

Due to globalization, corporations across the world are increasingly sourcing manufacturing and distributing on a global scale making their supply chains very complex for them to manage. Hence, they have to outsource their logistics activities to experienced third-party logistics (3PL) providers, who have global operations. As the concept has evolved over the last 10 years, it has become obvious that numerous logistics activities can be effectively managed by 3PL that specialize in select, or broad based logistics processes.

The range of effective logistics outsourcing strategies spans the continuum from traditional outsourcing of transportation or warehousing services to complete outsourcing of all logistics activities. Research indicates that warehousing, outbound transportation and freight bill payment and/or auditing are the most frequently outsourced logistics activities. Other logistics services that are gaining attention and growing in popularity include packaging and assembly operations, cross-docking, merge-in-transit, inbound transportation and freight consolidation.

Why use 3PL?

More and more organizations worldwide want to develop products for global markets and at the same time, they need to source material globally to be competitive. Focus on core competence, while getting the experts to take care of the non-core activities is what companies appear to be favoring in today's competitive environment. For instance, a manufacturing company is better off focusing on its manufacturing operations, rather than spending a lot of time and money on distributing it products, that could be outsourced to another company. And this is what is happening in companies across industries – outsourcing logistics or using 3PL to manage complex distribution requirements. With their sophisticated IT capabilities, state for the-art transportation, material handling equipment and warehousing facilities, today's 3PL providers offer complete supply chain solutions.

Contd...

While complementing the logistics activities where the corporations lack competency, 3PL also helps to increase the geographic reach. When a corporation expands business overseas, it may not be conversant with the customs duties, tax-structures, rules and regulations, import/export policies of the government, and culture of the foreign country. A 3PL provider, who has long been operating in that country, will be better able to carry out the logistics operations.

Logistics may not be one of the core activities of a corporation. So, inefficiency may creep in if it is looked upon as a secondary activity. By outsourcing logistics, corporations may focus on their core competencies. It may also reduce costs as the 3PL providers can get the advantage of the economies of scale which is otherwise not available to the corporations. By outsourcing logistics, corporations can reduce their asset base, and deploy the capital released for other productive usage. It improves cycle time and delivery performance, thereby increasing customer satisfaction.

Due to an incredible growth in electronic retailing since the late 1990s, many firms around the world with virtually no distribution systems rely heavily on the 3PL providers for delivery of the merchandise at the customer's doorstep. This has resulted in a significant growth in the order fulfillment sector of the 3PL service industry. Since the 3PL providers are now offering a number of value-added services such as customs clearance, freight forwarding, import/export management, distribution, after sales support, reverse logistics and so on, corporations can outsource all these activities, and concentrate on their core business operations.

Industry	Percentage
Chemical	39 percent
Metal Industry	14 percent
FMCG	13 percent
Cement	9 percent
Textiles	8 percent
Paper & Paper Industries	5 percent
Automotive	5 percent
Consumer durables	4 percent
Electrical Equipment	2 percent
Leather	1 percent

A wider reach

Third-party logistics (3PL) or logistics outsourcing is gaining importance as more and more corporations across the world, unable to manage their complex supply chains, are outsourcing logistics activities to the 3PL or logistics service providers. By outsourcing logistics activities, corporations are able to not only concentrate on their core business operations, but also achieve cost-efficiency and improve delivery performance and customer satisfaction.

Currently, the logistics cost around the world is about $ 2 trillion. For any country, the logistics cost is pegged between 9 per cent and 20 per cent of GDP. The 3PL market across the world is increasing at a rapid rate.

According to a recent survey of Fortune 500 companies conducted by Northeastern University and Accenture, 83 per cent of these companies use 3PL providers and nearly 60 per cent use multiple 3PLs. According to a survey covering Global 1000 companies conducted by the Georgia Institute of Technology and Cap Gemini Ernst and Young, major US companies spend 49 per cent of their entire logistics budget on 3PLs. Their large European counterparts devote 65 per cent of their logistics budget to 3PLs.

Contd...

According to a research firm IDC, the 3PL revenue was $141 billion in 2003, and it will touch $ 300 billion in 2006 growing at a compounded annual rate of 17 percent. The world's largest 3PL providers are headquartered in Europe, top seven 3PL providers in terms of revenues are European-based, the UK-based Exel plc being the largest in the world with $ 8.3 billion in revenues, but the largest market is the US, which was about $ 80 billion in 2003 accounting for nearly 60 percent of the world market.

Focus India

In India, the 3PL concept has caught on in-the last three to four years but is restricted mostly to large consumer, goods companies. Firms in India still have a large in-house logistics division spending huge sums of money. The 3PL market here is highly fragmented, and there are very few service providers, who generate substantial revenues.

The TCI-MDI survey on SCM in India shows that the benefits of outsourcing logistics activities range from improved delivery schedules and reduced operating costs to expanded geographic reach and improved operational flexibility. The study also, showed that less than 55 percent of Indian companies subscribe to 3PL services, compared to more than 75 percent globally, which implies potentially, brisk market growth.

A survey conducted by Frost and Sullivan estimates the logistics market in India at $ 298.7 million in 2003 or 0.48 percent of the logistics cost in that year. Compare this figure with seven percent across the world and nine percent in the US, considering a GDP of over $ 10 trillion and 8.7 percent of the GDP being the logistics cost.

Revenues of the Indian logistics industry from the manufacturing sector were estimated at $ 13.46 bn in 2003. Chemical, metal and metal products, FMCG, cement and textiles are the top five revenue contributors for logistics. There is an immense potential for cost savings for India if it can bring down its logistics costs from the current level of 13 percent of GDP to 8.7 percent (level in the US). The savings would be around $ 20 billion resulting in a potential 4.3 percent cut in prices of Indian goods globally making them more competitive, a Logistics Institute Asia-Pacific study estimate.

Roadblocks In India

There are some operational and regulatory issues to the growth of the 3PL market in India. The Indian firms are still wary of outsourcing their logistics activities due to lack of trust and awareness. The 3PL activity is less than 10 percent of the total logistics operations in India, whereas the corresponding figures for the US, Europe and Japan are 57 percent, 40 percent and 80 percent respectively. According to a TCI-MDI survey, the mostly used 3PL services are inbound and outbound transportation and customs clearing and forwarding. Outsourcing of other value added services such as warehousing, inventory management, distribution and order processing is yet to pickup.

The poor infrastructure of India, acts as a deterrent for attracting investments for the logistics sector. The national highways constitute 1.4 percent of the total road network, but carry 40 percent of the total freight movement by roadways. Owing to a bad condition of roads and inadequate communications infrastructure, 3PL providers would not be able to provide quality service to their clients, and hence would not be able to attract business from the Indian firms. The unwillingness of the Indian firms to outsource logistics operations due to lack of trust and awareness and the unwillingness of the 3PL providers to bring in more investments due to a poor infrastructure constitute a vicious cycle and act as a major roadblock to the growth of the 3PL market in India.

The logistics firms offer limited services. In order to attract more business, they have to offer more value-added services, namely packaging and labeling, order management, order fulfillment, distribution, customer support, fleet management, freight consolidation, reverse logistics and logistics consulting.

The 3PL providers in India are also caught on the wrong foot because of the differential sales tax policy of the Indian Government. Currently, the 3PL providers have to set up warehousing facilities in a number of states to avoid double taxation, thus losing the advantage of the economies of scale. The

Contd...

Indian Government is working towards a uniform VAT regime. Once implemented, it will enable the 3PL providers to consolidate the warehousing facilities currently maintained in different states bringing in economies of scale.

Yet on the move...

Despite the problems mentioned above, the 3PL market in India is poised to grow at over 20 percent compared to the average world growth rate of 10 percent. Some of the large Indian corporate such as Reliance, Tata. Mahindra and Mahindra, TVS Group and Essar Shipping have already forayed into the logistics business. Initially, these corporate formed divisions to handle internal logistics, but sensing the potential of the market; they have started offering logistics solutions to other Indian corporate and have already turned these-logistics divisions into profit centres. Some large express cargo and courier companies such as Transport Corporation of India Ltd. (ITCIL). Gati, Safe express and Blue Dart also offer 3PL services. Owing to the large asset base and distribution networks that are already put in place, it was just a matter of time for these companies to venture into the logistics business.

There are various factors that will boost the 3PL market in the country. Indian firms are increasingly realizing the importance of reducing cost and staying competitive in the world market. One of the means of reducing cost is through outsourcing logistics, which also improves delivery performance and customer satisfaction.

Apart from this, the Indian GDP is growing steadily at high rate compared to the world GDP growth rate, which even beats the GDP growth rates in the US, UK and Japan. This eventually will translate into more outputs and more demand for specialised logistics services. Moreover, the Indian Government is paying more attention to infrastructure development with initiatives like the golden quadrilateral project of the National Highway Development Programme. These initiatives, which will connect all the four metros and will act as East-West and North-South corridors. It will give a boost to the road transportation network in India.

Almost all the large global 3PL providers have their presence in India doing mainly customs clearance and freight forwarding for their international clients. With the logistics market growing at a rapid rate and infrastructure developing, it is just a matter of time before global 3PL providers invest in domestic logistics. The possible routes may be acquisitions, quick and easy for the fragmented logistics market, and forming wholly owned subsidiaries or joint ventures.

In a nutshell

Logistics outsourcing is a clearly happening phenomenon world over and India is no exception. Currently the automotive, IT, hardware and FMCG companies are large users of 3PL services. Over the next few years industry segments like auto components, retail, pharmaceutical, and textiles are expected to be amongst large users of 3PL services. By 2009, this market is expected to generate revenues of $ 970.3 million. With Indian companies increasing focus on exports, superior logistics planning is crucial in order to remain competitive. 3PL provider will help them achieve this objective.

Source: This article has been authored by Priya Rao. It was published in **SEARCH-** The Industrial Sourcebook in the January 2006 edition. Copyright with Infomedia India Limited. Reprinted with permission.

Mind Power II: Fourth Party Logistics (4PL)-One-stop-shop

In today's industrial scenario, there has been an unprecedented increase in customer's demand for better service and on-time deliveries at reduced cost. This has put extra pressure on the area of logistics and supply chain management. The expectations of customers from the suppliers are continually increasing. This expectation and demand has been further augmented by the proliferation

Contd...

of Internet and the web-based technologies and the emergence of the latest phenomenon called convergence.

Traditionally, suppliers and big corporations have been meeting the demands by increased inventory, speedier transportation solutions, posting on-site service engineers and many times employing a third party service provider. However, these service providers, many a times, lack broad set of skills, integrating technologies, strategies and global reach.

To build up this strength, many third party service providers are going for collaborations mainly with consultancies and technology providers. Now corporations are outsourcing their entire set of supply chain process from a single organization which will assess design, make and run integrated comprehensive supply-chain solutions. This evolution in supply chain outsourcing is called fourth party logistics – the aim being to provide maximum overall benefit. Thus a fourth party logistics provider is a supply chain integrator that assembles and manages the resources, capabilities and technology of its own organization with those of complementary service provider to deliver a comprehensive supply chain solution.

Central to the 4PLs' success is the best of breed approach to providing services to a client. The development of 4PL solutions leverages the capabilities of 3PLs, technology service providers, and business process managers to provide the client organization with greater cross-functional integration and broader operational autonomy.

Stages of 4PL solutions

First key distinction between 4PL and current approaches to supply chain is that former should be considered in the broader context of improvements across the entire supply chain, which includes three phases of work: reinvention, transformation, and execution.

At the highest level of the 4PL solution is reinvention. Reinvention takes advantage of the traditional supply chain management consulting skills, aligns business strategy with supply chain strategy and is facilitated by technology that integrates and optimizes operations both within and across participating supply chains.

Reinvention, however, requires transformation. Transformation efforts focus on specific supply chain functions, including sales and operations planning, distribution management, procurement strategy, customer support, and supply chain technology. Transformation leverages strategic thought, deep analysis, process redesign, organizational change management, and technology to integrate the client's supply chain activities and processes.

At the tactical level is execution. A 4PL provider takes on operational responsibility for multiple supply chain functions and processes. The scope goes well beyond traditional transportation management, and warehouse operations logistics outsourcing. It covers transportation management, warehouse operations, manufacturing, procurement, supply chain, information technology, demand forecasting, network management, customer service management, inventory management and administration.

In summary, the 4PL responds effectively to the board complicated needs of today's organizations by delivering comprehensive supply chain solution. This solution is focused on all elements of supply chain management continuously updated and optimized technology and is tailored to specific client needs. To be successful, a 4PL leverages a full range of service providers (3PLs, IT providers, contract logistics providers, call centers, etc) along with the capabilities of the client and its supply chain partners. The 4PL acts as a single point of interface with the client organization and provides the management of .nultiple service providers through a teaming partnership or an alliance.

Contd...

A value proposition?

4PL has unique ability to deliver value to client organizations across the entire supply chain. The 4PL approaches the concept of supply chain integration through four key drivers of value like increased revenue, operating cost reduction, working capital reduction and fixed capital reduction.

Revenue growth by enhanced product quality, product availability, and improved customer service are all facilitated by the application of leading technology.

Operating cost reduction can be achieved through operational efficiencies, process enhancements and procurements. Savings will be achieved by complete outsourcing of supply chain functions and not just selected components. Synchronization of supply chain activities by supply chain participants leads to operating-cost reductions and a lower cost of goods sold, due to integration of processes, and improved planning and execution of supply chain activities.

Working-capital reductions of up to 30 percent can be realized through inventory reductions and reduced order-to-cash cycle times. The proactive use of technology, to manage order and Stock Keeping Units (SKU) movement throughout the pipeline minimizes the amount of inventory required, and increases item availability to reduce cycle times.

Fixed capital reductions will result from capital asset transfer and enhanced-asset-utilization. The fourth party logistics organization will own physical assets through freeing up the client organization to invest in core competencies (i.e. research and design, product development, and sales and marketing).

Companies, which may find 4PL an effective solution, are those where supply chain management is not a core competence in delivering competitive advantage, and where the supply chain is more complex than straightforward distribution and warehousing.

For large well-run companies, 4PL is unlikely to generate sufficient added value over conventional 3PL, particularly where routes are well defined and there are large volume movements. In addition, supply chain management is typically a more core activity than for example IT, which companies have become willing to outsource.

For smaller companies, there may not be enough value to share, and so any 4PL contract is unlikely to be economic for the 4PL service provider. In addition, restructuring of supply chains is removing some of the potential market by moving more companies into specialist integrator roles in which they manage all aspects of one flow in the chain including planning, purchasing, transport, as well as production operations.

Although 4PL offers many benefits, there also are some risks to consider. For instance, a company has to trust a great deal to the 4PL which may have no assets and so may be less robust financially. Both the 4PL and the providers of assets and services to them will need a fee, and interfaces and information flows may not be slick enough.

A land of opportunity

In a country like India, so diverse in its geographical landscape and cultural demographics, to provide logistics and supply chain services that are completely married to an organization's business process is indeed a mammoth task. Moreover, an integrated logistics network with value add-on services that facilitate a client's business is difficult to implement.

Indian distribution is multi-channel and multi-layered with inherent complexities of state permits and taxation rules governing the sales and distribution activities. The flow of products, services, information and financials across the closed border states and complex distribution channels require integrated and responsive supply chain architecture. 4PL services best fit the requirement in India as they provide the customer with the options to use various vendors and services through a single window facility. The most obvious advantage of using 4PL services in a country like India is the visibility of own supply chain through a highly technology driven SCM.

Contd...

Last but not the least, in a price sensitive market like India, it is critical that cost of doing business is constantly driven downwards. A 4PL provider has the ability to carve out a cost effective and operationally efficient supply chain for the customer. Use of a combination of a niche service provider, whose cost of operation is much lower in a particular location or for a specific route, as the backend of the customer's logistics activities will minimize cost instantly. At the same time, a single integrated front-end window from a 4PL service provider reduces the non-value added, non-core activities such as vendor follow-ups, shipment tracking, etc.

While 4PL market-is picking up in Europe and the US, it is still in a nascent stage in India. However, in future outsourcing of logistics functions is expected to increase in India, which in turn will offer immense opportunities for 4PL service providers. AFL, FedEx. Blue Dart and Gati are some of the major 4PL players in India at present.

As more and more companies outsource their logistics operations from HP to Compaq, from McDonald's to Wal-Mart, and as more and more players enter the market the 4PL services are here to stay. With the consultants like Mckinsey and Company and Andersen Consultancy also joining the bandwagon by setting up their own supply-chain practice cells, the market is poised to grow. With the current growth rate of 50 percent over the last few years, it is expected to become an Rs 500 crore industry in two years from current level of Rs 300 crore.

Given such a scenario the need for an integrated solution provider is indispensable and this is what will make the 4PL provider a winner in the evolving business paradigms.

The future

Globalization is expected to strengthen demand for 4PL due to the substantial lifting of market barriers and import tariffs. Suppliers require a vast network of genuine global logistic providers that can successfully integrate processes and information across geographical boundaries.

A more connected world results in universal access to sophisticated technology that allow 4PLs to efficiently manage complex supply chains and even modify supply chain networks and processes. For instance, technology advances, in wireless networking and RFID significantly increases productivity, customer satisfaction and ultimately profitability. Buoyed by these trends, the 4PL market as a whole is expected to witness considerable revenue growth from approximately Euro 4.7 billion in 2002 to about Euro 13 billion by 2010.

However, 4PL providers need to emphasize their unique value proposition to differentiate themselves from traditional 3PL providers. For instance, 4PLs have made a quantum leap from providing basic third party logistic services to being a centralized point of contact for the customer with the unique responsibility of monitoring supply chain performance. Simultaneously, they have provided solid cost reductions coupled with measurable and sustainable shareholder value. Also non-core activities requiring end-to-end outsourcing offer immense potential to 4PL providers.

End note

Emergence of 4PL is a new concept in supply chain outsourcing. With conventional service enhancement approaches such as expedited transportation, managed warehousing and distribution yielding only limited results, 4PL has thrown open new avenues in logistics that are being actively explored. Also the rapid advancements of technologies will make it easier to reap the benefits of fourth party logistics concept. Thus 4PL is the future of supply chain management.

Source: This article has been authored by Priya Rao. It was published in **SEARCH-** The Industrial Sourcebook in the January 2006 edition. Copyright with Infomedia India Limited. Reprinted with permission.

QUESTIONS FOR DISCUSSION

1. How do you differentiate between "logistics and SCM"?

2. How do you determine the level of customer services to be offered?

3. What are the factors would you consider before having a warehouse?

4. "Reducing the level of inventory is one of the challenges that industrial manufacturer face"- How can Logistics and SCM, aid the manufacturers to achieve the objective?

5. "Transportation of goods are getting costlier". How do industrial marketers deal with such increasing costs?

6. How does SCM act as tool for competitive advantage?

7. "Supply chains success is in information sharing and cooperation". Discuss.

chapter TWELVE

Industrial Salesforce: Developing and Managing Them

COMPANY PROFILE 12: HAL (HINDUSTAN AERONAUTICS LIMITED)

Hindustan Aeronautics Limited (HAL) came into existence on 1st October, 1964. The Company was formed by the merger of Hindustan Aircraft Limited with Aeronautics India Limited and Aircraft Manufacturing Depot, Kanpur.

The Company traces its roots to the pioneering efforts of an industrialist with extraordinary vision, the late Seth Walchand Hirachand, who set up Hindustan Aircraft Limited at Bangalore in association with the erstwhile princely State of Mysore in December 1940. The Government of India became a shareholder in March 1941 and took over the Management in 1942. Today, HAL has 16 Production Units and 9 Research and Design Centres in 7 locations in India.

The Company has an impressive product track record – 12 types of aircraft manufactured with in-house research and development and 14 types produced under license. HAL has manufactured 3550 aircraft (which includes 11 types designed indigenously), 3600 engines and overhauled over 8150 aircraft and 27300 engines.

HAL has been successful in numerous research and development programmes developed for both Defence and Civil Aviation sectors. HAL has made substantial progress in its current projects:

- Dhruv, which is Advanced Light Helicopter (ALH)
- Tejas - Light Combat Aircraft (LCA)
- Intermediate Jet Trainer (IJT)
- Various military and civil upgrades.

Dhruv was delivered to the Indian Army, Navy, Air Force and the Coast Guard in March 2002, in the very first year of its production, a unique achievement.

HAL has played a significant role for India's space programmes by participating in the manufacture of structures for Satellite Launch Vehicles like

- PSLV (Polar Satellite Launch Vehicle)
- GSLV (Geo Stationary Launch Vehicle)
- IRS (Indian Remote Satellite)
- INSAT (Indian National Satellite)

Apart from these three, other major diversification projects are Industrial Marine Gas Turbine and Airport Services. Several Co-production and Joint Ventures with international participation are under consideration.

HAL's supplies/services are mainly to Indian Defence Services, Coast Guards and Border Security Forces. Transport Aircraft and Helicopters have also been supplied to airlines as well as State Governments of India. The Company has also achieved a foothold in export, in more than 30 countries, having demonstrated its quality and price competitiveness.

The Company scaled new heights in the financial year 2004-2005 with a turnover of Rs. 4534 Crores and export over Rs. 150.05 Crores.

Source: www.hal-india.com

Mind Power I: Cost Reduction within Marketing and the Sales Process

Yes, there is pressure throughout firms today to reduce costs-and the sales department is not exempt. The paradox is that during slow times there is an even greater need for the work done by sales and marketing. In an ideal world, firms would increase their investments in lead generation. In spite of cost-pressures, so that new business development could offset business cycle weakness. The question is... how?

First, recognize that sales and marketing costs decrease as a percentage of sales the more successful the sales effort is. Therefore, the focus needs to be on generating new, additional revenue. We may in fact increase the marketing budget-if funds are available-so that revenue can be generated, and the cost of sales can fall in percentage terms.

Here are 11 steps you can take that will help increase revenues and hopefully reduce costs:

1. *Eliminate the weakest direct salespeople:* Every organization has salespeople who perform with varying degrees of success. The "A" salespeople are the 20 percent of the salesforce that usually produces 70-80 percent of new business. Leave them alone. The "B"s are not as productive, but have the potential. They usually require motivation and support training to make them even more productive. The "C" group makes up the majority of the 80 percent of the salesforce that produces 20 percent of new business. They require extensive training and are open to learning. The "D" group is not capable of learning, has not tried that which has been taught them, and just cannot be carried any longer. The "D" group must be let go now.

2. Put the "C" group on notice that only the top half of them will survive, and set a deadline. You can't afford to carry Cs that won't move up to A and B levels in the coming months.

3. Separate customer service from new business generation and have some portion of the salesforce working only on new business development. Too often, taking care of existing customers keeps salespeople from also working on suspects and prospects.

4. *Outsource lead generation:* Most salespeople (97 percent) are not very good at cold calling and don't like to do it. The combination is costly. They waste away the time or don't do it at all. Recognize that cold calling requires special skills and personality types and the people good at making face to face calls will most likely not be good at cold calling. Outsourcing your lead generation can double the time that the business development people spend with prospects, face to face.

5. *Shorten the sales cycle:* Most companies have an inflated view of how much calendar time and what number of calls are required to close new business. We encounter very few companies that don't have the potential to cut their sales cycle in half. This can be done by analyzing the strategy of each of the calls, and determining how efficient the first, second and third calls are. This is often difficult for a company to do on their own. Consider hiring a consulting firm to assist. A two or three day audit of your sales process can usually identify the weakness.

6. Use a postcard for the next direct mailing to your database. Postcards have high response rates and cost less than "heavier" mailings.

7. Increase the size of your prospect database. Most companies we talk to have too small a database. Buying a list of a new niche or target market can often breathe life into an over used list of prospects. The new names also will enlarge the list to where the small, expected response rates have a chance to come home. (If mail produces a 1/2-of-one percent response, and you mail less than 200, you most likely will have disappointing results.)

8. Consider expanding the use of independent sales representatives. They only get paid when they produce new business.

Contd...

9. ***Rethink your sales presentation:*** Is it educational or persuasive? If too educational, you are experiencing too low a conversion rate of prospects into customers/clients. By increasing your conversion rate you will drop the cost of sales dramatically.

10. ***Begin to manage your sales pipeline:*** New software is available that allows top management and sales management to see "Into the funnel". This will enable you to know what specific training the salesforce requires, and when the sales manager should intervene to help. While contact management software makes you more efficient, and CRM software helps you store data on customer relationships, the new sales management software provides tools that help the salesperson manage his time better: and the sales manager manage his people more efficiently.

11. Do something – NOW! We see too many companies "waiting for the holidays to be over" or "waiting for a big new order to come in" prior to taking action. Investing in marketing and sales is like putting money into a savings account. The sooner you start is more important than the quantity involved. The time value of action is impressive. You have the time during slow periods to engage management other than sales to help in the sales process. The CEO, the head of quality, HR ...many of these folks should devote a percentage of their time to business development during times that their normal workload has been lightened by the business cycle.

Source: Productive Strategy Inc., with kind permission of Philip Krone- President of Productive Strategies Inc. Visit them at www.productivestrategies.com

Mind Power 2: The Rules of Selling Have Changed!

The old fashioned sales routine of cold calls, telemarketing pounding the pavement, knocking on doors, ignoring "No Solicitors" signs and trying to visit people who don't want to see you, is DEAD.

I spent nearly ten years of my life making unsolicited calls and visits, trying to beat down doors and windows, climbing over barbed wire fences, burning up shoe leather, and inventing excuses to go see people who didn't want to see me. Can you relate to this? You call the guy on the phone: "Hi, I'm going to be in the area next Tuesday and I was hoping I could drop by and see you" as though you being in his neighborhood constituted any sort of reason for him to change his plans for that day.

You only get one chance to make a first impression. If the customers' first impression of you is that you're just another sales guy who wants to take away his precious time, then you've got one foot in the grave before you've even started.

Prospecting = Obsolete Sales Technology

If you don't remember anything else from our time together, remember this: that type of selling is obsolete. Dead. Ancient technology Irrelevant. It's like vinyl records, 8 track tapes, carburetors and Disco.

Now Vinyl records still have their place in the world; some audio fanatics still think they sound better than CD's. There are still swap meets where 8 track tape aficionados smoke weed and remember the 70's. There's probably still a carburetor shop in the town where you live, and as far as Disco is concerned. Well, you never know.

But no sane person is going to build any kind of real business on those things. There are going to be times when you need to pick up the phone and find someone who will see you. But that should be the exception, never the rule. And if you're building your business on old fashioned, outdated, manual labor grunt work, then you're violating every trend. Which means you're wasting huge amounts of time and money, antagonizing potential customers and missing out on very significant opportunities?

Contd...

Ten years ago, a visionary woman named Faith Popcorn wrote a book called *The Popcorn Report*. She said the trend in the 1990s was 'Cocooning'-which basically means people don't want to be bothered! There's no question, if they were "cocooning" ten years ago, then today they're locking themselves in a fortress! Some people hide behind their computer, reading their e-mails all day long, but won't even answer the telephone.

You've probably got a lot of customers just like that, don't you? If you're going to effectively sell to them, you're going to have to find a way to get invited – not as an unwelcome pest, but as a welcome guest.

Who Finds Who First is Very, Very Important!

Imagine these scenes. It could be any two situations where there's a buyer and a seller...

Scene 1: A buyer has a problem and needs to solve it. You get lucky and just happen to call the buyer that same day. The buyer was on your 'list' and you were able to show him a solution to that very problem.

Scene 2: Same buyer. Has the same problem and needs to solve it. He starts keeping an eye out for a solution. Talks to a friend, or notices an ad, or looks in the yellow pages, reads an article in a magazine and hears about you. Calls you on the phone to see if you can help.

Which situation is most typical for you? Which one do you like more? Scene 1 or scene 2? Well, unless you enjoy making phone calls that are uncomfortable both for you and the guy on the other end of the line, you'd rather be living in Scene 2, wouldn't you? Of course you would.

But there's another factor that's very, very important: In scene 2, you ALSO have TWICE the chance of getting the buyer's business as you do in Scene 1.

Why? Because *the buyer found you first.* In scene 1 you were prospecting. In scene 2 you were *positioning* yourself. The buyer naturally has more respect for you in Scene 2 because everyone knows you must climb the mountain to find the guru. Gurus don't come down from the mountain hunting for disciples. Who calls who first is very, very important.

Source: Reprinted with the kind permission of Perry Marshall. Visit them at www.perrymarshall.com.

Mind Power 3: Prove its Paying off: by M. H. "Mac "McIntosh, CBC

Your boss wants to see evidence that the money and resources invested in the company's marketing activities are really paying off. You start to sweat.

Relax. It is surprisingly easy to prove that B2B marketing is contributing to your company's bottom line. Here's how.

Show the relationship between your marketing and revenue

Start by looking for sales and revenue that can be linked to marketing activities. Simply compare lists of new customers or invoices to companies or people in your marketing database and look for matches. You don't have to find every sale that resulted from your marketing activities. Sometimes all it takes is one big sale to justify a campaign.

If sales haven't closed yet, count the number of qualified leads and use estimated conversion rates and average sales sizes to quickly determine the sales potential of those leads. Or look at the forecasted sales in the company's CRM system and compare them to the database of prospects, inquiries or qualified leads.

You can also send "Did you buy?" surveys to inquirers and qualified leads, using their answers to show that the prospects being targeted by your marketing are buying from you or the competition.

Contd...

Ask if they bought, and if so, from whom. Ask why and how much they spent. If your sample size is large enough, you can also use the answers you receive to estimate the number of sales and the amount of revenue that are represented by all the inquiries and leads you've generated.

Show how much you saved the company

Just give it some thought and you'll probably come up with a list of things you've done to save your company money or time. For example:

- Printing and postage savings after cleaning the mailing list or delivering the company newsletter by e-mail.
- Savings accomplished by offering electronic versions of literature.
- The money you saved by eliminating non-productive marketing activities.
- Time and money saved by automating the capture of Web forms and eliminating some manual data entry.

Show other ways your marketing is more effective

This can range from showing how many more prospects you reached with your marketing messages to indicating the improvements that have been made in cost per impression, cost per inquiry, cost per attendee or cost per qualified lead.

List all the marketing projects your marketing team completed

Marketers often don't think about their own productivity when justifying the money the company invests in marketing. Unfortunately, people quickly forget what happened last month or last quarter. Or they simply have no idea what's involved in creating a mailing or designing a new Web site.

Pointing out the number of marketing projects completed, and all the work steps involved, can be a real eye-opener to others who aren't aware.

Always be ready to make your case

I recommend that you block out a couple of hours for all this every month so you'll always have up-to-date results at your fingertips. If you're pressed for time, use an intern or tempt to do it for you.

Your results may vary, but consider this...

A marketer I know recently reported to her management that awareness of their company and products among target prospects more than doubled, the cost per qualified lead delivered to sales by marketing dropped by nearly 40 percent, 58 percent of the opportunities in the sales pipeline were found first by marketing, and 48 percent of the sales closed and 62 percent of the revenue during the past 12 months came from marketing-generated leads.

The result – she got a bigger budget and senior management no longer doubts marketing's contribution to the company's success.

Source: Reprinted with the permission of M.H. "Mac" McIntosh. You can contact him at www.sales-lead-experts.com. Copyright with M.H. "Mac" McIntosh.

INTRODUCTION

Any organization whether it be a B2B or B2C, has salespeople for their organization. These salespeople form not only the primary contact but they speak a lot more than that. Whether it is a great product, a great advertisement, or a great promotional tool, but still the best few steps of the journey is covered by the salesforce. In industrial marketing also selling is one of the major primary component and a determination for company's success. As we have seen earlier, that a manufacturer has multiple ways to reach his market place. Be it through an agent or representatives or through personal selling. Personal selling as a part of the marketing mix, would however depend on a multiplicity of factors like nature and composition of the market, nature of product, competitors outlook, objective of the business market and most important the financial capability.

The expenditure per employee through selling is very high and thus business marketers are a bit extra cautious about the employment of salesforce. It will however depend on multiple factors and thus not fixed across all industries. The objective of personal selling to a business marketer should be to blend it into the function of marketing mix.

Salesperson form a key strategic blind in between the manufacturer and the buyer. As we have seen in the earlier chapters that the buying decision process in business marketing is a complex process and salespersons primary job is to go beyond the ordinary, to create an extraordinary relationship.

A salesperson gets to meet a lot of diverse personalities and building a strong interpersonal relationship, communicating effectively and analyzing buyers is one of their most important tasks.

Futrell defines this process of sales management as the attainment of salesforce goals in an effective and efficient manner through planning, staffing, training, leading and controlling organizational resources.[1]

The job of a salesman is a highly paying job across the globe. Generally a senior management position is always filled up by a salesman rising up the ranks, because he/she has a complete understanding of the business and the market.

It is estimated that about 55 per cent of total sales expenses in the US industry pertain to personal selling, 36 per cent to advertising and 9 per cent to sales promotion.[2]

Salespeople are different from others. They have peculiar desires and have certain characteristic quality which are probably very difficult to find in others. Business marketers must also understand that they are extremely vital and play a very crucial role in the success of a company. They also build a strong relationship with the firm and have different levels of approach.

CUSTOMER FOCUS

One of the ways by which a business marketer can reach its customers is with the help of the personal salesforce. Once the business marketer, segments the market and there is a target which has been selected, the salesforce then comes into the picture frame. The salesforce speaks of the image, reputation and need satisfying capability. The team designs on to the complete offering in line with the objectives set by the management. The salesperson is not only offering the buyer firm, with a set of ideas, recommendation and assistance but also provides with a strong guarded relationship for over years.

The job of the salesman does not end there. He is the "pulse- watcher" of the industry. He carries with him a set of experiences, which the business marketer should capitalize in developing its new products and offerings. They also form a key source of competitor intelligence.

RECRUITING AND SELECTING THE SALESPEOPLE

Organizations are known for their people and that is why organization exists. Organizations who recruit people, who are good, always have a leading edge over the competitors. A superior human resource team in any organization cannot be duplicated and that is what makes an organization unique. Success thus starts for any organization from the people they recruit and hire. This is no different for business marketers. Salespeople make the difference, with certain degree of personal touch to every sales call. Buying organizations some times do not buy the product. They buy the strong relationship that exists between an industrial buyer and supplier.

The problem today that persists severely in any industry is the pool of qualified and "employable" candidates. This is shrinking day-by-day. This discourages the business marketer, because if they compromise on the quality of salesperson, the product will not be able to stand in the market, howsoever good they might be.

The situation for business marketers also becomes very tough. With the cost of selecting, recruiting, training, developing, motivating and managing them are added up, the figures can be mind boggling. Any industrial salesperson that leaves the job, sometime after joining the job can cost the company to the tune of Rs 1 lakh and more. This figure is however a very rough estimate and thus the management should be careful in the right decision-making.

When an application is received, there are multiple ways in which an initial screening is done for the industrial salespeople. They are:

1. Personal interviews

2. Evaluation of an application

3. Previous qualifications & experience

4. Tests

5. Reference checks, in cases of selection from existing employee reference.

SELECTION OF A CANDIDATE

Whenever a business marketer has to recruit a new salesperson, he is looking in for certain characteristics. They are:

1. Team dynamism

2. Communication

3. Knowledge about his job

4. Background

However these criteria's are highly variable and differ from one organization to another. Some organizations look at the educational back ground, some industrial recruiters might focus only on personal interview performance. In some of the companies which I know off, pay very much attention to the grades that one has been receiving from his school days. However, which is more predictable and accurate is a big subject matter of discussion as well as debate.

Team dynamics form a very important characteristic because selling is although an individual effort but equal support from each member is very essential. Today in industrial marketing, there has been a concept of team selling which has been developed to provide the industrial buyer with better information, service and faster deliveries.

Communication and technical knowledge is very essential as the products could be complex and whether a candidate meets that kind of requirement. When a person has good communication skills and technical knowledge he is in a position to effectively use them for better relationships, better understanding and providing better solution to problems.

Business marketers look in for candidates who demonstrate commitment to customer satisfaction. The candidates would be able to balance the organization and interests of his customer and also should be enthusiastic, go getter and professional.

SOURCING OF INDUSTRIAL SALESPERSONS

There are a multiple sources, where a salesperson for an industrial organization can be sourced. But before doing that, certain factors need to be looked into. The number of people to be recruited, the potential to provide good people, budget available and easy approachability to the source. The different sources through which candidates are sourced are:

1. References by existing employees

2. Educational institutions

3. Advertisements

4. Placement consultancy

5. Recruitments within the company

Also a term which is frequently used is "poaching". It is picking up a salesperson from a competitor's company. It is also often seen that, when a person joins in at a managerial level in sales (especially if he was with a competing company) he pulls in some or most of his colleagues. We would not discuss the ethical aspects of it, but it is a trend.

PERSONAL IN-DEPTH INTERVIEWS

It is the most frequently used and least scientific amongst all the selection techniques that are available. Personal interview is a must. Even in cases, where in an employee from some other department wishes to come into sales are interviewed. Also if a salesperson wants to switch from one product to another, he is also interviewed. This complete exercise is to know whether a candidate is motivated and whether he has certain set of skills which the industrial organization is looking in for. Generally two or three interviews are done. This is basically to understand a person in-depth. However the validity of such an instrument needs to be determined.

The personal interview can be of various forms. It could be done by a single interviewer. The problem of biases always stays. Smaller organizations with limited resources may adapt to this. Industrial organization also conducts panel interviews, wherein there are people from various ranks and departments examining the candidate. There are also structured interviews that happen, wherein questions are constructed and all candidates are asked the same. There could also be stress interviews.

This process of personal interview, allows the organization to understand the candidate in-depth and the candidates can be compared. The recruitment and selection process also quite depends on the outlook of the company, its size and policies. The human resources department also plays a key role in determining whether the organization and the candidate would have harmony in their organizational objectives. They play a very critical role in selecting a candidate. To give an example, a candidate working with a family run business may find difficulties in cases if he is joining an MNC firm. Human resources also discusses on the compensation part with the candidate.

SELECTING OR REJECTING

Once the interviewing process is done, the question the industrial organization would have is whether a candidate is to be selected or rejected. What would be the possible fates of "border line candidates" who can be taken in? As we have said earlier, that the cost involved if an industrial salesperson does not perform and quit, is very high. This decision of "to select" or "to reject" becomes very critical.

It is also important to know that a candidate might get rejected, because of personal biases of an interviewer. Even if a candidate is good, the interviewer might have an altogether different opinion. So this process is definitely not the right way, to say whether a candidate is good or bad. However with increased experience, the interviewer can take strong ideas from his sixth sense and past experiences and take a judgment. But still, it is not leak proof.

In cases when the interviewer has any kind of doubts, about a candidate, he should be called back and interviewed with proper reference checks. However a system can be in place, which can keep records of successful salespersons and use the data in future selection of candidates. No psychological tests or any kind of tests can say that, "this" is the fittest of them all for sales profession. It is a different game altogether.

Rejection of a salesperson could be because of a multiple reasons. It could be as trivial as a "cold hand shake" or it could be a serious issue like an "immature and impoliteness". The reason for rejection cannot be told. It varies from interviewer to interviewer. The interviewers can have their own interpretation for rejecting a candidate.

It is often seen that after recruitment, the average ones are the salespeople who perform brilliantly and the best ones (for the interview) are the ones who stumble. Predicting the success or the failure of a salesman, his association with an industrial organization, just cannot be predicted.

In an industrial organization, who were manufactures of plastic products, observed that their salesperson who were below 7 months in service, were the ones who were more vulnerable to leaving the company. Once that period is over, they were staying on over three years on an average. No rationality or science can explain this behaviour, probably.

SALESFORCE SOCIALIZATION[3]

A salesman needs to be integrated to an organization. He must be able to gel with the people that are around him. The proper introduction of the recruit to company practices, procedures and philosophy and to the social aspects of the job is crucial in achieving a return on the sizable investment made during the recruitment and selling process. When a salesman is socialized, his understanding of the job increases and leads to a better job satisfaction for an individual. Anderson, Hair & Bush mention about two levels of socialization; namely Initial socialization and Extended socialization.

Initial socialization is the preliminary exposure to the firm, with the recruiting and the selling process and ends with the initial orientation of the salesperson to the firm's procedures & policies. Extended socialization concerns, making the new salesperson feel that he/she is an integral part of the company.

DEVELOPING AND TRAINING SALESPEOPLE

Industrial salespeople like other salespeople require training. They need to be developed, to perform at their fullest potential. Even if a salesperson for an industrial company has experience he still needs training to fine tune his skills and to understand about the policy that is approached by the company. Today all B2B organizations are spending lakhs in the induction, development and training of salesman. Industrial marketers are also speaking in terms of man days, that a person involves himself in training. One more important aspect that needs to be kept in mind as an industrial marketer is the high rate of technological obsolescence. To prevent this, salesperson must be constantly updated with the recent changes and trends in technology.

One trend in Indian industrial salespersons is that sales trainings often are taken lightly and it rarely yields results. Training happens at irregular and, in some companies, on an yearly basis. One thing that has to be kept in mind is that, training provides a great deal of motivation in a salesperson. He is able to identify his areas of improvement vis-a-vis his colleagues. Also newer changes in the market, addition of a new product or the new competitor in the market, make the salesman up to date. Not only that, new techniques to sell can also be discussed in such forums. Quite often, experiential learning from other colleagues also enriches ideas & thoughts.

Sales training can be defined as the effort put by an organization to equip its sales staff with certain set of skills, attitudes and knowledge so as to perform better and effectively in a dynamic business environment.

Today in industrial markets, things are changing fast. Probably in the past, the pace of change has never been so dramatic. Also, if organizations fail to keep their salespeople updated about changes happening, they would not be able to survive in the near future. Technology, competition, products, market place have seen a dramatic change and these are some of the areas, where a salesperson needs to be trained upon.

VARIOUS REASONS FOR SALES TRAINING

There could be various reasons for providing sales training. It can be:

1. To enhance skills of a salesman.

2. Orientation of a new salesman.

3. In cases of promotion, it could be team building and managing.

4. Increasing sales in a particular product or cross selling products from other divisions.

5. Improving knowledge.

Some words of caution and check before the sales training is on, is that salesperson with some kind of experience find it quite difficult to sit through the training modules and often consider it to be a waste of time. So the trainer should be very careful in understanding his trainees and keeping everyone involved. The ability or motivation of employee to undergo training reduces, as his age increases with the company. Also one of the major areas of concern is to provide feed back. Neither does trainer provide feedback to salesperson nor does salesperson give it to the organization as to whether he has been able to do the job better. Video taping the class room exercises, can the give salesperson to understand him better and make the necessary changes for him. Also experienced salesperson show certain levels of discomfort in grasping training, especially of new products.

SALES TRAINING

The success of any training programme, to quite some extent depends upon the trainer and his ability to transfer a set of knowledge, skills and attitudes to the trainees. Generally, the training is done by two sets of people. They are:

1.   The sales manager

2.   Trainer, who is a specialist in that area

Sales managers are generally the people appointed with quite some experience in that profession and thus they are able to deliver better. They are also immediate superiors and thus are very well aware of the problems and the areas of concern for each salesman. Sales managers are finally responsible to meet the branch targets and therefore have quite an interest in developing the salesperson. However the pitfall is that, there may be lack of seriousness and the tendency of the subordinates to try to impress him than real learning.

A slighter modification to this happens in relatively smaller companies or else in situations where a senior salesperson gives training to the junior executives and shares his experience. This generally happens as a part of the sales managers training for bigger companies. The problem here is that, often a senior salesperson do not want to share their "market success secrets", and also since they would be colleagues later on, they do not take him seriously. He also sees it as an unnecessary burden that is posted on him, which is practically a waste for him.

Trainers are hired by industrial organization for their sales executives. They are costly and they only allow a limited number of people at a particular point of time. Trainers could be a general trainer to improve the skills, attitude or communication or could be a sales trainer, exclusively for sales skills. This is done more frequently than the previous options. However, these trainers may actually find it quite difficult to address the specific problems of the sales executives, as selling across industries, geographical areas and products vary. Salespersons often treat training lightly as they often wait for the evening to take a dip in the swimming pools, in case it is organized in a resort. In case it is organized in the office, they would wait for lunch and snacks.

The costs involved in training are very high. Organizations which are large and have the capability have their own in house trainers for their people. Industrial organizations specify the number of days of training that each employee must undergo so as to have an improvement in his style of working and also to improve his efficiency levels. Training gives a lot of motivation to salesperson, to come back on a Monday morning and start afresh.

AREAS OF SALES TRAINING

As we have seen earlier, that sales training is important and areas where sales training are considered to be important are:

1.   Product Knowledge

2.   Company Knowledge

3.   The Role to be played by the Salespersonnel

4.   Advertising Sales Promotion & Channel of Distribution

5.   Customer (existing & prospective) and Competitors

6.   Industry

7.   Selling Skills

1.   *Product Knowledge:* Whether it is selling of a pin or an aeroplane or F-16, product knowledge is the foundation or the base of any sales. Salesperson must have an in-depth knowledge, about what he is selling, the features, benefits, technical specification. Industrial organizations should put a special stress on their product knowledge, because today is a technologically advancing society. Everyday changes are being made or innovations are happening. Not only that, the buyers are aware of their markets. If the interaction has to improve, between the buyer and the seller, product knowledge is very essential. A salesperson also needs to know whether the product range,

he is selling would be suitable to the industrial buyer. More over if the salesperson is poor in this area, handling objections from buyer would be a problem. The salesperson should know every detail about a product, like, performance, size, characteristics, operation, advantages & benefits and existing customers in the market place. Industrial buyers would never prefer to purchase or deal with a salesperson, who has slightest of the doubt about his product. Not only that, a salesperson must be taught to have confidence in his products. If by any chance a salesperson feels, that the competitor products are superior, dark days are about to begin for the company.

2. *Company Knowledge:* A salesperson, who is hired, is given a presentation about the company, and he is formally introduced to the company. The company policies relating to sales, quality, customer services, product, integrity, ethics and current operations. It gives them a sense of loyalty, and salesperson tend to take pride in the name of the organization they work for.

3. *The Role to be played by the Salespersonnel:* This is very true especially for new recruits straight out from the college; say an engineering graduate or a B-school graduate joining an industrial organization. When inexperienced people with sales background join the profession, find a series of roles contrary to their personalities; like hard selling, wrong selling, false promises etc... they should be trained and taught, how to handle such a situation. B2B salesperson need to be partners to buyers, otherwise relationship would never become long-term. "True selling" must be taught to the salespersonnel. It is important.

4. *Advertising Sales Promotion & Channel of Distribution:* Advertising and sales promotion is also equally important to be given a training for. They need to be told, to focus on a particular product say "A" with constant bombardment of advertisement and sales promotion. These advertisements and promotion give the buyer a lot of information and generate considerable sales. Also at later stage company salespersonnel can give their feed back about a particular advertisement campaign and also keep the organization aware about competitor's advertisement campaigns and sales promotions.

If an industrial product is distributed using channel members, it is important to know them, the product line that they carry. Pricing policies and how the products are purchased by the distributor. In cases of production delays and if the distributor is carrying some stock, it can be given to the industrial buyer. Such adjustments can be made only when the salesperson has a strong relationship with the channel members.

5. *Customer (existing & prospective) and Competitors:* The last rupee and poor follow up can result in loss of customers. Even competitors might be quite fast in grabbing opportunities, which probably a salesperson may not be able to prevent. Competitors are necessary evil. It keeps the salesman on toes as well as may make him lose business. Every move the competitor makes should be updated and counter attaching strategies must be formed immediately.

Also salespeople need to know which segments they would be selling, their prospective customers, profiles of such industry, trends, and data on prospects. Gathering data about prospects and market research data helps the salesperson.

Also salesperson needs to be given training on industry and market trend. This is to understand current business practices and micro level information of buyers, like buying decision makers, influencers etc. Many industrial organizations document such information, which forms a guideline for future salespersonnel. Salesperson should also be aware of future market potentials and trends. If the industry sales fall or the economy does not do well, then it has impact on salesperson's performance. They must be aware of it & should not be demotivated.

6. *Industry:* Salesperson must know about the industry, to keep themselves updated about changes and the possible impact on them. It could be in relation to anything that we have discussed earlier in this section.

7. **Selling Skills:** The buyer seller interaction in industrial markets are different from consumer markets and so are the selling skills involved. If an industrial organization is selling supplies, the skills required are very basic. For example selling of stationery. But, on the other hand, if let us say that an earth mover has to be bought from say BEML, it would involve quite some time before the deal is actually closed.

Also it involves quite amount of time, in understanding the purchasing pattern of industrial buyers. Human relations skill is very important in selling and forms an integral part. An industrial purchaser will make his decision to purchase, only when he is confident about the salesperson. Even the slightest of the doubt will deter him. Buying in industrial concerns is not always on the basis of pure logical reasoning, but on the basis of what the salesperson is, at least partially. Salesperson must develop the skill to "listen" and to "probe" so as to know the exact situation in the buying firm.

Another important aspect that the salesperson needs to be trained about is the negotiating skills. B2B selling is about partnerships. The greater the confidence, the greater chances of the buyer retaining the seller. Today, with multiple players into the market, industrial sellers are looking for agreements or partnerships which are mutually beneficial. Every contract with the buyer should be treated as a partnering relationship where both of them benefit from the contract.

Along with the selling skills, some amount of managing skills should be imparted to the salesperson. In industrial selling, the territories are larger to be covered by a salesperson (may not be true always). Now, he should know about his territory, the potentials, the forms, the paper work etc. They should also be taught to mange people below them, when they are taking charge of an area, with manpower below him.

Salespersons also needs to be trained with some personal productivity skills such as sales planning, tactics, presentations, managing of sales calls, etc. Today, they should also be taught to effectively communicate by means of letter and e-mails.

MOTIVATING THE SALESPERSON

Why do we need to motivate salespersons? The simple answer to this is stress. The biggest challenge to a salesperson is the level of stress that he undergoes throughout in a year. Every person in this world requires motivation Salespersons need it to a greater extent. Companies run, because salesperson are the anchor. They give in their days and nights, away from families, spending most of the month in hotels, trains and satisfying clients. They get paid for it, no doubt. Also, at the same time, one must remember that they are sandwiched in between customers and his company.

An industrial salesperson goes through a greater level of stress. Selling cycles are large and quite amount of time and energy is invested by salespersons for his customer. It might also happen at the end of the quarter or half year that many of his prospects have dropped. It might not be the fault of the salesperson. Could be a down turn of the industry. But the industrial salesforce suffer. One more issue, is customer satisfaction. Unlike selling a soap or shampoo, B2B buyers are very cautious. They have to be satisfied. Satisfaction is a very relative term and varies from person to person. Not only that, it consumes time and has to be balanced with search for new business. It is tough!!

One more problem that a salesperson goes through is the feeling of loneliness. Because if a sales deal goes through, he gets a pat, in case it does not, he hears the loud music. If buyers fail to renew orders or goes to the competitors the salesperson, had it. He is always stuck, in between the devil and the deep sea.

Also, salesman never has an "ok" day. It is either good or bad. He is exposed to multiple people, in a day or month or quarter with different ideologies, different moods and managing every one is a difficult task. He also has to change, as the situation demands for and act accordingly. He has to stay calm, even if the customer is yelling at the top of his voice. Most of the time, salesperson is not his actual self when he is on the job. It drains him. It is tough indeed. This is the single most reason, why he has to be and must be kept motivated. Industrial organization must understand that, however good a product might be or a promotion might be, or efficiency of the organization might be, it is salespersons who ultimately bring in the money. He must be kept motivated.

UNDERSTANDING MOTIVATION

We have a lot of motivation theories today, which we see in text books. Some of the most popular motivational theories are:

1. Maslow's need hierarchy theorem

2. Herzberg's motivator hygiene theorem

3. Victor Brooms expectancy theorem

4. Mc Clellands achievement theorem

The above are some of the classical theories which even today hold true for any workplace or person. Along with time, some new theories of motivation came up like the Japanese style of managing businesses, wherein management and workers come together for developmental purpose. A strong bond formed between the employees and employer can yield fabulous results.

In the earlier section, we have seen that motivation is very essential for industrial salesperson, because of the nature of job that he undergoes. Motivation, at the end of the year, to a salesperson could be a trip to Singapore (fully paid) or a Honda city car or probably a Rolex watch. People are different and so are their needs. Now there is a twist in this issue of motivation. Some industrial salesman always do not see material gifts as a motivator for oneself. Salesman could be interested by a pat in back, greater responsibility or a promotion. As an organization or as a manager one must try to understand:

1. What inspires a salesperson?

2. What directs his behaviour?

3. How can it be maintained over time?

Sales manager for industrial organization can always have a host of motivational tools. Some of them are:

1. Sales meetings

2. Contests

3. Non-financial tools like promotion, challenging assignments and recognition

Sales meeting are a part of every industrial organization. Sales meetings generally happen in a resort or outside the country. The objective of these meetings are two fold: one is to provide the salesperson with training, and initiate a two way communication amongst its employees. These salespersons are from various branches across a country and they get to meet once a year and share their views and opinion about a product or the company. It is here when the corporate marketing team, gets to meet the sales team and exchange of ideas happen.

Contests are one of the motivational tools that are used by sales organizations. But however they have their over pitfalls. Contests are generally introduced to increase the sales for a particular period of time or could also be for a year wide performance of the employees who are the best. However, the sales manager or his higher ups must design the contest goals and objectives very carefully; otherwise it can have negative impacts also. The prizes for the contests must be well designed, other wise it would not serve the purpose.

The pitfalls of this or any kind of contests is that many salesperson leave hope from the very first day. They surrender themselves and continue performing average. Some other salesperson think that it would be better to increase the pay, rather than spending money on only a handful. Some of the senior salesperson also feel below their dignity to participate in such contests. These contests can often become demotivators for those who lose it by a mere 0.5 percent, to 5 percent gap. Contests can have negative effects with salesforce pushing sales, and neglecting customer satisfaction.

Some other non-financial tools for motivating a salesperson is to promote him, and give him certain set of responsibility. Promotion generally means a hike in pay, but some may also defer from it. Responsibility of a salesperson when promoted to handle a bigger region or team increases. Some industrial organizations also believe in giving challenging assignments to some members of their salesforce. The challenge could be varied. It could be opening up a new branch, recruiting people promoting a new product line etc. Also recognition like sending letters to the family of the salesperson, about his achievements in the organization can add up to the motivational level.

COMPENSATING THE SALESFORCE

We all work in organization for money, be it in any field. Money acts as a big motivator for everyone. Salespersons earn a huge compensation. Monetary compensation for industrial salespeople should be well designed, the reason being primarily three. They are:

1. Attract the best talent of the industry

2. Motivate people to work

3. Retain people in the job

Some of the companies even go a little further in their vision, stating that the salesperson should be able to handle their business divisions into next ten years. Thus suitable opportunities should be given to them, in terms of recognition and growth opportunities.

Salary is nothing but a way to communicate to salesperson how well he is doing. Whenever we speak of salary in the Indian context, we mean a level of security. However students coming out of B-schools, often look in for higher compensation packages. But, it is always the salary which might not keep anyone motivated.

Any salesperson is generally rewarded by three basic means. They are:

1. Salary

2. Commission

3. Combination of 1 and 2

Generally salesperson is given a combination of salary & commission. But how the component of salary & commission is divided, quite depends upon the industry and the nature of product they are selling. A high involvement purchase would be generally over periods of month and therefore it becomes quite difficult, if the salespersons have only commission and less salary.

Also some of the companies also have this policy of giving a bonus or sometimes a group bonus which may be dependent on the profitability of the organization or branch. But, the important point is that whatever be the method that is applied, it should not lead to salesperson dissatisfaction.

Let us also try and understand that, in an organization and also amongst the salesforce there is a mix of people. There are people who believe in a high salary and do not stress on bonus or commissions. There are people on the other extremes who are highly "monetary oriented". They will calculate it to the last pie, that they have to receive.

As a sales manager of a company, it is next to impossible to design an incentive plan that keeps every one happy. The sales manager must consider multiple issues, before designing a compensation package for the salesforce. Some of the points that may be looked into are:

1. Requirements of the salesforce and the age profile of the sales staff

2. Industry patterns

3. Level of competition

4. Profitability of branch as against cost of sales

5. Nature of sales jobs and objectives of the management

Now whether it be a direct salary, commission or both, they have their own set of pitfalls and positives.

If it is only commissions: The advantage of this structure is correct for small organizations where in the available resources are very low. Also it means no work, no pay. Products have to sell. How far it is effective is a big question mark, because on a long-run, it would not work. Sales managers will have very little control, and the salesperson would tend to leave the job anytime he wishes to. This system can be highly complex, especially when the commission rates vary. In our country wherein people require a sense of security, working on commission basis is a no-no. Sales manager would have a tough time in retaining talent as they would move out.

If it is only salary: Sales manager have greater control over the workforce in terms of the work that they do. Sales managers also have freedom to work and nurture good salespeople. Salaries are easier to administer. Also for industrial selling, where the complexity of product is very high, and it may take a year to sell a unit, this is quite a good option. It also gives the salesperson, a sense of security. However the greatest problem with this kind is that performance may not improve drastically for salesperson. Also a sense of complacency would be developed amongst salespeople. Not only that, any better offer in terms of salary, he would be willing to take the jump.

A mixed compensation plan is definitely a better amongst the other alternatives available as higher performance can earn greater commission. One issue that needs to be kept in mind is that the salary and commission structures should be at par or better than industry to retain the best talents.

Anderson, Hair and Bush suggest that straight salary would work in the following circumstances:[4]

1. *Team selling situations:* Wherever there are more than two involved, it is an appropriate way to design a direct sales structure.

2. *Long negotiating periods:* Complex sales, involve a direct salary component Industrial purchasing is a complex process, and thus it would be useful with a straight salary.

3. *Initial learning periods:* When a salesperson joins the organization and he has to learn the business, a straight salary works for him.

4. *Missionary selling:* When non-selling jobs are done, like goodwill amongst customers by providing assistance and services.

COMPENSATING MANAGERS

How do we compensate mangers? This is generally decided by the national sales head. Since his responsibility is over a territory or a district or state, his job is heavily stressing. Generally sales managers or regional managers are compensated on two factors:

1. Their regional or branch performance

2. Individual sales performance of the members of the salesforce.

Managers are also given bonus based on company profitability and branch profitability. A combination of both regional performance and individual sales performance should determine his salary levels. The sales manager will thus try to nurture his weaker salesman and encourage the star performance to do better.

SALES EXPENSES

Sales expenditure is a must for the salesperson to carry out the necessary selling activities. It take into account the petrol expenditure, mobile bills, hotel expenses, travel expenses and others.

Whenever sales expenses are planned, certain things should be kept in mind:

1. It should be affordable

2. It should be flexible

3. It should be equitable

4. It should be simple

Generally industrial firms have limited reimbursement plan, which can be to certain amounts of money for a single day. However, industrial organizations are trying to keep their expenditure levels to as low as possible and are trying to control sales call costs. Industrial organizations are trying to get the best deals out of hotel, airline and train bookings. Also due to cheaper cost of communicating, more and more organizations are switching over to video conferencing.

CONCLUSION

Personal selling is the point of contact of the buyer and seller. It is a strong interface. Thus, the salesforce of an industrial organization should be very strong enough to build up a relationship with buyers. This would need a proper selection of the salesperson. Due to the nature of selling involved, some special characteristics like team dynamics, communication, background is very important. We have also discussed the interviewing pattern and the reference checks that are essential. Once a salesperson is inducted into an organization, he needs to be socialized with the organization.

Training and motivation of the salesforce is very essential for the success of selling. Any kind of sales training should be very well planned and organized. The training in an industrial organization is generally given either by the sales manager or a trainer who is generally hired from outside. Training acts as a big motivator to a salesperson and thus is given continuously in specific times as he progresses in the organization A salesperson also needs to be trained for his selling skills so as to sharpen his qualities and attitudes.

Salesperson also needs to be given motivation as it is a very stressfull job. One more issue that comes up is the compensation of the salesforce. This is generally to keep them motivated and going. It can be a salary, commission or a mixture of both. Both have them have their own shortcomings and positives. We also discussed on the issues of sales expenditure and how companies are trying to keep it low.

Salesforce is the base to the success of the organization. They form the pillar of success and they must be developed and nurtured over a period of time.

References

1. Futrell, *Sales Management – Teamwork, Leadership and Technology*, 6th Edition, Thomson South Western, pp 4.

2. Parker, Jr, (January – February 1975), *200th Year of Selling*, Marketing Times, pp A8.

3. Anderson, Hair & Bush, *Professional Sales Management*, 2nd edition, McGraw Hill International Editions, pp 248-253.

4. Anderson, Hair & Bush, *Professional Sales Management*, 2nd edition, McGraw Hill International Editions, pp 398.

Mind Power 4: How to Protect Your Good Accounts from the Competition

Question: *Because of the slowdown in my market, my competitors are trying to gain business anywhere they can. They are more active in my good accounts than ever before. How can I protect my good accounts from the competition?*

Great question. This is a major threat to your business. The Paretto Principle, also known as the 80/20 rule, dictates that for most salespeople, 20 percent of their customers produce 80 percent of their revenue. If that is true for you, it means that losing one of your good accounts to the competition can be devastating to your business. That should be enough reason for you to give special time and thought to this question

But losing a good account impacts your business in additional negative ways. The individuals within your good accounts are typically those people who provide you special insights into what your competition is doing and what is happening in the market. Lose one of those good accounts, and you lose some of that special insight.

Your good accounts are the first places you take your new products and services. They provide you ready acceptance and honest feedback for your new offerings. You hone your presentations and sharpen your approaches because of the feedback provided by your good accounts. Lose one of them, and that special function they provide is also gone.

And then, of course, we all knew that your good accounts are the places where you make the greatest financial return for your time invested.

So, it pays to think more deeply about how to vaccinate your good accounts from the competition's enticements. Here are four proven strategies to help you withstand competitive onslaughts.

Contd...

1. Deepen and broaden your relationships

It is difficult for your good friends to take their business away from you and give it to someone they don't know or trust as well. Not that it can't ever happen, but if you have great relationships with the key people in your good accounts, if you have turned them into friends and not just business acquaintances, you'll put a layer of protection between you and your competition. So, you need to focus on turning the contacts in your good accounts into friends by deepening and broadening your relationships.

To deepen the relationships means that you work at enabling the key people within your good accounts to know you and your company better. Take them to lunch, go to a ball game together, and create an opportunity for them to meet your spouse and vice versa. Turn them into friends.

Extend the relationship to include the rest of your company. If possible, bring a number of the key people in your good accounts into your facility to meet some of your company's other employees. Take your boss, operations manager and customer service people into the account to meet them. The more comfortable they are with your company, the more of your people they know, the less likely they are to seriously consider the enticements of a motivated competitor.

To broaden the relationships means that you make sure that you know more of the key people within your key accounts, and that they know you. Be methodical. Make a list of all the important contact people within a good account. Then carefully evaluate the state of the relationship you have with each of them.

If there are important people who don't know you fix that quickly. Make sure that you have positive relationships with your key contact's boss, and the boss's boss. Work as high up the hierarchy as possible.

While the depth and breath of your relationship isn't a foolproof vaccination against your competitors, it goes a long way to assuring that your good account will keep you informed of what is happening, and will probably give you an opportunity to respond to any especially appealing enticements. Its step one in protecting yourself from the competition.

2. Close any open doors

Your competitors will be looking for ways to gain a foothold in your accounts.

They'll search for cracks in the door that they can wedge into greater opportunities. Beat them to the punch by eliminating any opportunities. Carefully examine these issues:

a. *Pricing:* It is not at all unusual to find that some prices in your good accounts have crept up to the point where they are not nearly as competitive as they may be in other places. Review your prices, and make sure that your margin increases haven't put you in an awkward position. You may have to reduce some prices to prevent a competitor from making you look bad.

b. *Problems:* There may be some unresolved, lingering problems in your account. And, while they may not seem important to you, they provide an opportunity for your competitors to turn into an opportunity for them. Are there products that need to be returned? Invoices with discrepancies that need to be resolved? Items that need to be picked up? Training that was to have been done and never got scheduled? Information you were supposed to obtain for someone that you never did?

You've got the idea, if there are any unresolved problems in the account, a good competitor will find them and exploit them to his advantage and your disadvantage.

c. *Products:* You may have some product weaknesses that your competitor can exploit. For example, you may have available this year's version of some standard product. But your good customer is happy using an earlier version. You've never seen any reason to try to convert them to this year's model, when they are perfectly happy with last year's. However, last year's model may not stand up favorably to this year's version for your competition. In that case, you may

Contd...

look bad when your competitor brings in this year's hot new product, and compares it to an older model that you are supplying Shame on you. You should have detailed your version before your competitor got the chance.

3. Bundle up your products and services

You may be selling ten different items to one of your good accounts Rather then continue to sell those ten as separate issues, package them together and write a contract that addresses all of them as a package deal. Get your good customer to acknowledge the package. That way, if your competitor tries to pick out one of the items you're selling, they can't because the price and service on one item impacts the others. The more you can bundle items together into packages the more difficult it is for your competition to dislodge you on one of those items.

4. Formally communicate your value

Arrange for quarterly meetings between your good customer's key people and you and your boss. At these meetings, bring reports detailing aspects of your service, how much money you've saved that customer, the training you've done, the information you've provided, etc. Don't be afraid to identify other areas that you could impact in the same way. This formal reporting raises your position in the customer's eyes from that of being just a vendor, to that of a valuable partner. This separates you from the competition, and makes it less likely that your customer will be attracted to the someone else.

While none of these strategies are guaranteed to put an impenetrable wall around your good accounts, the wise combination of them will make penetrating one of your good accounts an extremely difficult and frustrating project for your competitors. Sometimes the best strategy is a good defense.

Source: About Dave Kahle: The Growth Coach

Dave Kahle is a consultant and trainer who helps his clients increase their sales and improve their sales productivity. Dave has trained thousands of salespeople to be more successful in the Information Age economy. He is the author of over 500 articles, a monthly e-zine, and six books. Ten Secrets of Time Management for Salespeople was recently released by Career Press. His Kahle Way® Sales management System empowers sales managers to Instill accountability and communication in the salesforce. You can join Dave's "Thinking about Sales Electronic Newsletter" on-line at www.davekahle.com/mailinglist.htm.

For more Information or to contact the author, contact The DaCo Corporation, 3736 West River Drive, Comstock Park, MI 49321, phone 1-800-331-1287, fax 1-616-451-9412, Cheryl@davekahle.com or www.davekahle.com

Mind Power 5: Deal or no Deal

How to maintain your margins when battling low-ball competition

By Rich Vurva

Even a rookie salesperson can close a deal by offering a lower price. But unless your company has better buying power than all of your competitors, or you're prepared to accept dramatically lower margins on every sale, competing on price alone is a losing proposition.

Suppliers and distributors agree that distributor salespeople must be able to demonstrate what additional value their companies offer to justify a higher price. If not, they'll likely lose the price war every time.

"I learned years ago, when you compete on price alone, it only takes a competitor to reduce his price one penny and he can take away all your business. You've got to have something else to talk about," says Lee Carrier, vice president of sales for Daido Corporation of America, a manufacturer of roller chain with U.S. headquarters in Portland, Tenn.

Contd...

Sometimes, salespeople can draw attention away from product price by focusing on total overall cost. For example, a higher priced roller chain might provider longer wear life, which translates into less downtime, fewer repairs and lower maintenance costs.

"If you find people who understand the cost of uptime vs downtime, then you can explain your product's benefits and features that will extend their wear life," says Carrier.

That approach can work if the primary decision-maker is involved in maintenance, production or plant management. But if your only choice is to deal with a buyer who is trained to focus on purchase price, it's a tougher sell.

"The buyer is only responsible for doing one thing: procuring the product. But the plant manager may later have to keep replacing the chain because they bought on price, not on value. You have to sell those benefits and features," Carrier says.

It's often easier to convince someone in production or engineering to focus on total cost compared to a corporate purchasing executive, says Tom Miller, executive vice president and chief operating officer of Motion Industries, the power transmission distributor headquartered in Birmingham, Ala. Customers at the plant level understand the ramifications of unscheduled downtime.

"When the caster goes down in a steel mill at 2 o'clock in the morning, you better have the parts to get it back up and running," Miller says.

If you can't state your case to the right person in a plant, you might have to walk away from the sale, adds Rick Glauthier, CEO of Cunningham Supply Company, a cutting tools distributor in Akron, Ohio.

"We've made a conscious decision to not call on certain customers because they don't care what kind of value we bring. All they care about is price," he says.

Selling value rather than price requires a more sophisticated approach than simply demonstrating a product's features and benefits. Salespeople must be able to explain the added value they bring the customer, such as access to new products and technology from leading suppliers, or the importance of a dependable, experienced supply chain with applications expertise.

Cunningham Supply maintains "customer value files" that document all of the value-added services the company provides to specific customers. For instance, a file might document how Cunningham helped a machine shop shave 30 seconds in cycle time from a specific production process.

If a buyer later raises a question about price, the salesperson can bring out the value file to show how much Cunningham has benefited the customer.

"Price buyers usually come back with the question, 'Is that the best you can do?' We say yes, that's the best we can do. And we don't talk about it anymore," says Glauthier.

Two-pronged approach

Some distributors and manufacturers fight low-ball competitors by going to market with a two-pronged product approach. They carry high-quality, higher priced brands to satisfy customers who understand total cost and appreciate value-added benefits such as engineering expertise, inventory management and specialized services. They also offer a secondary, lower-priced product to target price buyers. For this strategy to work, however, salespeople must know when it's appropriate to bundle the products and services the customer is willing to pay for.

"You've got to understand your market and where you play in that market. You can't be everything to everybody," Carrier says.

Distributors that offer a value-added service such as assembling hoses and couplings can demand a higher price than a company that sells bulk hose to a customer who wants to assemble the product

Contd...

himself, Miller says. In that case, it's the salesperson's responsibility to make sure the customer understands he's paying more for the service, not the product.

"There are times when a salesperson loses an order because someone has a better price, but all too often, that becomes an excuse when he simply got outsold," Miller says.

Glauthier says a strong relationship is the salesperson's best defense against getting trapped in a price war.

"When you have a good relationship with an account, and they know you, trust you and believe you, chances are they're going to accept your price and not try to beat you up over it," he says.

Glauthier says it's critical for distributors to align themselves with the best suppliers. Suppliers that provide training and field support for distributor salespeople, and that continually introduce new products and technology, can help them compete successfully against low-priced competition.

"A new product can help insulate you from a price situation. If you switch out a product with a new one, it makes it harder for someone else to compete against you. The new product is something he hasn't seen," Glauthier says.

Selling commodities

Some customers also mistakenly believe all products are alike if they meet an industry standard. For example, Daido Corp's Carrier says customers sometimes assume if a No. 50 roller chain meets standards established by the American National Standards Institute (ANSI), then it's a commodity item.

"Just meeting the ANSI standard is only meeting the minimum. It says nothing about quality. ANSI is the lowest minimum standard that all chains must meet. It doesn't say if the chain is heat-treated, pre-loaded, lubricated or anything else," Carrier says.

The salesperson's job is to explain to the customer how his product exceeds the standard, and why it carries a higher price.

Many salespeople feel they're in a commodity business and therefore must sell on price, according to Bill Brooks, a sales trainer and author. "Selling a commodity doesn't mean you automatically must sell on price," he says.

By definition, a commodity is any item that cannot be easily distinguished from others in the marketplace and is in direct competition with a large number of other extremely similar products or services, Brooks says. But products and services are seldom, if ever, really equal. What if the customer doesn't like the salesperson? What if the vendor only has eight and the customer needs 12? What if vendor A can't ship the product until next month but vendor B carries it in stock?

"The product or service may be identical to others in the marketplace, but all the things involved in getting the product or service to the customer differentiate one vendor from all the others," says Brooks.

It's the salesperson's job to make sure the customer knows all of the details that make one option different from another. Salespeople who can't make a convincing argument establishing the value they bring to the market will continually find themselves losing deals to low-priced competitors.

QUESTIONS FOR DISCUSSION

1. Why do you think are there less sales women, in the field of B2B selling?

2. "Sound product knowledge, is very essential for a good presentation." Discuss.

3. A salesperson has six years of industrial selling experience. He joins with your firm, which sells different set of products. What are the factors would you consider, before your company gives him any kind of training?

4. "A salesperson is lonely at his work." What could be the possible reasons and how could you overcome that?

5. How do you design a compensation plan for the managers and for the sales executives? What would be the factors of differentiation?

6. "Experience is the biggest asset that a salesperson has." How much would it be true, when recruiting for an industrial manufacturer's salesforce?

7. How can motivational theories, be applied to salesman?

chapter

THIRTEEN

Industrial Salesforce: Planning, Organizing and Controlling

COMPANY PROFILE 13: BEML (BHARAT EARTH MOVERS LIMITED)

Bharat Earth Movers Limited is a premier ISO 9001-2000 Company in India and the second largest manufacturer of earthmoving equipment in Asia. A four-decade old multi-locational and multi-product company, BEML has vital applications in diverse sectors of economy such as coal, mining, steel, cement, power, irrigation, construction, road building and railway. It has expanded its product range to cover high-quality hydraulics, heavy-duty diesel engines, welding robots and undertaking of heavy fabrication jobs. A public sector undertaking, BEML commands 70 percent market share in domestic earthmover industry. Nearly 40 percent of its equity has been divested to financial institutions and public.

The company's units at Kolar Gold Fields, Mysore and Bangalore incorporate hi-tech manufacturing facilities with sophisticated CNC machines, arc-welding robots and FMS.

BEML manufactures a wide range of products to meet the needs of mining, Construction, Power, Irrigation, Fertiliser, Cement, Steel and Rail Sectors.

The Earthmoving Equipment includes Bulldozers, Dump Trucks, Hydraulics Excavators, Wheel Loaders, Wheel Dozers, Tyre Handlers, Pipe Layers, Rope Shovels, Walking Draglines, Motor Graders, Scrapers, Water Sprinklers, Aircraft Towing Tractors and Backhoe loaders. BEML has recently introduced Road Headers and side Discharge Loaders for underground mining applications.

Railway products include Integral Rail coaches, Electric Multiple Units, Rail Buses, Track Laying Equipment and Overhead Equipment Inspection Cars. BEML manufactures Heavy Duty Trucks and trailers and hydraulic aggregates for transportation sector.

The company also manufactures high power Diesel Engines and heavy duty Hydraulic Aggregates to meet specific customer requirements. The company plans to diversify into varied activities including underground mining equipment, underground storage for petro-products, leasing and financial services and joint ventures abroad.

BEML research and development achieved a record 85 percent average indigenization in the collaborated products. As many as 30 value added products have been developed in-house. Rs. 300 million research and development center with sophisticated laboratories in fluid power, material science, power line testing, structural engineering, Proto manufacturing shops, Proto Assembly shops and state of the art "CAD Centre" forms the nerve center of BEML.

BEML Technology Division is a strategic business unit of Bharat Earth Movers Limited, a pioneer and the leading manufacturer of heavy engineering equipment catering to the needs of construction and mining, earth moving, rail and Metro and defence sectors.

BEML Technology Division draws upon the extensive expertise and knowledge gained through technology transfer from global giants and also through captive development of a wide range of world class machines deployed for rail transportation including metro coaches, earthmoving, construction and mining and defence. Design and Development experience in an ISO 9001-2000 certified environment and strategic alliances with global partners have ensured a competence comparable with the best in the world. The company has a reputation for innovative products, robust designs and excellent customer satisfaction.

This department has developed and manufactured automotive, defence and rolling stock applications, defence trucks of power and speeds up to 324kW and 90 kmph for off highway terrain trains with the most modern features, to name a few.

Source: www.bemlindia.com

Mind Power 1: Setting and Exceeding Sales Goals through Key Performance Indicators (KPI)

What's your Magic Number

By Jeff Hardesty

The most successful business– and certainly, sales departments– have identified their Key Performance Indicators (KPI); individual gateways that directly effect the outcome of a particular process. Then they measure the competency ratios in line with them.

Have you identified the KPIs in your sales process?

A good KPI example in the sales process might be how many times you advance the first sales appointment to the next phase, whether that's a demonstration, a site visit, a survey or a proposal. Another KPI is how many times you gain a new customer once the first gateway is passed. And when you do gain a new customer, what's the average revenue you achieve? That's certainly an important KPI. Because if your average revenue per sale is 40 percent less than the average peer KPI, you might want to find out why and take focused action to improve it, as you're leaving money on the table.

And what about the length of a sales cycle in days? Is that conditional or do you have a degree of control over it? If you have a team member that has an average sales cycle 30 percent shorter than the peer group, uncover and assimilate those best practices out to the rest of the sales team. Less time, more results. That makes 'Sales Cycle' a valuable KPI.

On a practical level, KPIs can provide management prospect reactions to their service offering for feedback to marketing and product development, detect problem areas in sales performance and signal the need for strategic or tactical modifications even an all out intervention through pinpoint sales performance training.

Perhaps the most overlooked KPI is the individual 'Magic number'; how many new weekly sales opportunities must be generated based on neighboring KPI's. Think of the magic number as the fuel in your gas tank needed to get from point A to point B. It's directly proportional to how far a distance, how fast you drive and your average miles per gallon. Your sales process 'Magic number' is a derivative of your average revenue per sale, 1st appointment to proposal ratio, closing ratio and revenue goal. It's your 'Activity barometer' and it should be at 100 percent.

The following are some tips for improving several sales process KPI's.

If your current 1st Appointment to Proposal ratio is below 65 percent:

1. Internally define what your 'Next step' objective of the 1st appointment is; a demo, a site visit, a survey or a proposal. Then train to a process and measure the outcome.

2. Decide to start at the 'Top' with the authority that can 'Call the shots'.

3. Avoid 'Selling' your product on the 1st appointment. Instead, outline your diagnostic steps to evaluate the fit between your solutions parallel to their business objectives.

If your current closing ratio is below 65 percent:

1. Ask pertinent questions to what the prospect Company's decision-making process is, what the internal criteria for change is and what players need to be involved for evaluation.

2. Communicate a timeline and set a specific date for the 2nd appointment before leaving the 1st appointment. Encourage that all management players be present at the next appointment.

Contd...

3. Catalog risk factors for each management player and develop strategies, tactics, and tools for direct communication to them.

4. Have relevant industry and title reference letters available for 'Real-time' credibility.

If your current 'Activity barometer' is below 100 percent:

1. Announce the competency of converting conversations to appointments as a key performance Indicator for sales success.

2. Define an appointment setting training objective and set a realistic goal.

3. Develop a training process in line with prospecting scenarios and best practice communications.

4. Don't sell your 'Widget'; sell the Business reason to meet.

5. Partner with technology to transfer best prospecting practices into 'Intellectual Capital' promotion throughout your sales society.

Ultimately, sales trainers and management should work in concert to create a new culture by replacing random sales routines with specific KPI competency training.

Targeted and timely KPI can make a critical difference to your monthly revenue scorecard. In today's high sales performance culture migrate away from monthly and quarterly 'Quota' focus to daily routines and weekly goals. The opportunity rests squarely on switching paradigms from the required 'End result' to the necessary steps (KPIs) to get there routinely. Then build supporting tools for learning and application.

And don't forget your 'Magic Number'.

Source: Jeff Hardesty is president of JDH group, Inc, and the developer of the X2 sales system, a blended training system, that teaches sales professional the competency of setting c-level business appointments. Jeff can be reached at jeff@convertmoresales.com.

Mind Power 2: How well are your salespeople serving your customers?

Copyright 2000, by Dave Kahle.

That's right. Serving, not selling. I know you are concerned with sales. It's easy to determine how well your people are selling to your customers. That's what sales reports are for. But your customers are more concerned with how well they are being served by your salespeople.

Why is that important? Because you are in it for the long run. You don't want to just sell something to a customer, you want to build a relationship that lasts over time and results in years of sales. In one sense, your business is not really a sales business, it's a relationship-building business.

And when it comes to developing long-lasting profitable relationships, it is not how well your salespeople present features and benefits and overcome objections that counts, it is how they serve the customers' needs.

Which brings us to a couple of questions? First, what does it mean for a salesperson to serve the customer? And second, how do you know that it is happening effectively?

Salespeople serving the customer?

Clearly, you know what it means for your company to serve your customer. On-time deliveries, competitive prices, reliable service, competent CSRs, etc. But, what do your customers want from your outside salespeople? Ask each salesperson what it means to serve the customer, and you can expect to hear a variety of answers. Some define service as picking up purchase orders, others will define it as taking

Contd...

inventory, some will propose that following up on back orders or short shipments is part of it, while others will say that it involves visiting the customer on a predictable basis. That's the problem. Few companies have any consistent description of what it really means to serve the customer. Generally, salespeople are left to figure it out on their own, create their own definitions, and develop their standards.

I have yet to meet a salesperson who did not believe that he/she provided excellent service to their customers. Every salesperson perceives that they are doing a good job. Not once has a salesperson taken me off to the side at a break in a seminar I was teaching, and confide in me. "You know, Dave, I really do a poor job of serving my customers".

So, on one hand, we have vague and general definitions of what it means to provide good service to the customer and on the other, we have the often-inaccurate perceptions of the salespeople.

The result? Inconsistent service and lots of unmet expectations on the part of the customers.

I recently worked with one of my clients to gain a deeper understanding of what service means by, of all things, asking the customers! We gathered six of this client's brightest and most insightful customers together for a half-day focus group. I facilitated the videotaped discussion, and the client viewed the tape later.

What did we discover?

How customers define good service.

Here's how those customers defined "good service" from the outside salesforce.

1. ***Don't Waste their time:*** If there was one theme that popped up over throughout the day it was this: We have less time to do our job than ever before. So, you better not waste any part of it. In other words, don't come into my business unprepared. Have something of value to share or don't come.

    They need to see some value in the time they share with your salespeople, every time they see them, or they won't see them. Don't waste their time with idle chit-chat, don't take longer to do something then you need to, don't be unprepared, and don't waste their employees' time. If you don't have something important to do or something valuable to bring, don't visit.

    And when you do visit, make sure you have all the answers. Know what the product does or doesn't do, know what the pricing and terms are, and be prepared to answer all their questions.

2. ***Be empowered to handle things now:*** One customer talked about the salesperson as "victim". He was referring to the salesperson who spends time explaining how the truck broke down, or the manufacturer back-ordered the product, or it was recalled, or what ever. All of these were seen as the salesperson saying. "It wasn't our fault. We're the victims of someone else's mistakes." These customers weren't concerned with whose fault something was, nor were they concerned with the reasons why something wasn't as it was supposed to me. They only wanted solutions. "Don't be a victim", they said. "Bring us solutions now." One customer remarked that the Ritz Carlton hotel authorizes its maids to spend up to $ 2,000 to make a customer happy, while the salespeople who call on him cannot resolve a problem over a $ 50.00 can of paint without several phone calls and days of approvals.

    Good service, to these customers, meant that the salesperson could solve the problem immediately, on the spot.

3. ***Know my business:*** Don't waste our time or insult our intelligence by presenting products or services that we can't use. These customers expected the salespeople to know what their processes were, know who their customers were, know what their goals and strategies were, know the limitations of their facilities, budgets and timetables, and take all of that into consideration before they present some product or programme.

    "The best salespeople." One remarked. "Are like extensions of my business."

Contd...

4. ***Bring us solutions, not problems:*** These customers did not want to discover after the fact that a purchase would be back-ordered or short-shipped. Find the problems before we experience them, and then bring us solutions. Tell us what our options are, and we'll decide what to do.

In other words, the salesperson who says, "I'm sorry about last week's back order, " is not serving the customer. The salesperson who is serving the customer is the one who says. "Next week we're going to short ship this order. If you need the balance right away, we can do any of three things to help. Here are your options…"

While these weren't the only definitions of "good service" this group of customers volunteered, they represent a good starting point.

If you're like most of my clients, at this point you may be little queasy in your stomach. You may be doubtful that your salesforce is really serving your customers like want to be served.

Six initiatives: What to do? Here are six initiatives you can consider.

1. Make sure your salespeople are thoroughly prepared to present any new product or program. Don't think that just because someone presented a new product in Friday afternoon's sales meeting that the salespeople are fully equipped to thoroughly present it.

    Role-play a customer asking questions. Don't stop until everybody gets it right. Think through every possible question that a customer may ask, and make sure that every salesperson has an intelligent and thoughtful answer.

    Give quizzes on the new products and programs. Don't allow anyone to present it until they have passed the quiz.

    Hold the salespeople accountable for having accurate and thorough knowledge.

2. Insist that each salesperson have a plan for every sales call, and something of value to bring to the customer. Train them in this.

    Use your contact manager software to spot check sales call plans and reports. When you are your sales managers are traveling in the field with salespeople, check for their preparation.

3. Empower the salespeople to fix problems on the spot. Create some guidelines for the level of authority the salesperson has. For example, you may decide that a salesperson can issue a credit of up to $500.00 on the spot to fix any problem he/she needs to.

    Instill information systems that allow the salespeople to have on line 24/7 access to order status, inventory, pricing, etc.

4. Train and equip the salesforce to "know their customer's business."

    Create detailed account profile forms (either electronic or paper), and require the salesforce to use them.

    From time to time, ask a customer to come in and talk about his/her business to the salesforce.

    Hold focus groups like the one I mentioned, and show the videotapes to the salespeople.

    At sales meetings, instead of only discussing your products and processes, educate the salespeople on a typical customer's business.

5. Teach and equip the salespeople to become proactive problem solvers. Make sure they have the right information tools to proactively discover problems before they hit the customer. Train them in using them. When you and your sales manager ride with them, watch to make sure they are using them effectively.

6. Finally, ask your customers. From time to time, personally visit some of your customers, and ask them how your salesforce is doing relative to other salespeople, and relative to that customer's expectations. Take a form to make sure that you are thorough. Ask your customers to rate each of the issue mentioned above. Use that input to refine your system. And then, find out how else your customer defines good service.

Contd…

Do these things and you'll begin to field a salesforce that the customers view as valuable. You'll take a huge step forward in developing the kind of relationships you'll need to prosper in the 21st century.

Source: About Dave Kahle: The Growth Coach:

Dave Kahle is a consultant and trainer who helps his clients increase their sales and improve their sales productivity. Dave has trained thousands of salespeople to be more successful in the Information Age economy. He is the author of over 500 articles, a monthly e-zine, and six books. Ten Secrets of Time Management for Salespeople was recently released by Career Press. His Kahle Way® Sales Management System empowers sales managers to Instill accountability and communication in the salesforce. You can join Dave's "Thinking about Sales Electronic Newsletter" on-line at www.davekahle.com/mailinglist.htm.

For more Information or to contact the author, contact The DaCo Corporation, 3736 West River Drive, Comstock Park, MI 49321, phone 1-800-331-1287, fax 1-616-451-9412, Cheryl@davekahle.com or www.davekahle.com

Mind Power 3: Power Strategies for Distribution Salespeople

Copyright 2000, by Dave Kahle.

Selling for a distributor puts you in a unique selling situation. While many basic sales principles still apply to you, there are additional unique challenges rising out of your position as a distributor salesperson. For example, you probably sell many of the same things your competitor sells. Add to that your special potential for creative in-depth relationships with your customers, and multiply that by the number of vendors and products you sell, and you can see the extra complexity of your job.

To be successful, you need some guidance in mastering the unique challenges of your job. Here are some "Power Strategies" specifically designed to help you become more successful.

1. FOCUS ON RESULTS

At first you may think this to be common sense and self-evident, and to some degree it is. However, many distributor representative are guilty of "going through the motions" selling. In other words, you see "Customer A" on Tuesday morning because that's your habit. Instead of being driven by the objective you hope to achieve in that meeting (the results), you're driven by habit. You go where it's most comfortable rather than where it's most effective.

You can apply this strategy in almost every aspect of your job. If you focus on results, you rank your prospects and customers in terms of their potential, and spend the greater amount of your time with the highest potential accounts.

You create specific call objectives for every call, and annual objectives for every one of your key accounts, focusing on the results you want to achieve.

You view the products in which you choose to invest your selling time in the same light. Which products will bring you the best results? Those are the ones you promote, if you're focusing on results.

You manage your time and territory precisely, asking yourself daily, if not hourly, "What is the best use of my time right now?"

Put all this together and "FOCUS ON RESULTS" become an overarching strategy that affects everything you do.

2. GET IMPORTANT

That means get important to your customers, and get important to the manufacturers whose products you represent.

Contd...

In this rapidly changing world, new sources of competition are continually surfacing. It seems that pressures on price and margin don't ever stop. In that kind of environment how can you secure a spot for yourself that provides you a good income and some security?

The secret is to get important. When you're important to your manufacturers, you're able to provide them the one thing they need from you. And that's access to your customers. Think about it. Most manufacturers can warehouse and ship and bill from you. And that's access to your customers. Think about it. Most manufacturers can warehouse and ship and bill their products almost as well as you can. What they can't do as effectively as you get in front of your customers.

It's always going to cost them more to get to your customers because they have a limited number of products over which to spread their sales cost, while you can spread your costs over a much wider number of products. Thus, you should always be able to access to the customer at lower costs then the manufacturers. And the smart ones know that. So, your ability to get important to your manufacturers is directly dependent on your ability to provide them access to your key customers.

That means that you must GET IMPORTANT to your customers. You do that by becoming, in your customer's mind, an integral, almost indispensable part of their business. You can't do that if you restrict your activities to quoting the lowest price and picking up orders. Rather, you must systemically create relationship with the most important people within your key accounts; invest your time in learning about their business and getting to know them better than anyone else, and then providing creative solutions and systems that solve deep and systematical problems. When you do that consistently and effectively, you become, in the eyes of your customer, a valued part of your customer's business. And that makes you important to them.

3. THINK A LOT

It's easy to do your job by mindlessly going through the motions. You see the customers with whom you are comfortable, quote the stuff they ask you to, grumble about the paperwork, and complain about price competition.

That's easy. Unfortunately, it's also a prescription for eventual failure. The world is changing too rapidly today to do your job "mindlessly". Your customers are changing, products and vendors are changing and adapting, new competitors and technologies are springing up. If you go through your job mindlessly, you'll soon be outdated and ineffectual.

Do just the opposite. Commit yourself to the challenge of continuous improvement. Think about everything you do and examine ways to improve and writing more value out of it.

Challenge and question everything you do. Is this the best way to write up a quote? Should you be visiting this account, or would the other one hold more potential? Should you really be spending your time promoting this product, or is another one important? Should you really be lunching with customer or should you invest that time in another? Is this the best way to file your old quotes, keep track of customer contacts, and file product literature?

Got the idea? Never rest. Be discontent with every aspect of your job in order to provide the stimulation to improve on it. Think a lot.

These three strategies can be guidelines to help you master some of the uniquely challenging parts of your job.

Source: About Dave Kahle: The Growth Coach:

Dave Kahle is a consultant and trainer who helps his clients increase their sales and improve their sales productivity. Dave has trained thousands of salespeople to be more successful in the Information Age economy. He is the author of over 500 articles, a monthly e-zine, and six books. Ten Secrets of Time Management for Salespeople was recently released by Career Press. His Kahle Way® Sales Management System empowers sales managers to Instill accountability and communication in the salesforce. You can join Dave's "Thinking about Sales Electronic Newsletter" on-line at www.davekahle.com/mailinglist.htm.

For more Information or to contact the author, contact The DaCo Corporation, 3736 West River Drive, Comstock Park, MI 49321, phone 1-800-331-1287, fax 1-616-451-9412, Cheryl@davekahle.com or www.davekahle.com

INTRODUCTION

We have multiple ways to reach the marketplace. Industrial marketers have manufacturer's representatives, distributors, dealers amongst others to reach their products to the market. They also have strong tools like advertisement, sales promotions, participation in trade shows to reach the industrial buyer. But still, personal selling constitutes the strongest component to reach the industrial buyer. It forms a very strong interlink between the buyer and the seller. Whether be it selling a Boeing or an executive jet or a corporate insurance policy, salespersons form a very key link for the industrial marketer. The job of the industrial salesperson is to facilitate the selling process, by providing solutions to the industrial buyer. The salesperson uses his expertise, knowledge, negotiating skills, puts in his touch before a sales deal is actually closed. One aspect we must try and appreciate is that, no promotional tool would bring in automatic business. It is the salesperson who has to sweat it out. The promotional tool, rather acts as his aid.

To enter the marketplace, we have seen earlier that the industrial marketer has a lot of choices. But, whether he chooses a mode of direct selling or through the help of a distributor quite depends on multiple factors like financial capabilities, nature of market, competition, and objectives. This we have seen earlier but it is an industrial seller who is appointed by these channels finally to reach the ultimate buyers.

Lets understand, why salespersons are used. It is for three simple reasons:

1. Nothing can replace human skills.

2. Selling industrial products is a very complex issue, because it involves "multiple heads" buying the product.

3. The buyers are few in number, and are generally large.

This chapter would be dealing with the issues of planning, Organizing and controlling. We would be discussing, the structure of the salesforce organization, how do you plan it, all about sales calls, making a presentation, how to deal with national accounts, future of salesforce, salesforce automation, and how to evaluate the salesforce performance, and monitor them. The most important however is the making of a sales presentation. That will make or break your sale.

ORGANIZING THE SALES DEPARTMENT

We have seen earlier, that selling is a very important function of an industrial organization. Now, selling is a very costly affair, in terms of the efforts, the resources, the training and compensation which the organization is putting in. Also, at the same time, it is looking for minimum profitability from the sales, i.e., they should be used effectively and efficiently, resulting into greater profitability for the organization.

Any industrial sales organization can broadly be divided into four major categories. They are:

1. Geographic Organization

2. Product-oriented Organization

3. Function-oriented Organization

4. Market-oriented Organization

Thus, the center of focus has to be either, the region, the product, or the function. Now, the question that is in our minds, is where to use which type, so as to reduce costs and increase efficiency and effectiveness.

Geographic Organization

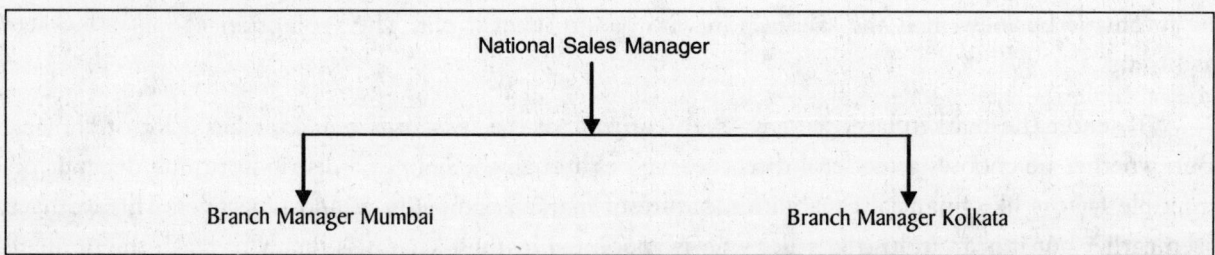

They are very common, but are generally used in combination with other organizational structure. A sales manager or branch manager takes care of the complete region, or area, and is generally responsible for all activities. The basic advantage is that, it is a decentralized form and there is sufficient amount of flexibility. Costs are more, and coordination with the central office, often becomes a problem. This form of organization is appropriate when industrial customers are geographically dispersed. Generally when industries tend to grow up in a particular region, or the regional behaviour of industrial purchasers vary. Industrial selling requires personalized attention, and geographically designed sales organization can serve it effectively.

Product Oriented Organization

In this type of organization, the salesperson are given a set of products to handle with. For example, there would a product team which would be selling PC's, one team for laptops and the other for accessories. This product-oriented organization is appropriate when products are complex, and there are differences in the product line. The marketing programme needs to

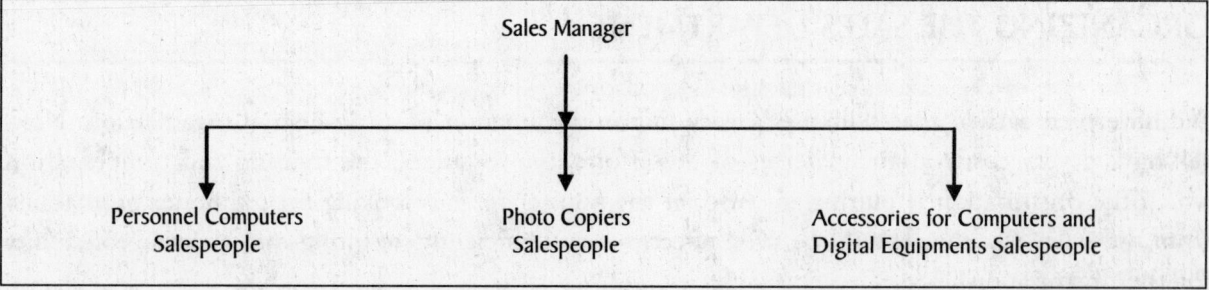

be well coordinated, and because of technological changes, products are updated frequently. Each product group brings in significant resources to the industrial organization and special care needs to be taken for all. There could be variations in product-oriented organizations. The biggest problem that is faced by such organization is the additional expense they have, mostly due to additional specialization and also industrial purchases, may be visited multiple times by salesperson from the same company. Some companies, also face the problem of brand image, with this structure.

Function-oriented Organization

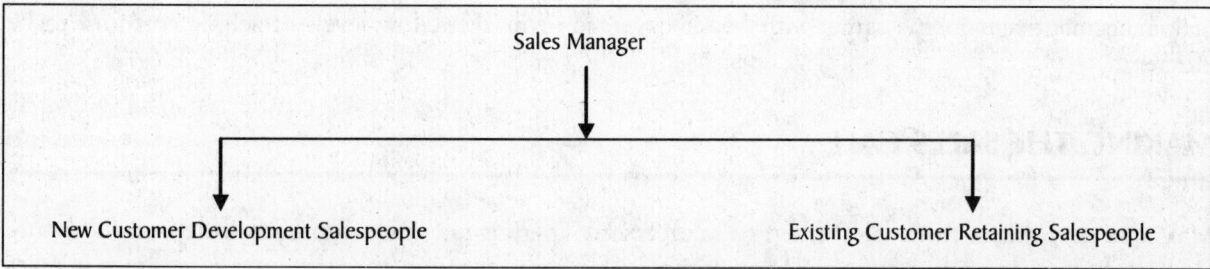

This is for only small and medium industrial organization, with simple product line up. They also have very few customers. This would be appropriate when functions can be justified. However, the major challenge is that salespeople on one side, believe the "grass is greener" on the other side. These organizations are not at all cost effective and with the growth of a small or medium sized industrial organization, changes have to be made in the function-oriented form.

Market-oriented Organization

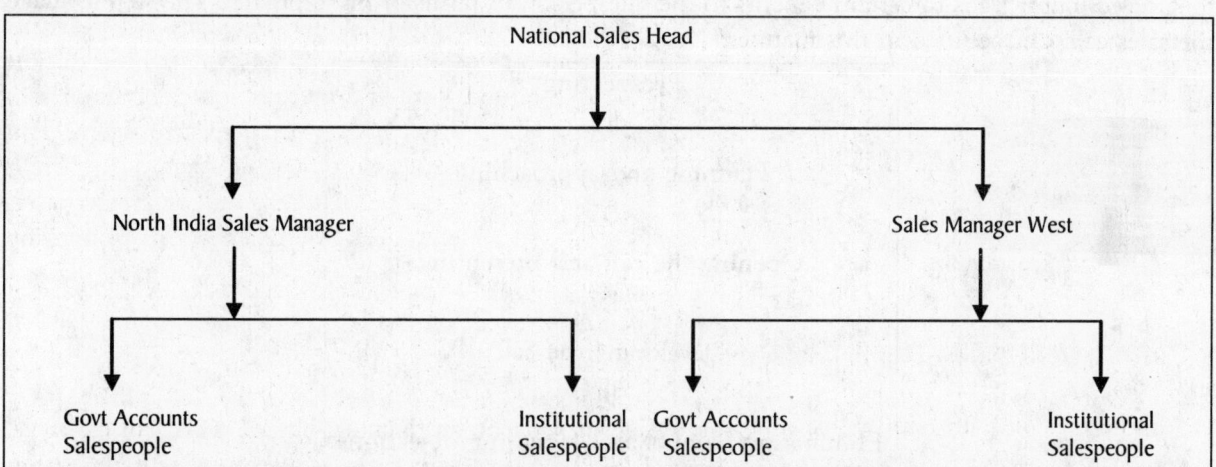

When industrial marketers have different set of customers with unique needs, market-oriented organizations are ideal. Generally, large industrial organizations would be having revenues from different accounts. So, these organizations divide their customer on the basis of markets, type of customers and usually classified by industry or channel of distribution or importance of that national account.

This type of organizational structure is appropriate when products are complex as well as unique. Industries vary widely as well as their needs. Some of the customers contribute a major chunk of the revenue.

Today, in industrial marketing with the huge onset of competition, serving large customers is being treated with great deal of sincerity and priority. We will look into this aspect a little while from now on.

This structure also have some disadvantages. Sales coverage of areas often become expensive, when customers are dispersed. There also is a need of different approaches for advertising and promotion to these various groups.

However, industrial marketing managers need not to watertight this component of dividing the department. Creativity can be applied and with a mix. Most companies purely do not follow one form of organization structure. They generally have a mix of forms. It could be a combination of geographic and product structure. Also, depending on the volume of business, profitability and potential for growth, the salesforce of the industrial organization needs to be organized. However, the basic principles of management remain the same, with better coverage of markets, low levels of selling cost and to be efficient.

MAKING THE SALES CALL

Making a sale, differs from salesperson to salesperson. There is no single approach which can be a sure shot guide to success in a sales call. Sometimes, sales come through the easy way, sometimes it takes quite a long time for a sale, actually to come through. Although every sales executive is given similar kinds of training, there performance would widely vary in all organizations. There is an unwritten law of "Sales aptitude" which makes a salesman successful. Some of them in the factor of aptitude, can be taught, some learnt with experience. There are also some salesman, who will charm the buyer, into a deal.

But while writing the textbook, sales charm probably would not help. Researchers, trainers, generally specify certain procedures, as to how to make a sales call. This is definitely not a sure shot way to succeed, but it leads to certain benefits to the salesperson in terms of his approach. The step to make the sales call, can be lined in this manner.

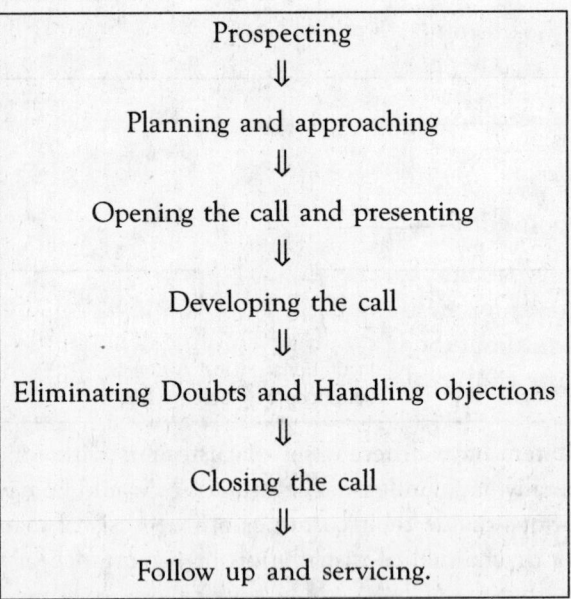

Prospecting
⇓
Planning and approaching
⇓
Opening the call and presenting
⇓
Developing the call
⇓
Eliminating Doubts and Handling objections
⇓
Closing the call
⇓
Follow up and servicing.

Prospecting is typically, a step when a business needs a particular product and they have the ability to purchase the product. This can be generated from multiple sources. It could be enquiries, references, online leads or it could be from the morning newspaper "tender" notices. Whatever be the sources of prospects, two most important aspects are:

1.   Salesperson could continuously look out for prospects.

2.   There should be sufficient "qualified prospects".

It has often seen that, once a particular month or quarters go on well with an industrial salesperson, he tends to neglect or forget about the quarter that lies ahead of him. If a salesperson has to perform brilliantly, he needs to do a great planning. Only then, he will do well. One more reason to have sufficient qualified leads is that, it does not result in any kind of wastage of time for the salesperson, specially in industrial selling, where selling cycles are long. Whenever a salesperson, needs to qualify a lead, he needs to mentally ask himself:

1. Is he willing to buy? Does he have the authority to decide?

2. Does he have the money to buy?

Once this is done, the salesperson can take over. This is where his skills would come in action. What is also important to know here is that, it is always good to be referred by someone. This increases the chance of the salesperson, to be easily accepted in the new customer's office.

The next most important step is planning and approaching. Never go out for a sales call without planning. Do your homework, before you ring the bell of the B2B prospective buyer. You must do your homework. You must know about his business (preferably more than he does), with data as backing. You must know his competitors, clients, and business in every minute detail. If you can, collect some personal information about the person, you are going to meet his likes and dislikes. Never leave your office without the homework done. When, an industrial salesperson goes with preparation, he is:

1. Confident.

2. Acting as a true professional.

3. Likely to develop trust and confidence.

Before approaching the customer, prepare a proposal as to how the industrial buyer is going to benefit. The features, advantages and benefits of the product you are going to sell. Have the objective of the sales call very clear in your mind.

Schedule for an appointment. Remember industrial buyer prefer not to attend to uninvited people. Don't say, "I was passing by, I just thought if I could visit you, probably". That's hara-kiri. Walk in only with an appointment.

When the salesperson goes and speaks to the prospective buyer for the first time that is "opening the sales call". The first few minutes are critically very important. At this point of time, the buyer will tend to develop a perception about the salesperson. This is very important as it is critically very important for the success or the failure of the sales. This initial impression on the salesperson depends much on the attitude and appearance of the salesperson. The salesperson needs to be trained as to manage himself in the very first few minutes.

The Great Presentation

The simplest key approach to presentation is to highlight the features, advantages and benefits and what is the industrial marketer offering to the buyer. The buyer need to be told, as to how he would benefit from this purchase. However, for a "new purchase" situation, the approach needs to be different. When an industrial buyer is purchasing for the first time and he has little knowledge about the product or service, relationship should be build before the presentation is made.

During the presentation by the industrial marketer, the job of the salesperson is to drive everybody's thought into the belief, that the product is the most appropriate for them. One word of caution for all industrial salespeople, is that presentations should not be loaded with data and information only. Generally, when presentations are made, testimonials of existing clients, can be shown to stress upon the added benefits that the industrial marketer would provide. While, the presentation is being made, doubts are being raised in the minds of the industrial buyer, which needs to be overcome. Today, more and more industrial organizations are using interactive media devices, multimedia to make presentations more effective.

It is very unlikely, that the industrial salesperson would meet all the members of the decision making unit at the same time. It would be quite possible, that he needs to present it, quite number of times.

Generally the presentations, are prepared by the sales managers. This can also be done with the help of trainers. However, at an individual salesperson level, when presentations need to be done, it can be modified and altered as required.

No presentation is great. Everyone would be having their own set of doubts. We would only come to know, that the presentation has been great, only when the industrial buyer gives a nod.

One of the major mistakes that often industrial salesperson do, is that they memorize the presentation and vomit it out. It definitely does not work. There has to be sanctity in the way, a presentation is done. However, researchers today speak of multiple sales presentation methods, like need satisfaction, AIDA approach etc.

Mind Power 4: Why "Countering Objections" Backfires, and what Stellar Salespeople do instead

In any sales situation, the seller wants the buyer to buy. The buyer, meanwhile, is considering the purchase and alternative courses of action. Most sales training gurus would call those alternatives "objections", and salespeople are trained to "counter" those objections.

But this usually backfires.

Here are some typical "alternative courses of action" that could be floating around in the buyer's mind as she listens to a sales pitch:

- I think I like the other company's product better.

- There are more important things to buy.

- I think I'd prefer a smaller/lighter/stronger/easier/cheaper version.

- A new, better version will probably come out next year.

- It's too confusing right now, too difficult to make a decision.

- I'd rather make it or do it myself.

Here's what happens in typical selling situations, when these issues come-up in the buyer's mind.

The least effective salesperson will talk and talk even though the buyer has made it clear, via body language and a sudden drop in interest level, that one of the alternatives has become more appealing as the salesperson prattled on. This salesperson has lost the sale, but continues to jabber, while the buyer is devising her exit strategy. "How can I get this person out of my office in the shortest amount of time and with the least amount of bother?" This is one of the most common situations in sales.

A slightly better salesperson will notice that the buyer is now crossing her arms and sitting back in her chair, and that she has started to frown. He will stop, and ask if she has a concern.

If it's too late, the buyer will pretend that there isn't a problem, immediately change her body language, and continue to devise her exit strategy as the salesperson resumes his pitch.

Contd...

If it's not too late, the buyer will express her concern.

And here is where we separate "Slightly better" salespeople from "stellar" salespeople.

The "slightly better" salesperson, as soon as the buyer expresses her concern, will start pitching again. He will treat the buyer as a silly child who just isn't aware of all the reasons why his product would be better than her alternatives. This will only alienate and irritate the buyer, who really did have a valid concern, and who will now regret that she shared her concern with the salesperson. "I should have kept my mouth shut," she will think. She will become more determined than ever not to give this salesperson her business.

The stellar salesperson will sense a concern, and stop pitching. He will actually turn off the presentation as soon as the buyer has expressed her concern. He will start to encourage the buyer to talk more about her concern, and will not sell during this entire exchange. He will agree with the buyer about her alternative courses of action. "Well, it's true, you could put this off right now," he will say. "Because you're right, if you wait a year or two, a new, better version will come out. We introduce new versions every six months, for example."

Then, the salesperson would *let there be silence*. This is the hardest thing for salespeople, and one of the main reasons that salespeople have so much trouble communicating with engineers, finance people, and anyone else who likes to compose their sentences in their heads before speaking. Not to mention buyers who are thinking over their alternatives. What will happen during this silence?

What will happen during this silence?

Whatever the salesperson said just before the silence will ring in the buyer's mind. "*We introduce new versions every six months, for example.*" The buyer will take this new information and add it to her thinking process. She will then ask a question: "If I buy from you, will I be able to upgrade for a reasonable price when you come out with a new version?"

Still sitting back, not selling, the salesperson will say, "Yes, we have an upgrade path. The cost of an upgrade is always about 1/3 the cost of the full program". More silence.

What is happening during this silence? The salesperson is letting the buyer go through her own buying process. He is not dumping more data on her, when she is not ready for it (which is what most salespeople do). He is not treating her as if she is stupid for considering alternatives. He is acknowledging that there could be alternatives, and he is letting her think them through.

Most importantly, he is taking advantage of a fact that is seldom, if ever mentioned in sales training materials: Buyers want to buy. Buyers want to purchase to be easy. It's easier to buy from a salesperson who is sitting in front of you than it is to keep looking. But it has to be the buyer's decision. The seller has to give her the time and space to make that decision.

The seller is also stepping back a little, letting the buyer come forward if she wishes. In the seller/buyer dance, the seller is letting take the next step. The buyer has now had time to consider her options, and has decided that her concern about obsolescence isn't that critical, because the seller has an upgrade path. She has now countered the objection in her own mind.

Now she will say to the salesperson: "Well, since you have a clear upgrade path, and I really do need to get this problem solved, I'm comfortable with this. Let's go back to the presentation."

The salesperson can now start pitching again, while keeping an eye on the buyer's responses.

Note that the stellar salesperson never countered the buyer's objections, but carefully listened to them and, if they made sense for the buyer, even agreed with them. Most importantly, he was willing to walk away.

I do need to note that this is not the *insincere agreement* so typical of telesales call techniques. "Oh, yes, Mrs. 'Zheerazho,' I understand why you would say that. I'm sure you are good at repairing your

Contd...

own computers. But wouldn't you still want a certified technician to come out and evaluate your current networked PCs and help you improve them?" This is not the same as the technique I just described. This is just manipulation, pure and simple, and it alienates and irritates the customer, who immediately thinks, "How can I get this creep off the phone as quickly as possible?"

Instead of countering objections, the best salespeople use the jujitsu method, where they don't fight the objection, they accept it and work with it. And, they are willing to walk away.

What's interesting is, when the seller is willing to walk away, the buyer often follows.

Source: By Kristin Zhivago on Jan 19, 2007. Visit her at www.zhivago.com or www.revenuejournal.com. Reprinted with permission. Copyright rests with the author.

The next important task for the industrial salesperson, is to handle objections and eliminate doubts. This is a very crucial step because, it will give the feel whether they will go or not go for the product.

It is very essential, to clear of the doubts, till the time the buyer is fully convinced. Very few presentations, will end successfully as the industrial buyer may not be easily convinced. It is the biggest test that salesperson face everyday, and has to come out of that successfully. If there are objections raised by the industrial buyer, it is a very good sign, which would indicate to the seller that, the prospect is interested, but needs to get certain doubts cleared before he strikes the deal. It takes a lot of courage for the salesperson to stand, before the industrial buyer, and handle objections. It is the last big hurdle. Objections could be of number of types. Typically, industrial salespeople will confront the following objections:

1. Postponing of purchase by industrial buyer
2. Price and payment terms
3. Competition
4. Image of the organization which the salespeople represent
5. Technical specifications and quality

Closing the sales call, is a big issue for many industrial salespeople. Some of them, just do not feel confident, and some do not know how to close and doubts on his ability, some wait for signals from the buyer, some salesperson are very scared, because of the idea of "rejection" that goes behind their minds. Trainers and sales managers should never neglect this part of the sales process. It is very crucial. Salesperson must be trained to handle it. An anecdote on this closing which says "Closing the sales, is like saying to your girlfriend.. "Will you marry me?" You might get rejected."

Once the sales is done, he is very happy. Within a few follow ups, the cheques has been issued by the client, and goods have been delivered to him. If you want to stay in the profession of sales, and you are not planning to leave the company, or industry, follow-up and give a "great" service. From my personal experience, if you do not that, you will meet that customer some other time, with bitter memories. In industrial marketing, the number of clients are very limited, a salesperson should never forget that.

Mind Power 5: The last thing to be Discussed is Price

The biggest fault while making a sales call is the discussion of price. Price is the last thing that needs to be discussed. While making a call inexperienced salespersons try and compete on price, which sometimes the buyer is not looking for. Buyers first look in for faith and confidence in the salesperson. Technical knowledge of the product and the business environment also helps the sales executive. Most often due to poor planning, salespersons do not plan their work. It leads to wastage of time. Studying a company also helps in the sales call, which gives an insight into the buying process. Unfortunately, most do not follow it and try and negotiate on the price front.

KEY ACCOUNTS

We have earlier seen the rule of 20-80 working for customers that an industrial organization has. 20 percent of the customers, will bring in 80 percent of the sales. These industrial buyers form a very important part for the industrial marketer. These large buyers have expectations from its suppliers in multiple respects. They would not only expect a genuine quality, price and service, but also value added services.

Whenever we are defining and trying to differentiate a key account to an ordinary account, we would see that there are some startling differences. They are:

1. They purchase in large volumes.

2. Key accounts expect value added service.

3. Their objective is to have "partnering relationship" and derive benefits out of such a relationship.

4. Key accounts participate in information sharing, with the industrial suppliers.

5. Multiple individuals take part in the buying decision process.

The typical feature that you see in a key account relationship, is the fact that there is a very close interaction and information sharing amongst the buyer and the seller. Key account management requires to be given a serious thought by industrial marketers.

Another school of thought by Shapiro and Moriarty[1] say that there is a difference between a major account and a national account. A major account is one when the customers purchasing potential is large, but the complexity involved in servicing such customers are low. A national account on the other hand requires, dealing with multiple people, is very complex and the potential to purchase is huge. They also mention that for a customer with small sales potential and relatively simple, a dyadic interaction is essential.

Dyadic interaction[2] as explained by Bonoma and Johnston is the interaction between the buyer and seller. In this case, not only goods are exchanged, but also information is exchanged to solve buyer problems. Both the buyer and the seller would have certain goals in mind before the process of selling begins. This interaction is very essential, as it builds up relationship for over the years.

Generally, the key account selling's are done with a team selling perspective. There are multiple people drawn from various departments, which may include branch manager, national accounts manager, engineer, logistics manager and the production manager also might pitch in. The objective is very simple "partnering relationships" to benefit both the buyer and the seller.

Mind Power 6: Key Account Management in a Competitive Market

– Sanjay Limaye

Key accounts are the heart of a business. How they are identified, developed and cultivated can mean the difference between a thriving enterprise and one that struggles to survive. With rapid change in the business environment, every organization needs to review its customer management process, especially for the profitable ones and who are expected to give repeat business.

The change drivers causing this rapid change in the business environment are;

- *Redefining marketplace:* Increasing commoditization of products and services, Greater and stronger competition, lower margins and saturated markets.

Contd...

- **Customer power:** More demanding and knowledgeable, Purchase behaviour strategic than tactical and higher expectations.

- **Rapid change due:** Shortening product and technology life cycles. Time based competition. Transient customer preferences.

- **Coping with globalization:** Suppliers are being differentiated by scope, bigger and innovative competition, lower margins, greater customer choice and larger-more complex markets.

What is a key account?

Key account is a customer in a business-to-business market identified by the selling company as being strategic importance. Typically the factors frequently used to identify such a customer are;

- Customers see value in product offering
- Prompt payments
- Hub/Focal company in a network
- Requirement of strategic alliances
- Customer hands over total responsibility
- Ease of doing business
- Regular flow of business stability
- Opportunity for cross selling
- Strategic/reference value
- Requirement of single point responsibility
- Requirement to innovate repetitive work

What is Key Account Management? (KAM)

It's an approach by a selling company aimed at building a portfolio of loyal key accounts by offering them, on a continuing basis, a product/service package tailored to their individual needs.

Key relationship development

Developing relationship for a KAM is of fundamental importance for mutual benefits. It consists of sharing knowledge and commitment to the exchange of goods and services, money, time and information. This business relationship needs to go through various stages before achieving significant trust and understanding. The typical stages are:

Exploratory- Basic – Cooperative – Interdependent and Integrated

The process, which leads to successful KAM, can be broadly classified as, KAM planning process and KAM implementation process.

KAM Planning processes are:

- KA Selection process.
- Analytical process.
- Process for determination of organization structure.
- Recruitment, allocation and development of K A Managers.
- Objectives and strategy definition.

Contd...

KAM implementation processes:

- Communication.

- Relationship development.

- Development/adaptation of product or services.

- Operational.

- Performance monitoring.

Communication, both within customer's organization and KA Managers own organization, is of great importance in KAM. Communication should be treated as a process itself rather than subcomponent of other processes.

Suppliers should expect to customize the product and (or) services for their key customers. The cross-functional teams need to seamlessly work and deliver the results for efficient customization. Similarly the underlying processes giving customized solution should work smoothly. Successful companies examine the customization requests they receive and learn from them, incorporating beneficial changes into their own standard practice.

As key accounts become more dependable on supply chain partners, they become more vulnerable to any failure and hence they need and expect high standards of performance from supplier's operations. While operations are not KA Managers responsibility, it is very much in his interest to ensure that robust and reliable processes are in place.

Performance monitoring is a crucial process. The monitoring of results is required to be rigorous and extensive.

In many of my interactions with organizations having successful KAM, I found basic four elements for their success. They are:

- High profile support from senior management

- Appropriate organization framework

- Well-rounded and highly focused KA Managers

- Customers with right attitude and approach to business

- Supportive, effective, dependable processes

Implementation is important rather than structure and strategy, for success of key account management.

Source: Copyright with Industrial Marketing Services, 2005. Reprinted with the kind permission of Sanjay Limaye. Visit him at www.inmas.com

DEPLOYING THE SALESFORCE

With increasing competition, salespeople are no more in their leisurely attitude, neither are sales managers from industrial firms are allowing them to. With rising costs, sales managers are very worried, to keep their costs down, so as not to reduce the profitability from a region or branch. Sales managers are today very worried about effective usage of time and territory management, by their salespeople.

There have been multiple models, softwares developed to deploy the salesforce. However still it remains a very untouched area. Not only that, it also requires large amount of collection and processing of data for effective deployment of salesforce. But before we do that, let us understand as to why we have sales territories.

They are:

1.   To increase the coverage of the marketplace and customers.

2.   Reduce cost levels to as low as possible.

3.   The dire requirement to improve servicing and customer relations.

4.   Evaluating salesperson performance and establish salesperson's jobs and responsibility.

5.   Make the sales team more effective.

6.   To coordinate selling with other departments better.

Market coverage is very important in industrial markets. It is not only about relying on existing business, but look out for new business opportunity which requires greater coverage. Once territories are assigned, the costs can be kept low, duplication of work is reduced and the sales team can be more effective. A particular salesperson can handle, maintain and service existing customers and search for new customers as well.

It is now clear to us that demarcating a sales territory is very essential. Now, the next question comes "How do we do it"? To designate a salesperson to a territory, there are a set of steps that an industrial marketer should follow. They are:

1.   Estimating the total market sales potential.

2.   Make an individual account analysis, to realize company sales, according to geographical areas.

3.   Develop a workload analysis, and determine how many people are needed to bring about the sales.

4.   Assign salesperson to territories.

The first step that we have mentioned is to estimate the total market sales potential. But before we do that, there is one more exercise that an industrial firm needs to take. It is to determine a "Geographical unit". The areas or the regions where the industrial marketer would be selling. We would see it as a process for domestic markets. Generally, a geographic unit is defined by states, cities, metropolitans, pin codes and trading areas. This is a job, which is generally done at a senior level, with data backup from industrial sources. These data may be secondary data, and in some industries, help of primary data is also taken.

Once the 'geographical unit' has been determined, the next step is to estimate the total market sales potential. This is done with respect to specific areas or branches. This job is also done by people top up in the organizational hierarchy.

The sales manager or branch manager is then given the charge to estimate, how much a particular branch is capable of. Sales managers then adjust the market potential, with reliable secondary sources and with contributions from their salespeople.

Let us say for a particular branch, there are three sets of customers. They are A, B, and C. The total market potential that has been estimated for them is as follows:

A → Rs 10,00,000

B → Rs 50,00,000

C → Rs 75,00,000

Now the salesforce, say, that about 60 percent of A, 30 percent of B and 40 percent of C can be achieved. It is also being accepted by the industry sources. The corrected market sales potential therefore is:

A → Rs 10,00,000 × 0.60 = Rs 6,00,000

B → Rs 50,00,000 × 0.30 = Rs 15,00,000

C → Rs 75,00,000 × 0.40 = Rs 30,00,000

However, we would not be getting the complete sales. This could arise because of multiple reasons like a new salesforce, poor promotional strategies, sales territory coverage is not there, due to lack of salesperson. There could be other reasons like high employee turnover, or could be industry downfall.

Let us say, the probability for Group A, B, C accounts are 50 percent, 20 percent and 30 percent. So, the expected values from each account are:

Rs 6,00,000 × 0.50 = Rs 3,00,000

Rs 15,00,000 × 0.20 = Rs 3,00,000

Rs 30,00,000 × 0.30 = Rs 9,00,000

Although the above is a hypothetical example, such an exercise would determine, how much of sales each account is going to generate and where the focus should primarily lie. Similarly other budgets, for that line needs to be decided.

The next important step is the "workload analysis", and determining how many people would bring in the requisite value of sales.

WORKLOAD ANALYSIS

Whenever we use the term "workload" we are trying to quantify the amount of work that needs to be done by a salesperson. This involves basically two things:

1.   The kind of market coverage that has to be done.
2.   The kind of product that is to be sold.

Now, the first step, that a sales manager needs to do, is to understand how many "effective sales call" a salesperson can make in a given time- say an year or half year. This requires the following data:

1.   The number of selling days available.
2.   The travel time.
3.   The length of time each call would require.
4.   Frequency of calls/customer.
5.   Non-selling time.

Let us say, the Bangalore Branch of an industrial manufacturer has 200 accounts to handle, across a certain radius. The customers are divided as follows:

Large	More than Rs 5,00,000 sales	30
Medium	Within Rs 1,00,000 to 5,00,000	50
Small	Below Rs 1,00,000	120
Total		= 200 accounts.

For the large customers, the sales manager feels that 1 call has to be made per month, for the medium customers 1 call every two months and for small customers, 1 call per quarter.

Thus, the number of accounts are:

Large = 30 × 1 call per month × 12 times = 360 calls

Medium = 50 × 1 call per two months × 6 times = 300 calls

Small = 120 × 1 call per quarter × 4 times = 480 calls.

= 1140 calls in a year.

Let us say, an industrial salesperson can make two calls per day. He works for 40 weeks in a year. Thus total calls he makes in a week is 10 calls, and in a year he makes 10 × 40 = 400 calls a year. Thus the number of territories required would be: 1140/400= 3 territories.

However, this is a very simple method. Not only this, a sales manager might bifurcate the calls into existing customers and new customers. Then, the possible accounts, number of calls and territories would increase.

This can be little more complicated, if we take into account the amount of traveling that each industrial salesperson has to do. Say for example, more the traveling you do, the lesser number of mandays you work. So, it would vary from each individual salesperson.

One more important aspect that also needs to be considered is the average length of call, that a salesperson spends with each of his customers. Also, 'unaccounted for' leaves, holidays, strikes, repeat calls and wastage of time unwillingly also needs to be accounted. This makes territory allocation a tougher task. Patty, speaks of profitability of salesforce allocation, with a concept of ROTI. (return on time invested).[3] It can be quite time consuming, and the sales manager is generally assisted by his colleagues to finish this territory allocations. However, softwares have slowly started replacing human brains in this territorial allocation.

The last step in the process of allocating territories to salesperson, is to assign the territories. Managers should be very careful and judgmental allocating areas. A "Tamil" speaking market, can be given to a salesperson who speaks that language. This is very true in India, wherein diversities are huge. Similarly, comparatively newer salesperson can be given smaller territories to handle. Also, managers should try and balance, the attachment one has towards his place of stay. For example, a person born is Chennai, can be given that location or preferably something nearest to him. Industrial marketing has limited set of customers, so messing up with them means business is doomed. Managers should be very careful in allocating such territories.

ORGANIZING THE SALESFORCE[4]

Dubinsky and Barry speak of the process of organizing the salesforce to achieve the goal set by an organization. How the salesforce of an industrial organization is arranged depends on a multiple factor. They are:

1. Nature and length of the product line

2. Markets segments served

3. Roles, intermediary plays

4. Competitor's salesforce

5. Buying behaviour encountered in each segment

They say, that the salesforce organization is generally done under the following groups:

1. Organizing by customer groups
2. Organizing by products
3. Organizing by territories
4. Organizing by functions

INTERACTION BETWEEN THE BUYER AND SELLER[5]

Jagdish. N. Sheth mentions that the interaction between the buyer and seller is very critical and crucial. The content of information and the style or mannerism affects the quality of interaction between the buyer and the seller. He refers to the "content" of communication, as the products, services, as well as individual needs. By style, Sheth refers to the "mannerisms and the way it is delivered to the buyer."

He speaks of a 4×4 matrix, with compatible content and style leading to a "Ideal transaction" and incompatible content and style leading to "No transaction". If either of them are incompatible, it leads to an "inefficient transaction".

According to him, three styles of interaction takes place. They are:

1. Task oriented.
2. Interaction oriented–which is more of socializing.
3. Self-oriented- which looks into the self-interest of a person.

An ideal transaction leads to business, but otherwise the interaction process would end, and in case sales happen, negative feelings remain.

MANAGEMENT OF TIME

Management of time is very essential. Proper routing, is essential to cut costs and improve productivity. Generally, new industrial sales trainees are helped by their immediate bosses, to prepare the routing plan. Some industrial salesperson, waste a lot of time in doing the wrong job, which adds up to the sales cost.

Salespeople should be aware of "time traps". Some common time traps are:

Common time traps:		
Poor planning of days activities	-	Putting in a short day's work
Calling on unqualified prospects	-	Taking of early on Friday afternoon
Following a hap hazard travel schedule	-	Too much chatting
Insufficient use of telephone	-	Too many coffee brakes
Taking long lunch hours	-	Inefficient use of waiting time
A lunch time cocktail	-	Too much entertaining of customers
Inefficiency in paper work	-	Walking in without an appointment
Staying out the touch too long with the home office so important messages are delayed.		

Source: Anderson, Hair and Bush – "Proffesional Sales Management" – 2nd edition - McGraw Hill International edition – pp 341

One more important aspect is the job of "routing". Routing is to set up a pattern for making calls. Routing leads to substantial cost savings. Generally when the job of routing is done carefully, it leads to substantial benefits. They are:

1. Less travel time

2. Reduce selling costs

3. Better territory coverage

Routing is also very essential for salesperson, new to an area. He should be given proper road directions and must plan himself effectively, so that he reaches to an appointment on time.

COSTS AND PROFITABILITY ANALYSIS IN INDUSTRIAL SELLING

Managers stress on the selling activities and volume, but neglect the cost control and profitability analysis often. But however, this idea needs to be changed, and proper data on customer segments, profitability, and information about accounts needs to be analyzed and understood. The evaluation of sales performance is part of the management control process. It is very essential to understand the difference between the original and actual, the possible reasons for differences, and make changes in the strategies for the next selling cycle. One more important aspect of this evaluation process is to understand the sales and cost analysis.

EVALUATING SALESPERSON

Regarding salesperson evaluation, some might ask, "Why is it so hard to evaluate their performance?" The problem stems from the difficulty of determining what creates profit for a specific company, a territory or is it service? Advertising and promotion? Technical assistance? Advice on inventory control? Further, traditional non-selling evaluation measures may be inadequate because of salesperson activities that do not result in actual sales output until months or even after they are performed.

There are certain problems while evaluating an industrial salesperson. The first problem arises from the fact that the salesperson work alone without their managers and it is quite difficult for them to evaluate at the end of the year. Another problem, that comes up is that, often sales managers fail to understand the problem his salesperson is going through. It might not be a problem of him, but sometimes whims and fancies of industrial buyers. Only figures in industrial selling, do not speak much. Quite a good amount of time goes into servicing customers and managing accounts.

Evaluating a salesperson, thus become a problem. But however, a performance standard needs to be maintained and established. But before, this is done, sales analysis needs to be done.

Sales analysis is nothing but collecting, classifying and evaluating data of an organizational sales performance. This is generally done at the end of the selling period, say a quarter, half yearly or sometimes an year. Generally, this data for sales analysis, is collected from:

1. Sales made during an year

2. Sales reports submitted by salesperson

3. Expenses of the salesperson

4. Customers and prospects

For the sales figures achieved by a salesperson in an year, the data is classified into:

1.   Total sales volume

2.   Total sales value

3.   Sales by territory

4.   Sales from customers

5.   Sales analysis by sales representatives

6.   Sales by product lines

INCREASED PRODUCTIVITY

Sales costs are rising, tremendous competitive pressures in the market and in such a situation, with increasing costs, it is not feasible to pass on some of the costs to the customers. Thus, salesforces requires to be kept trimmed and increase the level of productivity per person. Some of the approaches to increase productivity, that sales department employ are:

1.   Cutting down the size of the salesforce and their traveling

2.   Hiring manufacturer's representatives

3.   Use of technology

4.   Use of trade shows, mailers and advertisements

5.   Improving the SMIS – (Sales Management Information System)[7]

Salesforce is being rapidly cut down, and efforts increase productivity is being looked upon. The traveling of the salesforce is cut down with the use of technology, like cellphone, laptops, and videoconferencing so as to enable the salesperson perform more effectively. Sales managers and industrial organizations are today very keen on trade shows, especially because of the good quality of leads that are generated. Also usage of telemarketing, tradeshows and mailers are on the rise.

SMIS or sales management information system evolves with time. Most SMIS fall into one of the following stages, differing in terms of flexibility, complexity and question-answering power:

1.   Data storage and retrieval systems

2.   Systems for monitoring results of business activities

3.   Analytical systems for exploring and evaluating business alternatives[8]

Today industrial organizations are becoming highly cost conscious, and they are becoming more technology oriented. Increasing productivity of salesperson is highly essential so as to keep costs under control.

CHANGING WINDS OF SALESFORCE

Quite a number of times, we have been discussing that how difficult it is becoming for industrial marketers. Rapid changes in technology, competition not only from local markets, but across globe and huge costs have added to this difficulty. Now a part of cost cannot be passed down to the customers. So, organizations today are cutting costs, and trying to make the salesforce more productive.

The cost of making an industrial sales call and then following it up, realizing into final sales, and servicing can cost thousands. All these challenges have led to something called as "intrapreneurial philosophy".

Intrapreneurship is nothing but, becoming an entrepreneur within a large organization. This is done basically to inspire people and create a decision-making environment. An intrapreneurial philosophy can see the light of the day, only with constant support and encouragement from the top management. The objective of such an organization should be to innovate, and create new ideas, which would come from the employees. A classic example for it is the 3M "Post-It" notes. 3M has been a company of innovation. A large part of their product line is developed in their laboratories, and if it succeeds, the employees get a chance to head the division.

Today, with rising costs, most of the larger customers are approached by the national key accounts manager. The smaller accounts are mostly left to telemarketing to handle it and the middle-sized accounts are called upon. Today the job of a salesperson is "just not" to go and sell. It is much more. It is about being innovative, creative, flexible and knowledgeable.

Salesforce Automation

Salesforce automation also referred to as "SFA" is to manage the salesforce much more efficiently and effectively. It is to equip the salesperson with technology which helps better management of sales staff by their managers, make selling profitable and help sales staff become more profitable. It is to manage information much faster and more efficiently. Siebel systems, Oracle, PeopleSoft are some of the organizations helping marketers to be more effective. SFA is an integral part of customer relationship management and should not be treated separately. However, proper training to the salesforce is extremely essential for the successful usage of SFA softwares. However, one important thing, that needs to be noted is that, the cost involved in implementation is very high and often meets with objection from the salesforce. Salesforce must support it for its success. The salesforce must be willing to enter data into the SFA, to gain benefits and easy analysis from it.

SALES AUDIT[9]

Sales audit is an exercise that understands the sales operations. It covers the environment under which the organization works and the evaluation. It also addresses sales management planning and sales management functions.

It is typically a five step sequence. They are:

1. Examination of sales objective.

2. Review of plans and policies formulated in pursuit of these objectives.

3. Evaluation of methods, programmes, and procedures to implement plans.

4. Study of organization structure and staffing.

5. Development of recommendations for improvement based on the appraisal of objectives, plans, methods and organization.

CONCLUSION

The chapter started with a basic outline of organizing the industrial sales department. We then discussed how a sales call is typically made, the important steps involved and how objections are handled. Making a good presentation also forms a very essential part of the sales call process. Today, concepts of key accounts have been a subject of serious discussion in the industrial marketing scenario, and how key accounts are handled.

When, the salesforce needs to go out in the market, it has to be put in the right locations and with best allocational strategies, to increase efficiency and reduce costs. We saw how workload analysis is done to arrive at salesforce deployment.

Interaction between the buyer and seller, routing, costs and profitable analysis and how it has to be done was discussed. Today with technological changes, rising costs and global competition, industrial sales managers are forced to rethink on their strategies. The increased usage of SFA softwares validate it.

Selling today is not about profits. Its more than that. It is creativity, innovation, and flexibility that will keep driving the industrial salesforce.

References

1.   Shapiro and Moriarty, *National* (1982), *Account Management: Emerging Insights*, Cambridge Mass Marketing Science Institute.

2.   Bonoma and Johnston (1978), *The Social Psychology of Industrial Buying and Selling*, Industrial Marketing Management, pp 213-223.

3.   Patty (1982), *Managing Salespeople*, 2nd edition, Reston Publishing Company – A Prentice Hall Company.

4.   This section is based on Dubinsky and Barry (1982), *Survey of Sales Management Practices*, Industrial Marketing, Elsevier Science Publishing Company, pp 133-141.

5.   This section is based on Sheth (1976), *Buyer-Seller Interaction: A Conceptual Framework* in B.B. Anderson-Advances in Consumer Research, Vol III (Association for Consumer Research), pp 133-144.

6.   Johnson, Kurtz, Scheving, *Sales Management- Concepts, Practices and Cases*, 2nd Edition, McGraw Hill International Edition, pp 461.

7.   This section is based on Anderson, Hair and Bush, *Professional Sales Management*, 2nd edition, McGraw Hill International Editions, pp 514-516.

8.   This section is based on Anderson, Hair and Bush, *Professional Sales Management*, 2nd edition, McGraw Hill International Editions, pp 514-516.

9.   This section is based on Johnson, Kurtz, Scheving, *Sales Management – Concepts, Practices and Cases*, 2nd edition, McGraw Hill International Editions, pp 509-510.

Mind Power 7: Four Common Words that will Ruin your Sale

By Paul Johnson

Good news! When you say po-tah-toe, we both know we mean exactly the same thing. The trouble comes when a single word means different things to different people.

Contd...

Four words commonly used in marketing today can have a devastating effect on your sales results. We use these words to describe our offerings and assume the prospective buyer knows exactly what we mean. However, definitions vary widely and the end result of that type of miscommunication is disastrous.

These words lead to disappointed buyers and reversed sales. They cause unmet expectations on the part of the buyer and result in poor referrals. Using any of these four words is a sure way to generate negative references for what you sell. Let's take a moment to explore these four words and the impact of their use when selling.

What did you expect?

The first word to avoid is "value". All customers want good value, and all customer-oriented companies want to provide a good value. Yet, the seller should never claim to provide good value; that is entirely up to customer.

A good value is a transaction that provides us with more than we expect, more than we believe we paid for or bargained. The key word here is "Expect". A transaction either is or isn't a good value based on how well expectations are met. Unfortunately, expectations change almost daily.

For example, if I shop for a television set and choose a model that happens to comes with a one-year warranty instead of the usual 90 days, I'm pleasantly surprised. I feel as though I'm receiving good value for my investment. When I go to buy another television set, my expectation may be the inclusion of a one-year warranty. The manufacturer's idea of value may be a 90-day warranty and a lower price. The result: I'm disappointed if I don't get the one-year warranty, even if the price is lower.

The solution is to break a generic value statement into something more specific and meaningful to the targeted buyer. Where does the value come from? As a seller, you can point out where the value might come from so your buyer cannot overlook it. However, it doesn't have to be accepted by the buyer.

For example, perceived value may result from a lower price, or more standard features. It might come from lower cost of ownership due to extended reliability, or from lower maintenance costs. But I can't tell you that I am providing value. I can only tell you what I am providing and let you decide if there's value for you.

See "It" Yet?

The second common sale killer is the word "Quality". Many of us have a hard time defining quality, thinking "we'll know it when we see it". According to Philip Crosby, author of *Quality is Free*, quality is not a matter of opinion. Quality means conformance to requirements, and is defined by those characteristics that allow your purchase to do what you expect it to do.

For example, consider which is the higher quality automobile, Mercedes-Benz or Chevrolet? That all depends on the characteristics needed for quality. If I use my vehicle over an extended range, such as throughout the US and Canada, and up time is important to me because I depend on my vehicle to make a living, the Chevrolet may be the higher quality choice. Wherever I travel, I am never far from a Chevrolet dealer and the parts needed to fix my car. Chevrolet has over 15 times as many service locations as Mercedes-Benz in North America, and the parts distribution network to support them. It will almost take longer to get the Mercedes back on the road. If it's important to me that my car isn't tied up in the shop regardless of where I go, the Chevrolet is the higher quality product.

The solution is to describe the quality of your offering in terms of the fundamental characteristic that allows you to deliver that quality. For product characteristics might include the purity of the materials used, the precision with which they are built or assembled or the function it can perform service, quality may relate to speed of service delivery, a low error rate, or depth of service available.

Note that all of these are measurable and definable. By focusing on the characteristics of quality, quantity changes from a nebulous, I'll know it when see it" into a set of clearly definable and measurable requirements. Always remember that your definition of quality is not the same as the next person's even though we all think we know what it means.

Just Shut Up and Deliver

Third avoid the word "service". It's simply overused. It's just that like quality, everybody has a difference definition of what good service is. Some people associate good service with the sound of a human voice. Others actually seek one way solution of the problem. In fact, there are so many different ways to define good customer service that the topic has spawned an entire industry of customers and professional speakers to address the topic. If you haven't heard enough good and bad customer service stories already, give me a call and I'll be happy to share a few of my own.

Instead of talking about good service, just shut up and do it. Put some performance standards in place for your own organization and then deliver to those standards. Let your customers tell your prospects how you deliver service.

Jeff Multz of Atlanta, Georgia figured this out already. He read Ken Blanchard's hook Raving Fans and decided to create his own. Jeff would insist that his staff including him return all calls and acknowledge all e-mails within an hour. Not only did they have their service benchmarks on paper out they used software to help them deliver it, as well as report on it. Their computer would tell them if they are living up to the performance standards they set for themselves.

When talking to prospects about your offering, you won't have to mention a word about service instead, show them the testimonial letters you've collected from your happy customers. Encourage them to talk to your existing customer base. Show them the statistics from your customer satisfaction surveys that talk about responsiveness and service levels 'Your prospects will get the message'.

Now Compare This!

The last, and ugliest, word to avoid is "Price". Price doesn't usually come by itself. It's usually accompanied by another word. "low" As soon as you start talking about price, your prospects will be happy to compare it. Therefore, avoid making any claims regarding price in your advertising or other initial messages to your prospects.

You can never consistently win at the low price game anyway. To paraphrase Don Peppers of Peppers and Rogers group. "if you're competing on price you always have to underbid your stupidest competitor".

Price becomes a distraction in your customer's buying process. They forget about how important their purchase is in solving their problem, and instead become concerned with comparing "apples with apples". They quickly discount all the unique and significant attributes that make your offering a better solution. This concern over price reduces your offering to commonly status.

Of course, sooner or later everyone is going to need to know "How much?" and your offering needs to be priced in a range that is comparable with your competition. Just make sure the solution you're offering is worth much more to the buyer than the price you'll ask for it.

If your prospect jumps the gun and asks "How much?" before you've had a chance to help them establish value, explain with pride. "that's the best pan. I'll get to that in just a moment. "While you should be proud of your price, leading with it only makes your job more difficult.

Value, Quality, Service and Price will get you in trouble because they mean different things to different people at different times. While each concept is important, you must take care to explain and define each of these words if you choose to use them. Before you ever talk about value test the buyer's expectations. Before you mention quality, determine the buyer's requirements. Don't talk about service.

Contd...

Let others do it for you. And price you're really providing a worthwhile solution, price is the best part. Save it for last.

About the author

Mind Power 8: The Life and Times of Key Account Managers

By Lucie Benson, features editor

Key Accounts Management (KAM) revolves around strategic planning that goes beyond what we traditionally see as 'selling', in an attempt to satisfy the needs of today's powerful and demanding customers.

It plays a crucial role for many B2B companies because it dictates how they can maximize profits from their clients, and those key accounts have the ability to form a major part of the sales revenue. As such, it involves a great deal of relationship management and account planning.

A successful key accounts manager will understand the history of the account as well as where it is going in the future. It is therefore reasonable to expect that a KAM will face many challenges in their career, as well as successes. So what experiences have today's key accounts managers had? What were their aims and how have they set about achieving these? And what impact has KAM had on the company?

Alan Clark is strategic account director at RightNow, an organization that provides on-demand solutions to CRM. Clark says that KAM was implemented at RightNow because they wanted to focus much more on their key customers and develop their presence there.

"To do that, you need to have a wider view of the customer, in terms of what they do and what they are looking for," states Clark. "These customers are leaders in their particular field so that gives us a massive advantage of positioning ourselves with the leaders, therefore earning the right to go into the rest of that industry with some very strong success stories."

Through working as a key account manager, Clark has had to channel his focus significantly. "I have to get under the skin of the customer a lot more because my scope is shorter," he explains. "So rather than having a really wide territory, an inch deep, I have a very narrow territory, but I am going down into a lot depth".

Clark advises that the timing has got to be right, when companies are implementing KAM in their business. "The key account is absolutely vital in helping to mature the model. So once you have got a good, established company, I feel that you can go into that KAM getting closer to them, handling them better, and understanding them more. So you have to be established enough to have the access and the time to spend on those companies, and the proof at the end of it is really quite valuable."

Even though Clark believes that KAM can sometimes be limiting, by getting to know these companies better, you can actually deliver much more value to them. "The more companies work with their customers, the more they are working with you; the closer you are, the more likely you are to do even more business with them."

One of the challenges of KAM says Clark is getting over the notion that you are reducing your whole field of potential opportunities. "It is a bit nerve-wracking to start with, but I can't emphasise enough that if you actually focus and get closer, you can have absolutely phenomenal success with those organizations."

Contd...

Service, contact and communication

Sapiens UK is a provider of IT solutions to the insurance sector. In the early 1990s it was more technology-based, but towards the end of that decade it started to become more of a solutions provider. Raj Ghuman is director of account management for the UK and Europe at sapiens.

"Towards the end of the 90s, as an organization, we were not doing any form of account management and we needed to increase that function", he explains.

For Sapiens, the first step towards KAM was all about service, contact and communication. Then, over the proceeding one to three years, the model started to mature, "When you want to introduce KAM, you have to put in place the principles, the background and the infrastructure, to enable a slick service to be delivered", remarks Ghuman. "You must also ensure regular communication, so think about putting in place regular account review meetings.

"Over the initial 6-12 month period there was a bit of bedding down to be done, but ultimately in the long run, that reaped its own rewards and enabled us to penetrate the customer base," he adds.

After this initial period, Sapiens then introduced the commercial element of KAM. "From early 2000 to date, we have acquired significant new business," says Ghuman. "Today, 85-95 percent of our new business comes from our existing customer base and that is a significant shift from where we were."

Sapiens has now managed to ensure loyalty within its customer base, with some of the big insurance companies sticking with since the early 90s. This has, in part, been down to KAM, so it has therefore had a huge impact on the organization. For three years running, they doubled their turnover, year on year. "Our deal sizes began to increase from tens to hundreds of thousands in new business, to many millions," remarks Ghuman. "Obvious these deals aren't done in six months – they are over multiple years."

Ghuman adds that the impact has been nothing short of enormous. "It has changed our mentality, and, to look at today's climate, it is very difficult in the insurance sector to acquire new business. So we still need to acquire new names but our foundation is solid with our existing customer base."

Relationship Exploration

Chris Smith is currently director for Europe for risk solutions at Royal and SunAlliance. Prior to this, he looked after a team of key account managers in the UK risk solutions business. The European business is a couple of years behind its UK counterpart and Smith is now tasked with bringing key account managers into the European business within the next year.

Smith explains that, before introducing the KAM role to the UK business, they encountered many problems. "Our technical staff faced out to our customers, some of whom were not equipped to talk to customers," he explains. "We didn't change our approach based on how valuable the customer was, and we approached the customer on one line of business only."

This meant that the business missed opportunities to cross sell and left the customer with no idea how to access the complex organization. "We set about changing our approach by implementing pilot studies on eight of the accounts," he says. "We hand-selected key accounts which were allocated to each of these clients, and we were able to prove our case following impressive feedback from the pilot clients."

As a result of this, there have been significant differences in the way the business now operates according to Smith. "Eventually, all our customer touch points came within the control of this role, our competitors began to copy us and we had more focus on our most valuable clients," he adds. "Plus, reward and remuneration has driven by customer satisfaction and retention measures."

For KAM to be success, Smith adds that it is essential for senior management to be on board. "It needs buy in from the top of the organization because high level decisions will need to be made," he advises. "Also, ensure the KAM role covers all customer 'touch points'. And acknowledge that KAM isn't the answer every time– ask the customer what they want. Obtain good independent customer research and don't rely on what you think you know."

Contd...

Ghuman believes that, with KAM, it all boils down to relationships. "Make sure you are religious about keeping relationships intact. Existing customers for any business will be the bread and butter. If you take care of them, they will take care of you. For us, they are the foundation of our business."

And for Clark, it is the exploration of that relationship with significant benefits. "KAM allows you to work in areas you didn't initially realize you could, by having opportunities to work in other departments and getting to know the wider business. So it is moving around inside an organization and getting to know them more that is where the success comes from".

Source: Copyright with Sift Media 2007. Visit them at www.mycustomer.com. Reprinted with permission.

Mind Power 9: Dealing with Your Customer's Time Constraints

Copyright 2000. by Dave Kahle.

"My customers don't have as much time to spend with me as they used to."

That's a comment I'm hearing more frequently in my sales seminars. It's growing phenomena. Your customers used to be able to spend more time with you. But lately, it seems like they are on tighter schedules and are harder to see. You just can't spend as much time with them as you'd like, because they're pressuring you to move on.

This is a real information-age issue. You know how confused and pressured you feel these days. Your customers feel the same way. As pressures brought on by rapid change, growing competition and the need for every organization to become more streamlined and efficient have hit your customers, many of them have reacted by trying to make everyone more productive. As a result, your customers have too much to do and not enough time in which to do it, just like you. Some of your customers are walking around with day-planners under their arms today. When, just a couple of years ago, they didn't know what one was. Time, more than money, is the precious commodity of the information Age.

It's not that your customers don't like you, (although they may not) nor that they are not interested in your products and services. It's just that they have too much to do, and simply don't have as much time to spend with you as you'd like.

Implications...

This development is truly ominous because the implications strike to the heart of your ability to perform for your company. Let's think for a minute about the value you bring your company. Why do they employ you? What do they really need you and other salespeople to do? If you were to boil it down to its most fundamental level. You'd probably say that your company needs you to create relationships and spend face-to-face time with your customers.

Here's another way of looking at it. Suppose you were to make a list of all the things you do in the course of a week. Then look at the list, and ask yourself this question. "How many of those things can be done better or cheaper by someone else within my company?" If you answer honestly, most items on the list can probably be handled more effectively or efficiently by someone else.

But, the one thing that you do that no one else can do as effectively as you is interact with your customers. It's the face-to-face, person-to-person interaction with your customer that is the heart of your job, the core of the value you bring your company.

That's what makes this challenges ominous. If you can't spend quality time in front of the customer, your days as a successful salesperson are numbered.

Here's how to attack this challenge...

First, remember to respect your customer's time constraints. If you try to overstay your welcome, you'll only succeed in making him/her more irritated with you. Do unto him as you would have him do unto you, if you were in his place. Protect the relationship.

Then, focus on making the time that you do have with him more productive for both of you. Think of the issue being quality time, not quantity time. Here are three strategies that will work for you.

Contd...

1.   Focus on the quality of the time you have with your customer.

If you're not going to have as much time in front of the customer as you'd like, then you must concentrate on making the time that you do have as valuable and productive as possible. That requires you to spend more time planning and preparing for each sales call.

Gone are the days when you could just "stop in". Rather, make sure that you have at least three things prepared for every sales call:

❖   A specific objective—what do you want to accomplish in this call?

❖   An outline of how you're going to accomplish that objective and

❖   All the necessary tools you'll need to do it.

That way, the actual time that you spend with your customers will be more productive. Your customer will appreciate your organization and your respect of his time, too.

2.   Set an agenda—talk in terms of your customer's needs.

Begin every sales call with an agenda. Tell your customer what you want to cover and how you're going to proceed. Mention the needs and objectives in which he is interested, and explain how you're going to address them. This will relieve him of the worry that you're going to appropriate his time unnecessarily, and will allow him to focus on you.

For example, at the beginning of your sales call, you could say something like this:

"John I know you're interested in the cost payback of a possible investment in a new telephone system. I'd like to share with you some of the numbers that others have used to investigate this kind of purchase. After we go through these, I'll address any other questions you may have, and then we'll talk about the next step in this process. Does that sound reasonable?"

3.   Always have something of value to discuss.

This a longer-range strategy. As you consistently hold to this principle, over time you'll build up a certain expectation in the customer's mind. Don't expect an immediate payback from this strategy, but, nonetheless, stick to it for the long hall.

Think of the time that your customer does spend with you as an investment by the customer. Put yourself in his shoes, and see the situation from his perspective. Is he gaining something of value from you in exchange for his investment of time? You want the answer to that question to be "Yes".

In order to generate that perception in your customer's mind, make sure that every time you see him, you have something of value to share or to discuss with him. That means something that the customer is interested in. If you have nothing that the customer will think is of value, don't take his time. Wait until you do have something to see him.

After a few such calls, your customer will come to respect you and look forward to your calls, knowing that you're not there just to work some agenda of yours, but rather he'll come to expect to gain something from your sales calls.

You'll find it easier to make appointments and get time with your customers when you've built in them the expectation that the time spent with you will be well worth the cost of it.

Source: About Dave Kahle: The Growth Coach:

Dave Kahle is a consultant and trainer who helps his clients increase their sales and improve their sales productivity. Dave has trained thousands of salespeople to be more successful in the Information Age economy. He is the author of over 500 articles, a monthly e-zine, and six books. Ten Secrets of Time Management for Salespeople was recently released by Career Press. His Kahle Way® Sales Management System empowers sales managers to Instill accountability and communication in the salesforce. You can join Dave's "Thinking about Sales Electronic Newsletter" on-line at www.davekahle.com/mailinglist.htm.

For more Information or to contact the author, contact The DaCo Corporation, 3736 West River Drive, Comstock Park, MI 49321, phone 1-800-331-1287, fax 1-616-451-9412, Cheryl@davekahle.com or www.davekahle.com

QUESTIONS FOR DISCUSSION

1. "Key Account Management is becoming one of the discussed topics in industrial marketing". Discuss?

2. "Handling objections is one of the most crucial part of the presentation". Why?

3. "Salesforce automation" may not be feasible for smaller industrial marketers, Discuss.

4. What are the different methods, to organize the salesforce? When will you use the different methods of organizing the salesforce?

5. "Non-selling activities often kill the time of the sales executives". How can managers measure the productivity of non-sales activity?

6. How would you generate prospects, for industrial selling? What are the various sources to generate prospects?

7. "Sales routing is one of the major areas of discussions, today". Why is it gaining importance?

chapter

FOURTEEN

E-commerce

COMPANY PROFILE 14: BEL (BHARAT ELECTRONICS LIMITED)

BEL has over four decades of manufacturing experience. Bharat Electronics Limited has pioneered the professional electronics movement in India. With continuous upgradation of technology, commitment to quality and constant innovation, BEL has grown into a multi-product, multi-unit, and multi-technology company.

BEL has set up impressive infrastructure and manufacturing facilities in their nine ISO certified production units around the country.

BEL has also established two joint ventures – with General Electric Medical Systems, USA for X-ray tubes and Multi-tone, UK for paging systems and has a subsidiary company BEL Optronic Devices Limited for the manufacture of Image Intensifier tubes.

Total Organizational Quality Enhancement is the mantra being followed in BEL today. It is being imbibed into BELs culture through three phases: (1) Knowledge (2) Application and (3) Normalization.

Bharat Electronics Ltd., (BEL), a premier Professional Electronics Company of India, has established and nurtured a strong in-house research and development base over the years to emerge and remain as a market leader in the chosen areas of business in professional electronics. Each of the nine manufacturing units of BEL is having its own in-house research and development Division to develop new products in its field of operations. Besides, there are two Central Research Laboratories (CRL) located at Bangalore and Ghaziabad, to address futuristic technologies of interest to BEL.

Main areas of research and development activities at BEL include development of Military Radars, Naval Systems, Military Communication Products, Electronic Warfare Systems, Telecommunication products, Sound and Vision Broadcasting Equipment and Systems, Opto Electronic Products, and Electronic Components. CRL performs the dual role of carrying out blue sky research for the development of future technologies and supporting the D and E Divisions of BEL's nine units with state-of-the-art core technology solutions in areas like Embedded Computers and applications, Radar Signal Processing, VLSI designs, RF and Microwave Communication Technologies, Software modules, etc.

GEBEL is a joint venture between Bharat Electronics and General Electric Medical Systems. The facility based at Whitefield, Bangalore, India, manufactures X-ray tubes, for RAD and F and CT systems, as well as components such as High Voltage Tanks and Detector modules for CT system. The products are exported worldwide and meet the safety and regulatory standards specified by FDA, CE, MHW, AERB and the facility have been accredited with ISO 9001 certification. GEBEL also markets the conventional X-ray tubes made at Pune Unit of BEL.

BEL and Multi-tone, UK, offers state of the art Mobile Communication Products for the workplace. Multitone invented paging in 1956 when it developed the world's first system to serve the "life or death" environment of St. Thomas Hospital, London. With the strength of Bharat Electronics in the Radio Communications field and the technology of Multitone in the field of Radio Paging, the joint venture company is in a position to offer tailor made solutions to the Mobile Communication needs at workplaces in various market segments.

BEL Optronic Devices Ltd. is a subsidiary company of BEL for conducting research, development and manufacture of Image Intensifier Tubes and associated high voltage Power Supply Units for use in military, security and commercial systems.

Military Communications have been a forte of BEL even since its inception in 1954. BEL has been involved in providing state-of-the-art communication equipment to the Indian Army, be it handheld mobile radios and terminals, ground-based systems, airborne and even ship borne equipments and systems.

Source: www.bel-india.com

Mind Power I: B2B E-Commerce Hubs– Towards a Taxonomy of Business Models

Steven Kaplan and Mohanbir Sawhney–December 1999

Wherever you look, it seems like B2B is the place to be. In an earlier article, we introduced the concept of electronic Hubs (eHubs) in Business-to-Business e-commerce. Since we wrote that article, these eHubs have received a tremendous amount of attention. Ariba, Chemdex, Commerce One, Freemarkets, Internet Capital Group, and SciQuest.com have attained breathtaking stock market capitalizations. A torrent of research reports have been issued by Wall Street analysts. A robust community of "Net Market Makers" has emerged (*www.netmarketmakers.com*). And the venture capital community is racing to get in on the B2B action.

In our article, we defined eHubs as *neutral Internet-based intermediaries that focus on specific industry verticals or specific business processes, host electronic marketplaces, and use various market-making mechanisms to mediate any-to-any transactions among businesses.* We argued that eHubs create value by aggregating buyers and sellers, creating marketplace liquidity, and reducing transaction costs. We explained why we thought eHubs would proliferate and thrive.

In this article, we expand on and refine the ideas in our earlier article. We examine the dimensions on which B2B hubs can be classified. We use these dimensions to develop a taxonomy of business models for hubs. The taxonomy reveals important new categories of business designs that have yet to be exploited. The taxonomy also provides a deeper understanding of the relative merits and value creation potential of different business models, and the settings where different models are most appropriate.

We begin by describing the process of business purchasing on two simple dimensions – what companies buy and how they buy. We use these dimensions to create a taxonomy of B2B hubs along three key dimensions - (1) value creation mechanism (aggregation versus matching); (2) purchase situation (systematic versus spot purchasing); and (3) bias of the market-maker (one-sided/biased versus two-sided/neutral). This taxonomy offers insights into a new class of B2B hubs called reverse aggregators that are biased, and do not suffer from the "chicken-and-egg" problem in creating liquidity. The taxonomy also helps us understand where matching-based mechanisms (exchanges and auctions) are more appropriate than aggregation-based mechanisms (catalogs), and how these mechanisms differ on defensibility and value creation potential.

The Whats and Hows of Business Purchasing

To understand B2B hubs, it is useful to understand *how* businesses buy, and *what* they buy. Businesses buy a diverse set of products and services ranging from paper clips to computer systems, and steel to machinery. At the broadest level, business purchases can be classified into *manufacturing inputs* and operating inputs. Manufacturing inputs are raw materials and components that go directly into the manufactured product or manufacturing process. Manufacturing inputs tend to be *vertical* in nature, because the finished products that they go into are industry-specific. They are typically sourced from industry-specific suppliers and distributors, and they require specialized logistics and fulfillment mechanisms. For instance, UPS is not a good fulfillment provider for Hydrochloric Acid or High Density Polyethylene.

Operating inputs, on the other hand, are indirect materials and services that do not go into finished products. Operating inputs, sometimes called MRO (Maintenance, Repair, and Operating) inputs, include industrial supplies, capital equipment, services, and travel-related services. Unlike manufacturing inputs, operating inputs tend to be *horizontal* in nature (with the exception of capital equipment and some industrial supplies). For instance, every business needs computers, office supplies, and airline tickets. But an advertising agency does not buy steel, and a chemicals company

Contd...

does not buy semiconductors. Another important difference is that operating inputs are much more amenable to being shipped through 3rd party logistics providers like UPS. Operating inputs have been traditionally sourced from MRO suppliers like W.W. Grainger, who aggregate MRO catalogs for a diverse set of industries.

The other important distinction in business purchasing lies in *how* businesses buy products and services. Businesses can either engage in *systematic sourcing* or in *spot sourcing*. Systematic sourcing involves buying through pre-negotiated contracts with qualified suppliers. These contracts are often long-term in nature, so systematic sourcing tends to be relationship-oriented. A large proportion of manufactured inputs is purchased through this mechanism. In the semi-commodity chemicals, for instance, over 90 percent of purchasing is through prenegotiated catalog-based mechanisms. On the other hand, businesses can also buy commodity-like products on the spot market from anonymous sellers. Commodity trading for commodities like oil, steel, and energy exemplifies this mechanism. Spot sourcing is transaction-oriented, and rarely involves a long-term or ongoing relationship between buyers and sellers.

Classifying B2B Hubs based on Purchase Situations

This simple two-way classification – manufacturing inputs versus operating inputs (the "what"); and systematic sourcing versus spot sourcing (the "how") allows us to classify B2B hubs into four categories (see Figure 14.1):

- MRO hubs (operating supplies, systematic sourcing, horizontal focus)
- Yield managers (operating supplies, spot sourcing, horizontal focus)
- Catalog hubs (manufacturing inputs, systematic sourcing, vertical focus)
- Exchanges (manufacturing inputs, spot sourcing, vertical focus)

MRO hubs focus on improving the efficiencies in the procurement process for operating supplies for a diverse set of industries. Classic examples of these players are W.W. Grainger, Ariba, and Commerce One. These firms started out with an enterprise focus by licensing expensive "buy-side" software for Procurement to large enterprises. These MRO players are now scrambling to reinvent themselves as MRO hubs on the Internet, by moving from a licensed model to a hosted model for software, and by moving from an enterprise-centric model to a network-centric model, where all catalogs are hosted on a common hub that businesses connect into. Newer entrants who have started out with the hub architecture in this space include Bizbuyer.com, MRO.com, PurchasingCenter.com, and ProcureNet.com. These players are horizontal in nature, because operating inputs are common to a significant extent across a wide variety of industries. Given their horizontal nature, MRO hubs tend to use "horizontal" third-party logistics. Therefore, they can disintermediate existing middlemen in the channel, without having to replicate the fulfillment capabilities and assets owned by the current channel.

Yield managers focus on the spot procurement of operating inputs. Examples include human resources (Employease.com, Elance.com), utilities (Youtilities.com), capital equipment (iMark.com), manufacturing capacity (CapacityWeb.com), and advertising inventory (AdAuction.com).

These yield managers aim to insulate buyers and sellers from ups and downs in operations by allowing them to scale their operating resources upwards or downwards at short notice by participating in the spot market. They add most value in situations where there is high degree of price and demand volatility (e.g., utilities), or where there are huge fixed-cost assets that cannot be liquidated or acquired at short notice (e.g., manpower or manufacturing capacity). Yield managers tend to be more vertical in nature than MRO hubs, but are less vertical in nature than industry-specific vertical hubs like Chemdex or PlasticsNet.com.

Exchanges aim to create spot markets for commodities or near-commodities within specific industry verticals. These exchanges approximate commodity exchanges, and largely focus on transactional

Contd...

sourcing. The exchange maintains relationships with buyers and sellers, but buyers and sellers rarely have direct relationships. In fact, in many exchanges, buyers and sellers may not even know each others identities. Exchanges serve a yield-management role, because they allow purchasing managers to smooth out the peaks and valley in demand and supply by "playing the spot market". Examples of exchanges include E-Steel, Paper Exchange, and IMX Exchange.

Finally, catalog hubs streamline the systematic sourcing of manufactured input within specific vertical industries. These players start out by putting industry-specific catalogs online, and creating a large universe of supplier catalogs within the vertical. They aim to automate the systematic sourcing process, and create value for buyers by lowering transaction costs. These catalog hubs can be buyer-focused or seller-focused, depending upon who they create more value, for examples include PlasticsNet.com, Chemdex, and SciQuest. Catalog hubs need to work closely with distributors, especially on specialized fulfillment and logistics requirements for each vertical.

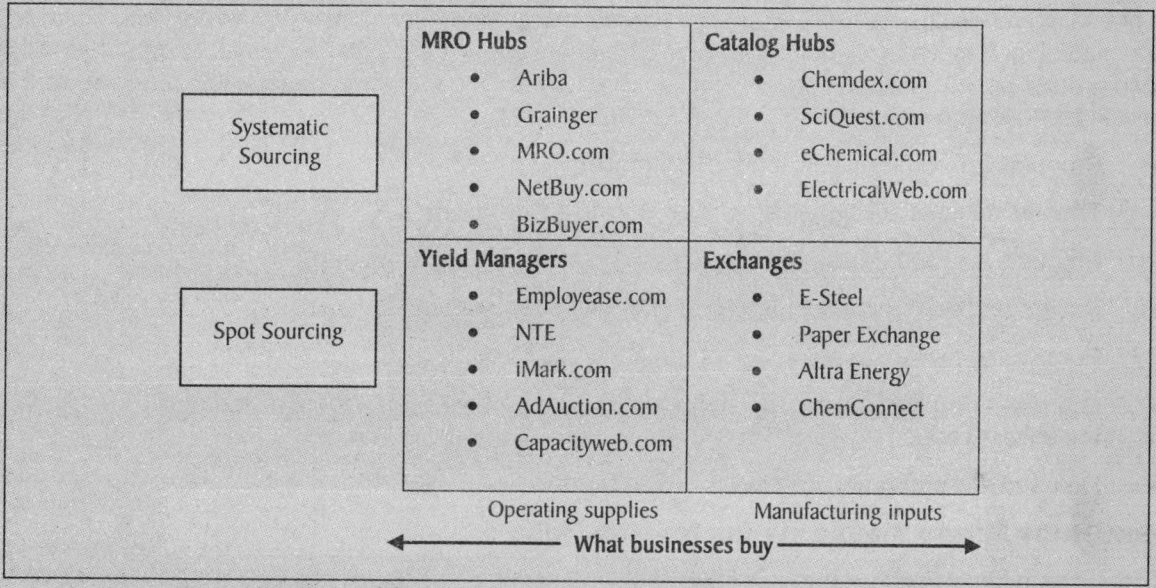

Figure 14.1: Classifying Business-to-Business Hubs

How Hubs Add Value: Aggregation versus Matching

As we think about the difference between systematic and spot purchasing, it becomes obvious that the market-making mechanism that is appropriate for catalog hubs is quite different from the market-making mechanism used by exchanges and yield managers. Fundamentally, hubs create value by two different mechanisms – aggregation and matching. The aggregation mechanism relies on bringing a large number of buyers and sellers under one roof, and reducing transaction costs by "one-stop shopping". For instance, PlasticsNet.com allows plastics processors to issue a single purchase order for hundreds of plastics products, and PlasticsNet.com sources these products from a diverse set of suppliers.

An important characteristic of the aggregation mechanism is that *adding another buyer to the hub only benefits sellers, and does not benefit other buyers.* This happens for a simple reason, buyers can never be sellers in a catalog aggregation model. So adding a buyer to the system only benefits sellers, and adding a seller to the system only benefits buyers. The aggregation mechanism is static in nature, because prices are pre-negotiated. The aggregation mechanism (also called the "catalog mechanism") works best in the following settings:

- The cost of processing a purchase order is high relative to the cost of items procured.

- Products are specialized and not commodity-like.

Contd...

- The number of SKUs (Stock Keeping Units) is extremely large.

- The supplier universe is highly fragmented.

- Buyers are not sophisticated enough to understand dynamic pricing mechanisms.

- Most purchasing is done on the basis of pre-negotiated contracts.

- A metacatalog of products carried by a large number of suppliers can be created.

The matching mechanisms is a trade mechanism that creates value by bringing buyers and sellers together to negotiate prices on a dynamic and real-time basis. For example, iMark.com brings buyers and sellers together in the market for used capital equipment, and Altra Energy makes a market in energy and electricity. In contrast with the aggregation mechanism, *buyers can be sellers in the matching* mechanism. So adding a buyer to the hub benefits *buyers as well as sellers*. The source of value creation in the matching mechanism is improved matching due to improved marketplace liquidity. While catalogs benefit only from the aggregation mechanism, exchanges benefit from both aggregation and matching. Because they benefit from both mechanisms, we think that successful exchanges will reap greater benefits from being successful first-movers. The matching mechanism tends to work best in the following settings:

- Products are commodities or near-commodities.

- Trading volumes are massive, relative to transaction costs.

- Products are relatively standardized and can be traded sight-unseen.

- Buyers and sellers are sophisticated enough to deal with dynamic pricing.

- Purchasing is often done on a spot/transactional basis.

- Logistics and fulfillment can be conducted by third-parties, often without revealing the identity of the seller or buyer.

- Demand and prices are volatile.

How Hubs Serve: Biased versus Neutral Hubs

There is one other dimension that is important in describing a B2B hub, its bias. B2B hubs can be either neutral or biased. Neutral hubs do not favor buyers over sellers or vice versa. All of the hubs listed in Figure 1 are neutral. Biased hubs, in contrast, favor either buyers or sellers. Neutral hubs, by definition, are faced with a "chicken-and-egg" problem, in that they need to get buyers as well as suppliers into their system, without compromising their neutrality. They need to be careful in taking equity investments from large buyers as well as from large suppliers, because they can be perceived as biased. The benefit that neutral hubs have is that they are true "market-makers", because they bring both buyers and sellers together.

There is another category of hubs that are one-sided and biased by design. These biased hubs either work for sellers or buyers, and help them to negotiate better terms or streamline the buying/selling process. Biased hubs (like neutral hubs) can occur both as aggregators in systematic markets and as matchers in spot markets. When they favor sellers, biased hubs act as forward aggregators or forward auctioneers. Examples include Ingram Micro in the computer industry, or e-Chemicals in chemicals. When they favor buyers, biased hubs act as reverse aggregators or reverse auctioneers. Examples include FreeMarkets.com (focusing on Fortune 500 companies with a spot purchasing mechanism), or FOB.com (focusing on demand aggregation for small buyers in chemicals and other verticals).

In Figure 14.2, we summarize this taxonomy of mechanisms for B2B hubs using a simple pictorial scheme. The direction of the arrow shows the bias of the hub (forward, reverse, or two-sided/neutral).

Contd...

The line versus the curve shows the nature of value creation (linear versus non-linear/exponential). This simple pictorial depiction allows us to classify hubs very parsimoniously on the mechanism they use, and who they serve (their bias).

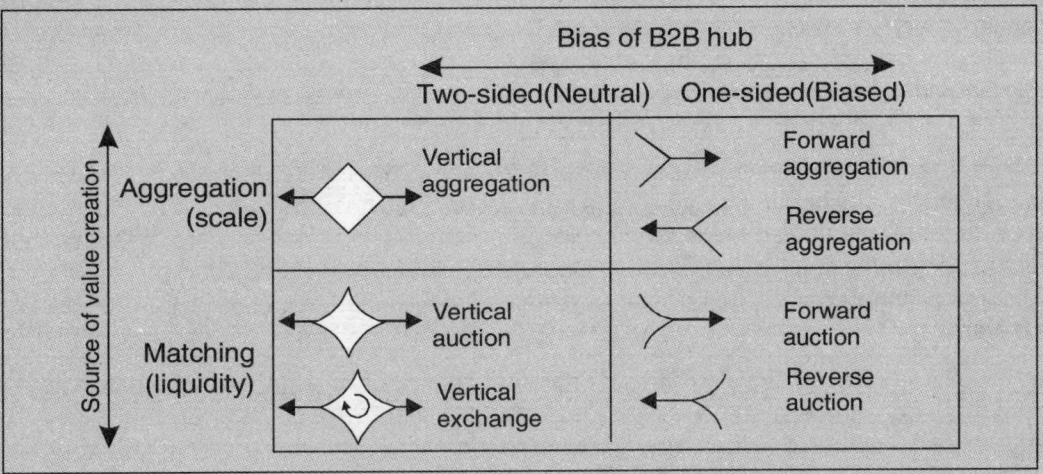

Figure 14.2: Taxonomy of Market Mechanisms

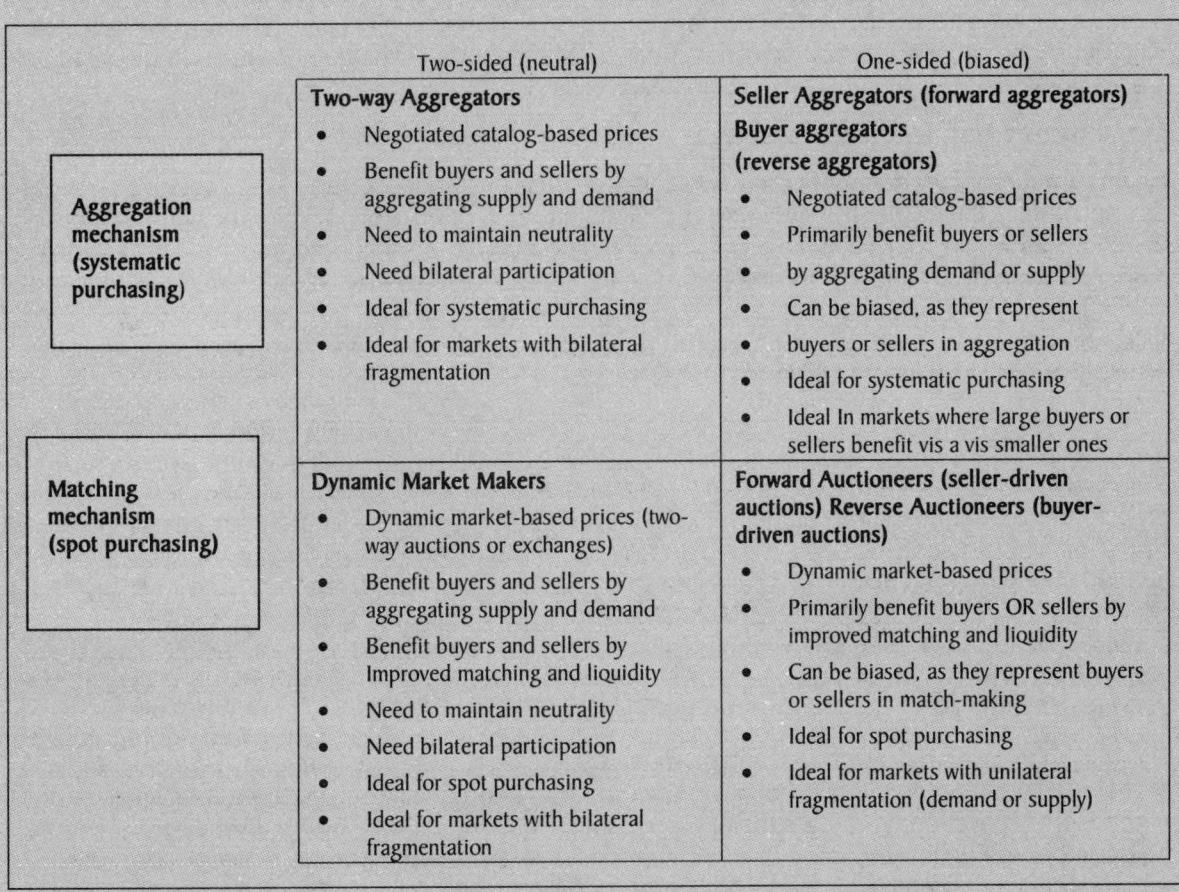

Figure 14.3: Taxonomy of Business Models for B2B Hubs

In Figure 14.3, we illustrate the different types of business models for B2B hubs, using this simple taxonomy the purchasing situation for which they are appropriate and their bias. Neutral hubs attempt

Contd...

to aggregate many buyers with many sellers. To do so, neutral hubs require two-sided liquidity. This creates a "chicken and egg" problem. Buyers do not want to participate unless there are a sufficient number of sellers; sellers do not want to participate unless there are a sufficient number of buyers. Neutral hubs also have to overcome the channel conflict that accompanies seller participation in many cases. When sellers sell through B2B hubs, they will do so at the expense of their normal distribution channels. This problem is particularly acute for two-way aggregators. Chemdex solved this conflict by partnering with a large cataloger – VWR. VWR promised to send all its business through Chemdex in exchange for an equity stake in Chemdex, as well as a concession that Chemdex not charge a transaction fee to VWR's largest buyers.

By their very nature, biased hubs do not need to worry about the "chicken-and-egg" problem, and can therefore hitch their wagon to one side of the transaction. This helps them to scale quicker than two-sided or neutral hubs. It also helps them to focus on smaller buyers or sellers, because they can aggregate demand or supply. Furthermore, biased hubs that represent buyers typically will not have to overcome channel conflict. This is true, for example, of Freemarkets, which organizes auctions for large buyers.

Neutral hubs and biased hubs also differ in one other important way. Neutral hubs are most likely to succeed and add value in markets that are fragmented on both the buyer and seller sides. In such markets, neutral hubs add value both by reducing transaction costs (aggregating) and improving matching (providing liquidity). If one side of the market is concentrated, these benefits are small or non-existent to the concentrated side of the market. Biased hubs, in contrast, can succeed as long as one side of the transaction is fragmented. In fact, reverse aggregators like FOB.com will add most value when the supplier universe is relatively concentrated, while the buyer universe is fragmented. In these situations, "leveling the playing field" for smaller buyers has significant value.

More about Reverse Aggregators: Enter the "Reverse VAR"

Reverse aggregators deserve some additional discussion, because they are a relatively recent development in the B2B arena. Reverse aggregators form groups of buyers of particular products or commodities within specific vertical or horizontal markets. Reverse aggregators reduce two major inefficiencies. First, by aggregating the buying power of many buyers – particularly, small and medium-size buyers – they can negotiate price reductions for those buyers. In some industries, volume discounts can approach 20 percent. Second, the purchasing hub can reduce procurement transaction costs by outsourcing the procurement function.

A vertical reverse aggregator pursues this buyer aggregation/purchasing outsourcing strategy in manufacturing inputs. FOB.com is pursuing this strategy in chemicals. BizBuyer.com and PurchasingCenter.com are a few of many firms pursuing this strategy in horizontal markets (MRO procurement). An interesting way to think about a reverse aggregator is that they act as "reverse VARs" or "Value-Added Re buyers" Traditionally, firms like Ingram Micro have worked as "forward aggregators" by aggregating selling power for small VARs (Value Added Resellers), by providing them with virtual back-office functions, and virtual economies of scale in purchasing (see Figure 4). In contrast, players like FOB.com are turning this supply chain on its head by reversing the direction of aggregation. They aggregate buying power for smaller buyers. In this way, they are exactly the reverse of Ingram Micro (see Figure 5 for an illustration of this).

Reverse aggregators have some advantages and disadvantages relative to neutral hubs for procurement of manufactured inputs. On the negative side, reverse aggregators will not be attractive to larger purchasers who already enjoy substantial volume discounts. Thus, unlike exchanges, reverse aggregators are unlikely to have all buyers as possible customers. On the positive side, reverse aggregators can potentially address both spot and systematic sourcing of inputs, in contrast with exchanges, who are largely tied to spot transactions. For example, a manufacturer looking for a long-term supply of steel is less likely to use e-STEEL than to negotiate directly with a steel manufacturer. Even in those instances where manufacturers do source inputs on the spot market, some fraction of

Contd...

that sourcing is still likely to be systematic and relationship-oriented in nature. Reverse aggregators will be able to aggregate buyers not only for spot purchases, but also to negotiate long-term contracts with suppliers. In many industries, we suspect that reverse aggregators will have access to at least as large a market as exchanges and catalogs.

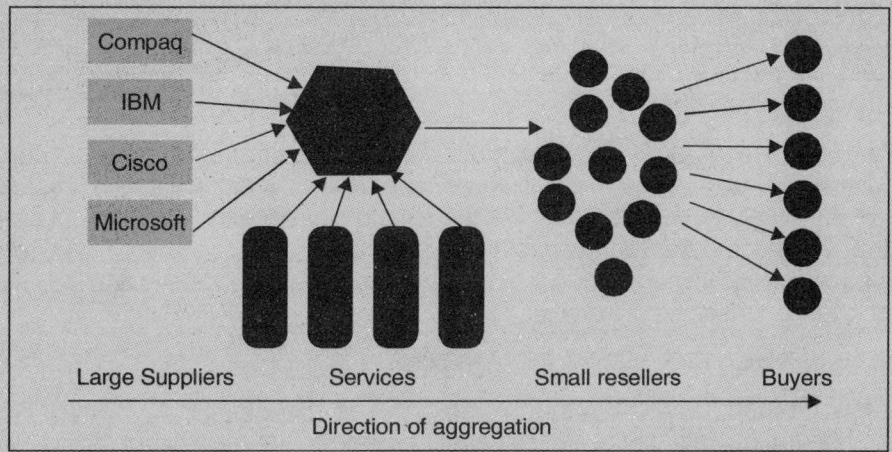

Figure 14.4: Ingram Micro as forward aggregator

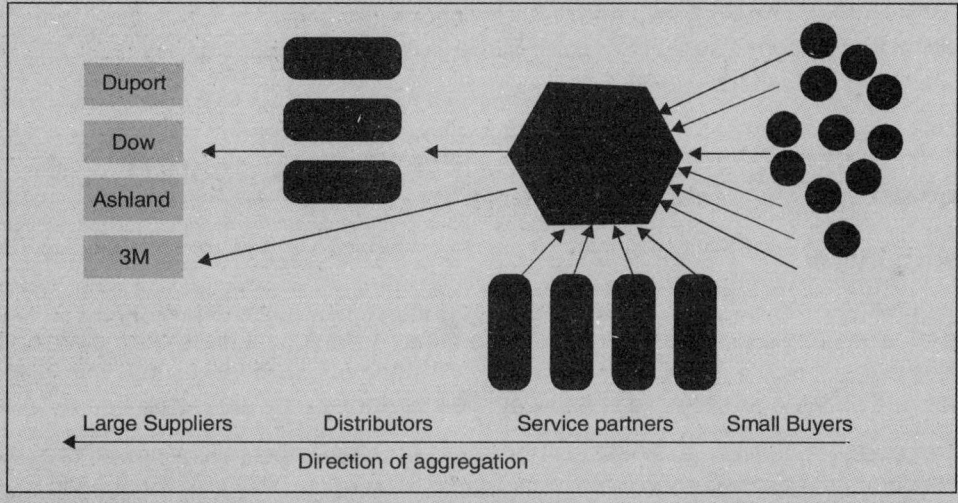

Figure 14.5: FOB.com as a reverse aggregator in the chemicals vertical

Where will we see reverse aggregators emerge? First, such hubs are likely to spring up in vertical and horizontal markets in which buyers are fragmented. As mentioned above, it is not necessary for the market to be fragmented on both the buy and the sell side. Second, the primary benefit that purchasing hubs provide is demand aggregation, so they will thrive in markets where there are a few large buyers and a large number of small buyers. In these situations, larger buyers enjoy significant volume discounts, while smaller buyers don't have the buying power to negotiate with sellers, especially with larger sellers. Third, purchasing hubs will be favored in products and services that can be more easily broken down into smaller orders. The smaller the lot size that the purchasing hub can deliver, the greater its value addition. Finally, they will add most value in product categories where the number of SKUs is not too large, because demand aggregation adds less value when product diversity is extremely high.

A logical concluding question to ask is – why does the reverse aggregator opportunity exist? Can't the neutral hubs (Chemdex, SciQuest, PlasticsNet) destroy these new entrants? Interestingly, we believe that existing neutral hubs in the relevant vertical markets or horizontal markets are unlikely to

Contd...

create reverse aggregators. First and most important, neutral hubs must provide effective neutrality between buyers and sellers to obtain the participation of both sides. If a neutral hub were to favor one side too heavily, it would risk losing its liquidity. Second, neutral hubs (especially exchanges) provide marketplaces for buyers and sellers to make spot purchases and sales. Exchanges are not designed to support systematic or contractual purchases. In other words, a manufacturer might use ChemConnect to find chemicals that it unexpectedly needs in the next month. That same manufacturer, however, is less likely to use ChemConnect for the chemicals that it buys under long-term contracts or through relationships.

In the din of the rapidly-evolving B2B marketplace, there is an enormous amount of confusion about what the different B2B hub business models are, where they add most value, and how profitable and defensible are they likely to be. We hope that the simple classification frameworks and taxonomy that we offer provides some clarity and direction as we see the landscape evolve. We also hope that the frameworks presented in this article will help entrepreneurs identify promising B2B hub business designs, and to better understand the what, where, why, and hows of B2B hubs.

Source: © 1999 Mohanbir Sawhney and Steven Kaplan. Reprinted with permission.

Steven Kaplan (steven.kaplan@gsb.uchicaao.edu) is the Neubauer Family Professor of Entrepreneurship and Finance at the University of Chicago Graduate School of Business, and the faculty director of the Entrepreneurship Program.

Mohanbir Sawhney (mohans@nwu.edu) is the Tribune Professor of Electronic Commerce and Technology at the Kellogg Graduate School of Management, Northwestern University, and heads the E-Commerce and Technology group.

Mind Power 2: Putting "e" in Distribution

by Richard Vurva

You've undoubtedly read the predictions and seen the hockey stick-shaped graphs depicting the coming explosion in e-commerce. If industrial and construction distributors don't develop Internet-based sales plans soon, warn the spin doctors, they'll stand on the sidelines and watch as dot-com companies and online marketplaces steal away their customers, by mouse click.

Despite the hype surrounding e-business and the sense of urgency technology providers try to convey, distributors shouldn't be concerned if their e-business strategy is still in the incubation stage, says Bob Segal of Chicago-based Frank Lynn and Associates. He says customers won't shift all of their purchases to the Internet overnight.

That doesn't mean distributors can ignore developing an e-business strategy altogether. Segal says large, publicly traded distributors must be able to articulate to suppliers and stockholders how they are formulating e-business plans, and small distributors must address the needs of customers who are early adopters in building an e-procurement process.

Before distributors align themselves with every dot-com company knocking on their door promising to help them join the digital revolution, Segal advises them to examine their own value proposition and their customer base. Unless a dot-com can demonstrate how its solution can either drive down a distributor's costs or ratchet up sales, don't take any techno leaps.

"The challenge for distributors and manufacturers is to truly understand buyer behavior," he says. "E-business doesn't change basic marketing principles." While Segal expects up to one-third of the industrial marketplace will be transacted over the Internet by 2004, it's not clear how much of that business will be directed through online marketplaces.

Contd...

"We originally thought that online marketplaces would account for about half of that e-commerce," he says. "We're a bit more bearish now, but we still think online marketplaces will be a big percentage of the industrial world."

Will buyers flock to online marketplaces to buy goods and services? If so, which marketplaces will succeed? What role will distributors play in a marketplace environment? No one knows for sure the answers to those questions. The ultimate winners will be those that merge the disparate needs of the marketplace, the distributor and the buyers.

What do online marketplaces want?

The goal of online marketplaces is to create a one-stop source where buyers will want to return again and again. One of the companies touting its method for aggregating buyers and sellers is TotalMRO.com, the newest Internet initiative of W.W. Grainger. Launched in March, the company lists 16 distributors in its growing network, including Grainger, Cameron and Barkley, Motion Industries, Wesco, Carlton-Bates, Precision Industries and Briggs-Weaver, and is negotiating with dozens of other distribution companies. TotalMRO.com president Liz Olig says the company's main revenue source currently is transaction fees paid by distributors.

For years, the MRO industry has been tagged with being a very inefficient, highly fragmented supply chain, Olig explains. Thousands of manufacturers interact with tens of thousands of distributors that range from local, small distributors to very large national players. They're all trying to serve the 8 to 10 million customers who use their products and services.

"We believe that through e-commerce there is a much more efficient model that leverages a Net market approach, she says. Bringing together and aggregating all of the information flows that exist within MRO, customers and distributors can much more efficiently interact at a much lower cost."

TotalMRO.com targets Fortune 1000 companies that have invested in Enterprise Resource Planning (ERP) systems and in e-procurement software from companies such as Ariba and SAP.

"Companies that have made a major investment are going to be committed to ensuring that this is how things are procured in the future," Olig says.

Few companies have successfully tied their indirect materials procurement processes to their ERP systems. The reason for the delay: most suppliers lack the technical sophistication to do so. Although the vast majority of industrial distributors and manufacturers have Web sites, Segal estimates that only 11 percent of manufacturers and about 7 percent of distributors offer fully enabled e-commerce technology. For sellers, market offerings such as TotalMRO.com offer a turnkey method for distributors to become enabled quickly. For buyers, it provides a source for one-stop shopping, if enough distributors can be persuaded to jump on board.

That's why TotalMRO.com is bending over backward to help distributors participate.

"We're working with distributors to collect their disparate sources of data," Olig says. "If one of our distributor partners only has paper catalogs and doesn't have their content in a database, that's no problem."

TotalMRO.com takes the separate sources of data, sorts and classifies it and puts it into a single database. Customers can then access a single user interface to search for product and service information and place their purchases. If a participating distributor has an existing contract with a customer, filters built into the technology limit end-user access to those distributors with prenegotiated contract pricing. When there are no pre-existing relationships, customers have access to any distributor on the site and can place orders accordingly.

"It's up to the customer to decide the best source given the situational need. Within TotalMRO.com, customers have access to all major MRO distributors such as Grainger, Wesco, and Motion Industries," says Olig. "The customer is going to drive who they buy from and how they buy from them."

Contd...

What do distributors want?

Distributors are looking for several things from online marketplaces. They want to be visible on the Internet, yet they fear doing so will make it harder for them to differentiate their value-added offerings. Ultimately, they fear, it will become easier for customers to shop them around for price. They want to utilize all that technology offers, yet they don't want to make huge cash investments. They want to be Internet savvy like the dot-coms, yet they're reluctant to change their traditional business model.

Ross Elliott, vice president and general manager for BuildNet, which recently acquired distribution software provider NxTrend, says distributors needn't fret about turning themselves into dot-com companies.

"Distributors need to consider how to make themselves 'dash' companies, not dot-coms," he says. He describes a "dash" company as a digitally aligned supply house. He says distributors should ask themselves, "How do I take my business and bring it into the digital world in a way that makes sense for my customers and my bottom-line profitability?"

Some dot-com companies offer to put themselves between the distributor and the customer by taking orders, billing and collecting payment from the customer and passing that money back to the distributor, minus their service fees. The distributor handles fulfillment.

"I'm not saying there's anything wrong with that model, but look inside your value proposition to determine if your logistics capacity is good enough to live on logistics alone," says Elliott. "Because that's what you're going to be competing on."

Elliott recalls a conversation he had with a distributor who said the single biggest challenge he faces in this new economy is to figure out how to be better at asset management. Eventually, if the dot-coms are successful at aggregating the buyers, the distributor's selling opportunity will be reduced. Buyers will simply shop for the lowest price.

"If this transparency concept is real, my ability to transmit information as a value-add is going to go down," the distributor said.

"So I have to become fantastic at managing the procurement process and managing the movement of goods through my warehouse. I have to make that my competitive differentiator."

Some distributors, like Winona, Minn.-based Fastenal, participate in more than one online marketplace. Fastenal e-business development manager Brian Fihn says Fastenal has made its catalog content available to about a dozen marketplaces, including iProcure, EqualFooting.com, PurchasingCenter.com and OrderZone.com, the horizontal marketplace founded by Grainger that recently merged with Works.com.

"Everyone takes a different approach to the way they display products, the way their Web site works, looks and feels," says Fihn. "Who is to say that every buyer out there is going to like the look and feel of Fastenal.com? We recognize that's not the case, so we came up with the strategy to put our data and our content wherever it made sense."

Like many distributor, Fihn becomes nervous whenever another company inserts itself between him and his customer. Even though he recognizes that some customers will like the convenience of a marketplace, he'd prefer they come to his site. So far, most of Fastenals sales via electronic commerce, on average about $2 million a month over the past few months, come from the company's own Web site, and from electronic data interchange relationships with large national accounts. Regardless of how orders are received, they all get routed through a central clearinghouse and pushed down to the branch level for fulfillment.

"Distribution occurs at our 850 locations," he says. "It's automatic, seamless integration into the point of sale."

Fihn doesn't believe Internet sales will ever totally replace the traditional salesperson. But he thinks it can be a valuable tool to get salespeople where they couldn't go before. For example, a Fastenal

Contd...

branch salesman on the East Coast used to call on a particular company once a month. Despite his efforts, he could never get past the gatekeeper or receptionist. The purchasing agent wouldn't give him the time of day.

"At 9 o'clock one night, a guy in the shop ordered a reamer from us," Fihn says. "The next morning, the salesman took the product and hand-delivered it. He walked past the receptionist and past the purchasing. Agent right to the shop guy who ordered the product. It turned into a minimum $1,500 a month account. So, the Internet is opening up some new opportunities for us."

What do buyers want?

Buyers want to be able to order products and services from their desktops or the plant floor. They also want price visibility (how much will it cost if I buy from Distributor A vs. Distributor B), yet they don't want to give up control of the relationship with valued suppliers.

"Most companies don't want their purchasing departments surfing the Net discovering new suppliers, for fear of jeopardizing their existing vendor relationships," says Bill Sullivan, vice president of industry marketing for PurchasingCenter.com, an e-solutions provider and creator of an online marketplace for industrial supplies. "What they really want is to utilize the Internet to further facilitate and nurture their existing supply chain."

What is required from buyers to become e-business enabled? First, they must adopt Internet-based business processes. They have to put down the phone, return the catalog to the shelf and boot up a desktop ordering system to place orders. They also have to define workflow. Who gets to buy what? How often? How much? From whom? What are the rules of engagement?

The promise of e-business technology is that it streamlines the buying process and eliminates costly procurement practices. Of course, you still have to convince end-users. It isn't easy to wean buyers away from a catalog, a phone or fax machine. And don't even think about telling a customer he can't do business with his favorite local distributor who saved his bacon last month when a production line went down and Joe got out of bed to deliver a critical spare part.

"This is still MRO," says Sullivan. "Local relationships are still viable as certain products are more readily and immediately available from your local supplier. Somehow, the Internet solution must accommodate for this reality."

Sullivan says traditional best practices are still relevant. Just because it's the Internet doesn't mean everything else goes away. Business process redesign, supplier consolidation and the importance of local relationships can't be ignored.

"Implementing technology is the easy part," says Olig. "The real work is in making users feel comfortable with the new process."

To help change end-user buying habits, TotalMRO.com holds cyber seminars on the Internet where users view an interactive demo, develops step-by-step instructions for use on the worksite and makes plant visits to explain to new customers how the system works.

Fastenal discovered that one of the most popular features of its Web site is the ability to print out a purchase order. Many customers like the convenience of online ordering, but still need to staple a purchase order to a materials requisition form and route it through the traditional approvals process.

"We also have a lot of users who go to Fastenal.com just for information about products and then fax orders or traditionally place orders," Fihn says.

Some might argue that's not totally seamless, integrated electronic ordering. But in many cases, it's all the customer wants.

The jury is still out on which companies (if any) have developed the best business model that satisfies the needs of online marketplaces, distributors and buyers. The market will undoubtedly continue to evolve.

Contd...

"Some dot-coms, e-marketplaces and exchanges will eventually fade away, as they have not developed a true value-add for buyer, distributor and manufacturer," Sullivan says. "What may have been a great idea on paper, that also generated venture backing, doesn't always translate successfully into the electronic world." Unlike traditional distribution companies, however, dot-coms are nimble and quick.

"They may not have the best business model today, but based on their backing and venture capital funding, they could change very quickly," says Fihn. Says Olig: "We're still in the early stages of the game, but the solutions that will win are those that are very customer-centric."

E-COMMERCE

Introduction

Till some year ago, distance used to be one of the key issues in the business and trade world. Manufactures, wholesalers, distributors, literally every one had to source from with a nation. The choices that domestic businesses had to offer were every limited. Trade and business were linked only to neighboring countries and an export or import was far beyond the reach of the businessman. Today at the onset of the 21st century things have changed. Businesses no longer runs in the same traditional fashion, but is facing stiff challenges from not only domestic markets but foreign shores.

Technology is rapidly changing for industrial marketers and so is the way how industrial markets run there business, E-commerce, Internet and all the other terms that keeps ringing in our ears have made a massive change in the way business is looked at today. The cost of sending message is virtually "zero" and the time taken is just one click of the mouse. Distance has been wiped off from the dictionaries of business houses, as proximity to one another is increasing. Today businesses are at a level playing field. Communication is not a problem, with no premiums attached.

E-Commerce is transacting of two companies, individuals for business. E-commerce is the movement of business onto the world wide web. However, it is only the bright side of e-commerce. There are also darker sides to it. This movement of e-commerce is broken-up in to two segments; B2B and B2C. We would discuss it in greater detail, as to how business has been influenced by e-commerce.

DEFINING E-COMMERCE

The phenomenal growth of electronic commerce can be attributed to the reduction of friction in business transactions over the network. This reduction has lead to improvements in the quality, service, customer care lower costs and faster execution of transactions. E-commerce is concerned with systems and business processes that support:

- Creation of information sources
- Movement of information over global networks
- Effective and efficient interaction between producers, consumers, intermediaries and sellers.[1]

Thus e-commerce can be defined as "business communications and transmissions over networks and through computers, specifically the buying and selling of goods and services, and the transfer of funds through digital communications."[2]

E-commerce serves certain great purposes. Today e-commerce is another way of communication, making payments. It also works towards the automation of business process and transaction. Customer servicing, a very essential component of industrial marketers can also be achieved with e-commerce. It would involve servicing existing customers, improving quality of good and faster and accurate delivery.

Dell today is considered to be the champion of e-commerce, because its sells more then US$ 50 million through its website every day. Similarly giants like Matshushita, Ingersoll-Rand, Tata Steel, Cisco System, Boeing have used this system very effectively.

Data on the scope and size of business to business transactions on the Internet provide perspective: B2B sales accounted for 94 percent e-commerce transaction in 2000. The manufacturing industry led all sector with total e-commerce shipments of $ 777 billion.[3]

NASSCOM figures reveal that the level of e-commerce transaction in India, was 1200 crores in 2001, with B2B transaction alone accounting for 1100 crores.

MAJOR ADVANTAGES OF B2B E-COMMERCE

B2B e-commerce has lot of advantages. Some of them are:

1. Interaction with customers, directly, effectively and efficiently. The communication patterns have changed in B2B. It has become paperless, and faster. The interaction between two organizations is purely on two computers.

2. Better promotional strategies.

3. Customer loyalty and customer relationship management.

4. Huge savings in distribution costs, better management of suppliers.

5. Better inventory management and control.

6. Secure payments and faster too!!

Some of the other advantages listed out are:[4]

- Economical, lower costs and higher margins.

- Better customer services.

- Easy comparison.

- Easy information sharing and teamwork.

- Higher levels of customization.

MAJOR DISADVANTAGES OF B2B E-COMMERCE

There are also problems associated with e-commerce. They are:

1. *Concerns of security:* Payments gateways, reluctance to give credit card numbers, serve as a big problem in e-commerce. Integrity of the buyer becomes a big question for an industrial seller. Not only that, there are also other concerns of hacking, corrupting accounts, illegally accessing somebody else's account is a reason for major concern.

2. *System scalability:* Now it is the two computers who are interacting. Now, with the increase in sight traffic, the need is to keep the site updated, maintain performance speed and a very less response time.

3. *E-commerce costs money:* Just a click does not result into a business. Neither it is cost free. There is a need for good monetary backing, to support the existing system, and to shift from the earlier system. Maintaining an e-commerce website is equally costly for business houses. Moreover, the size of the business, the increase in profitability, and the reduction in cost structures should justify setting up the system.

4. *Unwillingness among employees to handle e-commerce systems:* It is a potential problem. The complete organization should religiously bind itself to the e-commerce system. If the employees refuse to cooperate or halfhearted, the complete purpose of e-commerce is defeated.

Mind Power 3: Metaljunction adds 'bricks' to 'clicks'

Tata Steel and Metaljunction recently signed an agreement whereby Tata Steel entrusted the collection and selling of a range of their Secondary Steel Products, by products and Obsolete Capital Goods and Spares to Metaljunction. With the signing of this agreement, Metaljunction has taken over the complete end to end responsibility. This was so far the responsibility of the Secondary Products Division of Tata Steel.

With this step Metaljunction has added a new dimension to the services that it offers it clients. It now combines online selling over the Internet with a physical infrastructure of warehouses and the complete responsibility of logistics and payment collection. This ensures that whilst Buyers get efficient delivery of products, sellers get immediate cash collection.

For Tata Steel, selling of secondary steel products was not a 'core' activity and it sought to bring in a partner that could unlock value by using Information Technology and the Internet to provide a higher level of service to existing and new customers. The value that metal junction would create / unlock for Tata Steel are:

- *Reach:* The ability to rapidly roll out products across a large geographical area without the associated infrastructural costs.

- *Richness:* The ability to augment the sales effort without hiring new employees or financing the infrastructure necessary to support those employees.

- *Speed:* Service all existing customer relationships and add new customers without adding to costs.

Metaljunction presents enterprises the opportunity to grow sales through a number of unique online sales channels that lower distribution costs, develop new markets, increase customer loyalty and integrate payments and logistics to provide complete solution to the enterprise and its customers.

Coinciding with the taking over of the complete responsibility of selling which would involve warehousing and logistics, the 'bricks', metal junction has gone in for a name change which better reflects its new role. The company which was incorporated as "metaljunction.com private limited" has been rechristened "Metaljunction services limited". It has also become a public limited company. But this will not lead to any change in the shareholding pattern. The company will continue to be equally owned by SAIL and Tata Steel as a 50:50 joint venture.

Source: www.tatasteel.com

KEY ELEMENTS SUPPORTING E-COMMERCE

The most important element supporting e-commerce is the "Internet" and "world wide web". A research at the University of Texas, found out that Internet spans 250 million users, with 1,00,000 new users everyday. Internet traffic grows every three months. The Internet economy grew from US$ 5 billion to US$ 607 billion, from 1995 to 1999, with a growth rate of 212 percent. The GDP growth for that same period was 3.6 percent.[5] In India, also the growth percentages are phenomenal. As per a NASSCOM study, in the year 1995, there were just 0.01 million users, with 0.002 million Internet connections. In 2001, the Internet users were up to 8 million, with Internet connections of 2.5 million.

Internet is one of the strongest backbone, and a key element to support e-commerce.

The word Internet is a coined term from "Inter connected networks". It spans across the globe, and across all the countries. The environment surrounding the Internet has everything. It has EDI, e-mail videos, information publishing, voice, video conferencing and many others. The information exchange, is fast, comparatively cheap, zero marginal cost and very commonly available.

"The Internet began around 1965 when the US Department of Defense financed the design of a computer network to link a handful of universities and military research laboratories. Since then, this network linked by leased telephone lines, has mushroomed into a matrix of several thousand connections in over one hundred countries. So, in a short span of time, the Internet quickly became a front page story in every major newspaper; a cover story for magazines such as the "Business Week", "Time" and the "New Republic" a standing reference on CNN and inevitably, the inspiration for a "New Yorker" cartoon-two dogs at a key board, with one canine saying to the other, "on the Internet nobody knows you are a dog."[6]

We have come a long way, with hosts connected have passed fifteen million.

The e-commerce is built upon www or World Wide Web architecture. To provide a human analogy, think of the network infrastructure as the skeleton and the web as the flesh, veins and skin that shape the human body. Carrying the analogy further, the functions carried out by the human body would be the electronic commerce applications. In short, the web provides the functionality necessary for electronic commerce.[7]

INTRANET AND EXTRANET

As we have seen earlier, that the Internet today is one of the strongest driving force in B2B scenarios. There are two other elements that are integrated with the Internet technology. They are: intranet and the extranet.

Not being connected in the web, for a B2B marketer is of great shock and surprise. Today, most of the Indian B2B marketers, have a web interface. The important issue for a B2B marketer is not to sell the products directly to the buyer, but to maintain, integrate and sustain relationships. Buyers are looking in for more partnering relations than transactional ones. So, the need is not only to develop a relationship, but a sustainable long-run relationship.

B2B purchasing, does not mean, payments online, and the good reaches the industrial purchasers. It is about the integration of organizations, to capitalize on the strengths, and create a win-win situation for all. This in turn reduces inventory requirements, and there by creating better margins and profitability.

Intranets, are basically company specific and internal to an organization. This facility involves a lot of communication amongst employees across the globe. This also enables them, to share databases, information, interact, chat, view technical details, IPR's for effective business management. Boeing has an intranet, which connects all its employees across the globe. Even GE has an intranet in place for its employees and across divisions.

The intranet, thus plays the role as a corporate and product information center and is strictly a "within company" type of information exchange. This networked environment is restricted to internal employees and customers with firewalls to keep out non-employees. E-mail, replaces the traditional form of communicating messages. It helps in approvals, acknowledgements and other correspondences faster. Thus, the advantages of an intranet are:

1. Low development and maintenance costs.

2. Environmentally friendly, because it is company specific.

3. Availability and sharing of information.

4. Timely, current information.

5. Quick and easy dissemination of information.[8]

An extranet on the other hand is a shared intranet, using e-commerce for its vendors, suppliers and key accounts. These are also private networks, and not accessible to the people. When the intranets of two organizations are connected for better business efficiency and communication, extranet gets created. Extranets, allow business marketers to interact with their specific customers and customize information.

The success of e-commerce does not lie in creating more money for business marketers. It is in creation of value. Money is then a buy product, which would eventually follow through better margins and profitability.

ROLE OF E-COMMERCE

The importance of e-commerce is paramount, as we have seen earlier in this chapter. But with its gaining importance, e-commerce has a very crucial role to play for a B2B marketer. But, along with it comes certain words of caution. Managers, obviously have the tendency to get too much inclined for it, forgetting the basics of marketing. This should not be done at any circumstances. E-commerce serves as an instrument or tool to accomplish marketing objectives. Managers should however remember that it doesn't under any circumstances mean, that the basics of marketing should be neglected.

In terms of success in today's digital economy, the real asset is not money; money is just a commodity. The real asset is information and how it is used to create value for the customer. More than half of doing business no longer depends on the brick and mortar side of commerce; it depends on the core personnel of the firm and the customer. Having the employees be part of the organization and improving their skill sets, adds value and contributes to the success of the firm.[9]

There is a considerable myth existing among industrial organizations on e-commerce. Some of them are:

1. Internet marketing will steadily take over the marketplace, with little requirements for channel partners and basic marketing strategies.

2. E-commerce will be the only medium to attain new customers, as in the future, selling would stop.

3. E-commerce, cuts down expenditure of advertising and other promotional activities.

4. The level of skill required to introduce e-commerce is low, and the cost for such a setup is also low.

However, the above all are "myths", that marketing managers are bound to encounter. In reality, the Internet marketing concept is going to stay parallely with traditional selling. Complete removal is not possible. Neither would marketing channels be wiped off. This is because of a simple reason that some amount of training, credit facilities and logistics are managed by channel members. Also, not all industrial products would be profitable to be sold over the Internet.

Internet is an effective way to reach to the final customers, but not the ultimate way. For major industrial marketers, front to front talks are still needed. With a group of people taking a decision, to buy or not to buy, Internet will never replace personal communication.

Advertising and other promotional activities are still required to be in place, for creating awareness and brand building. A product will sell, only when buyers are aware of it. Basics should be perfect. Also, a common misconception, that e-commerce and Internet is a less costly affair, is wrong to be assumed. Not, only that, the complete B2B organization must be suitably geared up, to accept this change.

E-commerce and Internet does not mean changing the basic rules of the game of marketing and strategy. The objective is to facilitate the process of acquiring, maintaining and servicing customers. It has to be incorporated in the day-to-day functioning of the industrial marketer and create profitable customer relationship.

THE DIFFERENT FORMS OF B2B E-COMMERCE[10]

Internet brought about a lot of changes in the way industrial marketing business is carried on. It has quickened the process of B2B transactions and has successfully eliminated many of the difficulties that B2B marketers would traditionally encounter. Mostly, working on the Internet is about viewing and entering data. However, this process is on a shift of change. The industry is slowly moving to an interactive form of Internet, but also makes active use of data. Thus, the business would evolve from a supplier-centric to customer-centric systems. Monczka, Trent and Handfield, identifies four stages of progression towards increased integration buyers and suppliers via B2B electronic commerce. They are:

1. Web presence

2. E-Commerce

3. Data Delivery

4. Automation

1 and 2 is supplier centric, while 3 and 4 are customer centric.[11]

Web Presence

This is when manufacturers have a website and the industrial buyer can go and visit the web space for queries or product details. A basic form of providing product and service information. This is called as "disintermediation". The advantage is that, a manufacturer can directly be in touch or communicate with his buyers.

E-Commerce

This is a higher level of integration that goes beyond the web presence, where in products and services are not only displayed, but allows buyers to place their orders directly by linking to their internal line of business systems. This is a higher step than web presence.

Data Delivery

This is customer centric, wherein suppliers will deliver personalized data directly to customers. The supplier might supply a component that automatically updates the customer's spreadsheet, whenever an order status changes. It allows the customer, to take proactive steps to deal with issues like inventory shortage or missed delivery.

Automation

It is the integration between the decision-making systems of the business and their suppliers and customers becomes bi-directional and integrated. More intelligent business decisions can be taken as it involves customers and suppliers business systems.

BUSINESS TO BUSINESS TRANSACTIONS AND MODELS[12]

B2B models as described by "Joseph" are:

1. Aggregators
2. Hubs or process integration
3. Community or alliance
4. Content
5. Auctions or dynamic pricing markets.

The B2B models can be divided into three basic subdivisions, depending on who controls the marketplace. They are:

1. Buyer oriented B2B
2. Supplier oriented B2B
3. Intermediary oriented B2B.

Buyer Oriented B2B: A Buyer oriented B2B is typically a scenario, when the buyer has to purchase multiple products, and he uses the Internet, inviting suppliers to do the bidding. Generally the manufacturer, puts all the products on the Internet, he is looking in for, and waits for suppliers to bid in. For, bidding across nations, the product specifications need to be clear, for the supplier to bid.

Supplier Oriented B2B: A supplier oriented B2B is where a supplier invites business customers as well as individual customers to buy products over the Internet. The best example is Dell, who sells its computers over the Internet, and it represents 80 percent of its sales.

Intermediary Oriented B2B: An intermediary oriented B2B is for a buyer and seller to strike a deal, which involves setting up of an electronic market place by an intermediary company.

Another unique feature is electronic auctions. An item is put up for sale, and buyers offer their price. This goes till the price matches the requirement of the seller, and goes on until the bids are closed. Three variations of these electronic auctions are: forward auction, reverse auction and Internet exchanges.

A forward auction happens, where there is unpredictable demand, and there is excess stock. Seller entertains bids from multiple buyers. A reverse auction on the other hand is controlled by the buyer. The buyer asks for bids and the lowest bidder wins. This is a very good alternative for industrial buyers, with strong market commanding powers. In an effort by suppliers to submit competitive bids, prices are lowered. An Internet exchange auction is a third party operated exchange, where multiple buyers and sellers put in their bids and offers. From pins to aeroplane can be sold through the auctions, and the intermediary takes up the role of credit certification of the buyer and seller involved.

FORMULATING E-COMMERCE STRATEGIES

As we have seen earlier in the strategic management chapter, that formulating a business strategy would involve understanding business environments, current scenario, product lines, competition, resources and operations. Here also, we require to understand the similar things in a different format. But, one thing we must keep in mind is that devising a business strategy, is quite similar to an e-commerce strategy.

What, we need to be understanding is that, the power of Internet and e-commerce is limitless, but the resources of the business marketer are limited. Say for example, a hundred crore company, tries to buy Nucor or any other steel giant. Practically impossible. So, Internet or e-commerce will have certain restrictions, specific to an organization under which it would function.

Often, the top management feels that e-commerce will dramatically change the way, the industrial organization does its business. Half of the sales force can be cut, costs would be down, and profits would show from day one of implementation. That is a worse thought than a nightmare. Nothing, of that kind is going to happen. What will happen is facilitation of the business process. It would be a complimentary tool given to industrial organizations to improve efficiency or reduce costs or do both. Some of the key points that need to be looked into before formulating e-commerce strategy are:

The 8 Hows

1. How is it going to improve customer service?

2. How is it going to improve, the distribution channels of our organization?

3. How is it going to change our business? In case we do not implement it, is it going to dramatically affect the business?

4. How are we going to be placed against our competitors? Will the technology make us superior or similar to our competitor?

5. How capable are our people to handle Internet business?

6. How is it going to affect the cost structure as against efficiency?

7. How do we equip the "employees" to handle the change, in our way of working?

8. How can we cut costs and improve efficiency?

EDI: ELECTRONIC DATA INTERCHANGE

Traditionally the information exchange process is a very lengthy process and it comprises multiple steps from the time the order is taken, till the time the goods are delivered and serviced. However, this has changed in a new technological front called as EDI or Electronic Data Interchange. It is a communication tool, which is used to handle the entire communication between the seller and the buyer.

In EDI, one computer system, communicates with another in an electronic format. It is a standardized format. Earlier, before its existence, there were a lot of information flows that had to be done. It included product specifications, submission of bids, inspection of documents and making of payments. The problems however with this system were many. Time to transact, negotiate, human errors, low accuracy, poor efficiency and delays in processing.

However, with EDI, the complete scenario changed, in the way information was exchanged earlier. Today, more and more industrial organizations are inching towards EDI systems.

EDI has four components. They are:[13]

1. *Inter Business:* Transmission of data between businesses. Because there is little standardization, most companies using EDI use a third party service provider or Value Added Networks (VAN) as a communications intermediary. Such a provider handles the various communication protocols, line speeds, and performance on a regular basis.

2. *Computer-to-computer:* Data communication from one computer to another. This means providing online links between a buyer's and a seller's business application, with no human intervention at the receiving end. Delivery to the receiver is by electronic transactions. The receiver simply passes the transaction to the receiving computer application for processing.

3. *Standard Transactions:* Electronic versions of standard business forms. In EDI, a computer programme, not a human being, processes all data. EDI is designed to allow the receiver to handle a standard business transaction (e.g. billing a customer) in machine readable (not human readable) form between trading partners computers.

4. *Standard Format:* Transactions must be transmitted in a pre-defined form.

HOW DOES EDI WORK?

Prior to EDI coming into business, it was mostly manual work that used to go in. Work was not possible 24 × 7. More reliance was on fax and telephones. But however, with the communication style improving, it has drastically changed the scenario.

The computer of the industrial buyer, checks the inventory status of the item to be purchased. It can either be a single product or multiple products. A purchase order is created by the computer, with an amount and is sent to the industrial manufacturer. The manufacturers EDI system receives it and translates it into his own format. An acknowledgement is immediately given to the industrial buyer. Once the manufacturers EDI works on the purchasing order, multiple transactions take place. The order is created and sent to the ware house. A shipping notice is created and transferred to the industrial purchaser. Once the invoice and the shipping notice are received by the buyer's computer, it is translated into buyer's format. Payment authorization is electronically created and payments are made from the industrial purchaser's account to the manufacturer's account. An electronic remittance slip is transmitted to the industrial manufacturer.

In the complete process, the human component is very negligible. It increases efficiency, reduces paper work and saves a lot of time. There are also no clerical errors, or transmission delays.

Thus some of the major advantages of EDI are:

1. Reduction in costs and human errors.

2. Faster transactions and improved relationships with buyer.

3. Increase efficiency with accuracy.

The drawbacks of the EDI system are:

1. It requires huge investments to launch, maintain and update.

2. Still many industrial organizations in India, do not have such facilities.

3. The employees must be well-trained to handle such a system. Training is costly.

4. EDI requires special hardware and software, which costs money.

E-PAYMENTS

Business transactions over the Internet are growing at a very rapid pace. How, industrial organizations must be ready to conduct business in this environment, where transactions are moving towards the e-form. One of the most important issues in conducting business over the Internet is the payment for goods and services. The e-payment issue is one of the major blocks in conducting business. Issues relating to security, integrity, ease of use come up. However, e-payment systems are becoming central to e-commerce as more and more B2B companies, are looking into serving their customers efficiently and better. We will look into the issues and modes of e-payments under this section.

THE PAYMENT SYSTEMS

There are various ways of making a payment over the Internet. Some of them are traditional system and some are new generation payment systems. We would discuss some of them:

1. *Electronic Fund Transfer (EFT):* It is making of payments through electronic terminal like a computer or a telephonic instrument, authorizing a financial institution to debit or credit an amount.

2. *Credit Cards:* One of the most popular methods of payment over the Internet. There are a plethora of banks and companies, who handle the infrastructure of the credit cards. However, the problems with credit cards are high transaction cost, and security issues.

3. *Smart Cards:* First produced by Motorola in 1977, it handles a variety of applications. Units of prepayments or currency values are stored in an IC chip. The benefits of smart cards will rely on "smart card readers" that communicates with the chip in the smart card.

4. *E-cash:* E-cash is based on digital signatures, with a pair of public key and private key. It has embedded security privacy in it. Before e-cash can be used to buy products or services, it must be got from currency servers.

5. *Electronic Cheques:* These are quite similar to traditional cheques. It contains details of the payer, financial institutions, account number of the payer, and the amount. Digital signature used to be affixed on e-cheques.

Some of the concerns relating to e-payments like security, transparency, implications on small and medium sized business, and evasion of taxes still remain.

E-SECURITY

The problem with technology and development is common. Both have its "darker sides". Raising concerns, over doing business on the Internet, would probably be the biggest challenges that would be encountered by business marketers. Some of the concerns that exist in e-commerce are:[14]

1. Fraud, resulting in financial loss.

2. Theft of confidential, proprietary, technological or marketing information belonging to the firm or to the customer.

3. Disruption of service, resulting in losses to the business.

4. Loss of confidence due to illegal intrusion.

Mind Power 4: The World's Largest Office

By Naseem Javed

As the free-floating, nonrestrictive nature of streamlined Internet access and efficiency continue to grow, the Internet community will slowly render the traditional functionality of the office obsolete. Bye-bye cubicles and bye-bye water coolers.

The scene opens in a master bedroom, when the sun is not out yet but ticklish feet are searching for lost slippers, as rested fingers stretch and get ready for a frantic tap dance on the keyboard. A few clicks later and the worlds largest office opens. Welcome to Google. The big-mama of all connectivity, enabling the searching of the entire globe, connecting to millions via Gmail, offering calendars, shared schedules, spreadsheets, aerial surveillance, videos and dozens of other nick-nacks necessary to launch a major attack on any business or a personal quest.

This access to an omnipresent, fully functional office is so perfect, that it seriously threatens the world order of bureaucracy, whose red-tape processes have not only stifled progress with unnecessary functionalities, but continue to promote a mindset of dysfunctional square cubicles, dark elevators, and staled-air offices, where there are hourly meetings being held to determine why such meetings are required in the first place. As the free-floating, non-restrictive nature of streamlined Internet access and efficiency continue to grow, the Internet community will slowly render the traditional functionality of the office obsolete. The World's Largest Office is now open; all that's missing is the water cooler.

Bravo Google, your skateboarding through the corporate corridors over boardroom backstabbing is certainly paying off. All that's missing from Google are some additional services, like G-banking, job searches and so on. Did someone say office? What office? In the near future, you will be able to visit the full blown office exhibition at the Museum of Natural History, where young children can relive the rise and fall of the office hierarchy, the disappearance of three hour dry Martini lunches, the final revenge of Dilbert's armies and their breakdown of the cubicles, and the ultimate elimination of water coolers.

Eventually, the prospect of having an office may dissipate, as they are rapidly being replaced by rooms creatively constructed to look like safari camps, art galleries, solariums, fish tanks, kitchens and do not forget the master bedrooms. Offices of the past have done wonders, defined and pioneered by the great corporate leaders who laid the rules of hierarchy and delivered us the hard and soft goods

Contd...

leading to where we are today. A major transition where we are today, where grey flannel meets the colorful cotton, where the mahogany meets rattan and where four walls do not make a prison, nor "in" and "out" trays a cage. Freedom at last surpasses the conventional 9-5 model and daily traffic grinds.

Old mainframes first shrunk into micros, then to laptops and now to cigarette- sized USB drives to enable high data portability with several gigabytes in storage capacity. These tools, combined with the external accessibility of Google and dozens of other runners in this space, witness a major office revolution, the portability of the business is on the move and the days of stationary offices are numbered.

This change now incubates from a basic e-commerce approach to an end and new global e-commerce lifestyle dawns. By simply providing free Internet and computer access to an entire nation, the economical landscape can be dramatically altered. The prevalence of such turnkey Internet solutions such as Google, and Wikipedia further emphasizes easy accessibility for mass-connection. Harnessing the same logic behind this principle could bind together an entire city, nation, continent or region within a network of streamlined interconnectivity and unforeseen efficiency, holding the potential to shake the foundations of a nation and boost its GDP significantly. The old notion of hard wiring the entire nation for computer access at a mega cost is now being replaced to setting large Internet cafes at every street corner and let the office-less society become fully accessible worldwide. Hard to imagine phenomena in the making as these young players of e-commerce, move up to image and branding issues and kick start cyber-branding to tackle global commerce.

This is precisely what IBM achieved with its introduction of the Selectric typewriter, which boosted the efficiency of corporate communications amongst companies, as the art of letter writing amongst businesses blossomed. Since the dark ages, businesses have always sought to improve the means and quality of connection between buyers and sellers, by introducing a new medium at every age. From telegrams to faxes to the onset of online directories and vast, community based networks, each nation should strive to maximize this power, which, although free and easily accessible to all, still remains overlooked.

It is now high noon, I am still in the master bedroom and the leading publisher of top world class magazine "Office" wants to do a cover story with this piece, and then quit, later to join some of us in the local park. Please come with the birdfeed.

Source: Naseem Javed is recognized as a world authority on image building and creating global name identities. He introduced The Laws of Corporate Naming in the 80s and also founded ABC Namebank International in Toronto and New York a quarter century ago. Currently, Naseem is on a lecture tour in Asia and can be reached at nj@njabc.com

IMPLEMENTING MARKETING STRATEGY FOR THE INTERNET

In the last few pages, we have seen about e-marketing, e-commerce. The rational behind doing business over the Internet and the payment and security process. Now, what a business marketer has to do is to device a strategy for the Internet. Like other marketing processes, we must address issues on product, price, channels and promotion. One fifth 'P' in e-marketing is personalization. It is a combination of promotion and product, so that customers receive personalized information or visit a home page "customized" for them. It is a bit of "artificial intelligence" incorporated into the Internet marketing.[15]

Internet Product

Before we discuss more about the Internet product, it is important to realise that the website is the interface of the industrial buyer and manufacturer. Then, post the website comes the issues of e-commerce, hardware, software, services and information. While designing the website, one of the most important things that the management needs to understand, is what objectives the website must fulfill.

Developing the web content is another important aspect. On one hand the objectives must be met and on the other hand, it should be easy for the user to browse through. Giving a feel of the product is very important. What kind of product is the buyer interested in, how does it look, is what the buyer would be interested in. Content attracts users and keeps them returning. It has to be well-organized content.

Vicki August (2001), offers these five tips for "screaming content":[16]

- *Stay Fresh:* Update the site every day and at least once on the weekend.

- *Be relevant and unique:* Deliver highly focused content that is differentiated from competitive site content.

- *Make it easy to find:* Users want to find information or products immediately. Also don't include hyper links to other sites for content because users don't often return after they leave.

- *Serve a smorgasbord of content:* Integrate current news and facts with longer features and commentary. Include interactive material relevant to the site, such as quizzes, calculators, searches and so forth. Vary the format to include multimedia.

- *Deliver content everywhere:* This includes websites, wireless devices and special networks.

Another important aspect for business marketers is to develop e-catalogs. The catalogs will enable the industrial buyer with easy to access information, reduce the time required to search products, increase efficiency of the buyer. Developing Internet catalogs will help the buyer save, going through pages of data of specifications and details.

PRICING ON THE INTERNET

Previously industrial sellers who had the advantage of location and lack of competition used to make quick money. But today with easy accessibility to information and opening up of the marketing globally, the prices have been pushed downwards. Previously "commodities" like raw material supplies that could fetch high returns, are less profitable today. These products need to be sold and priced very carefully on the Internet, so as to be more effective in differentiating themselves. Internets also have increased in the bargaining powers of the buyer by greater access to information and that has led to industrial marketers control over price.

Marketers today can employee three types of pricing strategies. They are:[17]

1. Fixed pricing
2. Dynamic pricing
3. Barter

Fixed pricing is when the buyers must accept the price or leave the product. It is also called as menu pricing. Dynamic pricing is the strategy of offering different prices to different customers. Barter is when goods or services are exchanged for other products rather than cash.

CHANNELS ON THE INTERNET

Internet can bring about some dramatic changes in the channel structure, and business marketers must appreciate the importance of such changes. Once a target market has been decided by the industrial marketers, one important issue that needs to be understood is that, Internet is not the only means to reach the target market. The traditional channels should be supported with Internet presence. Software is one of the areas where Internet brings in a good deal of business, over the Internet. Companies like Adobe, Microsoft, McAfee uses Internet to their advantage, as a channel of distribution. Any information or product that can be transmitted over the Internet, has an advantage to the marketers, on having Internet as a channel of distribution:

Three major advantages of digital channels are:

- 24 hour accessibility
- Plenty of resources
- Customization for each buyers need

The huge amount of paper work that was involved previously in dealing with each channel number is zero, with Internet. Channels perform more effectively and efficiently. Inventory levels and flow of goods can easily be monitored. Reduction in costs of inventory and better performance to industrial buyers can also be achieved over digital channels.

COMMUNICATING TO BUYERS ON THE INTERNET

The major advantage over Internet is the availability of updated, low cost and quick information. Quick changes can be made on existing databases, by the industrial manufacturer. E-catalogues provide a plethora of information for industrial buyers. Internet also helps the sales representative to be much more effective in solving customer problems and building stronger relations. Internet provides a platform to customize for every individual, the business offerings. By promoting products through websites, marketers would be able to react to individual buyer needs. Thus each industrial buyer can be served in a different way. In the traditional medium like journals and business magazines, cannot get immediate feed back on customer's reaction. This problem however is well addressed on the Internet.

CONCLUSION

In this chapter we have seen how industrial marketers have changed, with the usage of technology. The traditional marketplace and ways to do business have dramatically changed with the introduction of the Internet. Doing business over the Internet has been continuously growing and manufacturers, distributors or other kinds of service providers are getting hooked to the Internet business.

E-commerce is about business communications and transmission over networks, doing business and transfer of funds. There are a plenty of advantages, while doing business over the Internet. They are savings, customer loyalty, better communications and faster secured payments. They also have their own set of disadvantages.

We also saw vertical markets, trading hubs, auctions, reverse auction and B2B exchanges providing with a new dynamicity in how B2B functions. The role of e-commerce and how new technologies are changing the rules of competition are worth noting.

The various forms of B2B e-commerce, the supplier centric and the customer centric forms starting from just a web presence to automated inter business process.

The e-commerce must be well crafted with a focus on the objectives. The last part of this chapter was marketing strategy for the Internet. We discussed some key issues relating to product, price, channels and communication issues. How communication over the Internet has become personalized in B2B markets and how Internet strategy should be integrated with other promotional strategies, were discussed.

References

1.   Bhasker, *Electronic Commerce-Framework, Technologies and Applications*, Tata McGraw Hill, pp 3.

2.   Good, Schultz (2002), *E-Commerce Strategies for Business-to-Business Service firms in the global environment*, American Business Review 14, pp 111.

3.   Hutt and Speh (2002), *IE Solutions 34*, no5. pp10. Adapted from, *"Business Marketing Management"*, Thomson South Western, pp 118.

4.   Awad, *Electronic Commerce – From Vision to Fulfillment*, Prentice Hall of India, pp 13-17.

5.   *Working Paper-Center for Research in Electronic Commerce*, University of Texas, 1999.

6.   Kalakota and Whinston, *Frontiers of Electronic Commerce*, Pearson Education Asia, Chapter 3, pp 85.

7.   As above, Chapter 6, pp 227.

8.   Awad, *Electronic Commerce- From Vision to Fulfillment*, Prentice Hall of India, pp 28-30.

9.   As above, chapter 1, pp 31.

10. Monczka, Trent, Handfield, *Purchasing and Supply Chain Management*, 2nd Edition, Thomson South Western, pp 645- 649.

11. George Moakley (1999, 1988-90), *E-Commerce Requires Intelligent Supply Chains, in Achieving Supply Chain Excellence through Technology*, Anderson Consulting, Chicago, II- Adapted from Monczka, Trent, Handfield, "Purchasing and Supply Chain Management," 2nd edition, Thomson South Western, pp 645.

12. For more on this read the section PT Joseph, *"B2B Transaction and Models"*, E-commerce: A Managerial Perspective, Prentice Hall of India, pp 38–39.

13. Awad, *Electronic Commerce from Vision to Fulfillment*, Prentice Hall of India, pp 393-394.

14. As above, pp 243-244.

15. As above, pp 322.

16. Strauss, El-Ansary, Frost-"E-marketing, 3rd edition, Pearson Education-Chapter 10, pp 284-285.

17. As above, Chapter 11, pp 321-326.

Mind Power 5: How to Make Sure your Website sells your Products

By Kristin Zhivago

The most important function of your website is the effective presentation of your products – whether you sell online or through a distribution network. Having just gone through a bunch of sites in the analysis of a buying process, and after doing a lot of research for clients on this subject in the course of website redesigns, I've come to some conclusions.

1.   First, answer their questions. Buyers come to your website looking for answers to their questions. The more complex the buying process (the more scrutiny they apply to the purchase), the more questions they have. You must know what their questions are, and your answers must satisfy their concerns in the order that those concerns arise in the customer's mind. If your website fails to do this, your website is a failure.

   Most sellers guess which questions are important and assume they know which answers will satisfy. I guarantee that this method will keep you from making sales. If you want to zoom ahead of your competition, you will interview your current customers – people who have already

Contd...

bought from you. They will have shifted from the skeptical buyer playing their cards close to their chest to someone who has a vested interest in your continued success. They will answer all of your questions. They will tell you what they were thinking during their buying process, what really mattered to them, what their issues were, and even how well or poorly you addressed those issues. They won't mind giving you this information. They will even be flattered that you cared enough to ask.

2. Save the fancy stuff for later in their buying process. Those PTNR (pony-tail, nose-ring) designers can easily get you all excited about beautiful flash animations at the entrance to your site. You will be convinced that it will make you look sophisticated and sexy. Meanwhile, your prospective buyers will be seriously irritated that they are being accosted by clowns as they try to enter your store. They have already seen and been irritated by plenty of equally flashy landing screens.

It's not a question of whether you should do something fancy. It's a question of when you should do something fancy. Save your fancy graphics for the "experience" part (see #6) which comes after you've given the buyer immediate access to product information and answered the questions they had in mind when they came to your site.

First you give them basic information, and then you can let them choose to be entertained as they drill down. Don't force-feed entertainment on them at the beginning of their session on your site. People love to shop online because they can find exactly what they want in a matter of seconds. They are determined to spend the right amount of money on the best product choice. Don't let your ego stand in their way.

3. Use thumbnails for product pictures. For fairly simple products, each product page should include a couple of thumbnails. The buyer should be able to click on and enlarge each one. For more complex products, you should have a photo gallery, which displays many thumbnails, each about an inch square. Again, they should be able to click on a thumbnail to see a larger image in a new window.

When they click on a different thumbnail, that new image should appear in the same popup window. In other words, don't clutter their desktop with a stack of popup.

So they can easily get back to the page with thumbnails, they should be able to click on a "return to thumbnails" button on the popup window, which will take them back to the thumbnail page.

The larger images should include a caption. No one does this, and they should. The caption should relate to what is being shown in the image and point out important features that the customer would find particularly valuable.

Virtual tours are useful, but not necessarily worth the expense. A series of good photos is just as good. And do yourself a favor: Hire a professional photographer. Yes, you understand all of the buttons on your digital camera, but it is lighting that makes the difference between a photo that answers questions and one that does not. Photos play a significant role in the question-answering process. Plus, if the photo is substandard, your buyer will assume that your product is, also substandard.

4. The more pictures, the better. You can never have enough pictures of your product. Think about your own experience as a buyer of online products. How often have you gone to a site, and clicked on the two or three pictures available, and thought, "Darn, this still doesn't answer my question." Maybe you want to see inside that computer case. Maybe you want to understand how big something is, but the picture offers no frame of reference. Maybe you want to see what the item is made out of, and would have made the purchase if you could have seen a close-up of the product components. Maybe you wanted to see the end of the item, the bottom of the item, the handles on the item, the closure on the item, and on and on. Your buyers want to know. If you don't provide this information, they'll simply go back to Google and go to the next site in the search results. In a matter of seconds, you will have lost another sale.

Contd...

5. Include photos, short and long descriptions, specs, and the price on the same page. Your interviews with customers will tell you which questions they want you to answer. But there is also basic information that should be on every product page. I'm shocked, frankly, at the number of companies that fail to include these basics, even though we've all had more than ten years to get this web stuff right.

Your product page should include at least one photo, at the top, with links to other photos via thumbnails (or a link to a gallery, for more complex products). Next, your product page should display a short, bulleted list of essential features and functions, and then a longer description. The description should be factual, personal and verb-heavy rather than adjective-heavy. "You can store up to 50 soda cans in this thermo-electric cooler" will lead to more sales than "this convenient thermo-electric cooler provides optimum carrying capacity."

The price should be prominently displayed on the page. Price is one of the biggest questions and often one of the first questions. Don't be coy. The price is the price. Answer the question, right up front. If you hide the price, they will assume it's too high, and they will also wonder what else you're hiding from them.

6. Do everything you can to help the customer "experience" your product. After you have created product pages that answer the basic questions with your copy and your images, and you still have the budget and the desire to get fancy, go ahead. This is the right time in the buying process continuum to help your buyer "experience" the product. Your buyer has got her basic questions answered, and is still there, interested. The buyer is now more than happy to mentally "try on" the item. This is when the buyer will click on the item to change its color, or watch a video of the sailboat in action, or take a virtual tour of that house for sale.

7. Put the buyer in the driver's seat. You can't make a sale if your buyer can't make a purchase. In other words, your buyer's purchasing process is more important than your selling process. If you don't support their buying process, you won't make the sale.

What do they want to know? How do they want that information presented? What matters to them most? How do they want the site to be organized? Where would they expect to find certain types of information, and how would they like that information to be presented?

Don't guess. Don't depend on website designers to tell you. Trust me, they don't know. Most website designers have only worked on the web, and have very little personal experience in other aspects of business. So their idea of what a customer would want, or what one of your selling partners would need, could easily be wrong.

All of this matters a lot. The web is not like a static brochure. It's a place where people interact with your information. If your information isn't holding up its end of the interaction, you will lose sales. And if you try to get fancy before you get the basics right, your website will be like a salesperson who only speaks gibberish whenever a customer asks a question.

Source: The article has been written by Kristin Zhivago. You can visit her at www.revenuejournal.com or www.zhivago.com. Reprinted with the permission of the author. Copyright rests with the author.

Mind Power 6: Is your Web site helping prospects move forward?

By M. H. "Mac" McIntosh, CBC

Your web site is often the first place somebody looks to learn more about your company and its products or services. Is your site helping prospects move forward in their consideration and buying process? Here's a checklist of questions to ask yourself:

Contd...

Does your web site make it immediately clear what your company does and who it serves?

Does it clearly spell out

- The products or services your company sells?
- The most common applications for your products or services?
- The types of businesses or institutions you serve? business? education? government?
- The size of organizations your company serves– large, medium or small.
- The geographic areas you serve – local areas, states, countries, regions of the world.

Is it easy for your prospects and customers to find their way around your Web site?

- Are there clear, consistent and well-organized menus?
- Is there a functional search mechanism?
- Are text links to related or in-depth information included?
- Are graphics clickable?

Does your Web site quickly communicate your company's unique selling proposition?

Does it clearly

- Explain why your company is a better choice than the competitor?
- Address your prospective customers' needs from their point of view?

Does your Web site back up those claims?

- Explaining the experience and expertise of your people, their depth of industry experience, their education and industry credentials?
- Listing a sampling of the companies and institutions your company serves. Providing testimonials from happy customers and case studies explaining how you solved your customers' problems.
- Showing the certifications and awards your company has won from customers and industry groups?

Does your Web site explain the additional resources you can bring to bear for your customers?

Does it give details about

- The pre and post-sales support services you offer your customers?
- The companies you partner with to bring value-added solutions to your customers?

Does your Web site contain lots of offers designed to engage prospects and start sales-winning relationships?

Are there multiple offers

- Appropriate for both business and technical decision makers.
- For each stage of the prospects' buying cycle – early, middle or late.
- Being made on every appropriate page of your site?

Contd...

Does your Web site make it easy for your prospects and customers to take the next steps in their consideration or buying process?

- Does every page of your Web site include strong calls to action?

- Is your company's contact information easily found on every page?

Does your Web site make it easy to place an order?

- Is entering orders as easy as it should or could be?

- Does the shopping cart work as smoothly as it should?

- Do your ordering processes and forms avoid making the customer start over if they make a mistake?

- Do you allow visitors to save shipping and payment information for future visits?

Are there multiple ways for prospective customers to request assistance or additional information about your company and its products or services?

Can they request this information by

- Phone

- Text chat

- Email

- Requesting a callback

- Downloading a document

- Filling out a form

Source: Reprinted with the permission of the author M.H. "Mac" McIntosh. You can contact him at www.sales-lead-experts.com. Copyright with the author. All rights reserved. Reprinted with the permission of the author.

QUESTIONS FOR DISCUSSION

1. How is Internet and e-commerce changing the industrial marketplace?

2. "Will e-commerce wipe out the intermediaries in industrial marketing"? Discuss.

3. What are the various departments that are affected with the influx of e-commerce and the Internet?

4. Do a study on "Cisco Systems", to find out, how are they using the Internet to support their selling activity?

5. "Will Internet marketing, change the face of industrial marketing? Can we imagine a day, when there would be no salesman?

6. How are prices being driven down with Internet usage?

7. How are online market places changing the face of industrial buying and selling?

chapter

FIFTEEN

Industrial Marketing Communication: Advertising, Sales Promotion and Publicity

COMPANY PROFILE 15: JINDAL STEELS

Jindal is one of the leaders in Steel Manufacturing and Power Generation in India. They have a passion for excellence and a never failing commitment towards their customers, employees. Part of the US$ 4 Billion Jindal organization, they believe in the concept of self-sufficiency. Through backward integration from captive coal and iron-ore mines to production of economical and efficient steel and power, they have been passing the benefits to the customers. Today, they are the largest private sector investor in the State of Chhattisgarh with a total investment commitment of more than Rs. 10,000 crores. They are also setting up a 6 million tonne steel plant in Orissa with an investment of Rs. 13,500 crores and a 5 million tonne steel plant in Jharkhand with an investment of Rs. 11,500 crores. Jindal Power Limited, wholly owned subsidiary of JSPL, is setting up a 1000MW OP Jindal Super Thermal Power Plant at Raigarh, with an investment of over Rs. 4500 crores.

JSPL offer customers worldwide, a manifestation of Steel and Power products. Steel, the very foundation of Jindal's growth and diversification, is available as Carbon Steel and Alloy Steel. It confirms to various National and International Standards (like SAE, AISI, DIN, IS and ASTM) and is produced in the form of billet, bloom, round and slab. Enhancing safety, increasing reliability and ensuring a prolonged rail life, they have set-up a Rail and Universal Beam Mill producing world's longest 120 meter long finished rails for the first time in India. The plant is also equipped with a flash Butt Welding Plant for welding of rails from 240 meters to 480 meters long rail panels. Available in normal grade as well as wear resistant grade, Jindal steel is certified by BSJ-London for Quality BS: EN 9002:2000 and BS : EN 14001:1996 for Environmental Management System.

Their H-beams, hot rolled parallel flange beams and columns are available in a comprehensive size range, from small and medium to larger sizes (Universal Beams: 200×100 to 700×300 mm and Universal Columns: 150×150 to 350×350 mm). For H-Beams, BIS Code No.1 is available for sizes up to 600×220 mm and is under review for the inclusion of sizes up to 900×300 mm. Jindal has pioneered the production of medium and large size hot rolled parallel flange beams and columns, in India and these confirm to the international specifications.

Power is another core operational area and expertise in it has made JSPL one of India's most economical power producers in the private sector. They are utilizing this power for captive purpose and also supplying it to Chhattisgarh State Electricity Board and to industrial units in the Industrial Estate. Having an undeterred and sharp focus, JSPL are poised for a quantum leap in this sector and are also setting up a 1000 MW O.P. Jindal Super Thermal Power Plant at Raigarh in the State of Chhattisgarh, thereby contributing to the growing power needs of our nation.

JSPL has added a new dimension that of exploration and mining of high value minerals and metals, like diamond, precious stones, gold, platinum group of minerals, base metals, tar sands etc.

Initiation has been made in exploration for diamond, gold and associated minerals under Reconnaissance Permit (RP) over 2500 sq.km in Jahspur district of Chhattisgarh State. Another area of 3009 sq.km in the adjoining parts of Jharkhand State has been allotted for exploration for diamond, gold, base metals, etc.

Jindal Rex Exploration Pvt. Ltd. has been incorporated under a joint venture with Rex Diamond Mining Company with the headquarters in Canada and the operational centre at Belgium.

The Indian ethos has always incorporated the concept of giving. Companies have an impact on society and the environment through their operations, products and services. Since beginning, Jindal have always recognized the responsibility, which corporate should have towards the wider communities they operate in. The Social Accountability, SA 8000, initiated by JSPL is a rock solid step towards maintaining corporate awareness and conscientiousness.

Source: www.jindalsteelpower.com

Mind Power I: End of Interruption Marketing: B2B Marketing Response

Market when customers give their attention

There are points in every buying cycle when the customer is actively seeking information. From typing something into Google to begin research to putting together a short list to building an ROI justification, buyers want trusted information to help them. This is why search engine marketing is so critical. Because the buyer is searching for information, the company that provides it is in the best position to be considered a trusted partner. The implication is that B2B marketers need search terms and landing pages designed to provide useful information to each stage of the customer buying cycles.

Build trusting relationships

If a marketer calls me in the middle of my day, I feel interrupted. If a good friend calls me, I pay attention to what he has to say. The difference is trust, built over time.

B2B marketers can build trust with their prospects in the same way that trusted relationships are built "in the real world".

1. *Expert advice:* B2B purchases are, by their nature, complex. Buyers often need help to see possibilities and issues they wouldn't think about on their own, if you can help frame the discussion. You will be seen as a trusted advisor and thought leader. This will help buyers believe that your company understands their problems and knows how to solve them.

2. *Not self-serving:* You need to have the buyer's best interests in mind. Marketing messages that are self-serving will be painfully apparent and could damage rather than build trust.

3. *Long-term view:* Trust is built over time, and needs to be nurtured across a series of interactions. This requires a long-term view of your marketing investments.

Nurture a community where people can discuss your solutions

Customers trust other customers more than, they trust marketers. This is as true in B2B as it is in consumer marketing. Marketing Sherpa's recent Business Technology Buyer's Survey found that word of mouth is by far the most common factor influencing purchasing decisions (48.3 per cent mentioning they were impacted by the tactic, as opposed to webinars which came in at 18.4 per cent and cold calls which came in at 2.8 per cent).

So what can B2B marketers do to take advantage of social media-based marketing techniques? The answer is to engage in and nurture the online communities, conferences, discussion groups, and blogs that your customers, prospects, partners, and influencers are already using.

Doing this successfully requires changing the traditional marketing mindset. B2B marketers are used to thinking they have control over the message, but with community-based marketing this is no longer the case. Put another way, marketing is no longer about putting on a show in which the audience (your community) watches passively; it is more like throwing a party and encouraging the attendees to interact. In this world, marketing's job is not to control the message but to ensure that their "party" is the most interesting and useful one around.

What do you think?

How is the role of the B2B marketer changing in a world where traditional marketing messages are ignored and buyers talk to each other to get their information? What strategies and tactics have you found that work?

Source: Posted by Jon Miller on August 21, 2006 in Interruption Marketing. Copyright 2007, Marketo Inc. You can visit the web at www.marketo.com. Reprinted with the permission of Jon Miller.

Contd...

Mind Power 2: Stop being a Cost Center

Too many CEOs and CFOs think of marketing as a cost center. Left unchanged, this attitude makes it almost impossible for a CMO to succeed. Take the following example, courtesy of Anne Holland at MarketingSherpa.

A B2B marketer started the year with an average cost per lead of $40. Determined to improve performance, he embraced online channels and created best-practice landing pages that quickly engaged prospects and gave them good reasons to register. As a result, the marketer improved lead quality and simultaneously reduced cost per lead to $10. Thrilled with the results, he went to the CEO to approve increased spending on this highly successful programme.

Did the marketer get his budget? No. The CEO decided that since leads now cost only $10, marketing can deliver the same results with less budget. Instead, she cut the marketing budget and used the extra funds to hire new sales people.

What went wrong here? The marketer had great performance, but did not connect his marketing results to bottom-line metrics that mattered to the CEO. By framing the discussion of marketing results in terms of costs, he perpetuated the perception that marketing is a cost center. With this framing, it is only natural that the CEO would try to reduce costs and put the extra budget to a "revenue generating" department such as sales.

As I wrote earlier, B2B marketers can defend against this framing the issue of marketing spending and marketing results in terms of hard metrics like revenue and growth. Marketing budgets must include revenue forecasts, and marketing plans must have business cases that show how the activity will drive revenue. Only by demonstrating how their efforts directly influence revenue can B2B marketers position Marketing not as a cost center but an asset that drives revenue.

I should note that making the connection between marketing activities and revenue is not always easy, but that doesn't mean you shouldn't try. It is too important to ignore, and even small steps can help show the value and give the motivation to keep trying to do it better.

Source: Posted by Jon Miller; Copyright 2007, Marketo Inc. You can visit the web at www.marketo.com. Reprinted with the kind permission of the author.

Mind Power 3: Sense and Nonsense in Business-to-Business Advertising— Just the Facts, Ma'am By Perry Marshall.

Anybody who's had anything to do with magazines lately knows that the last couple of years have been awful. Publications have gotten skinnier and skinnier as advertising revenue has dropped off. One editor told me, "As soon as a book gets small enough to fold up and stick in your shirt pocket, you can kiss it goodbye."

And indeed, as the economy has wobbled during 2001 and 2002, quite a few magazines have folded or consolidated. This is due to the facts that vendors have slashed their ad budgets, and revenue for the publications has plummeted.

When the economy is going backwards, there's a vicious cycle that everyone feels helpless to fix: Customers buy less, so there's less money for marketing, which means there's less money to persuade customers to buy in the first place, and eventually the whole industry is gasping for breath. It's just bad for everybody.

Contd...

But wait a minute — if advertising is often the first point of contact for new business, why would you cut back on it during a recession? Wouldn't you do more?

Sure you would, but only if you were, certain it worked.

The reasons people don't buy more in a recession is because they're not even sure it works in the first place.

So I have a' solution for the problem:

Fix the bad advertising and the problem will go away.

Before you write me off as an arrogant blowhard, let me pass this along from the late David Ogilvy, one of the great advertising geniuses of the 20 century. This is a story from his book *Ogilvy on Advertising*:

Do you think advertising gives you enough information about products?

I don't.

Recently, I smashed my car beyond repair and had to buy a new one. For six months I read all the car ads in search of *information*. All I found was fatuous slogans and flatulent generalities. Car manufacturers assume that you are not interest in facts. Indeed, their advertising is not aimed at consumers; its purpose is to win an ovation when it is projected on the screen at hoopla conventions of dealers. Showbiz commercials have that effect. Sober, factual advertising does not. If their engineering was as incompetent as their advertising, their cars would not run ten miles without a breakdown.

When I advertised Rolls-Royce, I gave the *facts* — no hot air, no adjectives. Later, my partner Hank Bernhard used equally factual advertising for Mercedes. In every case sales went up dramatically — on peppercorn budgets.

I have written factual advertising for a bank, for gasoline, for a stockbroker, margarine, foreign travel and many other products. It *always* sells better than empty advertising.

Before I started writing advertisements, I spent three years selling Aga cooking stoves to Scottish housewives, door to door. All I did was give my customers the facts. It took me 40 minutes to make a sale; about 3,000 words. If the people who write Detroit advertising had started *their* careers as door-to-door salesmen, you and I would be able to find the facts we need in their advertisements.

Remember, Ogilvy is talking about *cars*. We all know people often buy cars for very vain reasons, but the fact remains that a lot of solid information has, to fall in place before most of us will part with twenty or thirty grand for a new automobile.

How much more true, then, when the audience is engineers who are selecting controllers, drives, networks, I/O, sensors, data acquisition systems, software, motors and displays?

Right now I'm flipping through an industrial product rag from the U.S. An advertiser paid handsomely to be on the front cover. 40 per cent of his expensive placement is devoted to a big smiley face.

Gee, isn't that smart. Engineers always buy stuff when it has smiley faces.

On the back page (very typical, as you all know): A full-page ad with an out-of- focus picture and about sixty tiny words of vague puffery at the bottom. Boasting and bragging, but no specific information or story.

Admittedly most ads do try to squeeze in some important information, but most of the time the real story is still buried in the middle somewhere — or not told at all. You have to read it very carefully to discern what's really unique about the product.

Ads like that don't produce nearly as many inquiries as they could, because nobody's going to scour an ad just in case it might contain some kind of important message.

Contd...

But let me tell you a secret: If you tell the real story, in an interesting, relevant way, people will read all of it. Sometimes they'll read it over and over again.

Back when I was a teenager drooling over stereo equipment, each month I'd get my copy of Audio or Stereo Review and devour it. At the time, Carver had a product called the "Magnetic Field Power Amplifier" that they advertised with full page ads, full of text from top to bottom. These ads told the whole story behind their amps. They used very simple illustrations to show how the power supply in a traditional amp is like a bathtub full of water — a reservoir that must be filled before it can be emptied, and with finite capacity. The ad explained how their Magnetic Field amplifier, by contrast was like a faucet bolted onto a water main — all the power you need, available instantly. The ad went on to describe how this results in less heat, fewer failures, less weight, smaller packaging, and... well, awesome sounding bass and hi-fi nirvana.

Some might say "nobody's going to read an ad that's 1000 words long."

But I probably read that entire ad every time I saw it. I wanted one of those amps.

The people who aren't interested in buying your product won't read your ad no matter how long or short it is. But I can promise you, anybody who's worth one hour of your salesperson's time *will* read the ad, because he's looking for facts. And every fact you give them that a competitor leaves out is a vote in your favour.

If it costs you several hundred dollars to send a salesperson on a sales call (it does) then wouldn't you want him or her to only see people who are looking for the facts?

If slogans and vague generalities are lost on Joe Average, you can be that the engineer tunes 'em out in a nanosecond. Engineers are a literate bunch, probably in the top 5 to 10 per cent of the population in that regard. And engineers have insatiable curiosity. Pique that curiosity with some attention-getting facts and we're all ears.

Mr. Advertiser, I want to know the facts. I want to know why your product—the one that you spend forty or fifty hours a week selling, the one that you spent millions of dollars developing — I want to know what it will do for me. I want specifics. Does it save my money? How much? Is there a decision-making process? What is it? Was there an interesting discovery that made this product possible? Tell me the story behind the story. And just the facts, ma'am.

Source: Perry S. Marshall is an author, speaker and consultant in Chicago. Perry S Marshall and Associates and CLB Media Inc., the publishers of manufacturing AUTOMATION magazine. Reprinted with the permission of the author. Visit them at www.perrymarshall.com

INTRODUCTION

We need to communicate to our customers, both existing and potential. Although personal selling is the best mode of communicating to industrial marketers, which most of them follow, but still advertisement is required to sell the product. With industrial and consumer marketers, bombarding their target segments with their "punch lines", the industrial marketer should try and create a space for itself in the marketplace. The best of the products would require advertisements. We need to "tell" our customers, this is what we have to offer you, something unique. As industrial marketer, we must communicate to our customers, what we have to offer and what is so unique about our products. Not only is communication, the only motive it also helps the industrial marketer, to build a brand of its own, and to reach potential prospects.

There is a great deal of complexity, longer negotiation times while handling industrial purchasers. Most researchers thus agree to the fact that personal selling forms the key link to industrial marketing

Cost, is a moving target, and thus determining cost and fixing it at a certain level is difficult. Often, while fixing the cost, some assumptions are made which are absurd. Now, a higher mark up would definitely increase the price and there by reducing sales and lower profits. "Cost plus pricing leads to overpricing in weak markets and under pricing in the strong one exactly the opposite of a prudent strategy."[13] Therefore, there is a need to move away from cost based pricing, which are more product driven to value based pricing, which are more customer driven. In the former, the product generates the cost and the price, which the customers have no other option but to accept, but in the later case, it is customers, who determine the value, which determines the price of the product.

"From Marriott to Boeing, from medical technologies to automobiles, profit leading companies now think about what market segment they want a new product to serve, determine the benefits those potential customers seek, and establish a price those customers can be convinced to pay. Then companies challenge their engineers to develop products and services that can be produced at a cost low enough to make serving that market segment profitable."[14]

ASKING THE RIGHT QUESTIONS ON PRICING?[20]

Often, marketers juggle around, with prices and follow hit and trial mechanism to pricing. However, it shows a shoddy work on the part of the marketer. Understanding the costs, customers, competition, financial implications are very essential for right pricing decisions. Nagle and Holden, suggests that proactive, strategic questions need to be asked by the marketer, to get the pricing right.

1. What sales change would be necessary or tolerable for us to profit from a price change?

2. Can we deploy a marketing strategy that will keep those sales changes within acceptable ranges?

3. What costs can we afford to incur, given the prices achievable in the market, and still earn a profit?

4. Is our price justifiable given the objective value of our product or service to the customer?

5. How can we better communicate that value, thus justifying the price?

6. How can we convince the customer that our pricing has integrity and was measured against value?

7. How can we better segment the market to justify pricing differently when the value is different?

8. What level of sales or market share can we most profitably achieve?

9. What marketing tools should we use to win market share most cost effectively?

Analyzing costs and setting up of right prices would be a challenge that would haunt the industrial marketer. As industrial marketers, we need to relook as to what would be the pricing strategy that the customer is comfortable with. The faster we change the way we price, the better would it be.

TYPES OF PRICING

Here in this section, we would discuss the various ways in the industrial markets with relation to price quotations. The industrial buyers are spread across the nation and often across the globe. Also the need of industrial buyers varies considerably. The variations could be in terms of the volume of purchase, locations and thus bringing them at the same platform is very essential. Various kinds of terminologies are used, such as list price, net price, discounted prices and geographic pricing. We would discuss each one of them in detail.

List Prices: When we pick up any catalogue of an industrial marketer, we would see that the product specifications and technical details are given, but however no prices are mentioned in the catalogue. The prices are carried separately by the manufacturer representatives or salesperson in a printed format separately. This is because, in cases of price fluctuation or any changes that need to be made, only a single sheet for price, needs to be reprinted. This saves cost. Also, for industrial products, a lot of negotiation happens before a deal goes through. For initial proposals forwarded to the buyer by the seller, the list price is mentioned. From this list price, a wide variety of discounts can be subtracted to arrive at the net price. List prices are very rough estimates and negotiations over these prices happen to reach the final figures.

Net Prices: It is the final price quoted by the seller to the buyer, below which the seller cannot offer its products or services for. The net price gives the final figure after discount.

The discount could be in the form of:

1. Trade discount

2. Cash discount

3. Quantity discount

Trade discounts are reductions from the list price. This is for the intermediaries of the industrial marketer and for other groups of customers. The discount given should cover the type of function provided by the intermediary. It should help the distributor in covering the services effort and the sales effort that they undertake. Trade discount must be non-discriminatory and as per provisions of MRTP act. It is also an incentive for the distributor; therefore care should taken, so that competitors should not offer better discounts for similar product lines.

Cash discount is an incentive for the buyer to pay up early, after a sale goes through. Generally a payment term of within ten days is given a cash discount and above thirty days is charged with an interest. Generally, any payments made within ten days, would attract a cash discount of up to 2.5 per cent. Now the problem is for large accounts, wherein "pushing" for payment is a no-no. Such companies often due to procedural delays take time to pay and also cut the 2.5 per cent discount.

Quantity discounts are for industrial buyers to order in large quantities. There are price volume breaks that are given by the seller. This is given by the seller, because cost of handling, transporting and order processing would be higher if we ship 50 units of any industrial goods and comparatively lower if we ship 1000 units. The ideal way to do this is to study the purchasing pattern of the buyer, and preparing the quantity discount breaks. There are also non-cumulative discounts which are to encourage large orders, reduce storage and transportation costs. The cumulative discounts take into account the complete volume and "locks in" a buyer's interest for a longer period, there by providing guard against competitors.

All the above discount measures are for three major purpose. They are:

1. Encourage bulk purchase

2. Encourage faster payments

3. Cover up costs of dealing with different customers

Geographic Pricing

Geographical factors play an important role, for both the industrial buyer and the seller. The buyer would be interested in the cost of transportation. There are generally three ways of pricing the products.

1. **Ex-factory:** The prices at the factory gate of the manufacturer. The industrial buyer has to take the responsibility of insurance, and freight charges from the factory gate.

2. **FOB destination:** When the price is quoted by the manufacture as "FOB destination", it means the freight changes are borne by the seller. The seller arranges for the transportation.

3. **CIF:** It stands for "customs, insurance and freight". One of the most commonly used ways of paying. CIF includes FOB plus all domestic charges, transportation charges and other costs. The insurance is also paid by the seller. This is quoted at the port of destination. From the port of the destination, to the buyers godown is his responsibility.

LEASING

Till now, we have discussed about pricing and how it affects the industrial buyer. Often, it happens that due to cash shortages or frequent technological changes, the industrial buyer opts for what is called as leasing. Leasing is an alternative to selling capital equipment. Leasing not only has economic benefits, but also accounting benefits.

The advantages of leasing are:

- Disposing of equipments is not a problem
- Preventing the risk of obsolescence
- Investing cash for purchase and arranging of finance
- More working capital available.

Leasing has been gaining momentum in the industrial markets especially with high risks involved in buying. It is a very suitable alternative to purchasing and therefore business marketers can look in for the leasing market, than the decision to make an outright sale. For example, the use of a "truck" for transportation, the buyer requires only 1 number. Rather than investing 20 lakhs for a truck and making an one time investment, he would prefer to go in for a lease. One problem that the industrial marketer might face is, the financial aspects of leasing may not be easily understandable to a salesperson. So as to avoid this, a specialist can be recruited for the same.

There are two kinds of leases. The first one is a financial lease which is long-term, non-cancellable and fully amortized. The payment that one makes exceeds the original purchasing price. The buyer is given the option (often) at the end of the period to buy the asset. The buyer is responsible for operating and maintenance of the equipment. The other type of lease is the operating lease, which is a short-term, cancellable agreements and not fully amortized. The purchase option, at the end of the period like financial lease is not given. The lessor provides the maintenance and service.

BIDDING

In industrial marketing, a large chunk of the business happens through bidding. Now, this is true for all the three categories of buyers, and more importantly for the governmental markets. Bidding refers to a situation when the buyer asks two or more suppliers to submit bid prices, on a purchase that the buyer wants to make. Bidding is often for non-standardized products and products whose design and manufacturing methods may vary considerably. If sufficient number of suppliers is available and the industrial buyer has adequate time, bidding is used.

The reason for bidding is to obtain a price, which is very reasonable. Not only that, in case of complex purchases, wherein designs vary, the buyer has the option to choose. In cases of "new task" purchases, buyers can get information, on the market trend for prices and for "straight rebuy", the buyer can collect information as to whether the existing supplier, is supplying at a competitive price. When, the industrial buyer cuts down cost, it affects the profitability of the buyer.

Bidding always does not mean, searching for the lowest price. If the prices are the least, there would be higher chances that the quality and servicing suffers. So many companies often do not go in for the lowest and the highest bid.

Bidding is of three types. They are: open, closed and informal. Open bid is more of a formal process. Suppliers submit written tender documents. There can be changes made in the prices, before the final date and the buyer can examine it. The problem of open bid is that, the buyer may disclose it to suppliers, and also expect them to match the lowest bids. A closed bid is when the supplier submits a proposal in a sealed envelope, with specific deadline. All the bids are opened at a prefixed date and time. Generally the supplier with the lowest bid wins. The informal bidding is generally for casual jobs like printing work, stationery etc. These are generally for relatively simple purchases.

The Bidding Process

The bidding process starts with what is called as a "Request for Quotation" (RFQ). This is when the industrial buyer wants the bidder to be from the existing suppliers or previously associated with them. Otherwise, the buyer selects vendors or gives an advertisement for interested bidders, to apply for bidding. The details of the project, earnest money required, specifications, terms and conditions are mentioned. The date for the opening of the bid is mentioned for closed biddings.

For, all government contracts, certain amount of guarantee needs to be deposited before bidding.

The Bidder

To bid or not to bid is the greatest and biggest question. The industrial marketer should be able to understand the objectives, at the time of bidding. For example, if a plant of an industrial marketer is running at 90 per cent capacity and the new bid involves additional expenditures, to build in more capacity, the industrial marketer should rethink about bidding. Same plant if it runs at 40 per cent capacity, the industrial marketer, would try and get the contract at any cost and would price his products in such a way, so as to cover the variable costs.

The marketer may have other objectives. It could be:

- Gaining entry into new markets
- Full utilization of plant capacity
- Keep the labor force and the plant operating
- Maintain corporate image
- Greater price stability.

Bidding is not only about your company and your products. A great amount of information needs to be collected about what exactly the industrial buyer is wanting. The industrial buyer would look in for factors like service and delivery which may not be mentioned in the "RFQ" before bidding. The other factors which an industrial marketer should research about are:

1.   Competitor strategies, bids, plant capacity, plant utilization.

2.   The chances of winning "follow on" contracts. Follow on contracts are repeat orders.

3.   Previous bids by competitors.

4.   A check by the industrial marketer on himself, whether he will be able to fulfill the obligations.

5.   Buying Influencers.

A significant amount of money should be allocated to preparation of bid. Once all the data, has been collected, the bidder must find out the probability of wining the contract at various price. If the "bid price" is high, then chances of getting the contract would be low, and if "bid price" is low, then the chances of getting the contract would be high, but profitability would suffer. To determine this, there are several approaches (quantitative). However, managers might often use the power of intuition and experience to quote the bid price.

NEGOTIATION

Negotiation on pricing is very common for industrial markets. Negotiations may not be necessarily be based on prices but also on other factors like delivery schedules, technical assistance, quality, etc. Industrial purchasing is complex and there is lot of time lag, from the point of acceptance by the buyer, to the point the relationship finally builds. Negotiation should be beneficial for both the buyer and the seller, in terms of profitability building, relationship building and finally meeting corporate goals.

Generally, companies have different outlook to negotiation. Some of the companies give full responsibility to the salesperson for the negotiation purpose. However, some companies do not and require higher approval for any kind of decisions. How rigid or flexible the policies are of a seller firm, will give an advantage or disadvantage to the industrial salesperson.

Some of the top management feels that if power is given to an industrial salesperson he may cut down the price, to make a sell and the company would thereby lose money. So some of other companies set a "floor level" of price, below which a salesperson cannot go; in case of further negotiations, higher authority permissions are necessary.

Some last words of advice are that when to walk out of negotiation is an art. If an industrial buyer is stressing more on price, and sees it only from a single transaction point of view, it is better to walk off from the deal. In the future, further pressures relating to cutting down the price, may be put forward by the buyer. So, the industrial marketer should be careful, in choosing his customers.

CONCLUSION

In this chapter, we discussed the markets, the factors influencing the pricing strategy of an industrial marketer. How value being provided to the customer is very essential in the determination of price. The industrial marketer should do a through study on the cost and profitability analysis of particular product, the concepts of marginal cost and marginal revenue.

Analyzing costs is an essential component of industrial marketer, to arrive at prices and how various factors affect the cost structure. We went through the concept of learning curve, economies of scope and economies of scale. Viewing the price from a customer's point of view is essential.

We also saw how to price a product across the PLC, and analyzing pricing decisions and setting-up of prices. We studied the various methods to analyze and set prices like cost plus, ROI, perceived value pricing.

The types of pricing structure are essential for quotations and the kinds of discounts and pricing terminology in the industrial markets was discussed. Leasing as an important alternative to purchase of an equipment was discussed.

Industrial marketing often involves competitive bidding, especially from the governmental contracts and a broad idea on bidding was discussed. Finally, we saw the negotiation strategies, and the ways the industrial marketer should deal with each situation, effectively.

References

1. Dolan and Jeuland (1981), *Experience Curves and Dynamic Demand Models*: Implications for optimal pricing strategies", *Journal of Marketing*, 45, pp 52-62.

2. Gross, *Insights from Pricing Research - in Pricing Practices and Strategies ed, Bailey* (NY: The Conference Board 1978), pp 34-39.

3. Dolan, *How do you know when the price is right*, pp 178-179.

4. Cooper and Slagmulder (1990), *Develop Profitable New Products with Target Costing*, Sloan Management Review 40, pp 23-33.

5. Nagle and Holden, *The Strategy and tactics of pricing – A guide to profitable decision making*, 3rd edition, Pearson Education, pp 306-315.

6. Nagle and Holden, *The Strategy and Tactics of Pricing – A Guide to Profitable Decision Making*, 3rd edition, Pearson Education, pp 306.

7. Day and Montgomery, "Diagnosing the Experience Curve", *Journal of Marketing*, 47, (1983), pp 44-58.

8. Nagle and Holden, *The Strategy and Tactics of Pricing – A Guide to Profitable Decision Making*, 3rd edition, Pearson Education, pp 313-315.

9. Nagle and Holden, *The Strategy and Tactics of Pricing – A Guide to Profitable Decision Making*, 3rd edition, Pearson Education, pp 8.

10. Corey, *Industrial Marketing: Cases and Concepts*, 2nd edition, Prentice Hall: Englewood Cliffs, N.J., pp 157-178.

11. Nagle and Holden, *The Strategy and Tactics of Pricing – A Guide to Profitable Decision Making*, 3rd edition, Pearson Education, pp190-192.

12. Eckstein (1964), *A theory of the wage price process in modern industry*, Review of Economic Studies, 31, pp 267-287.

13. Nagle and Holden, *The Strategy and Tactics of Pricing – A Guide to Profitable Decision Making*, 3rd edition, Pearson Education, pp 3.

14. Nagle and Holden, *The Strategy and Tactics of Pricing – A Guide to Profitable Decision Making*, 3rd edition, Pearson Education, pp 4.

Mind Power 3: Is your Salesforce a Barrier to more Profitable Pricing ...or is it you?

By John Hogan and Tom Nagle

One of the most difficult pricing challenges facing marketers is how to maintain consistent, value-based street prices in highly competitive markets where every deal is seemingly at risk. For many, the temptation to maintain flexible pricing policies in order to negotiate customer-specific deals is too

Contd...

much to resist. Like a dieter trying to lose weight, these marketers try to "cheat" by treating themselves to a one-time price discount to close a particular deal. However, just like the dieter who must face the reality of the scale at the end of the week, price cheaters must face the reality of their bottom line. Unfortunately, that reality all too often is characterized by increasing price erosion and decreasing margins.

Companies that do not manage their pricing by policy will, in most markets, lose control of it. In the process, they risk alienating their best customers, slowing the sales process and eroding profitability. It happens because customers' willingness to pay for a product or service depends not only on their perceived value of it, but also on the expectations customers form about the need to pay for the value they receive. Sound policies create expectations on the part of each customer that the price they are asked to pay is determined objectively and has some relationship to the value received and/or the cost to serve. Unsound or nonexistent policies lead buyers to expect that they can manipulate information or their own behavior to win discounts without giving anything of value in return.

A common fear for managers who are replacing ad hoc discounting with transparent and consistent pricing policies is that sales representatives will not accept the change. While a minority might not make the transition, most will accept the change if it is implemented well. Sales representatives don't like being beaten up over price, don't like the long sales cycles that reactive price negotiations cause, and don't like having to spend their time making the case for discounts internally. Sales representatives are motivated when management stands with them in resisting bad deals, and empower them with the authority to cut good deals consistent with pre-approved policies. Interestingly, neither do most customers enjoy manipulative, drawn out price negotiations. They do it to survive suppliers whom they believe will exploit open, loyal customers.

When companies fully define pricing policies, their sales representatives can have full authority to offer even the deepest discounts, subject to rigid constraints based on the customer characteristics and behaviors allowing a customer to qualify for them. For example, when confronted by a customer demanding a lower price to meet competition from an Asian supplier, the policy-empowered sales representatives would not need to appeal to a higher level of management to authorize a lower price, thus delaying the sales process and risking the deal. Instead, the representatives could say, for example, that the company would grant a discount of 20 per cent if the customer committed to volumes months in advance, just as the Asian supplier would require. Perhaps the customer might still decide to fill most of his needs from Asia, but would want a contract with the company to cover just the amounts that might be required to meet short-term variations in demand. In that case, the sales representative would inform the customer of his company's policy to supply product in those situations only at spot prices, sympathizing with the customer but assuring him that price commitments require corresponding volume commitments.

The effects of pricing by policy are almost universally desirable. Customers learn that there is no reward for simply beating on the supplier, and that there is no need to fear that a competitor is getting a better deal. Consequently, customers lose the incentive to keep sellers in the dark about their true needs and the value of them. They also learn that there are trade-offs between the prices they pay and what they get. This process of "give-get negotiation" forces customers, even purchasing agents, to learn what their organizations really value. If policies are designed well, they drive changes in customer behavior that reduce your cost to serve them.

Good policies will make it easier for sales representative to resist pure price negotiation and to align price paid with value received. Sales representative, however, need to believe that those are necessary and valuable objectives for them, not just for their company. The first step in that direction, even before policies are in place, is to measure and reward salespeople for driving profitability, not just revenue. Many companies reward salespeople for making larger and more frequent sales, not for making more profitable sales. Unfortunately, giving salespeople revenue-based incentives and empowering them to negotiate prices is a toxic combination that poisons their motivation to sell value.

Contd...

Consider the dilemma facing sales representatives who are compensated as a percentage of sales. Say that the company's margin is 10 per cent on high-volume deals. A sales representative who invests a great deal of time with the account, selling value and/or getting the customer to change behaviors that drive up costs, might at best be able to increase the profit earned on the deal by an additional 10 per cent of sales, doubling the profitability. Even if all that increase is in price, however, his revenue-based commission increases by, at most, 10 per cent. In contrast, instead of trying to sell value, one of his colleagues spends the same amount of time selling two deals of equal size with only a 10 per cent margin. As a result, the colleague's effort increases the company's profit contribution by the same amount, but he earns twice as much commission for doing so. Even if the colleague has to cut the price by 5 per cent to win the deal, reducing the profit by half, he gets a bigger commission than the first sales representative who spent time selling value rather than volume, and as a result has to hear about his failure to keep pace!

Until you fix these perverse incentives associated with revenue-based measurement and compensation—driving revenue at the expense of profit—it will be difficult to get sales reps to do the right thing. The key to aligning sales incentives with those of the company is to link compensation with profitability using a contribution margin-based *profitability factor*. More than just theory, paying for profitability provides mutually beneficial sales incentives, and it encourages salespeople to pay more attention to value drivers beyond price such as innovative product features, quality defects and delivery speed. Once the company aligns sales incentives, salespeople will begin clamoring for the other things they need to succeed. At one company, for example, sales reps traded in their company sedans for vehicles in which they could transport product to new customers with an urgent need.

Creating a Sales Incentive to Drive Profit

The key to inducing the salesforce to sell value and maintain price discipline is to measure their performance and compensate them not just for sales volume, but for profit contribution. Although some companies have achieved this by adding Rube Goldberg-like complexity to their compensation scheme, there is a fairly simple, intuitive way to accomplish the same objective. Give salespeople sales goals as before, but tell them that the sales goals are set at "target" prices. If they sell at prices below or above the "target," the sales credit they earn will be adjusted by the profitability of the sale.

The key to determining the sales credit that someone would earn for making a sale is calculating the *profitability factor* for each class of product. To encourage salespeople to maximize their contribution to the firm, actual sales revenue should be adjusted by that profitability factor (called the sales "kicker") to determine the sales credit. Here is the formula:

> Sales Credit = [Target Price − k (Target Price − Actual Price)] × Units Sold
>
> where k is the profitability factor (or "kicker")

The profitability factor should equal 1 divided by the product's percentage contribution margin at the target price, in order to calculate sales credits varying proportionally to the product's profitability. For example, when the contribution margin is 20 per cent, the profitability factor equals 5 (1.0/0.20). When a salesperson grants a 15 per cent price discount, the discount is multiplied by the profitability factor of 5, reducing the sales credit by 75 per cent rather than by 15 per cent had there been no profitability adjustment. Consequently, when $1,000 worth of product is sold for $850, it produces only $250 of sales credit. But when $500 worth of product is sold for $550 (a 10 per cent price premium), the salesperson earns $750 of sales credit ($500 + 5 × $50). Obviously, the importance of this adjustment is directly related to the variable contribution margin. The larger the margin and, presumably, the greater the product's importance to the firm, the greater the profitability factor's ability to align what is good for the salesperson with what is good for the company.

Conclusion

Profit-based sales incentives are not merely theory. As companies have moved toward more negotiated pricing, many have adopted this scheme in markets as diverse as office equipment, market research

Contd...

services, and door-to-door sales. Although a small percentage of salespeople cannot make the transition to value selling and profit-based compensation, most embrace it with enthusiasm. However, senior managers must lead this change; sales will not do it on their own. Company leaders must develop the appropriate policies, metrics and incentives that align the salesforce to measures of profitability. In making this change, however, managers should also be prepared for some unexpected consequences as salespeople begin to focus more on profits and less on volume. Now, salespeople who previously fretted about the company's high prices will begin complaining about slow deliveries, quality defects, lack of innovative product features, and the need for better sales support to demonstrate value. The salesforce's attention will move from reflexive complaints about price to legitimate concerns about value drivers the company does or (does not) provide to customers. It will be a change so conspicuous you'll know you're on the right track.

Source: SPG Insights is a quarterly publication of Strategic Pricing group, a member of Monitor Group. In each issue, we take an in-depth look at current value based marketing challenges and provide practical solutions and insights for executives in marketing, sales and management. Visit the website at: www.strategicpricinggroup.com. This article was published in the Fall 2005 of the SPG Insights. Reprinted with permission.

Mind Power 4: Packaging adds Cost – A myth or Reality

Each side justifiably argues its stand. There are companies that develop packaging; with the sole aim of cutting costs. However, this may have dangerous fallouts, as it reflects negatively on packaging purchasers.

A low-cost packaging may appear to be cutting costs, however, in a broader perspective it is rarely the case. A low-cost packaging may provide inadequate protection leading to product damage or probably project a down market brand image.

On one side, packaging technologies are reaching new heights. On the other side, there is huge growth potential. And the constant demands for innovations, creative and increasing responsibility is another angle and a balance of these three parameters determines the dynamics of packaging. The confluence of these three can be looked upon as a Eutectic point, where-all the three responsible interests meet. And any variation, however minimal is bound to disturb the eutectic character affecting the co-existence.

The protagonists here are the Raw Material (RM) suppliers, converters and the packaging users. Often the latter makes demands on the converters for packaging at cheaper rates. With the cost of raw materials on the rise, the pressure is on the converters to supply packaging at low costs.

E-tenders, which are considered, modern means of purchase technique, claims to be open-ended but how this influences the supplier negativity gets into the background.

Yet another strategy employed by the packaging users is to enforce a methodology of calculating the cost based on raw material costs. They often demand packaging at costs, which they arrive at put adding up input and process cost and what is considered a reasonable markup. This markup is often based on technology level, infrastructure level, and on whether the company is an SME or belongs to the organized sector.

However, this method is not very accurate, as all these are intangible parameters. As technologies differ, so does the processing cost and markup. To calculate packaging costs on the above basis is not exactly accurate.

Also, the packaging user needs to bear in mind to soaring costs of raw materials, and compensate the converters accordingly. The other aspect is the condition of raw material sources for pre-payment and fluctuating supply schedule. Only if the three protagonists can find a workable solution that takes care of all parties involved, then the eutectic point can be reached and the equilibrium maintained.

Contd...

Cost vs Benefit

Cost optimization and savings have become the buzzword, and companies are looking for different avenues to slash cost. And at the same time product improvement, introduction of new products, alternates and substitutes with value addition and product branding is the order of the day. Amidst all these business demands, packaging has emerged as a key parameter. However to use packaging as the unique selling point, a company needs to rely on the newest technologies and novel material choices. Reducing losses, improving productivity and continuous research and development are also equally important. The package development exercise today has become a specialization. Also it is the joint effort of the supply chain and the product developers along with packaging specialist. The underlining principle should orient around rapid technology changes, search for flexibility, and greater competencies and globalization. This should help in organizational focus and facilitate changes. Most companies today outsource the expertise. The reason behind outsourcing is often not only to economize but to gain on time and service with greater access to broader resources. The in-house packaging professional however should not consider this as a threat. Working with external resources also benefit from reduced overheads, availability of broader skill and flexible times.

Approaches

The approaches to 'cost benefiting' can be many and varied. They can be traditional as well as sophisticated ones. Unlike conventional isolated approach, the strategy today is systems approach and takes into consideration several activities and their contribution individually and as a sum-up.

The analysis would essentially involve an in-depth value assessment of the current system - component wise, material-wise, process-wise, market-wise and possibly consumer-wise. A large number of factors like absence or inadequate specification, part or negligible quality control facilities and quality assessment, over-packaging, absence of information and or understanding of materials and development, under specification, pre-estimated level of cost of packaging all could lead to cost increase or product package damage/loss. For a systems approach, all these are either to be rectified.

A critical question is often raised – "Should the package development be initiated after the product is made ready" or 'conceptualized at the time of product design itself'?

If the latter is true then the stages need to be reviewed. If the former is true then one might like to revert back to the process itself. In either case, the industry should aim to get the maximum economic benefit through the complete package development and its role in supply chain management.

It is however important to remember that, the product-package movement distribution system and market practices determine the exact functional and POP responsibilities of a package.

Riding the Technology Wave

These are two significant vehicles available to the technologists to identify possible alternates that would help in optimizing the cost-effective system, both in terms of materials and process. A variety of new and improved barriers are today available that could replace the conventional ones with benefits of material inputs, better specification, better performance and cost reduction. The new material(s) can also be amenable to newer technologies of packaging systems, better machine performance and increased productivity. Lower grammege board with increased stiffness, improved temper tinplate and hence adoption of lower basis weight, higher impact resistance glass for regular type glass, higher denier of strand with lower mesh of fabric, reground and virgin combinations against pure virgin layers, and scores of such newer or improved materials offer specific possibility to better performance advantage with cast benefit.

The package development resources today also have the benefit of a large number of technology developments as effective tools in their exercises to identify the package type for cost reduction. Technology movements have seen from normal packaging to vacuum to gas flash to CAP/MAP system.

Contd...

Principles of Value Engineering

In any developing economy, most packaging systems in use are by evolution rather than by a systematic approach and design. Package placement and orientation, quantity per bulk, review of packaging components, alternates and substitutes, multiple packs, reinforcements and unitization are a few that could be the basis for the analysis. In quite a few instances alternate/substitutes not only help in material advantages but also help improve productivity besides inventory management and maintenance. A large number of case studies can be sited suffice to reflect the benefit of deployment of value engineering. Use of pressure sensitive label in place of pre or on-line glued label can be just an example. One gets a faster application, with reduced and near-zero wastage. More often, most packages are provided with reinforcement straps, angles, tapes, etc.

It may be wise to review the specification and explore if it is possible to eliminate any of the components or reduce the specification, either of which will result in cost cutting. It is not uncommon that wooden cases/ containers and crates are excessively strapped - both in number and strength, and this provides an area of cost reduction. Rigid containers to stand-up pouch and flexible bottles are typical examples, which can be used as effective substitutes and alternates. Increased productivity can be easily possible by using a self-locking bottom in a carton instead of tuck-n-type. Similarly with respect to strapping - metal or synthetics, a self-sealing (by heat of synthetic strap) and clinching of overlap of metal straps help to avoid the metal clips and an additional operation. These steps help in cost reduction in terms of material procurement, inventory maintenance, and other related administrative and stores activities.

The underlining principle in all such studies is to list all possible factors that could be the causes for unproductive-package and/or product failures. The analysis of the system through value analysis would also help identify areas leading to excessive costs.

Package Failure Factors

A large number of factors could be responsible for package failure. These could include failure to appreciate the importance and value of packaging, inadequate and lack of information and specification, and insufficient quality assessment knowledge and facilities. Specification, though important, often remains on paper. Acceptance and use of materials and packages without quality control clearance and quite often settling prices subsequently with reduction in price are some of the other common reasons for failure. Others include poor material planning and procurement becoming on urgency basis. Acceptance of materials under such circumstances can be the best example of 'specification for de-specification'. Another bad practice, which is unfortunately still prevalent is procuring materials/ packages against samples and in any packaging cost exercises — package components becoming the first source of cost saving.

Excessive Cost

In the zest to offer more protection, packaging has allowed additional costs to creep into the system. Some of the factors that lead to excessive or unnecessary cost can be identified as... inadequate information; lack of ideas; the habit and inertia revolving round safety; and safety resulting in excessive tolerances. Lack of capability, technology strength and back up, and shortage of time are others that add costs. Lack of facilities and responsibilities, and reluctance to obtain resources of appropriateness always result in excess cost and/or product, damage and loss.

Cost: The Ultimate Factor

The concept of cost has undergone a tremendous change, today. It has been established that packaging cost and its constituents need better understanding, and that too not in isolation or as a disintegrated activity. Today, packaging is a part of overall economic activity in the total supply chain management. It has relevance in many functions internal to the organization and external to distribution and marketing. And if used smartly, it is a resource that can work as a profit centre for an organization. The subject

Contd...

is a mixture of science, technology, engineering, business and management. But no means it is a cost without value. Only thing is that the subject needs to be understood in its rigid perspective to reap the benefit. The potential of packaging is enormous, and its impact far reaching, as it can trigger a chain reaction that could affect the entire dynamics of a business.

Source: This article has been authored by P V Narayanan. This article was published by Modern Packaging and Design, in the Nov-Dec 2006 edition. Copyright with Infomedia India Limited. Reprinted with permission.

Mind Power 5: Cost Management: Inter-organizational Impact on Cost

To manage costs across the supply chain, one should take into account the cost that can be viewed as costs incurred within the organization, costs incurred upstream and costs incurred downstream. This has been represented in Figure 16.1.

Further, these costs should be viewed not in isolation; rather one should look for ways to improve the cost structure looking at the buyer-supplier interface. Hence, the costs should be understood at three levels:

- Direct costs (material and directly traceable conversion costs)

- Activity-based costs (structural costs incurred at the individual organization level to support the business)

- Transaction costs (costs arising out of buyer supplier interactions)

These costs should be managed by understanding the possibilities of buyer supplier interface. Three key questions that can help in addressing these costs include:

- **Can the cost of products be reduced by taking advantage of inter-organizational synergies of product development?**

This concept can be understood better by looking at the automotive value chain (Figure 3). In the case of Indian auto majors like Tata Motors, Maruti and Mahindras, the supplier – primarily family members – get involved at the design stage itself. This approach drastically reduces the design and development cycle time.

Depending upon the criticality of the component and the capability of the individual supplier to design the product, outsourcing decisions are taken. The level of outsourcing too is determined on the same basis.

- **Can the cost of products be reduced by taking advantage of Inter-organizational synergies in manufacturing?**

In such a scenario, competencies of the individual supplier in manufacturing can be utilized better. Improvement to the supplier's facilities as well as process parameters can help to improve the overall cost of the supply chain. Engineering expertise of the suppliers is used to survive the cost pressures.

- **Can interfaces with our buyers and suppliers be made more efficient?**

Here, one will have to look for opportunities initiated either by the supplier or buyer or both together. Suppliers and buyers will have to look for actions to reduce the overall costs of the chain. Similarly, they will have to look for joint actions to be taken to reduce the overall costs.

Inter-Organizational Cost Management (IOCM) through buyer-led initiatives

Larger kingdom or barony buyers can help their supplier base to reduce the chain cost in various ways. For example, buyers can cluster their suppliers, introduce them to the best practices in the industry, provide training to improve their processes and thereby realize a better-cost advantage. There are a few companies in India that have started training their suppliers on various quality tools and management techniques.

Contd...

Buyers, who can boast of higher volume capabilities, can give their suppliers access to group savings. This can be done by representing the buyers to the common supplier or by grouping the component requirement and thus get a better deal from the supplier.

IOCM through Supplier-led Initiatives

Apart from focusing on giving a cost advantage to the ultimate consumer, there are various ways a supplier can lead the IOCM initiative:

- Suppliers focusing on improved on-schedule deliveries can reduce buffer inventories at buyer's end. Thus redundant stock can be reduced greatly.

- Suppliers reducing delivery cycle times can also lead to reduction of order to delivery time. Buyers can place orders later in the cycle. Thereby, the overall inventory in the system can reduce greatly.

- Suppliers initiative to improve their Overall Equipment Effectiveness (OEE) can also help to reduce the production cycle time. Thus, there will be tremendous reduction of uncertainty for the buyer. This too can reduce the overall inventory in the system.

- Extensive information sharing like sharing information on defect levels, cycle times and on-time delivery status can help the buyer to plan better.

- Passing on the benefits of improved inventory handling automated replenishment, vendor-managed inventory and direct on-line delivery are a few examples of this.

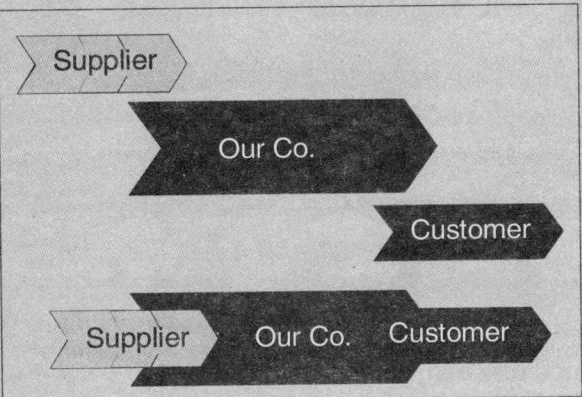

Figure 16.1: Looking beyond the organisational boundaries

Cost Advantages of IOCM

There are two specific benefits of better buyer-supplier interface. The improved interface efficiency leads to:

- Reduced inventory levels and

- Reduced transaction costs

Reduced inventory levels lead to a host of cost and competitive advantages like reduced obsolescence, released capacity in the plant, improved response to market and an improved bottom line.

Contd...

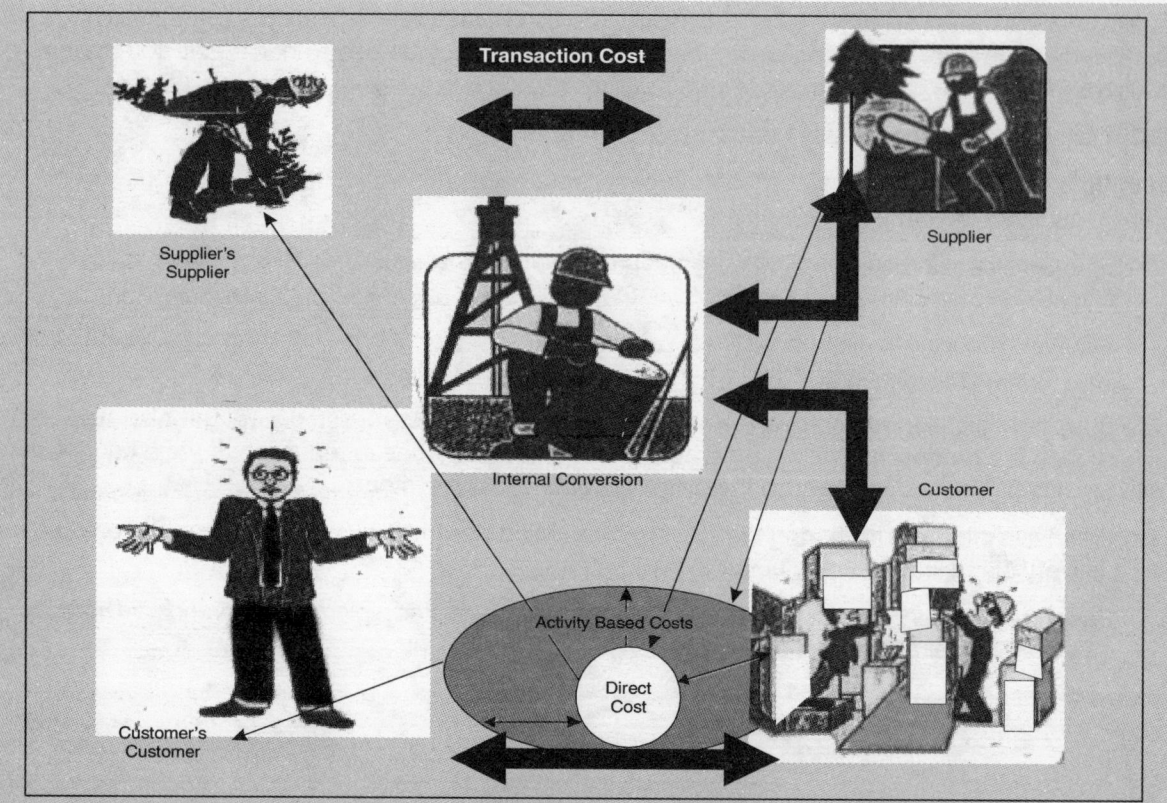

Figure 16.2: Supply Chain Costs

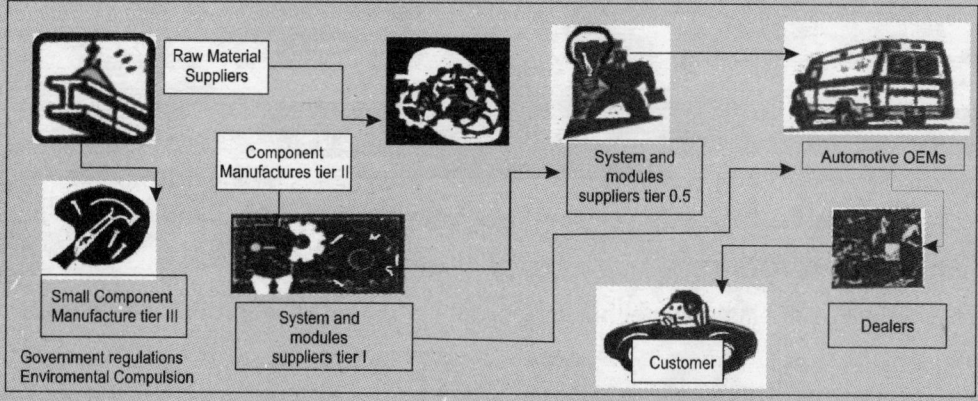

Figure 16.3: Automotive Value Chain

Reducing Uncertainty through Collaborative Forecasts

Dynamism and chaos are not synonyms. One of the major complaints against the OEM's is their constantly fluctuating daily requirement. In such a scenario, the supplier has to build stock to meet the ever fluctuating customer requirement. The process of planning is founded on uncertainty. One of the greatest advantages of improved buyer supplier interface is reduction of this uncertainty. Planning for a shorter time horizon is always more certain than planning for a month.

The changing customer requirement thus instead of becoming a planning nightmare, can improve the utilization of the supplier's resources better. Reduced uncertainty leads to reduced inventory levels through the supply chain. IOCM also calls for extensive information sharing, which can lead to

Contd...

collaborative forecasts. In an adversarial supplier relationship, both the parties try to plan for the inefficiencies of each other – supplier for the planning inefficiency of the buyer and the buyer for the inflexibility of the supplier. Collaborative forecasts can thus lead to reducing uncertainty. Reduced uncertainty leads to reduced inventory levels in the system.

Improving Flexibility

Of the three causes of bottom-line impact – revenue, cost and investment – CEOs tend to get fascinated by top line and investment. Both are perceived to indicate growth. Discussing cost is normally associated with struggle and survival. In the process, the third factor gets a backseat and the bottom line becomes red.

While attending a CEOs conclave of an industry association, the author came across several questions that were posed to the CEOs. One of the questions was, 'Should our industry invest more?' And, the response of all the panel members as well as the audience was a resounding 'yes'. However, the point that was missed out in all this commotion was that the Indian industry had enormous hidden capacities. For example, even though factories and plants are strained with excess loading, authorities claim that there is capacity in these plants.

But one should remember that capacity is not to be looked at from the point of view of what one produces but what he sells. Without policies of batch sizes, sequencing and other planning inefficiencies, he ends up producing for tomorrow and the day after, but forgets about the present. And, how many times has it happened that one oscillates between excess stock and stock out at the same time!

Flexibility comes from improving the cycle time - elimination of the *muda* of waiting time, non-operating time, reducing speed losses and quality rejects. These efforts release the capacity and improve the flexibility of the plant.

Improving Transaction Efficiency to reduce Transaction Costs

In an adversarial supplier relationship, one ends up doing redundant activities. For example; inspection is done by the supplier as well as the user. A host of activities to validate the quantity, quality and specification is done at both ends. This leads to commitment of resources for wasteful activities also increases the cost in the total supply chain. Identifying the activities that are performed at both ends to a larger extent can also reduce the transaction costs.

The second focus area for reducing transaction costs has to be simplification of transactions.

Further, e-intervention has led to tremendous improvement in the information sharing protocol along the supply chain. Standardizing transactions by e-enabling them can impact the transaction costs to a great extent. For example, key suppliers accessing the inventory database of the user to get the demand has started in a big way in India. A classic example of this is the e-Choupal of ITC.

Conclusion

Buyer-supplier interface is the most critical part of cost management initiatives. Effectiveness of this interface depends on mutual trust, interdependence and the extent of information sharing across the supply chain partners. IOCM can only be seen as a lip service as long as customers and suppliers view each other as someone out there to exploit.

Source: This article has been authored by M Hariharan. He is the director of Savoir Faire Management Services, Mumbai. This article was published with Modern Plastics and Polymers, in the December 2006 – January 2007 edition, published by Infomedia India Limited. Copyright with Infomedia India Limited. Reprinted with permission.

QUESTIONS FOR DISCUSSION

1. Pricing is the most important area, which effects the industrial marketer the most? Discuss.

2. "Why do most manufacturers prefer the cost plus pricing?" Discus it in light of other pricing techniques?

3. "Costs can never be accurately determined, as it is a moving target." Discuss.

4. How can an industrial marketer use the experience curve to its advantage?

5. Why is negotiation an important aspect of industrial marketing?

6. "Leasing is becoming an important alternative to selling industrial goods?" Discuss.

7. "Prior experience is very essential for industrial bidding". Discuss.

chapter
SEVENTEEN

Industrial Marketing for Global Markets

COMPANY PROFILE 17: AMARA RAJA BATTERIES

Amaron Hi-life, brought to you by Amara Raja Batteries Limited (ARBL), the largest manufacturers of Stand-by VRLA Industrial batteries in the Indian Ocean Rim and Johnson Controls Inc, USA; the global leader in Interior experience, building efficiency and power solutions. Amaron Hi-life batteries are made in QS 9000; ISO 14001 and TS 16949 certified using world class technology and stringent quality control parameters that make them last long. Some of the other features that add to making the Amaron Hi-life so good: longest life, patented BIC vents for enhanced safety, the highest cranking power and a completely unnecessary 36-month warranty.

Amara Raja supplies automotive batteries to almost all names in the country including Ashok Leyland, Fiat, General Motors, Hindustan Motors, Honda, Hyundai, Mahindra and Mahindra, Maruti and Tata Motors. The company is an exclusive supplier to Daimler Chrysler, Ford and Maruti-Swift platform.

Amara Raja received Ford India's highest recognition for supplier quality– the prestigious Ford Q1 awards and has also won the Ford worldwide Excellence award, one of the 24 companies, making it eligible to supply batteries to Ford worldwide. With the quest for growth and expansion of business beyond Indian shores, Amara Raja is poised to become a global player in the coming years.

Amara Raja's Industrial and Automotive batteries are exported to Singapore, Malaysia, Indonesia, Taiwan, Philippines, Greece, Australia, Kuwait, Dubai, China and Japan. In Singapore, Amaron supplies to the entire fleet of 'Comfort Delgro' cabs and had done an extensive branding of the taxis to enhance visibility thus capturing a sizeable market share; Amaron has proved to be the only battery that has twice the life when compared to any other battery even in the dry and humid desert conditions of Northern Australia. By virtue of its superior quality, Amaron has asserted itself under private labels in Japan, where stringent Quality and Technology are firmly adhered.

Amara Raja has also built a Battery Excellence Centre – the first of its kind in Asia. This research and engineering centre has been conceived as a completely self-sufficient facility with a full range of testing equipment. The centre incorporates all the latest gadgetry for battery performance evaluation, design and life testing and also has capabilities for application engineering, vehicle systems study, simulations and computer-aided design including a full calibration laboratory on site.

As a result, Amara Raja is uniquely placed to offer substantial benefits on sizing of batteries and electrical systems to its industrial and OEM customers and will be able to effect valuable improvements in product performance and manufacturing techniques. Furthermore, this centre will not only serve the needs of the domestic market, but also be a resource for alliance research and development projects.

Amara Raja's plant is located in Karakambadi, a village 12 km from the temple town of Tirupati. The existing facility is ISO 9001, QS 9000 and TS 16949 certified by RWTUV Germany. The plant is part of the most completely integrated battery manufacturing facility in India with all critical components, including plastics sourced in-house from existing facilities on-site. This gives Amara Raja complete control over inventory and product quality.

Amara Raja believes in taking responsibility for whatever we do within and without the company. It's what responsible leaders are expected to do. Our vision is to create communities that are economically and socially vibrant enough to stimulate growth and self-reliance; within and without the company. They have committed themselves in the fields of: education, infrastructure, village development, and environment.

Source: www.amararaja.co.in

Mind Power I: Potential Problems and Solutions when Hiring and Training a Worldwide Sales Team

Earl D. Honeycutt Jr, John B. Ford and Lew Kurtzman

Introduction

Currently, many US corporations are expanding their sales teams into the markets of East Asia, Eastern Europe, and the former Soviet Union. In addition, US firms continue to increase total sales to the European Union, NAFTA and Japan. Each of these areas has a very distinct culture which influences company business practices. The challenge for the international sales manager is to work closely with persons of different backgrounds, rather than attempting to impose his or her culture on them, to create teams of individuals who can reach company goals.

The purpose of this article is to point out the consequences of insensitivity to cultural differences encountered in international sales management situations, and to offer managers hiring and training suggestions which will improve their worldwide operations. To accomplish the article's purpose, alternative salesforce organizations, potential categories of salespersons, hiring criteria and sales training approaches are reviewed. Throughout, realistic examples that portray cultural problems encountered by US firms in global sales management situations are presented. Many of these examples were directly observed by one of the authors during years of international consulting.

Background

Salespeople are often hired according to the standards of the sales manager who has been successful in their native country. But when companies expand into global markets these same managers take on sales responsibilities outside the familiar business arena. For example, this phenomenon occurs when a US national sales manager becomes accountable for North American sales. Suddenly, Canada, Mexico, and Puerto Rico markets which are geographically close, but culturally diverse – are included in the area of responsibility. Because of these differences, hiring and training salespeople in each of these countries is considerably more complex than accomplishing these tasks within the USA. Customer expectations differ significantly by market, so the sales manager must now hire and train based on customer, rather than his or her own, expectations. Failure to do so can not only be embarrassing, but it can be extremely expensive and time consuming for firms that must constantly replace sales personnel and attempt to repair strained relationships. The following example illustrates this point:

A highly competitive and aggressive US sales manager, who believed that "winning was everything" regardless of the risk, was assigned to Canada and given a mission to hire a Canadian salesforce within a few months. He quickly hired the most aggressive, competitive people he could find. While this approach would probably have been a mistake in the US, it was disastrous in Canada, where customers expect to be treated with respect and not be pressured into a decision. The cost of lost business was high, as was the expense of rehiring and retraining both a new sales manager and a Canadian sales team.

Besides making decisions about hiring a direct sales team or selling through a distributor, sales managers must also decide how the selection process should be accomplished. To reduce the unknown factor of making these decisions in a global market, a number of firms have entered joint ventures (Jeannet and Hennessey, 1995). This article focuses on hiring and training problems faced by firms that export directly, use foreign sales subsidiaries, and/or establish local operations.

Companies that are actively engaged in global marketing can attempt to conduct all hiring and training activities. A number of firms, however, have found that utilization of a placement service in the new territory may be a wise and cost-effective alternative to trying to figure out the "right fit". Such a

Contd...

service can assist the international sales manager with the "do's and don'ts" of hiring and training within a geographical region. Currently, numerous US and European companies rely on these international recruiting/training services to reduce the costly mistakes described in this article.

Organizing the Global Salesforce

In international markets, where innumerable differences exist, firms often organize their salesforces similarly to their domestic structure around some aspect of geography, product, or customer (Hill and Birdseye, 1989). A single salesperson can be assigned to a specific geographical area of a developing market, with small sales volumes and similar languages or cultures. However, if the market is more complete, large, established, and multi-language/cultured then more specialized salesforce structures are required. Table I provides managers with a starting point for assigning their international salesforces.

Most global companies also include culture, as defined by the homogeneity or heterogeneity of languages spoken in the targeted market, when determining the appropriate organizational structure. For example, Belgium is often divided by language – French to the south and Flemish in the north, while Austria and Germany are combined because of each group's usage of the German language.

However, commonality of language is only one piece of a cultural mosaic, as the next example illustrates and, on its own, is incomplete at best:

Table I7.1: Organizational Structure

Structure	Appropriate Conditions
Geography	Undeveloped markets
	Small sales volumes
	Similar language/culture
	Single product line
Product/	Established market
Customer	Broad product lines
combination	Large sales volume
	Large/developed markets
	Distinct language/culture

Because of Spanish language skills, an international company assigned a salesperson from Puerto Rico to Mexico although many cultural similarities exist between the two countries selling in Mexico is quite different from selling in Puerto Rico. In Mexico, business is conducted over long, casual lunches that encourage the leisurely discussion of sports, food and family and the development of personal relationships. Once a friendship is established, then the business agenda is developed. Because of an inability to adapt to a slower selling pace and different relationship structure, the Puerto Rican salesman was unsuccessful and was terminated by the company.

In this circumstance, the sales manager wrongly assumed that Latin American markets were the same and that fluency in a language was a sufficient reason to assign the salesperson. Proper selection and training would have increased the likelihood that the manager understood the marketplace culture, felt comfortable in this new business environment, and could adapt to the new environment. However, in this situation, appropriate training was not provided.

Global Sales Organizations

A global firm has the option of using either independent sales agents or company salespeople. Outside the USA, about three-quarters of global firms use independent sales representatives (Hill and Still, 1990). When a company enters a developing market, agents are the economically prudent choice, although they generally receive a higher incentive commission rate because they are cost

Contd...

effective as long as sales levels remain low. Sales agents are expected to possess an excellent working knowledge of the respective market's supply/demand and customer base. However, there may be problems ensuring agents' loyalty to the company, especially when local firms are also represented.

A number of possibilities exist if management determines that a company salesforce is more advantageous. First, sales managers must determine who to hire for sales positions: expatriates, host-country nationals, or third-country nationals? Each category of salesperson will now be examined.

Expatriates as Salespeople

Expatriates are home-country salespeople and are favored by technical companies because of their high product knowledge level and ability to provide follow-up service. Many "big ticket" products are sold directly from the home office and automatically involve the use of expatriates. Overseas duty also provides companies with opportunities to train managers and prepare junior executives for promotion. Likewise, expatriates enable a global firm to maintain a physical presence and degree of control over international marketing and sales activities.

However, hiring and maintaining a first-class expatriate salesforce in the international arena represents a serious challenge. While the excitement of travel lures many into accepting international assignments, significant numbers of expatriates fail to complete their tour (Tung, 1982). Companies have found that, owing to poor selection practices, as many as half of those sent overseas are either ineffective or only marginally effective (Copeland and Griggs, 1985). Expatriates are also more expensive than local equivalents (Harvey, 1983). For example, the cost of maintaining a US employee overseas can reach $300,000 per year (Black, 1988). Finally, almost one-fourth of all American expatriates leave their companies within a year of returning to the USA (Gregersen and Black, 1992).

It is therefore extremely important to

- Confirm the level of expatriate commitment before individuals are sent overseas.

- Ensure expatriates are given sufficient incentive to stay with the company once they return home.

Appropriate hiring procedures can increase management's understanding of expatriate commitment and effective career counselling will communicate future planned responsibilities to the expatriate.

Host-country Nationals as Salespeople

Companies have a second option: hiring host-country nationals who bring extensive market and cultural knowledge, language skills, and familiarity with local business tradition to the sales position. Because of the abundant labor supply in most developing countries, it is often easier and less expensive to hire locally. And, in certain countries, laws exist which require companies to employ host-country citizens. Local sales personnel also permit a company quickly to become active in a new market, since the adjustment period is eliminated and potential difficulties caused by cultural alienation or language are minimized (Onkvisit and Shaw, 1993). As a result of these advantages, usage of host-country nationals has increased significantly over the past 15 years (Boyacigiller, 1990).

There are, however, several drawbacks to using host-country nationals: first, local hires normally must receive extensive product knowledge and be enculturated about the company history.

Second, trying to educate host-country nationals to change their behavior in favor of greater efficiency or a faster pace may defeat the purpose of hiring from this group. Behavioral expectations that are in conflict with long-standing customs will not be attained, and will probably cause friction between the manager and national sales organization. Therefore, considerable attention must be given to training within the cultural boundaries of the region.

Contd...

Third, in many cultures salespersons are not held in high esteem. In Europe, for example, selling is not considered to be an honored profession. Similarly, in the USA salespersons are often disguised as account executives and regional vice-presidents; French salespeople are routinely referred to as "consultants" or "commercial attaches" (Flynn, 1987). In Asian countries such as Thailand, Malaysia and India, this negative perception restricts the sales process between persons of different social strata (Hill, Still and Boya, 1991).

However, when business interaction does take place, the role of the salesperson is different from that in Western countries. For example, in India it is not uncommon for a salesperson to simply spout off product specifications to the buyer. When business agreements must be negotiated with someone of higher social status, such as the managing director or business owner, global companies may need to bring in an upper management representative.

In one situation an Indian buyer, who would not talk with local salespeople, welcomed a US manager to his facility and spent over three hours enthusiastically describing his requirements for some expensive process equipment. Knowing these requirements, it was easy for the US manager to make a recommendation for a full system. The final step was to negotiate a price with the Indian joint venture partner.

In many developing countries, the most coveted jobs are found in government or the professions. This attitude has forced global companies to consider sources other than university graduates for sales positions. In Central and Southern Africa, global companies have found that the army is an excellent source of sales recruits because administrative skills, discipline and steady work habits are stressed (Samli, 1993).

Fourth, the increased usage of English in business transactions has decreased the importance of local hire language skills except for certain industries, such as textiles (Linen, 1991). Although hiring globally is a complex process, assistance for managers in navigating regional laws and customs is available through reputable recruiting agents.

Third-country Nationals as Salespeople

The last option available to global companies is the hiring of third-country nationals. Similarities across markets within a particular region allow global companies to take advantage of third-country nationals' cultural sensitivity and language skills and gain access to skilled and/or less costly workforces not available in potential overseas markets. In many cases, third-country nationals are an effective compromise between expatriates and host-country nationals.

Several dilemmas are encountered by third-country nationals, however, including identity difficulties. The problem is that the nationalities of third-country salespeople have little to do with where or for whom they work (Cateora, 1993). Also third-country nationals experience other obstacles such as blocked promotions, transfer anxieties, income gaps and unfamiliarity with, and difficulty in, adapting to new environments (Zeira and Harari, 1977).

Selecting and Training the Global Salesforce

Given the morass of cultural pitfalls discussed above, it is extremely important for international sales supervisors to address properly the management activities of sales selection and sales training. Too often, sales managers assume that the fundamental skills of probing, presenting benefits and closing apply everywhere. The notion of hiring "closers" is an American inclination which is offensive to most Asian, as well as many European business people. The necessity of developing trusting relationships and negotiating agreements is far more important in most countries than the aggressive competitiveness cherished by many US sales managers.

It is also vitally important for sales managers to understand the great impact of cultural influences on both of these activities. In the best of situations, US managers try to overcome cultural influences in

Contd...

favor of higher efficiency or proven techniques for closing a sale. In the worst of situations, global managers find themselves in disastrous scenarios due to their cultural insensitivity!

For example, an American international sales manager tried to convince a Japanese sales team that they should always ask buyers "why" they had decided to buy from a competitor. The Japanese sales team viewed this action as challenging buyers to justify their actions and as an accusation of poor judgment consequence, it was not done!

Sales Selection

Selecting salespersons for international markets is much more complicated than it is for domestic markets. Worldwide companies report using educational levels, interviewing skills and previous experience to select international sales personnel (Hill and Birdseye, 1989). However, sales managers must also be aware of other situationally specific, cultural factors—such as religion and social class—when selecting international salespersons. The country of Malaysia offers an example of how cultural factors complicate sales encounters. First, tensions exist between the Chinese, who dominate commerce, and Malays. Second, cultural differences are accentuated by religious differences (e.g., Muslims versus Buddhists). And, finally, because society is highly stratified, Malays are not comfortable when social positions have not been clearly defined (Hill and Birdseye, 1989).

Sales management must also clearly define the employment opportunity to potential sales personnel, without over or under-selling the job. Formal job analyses and job descriptions, with special requirements identified for each target market, greatly improve the selection process. These steps also aid in identifying, early in the process, the appropriateness of expatriates or foreign nationals for the position. An extensive list of interview criteria is available for managers to use when interviewing international candidates (Noer, 1975).

Most technical companies hire salespeople based on their technical background and experience (Harzing and Ruysseveldt, 1995). For instance, it is common practice in Germany to hire PhD scientists as salespersons for chemical equipment. The rationale is that, to gain credibility and be viewed as competent, the salesperson must hold educational credentials similar to those of their customers. However, technical sales personnel are seldom effective without receiving extensive sales training immediately after being hired. Without sales training, the technical salesperson has a natural tendency to migrate back to the laboratory with the intention of solving the buyer's problems. The result is that too much time is spent focused on long-term technical projects rather than on sales goals. Additionally, the buyer can become overly dependent on the salesperson for free technical support.

In Germany, a salesman with a PhD in Chemistry helped a customer solve a chemical separation problem in the process of selling some analytical instrumentation equipment. After the purchase, the salesman was expected to continue to work on the research project by the customer, at the expense of developing new business and spending time with customers with less interesting projects.

A large portion of the hiring and training process must be the selection of technically knowledgeable candidates who can be trained to perform business in accordance with the culture of his or her customers. Since technical information is factual, product training can easily transcend the cultural differences; whereas, sales training must be conducted according to cultural commonalities. An example of problems encountered in this area includes the following:

A US citizen was hired for his technical expertise and assigned to a sales territory in South America. His vigorous comparisons of apartheid and US segregation in the South earned him a swift transfer back to the United States, and reassignment to the laboratory.

Sales Training

Each culture views sales training differently and sales managers must move cautiously when attempting to transfer sales training methods from one country to another. For example, unlike US firms, European

Contd...

and Japanese corporations view international training as an important area of attention (Harzing and Ruysseveldt, 1995). To operate successfully in cross-national sales training requires patience and an appreciation of local culture and religions. Two interesting stories, observed by one of the authors, serve to illustrate this point.

One international company scheduled a sales training session in India during Diwali, a sacred Hindu holiday. The meeting was called by the general manager, an Argentine expatriate, and the president of the international division, a Frenchman. No Hindu employee was willing to travel to the resort city of Goa for the meeting.

At another product training session in India the instruction, which consisted of overhead projectors and VCRs, was interrupted by power cuts, which are common in India and can last for several hours. Although the Indian trainees were accustomed to the delays, the American and British instructors became frustrated and critical of the interruptions.

Since languages vary so dramatically, sales trainers must exercise caution when translating training manuals, and be aware of the role language has on thought and behavior patterns. Also, sales managers must understand that it may not be proper to teach their problem-solving techniques to global salespersons. This is especially true for American companies training Japanese or Chinese salespersons.

In another instance, a company president assigned a sales manager to Japan for a three-year mission to "show" the salesforce how to sell "American style". This plan immediately caused embarrassment to the Japanese general manager and a loss of face for the entire sales team. In this case, the American was perceptive and quickly took a backseat role and re-established himself as a consultant to the general manager. He listened carefully to the Japanese salesmen and learned their business customs. After the first year, he was accepted by the Japanese sales team as a competent business partner who was willing to share ideas about effective selling strategies. Although he failed to change the Japanese to American ways of selling, he succeeded in helping the Japanese to become better at selling "Japanese style".

Methods of instruction also vary by culture. For example, in Japan salespeople receive on-the-job training in a ritualistic formal setting which ensures that constructive criticism does not result in "loss of face" for the trainee (Hill, Still and Boya, 1991). An excellent, but costly, example of management insensitivity occurred in Taiwan during an Asian training mission.

The American vice-president of Asia and his staff visited Taiwan to assess the training needs of distributors. The Taiwanese group had been struggling for over a year, and it was agreed the company would provide them with training. The Taiwanese were anxious to host and suggest ways the American group could help. Rather than listen to the Taiwanese, the vice-president presented sales figures proving they were "the biggest problem in Asia". They were subsequently told that training would be withheld until they "shaped up". The loss of face was devastating and resulted in emergency measures to repair the damage. It took years of apologies by senior management and negotiated concessions to undo the bad feelings. One of the first concessions was the replacement of the vice-president with someone who possessed more tact and understanding of Asian culture.

If a company selects expatriates to represent them in overseas markets, they must be carefully trained and sensitized to the culture of the overseas market. This responsibility includes a basic knowledge of the area's language and culture (Honeycutt and Ford, 1995). No matter how loyal to the company or knowledgeable of its products, cultural alienation renders an expatriate salesperson ineffectual. For example, a salesperson who discusses business over lunch in Switzerland, fails to display appropriate levels of modesty in Japan, or someone who touches a Thai customer on the head, will probably not be successful with their clients (Hill and Still, 1990). Other ways expatriates can offend through cultural faux pas include failing to understand that Canada and Puerto Rico have their separate identities, for example. One North American sales manager met with his Canadian

Contd...

sales team, and immediately offended them when he exclaimed that: "Canada was the fastest growing territory in the United States!"

Sales managers must remember that Puerto Rico is a US Commonwealth. Although citizens of Puerto Rico do not vote in presidential elections, they are US citizens. One way to lose the confidence of the Puerto Rican sales team is to treat them as a foreign country or "banana republic". Not only is Puerto Rico a significant market for many companies, but payment in US dollars is guaranteed.

Sales personnel should receive training in such areas as how to sell in the new global market (even if they have extensive domestic selling experience), company policies and procedures, product line and performance information, and local market conditions, particularly as they pertain to the level of competition and customer base (Honeycutt and Ford, 1995; Erffmeyer et al., 1993). Trainees must also fully understand their clients' culture and how international sales are accomplished in the marketplace. It is also important, in order to reduce early burnout after reassignment, to include the spouses and children in the cultural and language portions of the training programme (Noer, 1975).

Implications for Managers

When sales managers must make decisions about selecting and training an international salesforce, they should contemplate the guidelines presented in this paper for increasing the objectivity of their managerial decisions. Specifically, sales managers should consider the following points.

Carefully examine the cultural differences that exist between the home and global markets.

Managers should thoroughly compare and analyze the different cultural elements which exist in the home and potential markets. By expanding on the conceptual model of Terpstra and David (1985), the cultural elements to be considered are:

- language
- religion
- level of education
- politics
- law
- the concept of time
- aesthetics (or what the culture believes is beautiful)
- social organization
- values and attitudes and
- technology (or material culture).

The purpose of this examination is to determine the similarity or dissimilarity, when compared to the home market, of the markets to be served. Analytical results allow the sales manager to predict more accurately needed modifications of home country management practices. A recent practical example of the need for cultural sensitivity involved a US company conducting business in Japan.

Despite being warned that managers in Japan were appointed based on seniority, a US international sales manager felt that a 32 year-old salesperson had earned a promotion to president of the subsidiary. This manager never had a chance and immediately suffered severe problems. To rectify the situation, the US manager next sent an American senior manager to Tokyo to assist the president – which only worsened the problem. After a nervous breakdown and a divorce, the young man resigned.

Carefully examine the nature of the products to be sold in the prospective foreign markets

The types of products appropriate for prospective foreign markets are dictated by the nature of the cultures involved. The elements of culture most appropriate for this analysis are level of education,

Contd...

technology, values and attitudes, and language. These elements may dictate a different type of sales-force than that which the company has used in its home markets, as well as provide a good means for determining which of the home product assortment are appropriate in the prospective foreign market. Potential customers may not be technically literate enough to be able to use some of the company's more advanced products or, if they are more technologically advanced, company products may already be obsolete in the prospective market. For example, this potential problem was evidenced in Apple Computer's early foray into China.

Apple Computer was one of the very first computer companies to develop a presence in mainland China; however, the early purchasers of the products were government officials who did not know how to use the products, but only wanted to have them on their desks. It would be years before the newly computer-literate Chinese consumers would constitute a large enough market to be cost effective (this story was related to the authors by a visiting dignitary from the Chinese Ministry of Finance).

Carefully examine the nature of the customers to be served in the prospective foreign markets

Knowledge of the customers also greatly influences the appropriateness and effectiveness of the salesforce in the prospective markets. Determining the needs and motivations of potential customers allows the sales manager to choose the right type of salesperson and the right type of product mix for them to sell. When dealing with the foreign customer and his or her wants, needs, and motivations, all aspects of the cultural elemental mix should be assessed so that no important element is overlooked. This potential problem is apparent in the following true story.

After four years of design and development, a chemical analyzer was put on the worldwide market. The controls for the instrument were located on the top panel of the analyzer. While this was appropriate for tall operators, it was a strained reach for anyone under six feet tall. The product was redesigned once it was discovered that most Asian operators needed a step stool to turn on the analyzer. By the time the analyzer was redesigned and remarketed, however, competitors had made significant advances in Asia. The product died within a year.

Understand that sales management practices will be dictated by the culture of the foreign markets which will be served

All aspects of sales management (selection, hiring, training, promotion, motivation and dismissal) will need to be modified to accommodate the foreign cultures involved. The extent of that modification will, of course, be dependent on the degree of the dissimilarity to the home market. It is important to determine whether a regional orientation allows economizing of the salesforce organization. For instance, are the different countries in that particular region of the world similar enough in relevant cultural considerations to allow economies of standardization? In many cases, total localization is cost prohibitive and total standardization produces cultural insensitivities. Conversely, regionalization allows a certain amount of cost-effective standardization and economies of sales management. This need for cultural awareness and sensitivity is evidenced in the motivation of a Japanese salesforce by a non-Japanese company.

Team achievement is a national obsession in Japan. An individual's accomplishments are seldom announced, much less publicly celebrated. It is a mistake to have an international awards banquet and cite a single Japanese salesman as "Top Achiever". Japanese modesty and group orientation is rooted so deeply that Western managers must be prepared to invite the entire Japanese sales team to receive awards and citations.

Do not decide on the type of salesforce or training to be used in the prospective global markets until all previous checklist steps have been completed.

The international sales manager should not attempt to determine the composition of the salesforce for the prospective foreign market(s) until all of the previous issues discussed above have been addressed. If any one of these steps is left out, the mistakes which may result could be disastrous.

Contd...

The amount of work required of sales managers, however, is not necessarily onerous. It does require a thorough process of intelligence gathering that will take time and require patience.

The sales manager should visit the countries involved and experience them first-hand. Discussions should likewise be conducted with salespeople currently doing business in the country. Country experts, such as international recruiting and training services, can be retained to provide guidance for dealing with hiring and training issues. Sales managers should also attend trade shows in prospective markets and collect helpful information from other sales managers and salespeople in their particular industry. Finally, the US Department of Commerce has extensive foreign trade show experience and can easily arrange for sales managers to attend key industry events. If the pitfalls inherent in dealing with sales management issues in foreign markets are to be avoided, strict attention to intelligence gathering is a necessity.

Conclusion

International sales managers may appear to face similar situations that exist in domestic markets; however, appearances are often misleading. The differences encountered in the global marketplace are extraordinarily complex and require extensive cultural understanding and sensitivity if correct decisions are to be reached. A company's movement towards globalization can be fraught with disaster unless the sales manager realizes that an in-depth knowledge of culture is an absolute necessity. Sales managers must consistently view global situations from this new perspective rather than clinging to old and familiar domestic paradigms that are inapplicable. In order to reduce the probability of managers incorrectly handling selection and training opportunities for their international salespersons, this article has identified common problem areas, supported by real-world examples, routinely encountered by managers.

Throughout this paper references have been made to the high cost of insensitivity to differences in global social and business practices. With the best of intentions, managers intensely try to create change by getting people to do things their way. However, the international manager can only be successful by allowing people to accomplish company goals their own way. Otherwise, international sales management is truly an oxymoron.

Source: This article has been authored by Earl D. Honeycutt Jr, John B. Ford and Lew Kurtzman. Earl D. Honeycutt Jr and John B. Ford are Associate Professors, both at the Old Dominion University, Norfolk, VA, USA. Lew Kurtzman is President of Grown Resources Associates, Wilmington, NC, USA.

This article was published in Journal of Business and Industrial Marketing, Vol 11 No 1, 1996 pp 42-54. Copyright with MCB University press. Reprinted with the permission of the author.

INTRODUCTION

Today, doing business in India has changed. We are no more a part of the "conservative" society, but are exposed to the global marketplace in terms of our business. Prior to 1990, when business in India was mostly a domestic affair with few firms opting for overseas offices, things have changed drastically from then on. Today with the opening up of the marketplace and with encouragement of free trade we have seen a lot of ups and downs. Indian marketers that were nationally oriented have shed their image and have gone out to conquer the global marketplace.

Doing business in the global markets is not only a challenge but also has a great deal of hidden opportunity attached to it. The business environment drastically varies from country to country and the challenges are unique in each country with some marketers being able to cope up with the global pressures, others have not and have eventually been wiped out of the market.

The global business is divided into two fronts. On one hand, we have highly specialized, technically-oriented and capital intensive developed countries (USA, UK, Japan, EU) and on the other hand we have labour intensive developing countries (India, China). Each of the 'fronts' has their own set of advantages and disadvantages, with labour being cheap in the Asian and African countries, a lot of the manufacturing and assembling works are being outsourced and even companies from developed markets are opening their bases in the developing countries.

Moving into global market has its own set of advantages and disadvantages. As we have said earlier, the environment under which an industrial marketer would work, would be entirely different from the one he encounters in the domestic market.

In this chapter, we will see the following aspects of international marketing:

- International marketing environment.

- How does a business market expand and how to enter into it?

- Marketing research and marketing intelligence in global markets.

- Segmenting, targeting, positioning in global markets.

- Product, price, channels and promotional decisions in the global markets.

Mind Power 2: Singapore Used As a Conduit for Credit Card Fraud

If you receive a credit card order from Singapore, check it out before you ship. The Commercial Service of the U.S. Embassy in Singapore has received ongoing complaints from firms that have been defrauded by companies and individuals in and around Singapore using stolen credit cards.

What to look for?

The orders normally range from US$ 5,000 to US$ 30,000 using one or several credit cards. The "buyer" places the order for everything ranging from bicycle parts to medical equipment using the credit cards for payment and then requests immediate air shipment. The exporter processes the payment and ships the goods immediately as per the "buyers" request. Sometimes the "buyer" even places a second order if the first one processes without a problem. A couple of days later the bank informs the seller that the credit card(s) were fraudulent and the amount is charged back. Since the goods have already been shipped the seller has neither the money nor the merchandise. Frequently the "buyer" asks the shipment to be sent to a freight forwarder located near Changi Airport, Singapore's main airport. Once received, the goods are likely sent to neighboring countries making the items very difficult to trace or recover.

Source: United States of America Dept of Commerce: www.buyusa.gov

INTERNATIONAL MARKETING ENVIRONMENT

International marketing is a much more challenging role for an industrial or consumer marketer, because of certain uncertainties in the international marketing task. Now, in the domestic market, the marketer has certain controllable factors, i.e., the product, price, channels of distribution and research. But there are certain uncontrollable factors in the domestic environment. They are:

1. Potential/Legal forces

2. Competitive structure

3. Economic Climate

Every foreign country, in which a company operates, adds its own set of uncontrollable factors. In the foreign environment, the uncontrollable factors are:

1. Economic forces

2. Competitive forces

3. Level of technology

4. Structure of distribution

5. Geography and infrastructure

6. Cultural forces

7. Political/legal forces[1]

Economic development, policies, monetary, taxation structures, legal and political factors also play a very important role in the uncertainty of international business operations. The cultural factors although do not play an important role for industrial goods, but is important to be understood for negotiations with international partners. Recognizing, understanding and appreciating the changes surrounding the industrial marketers in global markets are very essential. Once it is done, the basic principles of industrial marketing remain the same. A word of caution here is that, the slightest of mistakes can cause huge losses to the industrial marketer and therefore careful steps needs to be taken for the foreign market operations.

POLITICAL AND LEGAL ENVIRONMENT

While we speak of international marketing environment, the first thing that we need to discuss is the potential and legal environment. The stability of the states is a major factor of influence for international industrial marketers. The state of politics, in a particular country, would determine two major things:

1. How should an industrial marketer enter the particular country, i.e., what would be the ideal mode of entry.

2. Should the marketer enter into the particular country concerned? What are the risks associated with such countries?

Now, the international marketer should be cautious of certain factors in the international political environment. They are:

1. *Restriction of trade and other monetary controls:* Protection to domestic trade is one of arguments that are given by developing nations. Not only that, any country would possibly be interested in their own development and protection, than allowing goods to be entering their stores. Therefore to restrict the flow of imports countries put in barriers, in terms of tariffs, quotas and voluntary agreements. Although the purpose of tariff is monetary income to the government, however quotas are for restrictions. Countries with unfavorable balance of payments or suffering from inflation or unemployment or stagflation impose barriers to protect the domestic economies. The restriction to trade does not end here. There are other forms of restrictions like VER (Voluntary Export Restraints) and boycotts. Japan has a VER on its automobiles to the United States not only that United States has banned products from Iran, Iraq and Cuba.

Governments also restrict monetary controls on "foreign companies" to protect their domestic environment. The restrictions could be in terms of:

❖ Repatriation of profits to parent foreign companies

❖ Technology transfer restrictions

❖ Usage of home country products for assembling or manufacturing

❖ Restriction of sale on particular products

❖ Price ceilings, differential taxations for foreign companies

❖ Restrictions on investment in particular sectors, specially the ones at a very nascent stage of development.

❖ Restrictions on expatriates working for a company.

All these restrictions have for a number of times caused problem to foreign companies. This was obvious specifically during the prime ministership of Indira Gandhi that IBM and Coca Cola had to leave Indian shores.

2. *Political risks:* It is ideal for any marketer to have a stable and friendly government. However it always does not remain the same way and there exists a lot of difference in the outlook of the political parties. The government philosophy undertakes a change, when there is the opposition party coming into power and there are conflicts, which raise big doubts on the stability of the marketer. Take the example of India post-liberation and how many governments and their ideologies have changed over a period of seventeen years.

This is also aggregated with other problems like tax controls, price controls labour problems, political sanctions, violence and terrorism. The worst probably of all the political risks is confiscation in which a company's assets are sized, without paying them a single pie. This has happened in Cuba. The next risk is that of expropriation when the government seizes the investment but makes some kinds of payments. The last risk of all is domestication, when a foreign firm transfers all its control to local citizens.

It is almost near to impossible to completely reduce political risks but it is possible, if as an international marketer we appreciate them. The first thing that we must attempt to understand is that, how vulnerable is the product to the economic development, welfare of the people and the environment. Also, a company needs to assess the political risks and try to forecast the political risks. Although, it is next to impossible but the risk can be reduced to a great extent by foreign companies.

ECONOMIC ENVIRONMENT

Policies and economies are two brothers. They go hand to hand. Economy of a nation does not follow a straight path to growth. There are a series of ups and downs. Economic environment can cause severe damage to the industrial marketer in the international context. With the examples of the past with Indonesian Rupiah, Thai Baht, Korean Won and Ringit of Malaysia depreciating severely in the 1990s can be a serious cause of concern for the international marketer. Three major contributing factors which need to be looked into before stepping into the international markets are:

1. Balance of Trade and Balance of Payments

2. Exchange Rates

3. Trade Alliances

Balance of trade is the difference between the value of exports and imports of a particular nation, whereas balance of payments is a record of all economic transactions between residents of a country and rest of the world. The Balance of Payment (BOP) is divided into two parts.

- Current account which is a record of all trade in goods, services. It also includes gifts and public and private aids between countries.

- Capital account is a record of long-term investment portfolio investments, short-term capital flows and long-term capital flows and also reserves of bullions and foreign currencies with the central bank.

Both the current and the capital accounts have a receipt and payment side. When the payments are more than the receipts, there is a deficit in the balance of payments. When the situation is reversed, there is a surplus in the BOP. However the former is the case with most of the countries across the globe.

The figures in the BOP give a clear picture to the international marketer as to the feasibility of putting money in such economies. When deficits of the BOT or BOP are higher, with weak currencies and poor reserves, the marketer should be concerned and cautioned with establishing base in such countries. Exchange rates from the 1970s have been allowed to float. It was prior to this, that exchange rates were mostly fixed. With fixed exchange rates, it was very easy to make a payment or receive a payment from foreign nations. But with "float" coming in, and no one being able to ascertain the future value of the foreign currency, finds it difficult in international markets. This is true, specifically for organizations which are dependent mostly on overseas revenue.

Any firm with an overseas operation must monitor the foreign exchange fluctuation, to protect themselves. So, when the value of rupees is weak in comparison to the buyer's currency, companies generally employ cost-plus pricing. "When the rupee in India, depreciated significantly against the US dollar, PC manufactures faced a serious problem. Because the manufactures depended on imported components, their option was to absorb the increased cost or raise the price of PC's."[2]

The changes in the currency exchange rates are a cause of concern to most international marketers. So if an international marketer is looking in for a partnership in a foreign nation, for a longer term, the pricing strategy needs to reflect variations in currency rates.

One more radical change that has been seen in world trade is the interest amongst nations to have economic cooperations. This was probably imitated with the European Union and today we have multiple economic and regional cooperation amongst countries. Be it a simple preferential trade agreement or a full scale economic integration, countries have been able to draw mileage of such an agreement. The complexity involved in handling business across the globe is huge and one way to reduce such a risk is to focus on regional economic agreements.

Mind Power 3: Doing Business in BOSNIA and HERZEGOVINA

A multi-tiered and divided two-Entity government creates a confusing array of regulations, fees, taxation, and standards requirements. The two entities are the Federation (FBiH) and the Republika Srpska (RS). This confusion results in a lack of transparency and opportunities for corruption in business-government dealings. As a result, it is strongly recommended that US companies engage locally knowledgeable people to assist in business operations in BiH or contact the embassy in Sarajevo for assistance. The Commercial Service at the Embassy assists U.S. companies in exporting to Bosnia and Herzegovina by identifying local opportunities for the sale of US products or services, providing counseling on the market, and meeting the advocacy needs of US firms.

There is no single best way to do business in Bosnia and Herzegovina. New entrants to the market will most likely be displacing/supplanting nearby supplies such as from Croatia and Slovenia, as well

Contd...

as dominant EU member country exporters. Of course, a regional strategy can build on existing trading patterns and customers if the market does not justify a full-time presence.

Sales agents, representatives and distributors all have important roles to play in this market. Regardless of which channel is selected, sales support and after-sales service are critical. Financing is a key factor for a Bosnian company making a decision to take on a new U.S. product line.

For a new-to-market company, there is no substitute for a local partner. Make your selection based on his or her knowledge of the local market – your focus should be to support your partner with the proper training and sales materials.

Source: United States of America Dept. of Commerce: www.buyusa.gov

CULTURAL ENVIRONMENT

The effects of cultural environment are very strong for consumer goods industry as the requirements from country to country vary. But in the case of industrial goods it is not so. A car tyre manufactured by MRF and being supplied to Ford motors, would be quite similar to the car tyre supplied to Toyota in Japan. The products remain the same, however certain specifications might change.

The cultural environment becomes a greater issue in cases of personnel selling and negotiation. The negotiation could be at any stage. It could be while searching for a "joint venture" partner or in cases of a capital equipment purchasing. With cultural differences across nations, these become a cause of great problem for the industrial marketers in international environment. The nature of differences could vary, from timeliness, shaking hands, exchanging cards, written contracts or invitation for a dinner after the meeting. Thus expatriate salespeople and managers who go in for negotiations or for the purpose of selling should be careful about these issues.

The main elements of culture are:[3]

- Attitudes and beliefs
- Attitude towards time
- Attitude towards work and leisure
- Attitude towards achievement
- Attitude towards change
- Attitude towards job

Whatever we do or say or behave is purely due to our attitudes and beliefs. They vary from country to country and sometimes across regions. If we understand the attitudes and beliefs of a society, we as international marketers would find it very useful.

With different people coming in from different cultures, attitudes towards time would be different. Some countries are very time conscious, like Germany and USA, while some are not like the Asian countries. This attitude of timeliness varies to a great extent from country to country and within regions. Say for example; local trains of Mumbai and Howrah. They are poles apart. The Mumbai locals would maintain time to the last minute, whereas it is a rare phenomenon for the Howrah locals. Public holidays are also an issue in some countries, where people go on a tour on holidays, some of the people work extra hours in some countries on those holidays. In Latin America, for example, no business deal would ever take place till the time the buyer is not confident on the seller and should have at least met the seller three or four times on informal occasions.

People in industrial societies work for greater number of hours than necessary. Attitudes relating to security in life, steady income and the ability to take risk vary across countries.

Money always is not a great motivation across the globe. Countries with Buddhism, as the principle religion do not believe or have less faith in money as a motivating factor. Even, Japanese have similar perceptions on money.

Americans (North Americans) would stress on written explicit contracts. But the same is not true for Middle East Countries, Japan and even South America. In all of these countries, until you have commitment, friendship and interest developed in each other, business would not go ahead. Friendships for them are treated as social commitments.

In some of the cultures, which follow a set hierarchy, there is a tendency of avoiding personal responsibilities and following instructions from the top (India).

The people of this culture their attitudes and beliefs, percolate down their systems and the behaviour is quite similar in fashion. While working with international clients or expansion of business, these cultural considerations form a very essential part for the marketer to understand. Differences in verbal languages across nations and non-verbal communications (like time, space, agreements, negotiations, etc.) will make every selling and transaction unique. This is also a great challenge that an international marketer should bear in mind.

MODES OF ENTRY IN INTERNATIONAL MARKETS

When a firm has to go international, they must choose the way of entry. There are multiple modes of entry. They are:

- Exporting
- Licensing
- Franchising
- Strategic Alliance
- Joint Venture
- Foreign Direct Investment   Control   Ownership   Complexity of Business

As a marketer moves on from simple exporting to the foreign direct investment mode of entry, the control and ownership increases, as well as complexity involved in taking decisions as to foreign investment is higher than any of previous modes of operation. We would discuss each one of them in detail. But, before the marketer takes a decision as to what mode of entry needs to be chosen, he has to critically appraise each market. For implementing that six criteria must be followed:[4]

1. Market potential
2. Market access
3. Shipping costs
4. Potential competition
5. Service requirements
6. Product fit

When an industrial marketer wants to expand its base into the overseas market, the first and foremost thing the marketer should keep in his mind is the level of experience he has in overseas markets and the kind of risk he would be willing to shoulder.

Exporting

An industrial marketer has the first entry to international markets with exporting. Exporting can be generally of two forms, i.e., direct and indirect. In direct exporting, the industrial marketer sells the product directly to a foreign customer, whereas in indirect exporting, the industrial marketer sells it in his home country, to a buyer, who exports the products. Exporting means, the amount of commitment and risk is the least amongst all the methods of entry into a foreign market. If an industrial marketer is new to international markets, wants to reduce commitments, wants to minimize cultural, political and economic risks, this method is the ideal.

The biggest problem with exporting decisions is on the future issues of growth in a particular country. Also, due to lack of compete control, the strategies may or may not fall in place at certain points of time. This causes problem. Moreover, as we have discussed in our earlier chapters, that industrial marketing works better by building relationships. That is sometimes different with exporting.

"In Germany, exporting is a way of life for the Mittlestand, 2.5 million small and midsized companies that generate two thirds of Germany's GNP, and account for 30 percent of exports. For companies such as steel maker J.N Eberle; Trumpf, a machine tool manufacturer, and J. Eberspacher, which makes auto exhaust systems, exports account for as much as 40 per cent of sales."[5]

Licensing

It is a form of contracting, where a company permits another to use its intellectual property in exchange for a fee or royalty or licensee fees or some other compensation. The intellectual property as we know could be patents, trademarks, technology, brand name and even the industrial designs.

Licensing is a much more popular mechanism for market entry. But it would work only when the company has a brand image. The advantage for licensing however is that there is no investment and the commitment levels would be low and therefore for companies who are looking to establish bases, find licensing useful. It can also be used to enter into countries where the government regulations do not permit or the barriers are too high.

Franchising

It is a form of contracting and another form to licensing in which the franchisor or the parent company grants a franchisee, the right to conduct businesses in a specific manner. The franchisor gives the products, services and systems while the franchisee provides knowledge, capital and involvement. The parent company has a considerably higher degree of control and can regulate the franchisee in terms of its operations. It could be selling of a product or method to produce or could be a business approach. There is also another form of contractual entry, called as the "contract manufacturing". It involves sourcing a product from a manufacturer in a foreign country for selling there or in other countries.

The last form of contracting is called as "management contracts". In management contracts, there is a bundle of skills that are provided to the client.

Strategic Alliances

It is a mode of entry into international markets, when a relationship is formed by two or more companies to cooperate due to mutual needs and share the risks. Strategic alliance is used when the partnering companies want to enhance their competitive positions, by leveraging from the resources of one another.

The problems for strategic alliances are seen, when:

1. Trust and coordination become a big issue and cause of concern for both the partnering companies.

2. For industrial marketers where rate of obsolescence is higher, strategic alliance may not turn out to be fruitful after sometime.

Often, strategic alliances become an issue of concern and implementational issues come into the picture within a short period of time. So careful selection of partners is very essential for successful strategic alliances. Effective coordination, amongst partners and focus on global customers should be of paramount importance.

Joint Ventures

The level of involvement is higher in international joint ventures than in any of the methods discussed above. When there is a local partner working, the political and cultural risks are minimized. Joint ventures are a better way than acquiring a company in the international markets. Joint ventures are thus an agreement to produce and/or market goods in a foreign market. In strategic alliances, the individual identity of the firms remains, but in a joint venture there is a formation of a separate legal entity.

Joint ventures are a form of access in many of the developing countries. For example in India, in life insurance governments have a policy for foreign players to enter into Indian markets with Indian partners. In some of the cases, both partnering companies are jointly able to pursue a large objective or goal. Also cultural and political aspects being taken care by home country, joint ventures give a certain breather to trickle the issues of new culture and policies.

The pitfall of joint ventures is that most of them fail. These are generally due to lack of clarity, choice of partners. There are also disagreements amongst partners on sharing of profits, key decision-making, and clashes in the style of management. Choosing the right partner is very essential for the success of joint ventures.

Consortia are an extension to joint ventures, where there are a large number of participating companies involved. Also, they operate in countries, where none of the partners are active. Financial and other resources are pooled in by various participating companies and one of the firm acts as a lead firm. The biggest consortia, however, is of Airbus, formed with four European companies coming together to fight Boeing.

Foreign Direct Investment

It is the most complex and highly risky venture. This involves a lot of key strategic questions to be answered by the industrial marketer and companies generally go for FDI, for the purpose of lower labor costs, attractive market opportunities, reduce cost of transportation and to gain access to raw material. For FDI, there are options of either investing in a local company or to acquire it (Tata-Corus) or probably start from scratch. Industrial marketers may want to access through FDI route, because of better access to markets, especially amongst countries with a trade agreement.

Whatever be the mode of entry, an industrial marketer chooses deep commitment is required at top management levels. Also the mode of entry into the market, getting the right kind of deals, matching of cultures amongst partners is very essential. Whatever is the form of entry, it costs money to the industrial marketer and it could pinch the marketer severely if it fails to work. It is thus necessary, at least in international markets not to expand till confident about the partners in business.

Mind Power 4: Making Appointments in Switzerland

Meetings are always by appointment.

The Swiss are perhaps the most punctual people on earth. You should arrive for any engagement at precisely the appointed time, not early–your counterpart may be unprepared–and certainly not late. This is especially true in the German-speaking areas, where arriving even five minutes late for a business meeting or a formal social engagement can cause offence. Although French and Italian speaking areas tend to be slightly more relaxed about time, punctuality is always the best policy.

Should you be invited to an informal social event at a Swiss home, you should aim to arrive 15 minutes after the given time in the German areas and up to 30 minutes late in the French and Italian speaking areas.

You must be well presented and remain polite at all times.

Source: www.executiveplanet.com

REGIONAL MARKETS

The economic factors are one of the strongest reasons as to whether an industrial marketer should enter into a particular comity. On the level of the economic activity, a particular country is having, the industrial marketer should align his marketing task. In markets, which are more rigid, the market patterns would be significantly different from more flexible and open markets. Markets which are dynamic and economies which are growing, give a special kind of challenge to industrial marketers and the activities relating to marketing must be matched with the changing needs and wants.

Before discussing the regional markets, it would not be very inappropriate to discuss Walt W. Rostow's, stages of economic development. He had spoken of five stages. They are:[6]

Stage 1: The traditional society: Countries in this stage do not have high levels of productivity. They are lagging behind in technology and science with low levels of development, infrastructure and literacy. Most of the people deal with basic commodities. Most of the African countries, especially the north and the east African countries are examples.

Stage 2: The preconditions for take off: Some sciences, which are in use in developed countries, are being used in some of the fields like agriculture and industrial production. The problems of traditional society have completely not gone, but some signs of improvement are being seen in telecom, construction, etc. Burma (Myanmar) and Vietnam would be examples of this stage.

Stage 3: The take off: Growth happens in these countries. Growth is a normal condition in such countries. There has been steady development in modernization and mechanization of industrial and agricultural sector. Russia and India would be examples of this stage.

Stage 4: Drive to maturity: Once growth is achieved, there is progress and the economy goes international. The quest to produce low cost goods starts. Modern technology captures all the fronts of business. South Korea is at this stage.

Stage 5: High mass consumption: There is a shift in leading economic sectors to consumer goods and services. Examples would be Japan, Germany, USA and Singapore.

It would be really difficult and beyond the scope in trying and analyzing all the countries. But to understand the regional markets a little better, what can be done is to group those countries into few clusters and try and derive some meaningful insights from it.

Mind Power 5: Business Customs in Spain

There is no substitute for face-to-face meetings with Spanish business representatives to break into this market. Spaniards expect a personal relationship with suppliers. Initial communication by phone or fax is far less effective than a personal meeting. Mail campaigns generally yield meagre results. Less than 30 per cent of local managers are fluent in English.

Spaniards are more formal in personal relations than Americans but much less rigid than they were ten years ago. The biggest mistake a U.S. businessperson can make is to assume doing business in Spain is just like doing business in Mexico and Latin America; Italy or France would be a better comparison. A handshake is customary upon initiating and closing a business meeting, accompanied by an appropriate greeting. Professional attire is expected. Business dress is suit and tie, and business cards are required.

Spaniards tend to be "conservative" in their buying habits. Known brands do well. Large government and private sector buyers appear more comfortable dealing with other large, established organizations or with firms that are recognized as leaders within their sectors.

Spain is a developed and stable democracy with a modern economy. Tourist facilities are widely available.

Source: United States America Dept of Commerce: www.buyusa.gov

---

Europe

It is one of the most prosperous and developed regions of the world. Europe can be divided roughly into two parts – the Western Europe and the Eastern Europe. The Western Europe consists mostly of people of the EU (European Union), with some of the highest per capita incomes. But still there exists considerable differences in the per capita income of Italy, Portugal, Switzerland and Norway. Some of the best industries with German engineering are widely known. Out of the Fortune 500 global companies, 9 chemical companies, 5 industrial equipment companies, 6 refining companies, 7 telecommunication companies are from the EU (The figures are of the industries where EU leads compared to USA, Canada and Japan).[7]

Eastern Europe, on the other hand, has been mostly politically turmoiled with the influence of communism. Their per capita incomes are comparatively low, compared to their Western counterparts. On one hand while countries like Poland, Hungary have higher per capita income, some of the other countries mostly fragments of erstwhile USSR are relatively very poor.

North America

It includes USA, Canada and Mexico. The GDP figures are at par with the European Union. All the countries are rich in natural resources; and have high per capita income, except Mexico. Mexico had been in turbulent time with growth rates less than 1 percent, with inflation levels touching 150 percent; however with changes in economic policies Mexico is undergoing massive changes. One interesting facet is that, over 25 percent of Canada's GDP is through exports. The three countries form a part of NAFTA agreement.

Latin America

South America or Latin America has some promising economies like Chile, while some others like Brazil are growing very fast. Countries like Argentina, Peru, and Columbia are still in the grip of problem with low growth rates and double digit inflations. Latin America is, however, growing with great recovery signs.

Asia Pacific

It is the biggest of all the continents, with huge diversities. On one hand, highly advanced economies of Japan, Singapore and on the other hand low-income countries of Pakistan, Nepal, and Sri Lanka. In the midway there are economies like China, India, Thailand, Malaysia and Indonesia. This zone of the world has over 50 percent of the world population but only 26 percent of global income.

Africa

It is one of the most underdeveloped regions with South Africa contributing the maximum GDP to this region. Widely diverse regions, still in primitive stages and often inflicted with civil wars. Some countries like Somalia, Ethiopia, Congo, and Eritrea are highly poverty stricken regions of the world.

Marketing industrial goods to all these regions of the world would definitely be challenging.

MARKETING RESEARCH

We have studied marketing research before, but here we would study it from an international perspective. When we conduct a market research for international markets, the environment being different across countries poses a challenge. Also another challenge as a researcher would be communicating across boundaries and require special skills, for example, translating into English to Mandarin and French.

Generally, for international markets research in carried out on three broad avenues. They are:

1. *General information about a particular country:* It might include features like economic, social, political climate, general markets conditions. In the general information, the marketer would try and understand the positives and negatives to do business in a particular country.

2. **Forecasting international market trends** is another area of research. For example, if Ashok Leyland wants to market its trucks to European countries, then what are the business trends within a particular country or a region?

3. *Specific Market Details:* The next area is about specific market details on products, pricing, channels and promotional strategy.

Now international research would follow quite similar steps of that of a domestic research, but some changes have to be made.

Step 1: Define the objective of the company and the nature of information required.

Step 2: Defining the problem.

Step **3:** Choosing units of analysis and determining the sources of information to fulfill the objectives.

Step **4:** Do a cost benefit analysis of the research.

Step **5:** Gather data from primary and secondary sources.

Step **6:** Analyze and interpret the data.

Step **7:** Present the data and findings to the decision maker.

The issues in international marketing research are plenty. It first starts from the fact that every country presents a unique feature and opportunity. Thus analyzing unique characteristic of every country or markets becomes a tough task. Also any kind of research activity has a limited budget and time. Industrial marketers would not be interested in putting too much of resource or budget for countries which "seemingly" may not be attractive.

Many of the countries like Russia, Eastern Europe and African countries have poor quality data or the data is inflated to show a very rosy picture. Sufficient proof on this has been found for the Russian economy. In our country also, availability of correct, accurate and comprehensive data is still a big challenge. In some countries like China and Japan, the researcher needs to have adequate knowledge to read, interpret and analyzes secondary data. Question on the reliability of data comes in for the international market researcher.

There is a problem often faced by a researcher, i.e., the comparability of data. For example, the technical requirements of electrical equipment would vary from country to country. Problems relating to socio-economic data also cause itch to a researcher. For cases of primary data collection, the problem may stem from ineffective translation or poor communication. The translation, as well as the researcher has to very apt in the languages in which the research being done. A poor translation of the questionnaire can result into poor data collection. The primary data collector can have problems when the respondent in some of the countries might not be willing to give information or could be problems relating to reaching the right set of samples.

Even with standard data gathering techniques, definitions differ around the world. In some countries, these differences are minor and in others they are quite significant. Germany, for example, classifies television sets purchase as expenditures for 'recreation and entertainment', whereas the same expenditure falls into the 'furniture, furnishings and house hold equipment' classifications in the United States.[8] So if you are a manufacturer of picture tubes and want to know the potential of it in the USA and Germany, comparing data would be difficult.

Researching on the Internet is seen as a growing phenomenon and an area of great interest for international market researchers. With Internet becoming a powerful tool, accessibility to data is becoming very easy and cost effective. Even some amount of primary research in international environment is being done by the Internet.

INTERNATIONAL PRODUCTS

The complexity faced by industrial markets in international markets would be comparatively lower than consumer goods industry, but certain points needs to be kept in mind. They are:

1. *Economic development:* Some pages back we had discussed Rostow's stages of economic growth,[9] with economies of each country undergoing five stages of economic development. They are:

   ❖ Traditional society

❖ Preconditions for take off

❖ Take off

❖ Drive to maturity

❖ Mass consumption

The level of economic development would be quite helpful for the industrial marketer in the international environment to determine the nature of goods and services required. However, drawing direct conclusions or generalizing would be difficult and would require further validation of data to predict accurately. Also, an important point to be kept in mind is the level of infrastructural differences that is predominant in many countries. "Load shedding" or "power failures" are a nightmare in the United States or Japan. Some of the countries have strong inland waterways, to transport goods, than roadways. These differences in infrastructure, need higher degree of product adaptation. A pilot project to test the amount of roughness that can be handled by a computer (which is low priced) for village students is ongoing. Some countries would require simplification of products. Also, due to availability of cheap labour, manual machines are more predominantly used in the developing countries. For example, for cutting wood, manual saws would be preferred in India.

Challenges, thus, for marketing an industrial good in developed and developing countries are different.

2. Cultural factors play a crucial role in determining the product strategy. In Middle East, all equipments have to supplied with extra electric coil and in some region, the electronic gadgets require local symbols. It will play a crucial role in industrial services, as there needs to be a lot of personal contact with the foreign company.

3. Political and legal factors play a crucial role in product design. The stringent norms like emissions from automobiles, designing of the engine, would be highly specific in the developed countries, wherein legal factors would be less specific in developing nations. However environmental norms are equally stringent in developed and developing nations.

4. Technological factors are quite related to the economic considerations that an industrial marketer must focus on. The need for high level of mechanization, due to high labor costs in the developed nations is dramatically different from the technological and mechanization requirements of the developing nations.

INTERNATIONAL PRICING

Although pricing practices tend to be the same, some differences are there in terms of governmental regulations, parallel imports, transfer pricing, counter trades and dumping.

Governments sometimes play a very critical role in the fixing up of prices. In some countries, government puts a ceiling; establish rules of margins and discounting, subsidies and price changes. Generally, the commodity market trade faces the maximum axe of the governmental regulations. Government also gives indirect loan facilities and manufacturing facilities, excise holidays, which affect the pricing decisions strongly.

Counter trade is a very important tool in the hands of the international marketer to achieve a competitive advantage. Counter traders are common in Eastern Europe, South America, China and Africa. Four variations of counter trading are seen in the markets — Barter, Buy back, Counter purchase and Compensation deals. Barter is the direct exchange of goods between two parties; buy back is when the seller agrees to accept partial payment and the rest output, or receive the full price and purchase a part of the output. Counter purchase is when seller agrees to sell his product at a price to a buyer. There is a second contract where the seller buy's the goods from the buyer for the complete amount, or a percentage of it. Compensation deals are the ones in which part of the payment is in cash and part is in goods.

Dumping is when goods are parked into foreign countries to dispose off excessive inventory at prices lower than costs. This is good for the purchasers of the dumped products, but is not good for the economy, as revenue earnings to the government and prices in the domestic market would fall. Government does have strong mechanism to prevent this. International marketers should take care to prevent this image.

INTERNATIONAL CHANNELS

Distribution is not only about moving goods across a country or region. It involves more functions like storage, handling, inventory carrying and packaging. Domestic distribution structure would be entirely different from international markets. Each country has a unique structure through which goods pass. With the Japanese distribution structure relatively complex due to presence of small middleman and controlling of the channels by manufacturers, while the West European countries have a fairly straight distribution structures.

The level of service that is offered by a middleman or the channel members vary considerably. Margins of the middleman and the breadth of goods a distributor carries vary from country to country. In the international markets, industrial manufacturers may also find problems, with relation to non-existent channels and blocked channels, wherein a channel is blocked from being used by an international marketer.

Any development in the international markets, in terms of new products or new technologies, is exported to other advanced industrial nations. Now the particular product gets spread to all developed nations. By this time the product is exported to less developed and developing markets. Here, most of the developing nations start producing the same goods and the sale of the goods starts falling in the origin country. At a later stage, the originating nation becomes the importing nation, because the good gets produced with simple tools and with labour-intensive methods. Industrial marketers can take advantage of this international PLC for their benefits.[10]

When a global industrial manufacturer is expanding its base to other nations he encounters two basic problems. The first one is in relation to existing stronger players in the market and the market structures may prevent an industrial manufacturer to establish the base. So either a better channel incentive system needs to be designed or else the manufacturer has to set up its own channels in the foreign country. However in such a situation, a direct salesforce is a viable option. But with sales not being able to cover up overhead costs it can act as a deterrent.

Mind Power 6: Making Appointments in Argentina

To conduct business in Argentina, it is necessary to obtain third party introductions through institutions such as law firms, consulting firms or banks.

Contd...

Should you need to reach a decision maker, you must go through his or her personal assistant or secretary. Politeness is essential when dealing with these intermediaries as they determine the order in which visitors get access to their bosses.

Appointments need usually to be scheduled one to two weeks in advance. Working hours differ; in Buenos Aires, people in decision-making positions may work non-stop from 10-00 AM to 5:00 PM with a short break for lunch at 1.00 PM [which may often be turned into a business lunch]. In the provinces, managers start earlier, have a break around 12:30/1:00 pm, resume work at 4:00/4:30 pm and then continue until 7:30/8:00 pm.

Punctuality is appreciated and expected from visitors to Argentina for all business related occasions. However, you may find your Argentine counterpart to be 15 to 20 minutes late! Guests to home invitations are expected to show up some 15 minutes late. For a dinner party, guests can arrive even 30 minutes late.

Source: www.executiveplanet.com

INTERNATIONAL PROMOTION

For industrial manufacturers in the international markets, personal selling is one of the strongest promotional tools. The challenge of using personal selling however, is from the fact that the buyer and seller meet from different cultures and the requirements are different. A buyer from the United States would prefer a written, contract, whereas a Japanese buying firm would focus upon oral agreements, trust and relationship building.

In 1993, a Malaysian developer, YTL corporation sought bids on a $700 million contract for power generation turbines. Siemens AG of Germany and GE were amongst the bidders. Datuk Francis Yeoh, Managing Director of YTL, requested meeting with top executives from both companies. "I wanted to look them in the eye to see if we can do business" Yeoh said. Siemens complied with the request; GE did not send an executive. Siemens was awarded the contract.[11]

Salesperson in the international markets can be of three types:

- Expatriates
- Local nationals of foreign country
- Third country nationals

While expatriates (who are from the parent company) have advantages like product and company information, they lack the cultural skills required for the purpose of negotiation. When products are highly technical and require exclusive application based knowledge they are the best. Often they add prestige to the product line in the eyes of the foreign customers.[12] They are also well-trained.

Local nations are preferred in cases when at sales, cultural factors play a strong role. Also maintaining local nationals are much cheaper than having expatriates. They also have a strong knowledge about the distribution channels of the country concerned.

Trade shows form another crucial role for international industrial marketers not only to generate sales lead but also good exposure in foreign countries. Also, a comparison of products can be done by the industrial purchaser. They also provide a great opportunity to establish relationship with agents, distributors and franchisees. Trade shows are unique and almost any kind of market in any country can be targeted through this medium.

Advertising for industrial products is not much discussed except for press advertisements, due to media coverage, governmental regulations and widely varying nature. However, direct mailers still are a more popular choice, if the contacts of the decision-making units can be strong enough.

CONCLUSION

For an industrial marketer international markets are a great challenge. The challenges are from the difference of cultural, political, social, and economic environment. Seeking business from only domestic markets or excessive reliance on only one market post globalization is not a feasible option, specially bearing in mind, the derived nature of industrial demand. In international environment, possibly every factor is uncontrollable with strong influences of political, economic and cultural forces. Problems relating to distribution, geography and infrastructure, competitive forces, level of technology play a crucial role.

We discussed the various modes of entry into the international markets and the level of control, ownership and complexity involved in each of the cases. Marketing research also plays a crucial role and the challenges are quite different from domestic markets.

At the last part of the chapter, we saw how the product, pricing, channels and promotional decisions are affected in the international environment.

References

1. Cateora and Graham, *International Marketing*, 12th edition, Tata McGraw Hill, pp 10-11.

2. Cateora and Graham, *International Marketing*, 12th edition, Tata McGraw Hill, pp 541.

3. Vasudeva, *International Marketing*, 3rd edition, Excel Publication, pp 259-260.

4. Keegan, *Global Marketing Management*, 7th edition, Pearson Education, pp 264.

5. Walt, W Rostow (1971), *The Stages of Economic Growth*, 2nd edition, London, Cambridge University Press, pp 10-11.

6. Onkvisit and Shaw, "*An examination of the international product life cycle and its application within marketing*", Columbia *Journal of World Business* (Fall 1983), pp 73-79.

7. Bruchli, "Looking East: Asia on Ascent, Is learning to say no to 'Arrogant' west", *The Wall Street Journal*, 13th April 1994, pp A1, 48, Adapted from Vasudeva, *International Marketing*, 3rd edition, Excel Publication, pp 407.

8. Cateora and Graham, *International Marketing*, 12th edition, Tata McGraw Hill, pp 504.

Mind Power 7: Mergers and Acquisitions: How to avoid the mourning after

Whenever you read an article about merger and acquisition, it's usually a lightly edited version of the official press release. What you don't read about are the bloody backstage battles that took place as the stakeholders maneuvered, and manipulated the detailed terms of the deal. Nor do you read about the mess after the deal.

Usually there's a big dog and a small dog, whether the parties involved admit it or not. The small dog is hoping to line his pockets, and the big dog is hoping to pick those same pockets.

Contd...

After the deal is signed, the revenues that were roaring along at the small dog company often come to a screeching halt. Partly because the revenues were pumped up unsustainably while the small dog was trying to get acquired, but mostly because of the problems that always plague mergers and acquisitions.

There is always a shake-up in top management; the founder often moves on, or gets pushed out, leaving a power vacuum. The managers, who are left, are consumed by the need to assert themselves and grab a good position within the new political structure. Employees become anxious and confused, because the only clear signal they're getting from management is that there are "overlaps" in infrastructure, and "cuts will be made". The best employees start checking out the job market.

Customers who are always leery of mergers and acquisitions anyway, defer buying decisions. They want to see if the new, combined company is going to continue to meet their needs.

This is a very dangerous time.

Here are some of the "back room" realities that are seldom discussed, and ways to deal with them.

Marketing: Who are we now? What promises should we be making?

Recognizing that your brand is the promise that you keep, not the one you make, takes us to the core problem with mergers and acquisitions. Each company has been making, keeping, and breaking certain promises. Customers, vendors, and business partners all know what to expect from the original two companies. Once the deal is done, all bets are off. It's a new ballgame.

Customers are asking themselves: Is it getting easier to get what we need from this company, or harder? Are the salespeople happy about the deal, or griping about it when they come to call? It's one or the other, and griping is more usual.

While customers are wandering if the new company is going to deliver on time, the marketing people and managers spending days in closed-door meetings with branding consultants, up with an "Image" for the new company. The result is a typical "exciting new company" campaign. Yawn.

They could save themselves a lot of money and hours if they simply called customers of the companies and asked them a simple question: "As you know, Company X just merged with Company Y. You have been doing business with Company X. In your mind, what promise they been keeping for you? What have you come to expect from them?"

The answers to these questions would point the way to the promises the new, combined should be making – and keeping. Customers would reveal the "essence" of what each company was known for, and what each company did best.

This customer-supplied information should serve as the foundation for the subsequent corporate and product positioning. At the early stages, it may be best to devise a message that mentions both promises, such as, "Company X service and Company Y products. The best of both." This will allow you to ride any positive momentum from before the merger, and give you some time to develop a new promise, as the combined company starts to develop its own character and capabilities.

Salespeople, the flag, and the hill

Salespeople are most productive when they know what their flag says and which hill they should running up. If they are uncertain about what their flag should say, or which hill they're supposed to conquer, your sales are going to suffer. If the confusion continues more than a few weeks after the deal is done, they will start looking for other jobs. You will lose your best salespeople and all the deals they had in the hopper - within months after the deal is done. The less-motivated, less-effective salespeople will only add to customer concerns about the new situation.

The customer interviews we mentioned earlier can help you create the right flag and choose the right hill. Then you must gather the salespeople from both companies into a room for an all-day meeting,

Contd...

where you hash out the details, including overlapping and conflicting account assignments. Companies that combine forces are often selling to the same customers, and sales turf wars are common and paralyzing. The salespeople will look busy, but they will really be concentrating on selling their internal rivals down the river. A salesperson will never pick up the flag and run up the hill when he is watching his back and has one hand on his wallet.

There should only be one sales manager over the new combined team, and that person should be given the power to make territory decisions. The sooner the salespeople know where the lines are, and what their assignment is, the sooner they can get back to running the flag up the hill. Even if they don't like the decisions being made, they will give it a try, just because they are optimists. But they must have clear direction.

Customer databases/support: Which will dominate?

After the deal is signed, you'll have two or more customer database systems, almost certainly incompatible. Should you scrap them and build a new system from scratch? Should you try to build that will integrate them?

No. Not yet. Now is the time to decide which the most efficient system is. That system is now the official system. Port the data from the other system into the official system, then shut down the "weaker" system. The people who understand the official system must then train the people who are coming over from the dead one.

If you scrap and replace both systems right off the bat, absolutely nobody will know how the new system works. There will be no one to turn to in case of a problem. Customer service will collapse.

Make the switch as clean as possible. It won't be perfect, but it will allow, you to keep taking orders and servicing customers. Use the same "sole survivor" method for your customer service and distribution infrastructure.

Over time, you will be able to improve your customer-serving systems, but doing so immediately after a merger or acquisition is asking for trouble. There simply isn't any way you can know, that early in the game, how the best system should work.

Culture: How is information communicated? How are decisions made?

Top management sets the tone for the company's culture. But there are also the day-to-day, worker-to-worker and manager/worker interactions, which boil down to two things: Communication and decisions.

Communication: Every company has its own communication style. Styles range from formal to informal; continuous to infrequent; spur-of-the-moment to rigidly scheduled; face-to-face or electronic. Normally, the new management team of the combined company is unaware of these differences. The result is a debilitating tension will undermine every meeting. Or, the big dog managers will try to impose their methods on everybody else. The problem with this method is that big dogs tend to drone along endlessly, whereas the small dog usually communicates more efficiently. The company should move more in the small dog's direction.

Managers need to have a meeting to resolve communication differences; right after the deal is done. They need to analyze what both companies have been doing and decide on an "official" meeting style going forward. They should agree on meeting purposes, players and schedules, and then communicate their decision out to the troops.

Decisions: Employees, customers, and partners will become discouraged and disillusioned if the new, combined company starts making decisions more slowly than the previous company. This is bound to happen simply because there are now three entities to consider in every decision (the two old companies and the new combined company).

Contd...

As with the communications style, most of the time this problem is pushed aside and the result is it intrudes on every single meeting for months. Instead, managers need to face the fact that it's a problem, and devote a couple of meetings to it. They will need to decide who is going to have the last say on certain subjects, based on that person's success in that area. They will also need to decide if they want to use the "open discussion and vote" method of making decisions, or the "expert presents, then the members discuss, then vote" method (which is usually more productive).

Revenues can get streaming again, soon after a merger or acquisition, if managers are aware of the pitfalls and address them head-on right after the deal is signed.

Source: By Kristin Zhivago on Feb 16, 2007. Visit her at www.zhivago.com or www.revenue journal.com. Reprinted with permission. Copyright rests with the author.

Mind Power 8: Doing Business in India

When doing business with Indians, Westerners sometimes have a hard time understanding their customs. This can lead to miscommunication and misunderstandings. However, growth can flourish if an effort is made to understand Indians ethnic values. It pays to follow the adage: "When in Rome, do as the Romans do." Read on for a primer on the formal and informal customs and conventions of India today.

1. *A perspective on time:* Indians are not particularly renowned for their punctuality; they are perceived as laid back people who only watch the clock when it's close to quitting time. While that may be true for a small percentage of the population, such as government servants, the vast majority follow a different strategy. For most of the world, time is precious; for the Indian, it's auspicious. One look at the Indian calendar should give you a clue–it's never complete without the list of auspicious and inauspicious times and dates, be it weddings, christenings, new ventures, C-section births, or just stepping out of the house for the first day on a new job. The average Indian allows auspicious times to dictate his activities. Don't dismiss this belief as superstitious nonsense. Remember that the West has its own superstitions: Friday the 13th, black cats and stepping on sidewalk cracks.

2. *Addressing issues of respect:* When compared to the numerous vernacular languages spoken in India, English is much less polite. Indian languages, unlike English differentiate between peers and those who are older and command respect. That's why the average Indian tends to address people as "Sir" or "Ma'am," or affix the title "Mr." "Ms," or "Mrs." before their names; they don't want to come across as disrespectful. English, on the other hand, is more informal. Americans generally prefer the use of first names. Remember that while most younger Indians will welcome the informality of first names, older ones may consider it an affront, especially if the speaker is much younger.

3. *Comfort zone:* A casual hug, peck on the cheek, or an arm thrown around a shoulder may not seem out of place in the West. However in India, even shaking hands with a member of the opposite sex is only in the process of being accepted. The exception to this rule is a handful of metropolitan cities. With the younger crowd drifting to the cities in search of jobs, multinational IT companies and call centres, they're adapting fast to the casual touch. However, spouses are often uncomfortable with this personal contact. Be mindful that your idea of touch may be too close for Eastern comfort.

4. *Strikes-even when the iron's not hot:* There are times in India when all activities come to a screeching halt: shops down shutters, people remain closeted in their houses, public transport is shut down, and private conveyances are stoned or pelted if they dare make an appearance.

Contd...

This strange phenomenon, termed a "bandh," is a source of bewilderment for the foreign business houses in the country. They're not sure if they should declare a holiday: if they do, their offshore work suffers, clients back home are furious, and precious time and money go down the drain: if they don't, they risk being the target of angry, irrational mobs. With political clout usually behind these bandhs it's best to go with the flow.

5. ***The creaky wheels of bureaucracy:*** One of the downsides of the great Indian adventure is the political parties that wield a huge amount of power. Industrial ventures are not easy to set up. At times, you'll need to grease their palms. And just when you think you've won them over, with your powers of persuasion and financial might, the next election rolls around and another party is lodged in the seat of power. No matter what progress you've made with their predecessor, it's back to square one for you. It's extremely frustrating, but that's the lay of the land.

6. ***Festivals: The flavor of sub-continental life:*** India has its fair share of religions, each of them with festivals. A few are short and sweet, but the rest are long, drawn-out affairs. Reasons for celebration range from the long ago slaying of mythical demons to the bountiful harvest that is reaped in the present. National holidays are declared for a few festivals that are celebrated by the majority, but there are others that often go unobserved. Overseas companies should anticipate and accept employees asking for vacation time around these days. It will be more appreciated at this time than around Western-centric Thanks giving, Christmas and the New Year.

7. ***Marriages are made in India:*** An Indian wedding, especially one that goes on for days, is one of those things that you have to see to believe. In India, marriages are occasions for large get-togethers. They include not only the immediate family, but also the extended cousins, aunts, uncles, grandmas, grandpas and new additions to the family. Keep in mind that it's not just the groom or bride who'll be asking for time off: even a distant third cousin will deem it imperative that he or she attend and enjoy this three or four-day affair.

8. ***Familial fraternization:*** The joint family system, prevalent in India for ages, is being nudged out by the nuclear family, a new discovery for the modern Indian. Even so there are many who still have aged parents and infirm relatives living with them. A good Indian son's duties include taking care of the elderly in the family. Understandably, a broken bone or heart attack will require the son's, and often daughter's, attention. Employers must be compassionate during these lines of family crisis,

9. ***Sometimes the office is taken home:*** Invitations to the home for business discussions are not uncommon. Don't be anxious if you're asked to lunch or dinner. Indians are very hospitable; the woman of the house will go to great lengths to prepare something she knows, you'll enjoy. On your part, you'll earn brownie points if you treat your host's family with courtesy and respect. A small gift is greatly appreciated when you're visiting a business partner's home.

10. ***Small talk is big:*** If you are hosting the business meetings remember that Indians are not as direct as their American counterparts. They generally start with small talk and relatively unimportant topics before migrating to the main issue. They also place importance on refreshments during the course of the meeting, either at the beginning, or in the middle during a break, depending on the time of day.

11. ***Going by the book:*** While Americans are generally more result-oriented, caring more about the end result, than the path taken to get there, Indians are sticklers for policy. They are used to following preset steps to arrive at a solution, usually because they do not want to get into trouble with someone above them in the hierarchy. Most of them are afraid of stepping out of line, but if encouraged to try new methods, they will be happy to do so.

12. ***Don't toe the line:*** The word "queue" has no significant meaning to the average Indian. The country has developed in leaps and hounds, but a few of its citizens still think that leaps and

Contd...

bounds are the way to go when asked to queue up at a public facility. Even the most civilized person can be reduced to fighting for his rightful place when others form a mass of people all jockeying to be first.

13. ***Call them more than cards:*** Indians place a lot of importance on business cards, handing them out even for casual occasions. A stranger will offer you his card, if you so much as ask him his name while you're traveling on the same train. He's not being pushy: it's just his way of packing his name, profession, and other details onto just one card.

14. ***Transport, traditions and travails:*** If you spend some time in India, you may be forced to test its public modes of transportation at some time or another. You'll find that your fellow passengers will be more than happy to help when you find yourself unfamiliar with the local lingo or have difficulty deciding where to get off. On the other hand, local auto rickshaw and taxi drivers may try to fleece you when they see you're not a native. Familiarize yourself with the local currency and the approximate transportation costs before you venture out on your own.

15. ***Is that English?*** It's the same language, but it's spoken with a distinctly different flavor in each part of the world. Every country adds to the language or takes words from it for its own tongue. In India, the English language is spoken with an Indian accent, although it is not as pronounced as some other countries. You'll find unusual expressions being used: "Cousin brother/sister" (cousin), "co-brother / sister" (brother or sister-in-law), and "What's your good name? Most Indians are familiar with the Western accent, but it helps to speak slowly. If you don't understand what they have said, don't worry-they don't mind repeating themselves.

16. ***Not too good with paperwork:*** Indians are not very big on documentation; they generally have to be taught to maintain proper records. Official correspondence is usually long-winded with pompous language that the ordinary person does not understand. E-mail has become a replacement for handwritten or printed documents, but there's a general ignorance of email etiquette. However, once shown the right way, Indians are adept at picking up any new technique.

17. ***The tower of Babel?:*** India has a potpourri of local languages, with most Indians fluent in more than just their mother tongue. If you come across a group conversing in the local lingo, don't take it as an affront; they aren't talking secretively about you. It's just their way of connecting to people who remind them of home,

18. ***Herd mentality rules:*** Most Indians are not very confident speaking in public. If you ask a group of Indians to raise pertinent questions during a meeting, you'll find that all the queries are posed once the meeting has broken up, by a small crowd that draws support from each of its members, and when the speaker is alone.

19. ***They mind their Ps and Qs, but differently:*** "Please" and "Thank You" are matter-of-fact for the polite Westerner, but an Indian may not feel the need to mention them. It does not mean that he's rude or impolite, Indians express their pleasure in a different manner: with a smile or a nod of the head.

20. ***Pecking Orders matter:*** Most Indian businesses have an order of hierarchy that's very important to those in the chain. When communicating with Indians, it pays to address the more important members first.

There's an Indian adage that says, "It takes two hands to generate applause." That's especially true when two cultures meet. Both should be willing to accept the idiosyncrasies of the other and work together to reach a common point of agreement. Keep these tips in mind when working with Indian people.

Source: Visit www.businessintelligencelowdown.com and www.biznichemedia.com. Reprinted with permission of Rich McIver.

QUESTIONS FOR DISCUSSION

1. What are the challenges in going global?

2. Why should companies go global?

3. When a research agency is working in the international industrial research, what are the possible challenges they would face?

4. How do the political factors impact industrial marketers, in an international environment?

5. "Do cultural factors really affect international marketers?" Discuss.

6. How would making a sales call be different across nations?

7. Which mode of entry to international markets is ideal?

c h a p t e r

EIGHTEEN

Business Ethics and Corporate Social Responsibility

COMPANY PROFILE 18: LMW (LAKSHMI MACHINE WORKS)

Lakshmi Machine Works Limited, a leading Textile Machinery Manufacturer in India and one among the three in the world to produce the entire range of Spinning Machinery. In 1962, LMW was founded to provide the Indian Textile Mills with the latest Spinning Technology. Today, LMW cater to around 60 per cent of the domestic market and have emerged as the leader in the Export of Textile Machinery in the country. LMW is today a global player and one among the three manufacturers of the entire range of Textile Machinery.

LMW's vision is to enhance customer satisfaction and our image globally and achieve exponential growth to leadership through world class products and services.

LMW's mission is to deliver greater value to our customers by providing complete competitive solutions through technological leadership and manufacturing excellence that are responsive to dynamic market needs.

History stands as a documented proof of LMW's Corporate and Financial success reflecting phenomenal growth since first year of operations. LMW diversified into CNC Machine Tools and is a brand leader in manufacturing customized products. LMW Foundry makes Precision Castings for industries the world over. The only company in Asia, outside Europe to manufacture OE products for Mikron of Switzerland. LMW's Global presence has grown over the years, with a market presence not only in developing countries, but also in Europe. LMW has won the Top Export Award in textile machine exports for the past seven years.

During 1988, LMW added to their formidable manufacturing resources, a new plant to produce CNC Machine Tools in technical collaboration with M/s. Mori Seiki Co. Ltd., of Japan. A plant that is one of its kind in India. A state-of-art foundry was added to the facility during 1993.

LMW Foundry Division manufactures Ductile Iron and Grey Iron Castings to demanding specifications in their state-of-the-art Nobake Foundry. Internationally renowned companies including General Electric, Siemens, MTU, and Wartsila have chosen LMW as their business partners for procurement of critical castings. LMW foundry has machined and value added castings for various applications. They manufacture Ductile Iron Castings, and Grey Iron Castings.

Lakshmi Machine Works Limited and Senthil Orthocare Hospital have conducted a Free Medical Camp on Orthopedic and General Medicine including diabetics and hypertension diseases at Government Higher Secondary School, Arasur, Coimbatore on 28th May, 06.

About 60 villages were informed about this free camp through various media like FM radio, local cable, banners, posters and door-to-door campaign. LMW true to its corporate policy always strive to achieve its social obligations to the needy people through such kind of value added health programmes.

FITEI and EEPC have bestowed LMW with the following awards:

- FITEI Top Exporter Award
- EEPC All India Award
- EEPC Regional Award

Source: www.lakshmimach.com

Mind Power 1: Ethics Centre

In 1995, The Merck Company Foundation entered into collaboration with the Washington-based Ethics Resource Centre (ERC) to establish a series of independent ethics centres in various regions around the world. The centres facilitate dialogue and action related to ethical business and organizational issues of importance in the countries where the centres are located.

The first centre to open was the Gulf Centre for Excellence in ethics in United Arab Emirates in 1998. Led by a local director, the Gulf centre developed a code of ethics for developed a code of ethics for the UAE Ministry of Health and has conducted educational seminars for military, government and corporate entities. In 2004, the UAE centre moved to Dubai and was renamed the Dubai Ethics Resource Centre. It is now housed within the Dubai Chamber of Commerce and Industry.

Along the way the Centre has overcome its share of challenges and setbacks associated with introducing new approaches to ethics in the region. Today, however, the Centre is rapidly becoming an effective voice for ethics in the UAE.

Since the Dubai Ethics Resource Centre first opened its doors, Merck has partnered with local organizations to launch additional ethics centres in South Africa, Colombia and Turkey. Each supports the work of governments, non-governmental organizations and the private sector in their efforts to foster a fair, transparent and open environment for business. The centres operate as facilitators of dialogue and action around ethical business and organizational issues of importance to the countries in which the centres have been established.

Although currently supported financially by grants from The Merck Company Foundation to the Ethics Resource Centre, each national centre is managed by an executive director who is independent of either organization and from any other organization representing either the public or private sectors.

Source: www.merck.com

Mind Power 2: The Higher They Go, the Stupider They Get

By Kristin Zhivago on May 2, 2005.

"What? He said that. "You're kidding." He actually said we have to do that. Starting tomorrow? Does he realize what he's asking? Oh, of course not. What an idiot! That means I'm going to have to drop everything I've been working on for three weeks and start running full speed in the other direction! I can't believe it."

This conversation, which takes place in millions of hallways across the world each business day, ends with everyone going back to their desks, carrying their cups of coffee, heads down, grumbling all the way.

Because of something a manager or manager's manager said, employees are going to be working on something that doesn't make sense, something that will mess up everything else they're working on, something that will probably inconvenience customers or worse, make customers shake their heads in disgust and go find a company who has a clue about what they need and how they want to buy.

Working on things that don't make sense – things that will hurt the company because they won't help the customer is, by far, one of the biggest problem in business today. It's an epidemic, and nobody talks about it. Scott Adams, the creator of Dilbert, owes a lot of his popularity to the sad fact that the stupidity of Dilbert's boss rings true for a lot of workers.

Contd...

Every minute an employee spends working on something that doesn't make sense is a wasted minute. You could even call it a "negative" minute, because (1) the job that should be getting done isn't getting done and (2) the employee's respect for the boss, and his belief in the company's future, has slipped down another notch.

Working on things that don't make sense is the single biggest source of job dissatisfaction. Who wants to work on something that is obviously going to fail? Who wants to fight traffic, spend 8 to 15 hours in a windowless office, answer another 200 emails, and sit through at least 5 boring meetings every day, just to do something stupid?

Employees are the happiest when they're working on something that is going to succeed. Something that they think customers will like, something that competitors can't do or won't do, something that "fits" with the company's set of promises (which as I explain in my book, a company's true brand). Something that makes them proud to be associated with a company that is doing the right thing.

Are these top managers really stupid?

Nope. The thousands of people I've worked with in top management were not stupid. They were intelligent and dedicated. But these same intelligent, well-meaning people make stupid decisions. Why? Because:

1.   They aren't personally talking to customers.

2.   Their employees don't tell them the whole truth.

3.   They have to answer to their own "bosses" who are also illogical. Let's take these one at a time.

1. They aren't personally talking to customers

Lou Gerstner is one of the best examples of a customer-centric CEO. If you're in management, and you haven't read his book, "Who Says Elephant Can't Dance"? you're missing a great read and insight into what made him so successful.

Before Gerstner came to IBM, he was an IBM customer, and a consultant to large companies. He knew the traps that CEOs can fall into. As a customer, he was fully aware of the stupid mistakes that managers make. When he first started his job as the CEO of IBM, instead of calling a bunch of meetings with employees and analysts to discuss His Grand Strategy, he horrified college professors and reporters by saying that the last thing IBM needed at that point was another "vision." Worse, he spent the bulk of his first three months visiting customers.

He continued to spend about 40 per cent of his time talking to customers during his tenure at IBM. How many CEOs can say they do that?

And I'm not talking about spending time with big-ticket prospects, closing the deal. When the CEO is acting as the company's Top Salesperson, the customers he's talking to, will be just as cagey and close-mouthed as they are with their regular sales person. The CEO won't learn anything useful in that situation.

What I am saying is that the CEO has to randomly call customers on a regular basis not to sell them, but to interview them. He needs to find out what drives them crazy. He needs to know, personally, what they really want. He needs to understand how they want to buy – the questions they need answered, how they need those questions answered, and in what order.

He needs to hear them tell him, in their own words, what they wish his company would do for them that it isn't doing now. What would they pay good money for? What makes sense to them?

If you're the CEO, all you have to do is pick up the phone and call. Start asking open-ended questions. "How's business?" What's driving you crazy right now? How do you feel about our product? Our service? What could we be doing better? Who else did you look at before you bought and what did

Contd...

you think of them? How did they sell to you? Was there anything about our sales process we could improve? What promise do you wish companies like ours would keep?"

These simple questions elicit the kinds of answers that can drive logical, market-conquering strategies. If you don't interview customers personally on a regular basis, you will fall victim to Agendaitis. Everyone has an agenda. Maybe they really do want to help the customer (there are more of these people, by the way, than most managers assume). Maybe they're trying to please or impress someone else a manager, a spouse, or even their mother-in-law. Maybe they're trying to do what only one customer wants (the main failing of sales-driven companies). And some, sadly, are just greedy and selfish, doing whatever pleases them.

When the CEO doesn't talk to at least several customers a month, she's going to do what makes sense to her based on what she hears from non-customers. Her main source of information will be her employees. That's a big mistake. Because...

2. Employees don't tell the whole truth

Here's a simple example. Let's look at a guy named Bill. Bill is in charge of a project. He's done the best he can with something he was asked to do, but it's not as good as he wanted it to be.

When Bill's boss asks how it's going, Bill says, "Good. We'll be able to meet the deadline."

What Bill doesn't say is that he isn't happy with how things are going, that some of the people who are supposed to be cooperating aren't cooperating.

Why isn't Bill telling his boss the whole truth? Here are just some of the possible reasons:

1. He doesn't want someone else to get into trouble.

2. He doesn't want to look like a whiner.

3. He is fighting a political battle with someone and he believes he is going to win. He doesn't want to say anything about it until it's obvious that he has to escalate.

4. He's afraid of being labeled a snitch, so he doesn't say anything about the people who are resisting.

5. He figures if he can't get the right people on board, he'll find another way.

6. It is taking longer than he thought to get certain information.

7. It is taking longer than expected to do some aspect of the project, but he thinks he'll be able to finish it if he can just get some uninterrupted time. Right. In fact, his day is filled with meetings and interruptions, so he never gets around to focusing on the big stuff.

8. He believes that someone is doing their part, when in fact their part either isn't being done or it is being done incorrectly. He will probably discover this when it's too late.

9. As the job is nearing completion, something changed-something that will have a major effect on the job. Bill doesn't know about the change. Or, worse, he knows about it but figures he can work around it. Or, worse, he knows about it and decides to ignore it because he can't figure out how to incorporate the change into what he is doing.

10. Bill screwed up somehow and is desperately trying to figure out how to make it right (or cover it up). Meanwhile, he isn't about to say anything about it to his boss.

11. The technology, employee, outside vendor, system, or process that Bill wanted to use for his project didn't work out. He is scrambling behind the scenes to find an alternative.

12. He's an eternal optimist, and in spite of all the obvious signs to the contrary; he believes the project will "turn out OK."

Contd...

We're up to reason #12 already and the list certainly isn't complete. Obviously, employees have many, many reasons to avoid telling their bosses the whole truth.

Bill doesn't tell his boss the whole truth, Bill's boss doesn't tell his boss the whole truth, and so on up the line until the story makes it to the CEO. The larger the company, the less truth is left in the story by the time it reaches the top. Plus, as everyone in the chain leaves out some of the truth, they add a little more fiction.

By the time the CEO hears the story, it bears little resemblance to reality. The CEO then makes a carefully considered decision, based on this filtered and embellished information, and delivers a decree. Bill gets the memo and thinks. "What an idiot!"

CEOs who depend entirely on their employees (or their kiss-up vendors) for the truth will always make stupid decisions. Smart CEOs make a point of looking elsewhere for the truth. They talk to customers on a regular basis, as we've already mentioned. This is the single most important thing a CEO can do.

A customer will say, "Well, I called customer service to solve my problem, but I was put on hold for 25 minutes, and then the representative couldn't solve the problem. So last week, when it was time to upgrade, I bought your competitor's product. And frankly, I've told others how terrible your service is." What did the customer service manager tell the CEO? "We're working on improving the phone system."

Many CEOs think they get the truth when they challenge these vague statements. "What do you mean, you're working on it? What's wrong? What are you doing?"

This leads to some answers, but the CEO will never hear this: "Well, the average hold time is 24.6 minutes, the system seems to cut off every 4th caller after they press '4,' and we don't have answers to 37 per cent of the questions we're asked."

Instead, he'll hear: "We need to hire more representatives to decrease the hold time, which is a little higher than I'd like. And we are testing the system because every so often it drops a call."

It's obvious that the CEO who gets this information is going to make stupid decisions, no matter how smart he might be. And he won't realize how much business he's losing because he's not getting the whole truth. Only his customers can paint that picture for him.

Meanwhile, his competitors will be having a field day exploiting his vulnerabilities. If he does interview customers and get the truth, he has to decide what to do.

Another barrier that will keep him from making the right decision is the stupid "bosses" he has to answer to. Which brings us to Reason #3?

3. They have to answer to their own bosses, who are also illogical.

Every CEO has a boss. In fact, every CEO has several bosses. At the very least, CEOs have to answer to the government. Regulations must be followed. Anyone who has tried to do his or her own taxes, or change something simple in their own town, knows that government regulations are neither simple nor logical. What makes sense to customers and to the companies that serve them may not have anything to do with what a CEO has to do to comply with government regulations, even if those regulations were created to protect consumers.

CEOs also answer to investors. In private companies, investors include family and friends, business associates, and venture capitalists. Each person has an agenda, which usually has little to do with what the customers want. Maybe the venture capitalists want to get to an IPO as fast as possible. Maybe they want to "flip" the company - grow it and sell it in the shortest amount of time. Maybe a relative or friend, who is advising the CEO, has been successful working in another company or industry, and wants to apply the lessons she learned in that previous situation to the current situation even if those lessons are inapplicable.

Contd...

In public companies, the stockholders, analysts, and press put pressure on the CEO. The CEO makes promises that he is expected to keep. When the numbers come out, if they're different than what the analysts expect, the stock price will suffer. This has a direct effect on the CEO's own net worth. which puts more pressure on the CEO. All of these brush fires can consume a CEO's working day, and still have nothing to do with what customers really want.

CEOs who have to answer to illogical demands placed on them by their "bosses" often fail to communicate that they are being forced into it by a poor policy. They don't want their bosses to find out they said negative things about the policy to their employees. They also don't like to admit that someone else is pulling their chain. But by protecting themselves, they are creating havoc and dissension in the ranks.

Better to say, "Look, I don't like this either, but I honestly haven't come up with a better alternative. We have to work through this right now, as efficiently as we can. This approach makes the employee feel he or she is part of the solution, rather than a victim of the problem. Employees who feel they are "in the know" are far more effective and motivated than those who feel they are treated like mushrooms (kept in the dark and fed BS all day). They also tend to sympathize with the CEO and even defend her because they understand what the real problem is.

This is far different than the employee who says to a customer, "Yeah, I know that's stupid. But what can I do? This is a direct order right from the top."

CEOs don't have to be stupid. They can know what is really going on, just by making a few phone calls to customers every week. They can make decisions that make sense to customers. They can tell employees and their investors – why they're making those decisions, and how those decisions will help customers. They can know when something has gone wrong, as soon as it starts going wrong, and take action before the situation gets out of hand.

Want to separate yourself from stupid CEOs? Call your customers.

Source: Visit her at www.zhivago.com or www.revenuejournal.com reprinted with permission. Copy right rests with the author. Reprinted with kind permission from the author.

INTRODUCTION

Why study ethics? Why Corporate Social Responsibility (CSR)? Although these two subjects are of discussion in any aspect of management today, it still remains one of the most discussed terms and least implemented. Although a company's top management might have ethical policies to post a good image in front of the stakeholders, often it is not the case at the ground. A sales person might not adhere to such standards, although he has the deepest of regards for such a policy. Environment, industry and often pressure put on employees keep ethical standard away from an employee. Also, when we speak of CSR, sometimes organizations and business marketers use this as a shield to protect themselves. Blow up the "little" good work that you are doing, and hide your sins under that.

Why should companies or business marketers follow ethical standards? What has a business marketer to give back to the society? Is there any relationship between business and society? This is what we are going to look in this chapter.

Ethical standard and its meaning, is what we need to understand. Ethics for one individual may not be ethical for another. Nor has anyone put the guidelines to be ethical. What is the thin line that divides ethical and unethical? Can we separate the two? We will also see in this chapter, that often unethical behaviour stems from organizational pressure.

Ethics as I believe (and CSR) in something which cannot be taught from books or models. For business marketer or any other marketer, ethical behaviour and the urge to help the society, should be infused in your blood. No models or diagrams can help making a person ethical or socially responsible. The need for every industrial marketer, is thus to understand, appreciate and implement such good practices.

WHAT IS BUSINESS ETHICS?[1]

As Peter Drucker have said, "There is neither a separate ethics of business, nor is one needed; for men and women do not acquire exemptions from ordinary rules of personal behaviour at their work or job. Nor do they cease to be human beings when appointed vice president, city manager and college dean. And there have been a number of people who cheat, steal, lie, or take tribes. The problem is one of the moral values and moral education of the individual, of the family, of the school".

Corporate ethics refer to a set of rules of conduct applied to a business which is acceptable to the society at large without any hitch/reservation.

Many students and industrial marketers might wonder that, for commercial organizations, profit maximization is the only goal. So why focus on a subject like "business ethics"? It often happens that the "bad" publicity spreads like wild fire, than "good" work done by an industrial marketer. If the marketer has engaged himself in dumping, cartels, scams, fixing of prices, dumping hazardous waste, polluting the air, or producing defective products, marketers fear that the "image" that is perceived in the marketplace may be destroyed.

The "image" of a business marketer which the society or people have, affects the way to which the society reacts in times of turbulence. When the "image" is strong and "positive", society still might be willing to forgive a company, in case the image being weak, then people would never be willing to forgive.

So what contributes this image?[2]

1. The attitude the business marketer has towards its customers, suppliers and employees.

2. Approach to living in the community.

The employees, who are on one hand, dealing with suppliers and on the other dealing with buyers, speak a lot about their industrial organization through their attitude. They are the 'forerunners'. Once the supplier or buyer derives a strong belief about the organization and its employees (a strong positive image) it becomes easy for the industrial marketer to sail through.

Maruti Udyog Limited called back all the 50,000 Maruti-800 cars sold during January-April 1997, as they suspected them to be made of inferior steel. Messerschmitt Bolkow Blohm (MBB) the biggest German Aerospace company, donated very expensive equipments to a Delphi Hospital for the homeless and provided drinking water, distributed books, stationery and scholarship to students in rural areas. Business ethics has, therefore, become a universal phenomenon, a cult with most of the progressive and future looking corporates.[3]

ETHICS: A BALANCE BETWEEN INDIVIDUAL, PROFESSIONAL AND ORGANIZATIONAL VALUES[4]

Business ethics are often about discussing, what is right and what is wrong. In the past, probably economic considerations were used to determine what is right and wrong. Business ethics are, however, a conflict of three standards. They are:

1. Ethics at an individual level

2. Ethics at an organizational level

3. Ethics at a professional level.

Every individual would have their own standards of ethics, which they believe are their levels of personal ethics. Similarly, organizational ethics are the levels of standard that is set by every individual organization and professional ethics differ from individual ethics by emphasizing the collective view point and acceptable practices of the members of the professions.[5] What is interesting to note here is that all of them try to balance each other and provide a check of each other.

CONCERN FOR THE SOCIETY

The job of marketing is no more than the one we have studied. Marketing is slowly evolving in a different format. The question comes up is that, should industrial marketers keep environment within their area of discussion, or should they forgo the societal aspects to marketing.

Many schools of thoughts can arise as to whether the ethical concerns and the societal concerns are a burden to the industrial marketer. Critics could be very anxious to point out the fact, which the ethical and social standards act as a barrier to the industrial marketer, and can easily lose its competitive strength. But however, marketing would also be treated as materialistic, if it is able to solve customer problems, satisfactorily and at the same time fails to serve the society in which the customer is a part.

With plethora of problems around, and industrial marketers using resources for the profitability of their company, should also at the same point of time, return back "something" to the society. Any kind of decision-making that takes place without keeping societal concerns in mind, is definitely a source of danger.

Prof. Philip Kotler has mentioned "societal marketing concept".[6] The role of marketing is no longer about knowing a customer need, satisfying it, being sensitive to the market and increasing profits, the need is also about societal concerns that the marketers should think. When we speak of societal marketing and products which are designed for the societal benefits, should have social, ethical and people consideration in it.

A question that can come up in mind is, "what is the role that the government is going to adopt or the role that an individual should have about the society?" Why should we as industrial marketers be concerned about life and society which does not fall under our purview? The job is to maximize revenue, and we should all work towards it.

We have seen the problems that are associated with tobacco and liquor companies. With these companies, the expenditure to basic health is definitely going to rise. These are the concerns. This has resulted into a negative image, about a product or company which is uncalled for. Business marketers, who pollute the environment, deplete natural resources, have no safety measurements for their employees, and are bound to face the axe from the government or their supplier and customers. Industrial marketing is about long-term partnering of two companies. A supplier, marketer or an employee would be more confident about an organization that is proactive and reliable. The products and the services it provides will carry that "unwritten faith" about its quality, reliability durability and safety. It will be then the supplier, marketer or the employee who will market the company image.

WHY THE DILEMMA?

Ethics is a pill, which is covered with bitterness outside and with sweetness inside. So when the top management takes the 'pill', the initial years are tough. It seems that decisions are getting tougher, due to ethical issues that the company is facing.

But over a period of time, the sweetness of the ethical decisions, that the company has been long standing for, comes. So, where is the dilemma? Why is the top management not keen enough to take the tough stand on ethical issues?

It is not true. Often, the top management binds ethics in its corporate vision and mission statements and is also a part of their corporate philosophy. But, there seems to be a gap, from the initial stages of planning to final implantation. Sometimes intuitionally, sometimes not knowingly, ethics is not viewed at all levels of management in the similar way. Some managers are very task-oriented and to them the 'end' matters and not the 'means'. This is where the difference lies and probably because of that, severe gaps or holes are formed in ethical decision-making process.

One more problem that the companies frequently face with relation to ethical dilemmas, is that too much of focus and importance is given to 'short-term' goals. Because of these goals (short-term), the focus on longer term switches over and profitability becomes the main cause of concern. Terminologies like EPS, share holders value, dividend declared are frequently heard. A goal in the short-term is achieved "at any cost" and if it is true, then one requires keeping ethics aside. In a market, with multiple players, it is nearly impossible, to meet the ethical standards as well as the short-term goals.

Another dilemma that comes up is that if the competitors are doing it, why should we not? If unethics is the order of the industry we live in, we can live with 'ethics' in such an industry?

A business marketer, who does not have ethical standards, as a part of the corporate philosophy, often finds himself in a 'temporarily' secure position. But it is the duty of the author to remind them of a company called as 'ENRON' here. Any organization that does not have a strong foundation cannot be built up. So why have not ethics as the foundation?

ETHICAL STANDARDS VARY

Ethical standards that are being set by the top management may not be followed by the one in the lower rung of the company. All employees often do not regard the single ethical standards that have been set by the top management of the company.

In spite of ethical standards being dictated by the top management, they often stay away from the purview of it. Receiving of kick backs, "small" gifts are often accepted, as a means to show favour. If the top management of a company indulges in such a practice, then what is wrong with salesforce spending more, and showing some extra expenditure?

Even, if we see that in international markets, some of the countries require huge kinds of bribe. In a country like Nigeria, it is said that even to move a truck out of your godown, you require to pay up. Why go so far? Take our country for example. If you have to bid for a government contract no scientific principles or experience works, it is often the "kick backs" that work. There is no rocket science involved in bidding for a government contract in our country. (Remember Bofors)

Ethical standards, thus, quite depend upon the managers who looks over a department or brand. But building pressures on manager, for performance in the short-run, always creates problem to balance between the line of ethics and unethics.

As management theorist, Peter. F. Drucker and many others have pointed out; there is danger in emphasizing only ROI. An overzealous pursuit of ROI can misdirect managerial attention and encourage some of the worst management practices, such as maximizing short-run, rather than long-run ROI.[7]

When the short-term focus becomes too much of importance, then the line dividing the ethical and unethical behaviour, breaks. Managers often break rules to maintain the security of the job or even to protect some employees from being sacked. In the paint and pharmaceutical industry often in the last week of a quarter, goods are "pushed" to the distributor (whether they want it or not) and billed for the next quarter, just to provide with satisfactory sales figures. As we have said earlier the "means" of doing a particular work does not matter, only the "end" does.

Ethical standards cannot be different for different people. When we use the word "standard", we mean "uniform". So how can ethics be differentiated, at different levels of the organization. This is a dilemma that many managers face. Often, the personnel background of an individual does not allow the person to behave in such a manner. But unfortunately, the pressure to perform is so high that ethical standards go down the drain. What remains is a "robotic human being", who is controlled by his superiors. These "robotic human being" are left with two options. The first is to flow with the tide, the second is to leave the job, and search for a new one.

The results of "ethics" cannot be judged on a short-term basis. It is a long-term objective. Not many stay to see the long-terms of a company. And this is when ethical standards get unbalanced.

Mind Power 3: Ethics in Action

We recognize that in our business, ethics and transparency are of critical importance to patients, health care professionals, our employees and investors and to our business success. We have strong policies and safeguards in place, and a long history of adherence to high ethical standards.

We know that it takes more than having the right mechanisms, standards and training in place to ensure an ethical business environment. Ethics is an integral part of how a company and its employees — from the executives and board level on down — conduct themselves everyday.

Every Merck employees is responsible for adhering to business practices that are in accordance with the letter and spirit of the applicable laws and with ethical principles that reflect the highest standards of corporate and individual behaviour.

Merck's traditions demand these high standards of corporate behaviour and Merck believes such behaviour is essential to the success of its business endeavours. Thus, the company will not accept anything less. Like integrity of product, integrity of performance is a Merck standard wherever we do business, and ignorance of that standard is never an acceptable excuse for improper behaviour. Improper behaviour cannot be rationalized as being in the company's interest. No act of impropriety advances the interest of the company.

Source: www.merck.com

ETHICAL ISSUES IN INDUSTRIAL MARKETING

A senior manager or the junior most executive working for an industrial marketer, often come through plenty of issues, which fall under the ambit of ethical decision-making. Gifts, commissions, kick backs, freebies, special favours or could even be a paid holiday trip to Singapore, would come under the purview of marketers, while fixing up a deal.

In this section, we will face some broad concerns of ethical issues in industrial marketing on products, price, channels and promotion. A special focus to ethical issues on selling of industrial products would be given.

American Marketing Association has established a code of ethics for ethical conduct for the marketers. It says, in part, "marketers shall uphold and advance the integrity, honour and dignity of the marketing profession by being honest in serving consumers, clients, employees, suppliers, distributors and the public".[8]

Ethical concerns for an industrial marketer can be from any part of the organization. They could be:

1. Ethical issues in STP

2. Issues in industrial marketing research

3. Issues with relation to technology

4. Issues with relation to production

5. Issues with relation to product, price, channels and distribution

6. Other ethical concerns

The start of ethical concerns for industrial marketers probably starts from day-to-day situations. Often managers are not kept informed by the executives and things go out of proportion, often. Especially, in industrial marketing, divulging out secrets of the company also becomes situational ethics. All these situational ethical situations are often a result of simple mistakes and can be corrected. You will often hear industrial salespeople say the following:

1. That is the norm followed by all of us

2. Every one does the same thing

3. We have done as the boss has told us.

It often happens in the organization that employees take the shorter route. If policies are followed, multiple objections may be raised by customers and buyers. So it is sometimes convenient to practice the short cuts to a task.

Consider this situation. The plastic division of one of the reputed business houses was sold off to a lesser known competitor. The division was in a state of turmoil as most of its employees had either started resigning or started hunting for jobs. The new management came to the office one morning and declared, "Any kind of payments has to be in the name of the new company". The sales guys came to know that this statement was a farce. It was still not published much, about the selling of this division. The sales guys closed some deals and collected the payments in the name of the old company. They feared, if they informed it to their customers they would lose business. They had started searching for jobs and they had nothing to lose. Did the salespeople behave ethically?

ETHICAL ISSUES IN INDUSTRIAL MARKETING RESEARCH

The ethical issues start from the marketing research department. Often it happens that the research agency does not disclose the actual problem to the client. It is often seen during research that the problem sources from a different point than what the company might be thinking. It is also often seen that research reports are generated which seems quite favourable to the management although in practice it might not be. For example, if a company has decided to launch a particular product in a new segment and the feasibility of the new segment is being researched on, but the researcher finds that it is unfeasible, presenting a report contrary to the top management belief would be an issue, which they need to tackle.

Another dilemma that the researcher might get into, is the availability of time that one needs to give to research. Cooking up data, submitting false data, extrapolating figures are issues, which they would face.

There could be a plenty of other issues that are related to marketing research.

ETHICAL ISSUES IN PRODUCTS

A silly mindset that often comes in front of industrial marketing is the launch or announcement of particular products in the market. Often these products are either not ready or properly tested. Due to huge orders that a product might receive some false claims or hyped up claims are also made. The products are launched to meet the competition face to face rather than with a definite strategy.

Often misleading claims, non-delivery are some of the problems that industrial products face. Claims made by advertisements about a "miracle" product are often not backed by justifiable performance. However when the buyer tests the products, the actual performance would anyway be out, but managers believe that the hype is still necessary.

Planned obsolescence is one more area where industrial products attract a lot of controversy. Even when the product has some demand, products are either sold off to a developing country or a new product is launched as it would generate more profits.

Safety standards, the quality of material used in manufacturing a product, or the emission standard are often not met. Issues like:

- Design of a product
- Quality control
- Material usage also form a key ethical concern

PRICING ETHICALLY

We have discussed it in this part of the chapter of pricing but certainly which require attention would be discussed here. Pricing practices could be unfair, deceptive and discriminative. Often, industrial marketers engage in cutting down of prices. Price fixations, cartels, charging excessively for products in shortage are causes of concern.

Often, it happens that non-value adding features (for example, safety) raise the price of the product, making the product unattractive and uncompetitive. This is often a big dilemma. So you need to make a choice between two objectives – safety with a greater price or no safety with competitive prices.

Pricing products to prevent entry of competitors in the market is also a decision that needs to be looked upon.

SOME OTHER ETHICAL ISSUES

The ethical considerations can vary and probably in everything that the industrial marketer does, lies a question of ethics. The issues and areas of discussing ethical behaviour are so much in number, that you have the opportunity to write a text book on that. Consider the following situations and see what you would have done.

1. You are working with an industrial marketer and want to know about your competition. A student from an MBA college is working on his projects in your organization. Should you pose him to extract information about your competitors?

2. You have just shifted to a new office in Gurgaon. The company has bought 50 laptops for the sales executives and about 30 computers for the office. Your manager calls you and offers you a scanner and printer at half the price of the market. You know it is a "gift" (read as kick back) from the supplier. Similar offers have been made to your other colleagues. What do you do?

3. Your company has a policy of not selling customer databases or divulging out information. One of your office people, you know, sells that database details to other competing companies. What do you do?

4. You sell bearing and tell your customers, they are the best value for money in the market. You know from the bottom of your heart "it isn't". Is it right to say that?

Ethical Issues in Selling

One of the latest and most debated topics is the question of ethics and unethical for a salesman. In our office, we had a saying that "everything is fair in love, war and sales". I do not know how far that is true, but somehow we must try and understand that industrial marketing is all about "building relationship" and whether we as industrial marketers do understand the meaning of ethics in selling, is the question.

THE GENESIS OF UNETHICAL BEHAVIOUR AMONGST SALESMEN[9]

Where did it all start the attitudes that those in sales, sometimes called salespeople or sale associates, are unethical or that being in sales would require one to do unethical things? I don't know if it started with the Trojan horse and Helen of Troy but I'm sure that it did not start then. Without going into ancient history and working our way through the ages and into today's business world, I will look at it from my era of some 50+ years in business and selling. Being been both salesperson and the recipient of others' selling activities, I believe I can see why this question of when did being unethical and being a salesperson come up. Putting being unethical and salesperson as being one in the same comes from, I believe the bargaining or negotiating over what something costs. It is not an activity many take easily. It is thought, by many, this is something other people do so if being unethical is to come into play, it is not I who is playing the game.

Let me state at the beginning, that being unethical is not exclusive to being a salesperson or as it said, "Being in sales." It is not exclusive because, from my approach to selling, anyone who asks others to buy, buy into, or accept and put to use any idea, information, skill, service or product, they are selling. It matters not what their job description is, for selling is something everyone does in both their personal and business lives from the time they able to communicate until they are laid to rest. While someone may not carry the title of salesperson, it is hidden inside where they believe it cannot be seen.

There was a time, when being a salesperson was seen as a profession. Almost universally, for salespeople and customers, being engaged in bargaining over price was not seen as a negative, it was a way of life. It was a form of social intercourse between two people who may or may not have known each other prior to that time. In some cultures it still exists. What the seller paid for it and what they wanted for it were only known to the seller. It was their decision to determine what something should sell it for. The salespeople knew their products and the customer knew the salespeople. There was a trust between the two and neither wanted to be known as taking advantage of the other. Sure, there were some that did not do business this way but the word got around fast and businesses failed due to being caught being unethical. So, it is happening of this day.

When we use the word "salesman" it is meant to be a generic one and includes both genders unless otherwise specified, and can be either singular or plural. The term "ethic" has many meanings. Dictionaries list the following:

1. The moral principles governing or influencing conduct.

2. Motivation based on ideas of right and wrong.

In all facets of business, not just for sales, these definitions fit. However, I will try to keep my remarks as they relate to sales and selling.

The term, "salesman ethics" is difficult to define as it can take on many meanings if not spelled out at the beginning. The term "ethics" when related to selling takes on many aspects and my comments will, hopefully, stay with these business situations:

- Salesman ethics as it relates the vendor firm.

- Salesman ethics as it relates to customers.

- Vendor ethics as it relates to sales staff.

- Vendor ethics as it relates to customers.

- Customers sales ethics as it relates to vendors.

- Customer sales ethics as it relates to salesman.

Each aspect will be different from the other due to the culture of where the vendor, salesman, customers reside or do business and this will affect how salesman ethics are seen.

Salesman Ethics as it Relates to the Vendor Firm

When one agrees to take on the job of salesman, if not written into an agreement or job description, it should be understood by the salesman that he will perform the job as required and that means he will follow the firm's policies and procedures. I list both with and without a job description because in many firms, there is no job description or, if there is, it is so generic that the job is not spelled out in detail.

There is still another facet to job descriptions that often confuses the picture. While the job description is spelled out and if it is read upon being hired that may be the only time the salesman reads it. As an aside, this is true of all employees and their job descriptions so in the case of salesman, not reviewing it from time to time is not unusual . . . not reviewing job descriptions is the norm in most businesses.

My point here, and this will certainly affect the other aspects, if the vendor does not give specific instructions or any job description, then it is they, the vendor, who are not following being ethical toward their salesman. Hence, very likely, salesman will end up as being seen by the vendor's management as not being ethical.

Vendor Ethics as it Relates to Salesman

Julius Zell, used to say that every boss deserves the employees they have. It sounds simple but it is not. Rather than blame themselves on hiring the wrong person, they will transfer the reason for the problem to the salesmen. This could be an example of the vendor being unethical.

One reason that salesmen are looked down upon is that they are seen as being an expense because their salary/commissions are listed on the books as an expense . . . a controllable expense. One of management's jobs is to control expenses and control usually means controlling the salary paid to the salesman but it also can mean controlling what, when, where and how salesmen sell.

Along this line, many businesses like to pay their salesman on commission or a base salary plus a commission because paying this way is directly tied to sales and this helps control sales expenses. Thus, low sales and the expense of paying salesman decrease. The management who fails to realize that commission selling never made a poor salesman a good salesman, or turn a good salesman into a great salesman. Great salesman, if they are truly great, will go out with the effort as long as they believe they are compensated fairly be it by commission, base plus commission or by salary.

When management believes that a salesman is making too much money, they begin to look to see what can be done to cut down on expenses and in order to control salary expense they do one or more of the following:

- The percentage of commission or bonus is lowered.

- The figure needed to get into the bonus category is raised.

- The territory or range, number of items/lines is decreased.

- The territory or range, number of items/lines is decreased, a new salesman can be brought in at a lower salary and this helps decrease salary expenses.

All four ways end up doing what management wanted but not the way they wanted. The myth management has brought into to justify these changes is that salesman would work harder in order to keep the same income. Their controllable expense may, in the end, increase because the above actions were disincentives to going out and selling more. It was hard enough before to make the income they were getting, now it will be more difficult so why do it? If a salesman takes this attitude, does that constitute salesman being unethical?

There is another reason for why a salesman is looked down upon. I'm not sure when it started but I believe it was when all jobs in a business, other than top management, were seen as functions . . . functions almost anyone could do. Salesmanship was one of those jobs. Why pay high salaries to people performing functions ended up by not following the "Rule of the 5 T's".

Take them-hiring

Train them

Task them – give them directions and realistic goals

Trust them – to do what they need to do as they see it

Thank them – for doing what they do/did

The result of not following the Rule was to inaugurate the "Management Rule of 2 T's"

Torture them if needed by saying not reaching goals was their fault, or, finally,

Terminate them

What is so surprising to me is that these very same people in management who believe salesman ethics are less than desired or expected, are the very same people that depend on the salesman to bring in the money that pays management's salary and provides the funds to run the business. If products and services are considered assets in business, isn't it logical that those that sell the firm's products and services should be looked upon as assets? Why is not this aspect of sales ethics pervasive in all businesses?

ETHICAL CONCERNS OF SALESPEOPLE[10]

Ethical concerns of a salesperson can be originated from four sources. So every salesperson should be made aware of four broad areas, where from ethical problems may stem in. They are:

1. Dealing with the Company

2. Dealing with the Workers

3. Dealing with the Customers

4. Dealing with the Competitors

Although the above list gives a very broad picture, there is industry specific and company specific ethical issues, that one must deal with.

CORPORATE SOCIAL RESPONSIBILITY

"By social responsibility, we mean the intelligent and objective concern for the welfare of society that restrains individual and corporate behaviour from ultimately destructive activities, no matter how immediately profitable, and leads in the direction of positive contributions to human betterment, variously as the latter may be defined."[11]

"Business has to take account of its responsibilities to society in coming to its decision, but society has to accept its responsibilities for setting the standards against which those decisions are made."[12]

Society and business are interdependent and the survival of one, without the help of another is not possible. Welfare and growth, also depends on this relationship. This is why CSR, is an important aspect that needs to be understood by any marketer.

There are five principal arguments against CSR. They are:[13]

- **Problem of competing claims (the role of profit):** Milton Friedman argues that the notion of social responsibility in business "shows a fundamental misconception of the character and nature of a free economy". Businesses function is economic and not social. However, this principle has been challenged by other management thinkers.

- **Competitive disadvantages:** Since any social action will have a price for the firm, it would have a competitive disadvantage.

- **Competence:** Milton Friedman asks, "If businessman do have a social responsibility other than making maximum profit for stockholders how are they to know what it is?"

- **Fairness (domination by business):** Milton Friedman asks, "Is it tolerable that these public functions of taxation, expenditure and control be exercised by the people who happen at the moment to be in charge of particular enterprises, chosen for those posts by strictly private groups?" This is fair argument against CSR.

- **Legitimacy (the role of government):** Social responsibility has to be taken care of by the government and not by corporations.

Although, all the arguments are true, but still the "corporates" need to have some basic obligations which must be done for the society.

CSR

CSR at Mitsui & Co.

Corporate Social Responsibility

Our ultimate guiding principles for the CSR-oriented management we aim to achieve are contained in the Mitsui and Co. Management Philosophy (Mission, Vision, and Values).
"Does our work really create new value and benefit society?"
"Can we always be proud of its processes and quality?"
In our business and in our social contributions, our CSR activities are always conducted with these questions in mind, and grounded in our management philosophy.

Mitsui & Co. Management Philosophy—Mission, Vision and Values

Mission — We will contribute to the creation of a future where the dreams of the inhabitants of our irreplaceable Earth can be fulfilled.

Vision — We aim to become a global business enabler that can meet the needs of our customers throughout the world.

Values —
- Making it a principle to be fair and humble, we, with sincerity and in good faith, will strive to be worthy of the trust society places in us.
- With lofty aspirations and from an honest perspective, we will pursue business that benefits society.
- Always taking on the challenge of new fields, we will dynamically create business that can lead the times.
- Making the most of our corporate culture that fosters "Freedom and Open-mindedness," we will fully demonstrate our abilities as a corporation as well as individuals.
- In order to nurture human resources full of creativity and a superior sense of balance, we will provide our people with a workplace for self-development as well as self-realization.

Basic CSR Policy

1 We will fulfill our role in the economy and continually strive to improve our corporate value by engaging in conscientious activities giving full consideration to the social significance of Mitsui & Co.'s presence and a strong awareness of our ties with the environment.

2 We will raise the awareness of each employer with regard to CSR and solidity our management base for practicing CSR through strengthening corporate governance and fully reinforcing internal control. We will also make efforts towards actively contributing to society.

3 We will place importance on interactive communication with our stakeholders. We will fulfill our accountability with respect to CSR and continually work to improve our CSR activities based on the responses of our stakeholders.

The Ten Principles of the UN Global Compact

Human Rights	1.	Businesses should support and respect the protection of internationally proclaimed human rights; and
	2.	make sure that they are not complicit in human rights abuses.
Labour Standards	3.	Businesses should uphold the freedom of association and the effective recognition of the right to collective bargaining;
	4.	the elimination of all forms of forced and compulsory labour;
	5.	the effective abolition of child labour; and
	6.	eliminate discrimination in respect of employment and occupation.
Environment	7.	Businesses should support a precautionary approach to environmental challenges;
	8.	undertake initiatives to promote greater environmental responsibility; and
	9.	encourage the development and diffusion of environmentally friendly technologies.
Anti-Corruption	10.	Business should work against corruption in all its forms, including extortion and bribery.

CSR-ORIENTED MANAGEMENT (ACHIEVEMENTS AND OBJECTIVES)

Mitsui remains close to the various issues affecting society today, through our global business activities and diverse business areas including Mineral Resources and Energy, Global Marketing Networks, Consumer Services and infrastructure. Our mission is to accumulate a track record of *good work* with sincerity and good faith, with every single Mitsui executive and employee fully understanding the role the company law has to play in resolving these issues and the expectations society places on us.

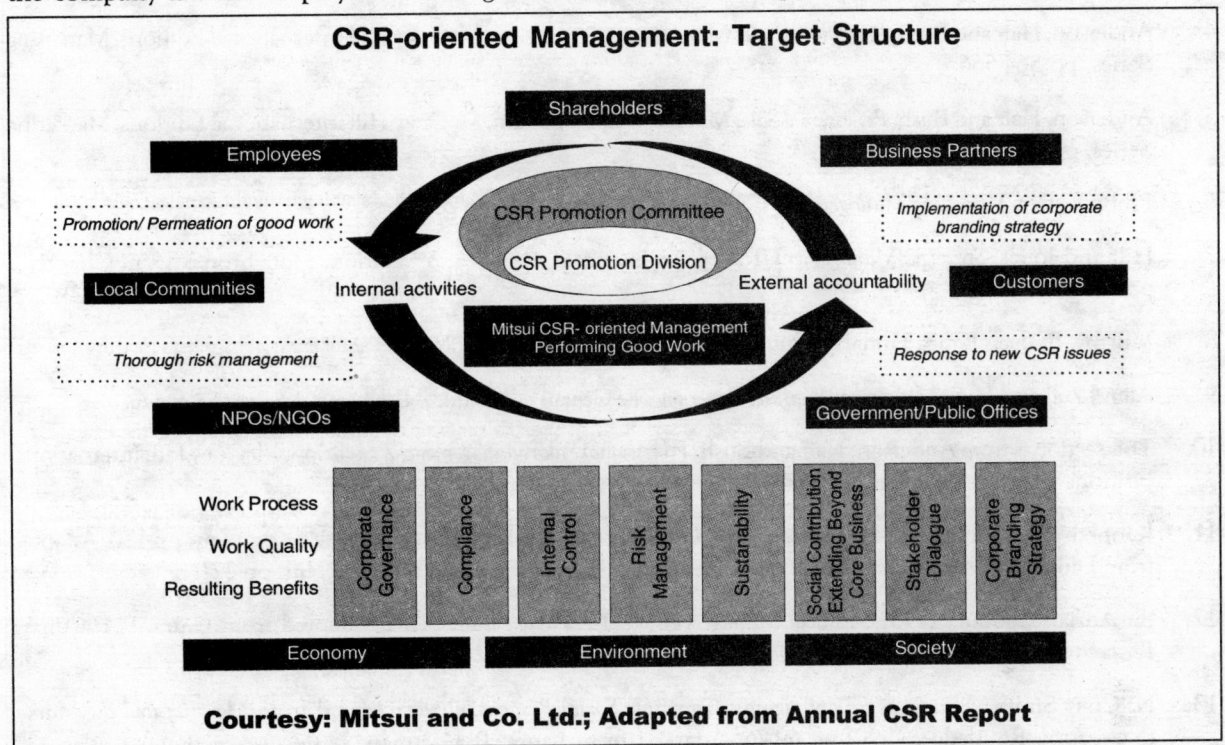

Courtesy: Mitsui and Co. Ltd.; Adapted from Annual CSR Report

CONCLUSION

Ethics and CSR, although most debated topics in management, but still implementation remains a cause of great concern. Although policies relating to ethics and CSR must be there in any company's corporate philosophy, implementation still remains a big question mark.

In this chapter, we first defined business ethics and how it assists companies to build a positive image around them. Ethics is a balance of profession, individual and organizational ethics, with each putting a pressure on one another.

We also discussed how the societal relationship with marketing is changing and how companies should try and change with the needs of society. Ethical standards in an organization vary and the philosophy at the top of the management may not be passed down to the bottom most in the organization. The pressure to perform and "at any cost" varies the focus on ethics.

The various issues on industrial marketing ethics were discussed in areas like marketing research, products, promotions, channels and selling. It was also discussed that why do salesman behave unethically.

At the end, we discussed CSR, the arguments against it and the CSR practices at Mitsui and Co.

The author believes that ethics and CSR cannot be taught, but needs to be practiced. It is obvious that the strength or foundation of individual value systems which give the right direction to ethics and CSR policies of a company.

References

1.   This section is based on – Dr. S. Singh, *Corporate Governance – Global Concepts and Practices*, Excel Books. pp 22.

2.   Vitale, Giglierano, *Business to Business Marketing-Analysis and Practice in a Dynamic Environment*, Indian Edition, Thomson South Western, pp 460.

3.   This section is based on – Dr. S. Singh, *Corporate Governance – Global Concepts and Practices*, Excel Books, pp 22.

4.   Anderson, Hair and Bush, *Professional Sales Management*, 2nd edition, McGraw Hill International Editions, Marketing Series, pp 564-566.

5.   Anderson, Hair and Bush, *Professional Sales Management*, 2nd edition, McGraw Hill International Editions, Marketing Series, pp 565.

6.   Philip Kotler, *Marketing Management*, 10th edition, Prentice Hall, pp 25.

7.   Hill and Jones, *Strategic Management Theory- An Integrated Approach*, 3rd edition, Houghton Miffin, Chapter2, pp 41.

8.   Murthy, *Business Ethics*, Himalaya Publishing House, Chapter 9, pp 247.

9.   Alan J Zell and H. S. Mukerjee, *Working Paper on The Genesis of Unethical Behaviour Amongst Salesman*.

10.   This section is from Anderson, Hair and Bush, *Professional Sales Management*, 2nd edition, McGraw Hill International Editions – Marketing Series, pp 567-570.

11.   Kenneth. R. Andrews (1971), *The Concept of Corporate Strategy*, Burr Ridge, IL: Irwin company, pp 120, Adapted from Laura P. Hartman, *Perspectives in Business Ethics*, 2nd edition, Tata McGraw Hill, pp 221.

12.   Sir Adrian Cadbury (1987), *Ethical Managers Make Their Own Rule*, HBR, Adapted from Laura, P. Hartman. *Perspectives in Business Ethics*, 2nd edition, Tata McGraw Hill, pp 220.

13.   N. Craig Smith, *Arguments for and against Corporate Social Responsibility* excerpted from *Morality and the Market* (New York: Routledge, 1990) pp 69-76, Adapted from Laura. P. Hartman, *Perspectives in Business Ethics*, 2nd edition, Tata McGraw Hill, pp 231-236.

Mind Power 4: The Ten Commandments for the Ethical Salesperson

Copyright 2001, by Dave Kahle

1. Don't intentionally misrepresent anything

Never, never, never lie to a customer. About anything. Ever. Period.

2. Fix any important misunderstandings that you can

It's possible that your customer will form incorrect ideas about some of the products you represent or the services that come with them. It's also possible that they will misunderstand things about your competitors, and about the needs and statements of other people who work in their organizations.

It's very tempting, when these misunderstandings work in your favour, to ignore them. However, that's not acting with integrity. When you become aware of any significant misunderstandings your customer has that impact the buying decision or the larger relationship, you need to correct them. Now, this doesn't mean that you need to set him straight on his political beliefs or his views on the controversial call in Sunday's football game. But it does mean that, on the important issues that impact the sale,

Contd...

allowing misunderstandings to exist is an act, on your part, of passive dishonesty. Correct them when you can.

3. Work hard for your employer

It's easy for a salesperson to give in to the temptation to cut corners when it comes to working a full day, every day. After all, who really knows if you hit your first call at 9 00 A.M. instead of 8:30 A.M? And who knows if you take a 30-minute coffee break between calls? And who knows if you make it home by 3:00 P.M. some days, and take a number of afternoons off to visit the golf course or the fishing hole during the summer?

All of these examples are ways of short-changing your employer that, in all probability, no one will ever know about except you.

And that's my point. You will know. A code of ethics is easy to live by when everyone is watching. But it's a real test of character when your ethics are tested in situations where no one else knows, and you know you can get away with it.

You owe your employer consistent, full days of your best efforts. Anything less is unethical.

4. Always be willing to trade a short-term loss for the sake of a long-term gain

This may be another definition of integrity – the courage and conviction to walk away from an unethical short-term gain in return for a long-term gain. In other words, always be willing to give up a sale or some immediate advantage if you must stretch the truth or act unethically to get it.

For example, you may have an opportunity to acquire a quick sale because your customer has misunderstood the specifications or features of your product. It's tempting to take the order and not say anything. But that would not be ethical.

The ethical salesperson will correct the customer and lose the immediate gain that the sale would have brought. The payoff, however, is the long-term gain in your reputation for integrity.

A long-term gain achieved ethically is always worth more than any short-term advantage.

5. Do what you say you are going to do

This isn't as simple as it sounds. One of the obvious implications of doing what you say you're going to do is that you must not say you are going to do something that you know you can't do. In other words, don't over promise. That's difficult to do when you're in the middle of a competitive situation over a nice piece of business, and you know the competition is over promising to get the sale. But, if you're going to be an ethical salesperson, you won't over promise, because you know you won't be able to do what you say you're going to do.

There's another implication — you must be organized enough to follow through on your promises. The most honest person in the world can be perceived as unreliable if he is not organized enough to follow through on his promises. If you say you're going to call a customer back on Thursday, make sure that you have a tickler file, day-time planner, computer programme, or some other system that will remind you to call them back when Thursday comes. It's not only good business, it's ethical.

6. Give liberally

As a distributor salesperson, you enjoy a challenging job with a lot of freedom and a substantial income level. The world is full of people who would love to have that. You're one of life's more fortunate people.

Contd...

I think that means that you have a greater than average responsibility to give back to society. Give of your money freely to charitable or religious causes, and give liberally of your time and expertise to the organizations that you can help. Your expertise, your time, your people skills, your organizational skills and your confidence and ability to get things done- all of these are assets you can bring to the Boy scouts, your church, the PTA and a thousand other organizations that can use your abilities,

Since you are more blessed with talent, time, and money than most of the population you have a greater responsibility to use it for purposes other than just your own edification. Give liberally.

7. Recognize those who help you

It's easy to get into the mindset that you alone are responsible for your success. After all you're out there all along fighting the battle every day. Nobody else knows what good work you did in getting that account or how hard it is some days when nothing goes your way.

In spite of this, you couldn't, do your job without the support of a whole group of people back at the office. Your manager gave you an opportunity and nurtured you along. The inside people have cleaned up more than a few of your messes and they have positively impacted many of your customers. The manufacturers you represent have put lots of time and energy into creating the products that ultimately provide your livelihood.

All of these people, and probably dozens of others, have contributed in significant ways to your success. It is just as dishonest to not recognize them as it is to misrepresent a product.

The ethical salesperson recognizes those people who have helped him.

8. Continuously learn and improve

You are not as good at sales as you can be. You have to reach your potential. One of the reasons why your employer hired you for this position is that he/she saw potential in you. I believe you have an ethical obligation, not only to your employer but also to yourself, to become as good as you can be to continuously improve yourself. When you decide that you are good enough that you know about all you need to know, you quit learning and improving and when that happens you rob yourself and your employer of that potential you have that will not be developed.

What a shame It's not good business. And besides, it's unethical.

9. Never give up

This may seem odd in a section on ethics but I believe that giving up is the same thing as going home early or taking extra days off without anybody's approval. Both shortchange yourself as well as your employer.

When you give up prematurely on a sale or you give up on yourself and give into negative thinking you're choosing to deprive yourself and your talent and time. That's unethical.

10. Don't speak badly about anyone

In my first sales position when I was selling amplification equipment there were 29 major installations purchased in my territory. I got 28. My stomach still gets a little tight whenever I remember one of my crucial sales calls with the #29 customer.

During the course of the conversation she stopped me and said, "You know I really don't like it that you're so negative about your competitors." I was stunned, embarrassed and flustered. I turned bit red and stumbled out an apology but that was the end of that deal.

All because I had spoken badly about my competitor. That was an intensely painful lesson for me. I resolved never to make that mistake again.

Contd...

As I matured, I realized that when you negatively judge anyone you really say more about yourself than you do about the other person. Speaking badly about a competitor, your boss, your company, or a manufacturer always makes you look bad. And besides, it's unethical.

Source: About Dave Kahle, The Growth Coach

Dave Kahle is a consultant and trainer who helps his clients increase their sales and improve their sales productivity. Dave has trained thousands of salespeople to be more successful in the Information Age economy. He is the author of over 500articles, a monthly e-zine, and six books. Ten Secrets of Time Management for Salespeople was recently released by Career Press. His Kahle Way Sales Management system empowers sales managers to instill accountability and communication in the salesforce. You can join Dave's "Thinking about Sales Electronic Newsletter" on-line at *www.davekahle.com/mailinglist.htm.*

For more information or to contact the author, contact The DaCo corporation, 3736 West River Drive, Comstock Park, MI 49321, phone 1-800-331-1287, fax 1-616-451-9412, *cheryl@davekahle.com or www.davekahle.com.*

QUESTIONS FOR DISCUSSION

1. "Either you quit or follow our policies" – You would often hear it. Do you compromise on your value system?

2. Why should ethics study and implement at all, when competitors are not behaving ethically?

3. Your competitors are propaganding false statements against your company. What do you do?

4. Are the arguments against CSR valid? Give examples to prove your point.

5. "The line dividing ethics and unethics is thin" – How do you define this line in your life?

6. Do a research on an Indian B2B company to find the CSR practices that they follow?

7. "Is CSR an act to shield the wrong doings of a company" Discuss.

Case Studies

Case 1

Consolidated Products: The Industrial Systems Business Unit

Consolidated Products is a $21 billion company headquartered in Atlanta, Georgia. The company's six business units, which offer a wide array of products and services, are the result of an aggressive strategy of mergers and acquisitions starting in the late 1980s. Exhibit 1 provides an overview of Consolidated Products and its six primary business units. The corporate staff is surprisingly small, comprises general management, legal staff, and human resources. Part of the reason for this small staff is due to the eclectic array of businesses housed within one corporate entity. A *Business Week* editor recently commented that "Consolidated Products could easily be broken up into six separate companies, since at one time it was six separate companies." The editor also said that if the company "ever learned how to leverage its size in the marketplace, Consolidated Products could be a Wall Street powerhouse!"

While Consolidated Products is a global corporation with facilities around the world, it operates each business unit as a highly independent and decentralized company. The corporate culture is best described as entrepreneurial, with each business unit being headed by an executive vice president who has complete profit and loss accountability.

Exhibit 1: Consolidated Products (2001)

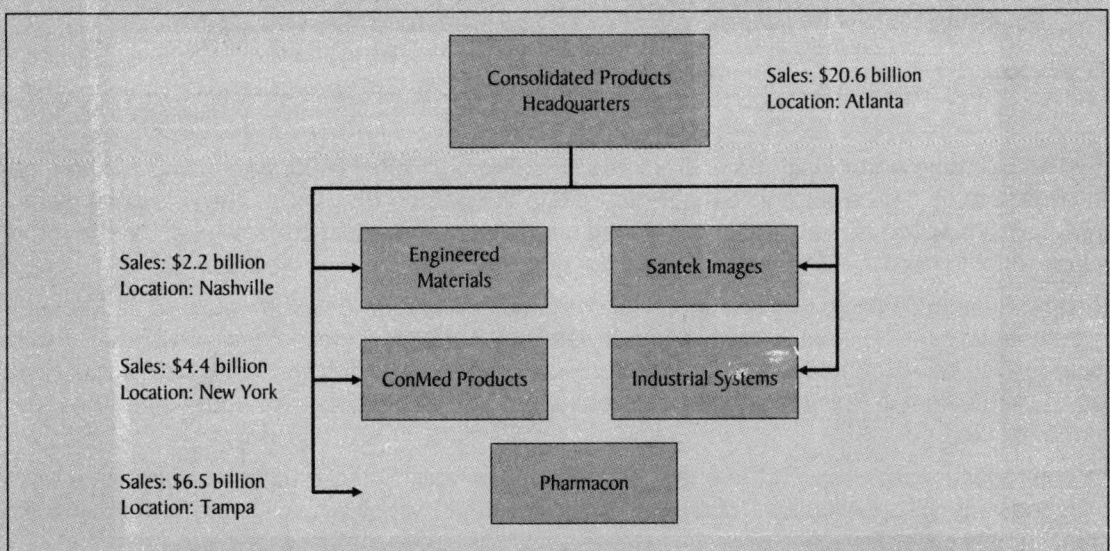

A review of the six units indicates that each faces a wide range of sourcing issues. Since sourcing is a process, it comes as no surprise that some of the issues are common to more than one unit.

Industrial Systems

Industrial Systems, a $5 billion business unit headquartered in Dallas, Texas, is developing a new line of industrial pumps. This unit will assemble pumps in its own facilities, but intends to outsource many of the key components and subassemblies, including the electronic control sensors that are becoming the accepted standard on new pumps and compressors. The decision to outsource the electronic sensors resulted from an executive-level study that concluded the cost to manufacture electronic sensors in-house was highly prohibitive.

Contd...

Marketing, which is responsible for forecasting and demand planning, estimates that first year demand for the new line of pumps, and therefore the control sensors that manage the operation and performance of the pump, would be approximately 500,000 units, with a 20 per cent growth expected for two year. Sensor demand depends totally on final product demand, which can be somewhat volatile.

Exhibit 2 details the monthly sales forecast for the new product line. The marketing director is responsible for forecasts, and he maintains that a 95 percent confidence interval around the actual demand will likely be between 400,000 and 600,000 units. Supplier responsiveness and ability to satisfy volume fluctuations will be critical.

Exhibit 2: Two-Year Pump Product Line Forecast

August 2002	50,000 units	August 2003	66,000 units
September 2002	55,000 units	September 2003	60,000 units
October 2002	50,000 units	October 2003	48,000 units
November 2002	50,000 units	November 2003	48,000 units
December 2002	35,000 units	December 2003	54,000 units
January 2003	35,000 units	January 2004	42,000 units
February 2003	35,000 units	February 2004	42,000 units
March 2003	40,000 units	March 2004	48,000 units
April 2003	40,000 units	April 2004	48,000 units
May 2003	35,000 units	May 2004	48,000 units
June 2003	35,000 units	June 2004	48,000 units
July 2003	40,000 units	July 2004	48,000 units

Industrial Systems is targeting the price of its pumps from $1300-$1800, depending on the model and configuration. The electronic sensor must be in the $125-$150 range. The company plans to introduce the new line of industrial pumps to the marketplace in August 2002. It must have inventory by June 2002 to begin process proving and pilot production.

Industrial Systems relies on cross-functional commodity teams to develop sourcing strategies for key purchased items. Executive management views this supplier selection decision as critical to the success of the new product line. Control sensor technology helps differentiate the final product in the eyes of the customer. This is important to counteract the perception that industrial pumps are a commodity item.

The commodity team has spent the last several weeks visiting three suppliers, and is currently evaluating various supply options. The team expects to begin negotiation with one or more suppliers within the next several weeks.

Five suppliers responded to the commodity team's Request for Proposal, which was forwarded twelve weeks previously. Although other electronic control suppliers exist, only five showed an interest in the proposal. An initial review of these proposals revealed that three of the five suppliers were cost competitive given the initial target cost.

The team visited three suppliers directly to collect detailed information. The visits ranged from one to two days each, with all three visits completed within a three-week period. These visits were time-consuming and exhausting, particularly since one of the suppliers was located in Asia. Unfortunately, Industrial Systems does not have an International Purchasing Office (IPO) to support its international procurement activities. Furthermore, no one on the team spoke Japanese. Fortunately, the other two suppliers, located in the U.S., were much easier to visit. In fact, one supplier was located only 50 miles from the buyer's assembly facility. The following sections summarize data collected during the commodity team's three supplier visits.

Contd...

Supplier 1: Control Technologies

Control Technologies, located in Nagasaki, Japan, was the largest supplier the team visited (sales of $6.25 billion). The plant covered 10 acres, with a wide variety of electronic components produced in the facility. Control sensors represent a large segment of the supplier's production (Control Technologies commits 50 per cent of total capacity to sensor production and derives 60 per cent of its revenues from sensors). Because of its size, however, the company seemed most interested in large contracts ($100 million or more annually). Geographic distance from Texas, along with the need to accommodate the needs of some large customers, made this supplier's quoted lead time the longest of the four suppliers being evaluated.

The highest-ranking manager that met with the commodity team was a sales manager, who took the team to visit various departments. The division vice-president and plant manager were in conference with a large customer, who the buying team found out had formed a strategic supply alliance with Control Technologies. The commodity team felt a bit "snubbed" at the facility, particularly the group's female member. The facility, however, was efficient, spotless, and modern.

When the team visited engineering, they spoke with a manager in sensor design. The engineer estimated, based on previous experience, that the ramp-up time to begin production that would satisfy product specifications would be about four months. Furthermore, tooling costs would likely be $2.75 million.

The sales manager was particularly proud of his company's new Internet-based Electronic Data Interchange (EDI) system. This system allowed direct communication with customers. He was also proud that Control Technologies was "the price leader" for the industry, and was producing sensors for several major companies. He also talked about the company's extensive investment in research and development. When the sales manager heard that the sensor order, based on 500,000 units in year one, would likely not exceed $65 million per year, he hesitated, saying that he would need to discuss the order with management. The economics associated with large orders is what made Control Technologies a low-cost producer. Relevant Control Technologies data include:

- Quoted price = $131 per unit (quoted at 120 yen to $1 U.S.)

- Delivery lead time = 9 weeks

- On-time delivery record = 94 per cent on-time (for large customers)

- Quality = 10,200 PPM defects

- Transportation costs from Asia to Industrial Systems = $22 per unit

- Current installed capacity for sensor production[1] = 97 per cent

- Duties and customs = $11.50 per unit

- Insurance = $2.50 per unit

- Frequency of shipment = Monthly

- Tooling costs = $2.75 million

- Ordering, inbound receiving, and quality inspection costs = $5.50 per unit

- Ramp-up time = 5 months

- Denomination of contract = Yen

---

1. *Note:* Current installed capacity indicates that portion of the supplier's sensor capacity that is currently utilized. For example, if current installed capacity is 98 percent, then this supplier is utilizing 98% of its production capacity and presumably has 2 percent of its capacity available for new business.

Contd...

Supplier 2: Techline

A second candidate for the contract is Techline, a smaller manufacturer located in Colorado Springs, Colorado. The company focuses exclusively on the design and production of electronic sensors for industrial pumps and compressors. The team discovered this company almost by accident. A team member was browsing a trade journal and saw Techline's advertisement. When the team visited the facility, the team was surprised at its small size and by the fact that it is located in an old warehouse. Techline's president met with the team in person. He explained that he was a graduate of Stanford in electrical engineering and had decided to start his own company after working for another supplier for 18 years. The company entered the sensor market 4 years ago and, during this time, has established a reputation for delivery reliability and innovation. The president explained that Techline's success was based largely on its commitment to develop new technology, especially technology that enhanced product reliability. He also claimed that he knew every customer personally.

Everyone in the plant seemed highly motivated. The president was particularly excited about the possibility of working with Industrial Systems, and promised to work closely with the company on this contract and for any new product lines. When asked if his firm would have any problem in meeting demand should they receive the contract, he hesitated before answering. He admitted that this contract would be the largest in Techline's relatively short history. He also indicated that several other buying teams were also going to be sending teams to evaluate Techline within the next several weeks. However, he assured the team that he would do whatever it took to maintain reliable delivery schedules if Techline received the contract. Interestingly, it appeared that the production lines were experiencing some problems during the team's visit, as they were shut down for nearly four hours! Relevant Techline data include:

- Quoted price = $142

- Delivery lead time = 4 weeks

- On-time delivery record = 96 percent on-time

- Quality = 12,500 PPM defects

- Transportation costs from Techline to Industrial Systems = $6.50 per unit

- Current installed capacity for sensor production = 92 percent

- Duties and Customs = $0.00 per unit

- Duties and Customs = $0.00 per unit

- Insurance = $1.75 per unit

- Frequency of shipment = weekly

- Tooling costs = $4.3 million

- Ordering, inbound receiving, and quality inspection costs = $3.50 per unit

- Ramp-up time = 6 months

- Denomination of contract = Dollars

Supplier 3: Sensor Link

The third supplier, a reputable manufacturer of electronic sensors, was located less than 50 miles from Industrial Systems. About half the company's sales came from electronic sensors. In fact, the firm was one of the larger producers of these units worldwide. In addition, the plant manager pointed out that the company has committed significant resources to setting up a JIT production system for the electronic sensor line. The buying team was impressed with the performance of the *kanban* signals and flow-through workstations. The plant manager also emphasized that because of their close proximity to Industrial Systems, they would have no problem delivering the product in two-day lot sizes "just-in-time." The manager was able to show reports that backed this claim. Sensor Link also had a solid reputation within the industry for working with its customers on future product development.

Contd...

Upon visiting the quality department, the quality manager seemed particularly preoccupied and "on edge." When the plant manager left for a few minutes to answer a phone call, the group asked the quality manager if the company had experienced any significant problems recently. He confessed that the last shipment of sensors had several quality problems, and the number of returns from large distributors had increased dramatically. This was creating some fairly severe disruptions to production scheduling and delivery. The most serious problem was an annoying shut down of the sensor when the pump was started. However, he assured the team that the design engineers were working full-time on the problem and that it would be solved well before Industrial Systems placed an order. When the plant manager returned, the quality manager made no further mention of the problem. Relevant Sensor Link data include:

- Quoted price = $139

- Delivery lead time = 2 weeks

- On-time delivery record = 97.5 percent

- Quality = 11,500 PPM defects

- Transportation costs from Sensor Link to Industrial Systems = $16 per unit (due to frequent deliveries of small quantities)

- Current installed capacity for sensor production = 95 percent

- Duties and customs = $0.00 per unit

- Insurance = $2.00 per unit

- Frequency of shipment = Every other day

- Tooling costs = $3.95 million

- Ordering, inbound receiving, and quality inspection costs = $3.25 per unit

- Ramp-up time = 5 months

- Denomination of contract = Dollars

Supplier Financial Data

The team also gathered financial data for each supplier. While the team believes the data for the U.S. suppliers to be reliable, several assumptions and estimates had to be made regarding the Asian supplier. The team also had to convert Japanese yen into dollars. Exhibits 3 and 4 summarize selected supplier financial data.

**Exhibit 3: Selected Supplier Balance Sheet Data (U.S. $ in millions)
for Period Ending December 31, 2000**

	Control Technologies	Techline	Sensor Link
ASSETS			
Cash	$105.9	$35	$75
Marketable securities	$152.5	$9	$115
Accounts receivable	$889	$54	$395
Inventories	$1177.7	$105	$183
Total current assets	$2,325.1	$203	$768
Investments at equity	$838.4	$26	$50

Contd...

Goodwill	$400	$38	$130
Total investments and other assets	$1,238.4	$64	$180
Property, plant, and equipment	$1,958.5	$155	$372
TOTAL ASSETS	$5,522	$422	$1,320
LIABILITIES AND SHAREHOLDERS' EQUITY			
Notes payable	$625.5	$21	$59
Accounts payable	$725.9	$95	$205
Taxes due on income	$270	$25	$63
Accrued payroll and employee benefits	$453.2	$50.5	$210
Total current liabilities	$2,074.6	$191.5	$537
Long-term debt	$1,643.5	$65	$266
Shareholders' equity	$1,803.9	$165.5	$517
TOTAL LIABILITIES AND SHAREHOLDERS' EQUITY	$5,522	$422	$1,320

Exhibit 4: Statement of Income Data (U.S. $ in millions) Year Ended December 31, 2000

	Control Technologies	Techline	Sensor Link
Net sales	$6,250	$600	$2,400
Cost of goods sold	$5,575	$401	$1,555
Selling, general, and administrative expenses	$450	$81	$630
Interest expense	$175	$35	$72
Costs and expenses	$6,200	$517	$2,257
Income before income taxes	50	$83	$143
Estimated taxes on income	$20	$40	$69.5
NET INCOME	$30	$48	$73.5

Additional Information and Assumptions

- Although Industrial Systems is buying an electronic sensor that has features defined by industry standards, extra design features and performance capabilities that will differentiate the end product will result in additional tooling requirements at each supplier.

- The company expects the line of pumps to have a two-year life cycle. The commodity team will allocate all supplier-related production costs, such as tooling, on a per unit basis over a two-year period. The company fully expects to introduce its next generation of pumps at the end of two years.

- Industrial Systems plans to maintain some level of safety stock inventory for the sensors, at least for the first year. Due to long material pipelines, Industrial Systems expects to maintain a one-month safety stock inventory if it utilizes an Asian supplier. For domestic suppliers, the company expects to maintain an inventory equal to two weeks worth of demand as safety stock.

Contd...

- Inventory carrying costs, which include storage, handling, obsolescence, taxes, and cost of capital are 16 percent of the inventory's unit cost. The company assumes carrying costs for safety stock material.

- For this analysis, assume the unit price quoted by each supplier is what Industrial Systems would pay for the sensor from each supplier. Subsequent negotiations will likely alter the quoted price.

- While tooling depreciation could be a cost consideration; this case does not consider depreciation.

- While Industrial Systems takes an active role in coordinating inbound transportation shipments, company policy prohibits assuming title to material until the material arrives at the receiving dock.

- On average, a quality defect costs Industrial Systems $400 in various charges to correct the non-conformance.

- Assume the date is currently January 2002 with first production by the supplier required in June 2002.

Case Assignment Questions

1. No supplier selection decision is without risk. Create a table for each supplier that identifies the various risks associated with the decision and identify ways to mitigate or manage the impact of each risk if it were to occur. For example, delivery variability with a foreign supplier is a risk that would require a plan to manage that risk.

2. Perform a financial analysis, using financial ratios, for each supplier. Indicate any strengths or weaknesses for each supplier as identified by the analysis.

3. Unit cost never equals the total cost of doing business with a supplier. Develop an expected total cost of ownership model for each supplier, considering unit cost, quality costs, inventory requirements, etc. Clearly state whatever assumptions you make during your analysis.

4. Develop and evaluate each supplier using a weighted-point supplier selection tool. Be sure to specify clearly the performance categories, category weights, and assessment scales used to score the supplier.

5. Supplier evaluation and selection is a critical process. Develop a supplier evaluation and selection process that the various units at Consolidated Products could employ during major supplier selection decisions.

6. Identify and discuss various ways to effectively reduce the cycle time required to identify, evaluate, select, and negotiate with a supplier.

7. The *Business Week* editor commented that if the company "ever learned how to leverage its size in the marketplace, Consolidated Products could be a Wall Street powerhouse!" Describe what leverage means as it relates to supply chains. Next, describe how an organization such as Consolidated Products can effectively leverage its purchasing power.

Source: This case has been authored by Robert J Trent of the Lehigh University. The case study has been reprinted with the permission of the author.

George Pappas, President and Founder of Lexington Supply Company (LSC), was becoming increasingly concerned over the future direction of the business. "Some how," he thought to himself, "I've got to learn more about how supply chain management is going to impact LSC. The discomforting fact is that such impact is probably going to arrive much sooner than either I or anybody else in this organization is willing to admit."

Company Background

Lexington Supply Company (commonly referred to as LSC) is a regional distributor of pipes, valves, and fittings located in Lexington, Kentucky. The owner and CEO of the company is George Pappas. George's father-in-law, Alex Gilardi, founded LSC in the mid-1950s; and George joined the company as its treasurer and CFO in 1963 after getting an MBA at Wharton. The business has grown significantly through the years and is now approaching $50 million in annual revenue. The company operates throughout the state of Kentucky, Southwestern Ohio, and Southern Indiana, but its core business is in the triangle formed by Lexington, Louisville, and Cincinnati. The main offices and warehouse are in Lexington, but there are branches in Louisville and Cincinnati.

LSC's main business is in the general market for maintenance, repair, and operating (MRO) supplies. Its principal customers are large factories or plants that purchase its principal product line (pipes, valves, and fittings, or PVF) mainly for facility and equipment upkeep.

The business originally focused on the Lexington market for small-diameter copper pipe (1″ to 3″ in diameter) used in residential and commercial plumbing applications. By I960, revenues had grown to over $1 million.

In 1962, medium-diameter pipe (4″ to 10″) had been added to the product line and LSC decided to open a branch in Cincinnati to focus on the southern and central areas of Ohio. Both the Lexington and Cincinnati locations inventoried a full range of products, and there were little or no inventory transfers between sites.

By 1965, revenues approached $5 million. In this year, LSC added large-diameter pipe (greater than 10″), including ductile iron and stainless steel, to its product line. Some of these were kept in inventory, but many were special order from the manufacturers.

In 1970, revenues reached $8 million. This was also about the time when fittings (essentially elbows, flanges, nipples, tees, "Y" connectors, and end caps) and valves were added to the product line in response to customer requests. Since some customers had locations throughout Kentucky and Ohio, this product line expansion precipitated the decision to open their third branch, in Louisville.

As the complexity of the business increased, an inventory analysis was performed that resulted in several key decisions being made:

1.   Only A and B inventory items for pipes and fittings were to be kept at Cincinnati and Louisville.

2.   All pipe with diameters of 10″ or greater were held in Lexington.

3.   Inter-branch transfers were now required between Lexington and the other two sites.

Contd...

Revenues hit $10 million by 1974 when LSC added large-diameter ball, gate, and butterfly valves to its product offering. Fast-moving valve products were located in all three locations, and the slow-moving (C) items were held only in Lexington. Expanding the product line, however, allowed many customers to consolidate orders, with the result being a dramatic revenue increase between 1974 and 1998.

Organization

As president, George Pappas has the following five key managers reporting directly to him (also see Figure 1). Each is based in Lexington; however, note that their subordinates may actually be located at one of the branches:

- Jamie "J. G." Curtis, purchasing manager

- Laura Ashton, Chief Financial Officer (CFO)

- Bob Packer, sales manager

- Callie Pappas, operations manager

- Sam Gilardi, inventory manager

Laura has responsibility for all billing, collections, and payment responsibilities for all three locations. These activities are centralized in Lexington and include four full-time and one part-time employee. For sales, LS.C is divided into four sales territories, each having its own sales representative located in the field and its own customer service representative at Lexington. These eight individuals report to Bob Packer. Callie oversees three distribution center (DC) supervisors, one transportation supervisor, and three transportation clerks. The DC supervisors and the three transportation clerks are located at the field locations. Sam has three inventory clerks reporting to him from the field locations. J. G. has a centralized purchasing operation consisting of three buyers, one for each product line.

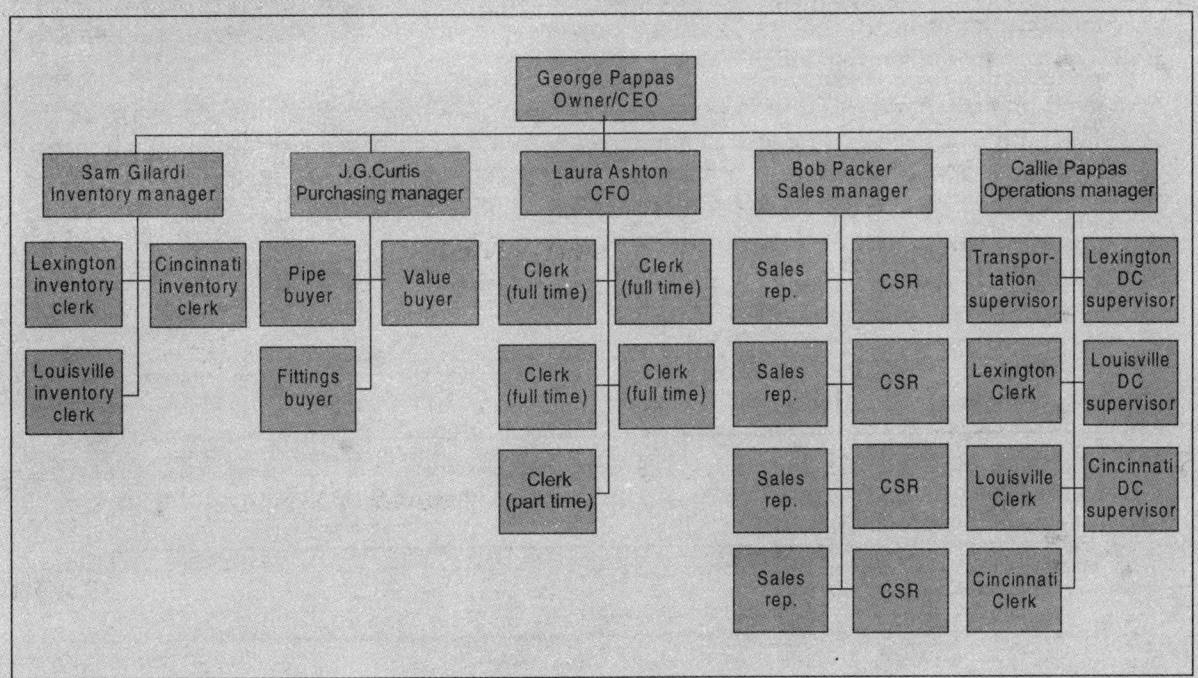

Figure 1: Organisation

Contd...

Supplier and Customer Bases

LSC suppliers are geographically dispersed across the United States. Suppliers for small and medium-diameter pipe are located in Pittsburgh, Green Bay, and Minneapolis; large-diameter pipe suppliers in Flint Michigan and Huntsville (Alabama); and valve suppliers in Cleveland (Columbia), Georgia (Philadelphia) and Birmingham (Alabama). Each supplier carries a full range of sizes. Fittings suppliers are located in Toledo; Topeka, Kansas; and Houston. Like the valve suppliers, these suppliers also carry a full range of fittings, including different diameters and alloys.

Shipments of small and medium pipe are either less than truckload (LTL) or truck-load (TL). Some of the TL moves are handled by 48" or 53" dry vans. Smaller-diameter pipe is loaded on returnable racks inside dry van trailers. LSC holds, the racks until a full TL can be returned to the supplier. Because inclement weather has little effect on pipe, flatbed trailers carry TL medium- and large-diameter pipe orders. Flatbed trailers are difficult to obtain during certain times of the year because of demand swings in such industries as construction where the movement of structural steel and precast concrete can consume much of the available capacity. All regular orders for valves and fittings are shipped to LSC by LTL carriers. Special order valves for oversize pipes may be shipped either by TL or flatbed trailers. The shipment terms for inbound product are FOB origin.

LSC's customers are industrial plant sites ordering PVF suppliers for general maintenance, operations, and repair. LSC's service area is defined by Wheeling (West Virginia) and Roanoke (Virginia) on the east, Knoxville and Nashville on the south, St. Louis on the west, and Indianapolis and Columbus (Ohio) on the north. However, 70 percent of sales come from customers within a 135-mile radius of each LSC location. Driving this concentration is LSC's guarantee of next-day delivery within this area.

Private fleets of trucks are maintained for customer deliveries and inter-branch transfers. The table below shows the kinds of vehicles, numbers of units, and base of operation. Tractor-trailer combinations each drive 50,000 miles per year at a unit cost of $1.45 resulting in $115,000 or $1,860,000 for the fleet when the cost of the additional five trailers is included. Seven straight trucks are also in the field for local deliveries of smaller orders. These are driven approximately 25,000 miles per year each at $0.85 per mile for a total cost of $297,000.

All routing and dispatching of LSC's fleet are done manually by the transportation clerks at the branches. A contract with a national LTL carrier is used for those customer shipments not made with the private fleet. Total cost per year of the contract is $150,000. The total combined inbound and outbound total annual transportation expenditures are $2,657,500 or about 5.3 percent of revenue.

Private Fleet Statistics

Location	Tractors		Trailers		
	Type	Units	Type	Units	Straights Units
Lexington, Kentucky	Tandem axle	3	48' flatbed	4	3
Louisville, Kentucky	Tandem axle	2	48' flatbed	3	2
Cincinnati, Ohio	Tandem axle	2	48' flatbed	3	2
Total units		7		10	7

Customer Interface

Customers place all orders by phone or fax through the customer service representatives (CSRs) in Lexington. There are currently no customers submitting orders by EDI.

Contd...

Upon arrival of an order, the CSR checks inventory availability at the designated shipping branch. Each branch takes inventory at the end of the day and reports it to Lexington each evening. If the inventory is available to fill the order completely at the primary shipping branch the inventory is allocated to that order. If only part of the inventory is available at the primary shipping branch, the CSR will look at inventory levels at other branches. In the case of C items, the CSR will always check availability at Lexington. If the C item is available in Lexington, it will be put on the next scheduled inter-branch transfer. If the vehicle reaches the primary delivery branch in time to match up the C item with the rest of the order, the complete order will be shipped to the customer. If it is not on time, the primary branch will deliver it as a split shipment.

If LSC does not have the inventory at any location (e.g., a special order pipe), a purchase order is created and forwarded to the buyer assigned to that commodity and supplier for placement. All customer orders and transfer orders are faxed to the appropriate branch each night.

Once the customer order is confirmed, it is sent to billing so an invoice can be created and mailed to the customer. Customers traditionally begin the payment process when their purchase order is matched with the delivery receipt and the invoice. If this matching process is successful, the customer will generate a check and mail it to LSC. If it is not, the customer calls the CSR to rectify the discrepancy.

Supplier Interface

Inventory control at the branches uses a min./max. system with ending inventories reported to Lexington nightly. Replenishment orders are generated by the branch inventory clerk but are typically placed by the appropriate buyer. LSC purchase orders are normally transmitted to the respective suppliers each morning by phone or fax. Special orders and emergency shipments are always telephoned. LSC has EDI capability for purchase order but only uses this with its largest supplier, Ajax Valve. Normal replenishment orders have specified lead times from each supplier. If the promised lead time cannot be met, the supplier will notify LSC of the actual delivery date. On special order and emergency shipments, lead times are given to the buyer who subsequently informs the CSR and/or the delivering branch of the expected delivery date.

LSC uses a payment process that is very similar to the one used by its customers. Invoices are generated based on as-shipped dates and mailed to LSC for processing.

Ajax Valve, the current exception, has begun using EDI to; send invoices to LSC and while developing the capability, cannot yet receive funds this way (EFT). When the LSC branch receives the shipment, the delivery receipt is compared to the purchase order. If they match, these documents are sent to LSC Lexington to be matched with the invoice. If all documents match, a check is generated and mailed to the supplier.

Stevenson Carbon Corporation

"I'm not surprised at what you're telling me," said Joe Cioffi to the group of consultants seated around the table in the conference room. "I know we spend a lot of time on supplies purchases and we apparently don't get it right too often either. Maintenance at all of the plants has complained about purchasing for so many years that I started to believe that it was just cultural."

Joe looked through the hard copy of the presentation one more time, took a deep breath, and finally said, "OK, we know we have a problem. Supplies purchasing costs us too much, and the service is poor. So what can we do about it?"

Background

Stevenson Carbon was founded in 1910 by Duncan Stevenson, a Scottish immigrant who had earned a degree in chemistry at Edinburgh University. Believing that there was a better, more economical method to manufacture asphalt and related products, he established his first plant near Pittsburgh.

Contd...

The Stevenson Process, as it was called in the patent, took prude tar, a by-product of steelmaking, and fractionally distilled it into asphalt, refined pitch, and a lesser range of benzenoid chemicals.

As it turned out, Stevenson's timing could not have been better. The growing U.S. population required improved roofing materials for its expanding cities; and, not too many years later, large quantities of asphalt were needed to support road-building, which used a new material invented by a fellow Scot named MacAdam.

Although growth had pretty much leveled off by the 1990s, Stevenson was a profitable firm with sales approaching $620 million annually. In addition to Pittsburgh, the company had plants, generally found in close proximity to steel mills-namely, in Gary, Indiana; Paducah, Kentucky; Baltimore, Maryland; and Birmingham, Alabama. Crude tar was purchased from Bethlehem, USSteel, LTV, and AK.

The process was essentially a closed one, but, because of the heat employed as well as the very nature of the material, it demanded significant and continuous streams of supplies to keep in operation. A breakdown of the categorizes and their respective annual corporate expenditures can be found in Table 1.

Organization

Each plant had a purchasing agent; but, despite the name, each was only in charge of supplies as raw materials were negotiated at the corporate level and released as needed by the plant manager. Similarly, capital equipment was specified, sourced, and negotiated by the plant engineer; although, in this case, purchasing did issue the confirming purchase order.

Table 1: Stevenson Carbon, Inc: Breakdown of MRO Expenditures

Pipe, valves and fittings	$ 5.2 million
Electrical supplies	1.2
Filters and strainers	1.2
Bearings	0.6
Welding & grinding supplies	0.4
Safety, health & environmental	0.2
Vehicle parts and tires	0.2
Misc. chemicals, cleaning, janitorial	0.1
Total	$9.1 million

Reporting directly to the plant manager, purchasing agents typically had four people working for them: usually a pair of purchasing clerks plus a pair of storeroom clerks, one of whom was considered lead clerk. This latter pair was responsible for receiving, put away, issues, maintaining inventory records, and occasionally delivering items to specific work sites.

Purchasing Process

Requisitions authorizing purchases arrive at purchasing from one of two sources: the storeroom or directly from the requisitioner. Direct requests are made when there is no known stock in the storeroom or when the requisitioner suspects that there are no stocks in the store but may not have checked.

Established practice for all items is over $500 to be placed only after three quotations have been obtained. The purchasing agent or more likely one of the clerks will obtain quotes for items of much lesser value when they believe that greater savings potential exists. While price is an import driver of purchasing decisions, delivery will take precedence when supplies are urgently required. Although occasionally attempted, purchasing will not compromise on specified quality unless substantial savings may be available by doing so. Usually, such a decision becomes the basis for major political battles between purchasing and engineering-battles frequently needing resolution at the plant manager level.

Contd...

Purchase order cycle time is an important consideration, and like many purchasing environments, most people "want it yesterday." The quoting process frequency slowed down cycle time as many times a supplier would need to make further inquiry and call the buyer back, or the buyer and seller would "play telephone tag"-all to the frustration of the maintenance technicians and all to the detriment of purchasing reputation.

But there was another source of irritation: maintenance felt that purchasing did not adequately understand the items they were being asked to buy; nor did they understand how those items were used within the plant. The problem-at least in the opinion held by the technicians-was that purchasing did not get out of its office to go learn these things. The purchasing agents more or less agreed with this view but claimed that they were too "snowed under" with work to be able to afford that particular luxury, however useful it might be.

Finally, there was the issue of supplier invoices. While Stevenson used a computerized, general ledger system, accounts payable remained archaic with manual matches of purchase orders, receiving tickets, and supplier invoices being made at each plant. If all three exactly matched, an online voucher screen was prepared and transmitted to Pittsburgh where checks were printed and mailed. In those instances where exact matches were not achieved, purchasing was instructed to resolve the discrepancies, arrange for revised documentation, and return everything to accounting for vouchering. Current estimates reveal that in excess of 20 percent of the match attempts fail on first try.

Storeroom Process

All inventoried items are kept in locked storerooms. Whenever maintenance technicians require an item, they go to the storeroom, submit an approved requisition for the item in exchange for its receipt, and return to their worksite, which in some situations may be close to a quarter-mile away. The requisition subsequently becomes true reordering authorization to replace the item in inventory that had been issued.

Frequently, however, the item may not be in stock, in which case the requisition is forwarded to purchasing where the item is sourced and an order placed. Other times, because of a pressing need, such as in the case of an emergency shutdown, the technician would request admission to the storeroom and attempt to "engineer on the fly" a solution to the problem from what appeared to be immediately available parts.

Some items in the storeroom are kept on the inventory system, but many have been in stock since before the system was implemented; hence, these records, some perhaps having been maintained on Kardex or others not at all, are unreliable at best. The result, of course, is that some items are found in two places in the storeroom: one where the system controls inventory; the other, where the old stores are kept. Either way, there appears to be much wasted effort in searching for items or for keeping unnecessarily large quantities on hand.

The Cost Meeting

"Look at this!" Geoff Staley, one of the staff consultants looking at MRO purchasing, exclaimed looking at the totals column on his computer spreadsheet. "It costs Stevenson over $251 per purchase order once we account for all the effort that goes into the total procurement cycle." (See Table 2).

"There has to be something wrong with that," came Joe's reply in utter disbelief. "We ran a similar analysis about two years ago and felt that $68 was pretty close to 'right-on.'"

Table 2: Cost elements of MRO Procurement cycle

Defining the purchase	$ 31
Defining the demand or need	
Prepare specification	

Contd...

Qualification of suppliers	
Determining if item in stock	$ 57
Search inventory record	
Physically look in storeroom	
Ordering	$ 47
Solicit prices and determine availability	
Place order and prepare documents	
Expedite orders	
Receiving orders	$ 26
Complete receiving ticket	
Contact requisitioner	
Put away in inventory	
Deliver/place item at jobsite	
Prepare payment	$ 32
Receive invoices	
Match documents	
Input voucher data	
Print checks	
Mail checks	
Resolve mismatches	
Stores inventory	$ 58
Inventory holding costs	
Put away costs	
Retrieval costs	
Record keeping costs	
Total	$251

But what did you include?" queried Bob. "Writing the requisition, submitting it to purchasing, placement of the order, receipt of the goods, and payment of the invoice?"

"That's- exactly the way we measured it. Costs of operating the purchasing department and accounts payable plus some portion of time for completion of requisitions by the user, but that didn't amount to much," said Joe.

"But how much time does the technician take looking for the stuff he needs or calling various suppliers trying to find something that may work. You have to take a look at purchasing as a process that many people do small parts of. It's not just a department with a name on the door."

"That's true," replied Joe.

"Geoff also included inventory considerations. There's a lot of stuff in the storeroom that has been obsolete for years, and there's even more that you carry too much in inventory. All that eats into working capital but also puts a demand on storeroom space-space that the clerks claim they don't have."

"And don't forget the informal inventories," Geoff reminded the two others. When maintenance guys strike out too often at the storeroom, they find ways to protect themselves such as building their own little cache of critical items. A friend of mine refers to these as the maintenance closets, but they're really located all over plant. It's like squirrels hiding nuts."

Contd...

"OK, you've made your point," said Joe. "What else does your analysis show?"

"Well," began Geoff, "of the thousands of purchase orders we've looked at, the median had a face value of only $158. That means Stevenson is paying $251 to place an order for S158! Doesn't sound like a very good deal to me, especially when your internal customers are complaining about the service?"

"I hear what you guys are saying, but what can we possibly do about it?"

"We've seen some interesting developments along this line. For one, some of the major oil companies such as Amoco have been implementing something called integrated supply. It takes purchasing out of the transaction loop by using some carefully selected suppliers who are connected to both you and to each other electronically. The idea is to simplify both the process and the supplier relationship to the point that they will maintain on-site inventories close to the point of use. The stocks are replenished on a pre-established schedule and summary billed to you monthly."

"You know, now that I think about it, there was an article in Purchasing Magazine about something like this being implemented at Bethlehem Steel," Joe thought out loud.

"That is one of the better-known ones," said Geoff. "But you already have a plant that's fooling with it but probably doesn't recognize it as such. Paducah has its pipe, valves, and fittings (PVF) wholesaler placing a locked trailer on the plant property. Each electrical foreman has a key and just takes what's needed. The supplier checks the usage and replenishes every Wednesday morning. Gus Schmidt (the Paducah chief engineer) seems to like it a lot."

"Let's see. What will it take to formally expand this into a formal programme encompassing a full range of items and ultimately implementing at all of our plants?" affirmed Joe.

Lexington meets with Stevenson

Bob Packer, sales manager for Lexington, in filling his role as the national accounts manager, called on Joe Cioffi at Stevenson's headquarters near Pittsburgh. The purpose of such a visit was (1) to maintain the long-standing relationship between the two firms, and (2) to gain a better insight for the potential demand that the Stevenson plants anticipated during the next calendar quarter or two.

"We're starting to rethink the process we use to purchase MRO," began Joe, catching Bob quite unaware. "We have too many suppliers, too many transactions, too many internal resources committed, and too few dollars expended. Something has got to give somewhere. We've already conducted some in-house seminars and developed a cross-functional team consisting of those individuals having a vested interest in the outcome, and held some exploratory meetings with some potentially interested suppliers."

"But we've been suppliers to Stevenson for years," responded Bob, admittedly a bit defensively. "Lexington has always, given you competitive prices and superior service. I can even remember taking phone calls at home in the middle of the night to keep Paducah running."

"True enough, Bob, and we really appreciate that, but we've got to find a better way," continued Joe. "We've got some consultants working with a team down at the Paducah plant. They're looking to find ways where we can work smarter-you know simplify the business-to-business processes and perhaps add some of the latest, and now much more affordable, information technologies. I think that they're going to be ready to issue a request for proposal in the not too distant future."

"Well, I can tell you, Joe. We have at least one supplier who seems to be thinking in that same direction. I'm sure we'll be in here again soon with some intriguing ideas."

"I don't want to sound threatening, Bob," began Joe, "but the market is changing. Those suppliers who can't come up with new relationships, new ways of doing business or approaches that add value all the way through the supply chain are going to be the ones to fall by the wayside. We just can't afford to do business that way any more."

Contd...

Bob, now furiously taking notes, was already formulating the wording for his call report. "It sure won't make George Pappas's day when he reads this one," he thought to himself.

Proposal for Supplier Collaboration

A few days ago, the principals of LSC had attended a major presentation from one of their leading suppliers, Ajax Valve Company, on the subject of "vendor-managed inventories." Sales of the Ajax line represent about 15 percent of LSC's overall sales. The presentation described a new to programme to allow for better information sharing and collaboration between LCS and Ajax based on a new concept called collaborative planning, forecasting, and replenishment, or CPFR. Ajax's programme was called FASTER, the acronym for forecasting and scheduling technique for efficient replenishment.

In addition to Ajax's presentation, George had also recently read about a CPFR programme called HOPS, which Heineken USA had implemented with its distributors. He had been impressed that Heineken had taken the initiative to develop the supply chain capability on behalf of its distributors and that, apparently, it was producing benefits for all parties.

Key features of FASTER are as follows

- Communications will be via the Internet and a Web browser. The main technology investment will be by Ajax, which will have to install a new server and collaboration software.

- The program will focus on the A items of Ajax that LSC carries. This would be approximately the top fifty SKUs that would represent 85 percent of sales.

- On a weekly basis, planners at Ajax and buyers at LSC would exchange sales, "on hands", and one-month and three-month forecasts for the items involved. Ajax would also forward the master production schedule for the following four weeks. Each would review the other's information for discrepancies.

- If there were discrepancies, the planner and buyer would exchange e-mail messages or phone calls to rectify.

- Based on the commonly agreed-to forecasts, Ajax would provide LSC with a weekly suggested replenishment order. LSC would review the order, add B and C items, and submit it.

- Order tracking would also be facilitated by the system.

- LSC sales info on B and C items would also be shared with Ajax. An expected future feature of the program would be for Ajax to take over warehousing and distribution of slow-movers.

Ajax's expectations were that FASTER would enable it and its distributors to reduce inventories, lower transaction costs, and cut lead times. A preliminary estimate of, the cost to LSC to join FASTER was about $20,000 for hardware, software, and communications expenditures.

Planning for the Future

George Pappas called together his executive team to discuss the integrated supply and CPFR issues. He realized that LSC was at a critical juncture in its history. In the past "arm's-length transactions" were the rule in their relationships with both customers and suppliers. The world was changing now, and George felt pressure from both customers and suppliers to work more closely together toward common objectives. Assembled were Laura Ashton, Bob Packer, Gallic Pappas, and J. G. Curtis and Sam Gilardi.

George: I appreciate your being able to join me on short notice. We are faced, with making some key decisions, and everyone's input will be important. As you know, one of our largest accounts, Stevenson, has asked us to develop an integrated supply capability and one of our largest vendors, Ajax, is pushing us to participate in a new collaboration program. I don't believe these are isolated situations. I feel they might be trends that will shape the way we will operate with most of our customers and suppliers in the future.

Contd...

Bob: I know that's true on the customer side. Many of our bigger customers are waking up to the opportunity to reduce their MRO purchasing costs. Through programs like integrated supply. We do have to do something now or it will soon be too late. You've seen my call report from Stevenson Carbon at Pittsburgh.

J. G.: The pressure is not as great from our suppliers, but it's there just the same. I believe Ajax is on the cutting edge with what they are proposing.

Callie: I have some concerns about the Ajax approach, but I, too, feel it's an opportunity we should look closely at.

George: What's bothering you?

Collie: Well, it's mostly technology adoption and partnering concerns. Are we really ready for this Internet stuff? Is the Internet ready? How will our roles change? Can we trust Ajax with the sensitive information we will be sending them? Do they really, have our interests at heart, or is this just another program for a vendor to push inventory and cost back on us? How will we know if the program is working? Our measurement systems-forgive my language-really suck.

George: Callie, my first thoughts on these programs are that they are "must dos," which should be justifiable from a financial perspective. I think we can afford them. Or, put better, maybe we can't afford not to do them. What do you think?

J. G.: We need to give it serious consideration because I'm hearing these things elsewhere. I had a conversation with one of our stainless pipe suppliers who told me about a partnership that's forming near Cincinnati called RTS Group, which means real time supply. As I understand it, it, too, uses an information technology solution to link noncompeting wholesalers together with a common business process. I think integrated supply is here right now.

George: Sounds like more evidence suggesting that maybe we need to look real hard about getting into this way of doing business.

Laura: George, you know it won't be easy. In particular, getting up and running with integrated supply will be expensive. My first thoughts, too, are that this will be a lot of effort and money for just one customer and one supplier. I think, also, that it would be prudent for us to do an informal cost-benefit analysis for both proposals. I think we have a good handle on what the costs are, but how about the benefits?

Sam: I realize that many of the benefits of integrated supply are soft, but I truly believe we will lose Stevenson and some other major accounts if we don't move forward. One of the "benefits" will definitely be avoiding lost customers and sales! Also, the window of opportunity with someone like this RTS Group might close pretty quickly on us. They might select another PVF distributor for this area.

George: As you know, we have a board meeting next week, and I would like to discuss these issues with Alex and the outside board members. But, first, we need to do some more thinking. As a team, I'd like to propose we do the following for both of the projects:

1.   Develop a list of the expected benefits.

2.   Develop a list of what we feel will be the problems or "down sides."

3.   Identify the key barriers that might be expected in implementing the programs.

4.   For the three most important barriers, create a list of initial action steps to overcome them.

Source: This case was prepared by William L. Grenoble. Robert A. Novack. and Richard R. Young, all of the Center for Supply Chain Research, The Pennsylvania State University. Reprinted with the kind permission of the author.

As J. Franklin, Managing Director of Burke Engineering, you have now completed the business plan. Action is now necessary to change the company from one providing a range of low margin general engineering services into a specialist of high value-added valve manufacturer. This will involve the company in operating in new areas, and you must identify the core operations of the firm those that it will carry out using its own personnel, and those that can be more effectively left to other organizations. Some of the areas that have historically been handled in-house are of particular concern. Initially you have decided to concentrate upon the following areas of operation: (a) Tool cutting, (b) Foundry operations, (c) Physical distribution, (d) Data processing, (e) Catering, (f) Security, and (g) Cleaning.

Tool Cutting

Because of the increasing complexity of valve design and construction, meeting customer demands would steadily become more costly. Currently, Burke's investment in tool cutting was limited to old style lathes and drilling equipment. Introducing the entire range of computer aided cutting equipment into the area would place a substantial cost burden on the company. The plan indicates that the tooling problems facing the company would inevitably increase, as both the number of customers and the depth of product range grew.

The entire department would also be under greater pressure with the reduced time that could be allowed in the tooling process. It was thought likely that the total number of tools required would rise from around 100 to over 500; the complexity of each tool would more than double, and tools would have to be available within four rather than six weeks. You had investigated the alternatives of using outside contractors to provide support in both areas. A number of suppliers could meet Burke Engineering's needs in the foreseeable future. There were advantages and disadvantages associated with each of these but three contractors had been identified as possible tool suppliers.

Panopil of Portugal: Panopil was heavily used by many companies in the toy industry, and was increasing its share of the engineering market in the West Midlands. It had a whole range of computer controlled cutting equipment in its plant near Lisbon in Portugal. It offered a comprehensive service for all types of tooling from the very small to the largest currently used by UK manufacturing industry. The speed of tool production varied according to the complexity and the urgency of the request, but were costed on an individual basis and the company did not require overseas companies to enter into any other contractual agreement. For Burke, the majority of their valve designs would require a two week turn round to which would have to be added the journey time from Portugal (an additional week). It was likely that Panopil could offer cost savings of around 35 percent on the current Burke tool cutting operation.

Driffield Toolmakers: Driffield Toolmakers were the leading specialist toolmaker in the Midlands. It had been established to service the requirements of the steel industry, but had, with the demise of most manufacturing in that area, been forced to diversify into automotive and other components. The company had some of the more sophisticated cutting equipment, but much of its work still used traditional machinery. The company had a high reputation for producing quality work. The costing system differed from Panopil. It required a fixed contract system whereby the manufacturer guaranteed a specific revenue over a two year period. This fixed contract covered all the costs of the standard range of items, which would be established at the initial discussions between Driffield and the manufacturer, special requirements would be additionally costed. The completion time for the typical Burke product would be around two weeks from the date of design despatch. Driffield Toolmakers required a minimum annual order and were likely to be around 10 percent more expensive than Panopil.

Contd...

Advanced Tool Design (ATD): ATD was a small newly established company, developed to provide tool cutting services for the specialist manufacturers servicing the Channel Tunnel. Although it had the latest tool cutting technology, as a new company it had not yet established a reputation and was eager to offer its services on a single project basis in a similar fashion to Panopil. Because of fluctuations in demand from the Channel Tunnel, it could not guarantee as fast a turn round as Driffield Toolmakers. Of the three potential suppliers the company offered the fastest potential turnaround of about 18 days (though this varied according to the complexity of the tool), there was no minimum order and the cost was likely to be between that of Driffield Toolmakers and Panopil.

Foundry

Though the foundry area was the most up to date part of Burke's production process, it was limited to temperatures up to 1500°C and could not handle the largest sizes of industrial valve which the company might be asked to produce. It was likely that around a quarter of total future production would require either higher temperatures or the ability to handle larger sizes, the current plant would not be able to cope effectively with the entire range of new products. As the most recently replaced equipment, cost savings on production of the current range would not be substantial, but the installation of a new system so soon after it had been initially installed would worry the major investors which had put up the money for the initial installation only 18 months previously.

With the decline in manufacturing industry in the Midlands, there were a large number of companies in the area that had excess foundry capacity and were keen to gain extra revenue by subcontracting. Because they were locally based none of the prospective subcontractors required any minimum order arrangement and would cost the work on a cost plus basis, the elements of which were clearly understood: size, complexity, temperature, and raw materials. Three local companies seemed likely to provide high levels of service.

Extruded Metal: Extrum was one of the largest metal manufacturing companies in the West Midlands with expertise dating back to the turn of the century. It had three large foundries, one was currently closed and the other two were operating between 66 and 78 percent capacity. Because of its large size and spare capacity, Extrum could offer a rapid completion of work with an average quoted delivery time of three days, but was more expensive than the other two alternatives, though around 10 percent cheaper than Burke's current manufacturing costs. It was also insisting on a fairly large annual commitment, though this appeared to be negotiable.

David Engineering: David Engineering was a medium sized engineering firm, with a turnover about 50 percent higher than Burke's. It specialised in the manufacture of high quality steel for the construction industry, especially the production of girders where high levels of purity and performance were required. It had one large foundry, which operated at around 75 percent capacity. David Engineering prices appeared to be around 5 percent lower than Extrum, though this and the lower minimum order requirement was to an extent offset by the substantially longer delivery periods of up to ten days.

Calsall Industries: A company very similar to David Engineering it had two large foundries which operated at around 60 percent capacity. It could provide a fairly rapid service, and though this was the first time that it offered subcontracting work, it decided against setting preconditions to the use of their foundry by outside firms. Though Calsall Industries were primarily concerned with the manufacture of pure metal components for other manufacturers, it had over the last five years moved increasingly into original equipment manufacture, including the production of more and more valves. Calsall Industries was the cheapest of all three companies contacted by a small margin (around 3 percent) and offered an average delivery period of eight days. They also required some form of commitment over the year to a minimum order level, but this appeared to be nominal.

Physical Distribution

The plan you have developed for Burke Engineering insists upon a major move away from submersible and general engineering into the manufacture of sophisticated valves, both in UK but increasingly overseas. The company's physical distribution system would have to reflect this shift towards the more rapid delivery of smaller weight items of higher individual value, and away from the movement

Contd...

of heavy products. It was likely that the number of customers would increase from around 200 to nearly 1,000 over 5 years; the company would become more and more international with average distances between the company and customers increasing from 50 to 250 miles; customers would be more and more demanding on rapid delivery schedules even though the average order would be likely to decline from around 250 to 75 kilos.

The implication of such a change was that total journeys would increase fivefold from 1,200 to nearly 6,000; mileage would grow from 35,000 to nearly 250,000, while the total tonnage carried would drop from 800 to around 200. It appeared from analysis that there would be three main transport requirements: orders of low weight but high value to UK customers, similar orders to international clients, and high weight but low value to UK customers. Currently the transport department employed five drivers, and used a variety of vehicles for different types of delivery. The cost of the current operation was about € 380,000 per annum, and with the far greater spread of overseas customers the forecast physical distribution cost using the same system of operation is around € 650,000, a fivefold increase in cost per ton.

Obviously the difference between the transport costs of general engineering, submersible equipment, and valves was considerable. The current method of covering the distribution costs across the entire range of Burke products made accurate costing on a single product group basis very difficult to achieve. However with the change to valves, the likely unit load would be around 35 kilos with an average order size of 8 units, with the result that a much greater control over distribution costs could be envisaged.

Various companies offering particular types of freight forwarding service had sprung up over the past ten years in the West Midlands. These ranged from freelance operators with their own lorries, to large and sophisticated firms that provided anything from local deliveries to international despatch. Each had different charging arrangements, minimum orders, and extra costs, and three companies had been approached for the details of the service that they provided.

Seacost Distribution: Seacost was a medium-sized company based in the Midlands. It had grown rapidly from providing a small local service to one that operated throughout the United Kingdom and offered international transport services to the EEC and other destinations. The costing system was based on one or more of three possible tariffs. One tariff was based on weight and guaranteed delivery within 48 hours within the United Kingdom; two international rates, one using air freight and the other offering consolidated loads for onward delivery to overseas customers. The UK tariff worked out at approximately € 2 per kilo on a national basis; EEC tariff were € 8 per kilo (air freight) and € 3.50 when loads were consolidated.

FDS Services: FDS was one of the major national firms with a local office near Burke Engineering. FDS provided contract hire vehicles for a range of transport requirements: from very large loads to small vans including drivers when required. Because it was a contract hire company, there was a standard charge associated with each vehicle, generally over a three year period. The contract hire cost, which included all driver and maintenance costs, but not fuel, ranged from € 17,000 for a small van to € 65,000 for the largest truck.

Advance Trucking: Advance Trucking was a small firm with offices only 2 miles from Burke Engineering which offered a highly flexible service. It would provide freight forwarding for overseas customers on the basis of € 5 per kilo throughout the EEC and national delivery on a sliding scale; with small deliveries below 200 kilos costing € 3 per kilo and deliveries above 1,000 kilo around € 2 per kilo, falling to € 1.5 per kilo for 20,000 kilo loads.

Catering

The plan involved both a considerable drop in the overall number of people employed by Burke, and a move towards 16 or 24-hour production from the single current 8 hour shift, with the factory changing from 5 to 7 day working. This would mean that the current catering operation would have to be drastically overhauled to meet the new demands being placed upon it. Daily lunches would drop from

Contd...

350 to around 95, and the company would also have to provide the same number of evening meals and breakfasts on a daily basis. Currently, catering costs were a major overhead cost to the company.

With the split canteen system, the subsidy per meal ranged from € 2.50 (managers), at an average cost of € 3.00 (a total estimated subsidy of € 80,000 per annum) and € 0.80 per shop floor employee at an average cost of € 1.20 (an estimated annual subsidy of € 70,000 per annum). The catering operation enabled the company to entertain in-house, a cost which would otherwise have to be borne by the individual departments. In the previous year there had been 350 visitors entertained in the management dining room, though the total number of potential customers entered in the sales log was only 80. You have asked for quotes from three catering organizations for their proposals to replace the current catering service, based on the creation of a single canteen for all staff.

Grand Picadilly: Grand Picadilly was a subsidiary of one of the national firms, with substantial experience in providing on-site catering for all types of industrial operation. It had quoted an inclusive fee of € 35,000 to provide the level of meals anticipated in the self service operation, but they would not be able to make any special provision for visitors. Meal costs would rise to an approximate € 1.50 for all staff.

Extra Catering: Extra Catering was one of the local firms that supplied catering services to the three factories nearest to the Burke Engineering site. It had come to inspect the current operation, and was of the opinion that it could provide a substantially better service at lower cost. First, it would introduce microwave cookers and self-service chilled cabinets with pies, hamburgers, and chips, which would provide the bulk of the meal demands. Staff requiring this service would pay the raw material cost of all the ingredients. Secondly, Extra Catering would provide a full service operation for those that did not want self-service fast food, with a range of menus, and if booked in advance a waitress service for guests. Extra Catering would provide all the raw materials and equipment, and price meals on a cost plus 10 percent basis. For the average meal this would mean around € 1.30. The quote for this service was € 20,000 per annum.

Speed Feed: SF was a national company that specialized in providing 24-hour catering cover for manufacturing and service companies. It offered the same type of service as Extra Catering with a whole range of prepared meals, either frozen or fresh, which could be heated at the time of consumption. The company made its money from the sale of products, rather than providing a full service function. It offered to install all the equipment free, provided the company could sign a three year contract. Cleaning costs would be carried by Speed Feed within the overall cleaning costs of the company. The average cost of meals would be € 1.70 per head.

Data Processing

Currently, the company employed four staff in the area of data processing (at an annual cost of € 55,000) and had installed a large computer, which was on an annual lease of € 35,000. The system had suffered from a considerable lack of expertise and delays in implementation, especially now that the data processing manager had resigned. It was possible that outside bureaux could provide a far better and more cost-effective service. The two companies approached had all substantial experience in the provision of data processing support for manufacturing companies: BDS and OnLine Processing.

BDS: BDS were one of the major regional data processing bureaux. They had invested in a large mainframe computer in late 1987 and so could provide one of the most rapid and comprehensive data processing services available locally. The company operated either a batch or an online service, with batch provision being considerably cheaper than online. With the batch service, the client had to provide all the data on specifically designed forms and deliver them to the company by messenger.

The likely total cost to Burke Engineering was difficult to define, but on the current data load the cost would be around € 25,000, though there was the proviso that this cost could rise if the complexity

Contd...

of the data or its volume increased. The online data processing service involved a basic cost of 10 per hour with additional processing time when and if required. It was likely that this would cost in the region of € 50,000 for the current data requirements of the company, though you have found that online access to data processing companies tends to substantially increase the amount of data processing that is carried out.

OnLine Processing: The major alternative was OnLine Processing. This company specialised in instant access. It offered tailor made management systems, creating software for particular applications within the client company. The cost of the creation of these programs depended on their complexity. OnLine estimated that with the current operation 20 programs would be required, each costing between € 500 and € 2,500. Once established the cost to Burke Engineering would vary according to the amount of access that the company required. With the current level of demand, OnLine estimated that access costs would be € 35,000 but should greater demands be made costs would inevitably rise.

Security

The current Burke Engineering security operation was limited to one security officer with six security guards on a 24-hour basis, costing € 35,000 per annum. You are aware of problems such as high levels of theft and damage to possessions and equipment throughout the factory and administration block.

Part of this was due to the poor physical security on the site. This was also the view of a firm of security consultants which had been brought into advise on safety aspects (memo provided in previous chapter). The poor physical security meant that Burke Engineering had to employ large numbers of security staff, even though some of these staff were used to meet staff shortfalls in certain key areas, such as local deliveries and collections.

There were a large number of alternative security firms in the area, three of which had provided quotations.

Dagmar Security: DS was one of the small operators in the area. They offered a mobile security service throughout the site on a 24-hour basis for around € 15,000 per annum. These mobile patrols would include dog handlers during the night to reduce the potential for theft throughout the site. They suggested that a two-hour patrol would be adequate throughout the day and night.

Prestige Security: Prestige Security was one of the large regional firms which had been established for over 20 years. They quoted for a fixed security presence during the day to monitor movements in and out of the plant, combined with a mobile patrol during the night. To meet the requirements they considered that the annual cost would be of the region of € 25,000.

Alpha Guards: Alpha Guards was one of the largest national firms. They suggested that a combined team of security guards at fixed points to monitor the movements of goods in and out of the plant, together with a roving patrol over the 24-hour period. Cost would be around € 32,000 per annum.

Cleaning

Currently the company employed around 10 part-time cleaning ladies. Because of the elderly nature of much of the plant they had not been able to make a great impact on much of the company, but they kept the administration block extremely clean and neat. The costs of cleaning were € 20,000 per year. You have received a number of quotes which are all surprisingly similar. All the main three cleaning companies have quoted € 15,000 per annum to provide a comprehensive cleaning service.

Action

Which of the areas that you as J Franklin has considered should be subcontracted? What problems do you think that the company is likely to encounter in subcontracting?

Case 4
Parker Instruments Ltd.

Overview

Parker Instruments Ltd. (PI) is a British firm that operates as a manufacturer and an importer/distributor. Its field is electronic instruments, and the imported products account for about 75 percent of sales. One of the companies Parker Instruments represents in the United Kingdom is Electro Industries (EI), a Canadian precision instrument firm. PI and EI have been working together for about ten years. The relationship between the two companies was good for a number of years. Then things started to go wrong, and this was accentuated by an accident that robbed EI of its top two executives. The time of the case is one year after the accident. George Parker feels strong ties to EI but is increasingly worried by the Canadian company's seeming indifference to its international operations in general and to the relationship with PI in particular.

George Parker locked the door of his car and walked across the parking lot toward the station entrance. Although it was a sunny spring morning and the daffodils and tulips provided welcome color after the grayness of winter, Parker hardly noticed. Within a few minutes the train from London would be arriving, and with it Bruce MacDonald, the export sales manager for Electro Industries-a Canadian firm that George's company represented in the United Kingdom. Parker would be spending the day with MacDonald, and he wondered what the outcome of their discussions would be.

Parker Instruments Ltd.

George Parker was managing director of Parker Instruments Ltd., part of a small, family-owned U.K. group of companies. The company gained its first sales agency in 1923 (from a U.S. manufacturer), which made it one of the most well-established international trading firms in electronic instruments. PI sales were equivalent of about $1 million, with 75 percent coming from imported distributed items and 25 percent from sales of its own manufactured items. The company had a total of 15 employees. PI was the U.K. distributor for 15 manufacturers located in the United States, Canada, Switzerland, and Japan. Like many firms, it found the 80/20 rule held true; about 80 percent of the import sales of $750,000 were generated by 20 percent of the distributorships it held. With current sales of $165,000, the Electro Industries distributorship was an important one.

Electro Industries

Electro Industries was a younger and larger organization than its U.K. distributor. Located in southern Ontario, it was founded in the mid-1950s and had current sales of $2 million and a workforce of 90 employees. EI had developed a strong reputation over the years for its high precision instrumentation and testing equipment, and this led to considerable market expansion. The company had moved in a number of new product directions. The original products were very precise devices for use in standard laboratories. From this base it had more recently established a presence in the oceanographic and electric power fields.

As a result of this expansion, 80 percent of sales arc now made outside Canada split evenly between the United States and offshore markets. In the United States, the company had its own direct-sales organization, whereas indirect methods were used elsewhere. In the "best" fifteen offshore markets, EI had exclusive distributors; in thirty other markets, it relied on commission agents.

Working Together

EI and PI first made contact in New York City, and the two companies agreed to work together. George Parker was on a business trip in the United States when he received a cable from his brother saying that a representative of EI wanted to get in touch with him. Parker and his wife met the senior executive in their hotel room and after initial introductions, settled down to exchange information. At

Contd...

some point, Parker, who had had a hectic day, fell asleep. He awoke to find that PI was now more or less EI's U.K. distributor, his wife having kept the discussion rolling while he slept.

The two firms soon began to prosper together. The distributorship gave PI a product line to complement those it already carried. Furthermore, the EI instruments were regarded as the "Cadillac's" of the Industry. This ensured entry to the customer's premises and an interest in the rest of the PI product line. As far as EI was concerned, it could hardly have chosen a more suitable partner. PI's staff was technically competent, facilities existed for product servicing, and customer contacts were good. Moreover, as time passed, George Barker's long experience and international connections proved invaluable to EI. He was often asked for an opinion prior to some new move by the Canadian producer. Parker preferred to have a close working relationship with the firms he represented, so he was happy to provide advice. In this way, PI did an effective job of representing EI in the United Kingdom and helped with market expansion elsewhere.

As might be expected, the senior executives of the companies got along well together. The president and vice president of marketing-EI's "international ambassadors"-and George Parker progressed from being business partners to becoming close personal friends. Then, after nine successful years, a tragedy occurred: the two EI executives were killed in an airplane crash on their way home from a sales trip.

The tragic accident created a management succession crisis within EI. During this period, international operations were left dangling while other priorities were attended to. Nobody was able to take charge of the exporting activities that had generated such good sales for the company. Although there was an export sales manager Bruce MacDonald, he was a relative newcomer, having been in training at the time of the accident. He was also a middle-level executive, whereas his international predecessors were the company's most senior personnel.

From Parker's point of view, things were still not right a year later. The void in EI's international operations had not been properly filled. Bruce MacDonald had proved to be a competent manager, but he lacked support because a new vice president of marketing had yet to be appointed. A new president headed the company, but he was the previous vice president of engineering and preferred to deal with technical rather than business issues. So despite the fact that MacDonald had a lot of ideas about what should be done internationally (most of which were similar to George Parker's ideas), he lacked both the position and the support of a superior to bring about the necessary changes.

While the airplane accident precipitated the current problems in the two companies' relationship, Parker realized that things had been going sour for a couple of years. At the outset of the relationship, EI executives had welcomed the close association with PI. Overtime, however, as the manufacturer grew in size and new personnel came along, it seemed to Parker that his input was increasingly resented. This was unfortunate, because Parker believed that EI could become a more sophisticated international competitor if it considered advice given by informed distributors. In the past, EI had been open to advice and had benefited considerably from it. Yet there were still areas where EI could effect improvements. For example, its product literature was of poor quality and was often inaccurate or outdated. Prices were also worrisome. EI seemed unable to hold its costs, and its competitors now offered better "value-for-money" alternatives. Other marketing practices needed attention also.

The Oceanographic Market

One area where EI and PI were in disagreement was the move into the oceanographic field. George Parker was pleased to see EI moving into new fields, but wondered if EI truly appreciated how "new" the field was. In a way, he believed the company had been led by the technology into the new field rather than having considered the "fit" between its capabilities and success criteria for the new field. For example, the customer fit did not seem even close. The traditional buyers of EI products for use in standards laboratories were scientists, some of whom were employed by government, some by

Contd...

industry, and some by universities. By and large they were academic types, used to getting their equipment when the budget permitted. As a result, selling was "gentlemanly," and follow-up visits were required to maintain contacts. Patience was often required, since purchasing cycles could be relatively long. Service needs were not extensive, for the instruments were used very carefully.

In contrast, the oceanographic products were used in the very demanding sea environment. Service needs were acute, due to not just the harsh operating environment but also to the cost associated with having inoperable equipment. For example, ocean research costs were already high but became even higher if faults in Shipboard equipment prevented taking sea measurements. In such a situation, the customer demanded service today or tomorrow, wherever the faulty equipment was located. The oceanographic customer was also a difficult type-still technically trained but concerned about getting the job done as quickly as possible. Purchasing budgets were much less of a worry; if the equipment was good, reliable, and with proven back-up, chances were it could be sold. But selling required more of a push than the laboratory equipment.

When EI entered the oceanographic field, a separate distributor was appointed in the United Kingdom. However, the arrangement did not work out. EI then asked George Parker to carry the line, and with great reluctance he agreed. The lack of enthusiasm was due to Parker's perception that his company was not capable of functioning well in this new arena. Because PI was ill equipped to service the oceanographic customer, it was thought that there could even be repercussions. In its more traditional field, Parker was unwilling to risk the company's established reputation in this way. However, while he preferred not to represent EI in the oceanographic field, he worried about a "one market, one distributor" mentality at EI.

The Current Visit

George Parker had strong personal sentiments for EI as a company. In his opinion, however, some concrete action was required if the business relationship was to survive, let alone prosper.

Parker recognized the good sales of EI products, but also took note of shrinking profit margins over the last few years due to the increased costs PI faced with the EI product line. Since EI was slow to respond to service and other problems, PI had been putting things right and absorbing the associated costs more and more frequently. However, these costs could not be absorbed forever. Parker had been willing to help tide EI over the last difficult year, but expected a more positive response in the future.

George Parker hoped that Bruce MacDonald would bring good news from Canada. Ideally he hoped to drop the oceanographic line and rebuild the "bridges" that used to exist between his firm and the manufacturer. A return to the close and helpful relationship that once existed would be welcomed. However, he wondered if EI's management wanted to operate in a more formal and distant "buy-and-sell" manner. If this were the case, George Parker would have to give more serious thought to the EI distributorship.

Source: The case was prepared by Professor Philip Rosson of Dalhousie University, Halifax, Nova Scotia, Canada, as a basis for class discussion rather than to illustrate the effective of ineffective handling of an administrative situation. The names of the companies and persons have been changed, but in all other respects the case study is factual. Copyright 1984 Philip Rosson. Reprinted with the kind permission of the author.

You as J Franklin have decided to visit Margerine SA with the sales manager D Grayson. This company is one of the largest potential clients in France for the new motorized valve. You were reviewing with D Grayson the information that was available on the company and its senior buyer, R Noyons, who you are to meet.

You are also interested in whether the company would be a potential client for the new "smart" valve. Two companies in Northern France are already testing the new products for Burke. Now that the dispute between the separate departments has been resolved by a re-organization of the company, it is likely that full scale introduction of the range can commence in 3 or 4 months.

The continuing drive into the highly sophisticated end of the market was creating strains within the organization as the company had originally been organized to service a single customer type requiring standard traditional engineering. Recently, Burke had been serving an increasingly sophisticated clientele as well as the old customer base. The division of the company along customer lines, with the formation of a high technology service department, is seen by you as a logical step to provide the support that the new customers require. The creation of such a new structure had been further supported by the interest that the US and Pacific rim markets had continued to show in the "smart" valve.

With the promotion of J Porter to the board of directors, the creation of a sales subsidiary to service those markets was also becoming necessary. With the separation of the company into customer based divisions, there was a need to re-organize the existing sales and marketing department, and their staff into standard engineering and high technology divisions. D Grayson seems an ideal candidate for the high technology division, as the appraisal in Appendix B indicates.

Margerine SA

Margerine Industries is one of the largest manufacturers of additives and flavours for the European food industry. Additives and fats were complex chemical products and required sophisticated control systems, including valves, throughout the large manufacturing areas. Margerine SA turnover had steadily grown over the years and it now employed over 5,000 staff on three sites. Turnover was now approximately € 250 million and profitability in the last year had reached € 18 million pre-tax. Both sales and profitability were on a growth trend.

In its core market, the company was well protected by the structure of French industry, which encouraged the major home market manufacturers to buy from French suppliers. With the steady removal of barriers due to the unified European market, the company was facing increased competition from other European companies, especially Dutch and German. It was predicted that the erosion of market share would tend to be slower than most forecasts anticipated. During the past 3 years, the company had moved from high volume but low profit fats and animal feeds, into an increasingly sophisticated area of manufacturing flavours, fragrances, and additives, which were much more profitable than the traditional fats or animal feed additives.

Fragrances now accounted for nearly a quarter of the profit from around 10 percent of turnover, with additives and flavours accounting for an additional 30 percent profit from the same percentage of turnover. The company was also becoming more international. It had established successful sales subsidiaries in Germany and Italy and was starting to develop in the United States. Here, the strengthening of the dollar against the European currencies had meant that the company had suffered losses during the past 2 years. Regardless of this increasing international outlook, the company was still dominated by French speaking engineers with a background in volume rather than specialist

Contd...

manufacture. Many individuals employed by the company were having difficulties with the demands of the new products.

As the company moved away from fats into fragrances and flavours, quality control became more important. Sophisticated products were also made in much smaller quantities, creating further production problems. A contributory factor had been the failure of some of the new, mainly French production control equipment and the effects of the limited maintenance program. The shortage of skilled manpower meant that Margerine were unlikely to be able to fully meet the demands of the new equipment within the next 18 months.

The company had been spending heavily on the re-organization and re-equipping of the three factories, to meet the demands of the new strategy, and this appeared to be having a severe impact on the cash flow of the entire group. The best estimates of the investment and the current age of the equipment, had been gained from the study of the companies annual report. Capital spending was now running at € 18 million a year, and was likely to remain this high for the next 2 years.

In comparison to other competitive manufacturers, much of the production plant was still very outdated, and the company was obviously under pressure to introduce new plant to improve the effectiveness of the production process. For example, the main competitors in Germany had an average age of plant of only 8 years; Swiss manufacturers 6.8, compared with an average of 11 for Margerine. The current suppliers of equipment were mainly from mainland Europe. It appeared that around 57 percent of the production control equipment was supplied by two French firms, one of which had caused substantial problems. Other contractors have also been involved two German, one Italian, with one Japanese and one American firm providing some of the more sophisticated equipment.

Burke had provided a variety of valves to the company for comparative test purposes, and had passed this initial quality threshold because of its keen pricing policy. Burke, as a result of the sophisticated manufacturing systems that had been introduced was able to offer these products at slightly below the market average price, even though the company was considerably smaller than the majority of suppliers to Margerine. It had not yet been formally informed of the technical acceptability of its product and this was undoubtedly one issue that would be used as a bargaining lever by Margerine.

Competitive Suppliers of Valve Products to Margerine SA

ACG: Major German manufacturer of precision valve and control equipment. Has provided specialised high pressure valves for the control of potentially dangerous reactions. It was one of the European manufacturers that was pioneering the development of 'smart' valves for sophisticated manufacturers of small batches of high added value chemicals. It had one of the leading reputations in providing rapid delivery and complete after sales service. The company's products, though excellent in quality, had become very expensive over the past 3 years and were approximately 50 percent above the market average. It supplied around 10 percent of Margerines requirements in control equipment. Its annual turnover was in excess of € 700 million. ACG was known to have very strict rules about providing extended credit, though all their price lists were provided in the local currency of the country in which they operated. The sales literature that the company provided was highly technical and was translated into all the major European languages.

Arkansas: This was the subsidiary of a manufacturer of machine tools that specialized in the production of computer controlled manufacturing systems. It had some experience in valve manufacture, but this made up only a small proportion of its total business. Its valve products were extremely expensive being double the market average, and suffered from having poor European installation and servicing arrangements. Margerine had placed an order 6 months ago which still had not been entirely delivered or installed. The result was that the company was unlikely to gain any further orders. As one of the larger industrial groups in the United States, with a turnover over € 4 billion, the company would be able to resource improved service and delivery, but appeared at present to have other priorities. The company provided very limited credit and always quoted prices in American dollars. Sales and

Contd...

installation literature was designed for the US market and only a small percentage was translated into the appropriate European language.

Isutsu: Isutsu was one of the new breed of Japanese suppliers of production control equipment, which had been making major inroads into the European market. It was another manufacturer of sophisticated valves, including 'smart' valves. The company was able to meet very tight production schedules and this, combined with the high quality work, had led to their increasing penetration of the European market. Its products were competitively priced at around 20 percent above the market average, though it suffered from problems in providing fully effective installation and after sales service. However, it had delivered three orders on time and specification to Margerine, and was providing around 20 percent of its control requirements. Isutsu had initially provided lengthy credit to all its European customers though recently this policy had been significantly tightened. The company always quoted its prices in the local currency. The technical leaflets provided varied enormously in quality. Some were very good while others were extremely poor.

Salice: Salice was French, fairly newly established, and based on a management buy out of a much larger broadly based engineering concern, which had been Margerine's main previous supplier. The new company continued to have problems with delivery dates and meeting quality standards especially in motorized valves. It did not as yet produce 'smart' valves and mainly relied on the sale of traditional valves for the bulk of its turnover. The company priced around 20 percent below the market average, and had in the past supplied over 65 percent of Margerine's requirements though this was falling. The company offered the longest credit terms available in Europe at 120 days. The literature that the company had so far produced, though in French, was poorly designed and presented.

Corrente: Corrente, the main French competitor to Burke, was one of the oldest established European valve manufacturers, with a record of supplying French industry that went back over 100 years. It had a sound reputation for producing basic valves of high quality, and was involved in supplying the majority of major French manufacturers. It was a long-term Margerine supplier. It offered credit to its long-standing customers of around 30 days. The literature that it provided was old and outdated.

R Noyons - The Buyer

R Noyons the Margerine buyer, a senior production engineer, was one of the senior members of the company. R was 52, had a degree in process engineering from one of the leading French universities, and had worked for Margerine Industrie for the last 15 years after being with Maxilink, the Anglo Dutch group, in their margarine businesses. R had authority to place orders of up to € 250,000 for process engineering equipment without referral to the main board. Typically orders for valves were placed in batches of € 30,000; once a satisfactory relation had been established, repeat orders would be forthcoming. R was well conversant with all the recent advances in valve design. R had spent a considerable amount of time in the Midlands with Maxilink and had a daughter currently studying social studies at the University of Brent.

R Noyons had studied the literature from Burke Engineering with interest. The Margerine buyer pointed out that it would be difficult to recommend the purchase of equipment which was so expensive. Having considered the Burke price list, Noyons felt that the prices quoted were far too high, and would need to be reduced by at least 30 percent before they could be seriously considered. Margerine was a major company and would be placing significant orders if Burke could pass the stringent technical requirements.

Burke Engineering Product Range

The Burke motorized valve came in three basic sizes, though there was substantial variation depending on customer specifications. The three sizes were priced around 10 percent below the market price delivered and installed. The company could offer delivery within 3 weeks from receipt of order and could arrange for training and other technical support depending on customer requirements. Burke would also be able to provide a full maintenance program should the customer require it.

Contd...

Credit had always been allowed to vary according to the volume of business and the ability of the sales representative, and though the very lengthy credit periods that had been offered to governments for submersible contracts were no longer permitted, credit of over 60 days was common.

Burke Engineering leaflets had been produced with simple graphics and detailed illustrations of operating methods and tolerances. They had all been translated into the main European languages.

Action

How do you as J Franklin assess the chances of achieving a sale to Margerine? What do you think are the important factors that are likely to motivate the buyer? What plan do you and the sales representative need to adopt?

Source: Used with the kind permission of IBIS Associates. IBIS Associates specializes in creating expert system for business planning and monitoring. You can visit them at www.ibisassoc.co.uk. All rights reserved. Copyright 2007 Alan West. Reprinted with permission.

Kevin Cage, general manager of Wind Technology, sat in his office on a Friday afternoon watching the snow fall outside his window. It was January 1991 and he knew that during the month ahead he would have to make some difficult decisions regarding the future of his firm, Wind Technology. The market for the wind profiling radar systems that his company designed had been developing at a much slower rate than he had anticipated.

Wind Technology

During Wind Technology's ten-year history, the company had produced a variety of weather-related radar and instrumentation. In 1986 the company condensed its product mix to include only wind-profiling radar systems. Commonly referred to as wind profilers, these products measure wind and atmospheric turbulence for weather forecasting, detection of wind direction at NASA launch sites, and other meteorological applications, (i.e., at universities and other scientific monitoring stations). Kevin had felt that this consolidation would position the company as a leader in what he anticipated to be a high-growth market with little competition.

Wind Technology's advantages over Unisys, the only other key player in the wind-profiling market, included the following:

1.   The company adhered stringently to specifications and quality production.

2.   Wind Technology had the technical expertise to provide full system integration. This allowed customers to order either basic components or a full system, including software support.

3.   Wind Technology's staff of meteorologists and atmospheric scientists provided the customer with sophisticated support, including operation and maintenance training and field assistance.

4.   Finally, Wind Technology had devoted all of its resources to its wind-profiling business. Kevin believed that the market would perceive this as an advantage over a large conglomerate like Unisys.

Wind Technology customized each product for individual customers as the need arose; the total system could cost a customer from $400,000 to $5 million. Various governmental entities, such as the Department of Defense, NASA, and state universities, had consistently accounted for about 90 percent of Wind Technology's sales. In lieu of a field salesforce, Wind Technology relied on top management and a team of engineers to call on prospective and current customers. Approximately $105,000 of their annual salaries was charged to a direct selling expense.

The Problem

The consolidation strategy that the company had undertaken in 1986 was due in part to the company's purchase by Vaitra, a high-technology European firm. Wind Technology's ability to focus on the wind-profiling business had been made possible by Vaitra's financial support. However, since 1986 Wind Technology had shown little commercial success, and due to low sales levels the company was experiencing severe cash flow problems. Kevin knew that Wind Technology could not continue to meet its payroll much longer. Also, he had been informed that Vaitra was not willing to pour more money into Wind Technology. Kevin estimated that he had from nine to twelve months (until the end of 1991) in which to implement a new strategy with the potential to improve the company's cash flow. The new strategy was necessary, to enable Wind Technology to survive until the wind-profiler market matured. Kevin and other industry experts anticipated that it would be two years until the wind-profiling market achieved the high growth levels that the company had initially anticipated.

Contd...

One survival strategy that Kevin had in mind was to spin off and market component parts used in making wind profilers. Initial research indicated that of all the wind-profiling system's component parts, the High-voltage Power Supply (HVPS) had the greatest potential for commercial success. Furthermore, Kevin's staff on the HVPS product had demonstrated knowledge of the market. Kevin believed that by marketing the HVPS, Wind Technology could reap incremental revenues, with very little addition to fixed costs. (Variable costs would include the costs of making and marketing the HVPS. The accounting department had estimated that production costs would run approximately 70 percent of the selling price, and that 10 percent of other expenses-such as top management direct-selling expenses-should be charged to the HVPS.)

High-Voltage Power Supplies

For a vast number of consumer and industrial products that require electricity, the available voltage level must be transformed to different levels and types of output. The three primary types of power supplies include linears, switchers, and converters. Each type manipulates electrical current in terms of the type of current (AC of DC) and /or the level of output (voltage). Some HVPS manufacturers focus on producing a standardized line of power supplies, while others specialize in customizing power supplies to user's specifications.

High-voltage power supplies vary significantly in size and level of output. Small power supplies with relatively low levels of output (under 3 kV) (1) are used in communications equipment. Medium-sized power supplies that produce an output between 3 and 10 kV are used in a wide range of products, including radars and lasers. Power supplies that produce output greater than 10 kV are used in a variety of applications, such as high-powered X-rays and plasma-etching systems.

Background on Wind Technology's HYPS

One of Wind Technology's corporate strategies was to control the critical technology (major component parts) of its wind-profiling products. Management felt that this control was important since the company was part of a high-technology industry in which confidentiality and innovation were critical to each competitor's success. This strategy also gave Wind Technology a differential advantage over its major competitors, all of whom depended on a variety of manufacturers for component parts. Wind Technology had successfully developed almost all of the major components and the software for the wind profiler, yet the development of the power supply had been a problem.

To adhere to the policy of controlling critical technology in product design (rather than purchasing an HVPS from an outside supplier), Wind Technology's management had hired Anne Ladwig and her staff of HVPS technicians to develop a power supply for the company's wind-profiling systems. Within six months of joining Wind Technology, Anne and her staff had completed development of a versatile power supply which could be adapted for use with a wide variety of equipment. Some of the company's wind-profiling systems required up to ten power supplies, each modified slightly to carry out its role in the system.

Kevin Cage had delegated the responsibility of investigating the sales potential of the company's HVPS to Anne Ladwig because she was familiar with the technical aspects of the product and had received formal business training while pursuing an MBA. Anne had determined that Wind Technology's HVPS could be modified to produce levels of output between 3 and 10 kV. Thus, it seemed natural that if the product was brought to market, Wind Technology should focus on applications in this range of output. Wind Technology also did not have the production capabilities to compete in the high-volume, low-voltage segment of the market, nor did the company have the resources and technical expertise to compete in the high-output (+10 kV) segment.

Potential Customer

Power supplies in the 3-10 kV range could be used to conduct research, to produce other products, or to place as a component into other products such as lasers. Thus, potential customers could

Contd...

include research labs, large end-users, Original Equipment Manufacturers (OEMs), or distributors. Research labs used an average of three power supplies; other types of customers ordered a widely varying quantity.

HVPS users were demanding increasing levels of reliability, quality, customization, and system integration. System integration refers to the degree to which other parts of a system are dependent upon the HVPS for proper functioning, and the extent to which these parts are combined into a single unit or piece of machinery.

Anne had considered entering several HVPS market segments in which Wind Technology could reasonably compete. She had estimated the domestic market Potential of these segments at $237 million. To evaluate these segments, Anne had compiled growth forecasts for the year ahead and had evaluated each segment in terms of the anticipated level of customization and system integration demanded by the market. Anne felt that the level of synergy between Wind Technology and the various segments was also an important consideration in selecting a target market. Table 1 summarizes this information. Anne believed that if the product was produced, Wind Technology's interests would be best served by initially selecting only one target market on which to concentrate.

Table 1: HVPS Market Segments In The 3-10 KV Range

Application	Forecasted annual Growth percent	Level of Customization/level of system integration*	Synergy Rating+	Percentage of $237 Million Power Supply Market++
General/University Laboratory	5.40	Medium/medium	3	8percent
Lasers	11.00	Low/medium	4	10
Medical equipment	10.00	Medium/medium	3	5
Microwave	12.00	Medium/high	4	7
Power Modulators	3.00	Low/low	4	25
Radar Systems	11.70	Low/medium	5	12
Semiconductor	10.10	Low/low	3	23
X-ray systems	8.60	Medium/high	3	10

* The level of customization and system integration generally in demand within each of the applications is defined as low, medium, or high.

+ Synergy ratings are based on a scale of 1 to 5; 1 is equivalent to a very low level of synergy and 5 is equivalent to a very high level of synergy. These subjective ratings are based on the amount of similarities between the wind-profiling industry and each application.

++Percentages total 100 percent of the $237 million market in which Wind Technology anticipated it could compete.

Note: This list of applications is not all-inclusive.

Competition

To gather competitive information, Anne contacted five HVPS manufacturers. She found that the manufacturers varied significantly in terms of size and marketing Strategy (see Table 2). Each listed a price in the $5,500-$6,500 range on power supplies with the same features and output levels as the HVPS that had been developed for Wind Technology. After she spoke with these firms, Anne got the feeling that Wind Technology could offer the HVPS market superior levels of quality, reliability, technical expertise, and customer support. She optimistically believed that a one-half percent market share objective could be achieved the first year.

Contd...

Table 2: Size and Marketing Strategy of HVPS Manufacturers

Company	Gamma	Glassman	Kaiser	Maxwell*	Spellman
Approximate Annual Sales	$2 million	$7.5 million	$3 million		$7 Million
Market share	1.00percent	3.00percent	1.50percent		2.90percent
Price+	$5,830	$5,590	$6210	$5,000-$6,000	$6,360
Delivery	12 weeks	10 weeks	10 weeks	8 weeks	12 weeks
Product Customization	No	Medium	Low	Medium	Low
System Integration Experience	Low	Low	Low	Medium	Low
Customer Targets	Gen.lab.	Laser	Laser	Radar	Capacitors
	Space	Medical	Medical	Power mod	Gen lab
	Univ.lab	X-ray	Microwave	X-ray	Microwave
			Semiconductor	Medical equip	X-ray

* Maxwell was in the final stages of product development and stated that the product would call in the $5,000-$6,000 range.

+Price quoted for an HVPS with the same specification as the "standard" model developed by Wind Technology.

Promotion

If Wind Technology entered the HVPS market, it would require a hard-hitting, thorough promotional campaign to reach the selected target market. Three factors made the selection of elements in the promotion mix especially important to Wind Technology: (1) Wind Technology's poor cash flow, (2) the lack of a well-developed marketing department, and (3) the need to generate incremental revenue from sales of the HVPS at a minimum cost. In fact, a rule of thumb used by Wind Technology was that all marketing expenditures should be about 9 to 10 percent of sales. Kevin and Anne were contemplating the use of the following elements.

1. **Collateral Material:** Sales literature, brochures, and data sheets are necessary to communicate the product benefits and features to potential customers. These materials are designed to be (1) mailed to customers as part of direct-mail campaigns or in response to customer requests, (2) given away at trade shows, and (3) left behind after sales presentations. Because no one in Wind Technology was an experienced copywriter, Anne and Kevin considered hiring a marketing communications agency to write the copy and to design the layout of the brochures. This agency would also complete the graphics (photographs and artwork) for the collateral material. The cost for 5,000 pieces (including the 10 percent markup for the agency) was estimated to be $5.50 each.

2. **Public Relations:** Kevin and Anne realized that one very cost-efficient tool of promotion is publicity. They contemplated sending out new product announcements to a variety of trade journals whose readers were part of Wind Technology's new target market. By using this tool, interested readers could call or write to Wind Technology, and the company could then send the prospective customers collateral material. The drawback of relying too heavily on this element was very obvious to Kevin and Anne-the editors of the trade journals could choose not to print Wind Technology's product announcements if their new product was not deemed newsworthy.

The cost of using this tool would include the time necessary to write the press release and the expense of mailing the release to the editors. Direct costs were estimated by Wind Technology to be $500.

Contd...

Table 3: Trade Publications

Trade Publication	Editorial	Cost per color Insertion(1 page)	Circulation
Electrical Manufacturing	For purchasers and users of power supplies, transformers, and other electrical products.	$4,077	35,168 non-paid
Electronic Component News	For electronics OEMs. Products addressed include work stations, power sources, chips, etc.	$6,395	110,151 non-paid
Electronic Manufacturing News	For OEMs in the industry of providing manufacturing and contracting of components, circuits, and systems	$5,075	25,000 non-paid
Design News	For design OEMs covering components, systems, and materials	$8,120	170,033 non-paid
Weatherwise	For meteorologists covering imaging, radar, etc.	$1,040	10,186 paid

Note: This is a partial list of applicable trade publications. Standard Rate and data Service lists other possible publications.

3. **Direct Mail:** Kevin and Anne were also contemplating a direct-mail campaign. The major expenditure for this option would be the purchase of a list of prospects to whom the collateral material would be mailed. Such lists usually cost around $5,000, depending upon the number of names and the list quality. Other costs would include postage and the materials mailed. These costs were estimated to be $7,500 for a mailing of 1,500.

4. **Trade Shows:** The electronics industry has several annual trade shows. If they chose to exhibit at one of these trade shows, Wind Technology would incur the cost of a booth, the space at the show, and the travel and incidental costs of the people attending the show to staff the booth. Kevin and Anne estimated these costs at approximately $50,000 for the exhibit, space, and materials, and $50,000 for a staff of five people to attend.

5. **Trade Journal Advertising:** Kevin and Anne also contemplated running a series of ads in trade journals. Several journals they considered are listed in the Table 3 above, along with circulation, readership, and cost information.

6. **Personal Selling:**

   (a) *Telemarketing (Inbound/Inside Sales).* (2) Kevin and Anne also considered hiring a technical salesperson to respond to HVPS product inquiries generated by product announcements, direct mail, and advertising. This person's responsibilities would include answering phone calls, prospecting, sending out collateral material, and following up with potential customers. The salary and benefits for one individual would be about $50,000.

   (b) *Field Sales.* The closing of sales for the HVPS might require some personal selling at the customer's location, especially if Wind Technology pursued the customized option. Kevin and Anne realized that potentially this would provide them with the most incremental revenue, but it also had the potential to be the most costly tool. Issues such as how many salespeople to hire, where to position them in the field (geographically), and so on, were major concerns. Salary plus expenses and benefits for an outside salesperson were estimated to be about $80,000.

Decisions

As Kevin sat in his office and perused the various facts and figures, he knew that he would have to make some quick decisions. He sensed that the decision about whether to proceed with the HVPS spin-off was risky, but he felt that not to do something to improve the firm's cash flow was equally risky. Kevin also knew that if he decided to proceed with the HVPS, there were a number of segments

Contd...

in that market in which Wind Technology could position its HVPS. He mulled over which segment appeared to be a good fit for Wind Technology's abilities (given Anne's recommendation that a choice of one segment would be best). Finally, Kevin was concerned that if they entered the HVPS market, promotion for their project would be costly, further exacerbating the cash flow situation. He knew that promotion would be necessary, but the exact mix of elements would have to be designed with financial constraints in mind.

1 V (kilovolt): 1,000 volts

2-Inbound refers to calls that potential customers make to Wind Technology, rather than outbound, in which Wind Technology calls potential customers (i.e., solicits sales).

Source: Ken Manning, Gonzaga University, and Jakki Mohr, University of Montana. © 1990 by Jakki Mohr. Reprinted with the permission from the author.

Case 7

Beta Pharmaceuticals: Pennsylvania Distribution System

Jack Sexton, manager of logistics planning, walked out of his boss's office with a frown on his face. He had just learned that the top management of his company, Beta Pharmaceutical, had been taking a closer look at cost levels in the company's distribution system. In particular, high transportation costs resulting from frequent minimum-size LTL (Less Than Truckload) shipments to customers and low-volume resupply shipments to the smaller warehouses were beginning to raise eyebrows. Total warehousing and material-handling costs had also been questioned.

When he got back to his office, Mr. Sexton sat back and thought the problem over. He recalled that the present plant, warehouse, and customer configuration had evolved during a period of high-growth years, without the systematic development of a master distribution plan. Warehouse location and customer service decisions were based mainly on marketing-centered recommendations, competitive pressures, and customer desires. Customer order frequency and shipment size had been largely in the control of the customer. Basically, Beta believed that to achieve and maintain industry leadership, it was necessary to meet customer demand 100 percent of the time. Thus the cost of customer service, inclusive of distribution, had historically been very high.

Several days later Mr. Sexton settled on a course of action. Calling in a logistics consulting firm, HLW and Associates, he asked that a pilot study be conducted to evaluate a portion of the present product logistics system for cost-service effectiveness. The state of Pennsylvania was determined to be a "typical" subsystem within the national distribution network and was designated by Mr. Sexton as the focal point for the study. An outline of the study proposal is shown in Table 1.[1]

Background – The Company

Beta Pharmaceuticals is a multidivisional manufacturer and distributor of a diversified line of medical care products. Manufacturing, sales, and distribution facilities are located throughout the world, with major operations existing in Europe, Africa, South America, Australia, Asia, Canada, and the United States. Products include intravenous solutions, artificial organs, disposable medical devices, clinical testing and diagnostic supplies and equipment, blood collecting and storage equipment, prescription drugs, and industrial and medical enzymes.

Beta has twelve production or research facilities in the United States, and markets its products through five customer-service or distribution-center regions. The company employs 13,600 persons throughout its worldwide system.

The backbone of Beta's strong marketing position in the hospital supply industry is a well-funded research and development program. New products, as well as improvements to existing products, are constantly being developed and exploited as a key element in market strategy and industry leadership. As a result of this philosophy, Beta increased the 1994 expenditures for research and development by 25.7 percent over 1993 for a total dollar investment of $46.7 million.

The aggressive competitive stance, supported by resourceful research and development, effective quality control, and customer-oriented distribution, has enabled the company to build a sixteen-year compound growth rate in sales and earnings per share of 20 percent. Its 1994 sales were $855.9 million, which represented a 27.7 percent increase over 1993. Earnings per share for 1994 were $1.95, a 23.4 percent increase over 1993.

Contd...

Table 1: Outline of the Study Proposal

Project Description

Project:	How should Beta Pharmaceuticals distribute products to customers in the state of Pennsylvania?
Background:	Beta currently distributes products to customers from public warehouses in Pittsburgh, Harrisburg, and Philadelphia.

- Cartage carriers are used in the three metropolitan areas.

- Common carriers are used in the balance of the state.

- Customers (hospitals) order both in patterns and randomly.

- Shipments are made within 24 to 48 hours of order receipt.

- Shipment sizes are small, from under 100 pounds to a few thousand pounds.

- The full product line is stocked in Philadelphia and Pittsburgh, but only a partial line is stocked in Harrisburg.

- Distribution costs are a significant element of total costs.

Objective:	Determine the best method to distribute products to customers, considering the effects on:

- Distribution costs (freight and handling).

- Levels of customer service.

- Inventory levels.

Scope:	The scope of the project should be restricted to the state of Pennsylvania to keep it manageable.

- Inventory policies and methods of replenishing warehouses should be ignored. However, the relationship between aggregate inventory levels and warehouse volume must be recognized.

- Customer order patterns can be assumed to be controllable within certain limits, to be defined. Customer contact will not be allowed.

- The number and location of warehouses should be determined.

- Methods of delivery should be determined, including such alternatives as (1) direct shipment or (2) scheduling of customer orders for pooled delivery, including contact with carriers for rates and feasibility.

The Distribution System

The current distribution system used by Beta within the state of Pennsylvania makes use of three public warehouses: Philadelphia, Pittsburgh, and Harrisburg. From these three warehouses, Beta is able to serve most of its customers in forty-nine of the sixty-seven counties in Pennsylvania; this service is supplemented by shipments from nearby out-of-state warehouses or by carload shipments direct from a Beta plant. The distribution responsibilities of the three Pennsylvania warehouses include shipments to out-of-state customers as well as to the Pennsylvania customers.

Beta maintains either a company-salaried customer service representative or a warehouse employee at each warehouse to handle orders and customer inquiries. Whenever an order is received, company policy dictates that it be filled and tendered to a carrier within forty-eight hours. Orders are received either electronically or by phone, direct at the warehouse or at company headquarters in Chicago. The forty-eight-hour service goal starts at the point the order is received within the Beta system.

Once the warehouse receives the order, two possibilities exist. If the items are in stock, a bill of lading is cut and the freight is tendered to a common carrier or a cartage carrier. Of those shipments tendered to common carriers, 95 percent are delivered by the second morning. This means a maximum order filling time-including transportation- of four days 95 percent of the time. If the customer is

Contd...

located within the commercial zone of the city and a cartage carrier can be used, total time from order receipt by Beta to delivery to the customer is reduced to two days, 95 percent of the time.

When sufficient stock is not available, the warehouse representative will contact the regional distribution center to which the warehouse is assigned. The regional distribution center will, review the inventory levels of the surrounding warehouses and assign the order to one of these warehouses. Transportation cost is used as the basis for which warehouse should receive the order. If the item is not available in any of the surrounding warehouses, it will be back-ordered and expedited from a production facility. Since Beta wants to maintain high customer service levels, every attempt is made to maintain inventories high enough to avoid the need of back ordering to Chicago.

The majority of Beta's customers are hospitals. As such, they have limited storage space. They also cannot afford to wait very long after ordering items because their inventory averages approximately one week's demand. Since Beta is the major supplier of medical products in the Pennsylvania area, it falls upon them to provide hospitals with the required service. Traditional performance and marketing pressure have forced Beta into the position of maintaining inventory for its customers. However, very few of the shipments made by Beta are on a life-or-death basis for a patient.

Preliminary Findings and Plans of the Consultants

Beta's present distribution system is structured around basic customer service objectives. Competitive stress and rapid growth contributed to the piecemeal development of the present structure, wherein the customer sets the rules. This resulted in a number of marginal, close-to-the-customer warehouses. Warehouse-to-customer shipments are made without consideration of economic order quantities or potential savings to be recognized by shipping in consolidated lots. Many customers avoid assuming inventory responsibility and cost by ordering frequently, often at random intervals and in varying order quantities. Beta provides twenty-four-hour delivery to all customers within the commercial zone of each warehouse, and forty-eight-hour delivery to other customers. This situation has necessitated the establishment of safety stock of nearly 100 percent at most warehouses.

The piecemeal pattern of development has presented coordination problems at the corporate level. Many problems common to several areas are still handled on an individual basis at the local level. Rarely is the experience and information gained at one point generalized for the benefit of other areas of the system. The nearly exclusive use of public warehouses compounds this situation, particularly when quality control, damage, or liability become the question. The use of public warehouses also complicates the information-gathering process and makes the control aspects of inventory more difficult to handle.

Even though growth potential remains high for Beta, a plateau has been reached in many areas. For example, the climb to leadership in the medical products industry has been achieved; a reputation for high standards, effective quality control, and an understanding for the specialized problems experienced by hospitals has been established; an impressive record of innovation and responsible research and development has been compiled. In essence, Beta has created a "pull" situation, in the marketing sense, for the products bearing the Beta trademark.

Beta presently has good information potential. Most operations-related facts are collected in the present system, but unfortunately those items not lost due to pure volume are presented in a manner that makes their usefulness limited and suspect. Feedback and information update is slow and complicated under the present system of hand tallies, verbal order placement at each warehouse, and conflicting loyalties (due to the nearly exclusive use of public warehouses). Control at the warehouse level is shaky at best.

The Pennsylvania Subsystem

The following information is available for the Pennsylvania subsystem:

1. **Monthly demand for Pennsylvania customers:** A computer printout for March 1995 gives demand by customers for each of Beta's major product lines. It shows how many bills of lading

Contd...

were cut and the number of cases per product line on each bill. Every order shipped within the state of Pennsylvania is included, with coded identification of which warehouse filled the order. There is a considerable amount of overlap in the territory served by various warehouses. Out-of-state warehouses appear throughout the printout, indicating service to cities also serviced by the Pennsylvania warehouses. The monthly demand information gives no indication of the timing throughout the month for the orders. It is easy to identify how many shipments a customer received but not when they were received. Finally, there is no indication that March 1995 was a typical month in terms of demand level. A quarterly demand schedule was requested but not provided. As a result, the assumption that March 1995 is a typical month had to be made.

2. *Quarterly transportation cost:* This is a summary of the air and truck costs incurred by each of Beta's warehouses on an outbound basis by product line only. It does show total pieces and weight of each product line shipped by air and truck, but it does not break total cost down past a total for air and truck. Since the total cost is a three-month figure for all shipments out of a warehouse, an average cost would not truly reflect the intrastate rate levels.

3. *March payments to carriers:* Beta provided a list of the total billings for transportation charges paid to carriers in March 1995. The charges are broken down by product line pieces and weight. The list is not very useful because it is for bills paid in March, not for shipments made during March. Also, no information was provided concerning the number of shipments each carrier handled or the destination of these shipments.

4. *Warehouse throughput:* Beta was able to provide estimates of the average monthly throughput in terms of total cases for the three Pennsylvania warehouses, as follows:

Philadelphia:	50,000 cases
Pittsburgh:	35,000 cases
Harrisburg:	9,000 cases

Warehouse capacity in both Philadelphia and Pittsburgh is large enough to handle the entire throughput of Harrisburg should that location be eliminated. Average monthly throughput would be useful in evaluating the methods of warehouse replenishment.

5. *Warehouse cost:* The three Pennsylvania facilities are public warehouses. Under the contract agreements with Philadelphia and Harrisburg, a single charge is assessed for each carton that comes into the warehouse. There is no annual rental fee, no quantity discount, and no penalty for falling below a minimum level. The single rate per carton includes storage, handling, stenciling, and anything else the warehouse people might have to do to the case. The charge in Philadelphia is 44 cents per case, while the Harrisburg charge is 43 cents per case. Pittsburgh, which does not have the same type of arrangements, pays an average of 46 cents per case. There is no indication of how this figure would vary with different inventory levels. An additional 10 cents per case is assigned by Beta to each case handled through the Pittsburgh warehouse due to the presence of a Beta customer service representative in that city.

6. *Warehouse replenishment policy:* Beta will not retain a warehouse unless it can be replenished at least once a month in carload quantity. The information provided by Beta concerning actual replenishment schedules is very sketchy. Philadelphia and Pittsburgh are replenished on a carload basis once a week. However, no information was available as to how many cars per week were used, whether they get the 40,000-pound or the 60,000-pound carload rate or whether additional demand would also move at carload rates. If Harrisburg is eliminated, inbound freight costs to Philadelphia and Pittsburgh will change. The Harrisburg replenishment schedule was stated to be once every two to three weeks and once a month.

7. *Average inventory level:* Both Philadelphia and Pittsburgh hold six weeks' demand in inventory, whereas Harrisburg holds eight weeks' demand in inventory. These figures were unfortunately subject to some uncertainty.

Contd...

8.   *Truck rates:* Evaluating configuration changes in the current system requires a comparison of total cost for both the present and proposed systems. Costing out a system requires a close estimate of the transportation costs generated by that system. In light of the restrictions of a linear programming algorithm in terms of homogeneous product and potential system requirement of over 2,000 rates, weighted rate per county was used. Since the three Pennsylvania warehouses service forty-nine counties in Pennsylvania, forty weighted rates were obtained. A weighted rate assumes that all freight destined to a specific county is going to the one city where the major customers demand is located. By selecting the city having the maximum flow of freight, variation from the actual rates is minimized. The weight break to that city is computed in terms of the average weekly tonnage coming into the entire county. This requires that a maximum of four shipments per month be allowed for any county. After one rate for each commodity group was established, the four rates were combined into one weighted rate, based on the percentage of the total weekly tonnage that the product line accounted for.

Propose several ways in which the Pennsylvania distribution system might be improved.

Source: This case was prepared by Harvey Boatman, Paul Liguori, and Gary Wiser under the direction of Professor Alan J. Stenger, The Pennsylvania State University. Reprinted with the kind permission of Prof. Alan .J. Stenger.

(1)-Pennsylvania represents a "mini model" of the local system in that it contains a three-warehouse configuration, two customer service areas, a customer service representative, and a dollar demand pattern consistent with the rest of the national system.

Product Positioning Case Study

PPM Computers

The board of PPM computers is reviewing the direction of the business having asked a group of junior executives to prepare a marketing plan for the future. The company currently sold a range of personal, networked and workstation computers through high street outlets, direct mail and specialised distributors and direct to its major customers. PPM had been hit by the overall decline in the growth of the personal computer market and the greater pressure on profitability. The trends in company sales and profitability are in Table 1.

Table 1: Sales and profitability of PPM Computers for the last 3 years (all figures in £ million, with year 3 most recent).

	Year							
	1		2		3			
	Sales	Profit	Sales	Profit	Sales	Profit		
PC sector	50	8		65	6		72	5
Network	10	2		12	2		14	2
Workstation	10	3		17	5		25	7

The decline in profitability reflected an industry-wide change in profitability and return on equity which had been below the average for manufacturing industry over the last 4 years. This compelled PPM to pay more attention to marketing. The PPM board were asking their expert team to provide a detailed analysis of where the company should concentrate. This marketing plan was to include specifications of customer segment, product benefit, distribution channels, salesforce numbers and skills, promotional planning and creative component, and product pricing. The team was also asked to provide an analysis of the likely return to the company from the marketing plan.

The International Market and Main Competitors

Though there had been substantial growth in all sectors during the last 10 years, certain market sectors had performed better than others. The workstation and Personal Computer (PC) sectors had grown most rapidly; mainframe and minicomputers sectors had expanded more slowly. Computers had become steadily more powerful as new microprocessor variants came available. Speed had increase from 0.1 MIPS (Millions of Instructions Per Second), to a projected 250 over a 10 year period. Microprocessors and memory storage had also continued to fall rapidly in price with memory costs falling 50 fold over the same 10 year period. The increasing power of microprocessors and the declining costs of memory had tended to blur the barriers between the sectors, with the increasing power of microprocessors meaning that the current PC has the power of a ten-year-old mainframe. Nevertheless particular market sectors with specific service requirements could continue to be defined. The main characteristics of each of the sectors are in Table 2.

Table 2: Main Segments of the Computer Market

Type	Characteristics	Customer	Software required
Super	V. high calc. speed	Military Govt institute	Tailor made
Main	Large storage many terminals	Big company. system/modified	Complex

Contd...

Mini	Data storage/ separate terminals	Division or medium firm	Specific package
Work- station	High speed calculations	Design/ Engineering	Package
PC	Small unit	Small firm/ individual	Standard package

Increases in processing power and declining data storage costs had also meant a substantial growth in applications. Some of the most rapid growth has occurred in software, peripheral devices of various types, and a considerable potential expansion foreseen in electronic publishing and multimedia, the interaction of computer and graphic systems. Total world markets for hardware were forecast to grow by around 10 percent, year on year, but software was likely to grow at around 25 percent per year. This suggested that the world market for software would equal hardware in the middle of the 1990s and then rapidly surpass it.

The total market for peripherals was also forecast to grow by around 25 percent per annum with increasingly sophisticated displays, data storage and printers creating a world wide market of $20 billion by the middle of the 1990s. Combinations of hardware, software and peripherals were likely to produce major new markets. By the mid-1990s, electronic publishing systems were likely to double from around $5.5 billion in the late 1980s; multimedia from $0.2 billion in the late 1980s to $12.0 billion by the middle of the Nineties with spectacular growth in the consumer sector - the expansion of virtual reality games, and major increases in business applications such as training and presentation. Surveys of the most required corporate software in the late 1980s, showed that graphics, communications, electronic mail, and design systems were the most asked for additional software.

Current Product Range

PPM computers sold the bulk of its computers in the UK. The company had considered export, but felt resources were too limited to effectively compete in world markets. Nevertheless, the percentage of export sales had grown from 1 percent 5 years ago to a current 6 percent. The structure of the UK market is shown in Table 3.

Table 3: Percentage Market Shares by Product Range in UK

Company	PC market	Network	Workstation
Amstrad	25	3	
Olivetti	10		
Tandon	15	5	
IBM	20	10	15
DEC	25	15	
HP	15	35	
PPM	5	3	10
Apple	10		
Xerox	6	15	

There was little seasonality in all sectors of the computer market with the exception of the summer period from June to September, when sales fell to very low levels. PPM had always planned around an 8 month year, and attempted to achieve their sales budget within this period. Such seasonality naturally had important implications for their promotional planning which followed the sales seasonality. The current product range consisted of the three core products, listed here.

Personal Computer: PC 640. Operating with 386 microprocessor, 1 disc drive, range of hard disk options from £899 in price.

Contd...

Network Computer: X912 486 microprocessor. Unix and MSDOS compatible, 1 disc drive, range of hard disk options from £1699 in price.

Workstation: Y4000. Pentium (double) 2 disc drive, range of hard disc options from £2999 in price.

PPM concentrated on maintaining a low price route to gain market share. The company used Far Eastern manufacturers for all product ranges and did not manufacture in-house. A worrying consequence of this was that the company saw significant fluctuations in stock and was often out of stock of the PC and workstation ranges. The comparison between PPM and its main competitors (PPM based 100) is in Table 4 which shows that PPM is substantially below the competition in pricing especially in the workstation segment. The marketing team has the freedom to suggest new price structures for all the ranges.

Table 4: Retail or Dealer Prices in UK on base of PPM =100

Company	PC market	Network	Workstation
Amstrad	115	130	
Olivetti	125		
Tandon	145	155	
IBM	165	185	225
DEC	180	200	
HP	175		185
PPM	100	100	100
Apple	205		
Xerox	165	175	

The company had a limited service network, its distribution outlets handled the majority of problems. Failure rates were low during previous years, but had risen steadily in the current year, and had become a particular problem for the PC range with rates rising to 5 percent in the final quarter. This limited service support was because the company used subcontractors for the majority of its servicing and manufacturing. It had continued to emphasize its sales and marketing departments as the key elements of the company. At present there were four company directors; the managing director and founder, a sales director, marketing director and distribution director. The managing director was responsible for liaison with the subcontractors.

Current Distribution

The three product ranges used different distribution channels. The PC range was primarily sold through high street outlets, whereas the balance of the networked system was handled through distributors. The physical distribution of the company was handled almost entirely by road haulage subcontractors. PPM continued to use mail order direct from the company for the workstation system. The importance and number of distribution intermediaries are in Table 5. The pattern of distribution for personal computers showed that the company was broadly in line with others in the personal computer market, the nationwide structure of which is reflected in Table 6.

Table 5: Distribution Structure of PPM

	PC	Network	Workstation
High street outlets	1000		
Percent total sales	85		
Dealer numbers	30	45	
Percent total sales	5	85	
Mail order outlets	15		
Percent total sales	10		
Percent direct from factory		15	100

Contd...

In comparison with competitors, PPM was weak in its dependence on dealers for the promotion and sale of network products, an increasing percentage of which were sold by the major companies on a direct basis. Apricot for example, achieved over 60 percent of its total sales on a direct basis. The reliance on mail order to establish contact with the main customers of the workstation range was another competitive weakness other companies had highly trained salesforces to demonstrate and install systems to customers' specifications.

Table 6: Distribution Patterns of Personal Computers by outlet and value by year. Percentage of total sales by outlet type

Type of outlet	1990	1995
Electrical goods retailers	25	25
Independent specialists	13	22
Specialist computer multiples	12	16
Mail order	4	3

Supporting the Distribution Channel

Each distribution channel required a specific type of support. The PC range was sold through both high street outlets and dealers. Of these, the high street retailers were the most straightforward. They operated on a gross margin of 40 percent, and demanded promotional investment in mainstream computer magazines. The dealers that handled PCs looked for sales support as the most important resource that the supplier could provide. The company had two sales representatives for these dealers and three that were responsible for negotiating with the high street multiples. Neither of these sales teams had been properly trained or integrated; the company was unsure how many sales representatives were needed in this area, and about the exact job description. Currently each of the sales representatives cost around £20,000.

The network range was mainly serviced through dealers. The potential market for the network product was firms with more than 200 employees: an estimated 12,000 outlets. Currently, the company employed three sales representatives in this area to support the dealer network; each cost around £25,000. Their exact job had not been properly defined and all three had limited training. In contrast, PPM's main competitors had spent considerable sums annually on training. It was estimated that new recruitment might be necessary to achieve the necessary skill effectively to service the dealer network. A small survey of the dealer network revealed that to service corporate customers effectively, the company must provide a sales representative for every 100 potential clients. The workstation range, sold direct to the potential customer, employed five sales representatives to service an estimated 3,000. Trade sources suggested that this was totally inadequate; the detailed nature of the selling task demanded that sales representatives concentrate on a limited number of customers, with 60 being the upper limit.

Sector Analysis

PPM had carried out detailed market research on the various customers that the company serviced, and their expectations for improved product benefits.

PC: The customer for the PC was the small business and home user. Typically the buyer was around 30, male, and had some computer knowledge. Customers were quite rapidly changing their computer products as new improved systems came along, but thought - in quite great detail - about the type of machine they required before making a purchase. The required product benefits were: simplicity of use, reliability, range of bundled software, comprehensiveness and usefulness of manuals, ease and range of attachments, price, and availability and speed of servicing and the supply of consumables (discs, printer ribbons). The comparison between the PPM product and the main competitors on these key criteria had also been analyzed and the results are in Table 7.

Contd...

To upgrade the performance of the PC would require a varying level of investment. The big decision that the company had to make was whether to upgrade the current microprocessor to either a 486 or a Pentium base.

**Table 7: Comparison of the PPM PC Product
Range with the Competition (1 best, 9 worst)**

Factor	PPM	Amstrad	Olivetti	Tandon	IBM
Simplicity	3	2	2	6	4
Reliability	6	3	2	3	2
Software	8	5	5	5	8
Manuals	7	4	2	3	2
Attachments	6	6	5	4	4
Consumables	4	4	3	3	3
Service	9	8	5	5	4
Price	2	3	4	5	7

The trend in the market was favored by a concentration on these faster machines, but there was the inevitable cost implication. Either of these ventures would mean discarding its low price policy to a certain extent. The estimated costs to modify the PC were as follows. Improved simplicity £0.5 million, reliability £0.6 million, software £0.5 million, manuals £0.1 million, attachments £0.1 million, consumables £0.1 million, service £0.5 million, 486 upgrade £0.7 million, Pentium upgrade £2.0 million. The simpler of these changes - such as improved manuals - could be rapidly introduced, but the re-engineering modifications required for the 486 or Pentium chip would take at least 6 months.

One option, not yet explored, was subcontracting the entire PC operation. Though PPM currently assembled all the computers sold, the company already sourced a range of components from the Far East. A possible option to improve costs would be to transfer the entire production to a Far East manufacturer and merely sell under a label. The implications of such a policy change would be considerable. The contribution of PC manufacture to existing manufacturing overheads were substantial and removing this production line might mean that other product ranges became less viable. Subcontracting would also mean that the company would have to commit to significant volumes to achieve adequate economies of scale, and would therefore be unable to rapidly modify products as market demand shifted. The company had also fallen behind the industry average in promotional expenditure as shown in Table 8.

The pattern of expenditure varied from company to company. Some - Tandon and Olivetti - concentrated on exhibitions and magazine advertising; others - Apple, Amstrad and IBM - spent a large proportion of their total budget on television. It was considered that press and magazine advertising were more appropriate for products aimed at the mass market; television was often thought important for the corporate sector. The company had also previously used exhibitions for the PC market. On average a national exhibition cost £15,000 per day, when all the costs were included such as stand, personnel and demonstration equipment. There were many exhibitions available to the company, with a total of 102 days per year in the UK alone. The sales effectiveness of such exhibitions had been difficult to estimate, as purchase decisions were made several weeks or months after the exhibition, and relied heavily on the salesforce for effective follow up.

**Table 8: Main Trends in Promotional Expenditure in £000.000 by
value, with year 3 the most recent**

Company		Year	
	1	2	3
IBM	15	22	37

Contd...

Amstrad	18	27	30
Olivetti	5	7	7
Tandon	8	9	7
Apple	15	18	20
PPM	10	7	5

The most commonly used promotional channels were magazines, of which there were over 40 by the beginning of the 1990s. A sample of the specialist channels included Practical Computer with a monthly circulation of 300,000 and a page, colour, price of £3000; Personal Computer with a monthly circulation of 470,000 and a page price of £4500; Computer World 250,000 (£2500); and Global Computer 150,000 (£2500). The company could also use other business magazines or general newspapers read by business personnel. The costs and frequency of such channels are provided in the case study in Chapter 1. None of the current companies used direct mail to promote their PC products; there were around 4 million households nationally in the target market with an average cost per mail item of £0.40. Sales promotion was becoming increasingly important in the industry. Many companies were providing product in bundles, combining printers and software to add value. Each additional item cost around £50.

PPM considered each of the three divisions a separate profit centre, with the unit pricing the product according to market conditions. Each unit shared a common central manufacturing fixed cost of £12 million (current estimates) and effectively 'bought' their products from the manufacturing plant at the variable manufacturing cost. For the PC market the costing and pricing structure for retail, wholesale and manufacturing cost was as follows: Retail 100; wholesale 65: variable manufacturing cost 35. The personal computer market was considered to have a relatively high price elasticity, of around 5. The degree of price competition in the market had tended to increase over the past 3 years as sales growth had slowed and product sophistication had expanded.

X System: The main purchaser of the network model was the medium sized company. Unlike the PC sector, different types of company required varying performance criteria, the most important are in Table 9. PPM concentrated on the provision of products to the financial services sector - this had been one of the most rapidly growing sectors of the market and the most likely to yield substantial profits in the future. But market research showed that PPM was failing to meet the key product requirements in this sector (Table 10).

Table 9: Key Purchase Criteria by Sector (OS=Operating System)

	Sector			
Rank	Manufacturing	Retail	Finance	Transportation
1	Power	Power	Service	Power
2	Service	Service	Power	Service
3	Easy to use	Network	Ease of use	Cost
4	OS	OS	OS	OS
5	Network	Ease of use	Network	Network

Table 10: Comparison of PPM with other companies in quality of service provision to financial services sector on 1-9 basis (1 excellent, 9 poor)

	PPM	Apricot	DEC	Xerox
Customer service	9	4	2	1
Performance	5	4	2	2

Contd...

Ease of use	4	5	1	3
Operating system	3	3	1	2
Connectivity	6	3	2	2
Price	2	4	4	6

PPM had carried out the same type of analysis as for the PC on the potential costs of upgrading the systems to meet the comparable competitors. The company found that it would cost around £0.3 million to improve customer service; £0.4 million to improve performance; £1.0 million to improve ease of use; £1.0 million to upgrade the operating system; and £0.5 million to improve the connectivity of the system to others.

Companies in this sector tended to spend little on media investment and concentrated on building an effective salesforce to convince sophisticated buyers of the benefits of their particular products, and to provide the specialist software programming advice they required. PPM lacked such support, which was largely responsible for the high costs of meeting the competitive profile. Nevertheless, the trend towards higher media and below the line investment had been marked over the last 2 years, and PPM's share had collapsed. Total expenditure had risen from £2.5 to £5 million over the last 5 years: PPM's expenditure had remained constant at £0.3 million.

There were a number of specialist publications that serviced particular sectors of the market, and a growing number of small exhibitions aimed a limited audiences. These had been particularly effective at identifying likely prospects and generating business. There were 12 main alternatives with circulations ranging from 80,000 with page costs of £3000, down to magazines with restricted specialist audiences of 3000+ where page rates averaged around £800.

Most companies used direct mail to potential customers. PPM had concentrated instead on the dealer network. With 12,000 or so potential customers in the UK, direct mail would not be expensive - about £0.80 per mail item (higher than the PC market because of the need for better quality print and response mechanisms). The X System division of PPM followed the same pricing policy as the PC division, though the structure was slightly different - dealers made a higher margin than PC retailers. To offset this, manufacturing margins were substantially higher. From a customer price of 100, and a dealer price of 58, the variable manufacturing costs would be 32. Price elasticities were much lower in the network market than in the PC sector. Customers expected to pay high prices for premium service. It had been estimated that the elasticities operating in the market were of the region of 2. No company currently used any sales promotional techniques.

Workstation: The workstation market was restricted to high speed engineering and design uses. A recent survey revealed that the prime requirements, in order of importance, were very different from those of the network system: speed, power of calculating system, reliability, specialized software, service support, and finally price. PPM had also completed a survey similar to the one carried out for the other two systems. This revealed that the company was suffering in relation to the competition in a number of key areas. These are summarized in Table 11.

Table 11: Comparison of PPM workstations with other leading companies in the workstation market from 1 to 9 (1 good to 9 poor)

Factor	DEC	HP	PPM
Speed	2	3	3
Power	4	3	6
Reliability	2	2	4
Specialised software	3	1	5
Service support	2	2	5
Price	5	4	1

Contd...

The PPM analysis on investment levels to improve competitive advantage revealed the following likely costs: improved speed £7.0 million; power of calculating system £0.8 million; improved reliability £2.0 million; specialised software £1.2 million; and service support £0.7 million.

The promotional channels used by competitors concentrated on a sophisticated and highly trained salesforce. Hewlett Packard, the market leader, considered that a salesforce/client ratio of 1:120 was the highest acceptable level. Because PPM sold all the workstations direct, it did not have to provide a margin for the distributor. But manufacturing variable costs remained high over the past 3 years, though they were likely to drop in the following year to provide a cost pattern of customer price 100, variable manufacturing cost 48. Price elasticity in the workstation market was low, and continued to be lower than for the network market.

PPM carried out intermittent market research but there was a general lack of information in key areas. An essential recommendation involves the creation of an effective marketing information system.

Action

1. As the marketing management of PPM computers, what segment should you be concentrating on?

2. What are the crucial product benefits that you should be supplying? How should you reach these customers?

3. What information should you have to control the progress of the marketing plan?

4. How can you build competitive advantage?

Insourcing/Outsourcing Case: The FlexCon Piston Decision

Introduction

This case addresses many issues that affect insourcing/outsourcing decisions. A complex and important topic facing businesses today is whether to produce a component, assembly, or service internally (insourcing), or whether to purchase that same component, assembly, or service from an external supplier (outsourcing).

Because of the important relationship between insourcing/outsourcing and competitiveness, organizations must consider many variables when considering an insourcing/outsourcing decision. This may include a detailed examination of a firm's competency and costs, along with quality, delivery, technology, responsiveness, and continuous improvement requirements. Because of the critical nature of many insourcing/outsourcing decisions, cross-functional teams often assume responsibility for managing the decision-making process. A single functional group usually does not have the data, insight, or knowledge required to effectively make strategic insourcing/outsourcing decisions.

Case Objectives

At the conclusion of this case, participants should recognize the importance of:

- Linking insourcing/outsourcing decisions to strategic corporate requirements, including the need to define core competencies.

- Recognizing the qualitative and quantitative considerations associated with insourcing/ outsourcing decisions.

- Performing a total cost analysis to support insourcing/outsourcing recommendations.

Flex-con's Insourcing/Outsourcing of Pistons

FlexCon, a $3 billion maker of small industrial engines, is undergoing a major internal review to decide where the company should focus its future product development efforts and strategic investment. Executive management is arguing that too much capacity and talent are being committed to producing simple, commodity-type items that provide small differentiation within the marketplace. FlexCon concluded that in its attempts to preserve jobs, it has insourced parts that are easy to manufacture, while outsourcing those that are complex or challenging. Producing commodity-like components with mature technologies is adding little to what FlexCon's customers consider important. The company has become increasingly dependent on suppliers for critical components and sub-assemblies that make a major difference in the performance and cost of end products.

Part of FlexCon's effort at redefining itself involves creating an understanding of insourcing/outsourcing among managers and employees. The company has sponsored workshops and presentations to convey executive management's vision and goals, plus educate those who are directly involved in making detailed insourcing/outsourcing recommendations.

One presentation given by an expert in strategic sourcing focused on the changes in the marketplace that are encouraging outsourcing. The expert noted six key trends and changes that influence insourcing/outsourcing decisions:

- The pressure to reduce costs is severe and will continue to increase. Cost reduction pressures are forcing organizations to use their productive resources more efficiently. A recent study found that over 70 percent of firms surveyed expect no change or a decrease in purchased material costs through 2000. As a result, executive management will increasingly rely on insourcing/outsourcing decisions to provide a way to effectively manage costs.

Contd...

- Firms are continuing to become more highly specialized in product and process technology. Increased specialization implies focused investment in a process or technology, which contributes to greater cost differentials between firms.

- Firms will increasingly focus more on what they excel at while outsourcing areas of non-expertise. Some organizations are formally defining their core competencies to help guide the insourcing/outsourcing effort. This has affected decisions concerning what businesses a firm should engage.

- The need for responsiveness in the marketplace is increasingly affecting insourcing/outsourcing decisions. Shorter cycle times, for example, encourage greater outsourcing with less vertical integration. The time to develop a production capability or capacity may exceed the window available to enter a new market.

- Wall Street recognizes and rewards firms with higher ROI/ROA. Since insourcing usually requires an assumption of fixed assets (and increased human capital), financial pressures are causing managers to closely exam sourcing decisions. Avoidance of increased fixed costs is motivating many firms to rely on supplier assets.

- Improved computer simulation tools and forecasting software enable firms to perform insourcing/outsourcing comparisons with greater precision. These tools allow the user to perform sensitivity analysis (what-if analysis) that permits comparison of different sourcing possibilities.

One topic that interested FlexCon managers was a discussion of core competencies and how they relate to outsourcing decisions. FlexCon management commonly accepted that a core competency was something the company "was good at." This view, however, is not correct. A core competence refers to skills, processes, or resources that distinguish a company, are hard to duplicate, and make that firm unique compared to other firms. Core competencies begin to define a firm's long-run, strategic ability to build a dominant set of technologies and/or skills that enable the firm to adapt quickly to changing market opportunities. The presenter argued that three key points relate to the idea of core competence and its relationship to insourcing/outsourcing decisions:

- A firm should concentrate internally on those components, assemblies, systems, or services that are critical to the end product and where the firm possesses a distinctive (i.e., unique) advantage valued by the customer.

- Consider outsourcing components, assemblies, systems, or services when suppliers have an advantage. Supplier advantages may occur because of economies of scale, process specific investment, higher quality, familiarity with a technology, or a favorable cost structure.

- Recognize that once a firm outsources an item or service, it usually loses the ability to bring that production capability or technology in-house without committing significant investment.

The manager or team responsible for making an insourcing/outsourcing decision must develop a true sense of what the core competence of the organization is, and whether the product or service under consideration is an integral part of that core competence.

The workshops and presentations have given most participants a greater appreciation of the need to consider factors besides cost when assessing insourcing/outsourcing opportunities. One break out work session focused exclusively on developing a list of the key factors that may affect the insourcing/outsourcing analysis at FlexCon, which appears in Exhibit 1.

Exhibit 1: Key Factors Supporting Insourcing/Outsourcing Decisions

Factors Supporting Insourcing	Factors Supporting Outsourcing
1. Cost considerations favour the buyer.	1. Cost considerations favor the supplier
2. A need or desire exists to integrate internal plant operations.	2. Supplier has specialized research and know-how, which creates differentials in cost and quality.

Contd...

3.	Excess plant capacity is available that can absorb fixed overhead.	3.	Buying firm lacks the technical ability to build an item.
4.	A need exists to exert direct control over production and quality.	4.	Buyer has small volume requirements.
5.	Product design secrecy is an important issue .	5.	Buying firm has capacity constraints while the seller does not.
6.	A lack of reliable suppliers characterizes the supply market.	6.	Buyer does not want to add permanent workers.
7.	Firm desires to maintain a stable workforce in a declining market.	7.	Future volume requirements are uncertain--buyer wants to transfer risk to the supplier.
8.	Item or service is directly part of a firm's core competency, or links directly to the strategic plans of the organization.	8.	Item or service is routine and available from many competitive sources.
9.	Item or technology behind making the item is strategic to the firm. The item adds to the qualities customers consider important.	9.	Short cycle time requirements discourage new investment by the buyer using existing supplier assets is logical.
10.	Union or other restrictions discourage or even prohibit outsourcing.	10.	Adding capacity at the buyer requires high capital start-up costs.
11.	Outsourcing may create or encourage a new competitor.	11.	Process technology is mature with minimal likelihood of providing a future competitive advantage to the purchaser.

The Piston Insourcing/Outsourcing Decision

FlexCon is considering outsourcing production of all pistons that are part of the company's "R" series of engines. FlexCon has machined various versions of these pistons as long as anyone at the company can remember. In fact, the company started fifty years ago as a producer of high quality pistons. The company grew as customers requested that FlexCon produce an ever broader line of products. This outsourcing analysis has generated a great deal of interest and emotion among FlexCon engineers, managers, and employees.

FlexCon produces pistons in three separate work cells, which differ according to the type of piston produced. Each cell has six numerically controlled machines in a U-shape layout, with a supervisor, a process engineer, a material handler, and 12 employees assigned across the three cells. Employees, who are cross-trained to perform each job within their cell, work in teams of four. FlexCon experienced a 30 percent gain in quality and a 20 percent gain in productivity after shifting from a process layout, where machines are grouped by similar capabilities, to work cells, where machines are grouped to support a specific family of products. If FlexCon decides to outsource the pistons, the company will likely dedicate the floor space currently occupied by the work cells to a new product, expansion of an existing product, or to a product being brought back "in-house," although a final decision has not yet been made. FlexCon will apply the work cell equipment for other applications, so the outsourcing analysis will not consider equipment write-offs beyond normal depreciation.

While different opinions exist regarding outsourcing the pistons, FlexCon engineers agreed that the process technology used to produce this family of components is mature. Gaining future competitive advantages from new technology was probably not as great as other process applications within FlexCon's production process. This did not mean, however, that FlexCon could avoid making new investments in process technology if the pistons remained in-house, or that some level of process innovation is not possible.

Differences over outsourcing a component that is critical to the performance of FlexCon's final product threatens to affect the insourcing/outsourcing decision. One engineer threatened to quit if

Contd...

FlexCon outsourced a component that could "bring down" the entire engine in case of quality failure. He also said "our pistons are known in the industry as first-rate." Another engineer suggested that FlexCon's supply management group, if given support from the engineers, could adequately manage any risk of poor supplier quality. However, a third engineer remarked that "opportunistic suppliers will exploit FlexCon if given the chance - we've seen it before!" This engineer warned the group about suppliers "buying-in" to the piston business only to coercively raise prices. Several experienced engineers voiced the opinion that they could not imagine FlexCon outsourcing a component that was responsible for making FlexCon the company it is today. Several newer members of the engineering group suggested they should wait until the outsourcing cost analysis was complete before rendering final judgment.

Management has created a cross-functional team composed of a process engineer, a cost analyst, a quality engineer, a procurement specialist, a supervisor, and a machine cell employee to conduct the outsourcing analysis. A major issue confronting this team involves determining which internal costs to apply to the analysis. Including total variable costs is straightforward because these costs are readily identifiable and vary directly with production levels. Examples of variable costs include materials, direct labor, and transportation.

The team is struggling with whether (or at what level) to include total factory and administrative costs (i.e., fixed costs and the fixed portion of semi-variable costs). Factory and administrative costs include utilities, indirect labor, process engineering support, depreciation, corporate office administration, maintenance, and product design charges. Proper allocation of overhead is a difficult, and sometimes subjective, task. The assumptions the team makes about how to allocate total factory and operating costs can dramatically alter the results of the analysis.

The aggregated volume for pistons over the next several years is critical to this analysis. Exhibit 2 provides a monthly forecast of expected piston volumes over the next two years. Total forecasted volume in Year One is 300,000 units and 345,000 units in Year Two. The team arrived at the forecast by determining the forecast for FlexCon "R" series engines, which is an independent demand item. Pistons are a dependent demand item (i.e., dependent on the demand for the final product).

Exhibit 2: Aggregated Two Year Piston Demand

	Year One Expected Demand	Year Two Expected Demand
January	30,000	34,000
February	30,000	34,000
March	30,000	34,000
April	27,000	31,000
May	25,000	28,000
June	25,000	28,000
July	23,000	27,000
August	21,000	25,000
September	22,000	25,000
October	23,000	27,000
November	23,000	27,000
December	21,000	25,000
Total	300,000	345,000

Although this is a long-term decision likely to extend beyond ten years, the team has confidence in its projections (including supplier pricing) only through Year Two. While maintaining piston production

Contd...

internally would require some level of process investment in years three through ten, the team believes any projections past year two contain too much uncertainty. (Conducting a net present value for expected savings from outsourcing, if they exist, is beyond the scope of this assignment).

Insourcing Costs

The team has decided that a comprehensive total cost analysis should include all direct and indirect costs incurred to support piston production. FlexCon tracks its materials and labor by completing production worksheets for each job. The team collected data for the previous year, which revealed the three work cells produced 288,369 pistons.

Direct Materials: FlexCon machines the pistons from a semi-finished steel alloy purchased directly from a steel foundry. The foundry ships the alloy to FlexCon in 50 lb. blocks, which cost $195 per block. Each piston requires, on average, 1.1 lbs. of semi-finished raw material for each finished piston. This figure includes scrap and waste.

The team expects the semi-finished raw material price to remain constant over the next two-years. Although FlexCon expects greater piston volumes in Years One and Two compared with current demand, the team does not believe additional material economies are available.

FlexCon spent $225,000 last year on other miscellaneous direct materials required to produce the pistons. The team expects to use this figure as a basis for calculating expected Year One and Two costs for miscellaneous direct material requirements.

Direct Work Cell Labor: The direct labor in the three work cells worked a total of 27,000 hours last year. Total payroll for direct labor was $472,500, which includes overtime pay. The average per hour direct labor rate is $17.50 per hour ($472,500/27,000 total hours = $17.50 per hour). As a rule of thumb, the team expects to add 40 percent to direct labor costs to account for benefits (health, dental, pension, etc.). Also, the team expects direct labor rates to increase 3 percent a year for the next two years. The team does not expect per hour production rates to change significantly. The process is well-established, and FlexCon has already captured any learning curve benefits.

Work cell employees are responsible for machine set-up, so the team decided not to include machine set-up as a separate cost category.

Indirect Work Cell Labor: FlexCon assigns a supervisor, material handler, and engineer full-time to the three work cells. Last year, the supervisor earned $52,000, the material handler earned $37,000, and the engineer earned $63,000 in salary. Again, the team expects to apply an additional 40 percent to these figures to reflect fringe benefits. The team expects these salaries to increase 3 percent each year.

Factory Overhead and Administrative Costs: This category of costs is, without doubt, the most difficult category of cost to allocate. For example, should the team prorate part of the plant manager's salary to the piston work cells? One team member argued that these costs are present with or without piston production, and therefore should not be part of the insourcing calculation. Another member maintained that factory overhead supports the factory, and the three work cells are a major part of the factory. Not including these costs would distort the insourcing calculation. She noted that the supplier is most assuredly considering these costs when quoting the piston contract.

The team divided the factory into six "zones" based on the function's performed throughout the plant. The piston work cells account for 25 percent of the factory's floor space, 28 percent of total direct labor hours, and 23 percent of plant volume. From this analysis, the team has decided to allocate 25 percent of the factory's overhead and administrative costs to the piston work cells. Exhibit 3 presents relevant cost data for the previous year. The team expects these costs to increase 3 percent each year.

Contd...

Exhibit 3: Total Factory Overhead and Administrative Costs

Cost Category	Previous Year Expense/Cost
Administrative staff	$1,200,000
Staff engineering	$900,000
Taxes	$120,000
Utilities	$1,500,000
Insurance	$500,000
Plant Maintenance	$800,000
Total	$5,020,000

Preventive Maintenance Costs: FlexCon spent $40,250 on preventive maintenance activities on the 18 machines last year, and expects this to increase by 10 percent in each of the next two years (due to the increasing age of the equipment).

Machine Repair Costs: An examination of maintenance work orders reveals that the 18 work cell machines, which are each 5-7 years old, required unplanned repair expenses of $37,000 last year. The maintenance supervisor expects this figure to increase by 8 percent in Year One and 12 percent in year Two of the analysis due to increasing age and volumes.

Ordering Costs: Although FlexCon produces pistons in-house, the company still incurs ordering costs for direct materials. The team estimates that each monthly order to the foundry and other suppliers costs FlexCon $1,500 in direct and transaction-related costs.

Semi-Finished Raw Material Inventory Carrying Costs: FlexCon typically maintains one month of semi-finished raw material inventory as safety and buffer stock. The carrying charge assigned to this inventory is 18 percent annually.

Inbound Transportation: FlexCon receives a monthly shipment of semi-finished alloy that the work cells use to machine the pistons. Total transportation costs for the previous year amounted to $31,500 (which resulted in 288,369 pistons produced).

The team expects transportation charges for other direct materials used in production to be $0.01 per unit in Years One and Two of the analysis.

Consumable Tooling Costs: The machines in the work cell are notorious for "going through tooling." Given the consumable tooling costs realized during the previous year, the team estimates additional tooling expenses of $56,000 in Year One, and $65,000 in Year Two.

Depreciation: The team has decided to include in its cost calculation normal depreciation expenses for the 18 work cell machines. The depreciation expense for the equipment is $150,000 per year.

Finished Piston Carrying Costs: Because FlexCon coordinates the production of pistons with the production of "R" series engines, any inventory carrying charges for finished pistons are part of the cost of the finished engine and are not considered relevant to this calculation.

Opportunity Costs: The team recognizes that opportunities may exist for achieving a better return on the space and equipment committed to piston production. Unfortunately, the team does not know with any certainty what management's plans may be for the floor space or equipment if FlexCon outsources piston production. The team is confident, however, that a use for the space will be found. If the facility no longer engages in piston production, then FlexCon must allocate fixed factory and overhead costs across a lower base of production. This will increase the average costs of the remaining items produced in the plant, possibly making them uncompetitive compared with external suppliers.

Contd...

Outsourcing Costs

The following provides relevant information collected by the team as it relates to outsourcing the family of pistons to an external supplier. While it is beyond the scope of this case, the team has already performed a rigorous assessment of the supply market, and has reached consensus on the external supplier in the event the team recommends outsourcing. This was necessary to obtain reliable outsourcing cost data.

Unit Price: The most obvious cost in an outsourcing analysis is the unit price quoted by the supplier. In many respects, outsourcing is an exercise in supplier evaluation and selection. Insourcing/outsourcing requires the evaluation of several suppliers in depth – the internal supplier (FlexCon) and external suppliers (in the marketplace). The supplier that the team favors if FlexCon outsources the pistons quoted an average unit price of $11.08 per piston (recall that this outsourcing decision involves different piston part numbers). The team believes that negotiation will occur if FlexCon elects to outsource, perhaps resulting in a lower quoted price. Quoted terms are 2/10, net 30. The supplier says it will maintain the quoted or final negotiated price over the next two years.

Safety Stock Requirements: If the team decides to outsource, FlexCon will hold physical stock from the supplier equivalent to one month's average demand. This results in an inventory carrying charge, which the team must calculate and include in the total cost analysis. While it is likely that FlexCon will rely on or draw down safety stock levels during the next two years, for purposes of costing the inventory the team has decided not to estimate when this might occur. Inventory carrying charges include working capital committed to financing the inventory, plus charges for material handling, warehousing, insurance and taxes, and risk of obsolescence and damage. FlexCon's inventory carrying charge is 18 percent annually.[1]

Administrative Support Costs: FlexCon expects to commit the equivalent of one-third of a buyer's total time to supporting the commercial issues related to the outsourced family of pistons. The team estimates the buyer's salary at $54,000, with 40 percent for fringe benefits. The team expects the buyer's compensation to increase by 3 percent each year.

Ordering Costs: The team expects that FlexCon will order monthly, or twelve material releases a year. Unfortunately, suppliers in this industry have not been responsive to shipping on a just-in-time basis or using electronic data interchange. While FlexCon would like to pursue a JIT purchasing model, the team feels that assuming lower volume shipments on a frequently scheduled basis is not appropriate. The company expects the supplier to deliver one-month of inventory at the beginning of each month. The team estimates the cost to release and receive an order to be $1,500 per order.

Quality-Related Costs: The team has decided to include quality-related costs in its outsourcing calculations. During the investigation of the supplier, a team member collected data on the process that would likely produce FlexCon's pistons. The team estimates that the supplier's defect level, based on process measurement data, will be 1,500 ppm. FlexCon's quality assurance department estimates that each supplier defect will cost the company $250 in nonconformance costs.

Inventory Carrying Charges: FlexCon must assume inventory carrying charges for pistons received at the start of each month and then consumed at a steady rate during the month. For purposes of calculating inventory carrying costs for finished pistons provided by the supplier, the team expects to use the average inventory method. The formula for determining the average number of units in inventory each month is:

((Beginning Inventory at the Start of Each Month + Ending Inventory at the End of Each Month)/2) x Carrying Cost Per Month.

For calculation purposes, the team assumes that ending inventory each month is zero units (excluding safety stock, which requires a separate calculation). The team expects production to use all the pistons received at the beginning of each month. The carrying charge applied to inventory on an

Contd...

annual basis is 14 percent of the unit value of the inventory. Appendix 1 and 2 will help in the calculation of monthly carrying charges associated with holding supplier-provided piston inventory.

Transportation Charges: While it is FlexCon's policy to have suppliers ship goods F.O.B. shipping point, the company does not accept title or ownership of goods until receipt at the buyer's dock. However, the company assumes all transportation-related charges. The team estimates that transportation charges for pistons will average $2,100 per truckload, with 14 truckloads expected in Year One and 16 truckloads expected in Year Two. The outsourcing supplier is in the U.S., which means the team does not have to consider additional costs related to duties or currency risks.

Tooling Charges: The supplier said that new tooling charges to satisfy FlexCon's production requirements would be $300,000. The team has decided to depreciate tooling charges over two years, or $150,000 per year.

Supplier Capacity: The team has concluded the supplier has available capacity to satisfy FlexCon's total piston requirements.

Appendix 3 provides a worksheet to help in the insourcing/outsourcing cost analysis.

Case Discussion

1.   Discuss what FlexCon should do with its family of pistons. Support your arguments with evidence gathered during case analysis.

2.   Discuss the primary reasons when and why insourcing/outsourcing decisions occur.

3.   A major challenge with an insourcing/outsourcing analysis involves gathering reliable data. Discuss the various groups that should be involved when conducting an insourcing/outsourcing analysis such as the one presented in this case. What information can each of these groups provide?

4.   Discuss the major issues associated with an insourcing/outsourcing analysis and decision.

Source: This case has been authored by Robert J Trent of The Lehigh University. The case study has been reprinted with the permission of the author.

---

1.   The 14 percent figure is less than the 18 percent figure applied to safety stock carrying charges. The supplier does not receive payment until at least four weeks after FlexCon receives the pistons. This makes FlexCon's working capital committed to financing production inventory somewhat less than the capital committed to financing safety stock.

Year One Inventory Carrying Charges Outsourcing Option

	Beginning Inventory	Ending Inventory	Average Inventory	Inventory Carrying Costs
January	30,000	0		$
February	30,000	0		$
March	30,000	0		$
April	27,000	0		$
May	25,000	0		$
June	25,000	0		$
July	23,000	0		$
August	21,000	0		$
September	22,000	0		$
October	23,000	0		$
November	23,000	0		$
December	21,000	0		$
			Total Inventory Carrying Costs	

Year Two Inventory Carrying Charges Outsourcing Option

	Beginning Inventory	Ending Inventory	Average Inventory	Inventory Carrying Costs
January	34,000	0		$
February	34,000	0		$
March	34,000	0		$
April	31,000	0		$
May	28,000	0		$
June	28,000	0		$
July	27,000	0		$
August	25,000	0		$
September	25,000	0		$
October	27,000	0		$
November	27,000	0		$
December	25,000	0		$
			Total Inventory Carrying Costs	

APPENDIX 3

Insourcing/Outsourcing Cost Factors Worksheet

Insourcing Costs Per Unit	Year One	Year Two	Outsourcing Costs Per Unit	Year One	Year Two
Direct Materials Semi-Finished Other			Purchase Cost		
Direct Labor			Transportation		
Indirect Labor			New Tooling		
Factory Overhead and Administrative			Administrative Support		
Preventive Maintenance			Inventory Carrying		
Machine Repair			Safety Stock		
Ordering			Quality-Related Costs		
Depreciation			Ordering		
Inventory Carrying			Other Costs		
Inbound Transportation			Total Outsourcing Costs Per Unit		
Consumable Tooling			Total Savings (I)		
Other Costs			Less: Taxes on Savings (40 percent)		
Total Insource Cost Per Unit			Net Outsourcing Savings		

(I) Total Savings = (Total Insourcing Costs - Total Outsourcing Costs) x (Total Volume). Note: The total savings could be negative if the analysis shows that outsourcing costs are greater that insourcing costs.

Developing a Sourcing Strategy at Medwell Pharmaceutical Corporation

By Robert J. Trent - Reprinted with the permission of the author.
Lehigh University

This case requires participants to develop a sourcing strategy that pertains to a critical chemical required to support the production of a recently approved pharmaceutical drug. Accomplishing this requires participants to:

- Develop a supplier selection process that guides the sourcing of a new purchase requirement.

- Perform a supplier financial analysis that becomes part of a preliminary supplier selection screening process.

- Develop a cost model that considers cost factors beyond unit price when estimating the total cost of sourcing decision.

- Create a weighted point supplier selection system that considers qualitative and quantitative supplier selection considerations.

- Develop a set of action plans to mitigate the risks identified with the sourcing decision.

- Create a time line to carry out the strategy recommendation.

Overview

Medwell Pharmaceutical Corporation (MPC), Inc. is a medium-sized (but growing) pharmaceutical company located in central New Jersey. The FDA has recently approved for commercialization the company's new drug, named Regenerix that helps delay and even reverse early symptoms of Alzheimer's disease.[1] Because several other companies also expect to win FDA approval for their Alzheimer's drugs over the next several months, MPC knows it must manage its product launch quickly and effectively. Once a patient begins taking a particular drug, he or she is unlikely to switch from that drug if it is effective and has relatively few side effects. Getting to market first is not only imperative from a humanitarian perspective, it is critical from a return-on-investment perspective.

Most pharmaceutical drugs, particularly complex drugs, are "assembled" in a series of steps that involve a build up of intermediaries or chemicals to form a final molecule. Intermediaries, which help form the foundation of complex molecules, are molecules or base chemicals that come together to support the creation of an ever more complex final molecule.

The final assembly of Regenerix is particularly complex. Most drugs are based on central hubs consisting of a carbon atom with four branches of various atoms attached. While these hubs naturally occur in nature, scientists have mastered the ability to create and link together multiple synthetic hubs, a challenging process for any pharmaceutical company. The molecular structure of Regenerix is appreciably more complex than any other drug that MPC has developed over the last 20 years.

While most medicines are based on one or two naturally occurring central hubs, Regenerix is more complicated because it has four such hubs, including two that are man-made rather than natural. The intermediary that is the focus of this case is essential to the production of one of the man-made or synthetic central hubs.

---

[1] Both Medwell Pharmaceutical Corporation and Regenerix are fictitious names. Any resemblance to an actual company or drug is coincidental.

Contd...

As a result of an earlier study conducted by corporate personnel and an external consultant, executive management has decided that the final production of the new drug will remain in-house rather than outsourced to a third-party. This decision was based partly on MPC's belief that manufacturing is a core capability of the company along with the complexity of the new drug. However, the decision was also made to outsource the production of various intermediaries. Executive management believes this will save investment dollars as well as time. It will also allow MPC to focus its efforts and investments in areas that the company feels most closely align with its core capabilities. This case focuses on the sourcing of a major intermediary code named Intermediary 331 by the product design team.

Medwell Pharmaceutical Corporation relies on cross-functional commodity teams to develop sourcing strategies for key purchased items. Executive management views the sourcing of the Regenerix intermediaries as a critical part of the product launch schedule. The commodity team responsible for sourcing Intermediary 331 has spent the last several weeks visiting potential suppliers, and is currently evaluating various supply options. The team expects to begin negotiations with one or more suppliers within the next several weeks.

It is currently August 2005. MPC plans for pilot production and ramp up to begin in early December with the introduction of Regenerix in the U.S. in January 2006. The product will be introduced to other countries as the company receives approval from the appropriate regulatory authorities.

U.S. Anticipated Demand for Regenerix

Exhibit 1 details the monthly sales forecast for Regenerix in doses or pills, which is the unit of measure the company uses to forecast final production requirements. Users of Regenerix will take one dose or pill a day. Because this drug is a totally new approach to fighting Alzheimer's, the demand forecasts are inherently subject to some uncertainty or variability. The ability of suppliers to respond quickly to demand changes will be critical.

Given the volatility of new product forecasts, as well as experience with other product launches the marketing group estimates first year demand at 350,000,000 with 95 percent confidence that actual demand will be between 300,000,000 and 400,000,000 doses or pills. This forecast can be affected greatly if a competitor gets to the market before MPC.

During final production of Regenerix one pound of Intermediary 331 will yield an average of 1,590 pills. So, expected production for the first year of 350,000,000 doses requires 220,000 pounds of the outsourced intermediary.

MPC plans to purchase Intermediary 331 in lot sizes of 2,000 pounds. The company expects to purchase 110 lots or containers to support annual demand requirements (220,000 pounds of Intermediary 331/2,000 pounds per lot = 110 lots or containers). The material will arrive in containers via truck, although foreign suppliers will also ship via ocean carrier to a U.S. port. This will have an effect on logistics costs.

Adequate supplier and final production capacity is a critical issue since the drug quickly loses its efficacy if a patient stops taking the drug. MPC Pharmaceutical must have strong assurance from its suppliers that they can increase the supply of the intermediary by 20 percent within four weeks of changing demand conditions and by 40 percent within eight weeks. Also, the supplier's ability to support higher initial production rates to get finished product into the distribution network in anticipation of product launch (as well as building some safety stock of Intermediary 331) is also essential.

Quality is a critical factor in the selection of an intermediary supplier. A non-conforming lot or batch of chemicals will render an entire batch of final product unusable. If defective chemicals work their way into final production, the consequences will not be known for at least five days. (A final batch of Regenerix takes five days to "cook"). Defective final products that make their way to the consumer

Contd...

can have catastrophic consequences on the user as well as the future of MPC. The company is well aware of the costs of litigation and class-action lawsuits.

Exhibit 1: Regenerix Year One Forecast

Date	Units or Doses	Pounds of 331	Lots or Containers
January 2006	63,600,000 units	40,000 lbs.	20
February 2006	47,700,000 units	30,000 lbs.	15
March 2006	38,160,000 units	24,000 lbs.	12
April 2006	22,260,000 units	14,000 lbs.	7
May 2006	22,260,000 units	14,000 lbs.	7
June 2006	22,260,000 units	14,000 lbs.	7
July 2006	22,260,000 units	14,000 lbs.	7
August 2006	22,260,000 units	14,000 lbs.	7
September 2006	22,260,000 units	14,000 lbs.	7
October 2006	22,260,000 units	14,000 lbs.	7
November 2006	22,260,000 units	14,000 lbs.	7
December 2006	22,260,000 units	14,000 lbs.	7
Total Annual	350,000,000 units	220,000 lbs	110 containers

Note: Early volumes are higher due to a need to fill the supply pipeline with finished inventory and to maintain safety stock of the intermediary.

The Supply Alternatives

Six suppliers responded to the commodity team's Request for Proposal, which was forwarded to prospective suppliers twelve weeks previously. Although other potential suppliers exist, these were the only six that showed any interest in MPC's initial inquiries. A review of these proposals revealed that three of the six suppliers were cost competitive given MPC's target price. Engineering supported the commodity team's preliminary efforts by evaluating initial product samples provided by interested supplies. This helped determine if the suppliers had a product that initially satisfied the company's expectations. Relying on product samples, while providing some insight into the technical capability of each supplier, was not sufficient to support a final selection decision. Hence, the need for direct visits by the commodity team became obvious.

The team decided to visit three suppliers to collect detailed information and interview managers. The visits ranged from one to two days each, with all the visits completed within a three-week period. These visits were time-consuming and exhausting, particularly since two suppliers were located outside the U.S. Unfortunately, MPC does not have International Purchasing Offices (IPO's) to support its worldwide sourcing activities. Furthermore, no one on the team spoke any foreign languages. The following sections summarize data collected during the commodity team's visits to each supplier.

Ninaka Materials

Ninaka Materials, located in Nagasaki, Japan, was the largest supplier the team visited (sales of $6.5 billion). The facility covered ten acres, with a wide variety of chemicals produced in the facility. Intermediary 331 represents a large segment of Ninaka's production (the company generates around 3 percent of total revenue from the production of intermediaries such as 331). Geographic distance from New Jersey made Ninaka's quoted lead time the longest of the suppliers being evaluated.

The highest-ranking manager that met with MPC's sourcing team was a sales manager, who took the team to visit various departments. The division vice-president and plant manager were in conference

Contd...

with a major competitor, who the sourcing team found out was interested in forming a long-term supply alliance with Ninaka. The commodity team felt a bit "snubbed" at the facility, particularly the group's female members. The facility was efficient, spotless, and modern.

When the team visited engineering, they spoke with a process engineer. The engineer estimated, based on previous experience, that the ramp-up time to begin production that would satisfy MPC's specifications and then distribute the product to MPC's U.S. facility would be about 4 months. Furthermore, additional costs to begin production of 331 would likely be $150,000.

The sales manager was particularly proud of Ninaka's new Internet-based Electronic Data Interchange (EDI) system. This system allowed direct communication with customers. He was also proud that Ninaka Materials was "the price leader" for the industry, and was producing important intermediaries for several major pharmaceutical companies. He also talked about the company's extensive investment in research and development. When the sales manager heard that MPC's order would total "only" 220,000 lbs. in year one, he hesitated and said he would need to discuss the order with management. Moreover, he indicated that the company typically was not interested in orders of less than 500,000 lbs. per annum, but that exceptions might be possible. Furthermore, the company only enters into contracts in yen and will not accept payment in U.S. dollars. The sales manager said the economics associated with large orders is what made Ninaka a low-price producer.

Relevant Ninaka Materials data include:

- Quoted price = $4.75 per pound (quoted at 108 yen to $1 U.S.)
- Delivery lead time = 8 weeks
- On-time delivery record = 95 percent on-time (for large customers)
- Quality yield during production = 97 percent
- Lot acceptance rate at receiving = 96.5 percent
- Transportation costs from Asian facility to MPC = $2,900 per container
- Current installed capacity for intermediary production[2] = 96 percent
- Duties and customs = 4 percent of unit price
- Insurance = $700 per container
- Frequency of shipment = Monthly
- Tooling and set up costs = $150,000
- Ordering, inbound receiving, and quality inspection costs = $300 per container
- Ramp-up and delivery time to lot one = 4 months
- Denomination of contract = Yen

Fase Chemicals Company

A second candidate for the contract is FASE Chemicals Company, a specialty chemical producer located in Baton Rouge, Louisiana. The company derives about 7 percent of its total revenue from the sale of 331-type intermediaries. The team discovered this company almost by accident. A team member was browsing a trade journal and saw FASE Chemical advertisement. When the team visited the facility, the team was surprised at its relatively small scale with relatively older process technology.

---

[2]   Current installed capacity indicates that portion of the supplier's production capacity that is currently utilized for the production on intermediaries such as 331. For example, if current installed capacity is 98 percent, then this supplier is utilizing 98 percent of its production capacity and therefore has 2 percent of its capacity available for new business. This does not indicate how many available pounds this represents.

Contd...

FASE Chemicals's president met with the team in person. He explained that he was a graduate of Stanford in chemical engineering and had decided to start his own company after working for Dupont for 15 years. The company entered the intermediary market four years ago and has grown steadily. During this time, however, FASE Chemicals has established a reputation for delivery reliability and innovation. The president explained that FASE Chemical's success was based largely on its commitment to develop new technology, especially technology that enhanced product reliability. He also claimed that he knew every customer personally. Customer relationships are one of his highest priorities.

Everyone in the plant seemed highly motivated. The president was particularly excited about the possibility of working with MPC, and promised to work with them closely on this contract and for any new product lines. When asked if his firm would have any problem in meeting demand should they receive the contract, he hesitated before answering. He admitted that this contract would be the largest in FASE Chemical's relatively short history. He also indicated that several other buying teams were also going to be sending teams to evaluate FASE Chemicals within the next week. However, he assured the team that he would do whatever it took to maintain reliable delivery schedules if FASE Chemicals received the contract. Interestingly, it appeared that the production lines were experiencing some problems during the team's visit, as they were shut down for nearly four hours! Relevant FASE Chemicals data include:

- Quoted price = $5.75 per pound

- Delivery lead time = 3 weeks

- On-time delivery record = 97 percent on-time

- Quality yield during production = 96 percent

- Lot acceptance rate at receiving = 97.5 percent

- Transportation costs from FASE Chemicals to MPC = $1200 per container

- Current installed capacity for intermediary production = 98 percent

- Duties and customs = $0.00 per unit

- Insurance = $300 per unit

- Frequency of shipment = every two weeks

- Tooling and set costs = $175,000

- Ordering, inbound receiving, and quality inspection costs = $350 per container

- Ramp-up and delivery time to lot one = 5 months

- Denomination of contract = Dollars

DMS NV

The third supplier, DMS NV, is a Dutch company. DMS NV provided the second lowest bid at $5.20 per pound. During the team visit the plant manager claimed that capacity was not an issue, and that the company would be willing to commit the required production capacity to the Medwell contract. Intermediary production similar to 331 requirements accounted for about 2 percent of DMS NV's $1.3 billion in 2004 sales.

The commodity team felt much more comfortable at DMS NV than at Ninaka Materials. While this supplier has minimal experience doing business with North American firms, the company seemed quite anxious for the contract. In fact, a contract with MPC would be the first with a U.S. company. At

Contd...

this time DMS NV has no U.S. facilities or support staff. The team had some concerns about becoming DMS NV's first major U.S. customer.

The company's product was excellent. Every chemical batch went through an extensive certification procedure that assured few problems would occur. In fact, DMS NV's process control and testing were more thorough than any other supplier the team visited. However, the combination of the testing process and geographic distance meant that delivery cycle times were much longer, up to 10 weeks per order, although the on-time delivery performance for the facility was excellent. The team was not sure if current delivery performance outside North America would be indicative of delivery performance to the U.S. The facility appeared well maintained, clean, and orderly. The team noticed that the facility that produces intermediaries like 331 was extremely busy and wondered if the plant manager's claim about adequate capacity was accurate. Industry experts viewed DMS NV as one of the most promising and dynamic companies in the industry. The ramp-up time for the delivery of the first shipment was quoted as 4.5 months. Relevant DMS NV data include:

- Quoted price = $5.20 per pound

- Delivery lead time = 8-10 weeks

- On-time delivery record = 99.0 percent

- Quality yield during production = 98.7 percent

- Lot acceptance rate at receiving = 99.5 percent

- Transportation costs from DMS NV to MPC = $2,200 per container

- Current installed capacity for intermediary production = 98.5 percent

- Duties and customs = 3 percent of unit price

- Insurance = $450 per container

- Frequency of shipment = Monthly

- Tooling and set up costs = $200,000

- Ordering, inbound receiving and quality inspection costs = $225 per container

- Ramp-up time = 4.5 months

- Denomination of contract = Euros or Dollars

Supplier Financial Data

The team also gathered financial data for each supplier. While the team believes the data for the U.S. supplier is reliable, several assumptions and estimates had to be made regarding the Asian suppliers. The team had to convert Japanese and Euro currencies into dollars. In some cases, the desired figures were not available, or the supplier showed no interest in providing the team with the requested information. In particular, this was an issue with Ninaka Materials. Exhibits 2 and 3 summarize selected supplier financial data.

Exhibit 2: Selected Supplier Balance Sheet Data (U.S. $ in millions)
For Period Ending December 31, 2004

	Ninaka Materials	FASE Chemicals	DMS NV
ASSETS			
Cash	$95.9	$35	$54.3
Marketable securities	$122.5	$9	$27.7
Accounts receivable	$889	$45	$174.5

Contd...

Inventories	$1057.7	$75	$135.4
Total current assets	$2,165.1	$164	$391.9
Investments at equity	$738.4	$21	$95
Goodwill	$300	$40	$80.4
Total investments and other assets	$1,038.4	$61	$175.4
Property, plant, and equipment	$1,734.5	$125	$412.5
TOTAL ASSETS	$4,938	$350	$979.8
LIABILITIES AND SHAREHOLDERS' EQUITY			
Notes payable	$525.5	$11	$35
Accounts payable	$525.9	$75	$125
Taxes due on income	$245	$23	$48
Accrued payroll and employee benefits	$484.2	$13.5	$139
Total current liabilities	$1,780.6	$122.5	$347
Long-term debt	$1,243.5	$55	$165
Shareholders' equity	$1,913.9	$172.5	$467.8
TOTAL LIABILITIES AND SHAREHOLDERS' EQUITY	$4,938	$350	$979.8

**Exhibit 3: Statement of Income Data (U.S. $ in millions)
Year Ended December 31, 2004**

	Ninaka Materials	FASE Chemicals	DMS NV
Net sales	$6,500	$550	$1,355
Cost of goods sold	$5,500	$407.5	$948.5
Selling, general, and administrative expenses	$475	$65	$250
Interest expense	$300	$12	$55
Costs and expenses	$6,275	$484.5	$1,253.5
Income before income taxes	$225	$65.5	$101.5
Estimated taxes on income	$100	$28	$55
NET INCOME	$125	$37.5	$46.5

Additional Information and Assumptions

- The commodity team will allocate all supplier-related production costs, such as tooling and set up charges, on a per unit basis over the first year.

- Medwell Pharmaceutical plans to maintain some level of safety stock inventory for the drives, at least for the first year. Due to long material pipelines, Medwell Pharmaceutical expects to maintain a safety stock of one month average demand if it utilizes foreign suppliers. For domestic suppliers, the company expects to maintain an inventory equal to two weeks worth of average demand as safety stock.

Contd...

- Inventory carrying costs on the safety stock, which include storage, handling, obsolescence, taxes, and cost of capital, are 24 percent of the inventory's unit cost. The company assumes carrying costs for safety stock material.

- Assume the unit price quoted by each supplier is what Medwell Pharmaceutical will pay directly per pound from each supplier. Subsequent negotiations will likely alter the quoted price.

- While FTC takes an active role in coordinating inbound transportation shipments, company policy states that FTC will not assume title to material until the material arrives at the company's receiving dock. This requires no additional carrying charge of inbound material.

Case Requirements

Your group is to analyze this case using the data provided. The output from your efforts should be a well crafted sourcing strategy, which includes identification of the selected supplier, a clear summary of why a supplier was selected or not, discussion of the type of contract to pursue, identification of key negotiation issues, and a timeline to implement your strategy.

To reach a decision, your group must perform various analyzes designed to support the supplier evaluation and selection decision. These analyzes, with supporting worksheets or templates provided, include

Financial Risk Analysis: While this case assumes that the cross-functional team visited three suppliers, organizations often perform a preliminary financial risk analysis to identify the suppliers that may not warrant further consideration due to excessive financial risk.

Total Cost Analysis: Unit price rarely, if ever, equals the total cost of doing business with a supplier. This analysis requires each group to identify relevant additional costs beyond unit price. This involves considering a combination of actual and estimated costs.

Supplier Evaluation and Selection Analysis: As organizations continue to rely on fewer suppliers, the supplier selection process takes on greater importance. The Supplier Evaluation and Selection Analysis is a robust tool used during supplier assessment.

Sourcing Risk Management Plan: Sourcing decisions invariably involve risk. This analysis requires each group to (1) identify the potential risks associated with a sourcing decision, (2) assess the possible magnitude of each risk to operations, and (3) identify ways to manage or reduce risk exposure.

Also, develop a timeline that clearly displays the actions your team and the supplier must take to support the product launch date. This timeline is to be presented with your strategy recommendation.

Please note that while this case does not explicitly ask, a rough calculation of pounds of capacity available at each supplier is possible. It is highly recommended that a rough calculation occurs before recommending your sourcing strategy.

Source: This case has been authored by Robert J Trent of the Lehigh University. The case study has been reprinted with the permission of the author.

Purchasers assess supplier financial health for several reasons. The most important reason involves managing supply base risk. The analysis may highlight difficulties that will interfere with the smooth and timely flow of material. A supplier may be experiencing capacity constraint problems, have difficulty meeting its payables, have too many receivables, have poor inventory management as revealed by low inventory turns, or have cash flow problems as noted by current liabilities exceeding current assets.

A supplier financial analysis is likely whenever a purchaser is attempting to reduce a pool of potential supply sources. If a supplier does not meet certain thresholds as defined by the purchaser, then the supplier will likely not move to the next level of consideration.

Financial ratios are a key part of a supplier financial analysis. Of course, the key to a supplier financial analysis is a purchaser's ability to obtain reliable and complete financial data, which can be a challenge when evaluating closely or privately held corporations.

Besides calculating and attempting to interpret the meaning of financial ratios, comparing ratio data can provide even greater insight into a supplier's financial condition. While no correct answers exist for financial ratios, a comparison of a supplier's ratios to published industry norms can help identify if further financial analysis is necessary. An analyst should also compare several years of supplier financial data, if available, to identify favorable or unfavorable trends. Another comparison involves comparing a supplier's ratios with specific competitors, which is likely when a purchaser has collected data from more than one supplier.

Please use the following template to calculate selected financial ratios for the suppliers being considered for the contract.

Supplier Financial Analysis Worksheet

Selected Financial Ratios	Ninaka Materials	FASE Chemicals	DMS NV
Asset Utilization:			
Asset Turnover = Sales/Assets			
Inventory Turnover = Cost of Sales/Inventory			
Receivable Days = Accounts Receivable/Sales X 360			
Payable Days = Accounts Payable/Sales X 360			
Capitalization:			
Leverage = Assets/Equity			
Return on Equity = Net Income/Equity			
Long-term Debt to Equity = Long-term Debt/Equity			
Long-term Debt to Assets = Long-term Debt/Assets			
Current Ratio = Current Assets/Current Liabilities			
Quick Ratio = (Cash + Short-term Investment + Accounts Receivable)/ Current Liabilities			
EBIT Coverage = Earnings Before Interest and Taxes/Interest Expenses			
Profitability Ratios:			
Contribution Margin = (Sales - Variable Cost)/Sales			
Operating Margin = (Contribution Margin - Base Cost)/Sales			
Profit Margin = Net Income/Sales			

Note: Shareholders equity includes stock and retained earnings. This value is also referred to as Net Worth.

Conclusions and Interpretation:

APPENDIX 2
Total Cost Analysis

This template requires each group to quantify costs that are in addition to the quoted unit price. Using cost information provided in the case for each supplier, calculate the estimated per unit total cost from each supplier for year one.

Total Cost Analysis Worksheet-Year One

Cost Category	Ninaka Materials	FASE Chemicals	DMS NV
Quoted Unit Price			
Transportation			
Tooling and set up charges			
Quality yield loss			
Lot rejection loss			
Duties/customs			
Insurance			
Inventory safety stock carrying charges			
Ordering, inbound receiving and quality inspection costs			
Estimated Per Pound Total Cost			

Calculations:

Note: Quality yield during production is an estimate based on historical figures provided by the supplier and estimates based on sample tests. The team has decided to include quality yield loss as an expense within the total cost calculation.

The team estimates that each rejected lot or container at receiving costs Medwell $5,200 in expediting, handling, disposal, and transportation costs.

Conclusions and Comments:

The development of a supplier evaluation and selection analysis follows a sequence of steps:

Step One: Identify Key Supplier Evaluation Categories

Supplier evaluations must include those performance categories that are relevant to the sourcing decision under consideration. Examples of supplier evaluation categories that a team or individual may evaluate include (but are not limited to):

- Management and personnel capability
- Information systems capability
- Process and technological capability
- Delivery performance
- Flexibility
- Previous history and performance
- Responsiveness to customer needs

- Cost competitiveness
- Quality performance
- Environmental compliance
- Longer-term partnership potential
- Volume capacity
- Supplier's supply management efforts
- Information system capability

While including the relevant performance categories is critical, each additional category adds a greater degree of assessment complexity.

Step Two: Weigh Each Relevant Evaluation Category

The performance categories included within the analysis receive a weight proportional to the relative importance of that category. With any combination of weights, the weights must sum to 100 percent.

Step Three: Identify and Weigh Subcategories

Step 2 defines the broad performance categories included within the evaluation. This step requires the user to identify performance subcategories, if they exist, within each broader performance category. Each subcategory receives a weight, the total of which equals the weight of the broader performance category. For example, assume that supplier quality performance is 20 percent of the total score. Within that category, a team may create subcategories related to process control systems (5 percent), total quality commitment (8 percent), and parts per million defect performance (7 percent). Please note that the subcategories sum to 20 percent.

Step Four: Define Scoring System for Categories and Subcategories

This step involves defining what each score means within a performance category. A clearly defined scoring system takes criteria that may be subjective and develops a quantified scale for measurement. The scoring metrics are reliable if different individuals interpret and score similarly the same performance categories under review.

Step Five: Evaluate Supplier Directly

This step requires that a review team or individual visit a supplier's facilities to assess supplier performance capabilities. It is common for a reviewer to meet with a supplier shortly after the initial evaluation to discuss findings, and to point out opportunities for improvement. The visit may also help identify future supplier development opportunities.

Step Six: Review Evaluation Results and Make Selection Decision

The primary output from this step is a recommendation concerning which supplier(s) should receive a purchase contract. As with any tool, the outcome from this analysis is only as good as the planning and effort put forth.

Step Seven: Continuous Review of Supplier Performance

After supplier selection, a purchaser's emphasis must shift form initial evaluation to evidence of continuous supplier performance improvement.

When developing an instrument to support supplier evaluation, keep in mind that effective instruments have certain characteristics. Effective supplier evaluation instruments should be:

Comprehensive: The evaluation considers all the performance categories or criteria considered important to the selection decision.

Contd...

Objective: Objectivity requires the use of a quantitative scoring system, such as a weighted point scale, with the meaning of each value on the measurement scale clearly defined. Objectivity requires the creation of quantitative scales to evaluate performance items and categories, some of which may be inherently subjective.

Reliable: Reliability refers to the degree to which different individuals or groups reviewing the same supplier performance category using the same measurement scales would arrive at the same conclusion. Evaluated items and scales must be clearly defined and unambiguous so users understand what each means.

Flexible: Flexibility means the user can modify the performance categories, subcategories, and assigned weights depending on the sourcing decision. For example, selecting a supplier to provide a key jet engine component may require a higher emphasis or weight placed on quality compared with other performance categories. On the other hand, an evaluation of a distributor that provides industry-standard items (with well accepted quality standards) will likely emphasize performance categories such as depth of inventory, cost, and delivery.

Mathematically Straightforward: The use of weights and points during the evaluation should be simple enough so that those involved in the assessment (including suppliers) understand the mechanics of the scoring and selection process.

Please complete this exercise after the group has made its selection decision. For the selected supplier, identify any concerns by Potential Concern Area and make note of your plan to reduce the potential risk.

Sourcing Risk Management Plan Supplier: _____

Potential Concern Area	Risk or Concern	Risk Reduction Plan
Management Capability		
Delivery Performance		
Quality Performance		
Process Capability		
Capacity		
Cost		
Technical Ability		
Logistics		
Financial Issues		
Other Issues		

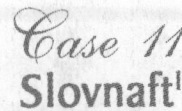

Case 11
Slovnaft[1]

Background and Objectives

Slovnaft, a.s., is a refinery and petrochemical company based in Bratislava, Slovak Republic. Since its privatization in 1992, the formerly state-run company has aggressively focused on modernization and adapting to Western European business practices. In 2000, it established a cross-border strategic partnership with MOL (www.mol.hu), one of Hungary's biggest corporations. In 2003, MOL acquired a majority stake. Slovnaft is now fully integrated in the international MOL Group, a leading company in the energy sector in Central Europe.

Since 1995, the Slovnaft Group has spent more than 625 million Euro on its retail marketing operations and on upgrading the refinery (Heavy Petroleum Residue Upgrading -HPRU), with a budgeted cost of about 445 million Euro. The HPRU became fully operational in late March 2000 and has resulted in a significant increase of the volume of lighter products (gasoline and diesel) in the Bratislava refinery, which is considered the most complex refinery in Europe.

Between 1995 and 1997, the company expanded its marketing operations by acquiring an 85.2 percent stake in Benzinol, a.s., Bratislava, the former state-owned retailer and wholesaler of refined products. The company has developed its own Slovnaft-branded network of service stations in the Slovak Republic. The company maintains retail operations in the Czech Republic, Poland and Ukraine, operated by its local subsidiary companies.

Slovnaft states its vision as "building our prosperity on integration within the oil industry in Central Europe by means of advanced technology, skills and knowledge of our employees". Based on this vision, and reflecting new managerial trends and the requirements of business reengineering, the corporate services focused its activities during the 1st quarter 2002 on the improvement of internal procurement processes, starting with e-procurement for chemicals and special equipment. The main objective to be achieved in this area was to improve the efficiency of processes by simplifying and reducing time and costs of the procurement process.

The achievement of this objective should be enabled by the introduction of electronic procurement. This included the integration of systems with suppliers and the implementation of an automated rating of suppliers. In accordance with these operational goals, it was decided that the centralization of procurement process for all commodities and services was a strategic requirement.

Activities

Starting from paper-based procurement.

The strategic plan to launch and implement an integrated e-procurement scheme in the company was prepared at a time when procurement activities of the company were still paper-based, typically consisting of the following steps:

- Slovnaft sent specification requirements to potential suppliers in the traditional way (by mail);

- On the basis of accepted quotations, the company started negotiations with suppliers;

- After selecting a supplier, the procurement manager sent a paper order;

- At the same time, the purchasing information had to be put into the enterprise information system for accounting, controlling, and stock control purposes;

---

1. This case study is a contribution from the Technical University of Košice, Faculty of Economics, researched and edited by Ing. Radoslav Delina, PhD, Ing. Viliam Vajda, doc. Ing. Tomas Sabol, PhD (contact: radoslav.delina@tuke.sk).

Contd...

- When the material was delivered, the invoice and the delivery order were produced and processed.

All these processes were slowed down by a lot of paperwork, for example filling in and signing warehouse receipts for goods delivered.

E-business Technology Implementation

The production process at Slovnaft is highly specific and requires a stable and efficient management system. Since growth in performance and demand was expected, and since consolidation of multiple servers to one platform was required, Slovnaft decided to upgrade its old Oracle Financials software to the e-Business Suite of the same make. The US based development centre of Oracle participated in this upgrading.

Based on the user requirements, the supplier provided applications and functionality which was - at that time - available for other customers only in the forthcoming version of its software.

Slovnaft defined its primary, long-term e-business strategy as to benefit from an integrated, centralized enterprise system and efficient collaboration with suppliers.

From January 2002 to February 2003, Slovnaft upgraded its enterprise information system GEMMS (Global Enterprise Manufacturing Management System). Since 1995 GEMMS had been supporting most of the firm's main processes. The upgraded system was called OPM (Oracle Process Manufacturing) and was a part of the Oracle e- Business Suite, which consists of almost 300 modules.

Upgrading the e-Business Suite contributed substantially to the integration of a large number of partial applications into the online central system. Although the specialization of the industry production is high, the amount of customization necessary could be significantly reduced in comparison to the preceding version of the suite. The system is based on an integrated relational multidimensional database (Oracle 9i) and uses Java technology with thin client applications.

As one of the major effects to be achieved, the purchasing process became digitally integrated at a satisfactory level. Procurement control was increased significantly and integrated from different systems to a central one for the whole company. Currently, the Oracle iProcurement and Oracle Purchasing applications are the basis for purchasing processes.

The integrated e-procurement solution electronically links production processes to procurement. Requests for supply goods are triggered right from the manufacturing processes. After needs identification, users can select goods or services from an electronic catalogue. After approval of the electronic requisition record, the system checks warehouse resources. If the goods are not available but covered by a general contract with a specific supplier, the system automatically generates an order.

Exhibit 1: Scheme of the eProcurement Process at Slovnaft

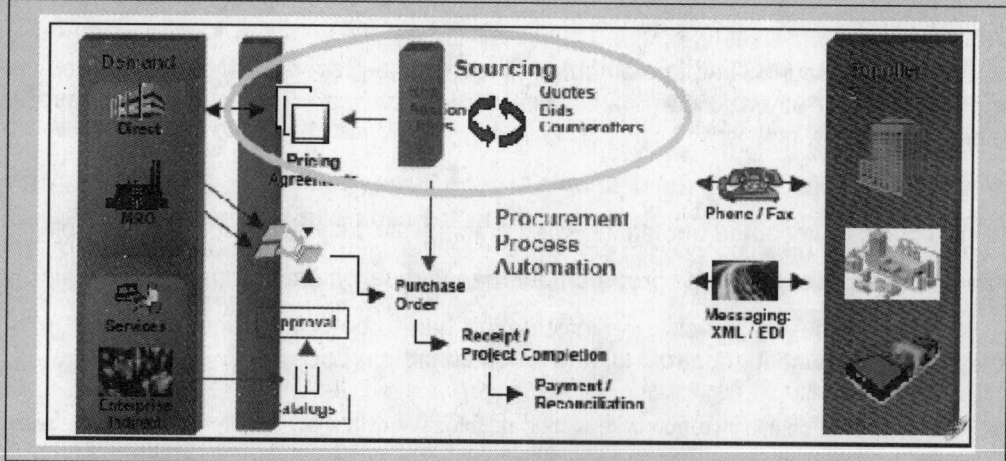

Source: SlSource: Slovnaft / Technical University of Košice, Faculty of Economics (2004)

Contd...

Electronic Tendering Procedure and use of B2B Marketplaces

While small orders are thus automatically processed, product orders which exceed a certain cost have to be purchased on the basis of a tendering procedure. In this case, potential suppliers have first to be selected and then invited to tender. Suppliers can be selected from a database of suppliers who cooperate or have already cooperated with Slovnaft. It is also possible to invite new potential suppliers through electronic marketplaces, from the Internet or from other sources.

As the ongoing search for new potential suppliers is important for Slovnaft, the enterprise's Oracle applications were integrated with ChemUnity.com, the first European vertical B2B marketplace in the chemical industry. In the field of horizontal B2B marketplaces, Slovnaft has decided to use Trade2B.com for eRFQ (electronic Request for Quotation) and for reverse auctions. In the case of RFQs, the purchasing department can use the Oracle purchasing application or external portals, for example Chemunity.com.

Use of Reverse Auctions

After the evaluation of the various offers received from potential suppliers, the purchasing department can select a single supplier or invite some of the suppliers to participate in a reverse auction. An auction needs to be carefully prepared, taking the following steps:

1. *Spend analysis:* Analysis of former costs on the same product, market analysis and impacts on price of purchased product.

2. *Strategy planning:* Identifying the period for the tender, its specifics and type.

3. *Request for information (from potential suppliers):* This is needed in case of complex requests, for instance if it is not possible to specify the product in detail.

4. *Request for price:* Asking for the first price offered by suppliers.

5. *Technical and commercial evaluation:* The auction can only be held if the technical offers and first offers are comparable. The fulfilment of requirements must therefore be evaluated beforehand.

6. *Auction:* call for participation and conduct of the auction.

It is important that the buyer can still decide whether to conduct traditional negotiations with suppliers or whether to go for a reverse auction procedure. In the case of reverse auctions, buyers have to carry out a rather complex evaluation beforehand in order to assure equal commercial and qualitative conditions before the auction begins. Otherwise, the auction cannot be held. Before launching a reverse auction, Slovnaft requires participants to submit authorization documents (for the auction participation) in paper form, including the name of a responsible person. The department then defines the start time, the auction date and possibly a starting price for the auction.

In a reverse auction, participants do not know each other. The auction is finished when there have been no new bids for 10 minutes. The winner in a reverse auction is the supplier offering the lowest price. The whole price negotiation process is carried out in an online environment among the suppliers, without any intervention of the purchasing department. According to Slovnaft, reverse auctions can reduce procurement costs and time, if the auction is well prepared in advance.

Lessons Learned

The upgrade to Oracle's e-Business Suite contributed substantially to integrating a large number of formerly separated applications into one central online system. Slovnaft estimates that it reduced the time for materials daily balancing[2] from two hours per day to 15 minutes, and for a calculation of the 10-days' production costs[3] from 15 to 2.5 hours.

---

[2] "Materials daily balancing" is the process of pricing outputs by inputs. The system monitors particular aspects and data related to inputs and calculates final product prices according to that data. The time needed to accomplish this process could be reduced by implementing the e-business system.

[3] Every 10 days, management performs some revisions and adjustments in the calculation of production costs taking into account externalities and internal process changes which are not reflected in the direct costs.

Contd...

The supplies purchasing process was successfully digitally integrated for the whole company. This resulted in a reduced purchasing time and created free capacity for so called value added activities of professional purchasers, such as market research, quality negotiations and improvement of the relationships with suppliers. These activities should in the medium and long-run result in even more substantial cost savings and are expected to positively influence the profit of the company.

Furthermore, the new system substantially substituted former paper-based workflows and helped to standardize and increase the transparency of the purchasing process. These objectives have also been accomplished.

Effectively, the former paper-based procurement process has been considerably streamlined by eliminating some phases, as illustrated in the exhibit below.

Exhibit 2: From Paper-based to Electronic Procurement at Slovnaft

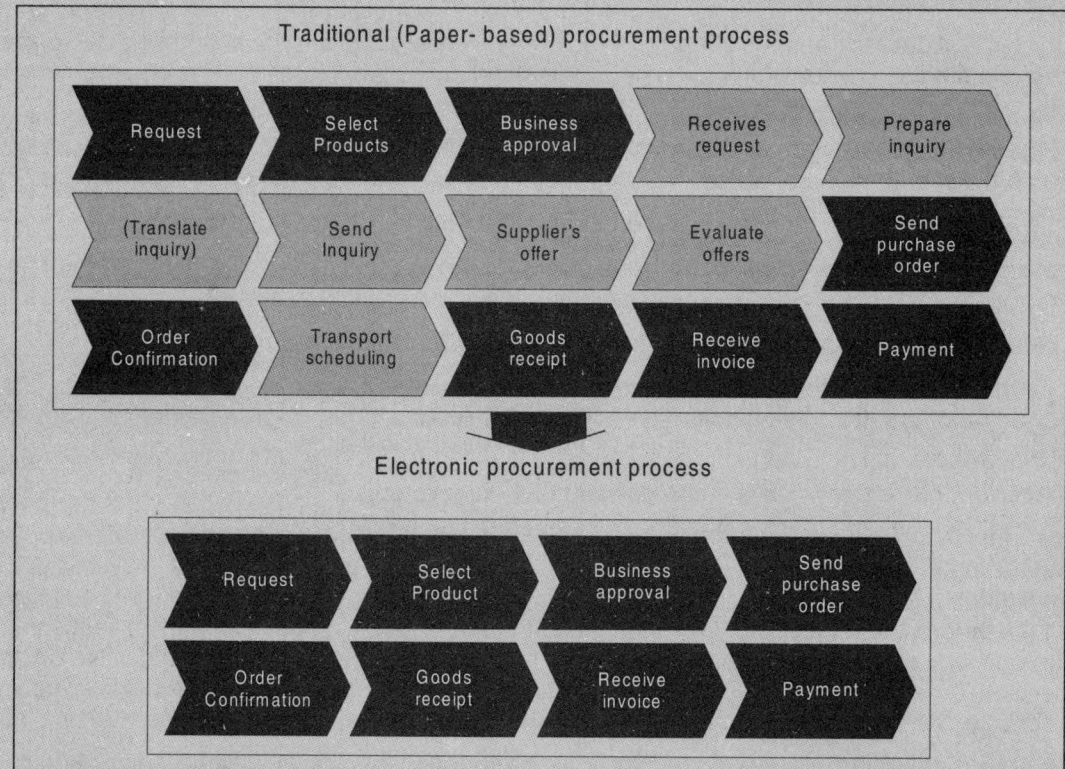

Source: Slovnaft / Technical University of Košice, Faculty of Economics (2004)

In general, the new system provides the following functions:

- Electronic requisition record and its approval directly in the information system. Generation of electronic demand

- e-Quotations

- Electronic approval of orders

- Sourcing

- e-catalogue of suppliers, products and services

- Automated matching of invoices with receipts and the purchasing orders.

In 2002, when the project started, Slovnaft purchased goods electronically for approximately 25 million SKK (625,000 Euro) and reduced procurement costs for these initial purchases by 12 percent

Contd...

on average. The total savings from eSourcing are presented in Exhibit 3. The minimum cost saving realized in a purchasing transaction was 3 percent, and the highest 35 percent. This auction with the maximum saving ran for 5.5 hours. During the last four hours, only two suppliers were bidding. From this experience, Slovnaft learned that the overall success of the auctions is significantly determined by their careful structure and preparation by the procurement department.

Exhibit 3: Cost Savings Due to the Introduction of eSourcing at Slovnaft

eSourcing		Vertical marketplace		Horizontal marketplace	
		2002	2003	2002	2003
No. of projects	eRFQ	80	93	2	77
	eA	0	0	34	63
		30.0 percent	12.7 percent	23.3 percent	14.2 percent

Source: Slovnaft/Technical University of Košice, Faculty of Economics (2004)

Setting Targets and Providing Incentives for Reaching them

One of the biggest challenges and problems of implementing e-procurement at Slovnaft was overcoming both internal and vendors' resistance. All users, internal as well as the purchasers, were trained to use the e-auction tools in special training sessions. There were separate trainings for the sourcing process and for using the system. Thereafter, experts from the e-procurement department were available for advice. Vendors received training manuals. In addition, the day before an e-auction is to take place, the vendor can test the system for over 5 hours if necessary. The e- procurement experts from Slovnaft assist vendors how to use the system. The responsible managers say that without good preparation of how to use this system the required acceptance by users would not have been achieved. This is a major lesson learned from the implementation experience.

In each of the departments, project managers were appointed with a clear responsibility to coordinate the electronic auctions and RFQs. One of the departments was appointed to co-ordinate the overall process and to assist the project managers, for example by explaining how to collect information, how to work out a strategy, and how to communicate with suppliers. During the whole process, clear objectives and targets had been specified and incentives were provided for reaching them. The required user training was supported by the software provider and representatives of the marketplace operators that were used.

The system has been in place for about two years and some experience has already been gained with using it. Slovnaft believes that it is a success story helping them to become one of the most IT-advanced companies in the chemical industry in Central and Eastern Europe.

Exhibit 4: Phases of eProcurement

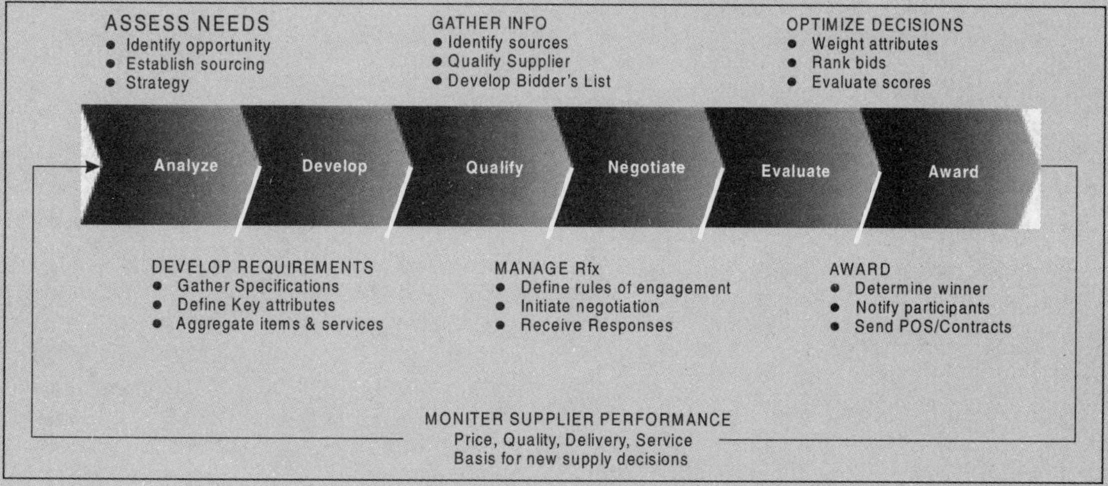

Source: Slovnaft/Technical University of Košice, Faculty of Economics (2004)

Contd...

Sources and References

- Interviews with representatives of Slovnaft: Ing. Dušan Valúch, Manager of the PR Department; Mgr. Silvia Brodanská, Expert for eProcurement and MGU Department. Interviews were conducted by Ing. Radoslav Delina, PhD, Technical University of Košice, Faculty of Economics, in May/June 2004.

- "Slovnaft successfully implemented ORACLE E-Business Suite", Slovnaft Press Release, 12 March 2003.

- Various documents provided by Slovnaft, www.slovnaft.sk

Contact

- e-Business W@tch, c/o empirica GmbH, Oxfordstr. 2, 53111 Bonn, Germany info@ebusiness-watch.org

- European Commission, Enterprise and Industry Directorate General, entr-ict-e-commerce@cec.eu.int

Source: This case study is a contribution from the Technical University of Košice, Faculty of Economics, researched and edited by Ing. Radoslav Delina, PhD, Ing. Viliam Vajda, doc. Ing. Tomas Sabol, PhD. The case study was prepared for e-business market watch. You can visit them at www.ebusinesswatch.org. Reprinted with the permission from the author.

Evaluating Sales Performance

On September 18, 2002, Mr. John Kee, vice president of agricultural sales, presented his newly conceived Dealer Marketing Plan and Evaluation Program to the president of ChemGrow, Inc., Mr. William Joseph.

Company History

ChemGrow is one of the largest fertilizer manufacturers in the world. It is basic in phosphate rock and manufactures phosphoric acid, anhydrous ammonia, and other mixed fertilizer products. In the past 10 years, the company's production characteristics have shifted dramatically from a manufacturer of specialized NPK (Nitrogen, Phosphates, and Potassium) materials in over 40 plants to the production of high-analysis fertilizers in a few very large capacity installations.

ChemGrow's major production facilities are in Florida, Louisiana, and Arkansas: They are located on or close to river or ocean transportation, and can therefore take advantage of low-cost barge transportation to large terminal points located to supply the market at the lowest possible cost (Exhibit 1).

During late 1999 and 2000, ChemGrow evaluated future fertilizer demand and found the need to develop a large-scale expansion program. The $260 million project included a new 425,000-ton-a-year anhydrous ammonia plant at Verdigris, Oklahoma (cost: $35 million), expansion of the phosphate rock mining facilities that it bought from Southern Gas at South Pierce, Florida, and construction of a 400,000-ton phosphoric acid plant near Donald sonville, Louisiana, as well as sulfuric acid, nitric acid, urea, and granulation facilities, and several formulating facilities.

Much of the ammonia made at Verdigris will start flowing early next year through ChemGrow's own 4,900-mile pipeline that runs from Oklahoma up through the fertilizer-hungry Midwest farm states and into North Dakota, Minnesota, and Ohio. ChemGrow's present expansion activities alone should boost its fertilizer output 50 percent over the 3.7 million tons of products it made in 2000.

The key to capacity growth for ChemGrow has been its control of its raw materials. ChemGrow has enough phosphate rock reserves to maintain its present phosphate production levels for 70 years. For the nitrogen side of its business, ChemGrow signed early last year a 17-year natural gas contract with Oklahoma Natural Gas Company. ChemGrow's expansion program also includes exploration for natural gas in seven offshore Texas and Louisiana tracts.

ChemGrow has been very optimistic about fertilizer growth, but there have been critics of the company-mostly competitors-who believe that ChemGrow's fertilizer expansion are atrociously ill-timed. They feel that after last year's boom, when buyers feared shortages and seized all the fertilizer they could find, the industry may now be on the verge of a worldwide glut, perhaps comparable to the agonizing oversupply of 1972-1974.

Contd...

Exhibit 1

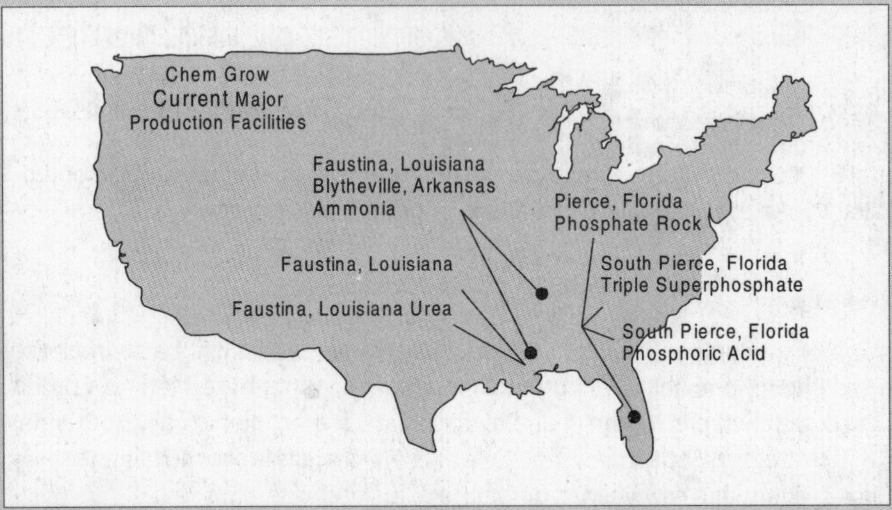

Management Team

At the headquarters of ChemGrow, Inc., in Tulsa, Oklahoma, Mr. William Joseph has built a winning managerial combination for an industrial empire. Mr. Joseph believes that when it comes to executives, the best are the cheapest for the company in the long run and that you don't make money by being a scrooge.

In selecting top people, he has looked for such qualities as initiative and drive; then he provides his people with the tools with which to work and with an incentive. Money is an incentive, but Mr. Joseph also believes they must have a pride in the company. The job of a chief executive includes creating the atmosphere that these people can operate in successfully. Mr. Joseph has built on the managerial philosophy that in order to succeed in any venture, you don't need a team of people, you need the right man to head up the effort and then he'll develop his own team.

Mr. John Kee, one of Mr. Joseph's leaders, is now in the process of reevaluating and developing his own marketing team. His first step was to define a basic outline for the Dealer Marketing Plan and Evaluation Program. Some of the major aspects of the plan are outlined below:

1. *State ChemGrow's marketing philosophy:* Includes various statements on channel trade goals, major emphasis products, customer classification and qualifications, and price strategy.

2. *Analyze present position:* Uses historical sales data, customer/product/territory profiles; define major and minor competition's supply network; describe ChemGrow's strengths and weaknesses compared to each competitor.

3. *Project future environment:* By product tons consumed per acreage, industry projections for product mix, favorable and unfavorable trends, and future competitive programs.

4. *Define marketing regions' goals:* Develop goals for product tonnage by account manager for the long and short-term; plan strategies to attain these goals by increasing customer growth, increasing the market share in the region by obtaining new customers, and locating expansion into new areas.

5. *Determine support required to obtain goals:* Include manpower requirements, supply and distribution requirements, marketing programs, training programs, and extra services needed.

Contd...

Mr. Kee felt that the overall basic plan for marketing was specific in terms of the company's primary interests for growth but too general for the region managers to put into action, so another outline was developed for the mechanics of the account manager marketing plan:

1.   Prior to customer call-outline your territory, locate and identify present customers and their trading area, locate competitor's supply points, and your own, and identify prospective areas of concentration for new customers.

2.   Steps to be completed with customers-complete sales forecast, update sales history for each customer, and complete customer profile with prospective customers.

3.   Steps to summarize territory marketing plans-prepare product profile for present customers, prepare marketing plan worksheet, and prepare sales volume forecast for the territory.

4.   Your territory plans- make up six-month time allocation schedule, make up a monthly calendar, prepare first call action plan for prospective customers, and get regional approval and support for plans and needed help.

Current Issues

Mr. Kee is pleased with the marketing plans which he has outlined, but he knows that getting the appropriate information to complete and implement the plans may be a problem. In the past, efforts at sales analysis had always been done on a "crisis" basis; whenever he absolutely needed a certain form of information, an analyst was assigned to the problem and the answers were developed on a one-time basis. But there was still little systematic evaluation of the sales data available in the company. Mr. Kee knows that this void needs to be filled if adequate information is to be available for decisions concerning sales effort planning and control.

Mr. Kee's general concern about the present quantitative evaluation program has recently been highlighted by an upcoming deadline. He knows that at the end of the month decisions need to be made involving (1) a special bonus plan for the most productive region, (2) a 1.0-day vacation to Mexico for the most outstanding salesperson in each region, and (3) a list of "most valuable" customers, who will be invited to participate in a luxury Dealer Council meeting. At the beginning of 2001, when Mr. Kee set up the program which offered these sales promotion incentives, he was intentionally vague about how the customers, salespeople, and regions would be evaluated in arriving at the award decisions. He knows that time is running short and that these evaluations must be made soon. Yet he is also sensitive to the fact that the salespeople and customers alike will be irritated if the award decisions do not appear to be fair. He wants whatever decisions are made to be objective and consistent.

Mr. Kee has expressed to several of his aides his frustration that he is in need of sales analysis information and that once again it must be assembled on a crisis basis. He said in his last staff meeting that he is placing high priority on developing a usable, accessible computerized information system so that problems of this sort do not arise in the future, and so that in the future ongoing sales analysis reports can provide systematic inputs for sales force decision making.

In recent years, all quantitative sales analysis has been done manually under the direction of Mr. Kee's assistant, Richard Evans. Richard never enjoyed these jobs in the past, feeling that he was spending much time on what appeared to be work that was clerical in nature or, worse yet, that could have been done more rapidly, accurately, and completely by computer. This time, however, Richard feels a new sense of intellectual challenge in the job. While he knows that he faces the immediate task of identifying the best performing territory overall, the best salesperson in each territory, and the list of key customers, he also sees that he can have inputs to the design of an integrative sales analysis system. He knows that he can work himself out of this recurring drudgery if he does a good job of figuring out what information is needed and in communicating that need to the computer personnel in the firm. In fact, Mr. Kee has told him that he wants a memorandum from Richard

Contd...

outlining his thoughts on what sales analysis reports they can request starting in the immediate future.

The Available Information

In preparing for his assignment, Richard has talked with several others on the sales management staff and he has been sensitized to the fact that his problem is not a simple one. For example, he has been reminded that each salesperson sells three different products and that each product has a different gross margin associated with it. Moreover, the sales department is concerned with its sales (and margin) growth over time, so Richard wants to be certain that he does not take a static view in evaluating performance.

Unfortunately, the information which he would like is not currently assembled at one place. From the accounting department he is able to get good estimates of the gross margin per ton of sales for each of the three major products (ammonia, phosphate, and potash) sold in this division. These gross margin figures are summarized in Exhibit 2.

Richard knows that different salespeople tend to sell these products in different proportions, however. In fact, several months ago this was raised as a concern. Mr. Kee felt that some of the salespeople were selling primarily the products that were easy to sell, rather than a complete product line in general and a profitable mix of products in particular. At that time, Richard had done an analysis on that issue, and it occurs to him that it might be useful for him to check his files for the report he prepared then. With the report in hand, Richard is reminded of what he had done. First, he had tabulated for each salesperson what proportion of his total ton sales were in each of the product lines. The summary table from his report is reproduced here as Exhibit 3. He also remembers that he had found the same information across different customers and during different time periods. Richard puts that report to the side, but makes a mental note that this information can be helpful to him in his current assignment.

Finally to get sales information on different customers, Richard goes to the accounting department, where he is told, in a pleasant manner, that right now they are in the middle of an audit and will not be able to respond to his requests until after immediate deadline. However, G.N. Leshades, the head of the accounting department, suggests that the distribution center may have some information he needs. At the distribution department, Richard does in fact find some helpful information: an alphabetical computer printout summarizing the total tons of products shipped to each customer in 1998, 1999, and each quarter of 2000. Back at his office, Richard's secretary volunteers to reorganize the information on the computer printout and to group the different customers according to the salesperson that sells to them and the region in which they are located. The secretary prepares a different summary for each region, and gives them to Richard. These are summarized in the Exhibits 4 to 7.

Case Exhibit 2 — Dollar Gross Margin Contribution for Each Product

Product	Gross Margin/Per Ton		
	1998	1999	2000
Ammonia	$ 8	$14	$20
Phosphates	12	12	12
Potash	16	9	5

Contd...

Case Exhibit 3 — Average Percentage of Total Sales for Each Salesperson

Region	Salesperson	Ammonia	Phosphates	Potash
Eastern	McFee	60%	35%	5%
	Collam	5	20	75
	Parks	80	10	10
	Dow	100	0	0
Central	Thums	80	20	0
	Cook	25	50	25
	Block	20	30	50
	Fowler	75	20	5
Northwest	Vans	70	20	10
	Sciffman	65	20	15
	Lukbore	80	10	10
	Wilkie	20	10	70
Southwest	Goodie	5	5	90
	Stubber	5	15	80
	Holden	0	0	100
	Macke	10	20	70

Case Exhibit 4 — Sales Analysis at the ChemGrow Company: Sales to Each Customer over Time—Eastern Region—Total Tonnage

Obs	Salesperson	Customer	Sales 94	Sales 95	1st Qtr 2000	2nd Qtr 2000	3rd Qtr 2000	4th Qtr 2000
1	Collam	EPF	6,523	4,800	2,800	3,000	2,635	2,635
2	Collam	FEV	3,018	4,550	4,740	10,000	0	0
3	Collam	FSC	1,565	4,100	3,685	5,000	3,035	3,030
4	Collam	HPC	3,251	4,850	3,000	3,000	683	0
5	Collam	M	6,028	13,000	5,000	15,000	3,000	584
6	Collam	PI	2,750	4,650	0	2,945	0	0
7	Dow	CSF	517	2,165	1,000	2,000	500	0
8	Dow	FSC	3,430	5,965	1,500	1,500	0	0
9	Dow	FSI	10,755	8,400	1,050	1,000	1,000	1,000
10	Dow	OSS	7,097	5,470	800	1,200	950	900
11	McFee	CFS	1,365	2,490	950	1,000	723	0
12	McFee	EGS	4,161	6,410	500	4,500	1,500	925
13	McFee	FCS	2,963	3,260	1,485	1,485	1,485	1,485
14	McFee	LAS	15,694	9,030	2,500	1,500	1,500	34
15	McFee	OI	10,076	7,000	1,785	1,783	1,780	1,780
16	Parks	JCS	427	2,800	500	500	500	35
17	Parks	LBC	1,373	7,120	1,605	2,000	500	500
18	Parks	MFS	5,628	4,395	900	1,200	800	170
19	Parks	PFF	12,400	0	3,000	10,000	415	490
20	Parks	SFM	193	3,350	0	1,535	0	0
21	Parks	VT	2,878	5,700	1,640	1,500	1,500	1,500
22	Parks	WT	3,663	6,600	0	0	0	0

Case Exhibit 5 — Sales Analysis at the ChemGrow Company: Sales to Each Customer over Time—Central Region—Total Tonnage

Obs	Salesperson	Customer	Sales 94	Sales 95	1st Qtr 2000	2nd Qtr 2000	3rd Qtr 2000	4th Qtr 2000
23	Block	CR	8,650	2,940	600	780	700	0
24	Block	LFS	17,350	7,549	200	1,480	1,060	350
25	Block	LSF	8,750	2,526	1,080	480	190	90
26	Block	TCF	5,100	1,623	0	0	0	0
27	Block	WDB	11,400	9,167	3,500	3,000	1,500	1,500
28	Cook	BFH	2,711	3,110	1,000	1,580	1,070	1,000
29	Cook	FFA	2,575	3,730	200	4,000	1,000	234
30	Cook	HD	3,170	3,465	1,500	2,780	2,070	1,500
31	Cook	JC	2,145	6,459	5,000	5,280	0	8,000
32	Cook	PF	1,680	1,190	0	455	0	0
33	Cook	RBR	2,880	1,275	600	875	510	500
34	Cook	TLA	3,375	2,036	3,000	3,865	0	0
35	Fowler	FGC	8,439	7,493	1,020	1,000	0	0
36	Fowler	GFS	9,164	5,094	450	4,345	1,085	800
37	Fowler	MSF	11,284	6,368	1,535	2,480	1,085	950
38	Fowler	RAP	3,843	12,175	0	1,680	0	0
39	Thums	FWM	1,084	2,700	1,260	2,120	1,000	300
40	Thums	WW	3,458	3,100	300	4,000	0	1,004
41	Thums	WWN	3,709	3,400	1,500	1,580	1,420	1,408
42	Thums	YP	18,315	8,960	4,500	9,000	1,200	588>>

Contd...

Case Exhibit 6 — Sales Analysis at the ChemGrow Company: Sales to Each Customer over Time—Northwest Region—Total Tonnage

Obs	Salesperson	Customer	Sales 94	Sales 95	1st Qtr 2000	2nd Qtr 2000	3rd Qtr 2000	4th Qtr 2000
43	Lukbore	BAS	6,200	7,444	2,875	3,596	2,485	74
44	Lukbore	MVF	4,800	7,603	1,650	1,550	1,550	1,710
45	Lukbore	SCF	9,300	5,648	2,500	2,500	1,380	0
46	Lukbore	WFL	5,500	3,555	0	6,050	1,460	0
47	Sciffman	HF	11,300	6,764	3,595	3,740	2,460	605
48	Sciffman	JN	2,100	4,194	0	5,000	0	380
49	Sciffman	LS	4,200	1,044	800	820	840	820
50	Sciffman	RM	4,300	3,890	2,160	564	2,010	66
51	Sciffman	VF	5,500	4,747	345	568	327	300
52	Vans	AGC	4,600	2,200	1,550	1,550	0	0
53	Vans	CF	5,900	5,400	1,875	1,875	1,875	1,875
54	Vans	DBI	2,200	2,100	1,265	864	871	0
55	Vans	ECG	8,500	4,629	2,467	3,495	2,140	898
56	Vans	OFC	2,800	6,080	6,591	3,140	719	100
57	Wilkie	ASI	4,800	5,230	2,100	1,565	346	1,889
58	Wilkie	BG	1,150	1,160	3,800	3,800	4,000	3,600
59	Wilkie	CF	4,100	3,700	0	2,600	0	0
60	Wilkie	CI	4,350	15,720	4,860	10,400	5,140	0
61	Wilkie	F&R	13,000	5,720	0	2,250	0	0
62	Wilkie	IO	8,750	2,690	1,200	1,240	1,200	1,200
63	Wilkie	LF	5,100	3,100	1,125	1,695	2,433	2,147>>

Case Exhibit 7 — Sales Analysis at the ChemGrow Company: Sales to Each Customer over Time—Southwest Region—Total Tonnage

Obs	Salesperson	Customer	Sales 94	Sales 95	1st Qtr 2000	2nd Qtr 2000	3rd Qtr 2000	4th Qtr 2000
64	Goodie	BSF	6,350	4,500	900	700	400	362
65	Goodie	GFF	6,540	8,350	2,465	1,245	1,240	2,500
66	Goodie	KMA	0	0	0	904	0	0
67	Goodie	LCS	3,650	3,840	1,105	1,365	750	981
68	Goodie	PGC	8,510	9,125	2,500	3,262	2,500	2,500
69	Goodie	RGC	19,290	7,240	4,750	20,000	300	671
70	Holden	AGS	2,324	2,505	1,125	3,685	1,038	662
71	Holden	FCS	3,150	5,370	0	5,500	0	0
72	Holden	GF	4,195	5,190	2,531	2,530	2,400	2,654
73	Holden	IFS	5,800	3,349	4,659	3,178	993	0
74	Holden	OFS	2,811	5,935	3,418	8,650	67	0
75	Macke	CE	4,600	2,505	621	652	262	0
76	Macke	CF	3,400	8,670	12,512	3,150	1,013	200
77	Macke	DG	5,900	2,765	850	855	850	855
78	Macke	FER	2,200	2,495	650	650	610	600
79	Macke	SCG	8,500	4,620	2,350	1,240	1,175	1,180
80	Macke	TMN	2,800	3,279	0	5,525	0	0
81	Stubber	BAC	4,505	4,820	1,000	1,000	1,080	1,080
82	Stubber	DPC	2,810	2,600	1,975	1,975	0	0
83	Stubber	GCC	8,125	8,150	5,000	5,000	775	0
84	Stubber	GSS	4,015	3,050	575	685	834	181
85	Stubber	HDS	6,050	5,530	2,475	3,156	1,004	240
86	Stubber	TPS	8,933	6,286	365	2,010	0	83>>

Richard knows that more information would be better, but it is not clear that he would be able to get more complete information, even if he had the time to wait. As he sits down to work on his analysis, he focuses on the immediate evaluations that he needs to have completed by the end of the month, but he also writes down his more general thoughts about what computer-generated reports the sales department will want in the future. In fact, he finds that in organizing some of his current analysis he is developing good formats and specifications for the reports that he will suggest in his memorandum to Mr. Kee.

Questions:

1. What decisions would you make with regard to which is the most productive region, who is the most outstanding salesperson, and who are the most valuable customers?

2. What computer reports should be generated on a regular basis to assist the managers in their evaluations?

Source: This case was developed by William D. Perreault, Jr., of the university of North Carolina at Chapel Hill and Kevin McNeilly of Miami University. The copyright is with the author. Reprinted with the kind permission of the author.

The Global Pharmaceutical Industry

The case looks at the development of the ethical pharmaceutical industry. The various forces affecting the discovery, development, production, distribution and marketing of prescription drugs are discussed as issues of corporate social responsibility in the industry and the strategies being followed by major pharmaceutical companies. Readers are then invited to consider trends for the future.

In late 2003, Britain's Guardian newspaper commented that, on the face of it, the global pharmaceutical industry 'looks like the epitome of a modern, mature industry that has found a comfortable way to make profits by the billion: it's global, hitech, and has the ultimate customer, the healthcare budgets of the world's richest countries.'[1] Pharmaceutical manufacturers certainly did not appear to be faced a looming crisis, yet, declared the newspaper, that was the alarming conclusion of a research report by analysts at investment bank Dresdner Kleinwort Wasserstein. The analysts argued that the world's largest drugs companies were operating a business model that was unsustainable and 'rapidly running out of steam'. The treatment they prescribed was further industry consolidation. This case explores some of the trends affecting the 'ethical' (research-based) sector of the industry and invites readers to prepare their own analysis and prescription.

Industry Evolution

As described in Box 1, the pharmaceutical industry is characterized by a highly risky and lengthy research and development process, intense competition for intellectual property, stringent government regulation and powerful purchaser pressures. How has this unusual picture come about?

The origins of the modern pharmaceutical industry can be traced to the late 19th century, when dyestuffs were found to have antiseptic properties. Roche, Ciba-Geigy and Sandoz all started out as family dyestuff companies based near the Rhine in Basel, Switzerland, which moved into synthetic pharmaceuticals and eventually became global players. Penicillin was a major discovery for the emergent industry, and during the 1940s and 1950s research and development became firmly established within the sector. The industry expanded rapidly in the 1960s, benefiting from significant new discoveries with permanent patent protection. Regulatory controls on clinical development and marketing were light and healthcare spending boomed as economies prospered.

The pharmaceutical market developed some unusual characteristics. Decision-making was in the hands of medical practitioners whereas patients (the final consumers) and payers (governments or insurance companies) had little knowledge or influence. As a result, medical practitioners were insensitive to price but susceptible to the sales efforts of individual representatives. This enabled numerous 'me too' drugs to achieve satisfactory returns on investment. Imitating a known drug reduced research and development risk considerably, while the market-place was open to products offering minor advantages such as a more convenient dosage form or fewer side effects, but with much the same therapeutic outcome.

There were two important developments in the 1970s. Firstly, the Thalidomide tragedy (where an anti-emetic given for morning sickness caused birth defects) led to much tighter regulatory controls on clinical trials. Secondly, legislation was enacted to set a fixed period on patent protection- typically 20 years from initial filing as a research discovery. This led to the appearance of 'generic' medicines. Generics have exactly the same active ingredients as the original brand, and compete on price. The impact of generic entry is illustrated by Bristol Myers Squibb's brand Glucophage, a treatment for diabetes, which generated US sales of $2.1bn in 2001. Following loss of the patent in January 2002,

---

[1] The Guardian, 12 September, 2003.

Contd...

brand sales plunged to $69m for the first quarter. Generics legislation had a major impact on the industry, providing incentives for innovation and a race to market. The time during which research and development costs could be recouped was drastically curtailed, putting upward pressure on prices. The introduction of generics, however, was very beneficial for society: valuable medicines became extremely cheap. Indeed, health economists have estimated that the social returns from pharmaceut- ical research and development exceed that appropriated by firms by at least 50 to 100 percent. By the end of the 1970s generic entrants and more stringent controls on clinical trials had led to substantial increases in research and development spending.

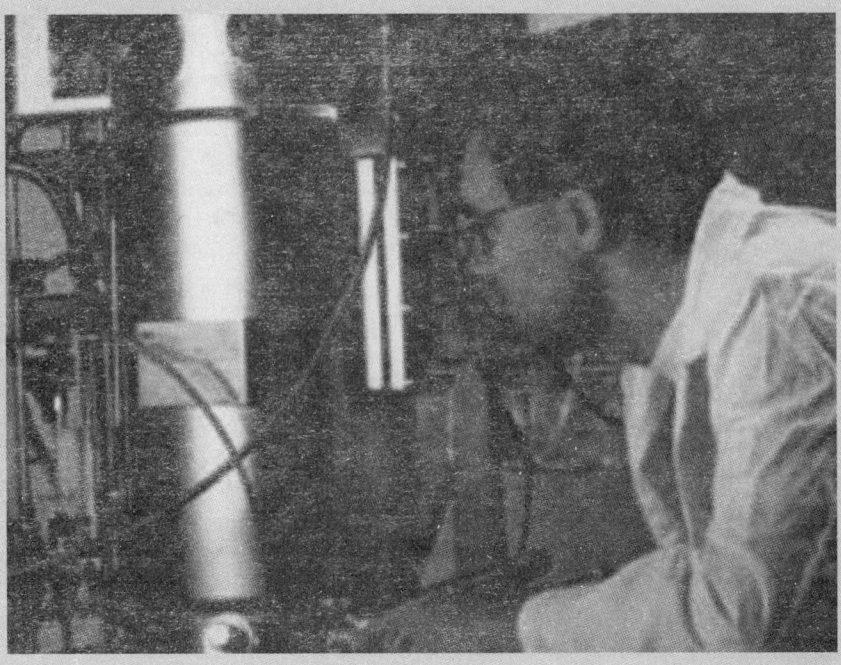

The pharmaceutical industry is unusual in that in many countries it is subject to a 'monopsony' -there is effectively only one powerful purchaser, the government. In the 1980s, governments around the world began to focus upon pharmaceuticals as a politically easy target in their efforts to control rising healthcare expenditure, although drugs typically accounted for less than a tenth of that expenditure. Many countries introduced some form of price or reimbursement control. The industry lacked the public or political support to resist these changes.

Entering the 1990s, worldwide economic recession reduced cash for provision of healthcare through tax-funded systems (Canada, Italy, Spain and UK); social security supported systems (France, Germany and Japan), as well as employer/privately-funded systems (US). Payers could no longer tolerate spiralling healthcare costs and created incentives for decision-makers to seek better value for money. In Germany in 1993, over- all pharmaceutical sales fell by 11 percent while the four leading generics manufacturers increased their sales between 10 and 63 percent. Pressure was put on the industry to deliver genuine product innovation rather than 'me too' drugs.

A new type of industry player appeared in the 1980s - small biotechnology start-ups backed by venture capital to exploit the myriad opportunities opened up by molecular biology and genetic engineering. By 2003 there were more than 600 publicly traded biotechs worldwide. However, biologicals were more complex to produce than traditional pharmaceuticals, causing a global shortage in production capacity. This drove up prices and often limited biotech applications to low-volume, high-need areas. Although sales doubled in the 5 years to 2002, at $27bn biologicals contributed only 7 percent of global market value. Many biotechs originally planned to integrate and perform all functions from research to sales. However, most biotechs lacked the finances to cope with the huge risks involved and by 2003 only three companies had achieved this goal, namely, Amgen, Biogen and Genzyme. Moreover, only 40 out of 1,466 biotech companies in the US were trading profitably. Amgen was the only serious global player, ranking number 17 in terms of sales during 2002. The other leading

Contd...

biotechs (Genentech, Chiron, Genetics Institute) were partly owned by larger firms. Biotechs had thus largely abandoned attempts to market drugs themselves (although they often sought to retain

BOX 1: The Drug Development Process

The pharmaceutical industry has long new product lead times, with period from discovery to marketing authorisation typically taking almost 12 years (Exhibit 1). New product development can be divided into distinct research and development phases. The research phase produces a New Chemical Entity (NCE) with the desired characteristics to be an effective drug for a targeted disease process. Development encompasses all of the formulation, toxicology and clinical trial work necessary to meet stringent regulatory requirements for marketing approval.

During all of these phases 'attrition' occurs, as promising agents fail particular hurdles, so most Research and development projects never result in a marketed drug. Of those that do, 80 percent fail to recoup their Research and development investment. The cost of developing and commercializing a new drug is now estimated at $500 - 800 million dollars. When the costs of all the projects that do not reach fruition are considered, it becomes clear that pharmaceutical Research and development is a very high stakes game.

Given the enormous risks and considerable investment involved, it is not surprising that pharmaceutical companies compete fiercely to establish and retain intellectual property rights. Only by securing a patent that can be defended against imitators can the value of all this Research and development be recouped. The patent clock starts from the moment that a promising agent is identified in pre-clinical tests and its chemical structure and synthesis filed with patent offices worldwide.

Once the patent application is made public, other companies are likely to try to create improved, patentable versions. Where genuine discoveries or inventions are made, patents can also be obtained for manufacturing method and even mode of administration. All of these supplementary applications can extend patent life and the earnings period for a new drug.

Pre-clinical development involves testing new agents against the target - for example, lowering cholesterol - to select the most promising leads. After further tweaking, these best candidates are evaluated in animal disease models to find the one with the best trade-off between efficacy and tolerability. Finally the lead agent is put through a battery of toxicology tests in animals and if successful put forward for clinical development in humans. Clinical development is usually divided into three phases. Phase I, trials determine whether the product is safe to use in humans. Phase II, trials aim to select dose and demonstrate efficacy. Phase III, trials are conducted versus the best current treatment, with the goal of proving superiority. Typically only 1 in 10 molecule survives from Phase I to launch, with late failures (Phase III) being more costly.

The industry is subjected to rigorous regulatory scrutiny. Government agencies such as the Food and Drug Administration (FDA) in the USA thoroughly examine all of the data to support the purity, stability, safety, efficacy and tolerability of a new agent. The time taken is governed by legislation and is at least six months. Every regulatory authority is different and while FDA endorsement is very helpful it does not guarantee approval in other countries.

US marketing rights) and instead used the global reach of the research- based multinationals to leverage return on Research and development through out-licensing and strategic alliances. As stock market funding dried up,[2] the sector began to consolidate to marry revenue streams with promising pipelines. In the UK, for instance, British Biotech merged with drug company Vernalis, while Celltech acquired Oxford Glycoscience.

Industry Sectors

At the turn of the millennium, prescription-only or 'ethical' drugs comprised about 80 percent of the global pharmaceutical market by value and 50 percent by volume. Ethical products divide into conventional pharmaceuticals and more complex 'biological' agents and vaccines. The remainder were 'Over The Counter' (OTC) medicines, which may be purchased without prescription. Both ethical and OTC medicines may be branded or 'generic'.

---

[2]   US stockmarket flotations of biotechs fell from 40 in 2000 to only 4 in 2001-2.

Contd...

Exhibit 1

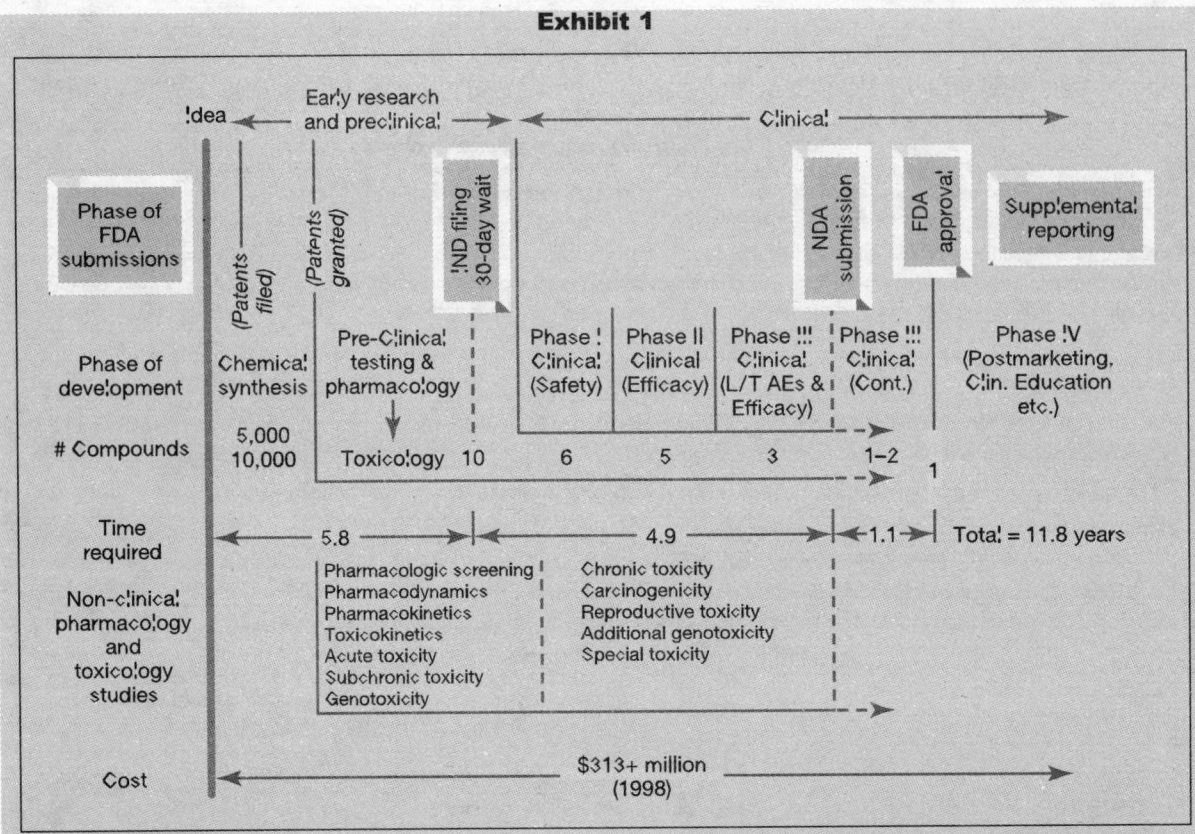

The typical cost structure at ethical pharmaceutical companies comprises manufacturing of goods (25 per cent), research and development (12 to 21 per cent), administration (10 per cent), and sales and marketing (25 percent). The key strategic capabilities at these companies are research and development and sales and marketing, and manufacturing historically suffered from low utilization, high fixed costs and low productivity. Growing pressure on margins became an incentive to restructure manufacturing, rationalizing the number of production sites and placing them in strategic locations offering tax advantages (e.g. Puerto Rico, Republic of Ireland). Companies also improved supply chain management to release the value trapped in high inventories.

However, manufacturing and distribution efficiency at research-based companies was not comparable with that of generics manufacturers, who competed on price. During the late 1990s, there was a collapse of generics prices in the US and a shakeout to determine cost leadership. In this environment, economies of scale proved decisive and the sector underwent consolidation. As a result the speed and aggression of generic attacks on branded products increased sharply. By 2002 generics captured 65 to 80 percent of new prescriptions within five weeks of US patent expiry on major drugs and overall accounted for nearly a third of US market volume. Given the number of major global brands with patent expiries looming and markets with untapped potential (e.g. Italy, Spain, France, Japan), the outlook for the generic sector was rosy. In 2002, nine of the top 10 fastest growing pharmaceutical companies were generics manufacturers and predicted compound annual growth rate of 12 percent was forecast to deliver $30bn in sales in 2004.

Thus by the turn of the century there were four broad types of industry player: ethical, OTC, generic and biotech. Each required very different strategic capabilities. Producers of branded prescription drugs required strong research and development and global sales and marketing infrastructure. Branded OTC drugs demanded direct-to-consumer marketing capability. Generics companies focused on supply chain management and manufacturing cost leadership. Biotechs needed to create and defend intellectual property in specialised research fields. Because of the different attributes and cost structures

Contd...

involved, multinationals which owned OTC and generics businesses generally operated them separately, frequently using another company name. Similarly, those that had acquired biotechs normally left them to operate fairly autonomously.

Business Environment

As key economies stagnated in 2002, challenges in funding healthcare advances remained. Ageing populations created further pressures, since the 'over-65s' consumed four times as much health- care per head as those below 65. This combined with more expensive high technology solutions and increasing patient expectations created an unsustainable situation. On the one hand, universal coverage systems (such as those in Spain and the UK) were slow or unable to introduce the latest treatments. On the other, insurance-funded systems (such as that in the US) were able to afford the latest innovations but were unable to share those benefits with an increasing part of the population. In 2002 the number of US citizens without health insurance rose by 5.7 percent to 43.6 million, the biggest single annual increase in a decade.

In response to these pressures, payers used a wide variety of methods to control spending on pharmaceuticals (see Exhibit 2). Some put the emphasis on the supply side - the manufacturer and distributor. Some emphasized the demand side- the prescriber and the patient. Other methods affected both. No country relied on a single approach. Types of control reflected deep-rooted cultural differences with supply-side measures were favored by more centralized, less market- oriented economies. The choice of strategy was also affected by the importance or otherwise of the national pharmaceutical industry as a contributor to GDP, balance of trade and employment.

Exhibit 2: Methods used to Control Pharmaceutical Spending

Controls on suppliers	Mixed effect	Controls to influence demand
Negotiated prices Average pricing Reference pricing Positive and negative lists Constraints on wholesalers and pharmacists	Partial reimbursement at price negotiated with manufacturer Generic substitution	Patient co-payments* Treatment guidelines Indicative or fixed budgets Incentives to prescribe or dispense generics or parallel imports Transfer from prescription-only to OTC

* Where the patient pays some of the drug cost.

In countries with supply-side controls, negotiating price or reimbursement approval could take as long as six months or a year. In countries with demand-side controls, there were similar delays in achieving market penetration, because of the need to negotiate product inclusion in formularies, or endorsement by bodies such as the National Institute for Clinical Excellence (NICE) in the UK. Generics posed a particular threat. Several important markets (Japan, France, Spain, Italy) featured low volume use of generics - no more than 6 percent. However, generics were being actively encouraged in all EU markets and rapid penetration was anticipated. Computer systems enabled prescriptions to be printed in their generic rather than branded form, enabling the pharmacist to supply the cheapest generic drug.

Pharmaceutical spending controls were designed to reward genuine advances. Price premiums and/or reimbursement levels were based on perceived innovativeness and superiority, penalizing 'me too' drugs. As a result, there was a race to market with each new drug class, since only the first to market would benefit. Competition was waged most fiercely at the level of drug class and being late to market with an undifferentiated product was a recipe for failure.

Contd...

The industry adopted a number of strategic responses to these challenges. Many pharmaceutical companies introduced 'disease management' initiatives.[3] Another common response was to conduct pharma-co-economic evaluations, studies that aimed to demonstrate the added value offered by a new drug as a result of improved efficacy, safety, tolerability or ease of use.

Government price controls created another challenge for the industry in the form of 'parallel trade'. The principle of free movement of goods across the Single European Market meant that distributors were free to source drugs in low price markets (Spain, Portugal, France, Italy and Greece) and ship them to high price markets (Germany, the UK, Sweden and the Netherlands), pocketing the difference. There was minimal benefit to governments or consumers, but a significant loss for the industry. Instead of being ploughed back into Research and Development, this arbitrage profit went to the parallel importers. Parallel imports were exacerbated when pharmaceutical wholesalers consolidated internationally through cross-border mergers and acquisitions, making it even easier to buy in one country and distribute in another. By 2002, parallel imports had gained 17 percent of the UK, 7 percent of the German market and were estimated to account for a 3.5bn of revenues a year across the EU. Furthermore, the enlargement of the European Union was expected to exacerbate parallel trade, as prices in Central and Eastern Europe tended to be low.

Parallel trade was also prevalent in the Far East and there was even a latent problem in the crucial US market given the price differentials with Canada. Canada had one of the toughest environments worldwide for the industry, with stringent and inflexible pricing and reimbursement criteria. In contrast, the US had no formal price controls and price increases were customary. Over time, this led to a wide disparity in prices (best-selling cholesterol-lowering drug Lipitor was $3.20 per pill in the US in 2003, compared with just $1.89 in Canada) that exposed the industry to sensationalist newspaper headlines such as 'Canada's Rx drugs pouring into USA'.[4] Cross-border trade was driven by the rapid rise in medication cost, the 25 percent of US seniors with no drug coverage, the economic slowdown, the ease of long-distance commerce over the internet and increased awareness of price disparities. By 2003, state governors and Congress representatives were proposing to institutionalise and promote imports, despite opposition from the FDA and the Justice Department. Storefront import pharmacies and drug-sale parties in care homes were appearing all over the US and grass-roots activism was rife. The real threat to the industry was not the actual level of imports ($800m in 2002), but the risk posed to free pricing in the US from the public backlash. FDA commissioner Mark McClellan declared that there was an impending global crisis. The situation where US citizens bore the lion's share of the global cost of pharmaceutical Research and Development through high prices appeared unsustainable. Either US prices would fall, damaging Research and Development investment, or other wealthy countries, such as Germany and Canada, needed to shoulder a fair share of the burden. But with their domestic pharmaceutical industries in decline, there was scant incentive for other governments to change their practices.

BOX 2: Globalization

A number of factors contributed to the globalization of the pharmaceutical industry. Chief among these was the international convergence of medical science and practice under the influence of modern communications technology and increased travel and information exchange. Well-funded US universities and hospitals generally led their fields, while conferences and specialist seminars in the US were the most prestigious platforms to learn about new discoveries. This may account for the fact that drugs first launched in the US gain far greater global market share and achieve twice the sales of those first launched elsewhere.

Regulatory processes were also undergoing international harmonization. In Europe the European Medicines Evaluation Agency (EMEA) was established to enable more rapid regulatory approvals across Europe through the 'centralized' procedure, which granted regulatory approval in all member states simultaneously. The creation of EMEA offered great benefits in terms of reduced costs and accelerated time to market for pharmaceutical companies, but also increased risk as more was at stake on one decision.

---

3.   These involved understanding the goals of the healthcare system in addressing a specific disease. The firm then aligned itself with the healthcare providers, trying to offer an integrated service that improved eventual disease outcomes, positioning its drugs as one part of the solution.

4.   USA Today, 7 October 2003.

Contd...

There was also a move towards global harmonization of standards for drug approval through the International Conference on Harmonization (ICH).

Further evidence of globalization could be found in the tripling of the number of blockbuster brands between 1998 and 2003. There were also clear signs that leading corporations were 'globalizing'. Most had a presence in all significant markets, with overall sales reflecting the market size of each country. Production sites had a global mandate and were selected by worldwide screening. Research and development was sourced from best place worldwide regardless of location, and that often meant the US. In 1990, the industry spent A8bn on research in Europe and A5.3bn in the US. By 2001, the US was receiving A26.4bn of spending compared with A18bn in Europe. GlaxoSmithKline, Europe's biggest drugs company, was being run from Philadelphia, while Novartis, the second largest, announced it was moving its research headquarters to Boston.

In 2003, the leading global industry players all originated from Triad countries - predominantly the US and Europe, as Japanese companies lagged behind. The strong US market enabled US companies to grow faster than their competitors and provided a springboard in achieving global ambitions. Pfizer, Merck and Johnson and Johnson recorded 2002 growth at or above 15 percent, while Novartis and Roche languished at around 7 percent. US companies even outdid their rivals in the EU market - of the seven top 20 companies that achieved double-digit growth in 2002, five were US firms. Multinationals from the US and EU also developed presence in Japan through acquisitions and in 2003 occupied four of the top 10 positions, where they were significantly outperforming domestic firms.

Key Markets

As described in Box 2, the majority of global pharmaceutical sales originate in the 'Triad' (US, EU and Japan), with ten key countries accounting for over 80 percent of the global market. The US has been by far the largest pharmaceutical market by volume and value ($192bn in 2002 - half of global sales), with the strongest growth among key markets, contributing 65 percent of global market growth. In 2002, the US accounted for a staggering 70 percent of blockbuster sales, compared with only 4 percent from Japan and 12 percent from the EU. Projecting out to 2007, the US was predicted to increase its share of the global market, while the shares of Japan and the EU would decline. Non-triad countries were expected to retain around 11 percent share between them.

Overall, the world market was set to become even more US-centric, leaving the industry heavily exposed to fluctuations there.

Following regulatory changes in 1997, pharmaceutical companies were permitted to market directly to US consumers. Direct-to-consumer (DTC) advertising transformed the marketplace and fuelled rapid sales growth. However, the US operating environment was getting tougher. Managed care, in which plan administrators set cost and reimbursement limits on healthcare services, was also changing market dynamics. In 1990, 63 percent of prescriptions were paid in cash by patients, but by 2001, 73 percent were paid by managed care plans. As companies' cost for providing drug benefits to employees increased 19 to 20 percent annually, MCOs began to encourage the use of generics through schemes where the consumer paid less if a generic was prescribed and extra for newer drugs. Furthermore, powerful bulk purchasers, such as the Veterans Administration with 6.9 million members, were able to extract prices even lower than those in Canada, so that average US prices paid were actually significantly lower than headline figures in the popular press suggested.

Japan had traditionally been the second largest market for pharmaceuticals, with sales of $47bn in 2002. The Japanese operating environment had historically been very different from that of the US or the EU. This divergence occurred at all levels, from medical practice, healthcare delivery and funding, to regulatory requirements, higher prices, the lack of generics, distribution, and the accepted approach to sales and marketing. Not surprisingly, relatively small domestic companies dominated the market. The Japanese pharmaceutical industry experienced significant environmental turbulence in the 1990s. Following a number of scandals, the system controlling clinical trials and regulatory approvals underwent a major modernization program, and many domestic companies were ill equipped to operate to the new standards. The economic recession caused tax revenues to fall, while the cost of treating the world's most rapidly ageing population was rising. This resulted in unprecedented price

Contd...

cuts, changes to healthcare funding and the introduction of stringent price controls. The upshot was very low pharmaceutical market growth of only 1 percent in 2002.

Europe made up the third part of the Triad, with the top five markets (Germany, France, Italy, UK, Spain) predicted to continue contributing around three quarters of EU sales out to 2007. European markets each had their own unique operating environments but they were generally characterised by strong payer pressures and consequently lower prices than the US or Japan. Combined with slowing economies, these pressures constrained EU market growth to 8 percent in 2002. Expansion of the EU, however, provided opportunities for growth, especially in Poland and central Europe, but also brought new challenges from generics and low-priced parallel imports.

Although growth prospects for emerging markets were considered modest in 2003, their enormous populations and high levels of unmet need offered significant long-term potential. Many had strengthened patent protection and liberalized equity controls. The pharmaceutical markets in Latin America had proved highly volatile, reflecting underlying economic trends. Nevertheless they had large numbers of wealthy consumers who were able to afford branded drugs.

Pacific Rim countries were becoming more important. Copy products were traditionally a significant issue in these markets, where patent protection was absent or very difficult to police. Pharmaceutical companies focused particularly on China, which had one of the fastest growing pharmaceutical markets. While Chinese herbal medicine remained a core part of healthcare, the use of Western medicines was on the increase, especially in booming coastal cities such as Shanghai.

Although least developed countries were not in a position to offer a significant market opportunity, they did present the industry with important strategic choices in the area of corporate social responsibility which had global ramifications. This is discussed further below.

Innovation

Ethical pharmaceutical companies establish competitive advantage by developing products that are innovative and differentiated, patentable, can be developed rapidly; and marketed globally. Moves away from the pharmaceutical 'core' have been made by various firms in the past, the results of which were mixed at best and usually weakened earnings and stock market performance. Companies with consistently high levels of research and development spending and productivity became industry leaders. For this reason, stock market valuations place as much importance on the Research and Development 'pipeline' (i.e. the products in development) as on the currently marketed products.

BOX 3: Genomics

Genomics is the study of human genes and through a joint multinational effort known as the Human Genome Project (HGP) has delivered a complete list, in order, of the chemical 'letters' making up the DNA in human cells, discovering the location and composition of all human genes. But sequencing the genome did not equate to fully understanding the function of the genes. It was essential to understand what genes were actually doing - so-called 'proteomics' - in order to identify new targets for pharmaceutical intervention. The total number of drug targets discovered up to the year 2000 amounted to well under 1,000. Proteomics had the potential to increase this by orders of magnitude, offering immense promise in the search for more effective and less toxic therapies.

The HGP provided only the 'plain vanilla' version of the genome, reflecting one individual's genetic make-up. Variations in genetic make-up (Single Nucleotide Polymorphisms or SNPs) were also of great interest. Understanding genetic susceptibility to disease could deliver improved screening tests and earlier intervention. Furthermore, 'pharmacogenetics' exploited genetic knowledge to understand why some patient populations benefited more than others from a therapy, or why some experienced specific side effects. A senior research and development executive at GlaxoSmithKline explained that 90 percent of drugs only work in 30 - 50 percent of people, and claimed that 'by eliminating the people that we predict will be non-responders we'll be able to do smaller, faster and cheaper drug trials.'* As a consequence, 'we will have better and better targeted drugs, better and fewer side effects', enthused a CEO.** This was likely to appeal to payers.

Some commentators predicted a dramatic increase in productivity at the early stage of research, and argued that while output would dip in the short term because of increased costs, it would soon take off again. Others believed that the HGP had led to irrational investor exuberance in 1999 -2000 and driven biotech valuations to an unsustainable peak.

* Allen Roses of GSK, quoted by the BBC News, 8 December 2003.

** Matthew Emmens, CEO of Shire Pharmaceuticals, quoted in The Guardian, 15 November 2003.

Contd...

Basic research is vitally important to probe into the causes of disease and identify new potential targets for pharmaceutical intervention. As well as conducting in-house research, many companies sponsored academic research, although it was becoming much more difficult and expensive to secure intellectual property rights from academia. Companies also sought research alliances with biotechs and genomics companies (see Box 3).

The holy grail of pharmaceutical research and development is the 'blockbuster'. Like 'killer applications' in the software market, blockbuster drugs are genuine advances that achieve rapid, deep market penetration. Because of their superlative market performance, blockbusters often determine the fortunes of individual companies. Glaxo went from being a small player at the beginning of the 1980s to the world number one, with a presence in 50 countries, on the strength of a single drug - Zantac for stomach ulcers. A blockbuster drug is typically a long-term therapy or a common disease that offers a step change in efficacy or tolerability and is marketed globally. Annual sales must normally exceed $1bn for a drug to earn this accolade.

While blockbusters made immense contributions to company fortunes and provided tremendous returns on Research and Development investment, they were few and far between. In 1998, only 40 products achieved over $1bn sales worldwide, while the average for all drugs was put at $186m. However, blockbusters rapidly increased in importance and by 2002 this number had tripled. Seeking a blockbuster was clearly a high risk Research and development strategy, but was fast becoming the only game in town, exposing an already high-stakes industry to even greater levels of risk. The 1995 industry pipeline had 450 drugs with average estimated peak year sales of $260m, while the 2001 pipeline had 209 with average estimated sales of $634m. However, over-dependence on blockbuster sales rendered companies highly vulnerable to generic competition at patent expiry. Between 2003 and 2008, 20 blockbuster drugs were due to lose patent protection. By 2002 global exposure to generics was already around $40bn, of which over 60 percent affected the top eight pharmaceutical companies. So even if the risky Research and development pipeline delivered a blockbuster, blockbusters vastly exacerbated the volatility of the corporate sales line.

Unfortunately for the industry, development times were lengthening and Research and development productivity was arguably in decline. The time taken for drugs to move from laboratory to market increased by nearly seven years from 1960 to 2000. Most of this increase occurred in the clinical development phase. The average number of trials and number of patients for each new drug application increased enormously, from 26 trials involving 1,500 patients in 1980, to more than 65 trials involving over 4,000 patients by 1995. As a consequence clinical trials became, by far, the most expensive element of the development process.

As clinical trials became ever more complex and costly, there was a sharp rise in Research and Development expenditure. The average fully capitalized resource cost (including research on abandoned drugs) to develop a new drug was estimated to be $1.4bn in 2003. The corresponding figure in 1987 was $231m and would have grown to under $500m by 2003 at the pace of general inflation. Research and Development spending by the major corporations reached $35bn in 2001, double the figure for 1997 and nearly triple the 1992 investment. But despite increasing average Research and development spend from 11 to 12 percent of annual sales to 16 or even 17 percent, pharmaceutical companies had not much more to show for it. The launch of 24 genuinely new drugs in the US in 2001 was considered poor and the 2002 figure dropped further to 17, the lowest for 20 years. The European Medicines Evaluation Agency received only 31 applications, down from 58 in 2001. While this could have been a natural consequence of blockbuster focus, half of the applications were for treatment of diseases with a limited commercial market.

Pharmaceutical companies endeavored to be both creative and efficient. Some argued that the secret of successful Research and Development lay in organizational competencies such as team-working, knowledge management and close relationships with external opinion leaders. Others emphasized 'lean and flexible' operations and outsourcing of all but core competencies. Some large

Contd...

companies attempted to rekindle innovation and productivity by reorganizing their Research and Development so as to create smaller and more nimble units - like internal biotechs. Others sought external innovation, entering alliances where technology was emerging, and only acquiring in- house capability once the technology was proven. For example, Aventis prided itself on managing a complex web of alliances with more than 300 universities and biotechs. In such companies, the management of alliances itself became a key competency. Not surprisingly, biotechs were contributing an increasing share of the industry's new products - a record 35 percent in 2001.

The organizational infrastructure required to deliver a new drug application had become large and complex. However, because of high attrition in new drug development, company pipelines could often be 'lumpy'. Many companies concluded that maintaining a high fixed-cost clinical development capacity did not make sense. Instead, they outsourced some clinical development to Contract Research Organizations (CROs). Typically it would cost more to conduct a trial via a CRO, but capacity could be switched on or off at will.

As the needs of patients with common chronic diseases became increasingly well satisfied by existing treatments, companies sought new research arenas. Some chose to pursue areas of high unmet need, such as cancer and Alzheimer's disease. Others focused on so-called 'lifestyle' conditions such as impotence, obesity and hair loss. It was not surprising that with drug targets becoming more challenging, increasing time to market and tougher regulatory hurdles, fewer new products reached the market.

Some questioned whether the levels of research and development investment could be sustained. For example, in 2002 there were 340 cancer drugs in development. With pressures on payers growing it seemed improbable that such enormous aggregate Research and development investment could ever be recouped. Overall the industry arguably faced substantial Research and Development over-capacity. Financially-tight biotech firms offered acquisition opportunities for cash-rich pharmaceutical firms. In 2003 Novartis acquired a 51 percent stake in Idenix, a biotech that had been forced to abandon plans to float. Licensing deals also provided an important source of promising new products. Two-thirds of the industry's total pipeline resided in small companies with 67 percent available for licensing. Alliances, however, required some sacrifice of sales margins and late stage deals (i.e. those where the product was close to reaching the market) were rare, costly and competitive.

Sales and Marketing

Sales and marketing capability became an increasingly important source of competitive advantage. A company that developed a strong global franchise with its customers could maximize return on its in-house products and was in a good position to attract the best in-licensing candidates. For example Bristol-Myers Squibb built the world's leading cancer business based entirely on in-licensed compounds.

The traditional focus of drug marketing was the personal 'detail' in which a sales representative (rep) discussed the merits of a drug in a face-to-face meeting with a doctor and often handed over free samples. Pharmaceutical promotion was subject to industry self-regulation. For example, in the UK, sales reps had to pass an examination testing medical knowledge within two years of going on the road. In some countries, government regulatory agencies checked that promotional claims were consistent with the data.

Payer efforts to influence prescribing in the 1990s gave rise to a belief that large salesforces were becoming obsolete and could be replaced by small numbers of specialist payer liaison sales- people. However, companies that also continued to increase their conventional salesforce size and resulting 'share of voice', such as Pfizer, found that it paid off handsomely. Experience taught firms that the more sales reps they deployed, the higher their sales. As a result the number in the US almost tripled from 1995 to 2002, reaching around 90,000, while the number of doctors rose only 20 percent to 850,000. However, doctors had less time to see sales reps with the average call lasting less than five minutes. More representatives selling fewer drugs resulted in returns from every dollar invested in marketing falling from $22 in sales in 1998 to $17 by 2001. Although cutting salesforce numbers would have made sense overall, firms were caught in a classic 'prisoners dilemma' - no one was willing to call off the arms race.

Contd...

Given the resulting squeeze on margins, maximizing salesforce effectiveness became crucial. Pharmaceutical companies became more sophisticated in the tools they gave representatives and in the targeting of their selling efforts. Novel communication channels such as e-detailing, where the doctor heard a presentation over a computer link, suited busy doctors' schedules and saved costs.

There were important differences in the marketing of 'primary care' and 'specialist' products. Office-based practitioners generally prescribed primary care products, whereas treatment with specialist products was typically initiated in hospitals. Sales volume, marketing spend and skills required differed for the two segments. Productled muscle marketing was the name of the game in the primary care sector, while specialist products involved targeted relationship marketing. A small number of companies built their strategies around under-served specialised customer groups, aiming to satisfy their needs on multiple dimensions. In other words, they developed a franchise. An example was Elan Corporation, which built a profitable niche business by targeting the needs of the neurology market.

In 2002, firms spent nearly $9.4bn on marketing in the US. A key factor that drove up costs was the growth in DTC advertising, where spending reached $2.7bn by 2002. Companies recognized that well-informed patients were prepared to ask for drugs by name, creating a powerful new 'pull' strategy. DTC could be very costly because of the vast target audience and expensive television advertising. It also required new marketing skills - both Pfizer and Novartis employed consumer marketers to smarten up their DTC promotion and branding. DTC also rendered drug advertising much more visible and risked creating a backlash against the industry.

Successful drug launches correlated strongly with product superiority, high prices and high promotional spend. An interesting trend began to emerge where drugs that were second to market were more successful than the original pathfinder drug. Evidently, it proved relatively easy to identify flaws in the first drug and deliver a follow-up positioned as 'best in class' or targeted at specific sub-populations. Exhibit 3 illustrates that the period of market exclusivity for first in class drugs was also shrinking fast.

The term 'high compression marketing' was coined to describe the approach adopted by leading companies to launch global brands. This involved simultaneous worldwide launches, global branding, and heavy investment in promotion and share of voice at time of launch. High compression marketing aimed to create a rapid take-off curve that would maximize return by creating higher peak year sales earlier in the product life cycle. A good example was the launch of Celebrex in 1999, which netted $1bn sales in the first nine months. Truly global branding was vital, with consistent brand name, messages, and visuals used around the world for maximum impact. Blockbusters launched between 1998 and 2003 typically reached $2bn in sales within 3.5 years, at least twice as fast as historical norms.

Exhibit 3: Number of years of market exclusivity enjoyed by selected drugs, 1965-99

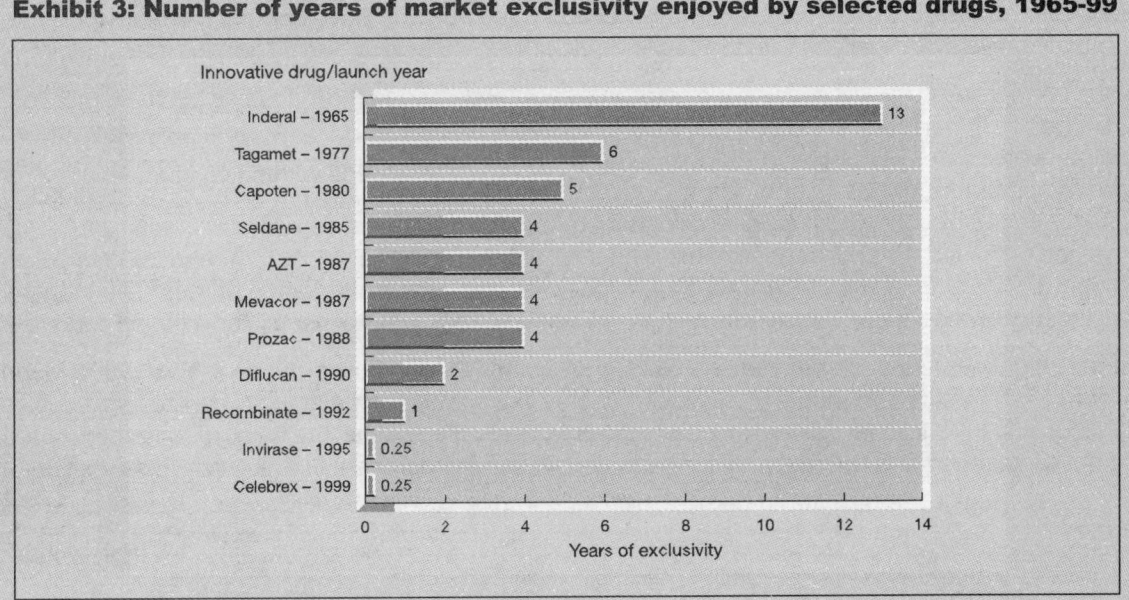

Contd...

BOX 4: Consumers and the Net

Increasingly vocal, well-informed and demanding consumers seemed inevitable. As the convergence of telephone, information technology and television accelerated, it was difficult to envisage how a ban on DTC in the EU could be maintained. Patients with internet access could obtain information on new products directly themselves. It was easy for non-US citizens to access US websites, and information on new drugs reached consumers via both company and independent web sites and through distribution of press releases to PR services. Health was one of the top two reasons for people to conduct searches on the Internet. In the US, up to 75 percent of those that searched for health-related information were likely to discuss that information with their healthcare providers (44 percent on average in the EU).

This trend was likely to increase patient demand for new effective, better-tolerated therapies, particularly in litigious countries such as the US. However, the internet also had the potential to raise awareness of international price disparities. Consumers were even beginning to purchase across borders, but with no guarantee that the drugs they received had been stored and shipped correctly and were not adulterated, contaminated, or counterfeit. The US FDA estimated that fake drugs accounted for over 10 percent of the global medicine market, generating annual sales of more than $32bn, with fake Viagra being an internet best-seller. More worrying, it was easy to purchase addictive painkillers and other potentially harmful drugs over the Internet, and rogue websites even offered miracle cures for cancer and AIDS. The pace of change was outstripping the capabilities and powers of regulators.

In addition to seeking an earlier, higher sales peak, marketers in pharmaceutical companies also aimed to extend the product life cycle. As a product approached patent expiry, effort might be invested in switching patients to new improved formulations with longer patent protection. Another strategy involved moving drugs from prescription- only status to OTC. The aim here was to encourage patients to recognize and buy a familiar brand. Consumer brand loyalty could then be used as a defence against generic competition. However, as described in Box 4, the increasing use of the internet has brought about interesting developments for the marketing of ethical pharmaceuticals.

Corporate Social Responsibility

During the 20th century average life expectancy in developed countries increased by over 20 years. A significant part of this improvement can be attributed to pharmaceutical innovation. Few other industries could claim to have done as much for the well being of mankind. So how did an industry that had delivered such enormous benefits acquire such a tarnished image and become an easy target for unpredictable government intervention?

One problem is that the market for pharmaceutical innovation has the characteristics of what economists describe as a 'public good' - i.e., expensive to produce but inexpensive to reproduce. The manufacturing cost of drugs is usually tiny compared with the amortized cost of Research and Development that led to the discovery. Setting prices that attempt to recoup Research and Development therefore looks like corporate greed in comparison with the very low prices that can be charged by generic manufacturers.

Some companies in the US and Europe acted in ways that damaged the industry's overall reputation. Sales details in particular were under increasing scrutiny. In Italy in 2003, 40 company staff and 30 doctors were under investigation for comparaggio - the prescribing of drugs in exchange for gifts such as computers and lavish trips. Many EU countries restricted the value of such gifts and voluntary industry codes of conduct were increasingly augmented with formal regulation. Similar problems emerged in the US: Pharmaceutical firms paid over $2bn in fines between 2000 and 2003 in cases brought by the US Justice Department, principally for pricing and marketing crimes. The industry also faced growing condemnation of its response to the enormous unmet need in developing countries.

An investigation by the United Nations Centre on Transnational Corporations in the 1980s found evidence for questionable industry practices.[5] Twenty years later campaigning organizations such as Health Action International claimed those practices were still rife and that the types of drugs consumed did not correspond with the real health needs of developing countries. In Thailand, consumption of

---

5. United Nations Centre on Transnational Corporations (UNCTC), Transnational Corporations in the Pharmaceutical Industry of Developing Countries, UNCTC, New York, 1984.

antibiotics was seven times higher than necessary, while drugs to combat tuberculosis, malaria and leprosy were under-used. Ineffective products such as tonics, vitamins and cough syrups were firms' best sellers in developing countries, some even containing addictive components. The marketing of unsafe drugs that had been withdrawn in developed markets was a particularly depressing finding. Dangerous products were among the best sellers in Argentina and Brazil and had increased the incidence of fatal childhood anaemia in Colombia. The image was of an industry prepared to break its own ethical rules when not properly policed on the fringes of the global economy.

Lacking adequate sanitation, nutrition and primary health care facilities for much of their population, developing countries relied on pharmaceuticals as the first line of defence against a wide range of infectious and parasitic diseases. Although for many diseases affecting millions of people, effective drugs and vaccines already existed, often their cost was beyond the means of the people who needed them. It was argued that leading pharmaceutical companies could make a significant contribution such as reallocation of Research and Development efforts in favour of major tropical diseases, the sale of low-priced essential drugs and technology transfer. According to a report by the International Federation of Pharmaceutical Manufacturers Associations (IFPMA), some global firms were rising to the challenge.[6] IFPMA claimed that in sheer size, spending by pharmaceutical companies rivalled that of the World Health Organisation (WHO) and programs benefited tens of millions of people in over a hundred countries. Examples included Pfizer's commitment to provide its antifungal medicine Diflucan free of charge and without time limits to people in the least developed countries living with HIV/AIDS and with cryptococcal meningitis and/or oesophageal candidiasis.

Questions around the purpose and ethics of the global pharmaceutical industry gained a high public profile as disputes over access to modern antiretroviral therapies for AIDS patients reached crisis point and threatened to jeopardize broader world trade agreements. AIDS was killing 3 to 4 million people annually, 2.3 million of them in Africa. The humanitarian efforts of major corporations were inadequate in the face of this immense need and according to campaigners, often came with unacceptable strings attached. Countries began taking matters into their own hands. Brazil halved the number of people dying of AIDS by providing patented anti-retroviral drugs to 150,000 people free of charge. It either made cheap, generic versions of the drugs itself, or obtained them cheaply from the patent-holder by threatening to do so. However, multinationals worried that supplying drugs free or at very low prices would flood higher priced markets with parallel imports. When the South African government proposed legislation to allow generic imports, a coalition of 39 firms took legal action. Given the tragic AIDS epidemic and the saintly figure of Nelson Mandela, this wasn't one of the best examples of corporate public relations.

Between 2002 and 2003 the CEO of GlaxoSmithKline (GSK), Jean Paul Garnier, helped negotiate the industry out of the South African court case and established clear principles of operation for GSK. The company would supply critical drugs to poor countries on a no-loss, no-profit basis. As for investing in research into 'not-for- profit' diseases, Garnier declared:

"We'll go after it. It's just that we've got to be street smart about the funding . . . There's plenty of money. . . to fund those initiatives and we've never been turned down. I talk to Bill Gates all the time.[7]

By early 2003 other companies were under pressure to follow GSK's example. A group of powerful investors stated publicly that the industry risked becoming the 'new tobacco' unless it cleaned up its act. Firms were accused of failing to prioritize cures for diseases prevalent in poor countries while concentrating on lucrative 'lifestyle cures' for prosperous ones. The group, with combined investments totalling $940bn, said if the industry did not shape up, its reputation would be destroyed and future profits put at risk. 'The statement came from a concern about the impact on shareholder value in the long-term,' commented one industry analyst.[8]

[6.]   Building Healthier Societies Through Partnerships, IFPMA, August 2003.

[7.]   The Guardian, 18 February 2003.

[8.]   BBC News, 24 March 2003.

Contd...

At the Doha trade talks in 2001, ministers stated that patents could be broken in cases of national emergency, such as AIDS or tuberculosis epidemics. Intellectual property rights should not prevent efforts to 'promote access to medicines for all'. The industry negotiated safeguards so that generic drugs would be labelled, packaged, shaped or embossed differently from the patented original, and importation could only be 'in good faith to protect public health' and not in order to 'pursue industrial or commercial-policy objectives'. However, corporations feared a broader threat to the hard-won intellectual property at the heart of their business model. Garnier portrayed the battle as an 'economic war' in which unscrupulous generics companies were using AIDS as a 'Trojan horse' to undermine the patent system. His concern was that those companies sought to pirate hard-won pharmaceutical discoveries and supply them to countries such as China and India, accounting for around 80 percent of the world's population. 'If the patents go away in those countries it's the end of the pharmaceutical industry as we know it.'[9]

The agreement valiantly attempted to balance the interests of the global industry with the public-health needs of the world's poor, but it remained to be seen whether it offered a workable solution.

Strategic Responses

While the pharmaceutical market remained relatively fragmented, with very large numbers of domestic and regional players, it was consolidating at the global level. No company held more than a 7.5 percent market share in 2002, but Pfizer's acquisition of Pharmacia took this over 10 percent in

**Exhibit 4: Leading Global Pharmaceutical Companies, 1997 and 2002
(Top worldwide sales, retail market share and major drug mergers in the late 1990s)**

1997		2002			
Company	Total sales ($bn)	Company	Total sales ($bn)	Share within global retail	Sales growth (2001 to 2002)
Glaxo Wellcome[1] (UK)	11.6	Pfizer[5] (US)	29.5	7.3 percent	11.4
Merck (US)	11.4	GlaxoSmithKline[6] (UK)	27.9	7.0 percent	7.0
Novartis[2] (CH)	11.0	Merck (US)	20.0	5.0 percent	6.6
Bristol-Myers Squibb (US)	9.3	Johnson and Johnson (US)	18.6	4.6 percent	16.1
Johnson and Johnson (US)	8.7	AstraZeneca[4] (UK/Swe)	18.1	4.5 percent	8.6
American Home Products (US)	8.4	Novartis (CH)	16.6	4.1 percent	12.8
Pfizer (US)	8.4	Aventis[3] (Ger/Fra)	14.3	3.6 percent	10.0
Roche (CH)	8.0	Bristol-Myers Squibb (US)	14.3	3.6 percent	7.4
SmithKline Beecham (UK)	7.4	Roche (CH)	12.5	3.1 percent	6.5
Hoechst (Ger)	7.4	Pharmacia (US)[7]	12.2	3.0 percent	8.1

Notes:			
Number	Created	Originating companies	
1	1995	Glaxo (UK)	Wellcome (UK)
2	1996	Sandoz (CH)	Ciba-Geigy (CH)
3	1998	Hoescht (Ger)	Rhône-Poulenc (Fra)
4	1998	Astra (Swe)	Zeneca (UK)
5	2000	Warner-Lambert (US)	Pfizer (US)
6	2000	Glaxo Wellcome (UK)	SmithKline Beecham (UK)
7	2000	Monsanto (US)	Pharmacia (US)

Source: The Economist, 21 November 1998; Financial Times, 6 April 2000, and own estimates.

---

9. The Guardian, 18 February 2003.

Contd...

2003. The top 10 players accounted for nearly half of global pharmaceutical sales and significantly only 2 blockbuster drugs were held outside the top 20 corporations. A strong trend was for previously diversified conglomerates to divest their non-healthcare businesses (e.g. agrochemicals), to focus purely on high-margin pharmaceuticals. Although the overall market appeared fragmented, this disguised the true level of concentration. Since both Research and Development and commercial franchises divided naturally along therapeutic lines, competition was fought at the level of therapeutic area and most intensely within specific product classes. The market leader within a franchise might hold a share as high as 28 percent (AstraZeneca in Gastroenterology and Metabolism in 2002) and 20 percent was not uncommon. The more successful companies led key franchises and competed in product classes that were large, fast-growing or had high unmet need. In 2002, the top 10 classes grew at 37 percent compared with overall market growth of 8 percent.

There was a strong belief that companies needed critical mass in Research and Development and global marketing presence in order to compete effectively. However, there were notable exceptions such as Sanofi-Synthelabo from France, and US-based Amgen, which ranked at 17 in terms of sales but grew at over 20 percent in 2002.

Exhibit 4 shows how the industry response to the need for critical mass had been a wave of mergers and previously unheard-of hostile acquisitions leading to amalgamation.

Mergers had resulted in the formation of Novartis, Aventis, AstraZeneca and GlaxoSmithKline, while Pfizer acquired Monsanto (Warner-Lambert) and then Pharmacia. Exhibit 7 shows how Pfizer overtook Merck, which followed an organic growth strategy throughout the 1990s. Leading companies were under pressure to consider further mergers after Pfizer's acquisition of Pharmacia. Eliminating duplicated costs remained one sure-fire way to keep profits relatively healthy.

But there was little conclusive evidence that mergers enhanced revenue or Research and development productivity. Successful mergers were based on strategic purpose and fit, rather than exacerbating weaknesses, and managing the process effectively had itself become a strategic capability.

A key rationale for mergers and acquisitions was to combine a company with a strong pipeline but weak sales and marketing with its converse. For example, the acquisition of Warner-Lambert gave Pfizer full marketing rights to the cholesterol- lowering agent Lipitor, which Pfizer then built into the world's best-selling drug.

Another argument for increasing size was to improve Research and development productivity, since it rested at least partly on 'technology platforms'. Companies had to invest in expensive new capabilities (such as High Throughput Screening) to keep pace with the industry leaders in speed to market. The larger the total Research and development program, the greater the number of individual projects that could benefit from the new capability, and amortize these costs. Pfizer's acquisition of Pharmacia gave the new entity an research and development budget of nearly $7bn, 50 percent greater than its nearest rival.

Others argued that mergers actually reduced Research and development productivity: More management layers resulted in greater bureaucracy, less freedom to innovate and a reduced research output. The success of biotechs in drug discovery suggested creativity was greater in small Research and development organizations. Portfolio management could also be problematic in merged companies. Cutting too many projects in the search for blockbusters could exacerbate risk. Cutting too few meant under resourcing potential winners and risked an over-stretched and unfocused organization. In one analysis, the median number of projects at merged firms fell from 85 in both pre-merger companies, to 56 by three years post-merger. Companies were either removing duplication and focusing on winners, or becoming less productive. Definitive evidence was years away.

Another argument for increasing size was to invest in larger sales-forces to secure greater 'share of voice' and to acquire global reach. Pfizer's acquisition of Pharmacia took the new entity from no. 4 in

Contd...

Europe and no. 3 in Japan to no. 1 across the Triad. Companies which lacked presence in key markets were obliged to make use of licensing deals, sharing the profit with another company. A strong global marketing capability was also vital in attracting the best in-licensing candidates and co-marketing deals, to strengthen the product pipeline. Supporters of organic growth claimed that marketing success came from combining the right skills, resources and competencies rather than sheer sales force size, pointing to the success of smaller 'franchise' players.

Some advocates of further industry consolidation emphasized that its purpose should be to create dominance in just a few therapeutic franchises, with non-core activities being sold off, making these huge corporations more manageable, and focusing research and development and sales and marketing efforts. Others proposed that the research and development and commercial functions could operate autonomously. The commercial organization would develop a product portfolio based on therapeutic franchises, using clearly defined business relationships with external Research and development partners. In turn, this would free in-house research and development to discover and to develop innovations beyond the commercial portfolio strategy.

An intriguing response to environmental change was adopted by managers at Roche, who positioned themselves as operating a new 'integrated healthcare' business model. Roche had a strong diagnostics division, owned much of the relevant intellectual property, and Roche's managers portrayed it as a complex business with high barriers to entry. Their strategic vision was to move from seller of instruments and reagents to a health information provider, offering value through better targeting of treatments, convenience and 'peace of mind'. Roche claimed to be the only company embracing these principles, having both requisite experience, and all the necessary tools to lead the paradigm shift in healthcare offered by genomics and diagnostics.

Summary

Many large pharmaceuticals companies are facing their toughest outlook in a decade. The industry has made a tremendous contribution to human well being, yet is vilified in the media and targeted by governments in their efforts to curb spiralling healthcare costs. Research and development and sales and marketing costs have risen sharply, while the product life cycle has shortened. Product approval, pricing and promotion are subject to increasingly onerous regulation, yet free trade allows wholesalers to extract a large chunk of value from the chain without adding anything back. Companies must balance shareholder return against the huge unmet need of developing nations. Exciting opportunities do still exist - more educated consumers, advances in genomics, regulatory harmonisation and of course unmet medical need. Industry consolidation is driven by the dominant belief that size is what counts, although a few players prefer to build focused franchises or offer integrated healthcare solutions. Ultimately, meaningful innovation is what matters most, but it is not clear that a business formula based on inventing and selling blockbuster drugs can continue to sustain double- digit growth rates.

Source: This case has been prepared by Bernardo Batiz-Lazo and Sarah Holland. It aims to foster discussion rather then present good or bad management practice. It does not necessarily represents the views of the authors nor of Astra Zeneca.

Case 14

Business and Human Rights: The Case of Hewlett-Packard

Introduction

Hewlett-Packard, headquartered in Palo Alto, California, is a technology solutions provider to consumers, businesses, and institutions. It operates in 178 countries and employs approximately 160,000 people across the globe. A distinct culture at HP, to be described in more detail, emanates strongly from within the corporation. Stanford University classmates Bill Hewlett and Dave Packard founded HP in 1939 in their Palo Alto garage. Their first product was an audio oscillator — an electronic test instrument used by sound engineers. One of HP's first customers was Walt Disney Studios, which purchased eight oscillators to develop and test an innovative sound system for the movie "Fantasia." Employees within HP claim to share a passion for satisfying customers, an intense focus on teamwork, speed and agility, and a commitment to trust and respect for all individuals.

The company of HP is divided into four businesses groups.

Table 1: HP's Core Business Groups

Enterprise Systems Group (ESG)	ESG focuses on providing the key technology components of enterprise IT infrastructure to enhance business agility, including enterprise storage, servers, management software and a variety of solutions.
Imaging and Printing Group (IPG)	HP is the leading provider of printing and imaging solutions for both business and consumer use. IPG includes printer hardware, all-in-ones, digital imaging devices such as cameras and scanners, and associated supplies and accessories. It also is expanding into the commercial printing market.
HP Services (HPS)	HP Services is a premier, global IT services team. It offers guidance, know-how and a comprehensive portfolio of services to help customers realize measurable business value from their IT investments.
Personal Systems Group (PSG)	PSG focuses on supplying simple, reliable and affordable personal-computing solutions and devices for home and business use, including desktop PCs, notebooks, workstations, thin clients, smart handhelds and personal devices.

Although its annual revenues for fiscal year ending October 31, 2002 were $72 billion USD and its scope and reach clearly span the globe, HP still revels in the "garage start- up" mentality of a company that is innovative, human-focused, and socially committed. Indeed co-founder David Packard stated in 1942:

Many assume, wrongly, that a company exists simply to make money...the real reason HP exists is to make a contribution...to improve the welfare of humanity...to advance the frontiers of science...Profit is not the proper end and aim of management - it is what makes all of the proper ends and aims possible...

Over 60 years later, current CEO Carly Fiorina re-states even more eloquently and expanded-upon in 2003:

We believe that the winning companies of this century will be those that not only increase shareholder value but increase social and environmental value... By developing products and solutions that are environmentally sound, by bringing the benefits of information technology to emerging markets, by holding our company to the highest standards of business conduct, and by giving back to the

Contd...

communities in which we operate, HP is contributing to a more sustainable future while also making HP a stronger company and the preferred IT solutions provider.

Through high-speed growth, mergers and acquisitions, down turns, new products, new management, and half a decade later, HP still appears to remain as committed to social responsibility and creating positive social impact today as they did when started in the garage of co-founders David Packard and Bill Hewlett.

HP states the following as its corporate objectives, which were first written down by the co-founders in 1957.

Table 2: HP Corporate Objectives

Customer Loyalty	To provide products, services and solutions of the highest quality and deliver more value to our customers that earns their respect and loyalty.
Profit	To achieve sufficient profit to finance our company growth, create value for our shareholders and provide the resources we need to achieve our other corporate objectives.
Market Leadership	To grow by continually providing useful and significant products, services and solutions to markets we already serve— and to expand into new areas that build on our technologies, competencies and customer interests.
Growth	To view change in the market as an opportunity to grow; to use our profits and our ability to develop and produce innovative products, services and solutions that satisfy emerging customer needs.
Employee Commitment	To help HP employees share in the company's success that they make possible; to provide people with employment opportunities based on performance; to create with them a safe, exciting and inclusive work environment that values their diversity and recognizes individual contributions; and to help them gain a sense of satisfaction and accomplishment from their work.
Leadership Capability	To develop leaders at every level who are accountable for achieving business results and exemplifying our values.
Global Citizenship	Good citizenship is good business. We live up to our responsibility to society by being an economic, intellectual and social asset to each country and community in which we do business.

HP and the UN Global Compact

In his address to The World Economic Forum in January of 1999, United Nation Secretary-General Kofi Annan challenged business leaders to join an international initiative - the Global Compact - that would bring companies together with UN agencies, labor, and civil society to support nine principles in the areas of human rights, labor, and the environment. The Global Compact's operational phase was launched at UN Headquarters in New York in July of 2000.

Through the power of collective action, the Global Compact seeks to advance responsible corporate citizenship so that business can be part of the solution to the challenges of globalization. In this way, the private sector - in partnership with other social actors-can help realize the Secretary-General's vision: a more sustainable and inclusive global economy. The Global Compact is a voluntary corporate citizenship initiative with two objectives:

● To mainstream the nine principles in business activities around the world.

● To catalyze actions in support of UN goals.

The Global Compact is not a regulatory instrument - it does not "police," enforce, or measure the behavior or actions of companies. Rather, the Global Compact relies on public accountability,

Contd...

transparency, and the enlightened self-interest of companies, labor, and civil society to initiate and share substantive action in pursuing the principles upon which the Global Compact is based. To this end, it has been largely criticized as "having no teeth" and as being fairly innocuous.

HP was one of the earlier US companies to become a participant in the UN Global Compact. This case will focus on HP's adherence to UN Global Compact principles one and two, which focus on human rights.

Table 3: UN Global Compact Human Rights Principles

Principle 1	Businesses should support and respect the protection of internationally proclaimed human rights within their sphere of influence.
Principle 2	Businesses should make sure that they are not complicit in human rights abuses

Human Rights and Business

Human rights are rights that individuals have simply because they are human. They are designed to respect the dignity and integrity of the individual. Human rights are fundamental principles that, if respected, ensure an individual can live a life of dignity, free from deprivation and abuse, free to participate in their community, and can express their beliefs. Human rights are recognized in international law. Although the rights are best achieved by action within a national legal system, such as the passing of laws and implementation of government programs, the national government is not the source of a person's human rights. It follows that the government cannot withdraw human rights at will.[1]

Human rights, as we know them today, grew out of the reaction against the horrors experienced during the Second World War. At the formation of the United Nations in 1945, one of the UN's stated objectives was to encourage respect for, and realization of, human rights. Not long after its formation, the UN produced the Universal Declaration of Human Rights, which was adopted by the nations of the world sitting in the General Assembly of the United Nations. The Declaration was adopted without a dissenting vote being cast, signifying an extremely high level of commitment to the principles contained in the Declaration. Since then numerous more focused and specific human rights documents have been drafted and accepted, but the Universal Declaration remains the foundational document in the human rights field.[2] The Universal Declaration contains a relatively comprehensive set of rights. It covers civil and political rights, as well as economic, social and cultural rights. Some of the main categories of rights covered by the Declaration include:

- Physical integrity

- Fair treatment before the law

- Equal protection

- Freedom of belief, speech, and association

- Political participation

- Access to education

- Just and favorable conditions of work

---

[1]   For more on the nature and sources of human rights see J., Donnelly, Universal Human Rights in Theory and Practice, Cornell University Press, Ithaca, 1989 pp. 14 - 19 and R., Higgins, Problems and Process: International Law and How We Use It, Clarendon Press, Oxford, 1994, pp. 95-110.

[2]   For more on the current system of human rights protection at the UN level see H., Steiner and P., Alston, International Human Rights in Context: Law, Politics, Morality, Oxford University Press, Oxford, 2000 pp. 137-141.

Contd...

- Adequate standard of living

- Participation in cultural life

A question is often raised concerning the scope of a firm's responsibility for human rights: If a business professes a commitment to human rights, do they become responsible for doing something about every human rights issue wherever it occurs? The answer is no. Businesses should think in terms of being responsible within their 'sphere of influence'.[3] A company's sphere of influence can be divided into four broad areas:

1. Core operations

2. Business partners

3. Host communities

4. Advocacy/policy dialogue

A company's core operations include issues that many companies are familiar with, such as labor rights, the regulation of the behavior of security forces, and independent monitoring, verification and reporting of company performance. In terms of relations with business partners, companies should ensure that business partners have an equivalent commitment to human rights and they should have some sort of monitoring and compliance verification processes in place. Effects of operations on the human rights of host communities should form part of the impact assessment performed by the company, and these communities should regularly be consulted on questions concerning human rights. Finally, companies should have a commitment to uphold international human rights standards in their dialogue with governments. A company might choose to achieve this by quiet diplomacy or advocacy, but whatever approach a company chooses should have some response to abuses such as the arbitrary detention of labor activists, unexplained disappearances of workers, or abuse committed by government-provided security forces operating at or around a company's location.[4] It can be seen from this discussion of issues that arise within a company's 'sphere of influence' that human rights extends beyond issues relating to how a company deals with its own immediate work force, although that remains vitally important. Human rights are also concerned with the broader impact that a company has in the communities in which it operates.

Following are some examples of ways in which human rights arise in the business context. Non-discrimination is required in all dealings. This includes interactions with employees, customers, suppliers, partners, and contractors. Human rights issues might arise in relation to the behavior of security guards in and around company facilities. Issues include excessive use of force by security guards in the performance of their duties, the implication of members of the security forces in human rights abuse in the area, and the use of security forces to shut down legitimate forms of protest by workers or community members against the company. In relation to communities, human rights issues could arise in the context of competition between the company and local populations over land and other resource use. These issues will be particularly acute where indigenous populations are involved. People may be deprived of their means of securing a livelihood (or practicing their religion or culture) by the location of, or demand for local resources by, the new enterprise, they may be forcibly removed by the government to facilitate the new venture, or their health might be adversely affected by the activities conducted by the facility. In dealing with employees, fair working conditions, freedom of association and collective bargaining, freedom from slavery, and health and safety need

---

[3] Amnesty International and the Prince of Wales Business Leaders Forum look in some detail at a company's obligations in terms of their sphere of influence. See Amnesty International and The Prince of Wales Business Leaders Forum, Human Rights: Is it Any of Your Business, April 2000, pp. 28-9.

[4] Amnesty International and The Prince of Wales Business Leaders Forum, Human Rights: Is it Any of Your Business, April 2000, pp. 28-9.

Contd...

to be ensured in relation to workers wherever they are located, irrespective of the level of protection those workers are afforded under national legislation.

NGOs have long been involved in the study and connection of human rights responsibilities to global business. For example, Amnesty International and the Prince of Wales International Business Leaders Forum have been engaged in an ongoing study that illustrates the geography of corporate risk within human rights segmented by industry. For the "IT Hardware and Telecommunications" sectors, into which HP falls, they believe the following four issues are under the human rights spotlight:

● Freedom of expression

● Forced labor

● Links to repression

● Access to knowledge[5]

However, it is not only major NGOs who appear to be engaged in corporations being involved positively in issues of human rights. In Global Issues Monitor, an ongoing large-scale study conducted by Environics International in 2003, which polled over 1,000 citizens in 20 countries, respondents cited "human rights" as the fourth highest priority for business, falling under "the rich/ poor gap," "biodiversity," and "basic education."[6]

Another study conducted by Edelman on Corporate Social Responsibility (CSR) which tracks attitudes towards business, media, government, and NGOs, the technology industry as a whole was viewed as the leading industry in CSR, leading consumer packaged goods, retail, manufacturing, pharmaceutical, publishing, automotive, financial services, and energy/ oil and gas industries.[7] Yet respondents were only 38 percent trustful that business as a whole was adequately addressing human rights issues. Finally, the Reputation Institute at Harris Interactive found that "Treatment of Human Rights/ Employees" was the most essential element of corporate citizenship in Europe, the U.S., and Scandinavia. So while the tech industry as a whole is seen as a leader in CSR in general, stakeholders are becoming increasingly engaged in and scrutinizing of human rights as a component of CSR in business.

Human Rights at HP

One senior manager from HP stated a compelling belief that the term "human rights" is largely an NGO term, not truly one that is used in business, and certainly not a term that has been used in the past at HP.[8] This was clearly confirmed in the interview process that was conducted for this study. A clear and succinct definition of human rights, as described above, was sent out to all interview respondents prior to the interviews. Even after that, a significant portion of each interview was spent detailing what is meant by the term "human rights," and fielding questions about the unbundling of the aspects of the term.

That is not to say that there is no attention paid to areas of human rights within HP; in fact, there is considerable commitment and attention. It is simply that within HP, treating employees fairly, not engaging in age or race discrimination or using hiring agencies that do, and not engaging with suppliers who do not comply with HP's Supplier Code of Conduct is not extrinsically viewed by HP managers as paying attention to human rights per se; it is simply good business and part the "HP way." HP has

5.   Business and Human Rights: A geography of corporate risk, Amnesty International and The Prince of Wales International Business Leaders Forum, November, 2001.

6.   2003 CSR Monitor, Environics International, March 2003.

7.   Edleman, Rebuilding Public Trust Through Accountability and Responsibility, address to the Ethical Corporation Magazine Conference, New York City, October, 2002.

8.   Interview with Senior Vice President, Corporate Affairs, HP.

Contd...

recently publicly aligned itself to the Universal Declaration of Human Rights[9]. HP upholds and respects human rights as reflected in the Universal Declaration of Human Rights. HP is also committed to fair labor practices and the respectful treatment of all employees, including the protection of workplace health and safety, and data-privacy protections.

HP has policies that deal with a number of human rights issues relevant to their operations (eg. privacy, accessibility and supply chain management) and it is active in terms of developing and supporting community development activities in parts of the world in which they operate.

Commitment to the Universal Declaration of Human Rights

A commitment to upholding and respecting human rights as reflected in the Universal Declaration of Human Rights has recently been included in HP's Commitment to Global Citizenship. The Global Citizenship Commitment goes on to set out HP's "Human Rights and Labor Policy" which focuses heavily on labor rights. The policy addresses forced, bonded or involuntary prison labor, child labor, minimum wages, working hours, non- discrimination, harsh or inhuman treatment, and freedom of association. For the most part the rights under this policy are expressed in a way that links them to compliance with local laws.

Supply Chain

HP recognizes that this is the area in which they have the most risk if human rights are not a focus; however, their efforts around supply chain and human rights are fairly nascent. The company currently contractually obliges its top 40 suppliers, which includes 100 sites and accounts for 80 percent of their spend dollars, to commit to HP's supply chain code of conduct. HP is in the process of increasing the number of suppliers it requires to make this commitment and strengthening the means by which it ensures compliance with the obligation. Eventually, this code of conduct will be explicit in all new supplier contracts, so compliance will be a necessity to do business. In developing their supply chain code of conduct, HP did their own extensive benchmarking and research, and worked with Business for Social Responsibility, a think tank and consultancy around CSR based in San Francisco, California. The Director of Supply Chain Services stated that they scoured the landscape of supplier codes of conduct, looked at the various international standards, even looked at the UN Global Compact- but none were satisfactory or entirely relevant to HP. So they developed their own code. They did find one company whose code they modeled and that was British Telecom. The BT code was derived from the Ethical Trading Initiative standard, which HP felt closely embodied the elements that were important to them.

The "HP Supplier Code of Conduct" professes to focus on compliance with local laws in the areas of environment, worker health and safety, and labor and employment practices, and intended to work in conjunction with management systems to measure, improve and communicate progress in these areas. The treatment of labor issues is fairly comprehensive and, despite the use of headings that refer to compliance with local laws, contains standards, for example, in relation to non-discrimination and prison labor, which may or may not be covered by local legislation. The focus on these issues is positive and its effectiveness will be greatly enhanced by the planned improvements in compliance monitoring. To meet HP's human rights obligations, the supplier code of conduct should be expanded to cover human rights matters beyond labor issues, matters such as performance and monitoring of security guards by suppliers; the impact on the local community of supplier operations; and the penalization of suppliers for corrupt or human rights-abusive regimes.

Currently, HP monitors its supply chain using a self-assessment questionnaire completed by HP's top 40 suppliers. HP then works collaboratively with suppliers to achieve the required standards in any area that is identified as falling below HP requirements. HP's Director of Supply Chain Services reports that HP's suppliers take this process very seriously given the importance to them of their

---

[9]   See HP's Commitment to Global Citizenship, 17 July 2003, http://www.hp.com/hpinfo/globalcitizenship/

Contd...

relationship and business with HP. HP is moving to expand and strengthen their supply chain monitoring. They are extending self- assessment beyond the top 40 suppliers to the suppliers HP regards as 'high risk'.

At the same time they are strengthening the monitoring of the top 40 suppliers by utilizing HP's own procurement auditing capacity to conduct site assessments of supplier performance, moving beyond the self-assessment model. In time, this model will also be extended to the high risk suppliers. Finally, HP is currently researching appropriate entities to conduct third-party assessment of supplier performance. Selective third-party assessment will be the final stage in the evolution of supply chain monitoring at HP.[10]

Privacy

HP invests considerable energy in the protection of information privacy for its consumers and its employees. HP has long had a policy dealing with employee information privacy stemming from HP's focus on 'doing the right thing' for their employees as part of the 'HP way'. From relatively humble beginnings as a one-person operation four years ago, the HP privacy program has grown considerably and now undertakes co-coordinated strategy on privacy for consumers and employees and conducts training on employee and customer data handling.

Since January 2001 HP has self-certified its privacy practices as consistent with U.S.- E.U. Safe Harbor principles on Notice, Choice, Onward Transfer, Access and Accuracy, Security, and Oversight/Enforcement. The Safe Harbor principles were designed in response to the prohibition in the European Commission's Directive on Data Protection on the transfer of personal data to non-European Union countries that do not provide 'adequate' privacy protection. HP also meets the requirements of the Council of Better Business Bureau's BBBOnLine Privacy Program. HP is a founding sponsor of the BBBOnLine Privacy Program, a privacy certification scheme that awards a privacy seal to businesses that have proven to meet standards relating to the following: posting online privacy notices; completing a privacy assessment; monitoring and review; and participation in the program's consumer dispute resolution system.

HP adopts the approach of applying a consistent global policy for privacy protection and complies with that policy or local laws, whichever are more stringent.

CSR

As Global Citizenship was outlined above as one of HP's seven core corporate objectives, HP has developed a well-integrated framework for this citizenship strategy:

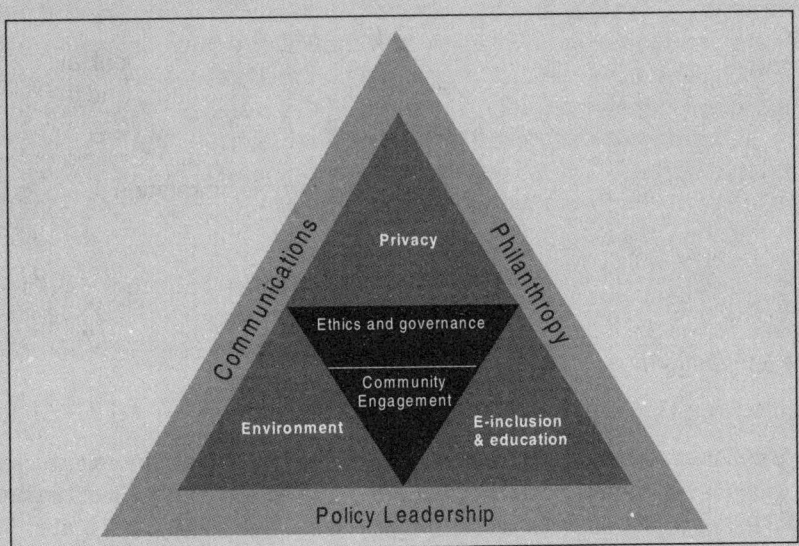

Figure 1: HP's Global Citizenship Framework

---

10. Interview with Director of Supply Chain Services, HP.

Contd...

Human rights, *per se*, is not explicitly one of the facets of this framework, although in language used to describe HP's commitment to global citizenship, the Senior Vice President of Corporate Affairs does explicitly speak of human rights:

Socially, HP upholds and respects human rights as reflected in the 'Universal Declaration of Human Rights'. HP is also committed to fair labor practices and the respectful treatment of all employees, including the protection of workplace health and safety and data-privacy protections.

HP has four separate policies that address these topics: the Environmental, Health and Safety Policy; the Human Rights and Labor Policy, the Privacy Policy, and the Supply Chain Commitment Policy. Each policy includes issues of human rights within them, ranging from employee health and safety to freely chosen employment to privacy of personal data.

There seems to be clear evidence, then, that 'human rights' as a term has not made it into the language of HP's business managers, but when the term is unbundled, evidence of careful attention to human rights is clearly visible.

Labor

Country human resources managers were very aware of human rights issues as they relate to employment, and seemed confident that HP was duly addressing human rights issues. For example, in Malaysia, HP's competitors tend to employ local indigenous employment agencies. It is standard in Malaysia for these agencies to both collect information on and use in hiring decisions data on age and race. There is no local law against doing so. However HP Malaysia has chosen not to use these local temp agencies for this reason, and instead uses global temp agencies which adhere to HP's Human Rights and Labor Policy. The Human Resources Manager believes that HP is ahead of the local country laws, and while she fully believes in this position and the "HP way", she also admits that HP undoubtedly loses business and pays more for labor than companies who use local employment agencies. HP has engaged with the local government in trying to improve local labor laws, but even being in Malaysia for 25 years and growing from eight to 1000 plus employees, the manager felt that HP was behind competitors like Dell and IBM in having enough presence and leverage to really force the government to change labor practices or law.[11]

There were slightly mixed messages received on whether local country laws are the standard or whether there exist higher and more consistent HP standards. One manager claimed that there is a global HP approach to treating all employees within their sphere of influence, with local law being relied on for only a few things, like pay and benefits. Yet another manager's understanding was that local law is the standard, and that documents like the Global Citizenship objectives, which claim to rely on local laws, also include some general standards that are likely above the standard of law in some of the countries in which they operate. An example of this would be 'discrimination on grounds of sexual orientation'- this is not a widely or globally understood concept, yet HP has it in their Global Citizenship policy. Ultimately there was some lack of clarity on how certain HP managers are about the standards they maintain. HP's Personnel Policy and Guidelines (PPG) is designed to provide the basis for decisions affecting HP personnel worldwide. HP's PPG are global in their application with some local variation based on local law and custom. It supports the decentralized organizational structure of the company by allowing local entity decision making, while still recognizing HP's dual objective of maintaining consistent treatment for its employees and complying with applicable legal requirements in the jurisdictions in which HP operates.

Recommendations for the UN Global Compact

There was a lot of discussion within HP of the UN Global Compact as being symbolically good for HP and fitting with their brand identity and commitment to global citizenship, but beyond that, it has little impact on how HP conducts its business. The managers interviewed felt that HP was already far beyond what the UNGC compels them to do.

---

11.   Interview with country Human Resources Manager, HP Malaysia.

Contd...

It seems that the value of the Global Compact for this, and perhaps for other North American companies, remains relatively unclear and largely symbolic. Perhaps further work, segmented by geographical areas, needs to be done to ferret out the clear value of the UNGC for segments of signatories, particularly in those regions in which the signatories are fewer. In fact, HP has already led in this direction, together with Pfizer. They organized a meeting in April, 2003, bringing together North American companies, both UNGC signatories and non-signatories, to discuss the UNGC and its usefulness and place within North American business. The Global Compact seems to serve best as a starting, or early point, for companies who are newer to the practices and strategy of corporate citizenship and issues therein.

Recommendations and Next Steps for HP

The following recommendations are relevant to HP's protection of brand identity as a leader in global citizenship, and are consistent with HP's public, consistent, and historical commitment to it. At this stage, they are leading the high tech industry with their Global Citizenship strategy and policy, and the industry has not had the intense scrutiny around human rights by NGOs that the apparel industry has, but there is belief inside the company that the risks and penalties of lack of human rights performance are very high, given what Nike and others have been through. HP can also increase its achievement of the principles of the Global Compact and the UDHR (in relation to which HP has stated its intention to respect as part of the Global Compact and as part of its Global Citizenship Policy).[12]

HP has a corporate culture that values 'doing the right thing', which is traced back to the original quote by David Packard in 1942. While this way was spoken about time and time again by each and every manager interviewed, this valuable manner of thinking about the impact of HP's business cannot be relied upon alone to achieve appropriate levels of human rights performance, particularly in this world of high-paced growth and mergers and acquisitions. It seems improbable that the newly acquired Compaq employees can fully embrace the "HP way" without more systemic and explicit standards and policies. While the four major policies do exist within HP, they could be better integrated into and aligned with the overall Global Citizenship strategy and framework. Across the company there is a need to:

1.   Identify and prioritize the human rights issues that are most likely to arise across the company's operations;

2.   Educate employees and management in the identification of these human rights issues; and

3.   Work to develop framework guidance on how to deal with the issues.

The HP tradition of 'doing the right thing' means that the company already operates with an eye towards the ethical and responsible dimensions of their work. This places HP in a perfect position to combine that commitment to ethics with education on human rights and guidance on how to handle the issues in order to strengthen their human rights performance by achieving a greater level of consistency across the various operations and locations. It is also risky to rely on the 'HP way' in a post-merger time when now 40 percent of the company are not pre merger HP employees, but rather came over from Compaq. The 'HP way' at this stage needs to be more explicitly stated and systemically measured for individual employee comprehension and performance.

HP should allocate responsibility for human rights across the company to a high level manager, or team of managers. More study is needed to understand who is doing this currently and what the best practices of this model might be. This will allow a comprehensive assessment to be made of HP's current human rights performance, identifying and prioritizing for HP the best way of addressing outstanding issues, and allowing the development of company-wide policy performance objectives and implementation plans. Such a company-wide approach is presently lacking in HP and is needed

---

[12]   HP's Global Citizenship policy, 17 July 2003, http://www.hp.com/hpinfo/globalcitizenship/

Contd...

to ensure that human rights are consistently addressed throughout the company's operations. It would also help facilitate awareness-raising within HP and allow the sharing of information and good practice among various parts of HP. Importantly, a centralized approach will allow a fast, comprehensive, consistent response to any human rights incidents that do arise. Such a next step is crucial to moving HP's commitment to human rights, as embodied in its Global Citizenship policy, into a living part of HP operations. It is imagined that, given HP's preference for decentralized structures, this company-wide activity would involve the close co-operation of regional and other managers as well as employees and would be best implemented by those close to the ground with a tangible understanding of the priority issues in their area.

HP should investigate how to strengthen its dual objective of maintaining consistent treatment for its employees and complying with applicable legal requirements in the jurisdictions in which HP operates.

This would include looking at timing and issues where there may be conflicts with local law and custom. This is already the practice in the privacy field where we understand arguments relating to the benefit of consistency and the ethics of providing the same level of protection to all regardless of their location were successful.[13] While an approach based solely on compliance with national laws may be valid for other considerations, it is not sufficient in achieving an adequate level of human rights compliance. Many countries have implemented laws that do not meet the standards required under international human rights law for the realization of particular human rights for members of their population. Other countries have no law at all on some human rights issues. The reasons for an absence of adequate law at the national level are many and may include pressure on governments of developing counties to attract and retain international investment, as well as historical and cultural factors.

HP is actively implementing internal and external monitoring systems for its supply chain systems. In addition to expanding the scope of issues considered by the supplier code of conduct, as discussed earlier, in order for this system to form an effective method for monitoring the human rights performance of suppliers it will need to evolve from the early self-assessment focused model to a model based on more effective compliance monitoring. HP's efforts in this regard are welcome.

Source: The case has been authored by Kellie A. McElhaney, Haas School of Business, University of California, Berkeley and Natalie Hill, Human Rights Center, University of California, BerKeley, Haas School of Business, University of California, BerKeley. Reprinted with permission.

---

[13]   Interview with Chief Privacy Officer.

Index